Not For Tourists Guide to **NEW YORK CITY**

2005

Not For Tourists, Inc New York

published and designed by:
Not For Tourists, Inc
NFT$_{TM}$—Not For Tourists$_{TM}$ Guide to New York City 2005
www.notfortourists.com

Publisher & Editor
Jane Pirone

Information Design
Jane Pirone
Rob Tallia
Scot Covey
Diana Pizzari

Managing Editors
Rob Tallia
Diana Pizzari

City Editor
Krikor Daglian

Writing and Editing
Cathleen Cueto
Krikor Daglian
Annie Holt
Diana Pizzari
Rob Tallia

Research
Erin Kreindler
Sherry Wasserman

Editorial Interns
Emily Bonden

Research Interns
Lauren E. Fonda
Beverley Langevine
Shilpa Raman
JoLisa Robinson

Graphic Design/ Production
Scot Covey
Ran Lee
Christopher Salyers
Galina Rybatsky
Sana Hong

Proofing
Jack Schieffer

Contributors
Sundeep Amrute
Aubrey Arago
Donna Blicharz
Amanda Bower
Peter Carbonaro
Glenn Cherritts
Rosalind Coffey
Esther Greenbaum
Kathrin Grotowski
Eric Hynes
Judith-Noëlle Lamb
Jennifer Lavenhar
Temah Mollison
Abel Montez
Ashley Regazzi
Matthew Waldman

Printed in China
ISBN# 0-9740131-5-3 $14.95

Dear NFT User,

Welcome to the 2005 edition of NFT—we're back for our sixth update of New York's many charms. For the uninitiated, what you hold in your hands is an extensive and all-inclusive guide to Gotham, put together by people who live in New York, work in New York, love/hate New York, and pretty much know it through and through. What we don't know, we get from the great and generous contributors listed on the opposite page, who sent in their suggestions and corrections to help make the book even better. As a result, NFT will help you in just about any situation, from finding a restaurant in an unfamiliar neighborhood to figuring out which train will get you out to Boonton, NJ. We think the book is amazing. So if you're reading this book in a bookstore or other shop right now, just go buy it.

And for owners of past editions, you might be interested to know that we've made a ton of updates from last year. The icons have been carefully sifted through, crosschecked by our supercomputers, and combed over by our dedicated staff to see that they're placed correctly. Assuming everything goes well, we hope to launch the NFT GPS satellite into space next year in the pursuit of even greater accuracy. Not willing to fall behind the times, we've expanded our listings to include even more modern necessities. We've added a page with **internet cafes & wi-fi hotspots**, a guide to the city's **yoga studios**, a full listing of the city's **places of worship**, some pointers for **finding bathrooms** in the city, and a guide to **activities and fun places for the kids**. And as we do every year, we've added listings in many categories, most importantly more **bars**, **restaurants**, and **shopping destinations**. If by some chance we've forgotten something, please visit our website at **www.notfortourists.com** and let us know, we'll be grateful.

As always, our appreciation goes out to the staff of NFT for their support and patience. I always marvel at all the hard work they put into making what's grown into a small army of titles. I know they'll always remember New York is #1.

Here's hoping you find what you need,

Jane Pirone, Publisher
Krikor Daglian, City Editor
Rob Tallia, Managing Editor
Diana Pizzari, Managing Editor

Subway Map/Address Locator
foldout, last page
Essential Phone Numbers
inside back cover

Table of Contents

Map 1 • Financial District

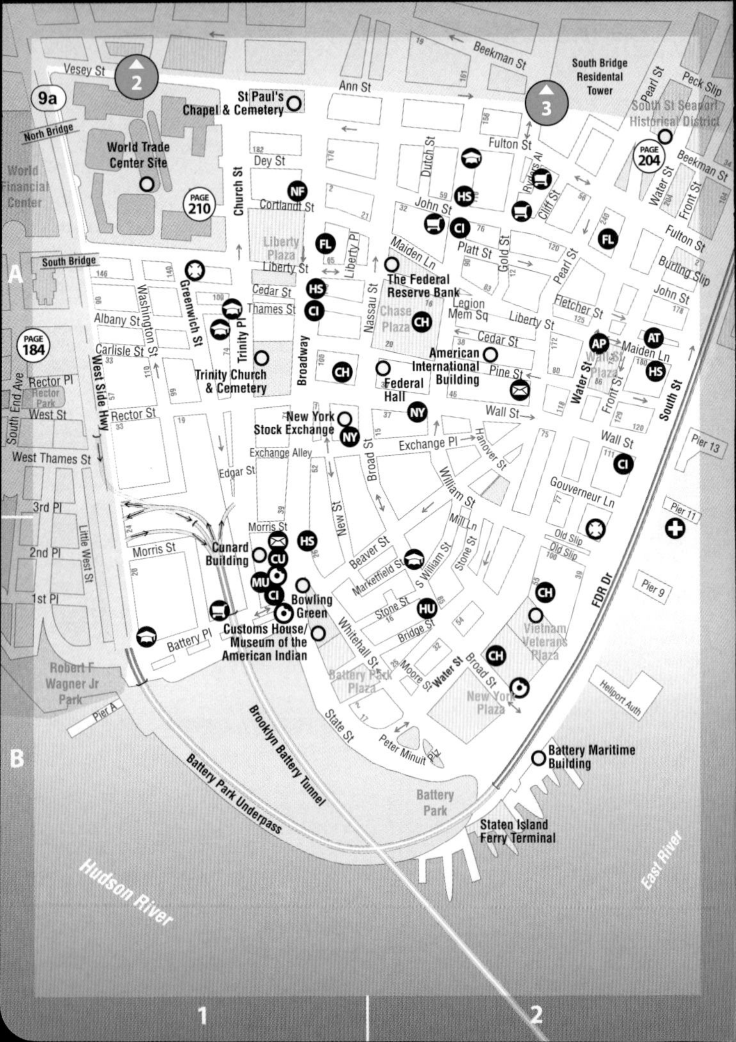

There are more closed streets and well-armed policemen, but overall downtown is now pretty much back in business, and construction on the new buildings at the World Trade Center site has begun. Skyscrapers are the main architectural eye candy down here, but look behind them to find such gems as Federal Hall, Trinity Church, the Cunard Building, and the Customs House.

ATMs

AP • Apple • Wall St Plz
AT • Atlantic • 15 Maiden Ln
NY • Bank of New York • 20 Broad St
NY • Bank of New York • 45 Wall St
CH • Chase • 1 Chase Plz
CH • Chase • 14 Wall St
CH • Chase • 4 New York Plz
CH • Chase • 55 Water St
CI • Citibank • 1 Broadway
CI • Citibank • 100 William St
CI • Citibank • 111 Wall St
CI • Citibank • 120 Broadway
FL • Fleet • 150 Broadway
FL • Fleet • 175 Water St
HS • HSBC • 100 Maiden Ln
HS • HSBC • 110 William St
HS • HSBC • 120 Broadway
HS • HSBC • 26 Broadway
HU • Hudson Union • 90 Broad St
CU • Municipal Credit Union • 2 Broadway
NF • North Fork Bank • 176 Broadway

Bagels

- **Champs** • 71 Broadway
- **New World Coffee** • 1 Broadway
- **New World Coffee** • 1 New York Plz

Fire Departments

- **Engine 10, Ladder 10** • 124 Liberty St
- **Engine 4, Ladder 15** • 42 South St

Hospitals

- **The Floating Hospital** • Pier 11

Landmarks

- **American International Building** • 70 Pine St
- **Battery Maritime Building** • 11 South St
- **Bowling Green** • Broadway & State St
- **Cunard Building** • 25 Broadway
- **Customs House/Museum of the American Indian** • 1 Bowling Green
- **Federal Hall** • 26 Wall St
- **New York Stock Exchange** • 20 Broad St
- **South Street Seaport** • South St
- **St Paul's Chapel & Cemetery** • Broadway & Fulton St
- **The Federal Reserve Bank** • 33 Liberty St
- **Trinity Church & Cemetery** • Broadway & Wall St
- **Vietnam Veterans Plaza** • Coenties Slip & Water St
- **World Trade Center Site** • Church St & Vesey St

Post Offices

- **Bowling Green** • 25 Broadway
- **Wall Street** • 73 Pine St

Schools

- **Drake Business School** • 130 William St
- **High School for Economics and Finance** • 100 Trinity Pl
- **High School for Leadership & Public Service** • 90 Trinity Pl
- **John V Lindsay Wildcat Academy Charter School** • 17 Battery Pl
- **Millenium High School** • 75 Broad St

Supermarkets

- **Associated** • 77 Fulton St
- **Jubilee Marketplace** • 99 John St
- **The Amish Market** • 17 Battery Pl
- **Vine Market** • 25 Broad St
- **Zeytuna** • 59 Maiden Ln

Map 1 • Financial District

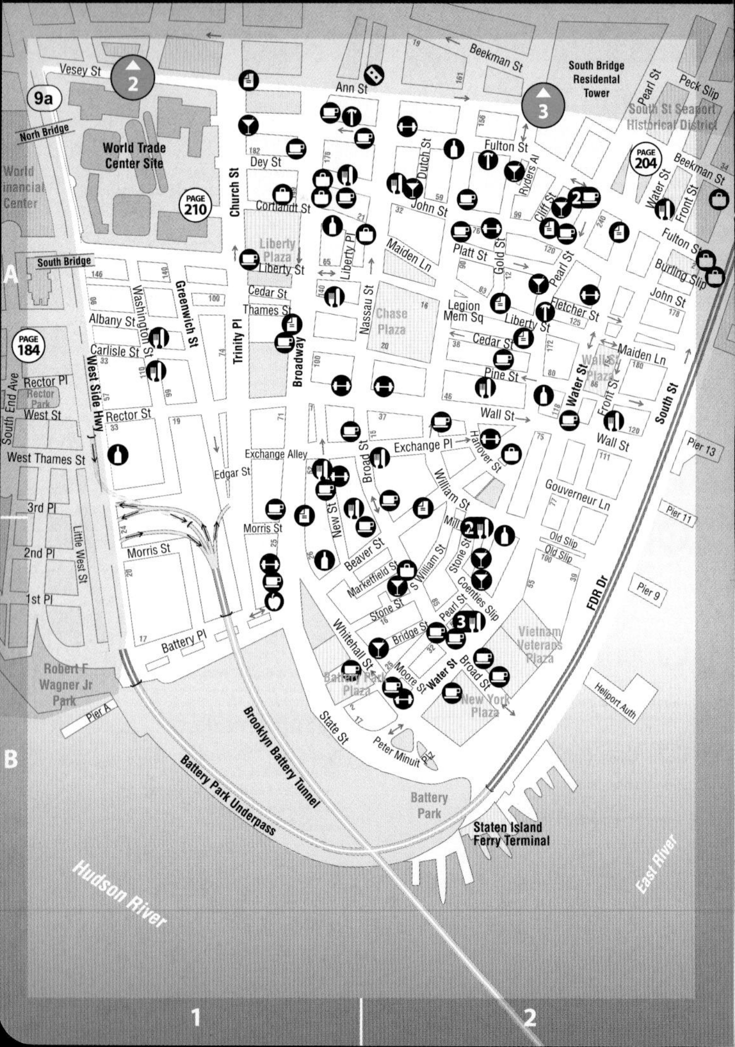

Vesey St
Ann St
Beekman St
South Bridge Residental Tower
Pearl St
Peck Slip
South St Seaport Historical District
9a
Norh Bridge
World Trade Center Site
World Financial Center
Church St
Dey St
Cortlandt St
Dutch St
Fulton St
Ryders Al
John St
Cliff St
Water St
Front St
Beekman St
Fulton St
PAGE 204
PAGE 210
Liberty Plaza
Liberty St
Liberty Pl
Maiden Ln
Platt St
Gold St
Pearl St
Burling Slip
John St
South Bridge
Greenwich St
Washington St
Albany St
Cedar St
Thames St
Trinity Pl
Broadway
Nassau St
Chase Plaza
Legion Mem Sq
Liberty St
Fletcher St
Cedar St
Maiden Ln
Wall St Plaza
Carlisle St
West Side Hwy
PAGE 184
Rector Pl
Rector Park
West St
South End Ave
Rector St
Pine St
Water St
Front St
South St
Wall St
Wall St
Pier 13
Exchange Pl
Hanover St
Exchange Alley
Broad St
West Thames St
Edgar St
William St
Gouverneur Ln
3rd Pl
Morris St
New St
Beaver St
Mill
Pier 11
Old Slip
Old Slip
2nd Pl
Little West St
Morris St
Marketfield St
S William St
Stone St
Coenties Slip
Pier 9
FDR Dr
1st Pl
Stone St
Pearl St
Bridge St
Whitehall St
Moore St
Water St
Broad St
Vietnam Veterans Plaza
Battery Pl
Robert F Wagner Jr Park
Battery Park Plaza
New York Plaza
Heliport Auth
Pier A
State St
Peter Minuit Plz
Brooklyn Battery Tunnel
Battery Park Underpass
Battery Park
Staten Island Ferry Terminal
Hudson River
East River
A
B
1
2

With very few and notable exceptions, everything closes before 8pm, even (especially) on weekends. The Jubilee Market on John Street remains the 24-hour must-go place for prepared foods and groceries, and they deliver if you're too lazy to go out yourself. Zeytuna, also on John Street, is an excellent gourmet grocery/deli, open until 10pm, on weekends as well.

Bars

- **Beckett's Bar & Grill** • 78 Pearl St
- **John Street Bar & Grill** • 17 John St
- **Liquid Assets @ Millennium Hilton Hotel** • 55 Church St
- **Ryan Maguire's Ale House** • 28 Cliff St
- **Ryan's Sports Bar & Restaurant** • 46 Gold St
- **Swan's Bar & Grill** • 213 Pearl St
- **Ulysses** • 95 Pearl St
- **White Horse Tavern** • 25 Bridge St

Coffee

- **Alfanoose** • 150 Fulton St
- **Andrew's Coffee Shop** • 116 John St
- **Au Bon Pain** • 80 Pine St
- **Claudia's Coffee Shop** • 125 Broad St
- **Donna Lynn's Coffee & Espresso Bar** • 30 Water St
- **Dunkin' Donuts** • 139 Fulton St
- **Dunkin' Donuts** • 196 Broadway
- **Dunkin' Donuts** • 20 Broad St/NYSE B1 Cafeteria
- **Dunkin' Donuts** • 29 Broadway
- **Dunkin' Donuts** • 48 New St
- **Dunkin' Donuts** • 50 Fulton St
- **New World Coffee** • 1 Broadway
- **New World Coffee** • 1 New York Plz
- **Pasqua** • 1 Liberty Plz
- **Roxy Coffee Shop** • 20 John St
- **Seattle Coffee Roasters** • 110 William St
- **Starbucks** • 1 Battery Park Plz
- **Starbucks** • 100 Wall St
- **Starbucks** • 100 William St
- **Starbucks** • 115 Broadway
- **Starbucks** • 195 Broadway
- **Starbucks** • 24 Pearl St
- **Starbucks** • 3 New York Plz
- **Starbucks** • 45 Wall St
- **Starbucks** • 55 Broad St

Copy Shops

- **Acro Photo Printing (24 hrs)** • 90 Maiden Ln
- **Big Apple Copy and Printing Center (8 am-6 pm)** • 115 Broadway
- **Complete Mail Centers Inc (8:30 am-7 pm)** • 28 Vesey St
- **Hard Copy Printing Inc (8 am-6 pm)** • 111 John St
- **National Reproductions** • 130 Cedar St
- **Perry Copy Center & Printing (8 am-6 pm)** • 50 Beaver St
- **Sol Speedy (8 am-7 pm)** • 26 Broadway
- **Staples (7 am-7 pm)** • 200 Water St

Farmer's Markets

- **Bowling Green Greenmarket** • Battery Park Pl & Broadway

Gyms

- **Crunch Fitness** • 25 Broadway
- **Equinox Fitness Club** • 14 Wall St
- **John Street Gym** • 80 John St
- **Lucille Roberts Health Club** • 143 Fulton St
- **New York Health & Racquet Club** • 39 Whitehall St
- **New York Sports Clubs** • 160 Water St
- **New York Sports Clubs** • 30 Wall St
- **Wall Street Boxing Fitness** • 76 Beaver St
- **Waterfront Boxing Club** • 44 New St

Hardware Stores

- **Dick's Hardware** • 205 Pearl St
- **Fulton Supply & Hardware** • 74 Fulton St
- **Whitehall Hardware** • 88 Greenwich St
- **Wolff Hardware** • 127 Fulton St

Liquor Stores

- **Famous Wines & Liquor** • 27 William St
- **Famous Wines & Spirits** • 40 Exchange Pl
- **Fulton Wines & Spirits** • 110 Fulton St
- **Maiden Lane Wines & Liquors** • 6 Maiden Ln
- **New York Wine Exchange** • 9 Beaver St
- **Water Street Wine & Spirit** • 79 Pine St
- **West Street Wine & Spirits** • 47 West St

Restaurants

- **Burritoville** • 36 Water St
- **Cassis on Stone** • 52 Stone St
- **Cosi Sandwich Bar** • 54 Pine St
- **Cosi Sandwich Bar** • 55 Broad St
- **Daily Soup** • 41 John St
- **Financier Patisserie** • 62 Stone St
- **Giovanni's Atrium** • 100 Washington St
- **The Grotto** • 69 New St
- **Lemongrass Grill** • 110 Liberty St
- **Les Halles** • 15 John St
- **New York Pizza Factory** • 30 Water St
- **Red** • 14 Fulton St
- **Rosario's** • 38 Pearl St
- **Roy's New York** • 130 Washington St
- **Sophie's** • 205 Pearl St
- **Sophie's** • 73 New St
- **St Maggie's Cafe** • 120 Wall St

Shopping

- **Barclay Rex** • 75 Broad St
- **Century 21** • 22 Cortlandt St
- **Flowers of the World** • 5 Hanover Sq
- **Godiva Chocolatier** • 33 Maiden Ln
- **M. Slavin & Sons** • 106 South St
- **Modell's** • 200 Broadway
- **Radio Shack** • 114 Fulton St
- **Radio Shack** • 75 Maiden Ln
- **South Street Seaport** • 19 Fulton St
- **Strand** • 95 Fulton St
- **The World of Golf** • 189 Broadway
- **Yankees Clubhouse Shop** • 8 Fulton Street

Video Rental

- **Ann St Entertainment** • 21 Ann St

Map 1 • Financial District

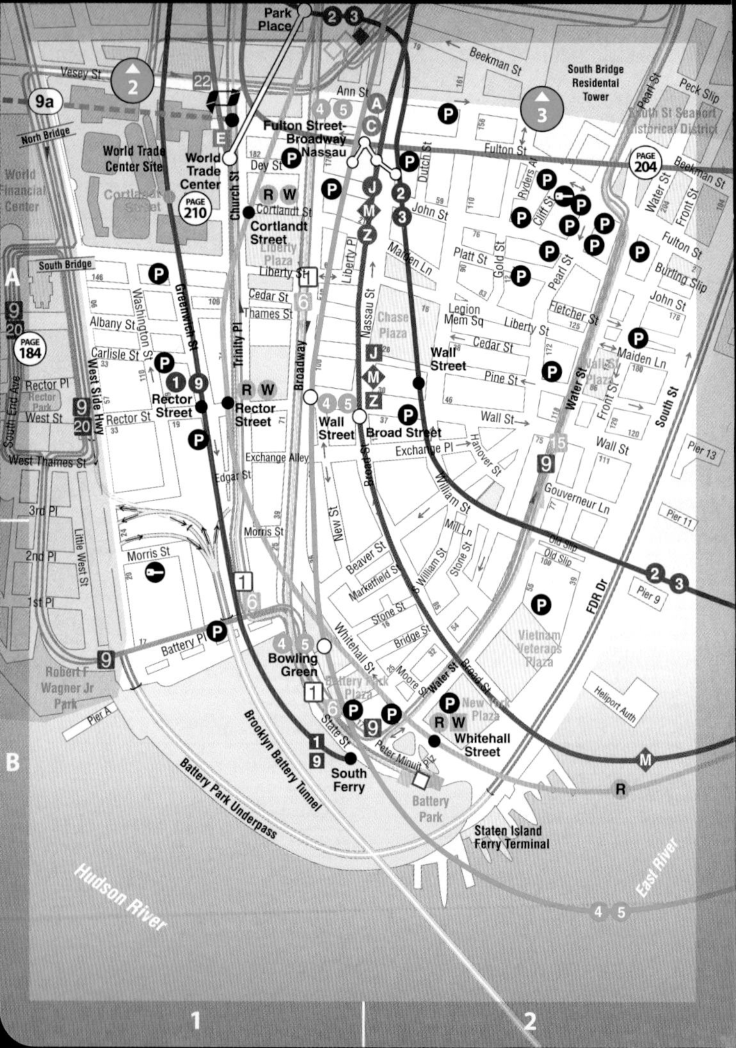

Park Place
Vesey St
Beekman St
South Bridge Residental Tower
Peck Slip
Pearl St
South St Seaport Historical District
9a
North Bridge
Ann St
Fulton Street-Broadway Nassau
Fulton St
World Trade Center Site
World Trade Center
World Financial Center
Cortlandt Street
Dey St
Church St
Cortlandt St
Dutch St
John St
Maiden Ln
Platt St
Gold St
Cliff St
Ryders Al
Water St
Front St
Fulton St
Burling Slip
John St
Liberty St
Liberty Plaza
Liberty Pl
South Bridge
Cedar St
Thames St
Nassau St
Chase Plaza
Legion Mem Sq
Liberty St
Cedar St
Fletcher St
Maiden Ln
Albany St
Washington St
Greenwich St
Trinity Pl
Broadway
Carlisle St
Wall Street
Pine St
Wall St Plaza
Rector Pl
Rector Park
West St
West Side Hwy
South End Ave
Rector Street
Rector St
Rector Street
Wall Street
Broad Street
Wall St
South St
Exchange Alley
Exchange Pl
Hanover St
Wall St
Pier 13
West Thames St
Edgar St
Broad St
New St
William St
Gouverneur Ln
Pier 11
3rd Pl
Morris St
Mill Ln
Old Slip
2nd Pl
Little West St
Morris St
Beaver St
Marketfield St
S William St
Stone St
FDR Dr
Pier 9
1st Pl
Stone St
Bridge St
Battery Pl
Bowling Green
Whitehall St
Moore St
Water St
Broad St
Vietnam Veterans Plaza
Robert F Wagner Jr Park
Battery Park Plaza
New York Plaza
Heliport Auth
Pier A
State St
Peter Minuit Plz
Whitehall Street
Brooklyn Battery Tunnel
South Ferry
Battery Park Underpass
Battery Park
Staten Island Ferry Terminal
Hudson River
East River

PAGE 210
PAGE 184
PAGE 204

1 2

Attempting to drive—or park—during the day down here can be maddening, but you can check out the lots underneath the FDR if you really must drive. Just remember that the fish market is still in business until the end of 2004 and South Street is closed until about 9:30 a.m. Subways are usually your best bet. The PATH Station at the WTC is now re-opened.

Subways

1 9 ...... Rector St
1 9 ...... South Ferry
2 3 ...... Wall St
4 5 ...... Bowling Green
4 5 ...... Wall St
2 3 4 5 A C J M Z ...... Fulton St-Broadway-Nassau St
E ...... World Trade Center
J M Z ...... Broad St
R W ...... Cortlandt St
R W ...... Rector St
R W ...... Whitehall St-South Ferry

PATH

- **World Trade Center Site**

Bus Lines

1 ...... Fifth/Madison Aves
15 ...... First/Second Aves
20 ...... Riverdale/246th St via Henry Hudson Pky
22 ...... Madison/Chambers St
6 ...... Seventh Ave/Broadway/Sixth Ave
9 ...... Ave B/East Broadway

Car Rental

- **Enterprise** • 56 Fulton St
- **Hertz** • 20 Morris St

Parking

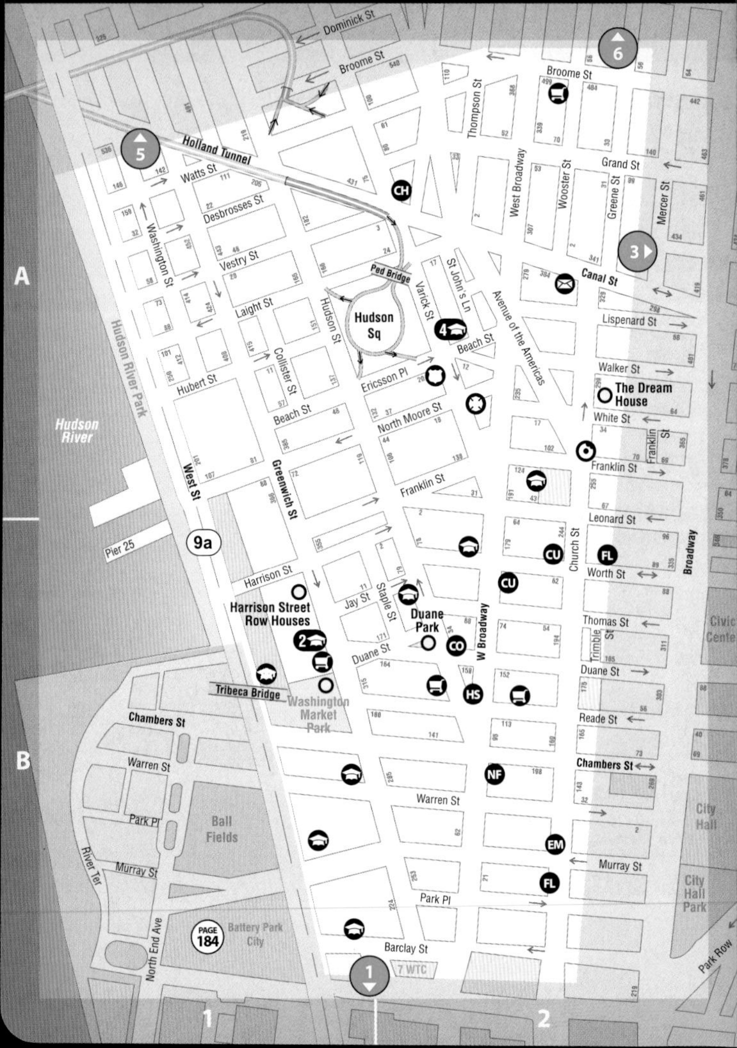

Map 2 • TriBeCa

Dominick St
Broome St
Holland Tunnel
Watts St
Desbrosses St
Vestry St
Laight St
Hubert St
Beach St
North Moore St
Franklin St
Harrison St
Jay St
Duane St
Chambers St
Warren St
Park Pl
Murray St
Barclay St
Washington St
Greenwich St
Hudson St
Collister St
Staple St
Varick St
St John's Ln
Ericsson Pl
Hudson Sq
Ped Bridge
Thompson St
West Broadway
Wooster St
Greene St
Mercer St
Grand St
Canal St
Avenue of the Americas
Lispenard St
Walker St
White St
Franklin St
Leonard St
Worth St
Thomas St
Trimble Pl
Reade St
Church St
W Broadway
Broadway
The Dream House
Harrison Street Row Houses
Duane Park
Washington Market Park
Tribeca Bridge
Ball Fields
Battery Park City
PAGE 184
Hudson River Park
Hudson River
Pier 25
West St
9a
River Ter
North End Ave
7 WTC
Civic Center
City Hall
City Hall Park
Park Row
A
B
1
2

TriBeCa's back—with a vengeance—as even more old warehouse buildings are being converted to multi-million dollar lofts that we can't afford. However, walking around and staring, and then taking a break at sublime Duane Park, keeps us happy for the moment.

ATMs

CH • Chase • 423 Canal St
CO • Commerce Bank • 25 Hudson St
CU • Municipal Credit Union • 40 Worth St
CU • Skyline Federal Credit Union • 32 Sixth Ave
EM • Emigrant • 110 Church St
FL • Fleet • 100 Church St
FL • Fleet • 57 Worth St
HS • HSBC • 110 West Broadway
NF • North Fork Bank • 90 West Broadway

Bagels

• **Bagel Masters** • 275 Church St

Fire Departments

• **Ladder 8** • 14 N Moore St

Landmarks

• **The Dream House** • 275 Church St
• **Duane Park** • Duane St & Hudson St
• **Harrison St Row Houses** • Harrison St & Greenwich St
• **Washington Market Park** • Greenwich St

Police

• **1st Precinct** • 16 Ericsson Pl

Post Offices

• **Canal Street** • 350 Canal St

Schools

• **Adelphi University** • 75 Varick St
• **The Art Institute of New York City** • 11 Beach St
• **Audrey Cohen College** • 75 Varick St
• **Borough of Manhattan Community College** • 199 Chambers St
• **College of Insurance** • 101 Murray St
• **College of New Rochelle DC-37 Campus** • 125 Barclay St
• **Metropolitan College of New York** • 75 Varick St
• **New York Academy of Art** • 111 Franklin St
• **New York Law School** • 57 Worth St
• **PS 150** • 334 Greenwich St
• **PS 234 Independence School** • 292 Greenwich St
• **Tribeca Learning Center** • 334 Greenwich St
• **Washington Market School** • 55 Hudson St

Supermarkets

• **Bell Bates Natural Foods** • 97 Reade St
• **Food Emporium** • 316 Greenwich St
• **Healthy Pleasures** • 489 Broome St
• **Morgan's Market** • 13 Hudson St

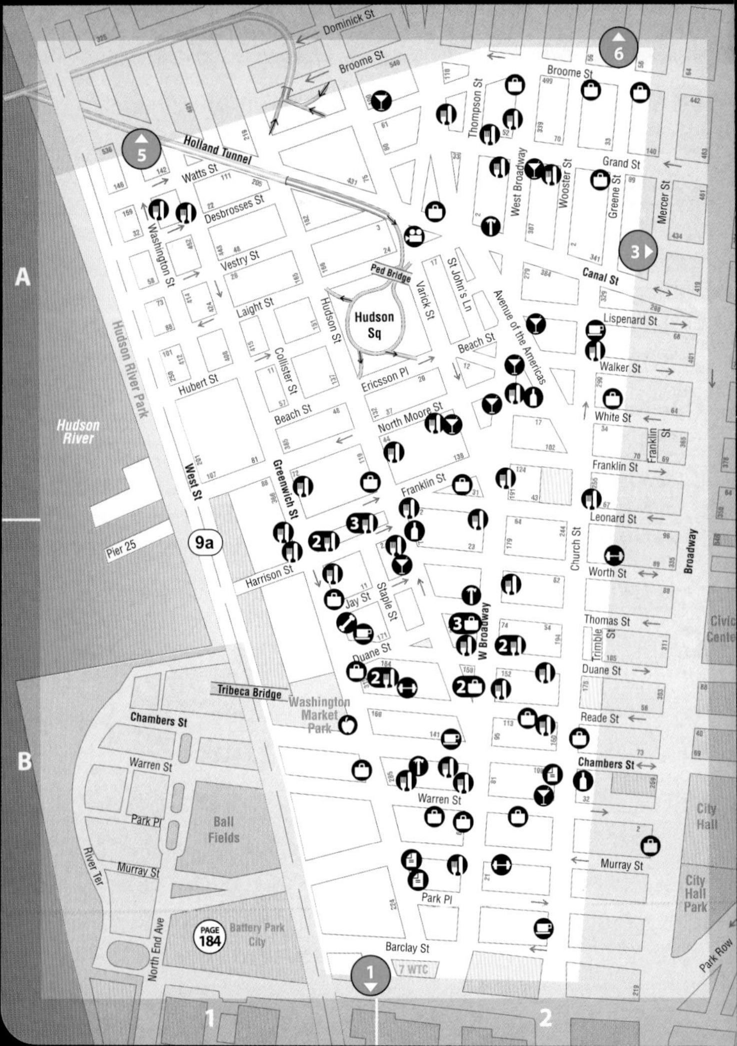

Map 2 • TriBeCa

Dominick St
Broome St
Holland Tunnel
Watts St
Desbrosses St
Vestry St
Laight St
Hubert St
Beach St
North Moore St
Franklin St
Harrison St
Jay St
Duane St
Chambers St
Warren St
Park Pl
Murray St
Barclay St
Thompson St
West Broadway
Wooster St
Greene St
Mercer St
Grand St
Canal St
Lispenard St
Walker St
White St
Franklin St
Leonard St
Worth St
Thomas St
Duane St
Reade St
Chambers St
Murray St
Washington St
Hudson St
Collister St
Greenwich St
Staple St
Varick St
St John's Ln
Avenue of the Americas
Ericsson Pl
Church St
Trimble Pl
Broadway
W Broadway
West St
Hudson Sq
Ped Bridge
Hudson River Park
Hudson River
Pier 25
9a
Tribeca Bridge
Washington Market Park
River Ter
North End Ave
Ball Fields
Battery Park City
7 WTC
Civic Center
City Hall
City Hall Park
Park Row
A
B
1
2

PAGE 184

For arts, Tribeca rocks—the film festival every year, the MELA Foundation's "Dream House," several galleries, and experimental music at Roulette. Stalwart bars such as Puffy's and Walker's can effectively wet your whistle while you're waiting to win the lotto so you can eat at Nobu.

Bars

- **Bubble Lounge** • 228 West Broadway
- **Circa Tabac** • 32 Watts St
- **Lucky Strike** • 59 Grand St
- **Nancy Whisky Pub** • 1 Lispenard St
- **Puffy's Tavern** • 81 Hudson St
- **Raccoon Lodge** • 59 Warren St
- **Tribeca Tavern** • 247 West Broadway
- **Walker's** • 16 N Moore St

Coffee

- **Downtown Delicious** • 327 Greenwich St
- **Starbucks** • 100 Church St
- **Starbucks** • 125 Chambers St
- **Westside Coffee Shop II** • 323 Church St

Copy Shops

- **City Copies Inc (8 am-7 pm)** • 158 Church St
- **Jean Paul Duplicating Center (8:30 am-7 pm)** • 275 Greenwich St
- **Mail Boxes Etc (8 am-7 pm)** • 295 Greenwich St

Farmer's Markets

- **Tribeca/Washington Market Park Greenmarket** • Chambers St & Greenwich St

Gyms

- **Equinox Fitness Club** • 54 Murray St
- **New York Sports Clubs** • 151 Reade St
- **Tribeca Gym** • 79 Worth St

Hardware Stores

- **Ace Hardware** • 160 West Broadway
- **CNL** • 378 Canal St
- **Tribeca Hardware** • 154 Chambers St

Liquor Stores

- **Brite Buy Wines & Spirits** • 11 Sixth Ave
- **Chambers Street Wines** • 160 Chambers St
- **City Hall Wines & Spirits** • 108 Chambers St
- **Downtown Liquor Store** • 90 Hudson St
- **Tribeca Wine Merchants** • 40 Hudson St
- **Vintage New York** • 482 Broome St

Movie Theaters

- **Tribeca Cinemas** • 54 Varick St

Pet Shops

- **Dudley's Paw** • 327 Greenwich St

Restaurants

- **A&M Roadhouse** • 57 Murray St
- **Bread Tribeca** • 301 Church St
- **Bubby's** • 120 Hudson St
- **Burritoville** • 144 Chambers St
- **Cafe Noir** • 32 Grand St
- **Capsuoto Freres** • 451 Washington St
- **Chanterelle** • 2 Harrison St
- **City Hall** • 131 Duane St
- **Danube** • 30 Hudson St
- **Duane Park Cafe** • 157 Duane St
- **Edward's** • 136 West Broadway
- **Felix** • 340 West Broadway
- **Flor de Sol** • 361 Greenwich St
- **Fresh** • 105 Reade St
- **The Harrison** • 355 Greenwich St
- **Il Giglio** • 81 Warren St
- **Kitchenette** • 80 West Broadway
- **Kori** • 253 Church St
- **Layla** • 211 West Broadway
- **Le Zinc** • 139 Duane St
- **Lucky Strike** • 59 Grand St
- **Lupe's East LA Kitchen** • 110 Sixth Ave
- **Montrachet** • 239 West Broadway
- **Nobu** • 105 Hudson St
- **Nobu, Next Door** • 105 Hudson St
- **Odeon** • 145 West Broadway
- **Palacinka** • 28 Grand St
- **Petite Abeille** • 134 West Broadway
- **Roc** • 190 Duane St
- **Salaam Bombay** • 317 Greenwich St
- **Sosa Borella** • 460 Greenwich St
- **The Sporting Club** • 99 Hudson St
- **Thalassa** • 179 Franklin St
- **Tribeca Grill** • 375 Greenwich St
- **Walker's** • 16 N Moore St
- **Yaffa's** • 353 Greenwich St
- **Zutto** • 77 Hudson St

Shopping

- **Assets London** • 152 Franklin St
- **Balloon Saloon** • 133 West Broadway
- **Bazzini** • 330 Greenwich St
- **Bell Bates Natural Food** • 97 Reade St
- **Boffi SoHo** • 31 1/2 Greene St
- **Canal Street Bicycles** • 417 Canal St
- **Commodities** • 117 Hudson St
- **Duane Park Patisserie** • 179 Duane St
- **Gotham Bikes** • 112 West Broadway
- **Jack Spade** • 56 Greene St
- **Janovic Plaza** • 136 Church St
- **Kings Pharmacy** • 5 Hudson St
- **Korin Japanese Trading** • 57 Warren St
- **Let There Be Neon** • 38 White St
- **Liberty Souveniers** • 275 Greenwich St
- **MarieBelle's Fine Treats & Chocolates** • 484 Broome St
- **New York Nautical** • 140 West Broadway
- **Oliver Peoples** • 366 West Broadway
- **Shoofly** • 42 Hudson St
- **Stern's Music** • 71 Warren St
- **We Are Nuts About Nuts** • 165 Church St
- **Willner Chemists** • 253 Broadway

Map 2 • TriBeCa

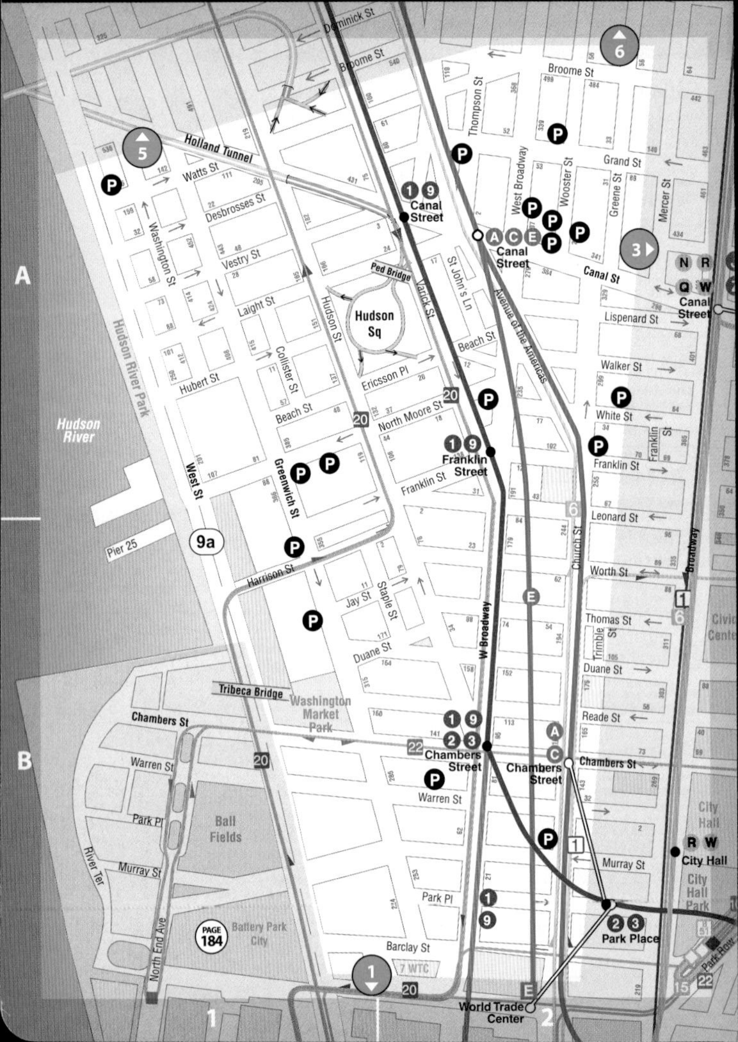

Hudson River
Hudson River Park
Pier 25
West St
Washington St
Greenwich St
Hudson St
Varick St
Holland Tunnel
Watts St
Desbrosses St
Vestry St
Laight St
Hubert St
Collister St
Beach St
North Moore St
Franklin St
Harrison St
Jay St
Staple St
Duane St
Hudson Sq
Ped Bridge
Ericsson Pl
St John's Ln
Avenue of the Americas
West Broadway
W Broadway
Thompson St
Wooster St
Greene St
Mercer St
Broome St
Grand St
Canal St
Dominick St
Lispenard St
Walker St
White St
Leonard St
Worth St
Thomas St
Trimble Pl
Reade St
Chambers St
Church St
Broadway
Franklin Pl
Warren St
Park Pl
Murray St
Barclay St
River Ter
North End Ave
Tribeca Bridge
Washington Market Park
Ball Fields
Battery Park City
7 WTC
City Hall
City Hall Park
Civic Center
Park Row
Canal Street
Franklin Street
Chambers Street
Park Place
World Trade Center
City Hall

PAGE 184

Transportation

Moving around and parking in Tribeca, especially in its northwest corner, isn't too bad, but the closer you get to City Hall and the WTC site, the more of a pain it is to find anything, especially during the week. But it's still a lot better than many other NYC neighborhoods.

Subways

2 3 .... Park Pl
1 2 3 9 .... Chambers St
1 9 .... Canal St
1 9 .... Franklin St
A C .... Chambers St
A C E .... Canal St
R W .... City Hall

Bus Lines

1 .... Broadway
20 .... Abingdon Sq
22 .... Seventh Ave/Sixth Ave/Broadway
6 .... Seventh Ave/Broadway/Sixth Ave
9 .... Ave B/East Broadway

P Parking

Map 3 • City Hall / Chinatown

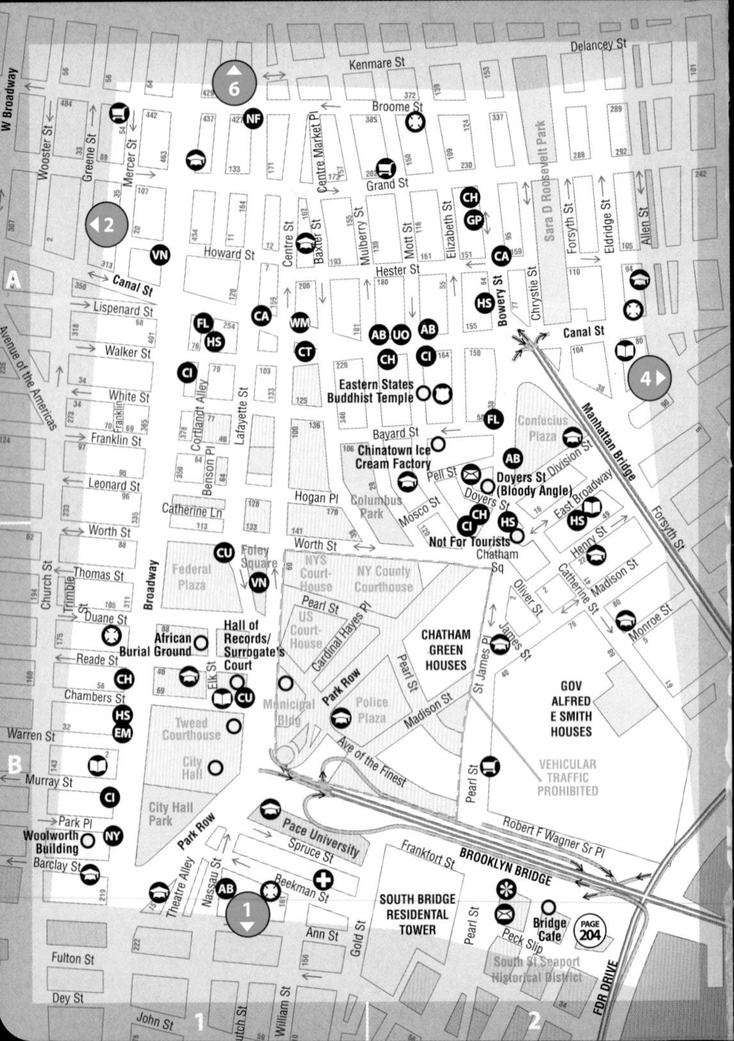

The post office on Doyers Street always has a hellish line—it's worth going somewhere else. The area's great civic architecture includes the Municipal Building, the Surrogate's Court, Foley Square, and City Hall Park. Canal Street is the major tourist area, but it's where I buy my $10 knock-offs.

ATMs

AB • **Abacus** • 116 Nassau St
AB • **Abacus** • 181 Canal St
AB • **Abacus** • 6 Bowery
NY • **Bank of New York** • 233 Broadway
CH • **Chase** • 180 Canal St
CH • **Chase** • 2 Bowery
CH • **Chase** • 231 Grand St
CH • **Chase** • 280 Broadway
CT • **Chinatrust Bank** • 208 Canal St
CA • **Chinese American Bank** • 245 Canal St
CA • **Chinese American Bank** • 77 Bowery
CI • **Citibank** • 164 Canal St
CI • **Citibank** • 2 Mott St
CI • **Citibank** • 250 Broadway
CI • **Citibank** • 396 Broadway
EM • **Emigrant** • 261 Broadway
FL • **Fleet** • 260 Canal St
FL • **Fleet** • 50 Bayard St
GP • **Greenpoint Bank** • 116 Bowery
HS • **HSBC** • 17 Chatham Sq
HS • **HSBC** • 254 Canal St
HS • **HSBC** • 265 Broadway
HS • **HSBC** • 27 East Broadway
HS • **HSBC** • 58 Bowery
CU • **Municipal Credit Union** • 2 Lafayette St
NF • **North Fork Bank** • 200 Lafayette St
UO • **United Orient Bank** • 185 Canal St
CU • **US Courthouse Federal Credit Union** • 40 Foley Sq
VN • **Valley National Bank** • 434 Broadway
WM • **Washington Mutual** • 221 Canal St

Community Gardens

Fire Departments

- **Engine 55** • 363 Broome St
- **Engine 6** • 49 Beekman St
- **Engine 7, Ladder 1** • 100 Duane St
- **Engine 9, Ladder 6** • 75 Canal St

Hospitals

- **NYU Downtown Hospital** • 170 William St

Landmarks

- **African Burial Ground** • Duane St & Broadway
- **Bridge Cafe** • 279 Water St
- **Chinatown Ice Cream Factory** • 65 Bayard St
- **City Hall** • Park Row & Broadway
- **Doyers St (Bloody Angle)** • Doyers St
- **Eastern States Buddhist Temple** • 64 Mott St
- **Hall of Records / Surrogate's Court** • Chambers St & Park Row
- **Happy Mazza Media** • 2 East Broadway
- **Municipal Building** • Chambers St & Park Row
- **Tweed Courthouse** • Chambers St & Broadway
- **Woolworth Building** • 233 Broadway

Libraries

- **Chatham Square** • 33 East Broadway
- **New Amsterdam** • 9 Murray St
- **NYC Municipal Archives** • 31 Chambers St

Police

- **5th Precinct** • 19 Elizabeth St

Post Offices

- **Canal Street Retail** • 6 Doyers St
- **Peck Slip** • 1 Peck Slip

Schools

- **French Culinary Institute** • 462 Broadway
- **IS 131 Dr Sun Yat Sen School** • 100 Hester St
- **Murray Bergtraum High School** • 411 Pearl St
- **New York Career Institute** • 15 Park Row
- **NYU School of Continuing and Professional Studies** • 14 Barclay St
- **Pace University** • 1 Pace Plz
- **PS 001 Alfred E Smith School** • 8 Henry St
- **PS 124 Yung Wing School** • 40 Division St
- **PS 130 DeSoto School** • 143 Baxter St
- **St James School** • 37 St James Pl
- **St Joseph School** • 1 Monroe St
- **Transfiguration RC School** • 29 Mott St

Supermarkets

- **C-Town** • 5 St James Pl
- **Dom's Fine Foods** • 202 Lafayette St
- **Gourmet Garage** • 453 Broome St
- **Italian Food Center** • 186 Grand St

Kenmare St
Delancey St
Broome St
Grand St
Howard St
Hester St
Canal St
Lispenard St
Walker St
White St
Franklin St
Leonard St
Worth St
Thomas St
Duane St
Reade St
Chambers St
Warren St
Murray St
Park Pl
Barclay St
Fulton St
Dey St
John St
W Broadway
Wooster St
Greene St
Mercer St
Centre St
Centre Market Pl
Baxter St
Mulberry St
Mott St
Elizabeth St
Bowery St
Chrystie St
Sara D Roosevelt Park
Forsyth St
Eldridge St
Allen St
Avenue of the Americas
Church St
Trimble Pl
Broadway
Franklin Pl
Cortlandt Alley
Benson Pl
Lafayette St
Catherine Ln
Hogan Pl
Columbus Park
Bayard St
Pell St
Doyers St
Mosco St
Chatham Sq
Confucius Plaza
Division St
East Broadway
Manhattan Bridge
Henry St
Catherine St
Madison St
Monroe St
Oliver St
James St
St James Pl
Federal Plaza
Foley Square
NYS Court-House
NY County Courthouse
Pearl St
US Court-House
Cardinal Hayes Pl
Park Row
Elk St
Municipal Bldg
Police Plaza
Madison St
CHATHAM GREEN HOUSES
GOV ALFRED E SMITH HOUSES
VEHICULAR TRAFFIC PROHIBITED
Tweed Courthouse
City Hall
City Hall Park
Ave of the Finest
Robert F Wagner Sr Pl
Pace University
Spruce St
Frankfort St
BROOKLYN BRIDGE
Beekman St
SOUTH BRIDGE RESIDENTAL TOWER
Theatre Alley
Nassau St
Ann St
Gold St
Peck Slip
South St Seaport Historical District
FDR DRIVE
Dutch St
William St

PAGE 204

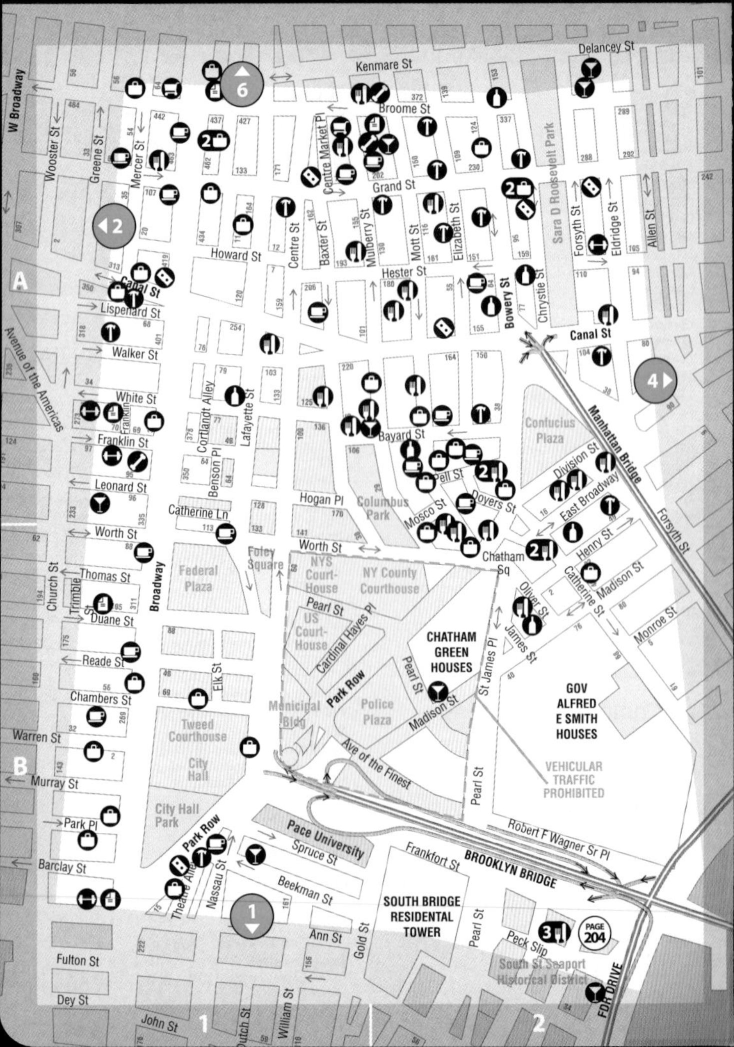

If you haven't had the crab soup dumplings at Joe's Shanghai on Pell Street, you should. Our favorite Vietnamese is Nha Trang, our favorite Thai is Thailand Restaurant; our favorite Malaysian is now closed; and our favorite Italian is Il Palazzo. If you're not in the mood for Asian or Italian cuisine, you're in the wrong area. While The Bowery is still the epicenter for discount kitchen supplies and lighting fixtures, more and more clubs keep sprouting up, complete with limos, burly bouncers, and red velvet ropes.

Bars

- **Beekman, The** • 15 Beekman St
- **Double Happiness** • 173 Mott St
- **Happy Ending** • 302 Broome St
- **Knitting Factory** • 74 Leonard St
- **Metropolitan Improvement Company** • 3 Madison St
- **Milk & Honey** • 134 Eldridge St
- **Paris Cafe** • 119 South St
- **Winnie's** • 104 Bayard St

Coffee

- **Cafe Palermo** • 148 Mulberry St
- **Dunkin' Donuts** • 321 Broadway
- **Ferrara Cafe** • 195 Grand St
- **Green Tea Café** • 45 Mott St
- **Ho Wong Coffee House** • 146 Hester St
- **Kam Hing Coffee Shop** • 119 Baxter St
- **Le Pain Quotidien** • 100 Grand St
- **Maria's Bakery** • 148 Lafayette St
- **Maria's Bakery** • 42 Mott St
- **Mee Sum Coffee Shop** • 26 Pell St
- **Mei Lai Wah Coffee House** • 64 Bayard St
- **Mini Coffee Shop** • 94 Chambers St
- **Nom Wah Tea Parlor** • 13 Doyers St
- **Sambuca's Cafe & Desserts** • 105 Mulberry St
- **Starbucks** • 111 Worth St
- **Starbucks** • 291 Broadway
- **Starbucks** • 38 Park Row
- **Starbucks** • 471 Broadway

Copy Shops

- **Blumberg Excelsior Copy (8:45 am-5 pm)** • 66 White St
- **Kinko's** • 105 Duane St
- **Soho Reprographics (8:30 am-7 pm)** • 381 Broome St
- **Staples (7 am-7 pm)** • 217 Broadway
- **Staples (7 am-7 pm)** • 488 Broadway

Gyms

- **Eastern Athletic / Tribeca Gym** • 80 Leonard St
- **New York Sports Clubs** • 217 Broadway
- **Peter Anthony Fitness** • 39 White St
- **YMCA Chinatown** • 100 Hester St

Hardware Stores

- **CK&L Hardware** • 307 Canal St
- **Carl Martinez Hardware** • 88 Canal St
- **Chinatown 25 Cents Store** • 7 Elizabeth St
- **Design Source** • 115 Bowery
- **East Broadway Appliance Hardware** • 59 East Broadway
- **General Machinery** • 358 Broome St
- **Lendy Electric Equipment** • 182 Grand St
- **Nelson Hardware** • 88 Elizabeth St
- **OK Hardware** • 438 Broome St
- **T&Y Hardware** • 101 Chrystie St
- **Walker Supply** • 61 Walker St
- **Weinstein & Holtzman** • 29 Park Row
- **World Construction** • 78 Forsyth St

Liquor Stores

- **Bowery Discount Wine & Liquors** • 133 Bowery
- **Chez Choi Liquor & Wine** • 49 Chrystie St
- **Mark's Wine & Spirits** • 53 Mott St
- **Royal Wine & Liquor Store** • 45 Madison St
- **Sun Wai Liquor Store** • 17 East Broadway
- **Walker Liquors** • 101 Lafayette St
- **Wine Wo Liquor Discount** • 24 Bowery

Pet Shops

- **Aqua Star Pet Shop** • 172 Mulberry St
- **Win Tropical Aquariums** • 169 Mott St

Restaurants

- **Bridge Cafe** • 279 Water St
- **Canton** • 45 Division St
- **Cup & Saucer** • 89 Canal St
- **Dim Sum Go Go** • 5 East Broadway
- **Excellent Dumpling House** • 111 Lafayette St
- **Ferrara** • 195 Grand St
- **Fuleen's** • 11 Division St
- **Goody's** • 1 East Broadway
- **Il Palazzo** • 151 Mulberry St
- **Joe's Shanghai** • 9 Pell St
- **Le Pain Quotidien** • 100 Grand St
- **Lily's** • 31 Oliver St
- **Mandarin Court** • 61 Mott St
- **Mark Joseph Steakhouse** • 261 Water St
- **New York Noodle Town** • 28 1/2 Bowery
- **Nha Trang** • 87 Baxter St
- **Pho Viet Huong** • 73 Mulberry St
- **Ping's** • 22 Mott St
- **Positano Ristorante** • 122 Mulberry St
- **Quartino** • 21 Peck Slip
- **Thailand Restaurant** • 106 Bayard St
- **Triple Eight Palace** • 88 East Broadway
- **Umberto's Clam House** • 129 Mulberry St
- **Vegetarian Paradise** • 33 Mott St
- **Wo Hop** • 17 Mott St

Shopping

- **Aji Ichiban** • 37 Mott St
- **Bangkok Center Grocery** • 104 Mosco St
- **Bloomingdale's** • 504 Broadway
- **Bowery Lighting** • 132 Bowery
- **Catherine Street Meat Market** • 21 Catherine St
- **Chinatown Ice Cream Factory** • 65 Bayard St
- **Fountain Pen Hospital** • 10 Warren St
- **GS Food Market** • 250 Grand St
- **Hong Kong Seafood & Meat** • 75 Mulberry St
- **Industrial Plastic Supply** • 309 Canal St
- **J&R** • 33 Park Row
- **Kam Kuo** • 7 Mott St
- **Kate Spade** • 454 Broome St
- **Lung Moon Bakery** • 83 Mulberry St
- **Mitchell's Place** • 15 Park Pl
- **Modell's** • 55 Chambers St
- **New Age Designer** • 38 Mott St
- **The New York City Store** • 1 Centre St
- **Pearl Paint** • 308 Canal St
- **Pearl River Mart** • 477 Broadway
- **Radio Shack** • 280 Broadway
- **SoHo Art Materials** • 127 Grand St
- **Tan My My Market** • 253 Grand St
- **Tent & Trails** • 21 Park Pl
- **Ting's Gift Shop** • 18 Doyers St
- **Two Lines Music** • 370 Broadway
- **Vespa** • 13 Crosby St
- **Yellow Rat Bastard** • 478 Broadway

Video Rental

- **323 Canal Video** • 323 Canal St
- **Charming Video** • 200 Centre St
- **J&R** • 23 Park Row
- **Laser Video Center** • 97 Chrystie St
- **Terence Video** • 282 Grand St

Map 3 • City Hall / Chinatown

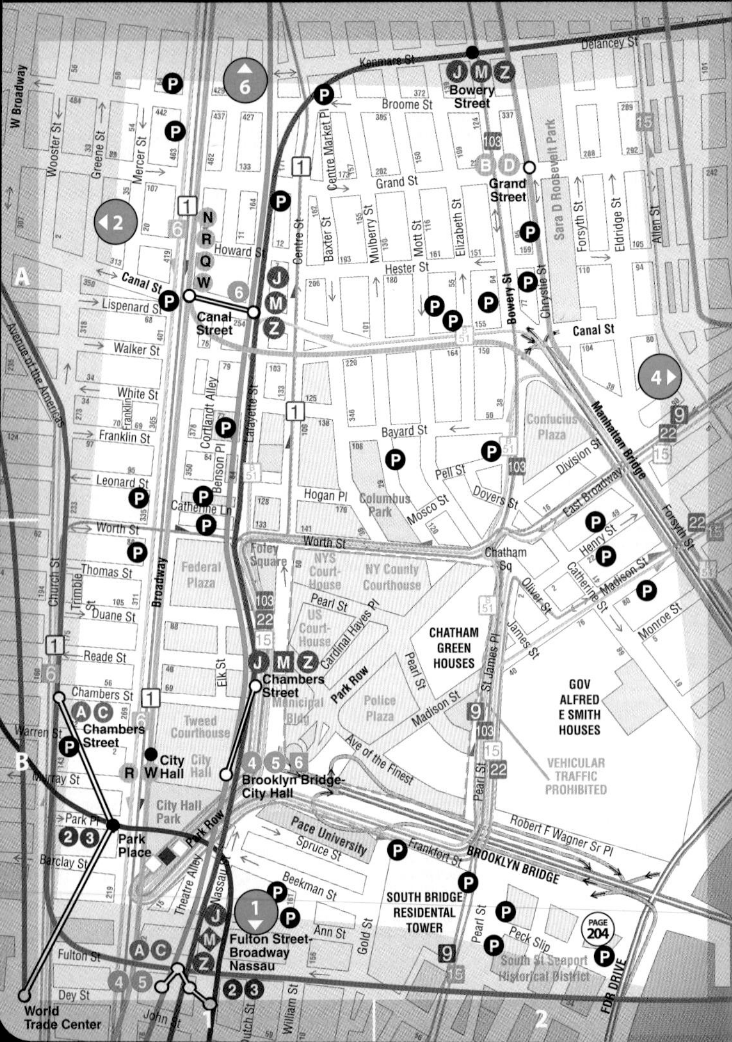

Delancey St
Kenmare St
Bowery Street
Broome St
W Broadway
Wooster St
Greene St
Mercer St
Grand St
Grand Street
Centre Market Pl
Sara D Roosevelt Park
Forsyth St
Eldridge St
Allen St
Howard St
Centre St
Baxter St
Mulberry St
Mott St
Elizabeth St
Hester St
Bowery St
Chrystie St
Canal St
Lispenard St
Canal Street
Walker St
White St
Franklin St
Cortlandt Alley
Lafayette St
Avenue of the Americas
Confucius Plaza
Manhattan Bridge
Bayard St
Division St
Pell St
Doyers St
East Broadway
Leonard St
Benson Pl
Hogan Pl
Columbus Park
Mosco St
Catherine Ln
Worth St
Henry St
Forsyth St
Chatham Sq
Foley Square
NYS Court-House
NY County Courthouse
Federal Plaza
Thomas St
Church St
Trimble St
Broadway
Duane St
Pearl St
US Court-House
Cardinal Hayes Pl
Oliver St
Catherine St
Madison St
Monroe St
CHATHAM GREEN HOUSES
James St
St James Pl
Reade St
Elk St
Chambers Street
Park Row
Pearl St
Chambers St
Municipal Bldg
Police Plaza
Madison St
GOV ALFRED E SMITH HOUSES
Tweed Courthouse
Warren St
Chambers Street
City Hall
Brooklyn Bridge-City Hall
Ave of the Finest
VEHICULAR TRAFFIC PROHIBITED
Murray St
City Hall Park
Pearl St
Robert F Wagner Sr Pl
Park Pl
Park Place
Park Row
Pace University
Spruce St
Frankfort St
BROOKLYN BRIDGE
Barclay St
Theatre Alley
Nassau St
Beekman St
SOUTH BRIDGE RESIDENTAL TOWER
Ann St
Gold St
Pearl St
Peck Slip
PAGE 204
South St Seaport Historical District
FDR DRIVE
Fulton St
Fulton Street-Broadway Nassau
Dey St
World Trade Center
John St
Dutch St
William St

The Brooklyn Bridge is best approached from Pearl Street. Be careful about driving east on Canal Street—you have to make a right on Bowery or else you'll drive over the Manhattan Bridge. (Canal Street is one-way going west between Bowery and Chrystie.) Forget about street parking during the day. Subways are running over the Manhattan Bridge again, meaning the end of the Grand St. shuttle, among other changes.

Subways

2 3 .... Park Pl
4 5 6 J M Z .... Brooklyn Bridge-City Hall-Chambers St
B D .... Grand St
6 J M Z N Q R W .... Canal St
R W .... City Hall
J M Z .... Bowery St
A C .... Chambers St
J M Z .... Fulton St/Broadway

Bus Lines

1 .... Broadway/Centre St
103 ....Bowery/Park Row
15 .... East Broadway/Park Row
22 .... Chambers/Madison St
6 .... Church St/Broadway
9 .... Park Row
B51 .... Lafayette/Canal Sts

Parking

Map 4 • Lower East Side

Essentials

The modern Lower East Side is an interesting mishmash of New York cultures, with the spillover from Chinatown abutting hipster-ville abutting bodega-ville, with the remnants of the Jewish population mixed in. Kossar's Bialys on Grand Street between Essex and Norfolk makes the best bialys ever, period. Check out Hong Kong Supermarket for Asian specialties.

ATMs

CI • Citibank • 411 Grand St
EM • Emigrant • 465 Grand St
FL • Fleet • 318 Grand St
CB • New York Community Bank • 227 Cherry St
WM • Washington Mutual • 270 East Broadway

Bagels

• **Kossar's Bagels and Bialys** • 367 Grand St
• **Toaster Bagel** • 197 Madison St

Community Gardens

Fire Departments

• **Engine 15** • 269 Henry St
• **Ladder 18** • 25 Pitt St

Hospitals

• **Gouverneur Hospital** • 227 Madison St

Landmarks

• **Bialystoker Synagogue** • 7 Bialystoker Pl
• **Eldridge St Synagogue** • 12 Eldridge St
• **Gouverneur Hospital** • Gouverneur Slip & Water St
• **Lower East Side Tenement Museum** • 90 Orchard St

Libraries

• **Seward Park** • 192 East Broadway

24-Hour Pharmacies

• **Rite Aid** • 408 Grand St

Police

• **7th Precinct** • 19 1/2 Pitt St

Post Offices

• **Knickerbocker** • 128 East Broadway
• **Pitt Station** • 185 Clinton St

Schools

• **Beth Jacob Parochial School** • 142 Broome St
• **JHS 056 Corlears School** • 220 Henry St
• **MCSS Day School** • 323 Grand St
• **Mesivta Tifereth Jerusalem** • 145 East Broadway
• **PS 002 Meyer London School** • 122 Henry St
• **PS 042 Benjamin Altman School** • 71 Hester St
• **PS 126 Jacob Riis School** • 80 Catherine St
• **PS 134 Henrietta Szold School** • 293 East Broadway
• **PS 137 John L Bernstein School** • 327 Cherry St
• **Seward Park High School** • 350 Grand St
• **University Neighborhood High School** • 200 Monroe St

Supermarkets

• **Pathmark** • 227 Cherry St

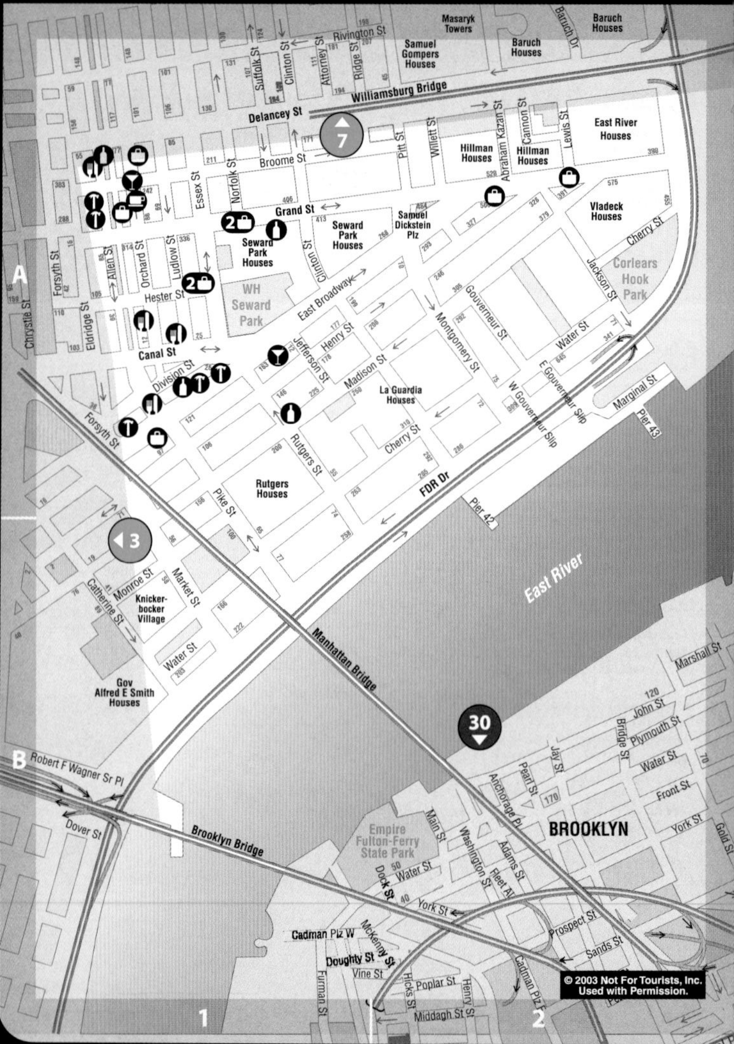

Map 4 • Lower East Side

Rivington St
Delancey St
Williamsburg Bridge
Broome St
Grand St
Hester St
Canal St
Division St
East Broadway
Henry St
Madison St
Cherry St
Water St
FDR Dr
Monroe St
Market St
Catherine St
Pike St
Rutgers St
Jefferson St
Montgomery St
Gouverneur St
Jackson St
Marginal St
Essex St
Norfolk St
Suffolk St
Clinton St
Attorney St
Ridge St
Pitt St
Willett St
Abraham Kazan St
Cannon St
Lewis St
Baruch Dr
Orchard St
Ludlow St
Allen St
Eldridge St
Forsyth St
Chrystie St
E Gouverneur Slip
W Gouverneur Slip
Pier 42
Pier 43
Masaryk Towers
Samuel Gompers Houses
Baruch Houses
East River Houses
Hillman Houses
Vladeck Houses
Seward Park Houses
Samuel Dickstein Plz
Corlears Hook Park
WH Seward Park
La Guardia Houses
Rutgers Houses
Knickerbocker Village
Gov Alfred E Smith Houses
East River
Manhattan Bridge
Brooklyn Bridge
Robert F Wagner Sr Pl
Dover St
BROOKLYN
Empire Fulton-Ferry State Park
Marshall St
John St
Plymouth St
Front St
York St
Bridge St
Jay St
Pearl St
Anchorage Pl
Main St
Washington St
Adams St
Fleet Al
Dock St
Prospect St
Sands St
Cadman Plz W
Cadman Plz E
McKenny St
Doughty St
Vine St
Hicks St
Poplar St
Henry St
Middagh St
Furman St
Gold St

Sundries / Entertainment

One key destination on the Lower East Side is Good World, a fabulous bar with excellent Scandinavian food. For great Jewish staples such as chocolate babka and sour pickles, check out Gertel's Bake Shop and Guss' Pickles, respectively.

Bars

- **Bar 169** • 169 East Broadway
- **Lolita** • 266 Broome St

Coffee

- **88 Orchard** • 88 Orchard St

Hardware Stores

- **Fung Chung Hardware** • 154 East Broadway
- **International Electrical** • 77 Allen St
- **Karlee Hardware** • 98 East Broadway
- **New York Home Center** • 71 Allen St
- **Weilgus & Sons** • 158 East Broadway

Liquor Stores

- **Madison Liquor** • 195 Madison St
- **Seward Park Liquors** • 393 Grand St
- **Wedding Banquet Liquor** • 135 Division St
- **Wing Tak Liquor** • 101 Allen St

Restaurants

- **Congee Village** • 100 Allen St
- **Good World Bar & Grill** • 3 Orchard St
- **Les Enfants Terribles** • 37 Canal St
- **Pho Bang** • 3 Pike St

Shopping

- **Doughnut Plant** • 379 Grand St
- **Frank's Bike Shop** • 553 Grand St
- **Gertel's Bake Shop** • 53 Hester St
- **Guss' Pickles** • 85 Orchard St
- **Hong Kong Supermarket** • 109 East Broadway
- **Joe's Fabric Warehouse** • 102 Orchard St
- **Kossar's Bialys** • 367 Grand St
- **Moishe's Kosher Bake Shop** • 504 Grand St
- **Sweet Life** • 63 Hester St

Map 4 • Lower East Side

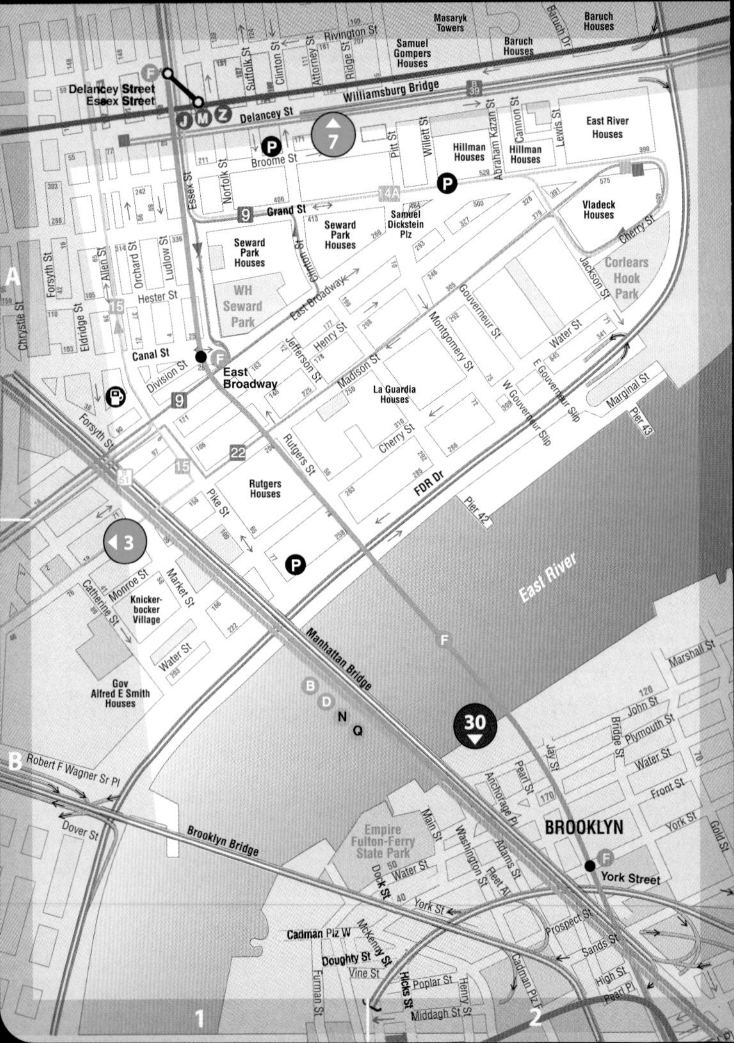

Rivington St
Masaryk Towers
Baruch Dr
Baruch Houses
Samuel Gompers Houses
Baruch Houses
Suffolk St
Clinton St
Attorney St
Ridge St
Delancey Street Essex Street
Williamsburg Bridge
Delancey St
East River Houses
Pitt St
Willett St
Abraham Kazan St
Cannon St
Lewis St
Hillman Houses
Hillman Houses
Broome St
Essex St
Norfolk St
Grand St
Seward Park Houses
Seward Park Houses
Samuel Dickstein Plz
Vladeck Houses
Cherry St
Jackson St
Corlears Hook Park
Forsyth St
Allen St
Orchard St
Ludlow St
Clinton St
WH Seward Park
Chrystie St
Eldridge St
Hester St
East Broadway
Gouverneur St
Montgomery St
Water St
Henry St
Jefferson St
Canal St
East Broadway
Division St
Madison St
E Gouverneur Slip
W Gouverneur Slip
La Guardia Houses
Marginal St
Pier 43
Forsyth St
Rutgers St
Cherry St
FDR Dr
Rutgers Houses
Pike St
Pier 42
East River
Monroe St
Market St
Catherine St
Knickerbocker Village
Water St
Gov Alfred E Smith Houses
Manhattan Bridge
Marshall St
John St
Plymouth St
Bridge St
Water St
Jay St
Pearl St
Anchorage Pl
Front St
Robert F Wagner Sr Pl
York St
BROOKLYN
Gold St
Dover St
Brooklyn Bridge
Empire Fulton-Ferry State Park
Main St
Washington St
Adams St
Fleet Al
York Street
Water St
Dock St
York St
Prospect St
Cadman Plz W
McKenny St
Sands St
Doughty St
Vine St
Cadman Plz E
High St
Furman St
Hicks St
Poplar St
Henry St
Pearl Pl
Middagh St

Take advantage of the reconstructed East River Esplanade off of South Street if you're biking, skating, or walking—it's got the best views of the bridges. The Williamsburg Bridge is now pretty much totally open for business, with a lovely new pedestrian/bike path to boot.

Subways

F .... East Broadway
F .... York St
F J M Z .... Delancey St-Essex St

Bus Lines

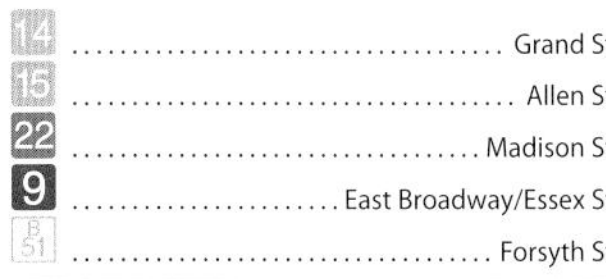

14 .... Grand St
15 .... Allen St
22 .... Madison St
9 .... East Broadway/Essex St
B51 .... Forsyth St

Gas Stations

• **Mobil** • 2 Pike St

Parking

Map 5 • West Village
MEATPACKING DISTRICT
W 16th St
W 15th St
W 14th St
W 13th St
W 12th St
W 11th St
W 10th St
W 9th St
W 8th St
Little W 12th St
Gansevoort St
Horatio St
Jane St
Bethune St
Bank St
Perry St
Charles St
Charles Ln
Christopher St
Barrow St
Morton St
Leroy St
Clarkson St
W Houston St
King St
Charlton St
Vandam St
Spring St
Dominick St
Broome St
Watts St
Grand St
Canal St
Ninth Ave
Eighth Ave
Abingdon Sq
Greenwich Ave
Waverly Pl
W 4th St
W 3rd St
Bleecker St
Seventh Ave S
Avenue of the Americas (Sixth Ave)
Washington St
Greenwich St
Hudson St
Varick St
West Side Hwy
Grove St
Commerce St
Bedford St
Jones St
Cornelia St
Carmine St
Downing St
St Luke's Pl
Gay St
Sheridan Sq
Washington Pl
Minetta Ln
MacDougal St
Sullivan St
Thompson St
Prince St
Renwick St
Jefferson Market Courthouse
Stonewall
Westbeth Building
White Horse Tavern
Chumley's
James J Walker Park
Hudson River Park
Hudson River
The Ear Inn
Holland Tunnel
9a
8
9
6
2
A
B
1
2

If you like quiet tree-lined streets (who doesn't?), then this is the neighborhood for you. The northwest and southwest parts are in the process of converting from manufacturing to residential and commercial areas, although services are still scant west of Hudson Street. The Hudson River Greenway is fantastic—we can't wait for the entire west side to be done. It's got a wonderful vibe, both during the day and at night.

ATMs

CH • Chase • 158 W 14th St
CH • Chase • 204 W 4th St
CH • Chase • 302 W 12th St
CH • Chase • 345 Hudson St
CI • Citibank • 75 Christopher St
EM • Emigrant • 375 Hudson St
EM • Emigrant • 395 Sixth Ave
HS • HSBC • 101 W 14th St
HS • HSBC • 207 Varick St
HS • HSBC • 80 Eighth Ave
NF • North Fork Bank • 403A W 14th St
WM • Washington Mutual • 340 Sixth Ave

Bagels

- **Bagel Bob's** • 434 Sixth Ave
- **Bagel Buffet** • 406 Sixth Ave
- **Bagel Restaurant** • 170 W 4th St
- **Bagels and Much More** • 70 Greenwich Ave
- **Bagels on the Square** • 7 Carmine St
- **Bread Factory Café** • 330 Bleecker St
- **Dizzy Izzy's New York Bagels** • 185 Varick St
- **Hudson Bagels** • 502 Hudson St
- **Murray's Bagels** • 500 Sixth Ave
- **New World Coffee** • 488 Sixth Ave

Community Gardens

Fire Departments

- **Engine 24, Ladder 5** • 227 Sixth Ave

Hospitals

- **St Vincent's AIDS Center** • 412 Sixth Ave
- **St Vincent's Hospital & Medical Center** • 153 W 11th St

Landmarks

- **Chumley's** • 86 Bedford St
- **The Ear Inn** • Washington St & Spring St
- **Jefferson Market Courthouse** • 425 Sixth Ave
- **Stonewall** • 53 Christopher St
- **Westbeth Building** • Washington St & Bethune St
- **White Horse Tavern** • 567 Hudson St

Libraries

- **Early Childhood Resource & Information Center** • 66 Leroy St
- **Hudson Park** • 66 Leroy St
- **Jefferson Market** • 425 Sixth Ave

24-Hour Pharmacies

- **Duane Reade** • 378 Sixth Ave

Police

- **6th Precinct** • 233 W 10th St

Post Offices

- **Village** • 201 Varick St
- **West Village** • 527 Hudson St

Schools

- **City as School** • 16 Clarkson St
- **City Country School** • 146 W 13th St
- **Elisabeth Irwin High School** • 40 Charlton St
- **Empire State College - State University of New York** • 225 Varick St
- **Greenwich House Music School** • 46 Barrow St
- **Joffrey Ballet School** • 434 Sixth Ave
- **Little Red School House** • 272 Sixth Ave
- **Merce Cunningham Studio** • 55 Bethune St
- **Our Lady of Pompeii School** • 240 Bleecker St
- **Pratt Institute** • 144 W 14th St
- **PS 3 The Charette School** • 490 Hudson St
- **PS 41 Greenwich Village School** • 116 W 11th St
- **PS 500 Unity High School** • 121 Sixth Ave
- **PS 721 Manhattan Occupational Training School** • 250 W Houston St
- **St Bernard-St Francis Xavier** • 327 W 13th St
- **St Joseph's Washington Place School** • 111 Washington Pl
- **St Luke's School** • 487 Hudson St
- **St Vincent's Hospital Medical School** • 153 W 11th St
- **St Vincent's Hospital School of Nursing** • 27 Christopher St
- **Unity High School** • 121 Sixth Ave
- **Unity High School** • 555 Broome St
- **Village Community School** • 272 W 13th St

Supermarkets

- **Associated** • 255 W 14th St
- **Citarella** • 424 Sixth Ave
- **D'Agostino** • 666 Greenwich St
- **D'Agostino** • 790 Greenwich St
- **Food Emporium** • 475 Sixth Ave
- **Gourmet Garage** • 117 Seventh Ave S
- **Gristede's** • 3 Sheridan Sq
- **Gristede's** • 585 Hudson St
- **Western Beef** • 403 W 14th St

Map 5 • West Village

The Corner Bistro has the best burgers in Manhattan, and the Ear Inn is one of our favorite all-time bars. We can't decide which we like most—Florent's food, Florent's vibe, or Florent's decor. Many gay and lesbian bars are in this neighborhood (duh). The meatpacking district is now hipper-than-thou, complete with unaffordable shops, too many French restaurants, and squawking between residents and developers. Recommended.

Bars

- **Art Bar** • 52 Eighth Ave
- **Automatic Slims** • 733 Washington St
- **Blind Tiger Ale House** • 518 Hudson St
- **Chumley's** • 86 Bedford St
- **Duplex** • 61 Christopher St
- **Ear Inn** • 326 Spring St
- **Henrietta Hudson** • 438 Hudson St
- **Red Light Bistro** • 50 Ninth Ave
- **Trust** • 421 W 13th St
- **Village Idiot** • 355 W 14th St
- **West** • 425 West St
- **White Horse Tavern** • 567 Hudson St

Coffee

- **Brewbar Coffee** • 13 Eighth Ave
- **Brewbar Coffee** • 327 W 11th St
- **Cafe Mona Lisa** • 282 Bleecker St
- **Cafe Sha Sha** • 510 Hudson St
- **Caffe dell'Artista** • 46 Greenwich Ave
- **Caffe Vivaldi** • 32 Jones St
- **Carpo's Cafe** • 189 Bleecker St
- **Coffee Sweet Heart** • 69 Eighth Ave
- **Cosi** • 504 Sixth Ave
- **Doma** • 17 Perry St
- **Dunkin' Donuts** • 536 Sixth Ave
- **Grey Dog's Coffee** • 33 Carmine St
- **Hudson Coffee Bar** • 350 Hudson St
- **Kenny's Coffee Shop** • 345 Hudson St
- **Longo Coffee & Tea** • 201 Bleecker St
- **New World Coffee** • 488 Sixth Ave
- **Odessey Coffee Shop** • 204 W 14th St
- **Starbucks** • 150 Varick St
- **Starbucks** • 378 Sixth Ave
- **Starbucks** • 510 Sixth Ave
- **Starbucks** • 72 Grove St
- **Starbucks** • 93 Greenwich Ave
- **Sucelt Coffee Shop** • 200 W 14th St
- **West Coast Coffee Shop** • 398 West St

Copy Shops

- **Copy/Com (9 am-8 pm)** • 70A Greenwich Ave
- **Elite Copy Center (9 am-7 pm)** • 52 Carmine St
- **Mail Boxes Etc (8:30 am-7 pm)** • 302 W 12th St
- **Mail Boxes Etc (8:30 am-7 pm)** • 511 Sixth Ave
- **Village Copy Center (8:30 am-7 pm)** • 520 Hudson St

Gyms

- **Crunch Fitness** • 152 Christopher St
- **Equinox Fitness Club** • 97 Greenwich Ave
- **Jeff's Gym** • 224 W 4th St
- **New York Sports Clubs** • 125 Seventh Ave S
- **Printing House Fitness & Racquet Club** • 421 Hudson St
- **Serge Gym** • 451 West St
- **West Village Workout** • 140 Charles St
- **YMCA McBurney** • 125 W 14th St

Hardware Stores

- **Barney's Hardware** • 467 Sixth Ave
- **Blaustein Paint & Hardware** • 304 Bleecker St
- **Colonial Hardware** • 163 Varick St
- **Garber Hardware** • 710 Greenwich St
- **Hardware Mart** • 151 W 14th St
- **Jonathan's Decorative Hardware** • 12 Perry St
- **Lock-It Hardware** • 59 Carmine St
- **Nanz Custom Hardware** • 20 Vandam St
- **The Lumber Store** • 71 Eighth Ave

Liquor Stores

- **Casa Oliveira Wines & Liquors** • 98 Seventh Ave S
- **Castle Wines & Liquors** • 168 Seventh Ave S
- **Christopher St Liquor Shoppe** • 45 Christopher St
- **Golden Rule Wine & Liquor** • 457 Hudson St
- **Imperial Liquors** • 579 Hudson St
- **Manley's Liquor Store** • 35 Eighth Ave
- **North Village Liquors** • 254 W 14th St
- **Sea Grape Wine & Spirits** • 512 Hudson St
- **Spirits of Carmine** • 52 Carmine St
- **Village Vintner** • 448 Sixth Ave
- **Village Wine & Spirits** • 486 Sixth Ave
- **Waverly Wine & Liquor** • 135 Waverly Pl

Movie Theaters

- **Film Forum** • 209 W Houston St
- **New York Public Library Jefferson Market Branch** • 425 Sixth Ave

Pet Shops

- **Beasty Feast** • 630 Hudson St
- **Beasty Feast** • 680 Washington St
- **Fetch** • 43 Greenwich Ave
- **Four Paws Club** • 387 Bleecker St
- **Groom-O-Rama** • 496 Sixth Ave
- **Pet Central** • 237 Bleecker St
- **Pet Palace** • 109 W 10th St
- **Pet's Kitchen** • 116 Christopher St
- **Petland Discounts** • 389 Sixth Ave

Restaurants

- **A Salt & Battery** • 112 Greenwich Ave
- **AOC** • 314 Bleecker St
- **Aquagrill** • 210 Spring St
- **Benny's Burritos** • 113 Greenwich Ave
- **Blue Ribbon Bakery** • 33 Downing St
- **Café Asean** • 117 W 10th St
- **Caffe Torino** • 139 W 10th St
- **Chez Brigitte** • 77 Greenwich Ave
- **Corner Bistro** • 331 W 4th St
- **Cowgirl Hall of Fame** • 519 Hudson St
- **Crispo** • 240 W 14th St
- **Day-O** • 103 Greenwich Ave
- **Dragonfly** • 47 Seventh Ave
- **Florent** • 69 Gansevoort St
- **French Roast** • 78 W 11th St
- **Grey Dog's Coffee** • 33 Carmine St
- **Home** • 20 Cornelia St
- **Ivo & Lulu** • 558 Broome St
- **Jefferson** • 121 W 10th St
- **Joe's Pizza** • 233 Bleecker St
- **John's Pizzeria** • 278 Bleecker St
- **Le Gamin** • 27 Bedford St
- **Lunchbox Food Company** • 357 West St
- **Mary's Fish Camp** • 246 W 4th St
- **Mirchi** • 29 Seventh Ave S
- **Moustache** • 90 Bedford St
- **One If By Land, TIBS** • 17 Barrow St
- **ONY** • 357 Sixth Ave
- **Pearl Oyster Bar** • 18 Cornelia St
- **Petite Abeille** • 400 W 14th St
- **Petite Abeille** • 466 Hudson St
- **Po** • 31 Cornelia St
- **Sapore** • 55 Greenwich Ave
- **Souen** • 210 Sixth Ave
- **Tea & Sympathy** • 108 Greenwich Ave
- **Two Boots** • 201 W 11th St
- **Yama** • 38 Carmine St

Shopping

- **Alphabets** • 47 Greenwich Ave
- **CO Bigelow Chemists** • 414 Sixth Ave
- **Faicco's Pork Store** • 260 Bleecker St
- **Fat Beats** • 406 Sixth Ave
- **Flight 001** • 96 Greenwich Ave
- **Geppetto's Toy Box** • 10 Christopher St
- **Integral Yoga Natural Foods** • 229 W 13th St
- **Janovic Plaza** • 161 Sixth Ave
- **Leather Man, The** • 111 Christopher St
- **Mxyplyzyk** • 125 Greenwich Ave
- **Myers of Keswick** • 634 Hudson St
- **Porto Rico Importing Company** • 201 Bleecker St
- **Radio Shack** • 49 Seventh Ave
- **Scott Jordan Furniture** • 137 Varick St
- **Urban Outfitters** • 374 Sixth Ave
- **Vitra** • 29 Ninth Ave

Video Rental

- **Evergreen Video** • 37 Carmine St
- **Vivid Video** • 100 Christopher St
- **World of Video** • 51 Greenwich Ave

Map 5 • West Village

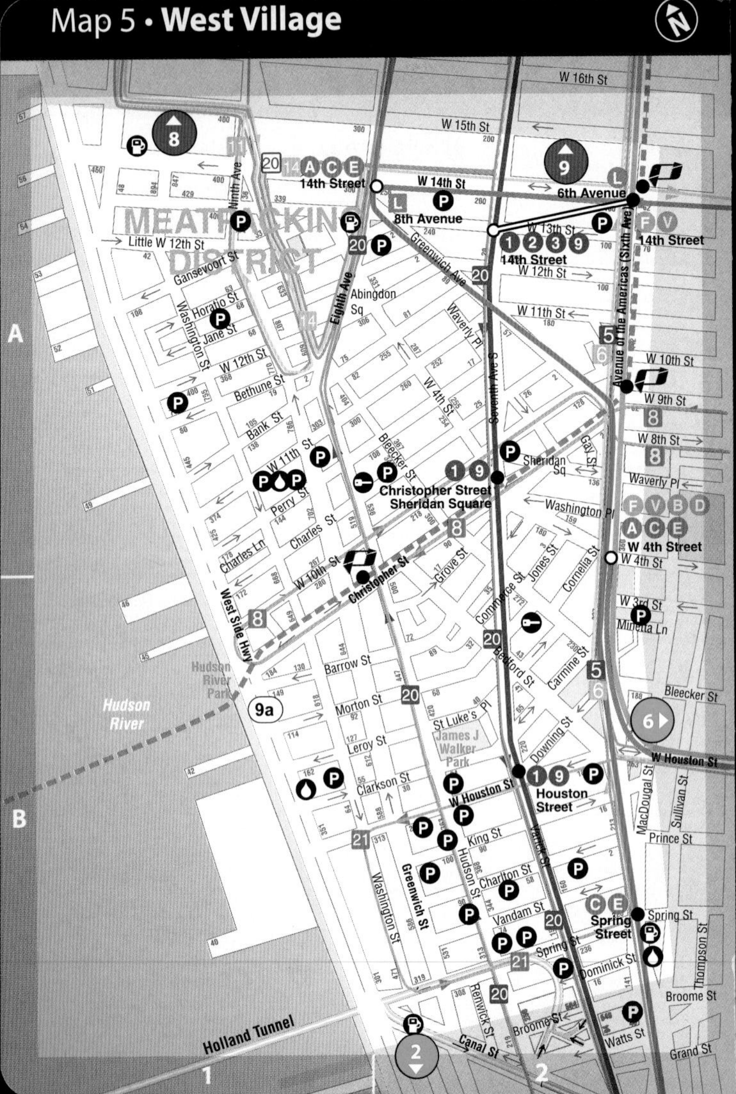

It's pretty tough to park anywhere east of Washington Street. All approaches to the Holland Tunnel suck. Thankfully, there is a great bike lane on Hudson Street, though the one on Sixth Avenue doesn't start until 9th Street. The Houston Street subway station might have the coolest mosaics of any station in Manhattan.

Subways

1 2 3 9 F V L .... 14 St-6 Ave
1 9 .... Christopher St-Sheridan Sq
1 9 .... Houston St
A C E F V B D .... W 4 St
A C E L .... 14 St-8 Ave
C E .... Spring St

Bus Lines

11 .... Ninth Ave/Tenth Ave
14 .... 14th St Crosstown
20 .... Abingdon Sq
20 .... Seventh Ave/Eighth Ave/Central Park West
21 .... Houston St Crosstown
5 .... Fifth Ave/Sixth Ave/Riverside Dr
6 ....Seventh Ave/Sixth Ave/Broadway
8 .... 8th St/9th St Crosstown

PATH

- **14 St** • 14th St & Sixth Ave
- **9th St** • 9th St & Sixth Ave
- **Christopher St** • Christopher St & Hudson St

Car Rental

- **Dollar** • 99 Charles St
- **Hertz** • 18 Morton St

Car Washes

- **Apple Management** • 332 W 11th St
- **Carz-A-Poppin Carwash** • 124 Sixth Ave
- **Village Car Wash & Lube** • 160 Leroy St

Gas Stations

- **Getty** • 63 Eighth Ave
- **Mobil** • 140 Sixth Ave
- **Mobil** • 290 West St

Parking

Map 6 • Washington Sq. / NYU / SoHo

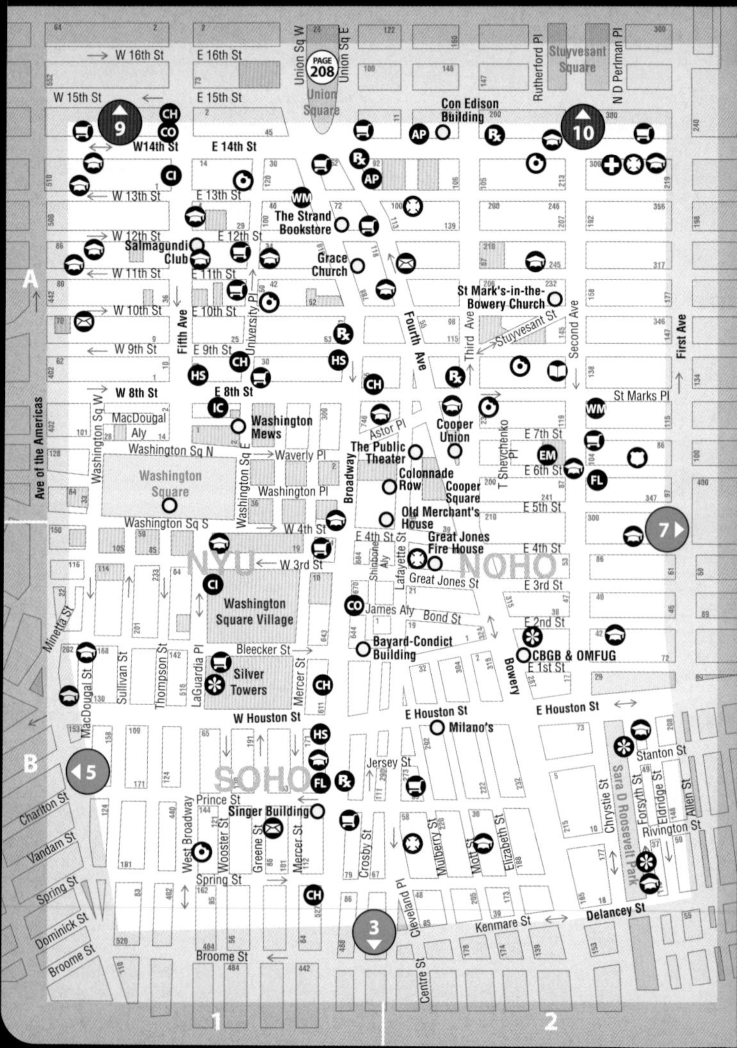

W 16th St
E 16th St
Union Sq W
Union Sq E
PAGE 208
Union Square
Rutherford Pl
Stuyvesant Square
N D Perlman Pl
W 15th St
E 15th St
9
Con Edison Building
10
W14th St
E 14th St
W 13th St
E 13th St
The Strand Bookstore
W 12th St
E 12th St
Salmagundi Club
Grace Church
W 11th St
E 11th St
University Pl
St Mark's-in-the-Bowery Church
W 10th St
E 10th St
Fifth Ave
Stuyvesant St
Third Ave
Second Ave
W 9th St
E 9th St
Fourth Ave
First Ave
W 8th St
E 8th St
St Marks Pl
Washington Sq W
MacDougal Aly
Washington Mews
Astor Pl
Cooper Union
E 7th St
Ave of the Americas
Washington Sq N
Waverly Pl
The Public Theater
T Shevchenko Pl
Washington Square
Washington Sq E
Broadway
Colonnade Row
Cooper Square
E 6th St
Washington Pl
E 5th St
Washington Sq S
Old Merchant's House
W 4th St
E 4th St
Great Jones Fire House
7
NYU
NOHO
W 3rd St
Shinbone Aly
Lafayette St
Great Jones St
E 3rd St
Minetta St
Washington Square Village
James Aly
Bond St
E 2nd St
Bleecker St
Bayard-Condict Building
CBGB & OMFUG
Silver Towers
E 1st St
MacDougal St
Sullivan St
Thompson St
LaGuardia Pl
Mercer St
Bowery
W Houston St
E Houston St
E Houston St
Milano's
Stanton St
5
Jersey St
SOHO
Charlton St
Prince St
Singer Building
Chrystie St
Sara D Roosevelt Park
Forsyth St
Eldridge St
Allen St
Rivington St
Vandam St
West Broadway
Wooster St
Greene St
Crosby St
Mulberry St
Mott St
Elizabeth St
Spring St
Spring St
Dominick St
Cleveland Pl
3
Kenmare St
Delancey St
Broome St
Broome St
Centre St
A
B
1
2

NYU has come to dominate this area in many ways, but Washington Square Park remains an interesting place to stroll through, regardless. Farther south, many great shops and galleries still abound in SoHo and on Broadway, even as the chain stores move in. The whole area is an architectural "greatest hits," which is fortunate since SoHo is becoming more like an upscale suburban mall every damned day.

ATMs

AP • Apple • 145 Fourth Ave
AP • Apple • 4 Irving Pl
CH • Chase • 32 University Pl
CH • Chase • 525 Broadway
CH • Chase • 623 Broadway
CH • Chase • 756 Broadway
CH • Chase • 90 Fifth Ave
CI • Citibank • 555 LaGuardia Pl
CI • Citibank • 72 Fifth Ave
CO • Commerce Bank • 666 Broadway
CO • Commerce Bank • 90 Fifth Ave
EM • Emigrant • 105 Second Ave
FL • Fleet • 589 Broadway
FL • Fleet • 72 Second Ave
HS • HSBC • 1 E 8th St
HS • HSBC • 599 Broadway
HS • HSBC • 769 Broadway
IC • Independence Community • 43 E 8th St
WM • Washington Mutual • 130 Second Ave
WM • Washington Mutual • 835 Broadway

Bagels

- **Bagel Bob's** • 51 University Pl
- **Dizzy Izzy's New York Bagels** • 250 E 14th St
- **Giant Bagel Shop** • 120 University Pl
- **New World Coffee** • 412 West Broadway
- **The Bagel Café/Ray's Pizza** • 2 St Mark's Pl

Community Gardens

Fire Departments

- **Engine 33, Ladder 9** • 42 Great Jones St
- **Engine 5** • 340 E 14th St
- **Ladder 20** • 251 Lafayette St
- **Ladder 3** • 108 E 13th St

Hospitals

- **New York Eye & Ear Infirmary** • 310 E 14th St

Landmarks

- **Bayard-Condict Building** • 65 Bleecker St
- **CBGB & OMFUG** • 315 Bowery
- **Colonnade Row** • 428 Lafayette St
- **Con Edison Building** • 145 E 14th St
- **Cooper Union** • 30 Cooper Sq
- **Grace Church** • 802 Broadway
- **Great Jones Fire House** • Great Jones St & Bowery
- **Milano's** • 51 E Houston St
- **Old Merchant's House** • 29 E 4th St
- **Salmagundi Club** • 47 Fifth Ave
- **Singer Building** • 561 Broadway
- **St Mark's-in-the-Bowery Church** • 131 E 10th St
- **The Public Theater** • 425 Lafayette St
- **The Strand Bookstore** • 828 Broadway
- **Washington Mews** • University Pl (entrance)
- **Washington Square Park** • Washington Sq

Libraries

- **Ottendorfer** • 135 Second Ave

24-Hour Pharmacies

- **Duane Reade** • 24 E 14th St
- **Duane Reade** • 598 Broadway
- **Duane Reade** • 769 Broadway
- **Walgreen's** • 145 Fourth Ave

Post Offices

- **Cooper** • 93 Fourth Ave
- **Patchin** • 70 W 10th St
- **Prince** • 124 Greene St

Schools

- **Alfred Adler Institute** • 594 Broadway
- **Benjamin N Cardozo School of Law** • 55 Fifth Ave
- **Cooper Union** • 30 Cooper Sq
- **Costume National** • 108 Wooster St
- **Eugene Lang College** • 65 W 11th St
- **Gateway School** • 236 Second Ave
- **Grace Church School** • 86 Fourth Ave
- **Harvey Milk School** • 2 Astor Pl
- **Hebrew Union College** • 1 W 4th St
- **Institute of Audio Research** • 64 University Pl
- **La Salle Academy** • 44 E 2nd St
- **Legacy School for Intergrated Studies** • 33 W 13th St
- **Little Red School House** • 196 Bleecker St
- **Nativity Mission School** • 204 Forsyth St
- **New School for Social Research** • 66 W 12th St
- **New York Eye and Ear Institute** • 310 E 14th St
- **New York University** • 70 Washington Sq S
- **Parson's School of Design** • 66 Fifth Ave
- **PS 751 Career Development Center** • 113 E 4th St
- **St Anthony School** • 60 Macdougal St
- **St Patrick School** • 233 Mott St
- **Third Street Music School Settlement** • 235 E 11th St
- **Tisch School of Arts - Dance** • 111 Second Ave

Supermarkets

- **Associated** • 130 Bleecker St
- **D'Agostino** • 64 University Pl
- **Dean & DeLuca** • 560 Broadway
- **Garden of Eden Gourmet** • 7 E 14th St
- **Gristede's** • 113 Fourth Ave
- **Gristede's** • 246 Mercer St
- **Gristede's** • 25 University Pl
- **Gristede's** • 333 E 14th St
- **Gristede's** • 5 W 14th St
- **Healthy Pleasures** • 93 University Pl
- **Met Food** • 107 Second Ave
- **Met Food** • 251 Mulberry St
- **Whole Foods Market** • 4 Union Sq S

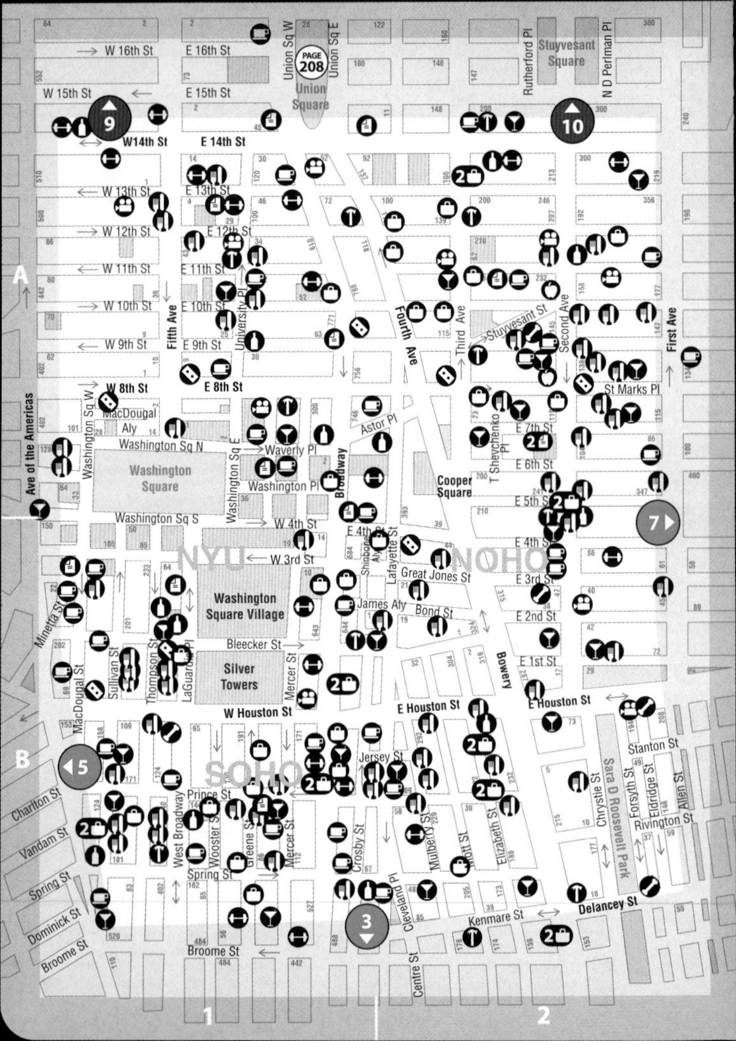

W 16th St
E 16th St
Union Sq W
Union Sq E
PAGE 208
Union Square
Stuyvesant Square
Rutherford Pl
N D Perlman Pl
W 15th St
E 15th St
9
10
W14th St
E 14th St
W 13th St
E 13th St
W 12th St
E 12th St
W 11th St
E 11th St
W 10th St
E 10th St
W 9th St
E 9th St
W 8th St
E 8th St
Fifth Ave
University Pl
Fourth Ave
Third Ave
Second Ave
First Ave
Stuyvesant St
St Marks Pl
Ave of the Americas
Washington Sq W
MacDougal Aly
Washington Sq N
Washington Sq E
Waverly Pl
Washington Square
Washington Pl
Broadway
Astor Pl
Cooper Square
T Shevchenko Pl
E 7th St
E 6th St
E 5th St
E 4th St
E 3rd St
E 2nd St
E 1st St
7
Washington Sq S
W 4th St
E 4th St
W 3rd St
NYU
NOHO
Shinbone Aly
Lafayette St
Great Jones St
Bond St
James Aly
Washington Square Village
Bleecker St
Minetta St
Silver Towers
MacDougal St
Sullivan St
Thompson St
LaGuardia Pl
Mercer St
Bowery
W Houston St
E Houston St
E Houston St
SOHO
5
Jersey St
Stanton St
Chrystie St
Sara D Roosevelt Park
Forsyth St
Eldridge St
Allen St
Rivington St
Charlton St
Vandam St
Spring St
Dominick St
Broome St
Prince St
West Broadway
Wooster St
Greene St
Mercer St
Crosby St
Mulberry St
Mott St
Elizabeth St
Cleveland Pl
Kenmare St
Delancey St
Centre St
3
A
B
1
2

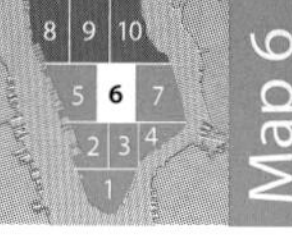

Dive bar? Milano's. Commies? KGB. Drunken Englishmen? Nevada Smith's. Coffee? La Lanterna. Liquor? Astor Wines. Movies? Angelica, Cinema Classics. Fondue and marrow? Blue Ribbon. Pizza? Arturo's. Bread? Sullivan Street Bakery. Soy Gouda? East Village Cheese. Manufacturing Consent? TLA Video, Kim's Video. Bored?

Bars

- **Bar 89** • 89 Mercer St
- **Beauty Bar** • 231 E 14th St
- **Blue & Gold** • 74 E 7th St
- **Burp Castle** • 41 E 7th St
- **Cedar Tavern** • 82 University Pl
- **Chez Es Saada** • 42 E 1st St
- **Decibel** • 240 E 9th St
- **Detour** • 349 E 13th St
- **Fanelli's** • 94 Prince St
- **Fez** • 380 Lafayette St
- **Hole, The** • 29 Second Ave
- **Holiday Lounge** • 75 St Mark's Pl
- **Josie Wood's Pub** • 11 Waverly Pl
- **KGB** • 85 E 4th St
- **Mars Bar** • 25 E 1st St
- **McSorley' s Old Ale House** • 15 E 7th St
- **Milano's** • 51 E Houston St
- **Nevada Smith's** • 74 Third Ave
- **Peculiar Pub** • 145 Bleecker St
- **Pravda** • 281 Lafayette St
- **Red Bench** • 107 Sullivan St
- **The Room** • 144 Sullivan St
- **Spring Lounge** • 48 Spring St
- **Sweet & Vicious** • 5 Spring St

Coffee

- **Au Bon Pain** • 684 Broadway
- **Caffe Dante** • 79 MacDougal St
- **Caffe Pane e Cioccolato** • 10 Waverly Pl
- **Caffe Reggio** • 119 MacDougal St
- **Chatham and Campbell Oriental Caffes** • 95 First Ave
- **Cloister Cafe** • 238 E 9th St
- **Coffee Cherries** • 13 E 4th St
- **Cosi** • 841 Broadway
- **Cremcaffe** • 65 Second Ave
- **Dean & DeLuca Cafe** • 560 Broadway
- **Dean & DeLuca Cafe** • 75 University Pl
- **Dunkin' Donuts** • 210 E 14th St
- **Esperanto Cafe** • 114 MacDougal St
- **Housing Works Used Book Cafe** • 126 Crosby St
- **Hugh Grande Cafe** • 126 Crosby St
- **Juice & Java Station** • 581 Broadway
- **Lanterna di Vittorio** • 129 MacDougal St
- **Mission Cafe** • 82 Second Ave
- **New World Coffee** • 412 West Broadway
- **Once Upon A Tart** • 135 Sullivan St
- **Oren's Daily Roast** • 31 Waverly Pl
- **Piece & Total** • 841 Broadway
- **Saint Alp's Teahouse** • 170 Bleecker St
- **Simone Espresso & Wine Bar** • 134 First Ave
- **Starbucks:**
  - 141 Second Ave
  - 21 Astor Pl
  - 21 E 8th St
  - 665 Broadway
  - 72 Spring St
  - 78 Spring St
- **Veniero's** • 342 E 11th St

Copy Shops

- **Advanced Copy Center (9 am-8 pm)** • 552 LaGuardia Pl
- **East Side Copy Center (8 am-11 pm)** • 15 E 13th St
- **King Photocopy (8 am-10 pm)** • 45 E 7th St
- **Kinko's** • 24 E 12th St
- **MacDougal Copy Center (9 am-6:30 pm)** • 127 MacDougal St
- **New York Copy Center (8 am-9 pm)** • 204 E 11th St
- **New York Copy Center(8 am-9 pm)** • 34 E 7th St
- **Prince St Copy Center (9 am-7 pm)** • 159 Prince St
- **Staples (7 am-7 pm)** • 769 Broadway
- **Staples (7 am-midnight)** • 5 Union Sq W
- **The UPS Store (8:30 am-6:30 pm)** • 111 E 14th St
- **Unique Copy Center (8 am-11 pm)** • 9 E 4th St
- **Unique Copy Center (8 am-11 pm)** • 252 Greene St

Farmer's Markets

- **St Mark's Church Greenmarket** • Second Ave & 10th St

Gyms

- **24/7 Fitness Club** • 47 W 14th St
- **Crunch Fitness:**
  - 404 Lafayette St
  - 54 E 13th St
  - 623 Broadway
- **Dolphin Fitness Clubs** • 94 E 4th St
- **Dolphin Fitness East** • 242 E 14th St
- **Hanson Fitness** • 63 Greene St
- **Hanson Fitness** • 826 Broadway
- **Lucille Roberts Health Club** • 80 Fifth Ave
- **New York Health & Racquet Club** • 24 E 13th St
- **New York Sports Clubs** • 34 W 14th St
- **New York Sports Clubs** • 503 Broadway
- **Physio Fitness** • 584 Broadway
- **Plus One Fitness Clinic** • 106 Crosby St
- **Sage Fitness** • 80 E 11th St
- **Sol Goldman YM-YWHA** • 344 E 14th St
- **Synergy Fitness Clubs** • 227 Mulberry St
- **World Gym** • 232 Mercer St

Hardware Stores

- **10003 Hardware** • 90 University Pl
- **14th St Hardware** • 211 E 14th St
- **Ace Hardware** • 130 Fourth Ave
- **Allied Hardware** • 59 Second Ave
- **Bowery Discount Hardware** • 2 Delancey St
- **East Hardware** • 79 Third Ave
- **Metropolitan Hardware** • 175 Spring St
- **Metropolitan Lumber & Hardware** • 175 Spring St
- **Mott Hardware** • 52 Kenmare St
- **Shapiro Hardware** • 63 Bleecker St
- **TS Hardware** • 52 E 8th St

Liquor Stores

- **Anthony Liquors** • 52 Spring St
- **Astor Wines & Spirits** • 12 Astor Pl
- **B&S Zeeman** • 47 University Pl
- **Crossroads Wine & Liquor** • 55 W 14th St
- **Elizabeth & Vine** • 253 Elizabeth St
- **Miat Liquor Store** • 166 Second Ave
- **S&P Liquor & Wine** • 300 E 5th St
- **Soho Wine & Spirits** • 461 West Broadway
- **Spring Street Wine Shop** • 187 Spring St
- **Thompson Wine & Spirits** • 222 Thompson St
- **Warehouse Wines & Spirits** • 735 Broadway
- **Washington Square Wines** • 545 LaGuardia Pl

Movie Theaters

- **Angelika Film Center** • 18 W Houston St
- **Anthology Film Archives** • 32 Second Ave
- **Cinema Classics** • 332 E 11th St
- **Cinema Village** • 22 E 12th St
- **City Cinemas: Village East Cinemas** • 189 Second Ave
- **Landmark Sunshine Cinema** • 141 E Houston St
- **Loews Village** • 66 Third Ave
- **NYU Cantor Film Center** • 36 E 8th St
- **Quad Cinema** • 34 W 13th St
- **Regal/UA** • 850 Broadway

Pet Shops

- **Creature Features** • 21 E 3rd St
- **JBJ Discount Pet Shop** • 151 E Houston St
- **Pacific Aquarium & Plant** • 46 Delancey St
- **Whiskers** • 235 E 9th St

Restaurants

- **Acme Bar & Grill** • 9 Great Jones St
- **Angelica Kitchen** • 300 E 12th St
- **Around The Clock** • 8 Stuyvesant St
- **Arturo's Pizzeria** • 106 W Houston St
- **Babbo** • 110 Waverly Pl
- **Balthazar** • 80 Spring St
- **Baluchi's** • 104 Second Ave
- **Ben's Pizza** • 177 Spring St
- **Blue Hill** • 75 Washington Pl
- **Blue Ribbon** • 97 Sullivan St
- **Blue Ribbon Sushi** • 119 Sullivan St
- **Bond Street** • 6 Bond St
- **Borgo Antico** • 22 E 13th St
- **Cafe Colonial** • 73 E Houston St
- **Cafe Habana** • 17 Prince St
- **Cafe Spice** • 72 University Pl
- **Canteen** • 142 Mercer St
- **Chez Es Saada** • 42 E 1st St
- **Cozy Soup & Burger** • 739 Broadway
- **Dojo** • 14 W 4th St
- **Dojo** • 24 St Mark's Pl
- **Eight Mile Creek** • 240 Mulberry St
- **Frank** • 88 Second Ave
- **Ghenet** • 284 Mulberry St
- **Gotham Bar & Grill** • 12 E 12th St
- **Great Jones Cafe** • 54 Great Jones St
- **Green Papaya** • 185 Sullivan St
- **Hampton Chutney Co** • 68 Prince St
- **Haveli** • 100 Second Ave
- **Holy Basil** • 149 Second Ave
- **Il Buco** • 47 Bond St
- **Iso** • 175 Second Ave
- **Jane** • 100 W Houston St
- **John's of 12th Street** • 302 E 12th St
- **Jules** • 65 St Mark's Pl
- **Kelley & Ping** • 127 Greene St
- **Khyber Pass** • 34 St Mark's Pl
- **Lupa** • 170 Thompson St
- **Melampo Imported Foods** • 105 Sullivan St
- **Mingala Burmese** • 21 E 7th St
- **Otto** • 1 Fifth Ave
- **Peep** • 177 Prince St
- **Penang** • 109 Spring St
- **Pravda** • 281 Lafayette St
- **Sammy's Roumanian** • 157 Chrystie St
- **Snack** • 105 Thompson St
- **Soho Steak** • 90 Thompson St
- **Spice** • 60 University Pl
- **Strip House** • 13 E 12th St
- **Time Cafe / Fez** • 380 Lafayette St
- **Tomoe Sushi** • 172 Thompson St
- **Zoe** • 90 Prince St

Shopping

- **Academy Records & CDs** • 77 E 10th St
- **Apple Store SoHo** • 103 Prince St
- **Blades Board and Skate** • 659 Broadway
- **Burberry** • 131 Spring St
- **Canal Jean** • 718 Broadway
- **CITE Design** • 120 Wooster St
- **Daily 235** • 235 Elizabeth St
- **East Village Cheese** • 40 Third Ave
- **East Village Music Store** • 85 E 4th St
- **EMS** • 591 Broadway
- **Footlight Records** • 113 E 12th St
- **Global Table** • 107 Sullivan St
- **Jam Paper & Envelope** • 111 Third Ave
- **Kar'ikter** • 19 Prince St
- **Kate's Paperie** • 561 Broadway
- **Kiehl's** • 109 Third Ave
- **Kim's Underground** • 144 Bleecker St
- **Kim's Video** • 6 St Marks Pl
- **Leekan Designs** • 93 Mercer St
- **Lighting by Gregory** • 158 Bowery
- **Michael Anchin Glass** • 245 Elizabeth St
- **Moss** • 146 Greene St
- **Nancy Koltes at Home** • 31 Spring St
- **National Wholesale Liquidators** • 632 Broadway
- **New Museum Store** • 583 Broadway
- **New York Central Art Supply** • 62 Third Ave
- **Other Music** • 15 E 4th St
- **Porto Rico Importing Company:**
  - 107 Thompson St
  - 40 St Mark's Pl
- **Prada** • 575 Broadway
- **Radio Shack** • 781 Broadway
- **Stereo Exchange** • 627 Broadway
- **Stuart Moore** • 128 Prince St
- **Sullivan Street Bakery** • 77 Sullivan St
- **Surprise, Surprise** • 91 Third Ave
- **Tower Records** • 692 Broadway
- **Utrecht Art and Drafting Supplies** • 111 Fourth Ave
- **Veniero's** • 342 E 11th St
- **White Trash** • 304 E 5th St

Video Rental

- **Blockbuster Video** • 774 Broadway
- **Couch Potato Video** • 9 E 8th St
- **Hollywood Video** • 46 Third Ave
- **Kim's Video** • 6 St Mark's Pl
- **Kim's Video III** • 144 Bleecker St
- **TLA Video** • 52 W 8th St
- **Tower Video** • 383 Lafayette St
- **Video World** • 138 W Houston St

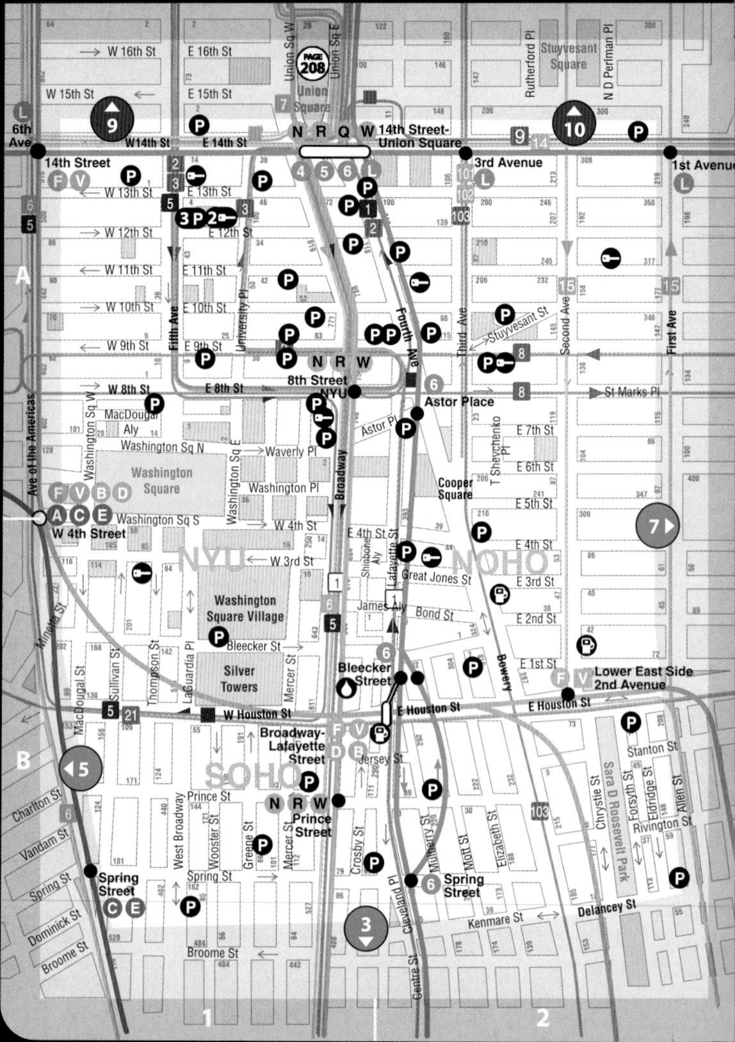
W 16th St
E 16th St
W 15th St
E 15th St
Union Sq W
Union Sq E
PAGE 208
Union Square
Stuyvesant Square
Rutherford Pl
N D Perlman Pl
9
10
6th Ave
W 14th St
E 14th St
N R Q W
14th Street-Union Square
4 5 6 L
3rd Avenue
1st Avenue
14th Street
F V
W 13th St
E 13th St
W 12th St
E 12th St
W 11th St
E 11th St
W 10th St
E 10th St
W 9th St
E 9th St
W 8th St
E 8th St
Fifth Ave
University Pl
Broadway
Fourth Ave
Third Ave
Second Ave
First Ave
Stuyvesant St
8th Street NYU
N R W
St Marks Pl
Astor Place
Astor Pl
MacDougal Aly
Washington Sq W
Washington Sq N
Washington Sq E
Waverly Pl
Washington Square
Washington Pl
Ave of the Americas
F V B D
A C E
Washington Sq S
W 4th Street
W 4th St
E 4th St
E 7th St
E 6th St
E 5th St
T Shevchenko Pl
Cooper Square
NYU
NOHO
W 3rd St
E 3rd St
Shinbone Aly
Lafayette St
Great Jones St
Washington Square Village
Bleecker St
James Aly
Bond St
E 2nd St
E 1st St
Bowery
Minetta St
Sullivan St
Thompson St
LaGuardia Pl
Mercer St
Silver Towers
MacDougal St
Bleecker Street
Lower East Side 2nd Avenue
W Houston St
E Houston St
Broadway-Lafayette Street
B D F V
Jersey St
Stanton St
SOHO
Charlton St
Vandam St
Spring St
Dominick St
Broome St
Prince St
Prince Street
West Broadway
Wooster St
Greene St
Crosby St
Mulberry St
Mott St
Elizabeth St
Chrystie St
Sara D Roosevelt Park
Forsyth St
Eldridge St
Allen St
Rivington St
Spring Street
C E
Cleveland Pl
Spring Street
Kenmare St
Delancey St
Centre St
Broome St
7
5
3
A
B
1
2

Considering how exciting and vibrant this section of the city is, parking should be way worse than it is. Contains one of the subway system's weirdest anomalies—you can only transfer to the B, D, F, Q from the 6 train's downtown track—there is no free transfer from the uptown side. For biking, use Lafayette Street to go north and either Fifth Avenue or Second Avenue to go south.

Subways

6 .... Astor Pl
6 .... Bleecker St
6 .... Spring St
F V .... 2 Ave
B D F V .... Broadway-Lafayette St
J M Z .... Bowery
L .... 3 Ave
4 5 6 L N Q R W .... 14 St-Union Sq
N R W .... 8 St-NYU
N R W .... Prince St
C E .... Spring St

Bus Lines

1 .... Fifth/Madison Aves
101 .... Third Ave/Lexington Ave/Amsterdam Ave
102 .... Third Ave/Lexington Ave/Malcolm X Blvd
103 .... Third Ave/Lexington Ave
14 .... 14th St Crosstown
15 .... First/Second Aves
2 .... Fifth/Madison Aves/Powell Blvd
21 .... Houston St/Avenue C
3 .... Fifth/Madison Aves/St Nicholas Ave
5 .... Fifth Ave/Sixth Ave/Riverside Dr
7 .... Columbus Ave/Amsterdam Ave Lenox Ave/Sixth/Seventh Aves/Broadway
8 .... 8th/9th Sts Crosstown
9 .... Ave B/East Broadway

Car Rental

- **A A Exotic Rentals** • 19 E 12th St
- **American Ways Rent-A-Car** • 33 Great Jones St
- **Autorent Car Rental** • 307 E 11th St
- **Avis** • 68 E 11th St
- **Big Apple Car Rental** • 220 E 9th St
- **Enterprise** • 221 Thompson St
- **Hertz** • 12 E 13th St
- **National** • 21 E 12th St
- **NY On-The-Go Rent-A-Car** • 741 Broadway

Car Washes

- **Broadway-Houston Car Wash** • 614 Broadway

Gas Stations

- **Exxon** • 24 Second Ave
- **Gaseteria** • Houston St & Lafayette St
- **Sunoco** • Bowery & E 3rd St

Parking

Map 7 • East Village

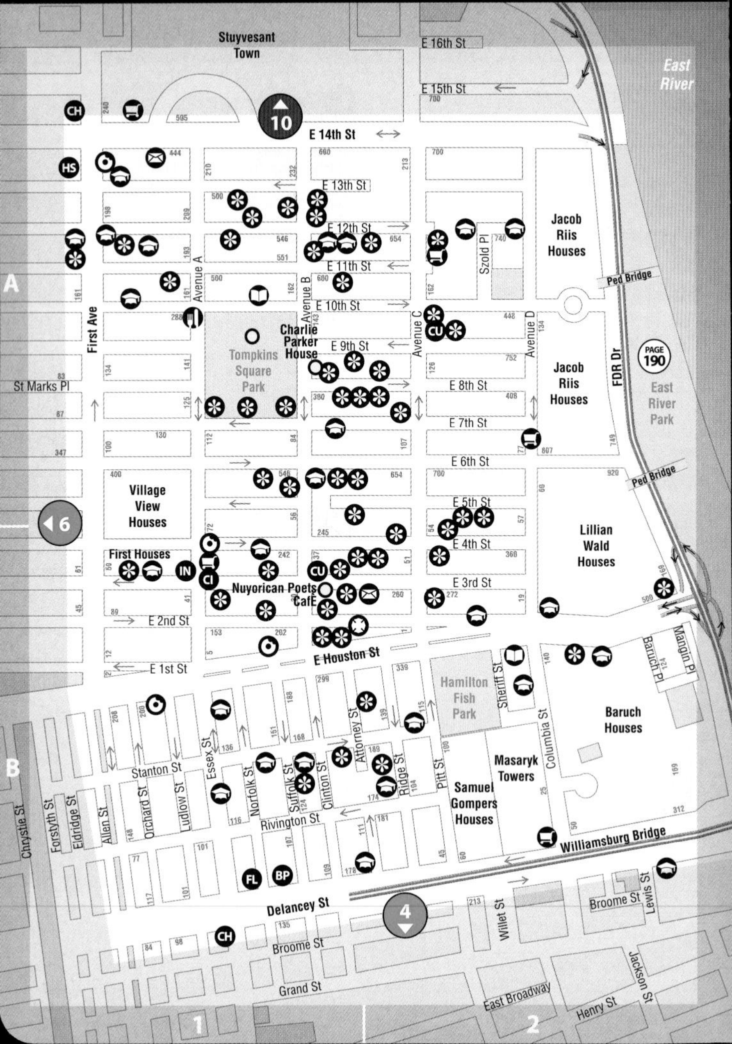
Stuyvesant Town
E 16th St
E 15th St
East River
E 14th St
E 13th St
E 12th St
E 11th St
E 10th St
E 9th St
E 8th St
E 7th St
E 6th St
E 5th St
E 4th St
E 3rd St
E 2nd St
E 1st St
E Houston St
St Marks Pl
First Ave
Avenue A
Avenue B
Avenue C
Avenue D
Szold Pl
FDR Dr
Jacob Riis Houses
Jacob Riis Houses
Ped Bridge
Ped Bridge
PAGE 190
East River Park
Tompkins Square Park
Charlie Parker House
Village View Houses
First Houses
Nuyorican Poets CafE
Lillian Wald Houses
Hamilton Fish Park
Sheriff St
Columbia St
Baruch Pl
Mangin Pl
Baruch Houses
Masaryk Towers
Samuel Gompers Houses
Williamsburg Bridge
Stanton St
Rivington St
Delancey St
Broome St
Broome St
Grand St
East Broadway
Henry St
Jackson St
Lewis St
Willet St
Pitt St
Ridge St
Attorney St
Clinton St
Suffolk St
Norfolk St
Essex St
Ludlow St
Orchard St
Allen St
Eldridge St
Forsyth St
Chrystie St
10
6
4
A
B
1
2

We think David's Bagels on First Avenue rocks. Ask Spectra for matte finish prints of your photos and a white border. Tompkins Square Park is a gated community for the rich and famous (this is what's known as "irony," for you literalists). The farmer's market on the southwest corner of the park does remind us of crunchier days, however.

ATMs

BP • Banco Popular • 134 Delancey St
CH • Chase • 108 Delancey St
CH • Chase • 255 First Ave
CI • Citibank • 50 Ave A
FL • Fleet • 126 Delancey St
HS • HSBC • 245 First Ave
CU • Lower East Side People's Federal Credit Union • 134 Ave C
CU • Lower East Side People's Federal Credit Union • 37 Ave B

Bagels

- **535 Self** • 203 E Houston St
- **Bagel Zone** • 48 Ave A
- **David's Bagels** • 228 First Ave
- **Houston's Bagel & Grill** • 283 E Houston St

Community Gardens

Fire Departments

- **Engine 28, Ladder 11** • 222 E 2nd St

Landmarks

- **Charlie Parker House** • 151 Ave B & Tompkins Sq Pk
- **Nuyorican Poets Cafe** • 236 E 3rd St
- **Tompkins Square Park** • Ave A & E 9th St

Libraries

- **Hamilton Fish Park** • 415 E Houston St
- **Tompkins Square** • 331 E 10th St

Post Offices

- **Peter Stuyvesant** • 432 E 14th St
- **Tompkins Square** • 244 E 3rd St

Schools

- **12th St Academy & East Side Community High School** • 420 E 12th St
- **CMSP- Marte Valle Secondary School** • 145 Stanton St
- **Connelly Center Education/Holy Child Middle School** • 220 E 4th St
- **East Villiage Community School** • 610 E 12th St
- **Immaculate Conception School** • 419 E 13th St
- **JHS 025 Marta Valle School** • 145 Stanton St
- **Mary Help of Christians** • 435 E 11th St
- **NEST+M** • 111 Columbia St
- **New Design High School** • 420 E 12th St
- **Our Lady of Sorrows School** • 219 Stanton St
- **PS 015 Roberto Clemente School** • 333 E 4th St
- **PS 019 Asher Levy School** • 185 First Ave
- **PS 034 F D Roosevelt School** • 730 E 12th St
- **PS 061 Anna Howard Shaw School** • 610 E 12th St
- **PS 063 William McKinley School** • 121 E 3rd St
- **PS 064 Robert Simon School** • 600 E 6th St
- **PS 097 Mangin School** • 525 E Houston St
- **PS 110 F Nightingale School** • 285 Delancey St
- **PS 140 Nathan Straus School** • 123 Ridge St
- **PS 142 Amalia Castro School** • 100 Attorney St
- **PS 188 The Island School** • 442 E Houston St
- **PS 196 Umbrella** • 442 E Houston St
- **PS 20 Anna Silver School** • 199 Essex St
- **St Brigid School** • 185 E 7th St

Supermarkets

- **Associated** • 409 E 14th St
- **C-Town** • 188 Ave C
- **C-Town** • 71 Ave D
- **Key Food** • 43 Columbia St
- **Key Food** • 52 Ave A

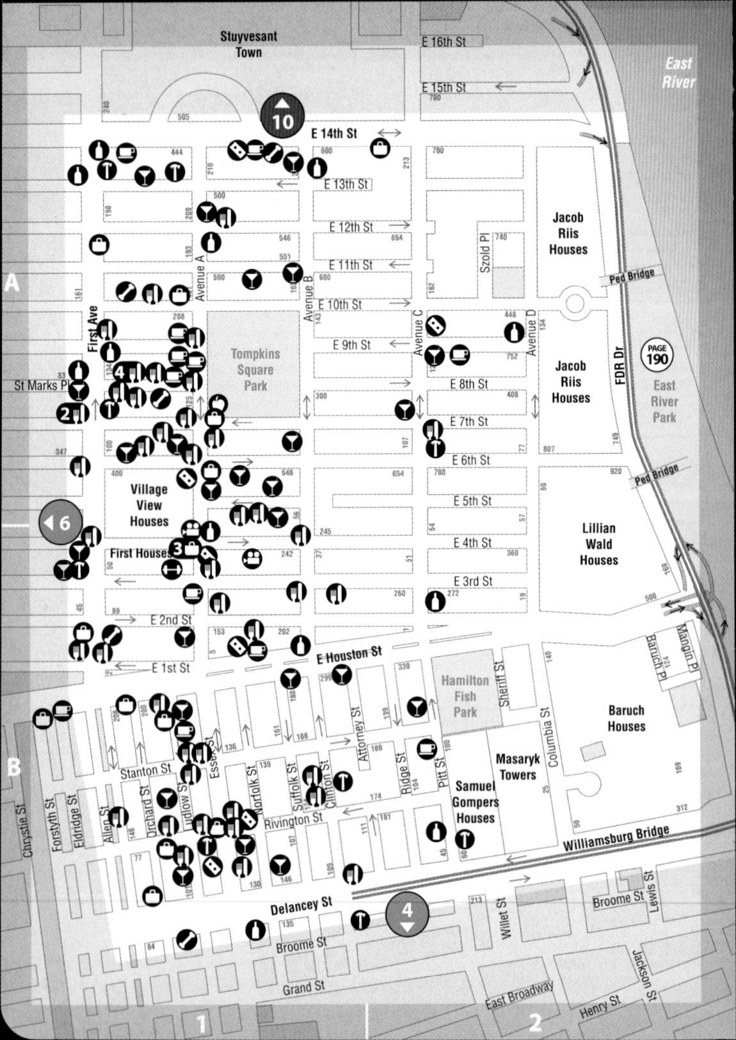

Stuyvesant Town
E 16th St
E 15th St
East River
E 14th St
E 13th St
E 12th St
E 11th St
E 10th St
E 9th St
E 8th St
E 7th St
E 6th St
E 5th St
E 4th St
E 3rd St
E 2nd St
E 1st St
E Houston St
St Marks Pl
First Ave
Avenue A
Avenue B
Avenue C
Avenue D
Szold Pl
Tompkins Square Park
Jacob Riis Houses
Jacob Riis Houses
Ped Bridge
Ped Bridge
FDR Dr
East River Park
PAGE 190
Village View Houses
First Houses
Lillian Wald Houses
Hamilton Fish Park
Sheriff St
Columbia St
Masaryk Towers
Samuel Gompers Houses
Baruch Houses
Baruch Pl
Mangin Pl
Attorney St
Ridge St
Pitt St
Clinton St
Suffolk St
Norfolk St
Essex St
Ludlow St
Orchard St
Allen St
Eldridge St
Forsyth St
Chrystie St
Stanton St
Rivington St
Williamsburg Bridge
Delancey St
Broome St
Broome St
Grand St
East Broadway
Henry St
Jackson St
Lewis St
Willet St
A
B
1
2

Kim's Video and Two Boots Video have the best selection of movies in Manhattan. Some favorite bars: 2A, 7B, Ace Bar, Bouche Bar, Mona's, Parkside, and Joe's Bar. First has great food and is open late and Banjara is by far the best of the 6th Street Indians. Mama's Food Shop on 3rd Street is one of the five reasons to never leave New York City.

Bars

- **11th Street Bar** • 510 E 11th St
- **2A** • 25 Ave A
- **7B** • 108 Ave B
- **Ace Bar** • 531 E 5th St
- **Barramundi** • 147 Ludlow St
- **Bouche Bar** • 540 E 5th St
- **Cherry Tavern** • 441 E 6th St
- **Clubhouse** • 700 E 9th St
- **DBA** • 41 First Ave
- **The Edge** • 95 E 3rd St
- **International Bar** • 120 1/2 First Ave
- **Joe's Bar** • 520 E 6th St
- **Korova Milk Bar** • 200 Ave A
- **Lakeside Lounge** • 162 Ave B
- **Lansky Lounge** • 104 Norfolk St
- **Max Fish** • 178 Ludlow St
- **Meow Mix** • 269 E Houston St
- **Mona's** • 224 Ave B
- **Motor City** • 127 Ludlow St
- **Parkside Lounge** • 317 E Houston St
- **The Phoenix** • 447 E 13th St
- **The Porch** • 115 Ave C
- **Sophie's** • 507 E 5th St
- **WCOU Radio Bar** • 115 First Ave
- **Welcome to the Johnsons** • 123 Rivington St
- **Zum Schneider** • 107 Ave C

Coffee

- **9th Street Espresso** • 700 E 9th St
- **Alchemy** • 106 Delancy St
- **altcoffee** • 139 Ave A
- **Café Cairo** • 189 E Houston St
- **Café Gigi** • 417 E 9th St
- **Café Pick Me Up** • 145 Ave A
- **City Market Cafe** • 131 Ave A
- **Des Moines** • 41 Ave A
- **Dunkin' Donuts** • 250 E Houston St
- **Dynasty Restaurant & Coffee Shop** • 600 E 14th St
- **J Coffee Shop** • 85 Pitt St
- **J&J Coffee Shop** • 442 E 14th St
- **Kudo Beans** • 49 1/2 First Ave
- **Pink Pony Cafe** • 176 Ludlow St

Farmer's Markets

- **Tompkins Square Park** • Ave A & 7th St - Sundays only

Gyms

- **Dolphin Fitness Clubs** • 155 E 3rd St

Hardware Stores

- **Ace Hardware** • 55 First Ave
- **Brickman and Sons** • 55 First Ave
- **CHP Hardware** • 96 Ave C
- **East Side Lumber** • 421 E 13th St
- **H&W Hardware** • 220 First Ave
- **HH Hardware** • 111 Rivington St
- **Rosa Hardware** • 85 Pitt St
- **Rothstein Hardware** • 56 Clinton St
- **Saifee Hardware** • 114 First Ave

Liquor Stores

- **6 Ave B Liquors** • 6 Ave B
- **Ave A Wine & Liquor** • 196 Ave A
- **Bee Liquors** • 225 Ave B
- **Bombay Spirits** • 224 First Ave
- **Fung Sing** • 138 First Ave
- **Gary's Liquor** • 141 Essex St
- **Jade Fountain Liquor** • 123 Delancey St
- **Loon Chun Liquor** • 47 Pitt St
- **Marty's Liquors** • 133 Ave D
- **Nizga Liquors** • 58 Ave A
- **Sale Price Liquor** • 24 Ave C
- **Wines on 1st** • 224 First Ave

Movie Theaters

- **Den of Cin** • 44 Ave A
- **Two Boots Pioneer Theater** • 155 E 3rd St

Pet Shops

- **Alpha Pet City** • 249 E 10th St
- **Animal Cracker** • 26 First Ave
- **Mikey's Pet Shop** • 130 E 7th St
- **Petland** • 85 Delancey St
- **Petland Discounts** • 530 E 14th St

Restaurants

- **1492 Food** • 60 Clinton St
- **71 Clinton Fresh Food** • 71 Clinton St
- **7A** • E 7th St & Ave A
- **B3** • 33 Ave B
- **Banjara** • 97 First Ave
- **Benny's Burritos** • 93 Ave A
- **Bereket Turkish Kebab House** • 187 E Houston St
- **Boca Chica** • 13 First Ave
- **Café Mogador** • 101 St Mark's Pl
- **Crooked Tree Creperie** • 110 St Mark's Pl
- **The Delancey** • 168 Delancey St
- **Dish** • 165 Allen St
- **Dok Suni's** • 119 First Ave
- **El Castillo de Jaqua** • 113 Rivington St
- **Esashi** • 32 Ave A
- **Essex Restaurant** • 120 Essex St
- **First** • 87 First Ave
- **Flea Market Cafe** • 131 Ave A
- **Flor's Kitchen** • 149 First Ave
- **Grilled Cheese NYC** • 168 Ludlow St
- **The Hat (Sombrero)** • 108 Stanton St
- **Il Bagatto** • 192 E 2nd St
- **Kate's Joint** • 58 Ave B
- **Katz's Delicatessen** • 205 E Houston St
- **Kuma Inn** • 113 Ludlow St
- **Kura Sushi** • 67 First Ave
- **La Caverna** • 122 Rivington St
- **La Focacceria** • 128 First Ave
- **Lavagna** • 545 E 5th St
- **Le Gamin** • 536 E 5th St
- **Lil' Frankies** • 19 First Ave
- **The Lite Touch Restaurant** • 151 Ave A
- **Mama's Food Shop** • 200 E 3rd St
- **Moustache** • 265 E 10th St
- **Odessa** • 119 Ave A
- **Old Devil Moon** • 511 E 12th St
- **Pianos** • 158 Ludlow St
- **Pylos** • 128 E 7th St
- **Raga** • 433 E 6th St
- **Takahachi** • 85 Ave A
- **Tasting Room** • 72 E 1st St
- **Teany** • 90 Rivington St
- **Two Boots** • 42 Ave A
- **Yaffa Cafe** • 97 St Mark's Pl
- **Zum Schneider** • 107 Ave C

Shopping

- **Alphabets** • 115 Ave A
- **Altman Luggage** • 135 Orchard St
- **Dowel Quality Products** • 91 First Ave
- **Earthmatters** • 177 Ludlow St
- **Economy Candy** • 108 Rivington St
- **Etherea** • 66 Ave A
- **Exit 9** • 64 Ave A
- **First Flight Music** • 174 First Ave
- **Gringer & Sons** • 29 First Ave
- **Lancelotti** • 66 Ave A
- **R&S Strauss Auto Store** • 644 E 14th St
- **Russ & Daughters** • 179 E Houston St
- **Spectra** • 293 E 10th St
- **Toys in Babeland** • 94 Rivington St
- **Yonah Schimmel's Knishery** • 137 E Houston St

Video Rental

- **Alpha Video** • 134 Ave C
- **Blockbuster Video** • 250 E Houston St
- **Crossbay Video** • 502 E 14th St
- **Kim's Video** • 85 Ave A
- **Two Boots** • 42 Ave A
- **The Video Store** • 128 Rivington St

Map 7 • East Village

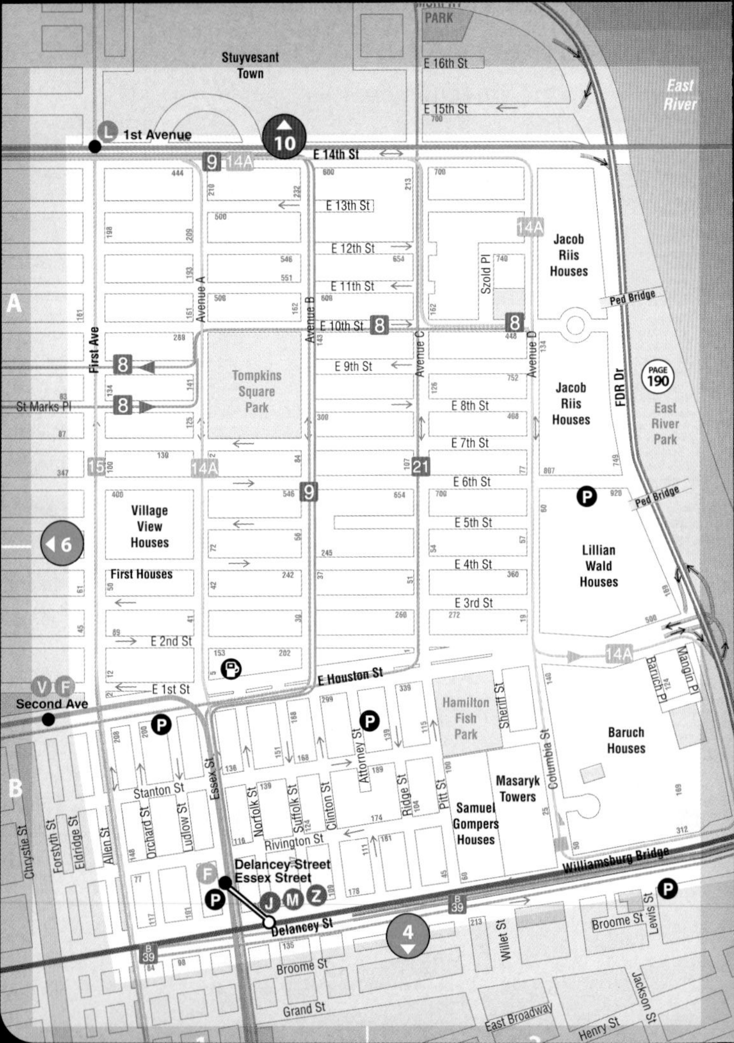
Stuyvesant Town
PARK
E 16th St
E 15th St
East River
1st Avenue
10
E 14th St
9
14A
E 13th St
E 12th St
E 11th St
E 10th St
8
E 9th St
St Marks Pl
E 8th St
E 7th St
E 6th St
E 5th St
E 4th St
E 3rd St
E 2nd St
E 1st St
E Houston St
First Ave
Avenue A
Avenue B
Avenue C
Avenue D
Szold Pl
Jacob Riis Houses
Ped Bridge
FDR Dr
PAGE 190
East River Park
Tompkins Square Park
21
15
6
Village View Houses
First Houses
Lillian Wald Houses
A
B
Second Ave
Hamilton Fish Park
Sheriff St
Columbia St
Baruch Pl
Mangin Pl
Baruch Houses
Masaryk Towers
Samuel Gompers Houses
Essex St
Stanton St
Orchard St
Ludlow St
Allen St
Eldridge St
Forsyth St
Chrystie St
Norfolk St
Suffolk St
Clinton St
Attorney St
Ridge St
Pitt St
Rivington St
Delancey Street Essex Street
Delancey St
Williamsburg Bridge
Willet St
Broome St
Lewis St
Grand St
East Broadway
Jackson St
Henry St
4
39

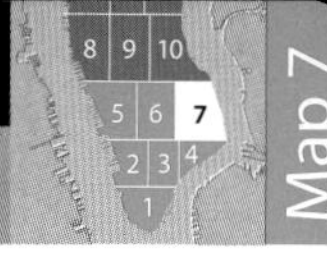

Parking is usually pretty good except for Friday and Saturday nights when the Bridge & Tunnel crowd invades. It looks like the L train will be in and out of service into 2005 and probably beyond. The East Village badly needs a subway line that has a Tompkins Square Park stop, but it will never happen, no matter how gentrified the neighborhood gets, so you can just forget it.

Subways

F J M Z .... Delancey St-Essex St
L .... First Ave
F V .... Second Ave

Bus Lines

14 .... 14th St/Ave A/Ave D
15 .... First Ave
21 .... First St/Ave C
8 .... 9th St/10th St
9 .... 14th St/Ave B
B39 .... Delancey St

Gas Stations

• **Mobil** • 253 E 2nd St

Parking

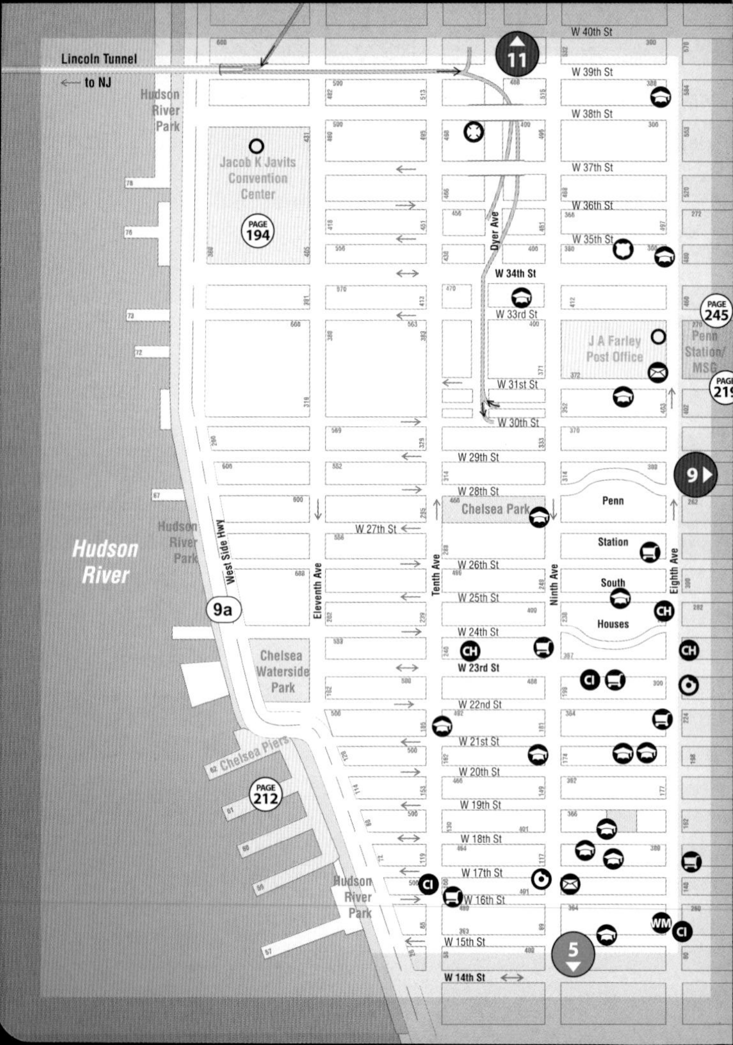

Lincoln Tunnel
to NJ
Hudson River Park
Jacob K Javits Convention Center
PAGE 194
Hudson River
Hudson River Park
West Side Hwy
9a
Chelsea Waterside Park
Chelsea Piers
PAGE 212
Hudson River Park
Eleventh Ave
Tenth Ave
Dyer Ave
Ninth Ave
Eighth Ave
W 40th St
W 39th St
W 38th St
W 37th St
W 36th St
W 35th St
W 34th St
W 33rd St
W 31st St
W 30th St
W 29th St
W 28th St
W 27th St
W 26th St
W 25th St
W 24th St
W 23rd St
W 22nd St
W 21st St
W 20th St
W 19th St
W 18th St
W 17th St
W 16th St
W 15th St
W 14th St
Chelsea Park
J A Farley Post Office
Penn Station/ MSG
PAGE 245
PAGE 219
Penn Station South Houses
11
9
5

Essentials

There are now roughly 200 art galleries in Chelsea, which has pretty much now deposed SoHo as the art capital of New York. However, more services are desperately needed, especially in the Javits Center area (unless you count the services of transvestite prostitutes as "essential"). Is this the future home of the Jets? Area residents certainly hope not...

ATMs

CH • Chase • 238 Eighth Ave
CH • Chase • 284 Eighth Ave
CH • Chase • 475 W 23rd St
CI • Citibank • 111 Eighth Ave
CI • Citibank • 322 W 23rd St
CI • Citibank • 88 Tenth Ave
WM • Washington Mutual • 111 Eighth Ave

Bagels

- **Murray's Bagels** • 242 Eighth Ave
- **Unbagelievable** • 75 Ninth Ave

Fire Departments

- **Engine 34, Ladder 21** • 440 W 38th St

Landmarks

- **J A Farley Post Office** • 441 Eighth Ave
- **Jacob K Javits Convention Center** • 36th St & Eleventh Ave

Police

- **Mid-Town South** • 357 W 35th St

Post Offices

- **J A Farley General** • 441 Eighth Ave
- **Port Authority** • 76 Ninth Ave

Schools

- **Bayard Rustin High School for the Humanities** • 351 W 18th St
- **Corlears School** • 324 W 15th St
- **General Theological Seminary** • 175 Ninth Ave
- **Guardian Angel School** • 193 Tenth Ave
- **The Lorge School** • 353 W 17th St
- **NYC Lab School & NYC Museum School** • 333 W 17th St
- **PS 11 William T Harris School & MS 260 Clinton** • 320 W 21st St
- **PS 33 Chelsea School** • 281 Ninth Ave
- **Satellite Academy Program** • 500 Eighth Ave
- **St Columba School** • 331 W 25th St
- **St Michael Academy** • 425 W 33rd St
- **Technical Career Institute** • 320 W 31st St

Supermarkets

- **Chelsea Market Assoc** • 460 W 16th St
- **D'Agostino** • 257 W 17th St
- **D'Agostino** • 312 W 23rd St
- **Gristede's** • 221 Eighth Ave
- **Gristede's** • 225 Ninth Ave
- **Gristede's** • 307 W 26th St

Lincoln Tunnel
to NJ
Hudson River Park
Jacob K Javits Convention Center
PAGE 194
W 40th St
W 39th St
W 38th St
W 37th St
W 36th St
W 35th St
W 34th St
W 33rd St
W 31st St
W 30th St
W 29th St
W 28th St
W 27th St
W 26th St
W 25th St
W 24th St
W 23rd St
W 22nd St
W 21st St
W 20th St
W 19th St
W 18th St
W 17th St
W 16th St
W 15th St
W 14th St
Dyer Ave
J A Farley Post Office
Penn Station/ MSG
PAGE 245
PAGE 219
Chelsea Park
Penn Station South Houses
Hudson River
West Side Hwy
9a
Eleventh Ave
Tenth Ave
Ninth Ave
Eighth Ave
Chelsea Waterside Park
Chelsea Piers
PAGE 212
Hudson River Park
11
9
5

Sundries / Entertainment

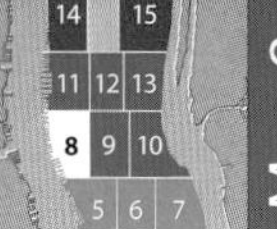

More and more excellent bars and restaurants are opening up, although some services are still pretty thin on Tenth and Eleventh Avenues. For food, the always amazing La Luncheonette is brilliant but pricey and Grand Sichuan International has some interesting dishes you might not even find in Chinatown.

Bars

- **Billymark's West** • 332 Ninth Ave
- **Blarney Stone** • 340 Ninth Ave
- **Blarney Stone** • 410 Eighth Ave
- **Chelsea Brewing Company** • Pier 59
- **Chelsea Commons** • 242 Tenth Ave
- **Freight** • 410 W 16th St
- **Glass** • 287 Tenth Ave
- **Kanvas** • 219 Ninth Ave
- **Openair** • 559 W 22nd St
- **The Park** • 118 Tenth Ave
- **Red Rock West** • 457 W 17th St
- **West Side Tavern** • 360 W 23rd St

Coffee

- **Big Cup Tea & Coffee House** • 228 Eighth Ave
- **Chelsea Coffee** • 140 Ninth Ave
- **Dunkin' Donuts** • 215 Tenth Ave
- **Dunkin' Donuts** • 269 Eighth Ave
- **Dunkin' Donuts** • 525 Eighth Ave
- **Java Works** • 309 W 17th St
- **Starbucks** • 124 Eighth Ave
- **Starbucks** • 177 Eighth Ave
- **Starbucks** • 352 W 30th St
- **Starbucks** • 494 Eighth Ave

Copy Shops

- **Document Express Inc (24 hrs)** • 75 Ninth Ave
- **Mail Boxes Etc (9 am-7 pm)** • 245 Eighth Ave

Gyms

- **Chelsea Piers Sports Center** • Chelsea Piers-Pier 60
- **New York Sports Clubs** • 270 Eighth Ave
- **Town Sports International** • 505 Eighth Ave

Hardware Stores

- **Diener Park** • 194 Eighth Ave
- **Friedlander Locksmith** • 307 W 37th St
- **Hardware Depot** • 399 Eighth Ave
- **Karmit Wholesale** • 529 Ninth Ave
- **Mercer Sq Hardware** • 286 Eighth Ave
- **MJ Hardware & Electric** • 520 Eighth Ave
- **NF Hardware** • 219 Ninth Ave
- **SGS Hardware** • 157 Eighth Ave
- **True Value Hardware** • 191 Ninth Ave
- **United Equipment and Supply** • 419 Ninth Ave

Liquor Stores

- **34th Street Winery** • 460 W 34th St
- **Brian's 336 Liquor Store** • 336 Ninth Ave
- **Chelsea Liquor** • 114 Ninth Ave
- **Chelsea Wine Vault** • 75 Ninth Ave
- **Chriskie Wines & Liquors** • 332 Eighth Ave
- **DeLauren Wines & Liquors** • 332 Eighth Ave
- **Kwang Koo Won** • 474 Ninth Ave
- **London Terrace Liquor** • 221 Ninth Ave
- **Metropolitan Wine & Liquor** • 486 Ninth Ave
- **Philippe Wine & Liquor** • 312 W 23rd St
- **US Wine and LIquor** • 486 Ninth Ave

Movie Theaters

- **Clearview's Chelsea West** • 333 W 23rd St
- **Gavin Brown's Enterprise** • 436 W 15th St
- **Loews 34th Street** • 312 W 34th St

Pet Shops

- **Barking Zoo** • 172 Ninth Ave
- **Blonde With Beagle** • 545 W 34th St
- **Petland Discounts** • 312 W 23rd St
- **The Dog Run** • 136 Ninth Ave
- **Towne House Grooming** • 369 W 19th St

Restaurants

- **Blue Moon Mexican Cafe** • 150 Eighth Ave
- **Bottino** • 246 Tenth Ave
- **Bright Food Shop** • 216 Eighth Ave
- **Burritoville** • 352 W 39th St
- **Chelsea Bistro & Bar** • 358 W 23rd St
- **Cuba Libre** • 165 Eighth Ave
- **Cupcake Cafe** • 522 Ninth Ave
- **El Cid** • 322 W 15th St
- **Empire Diner** • 210 Tenth Ave
- **Frank's Restaurant** • 85 Tenth Ave
- **Grand Sichuan Int'l** • 229 Ninth Ave
- **Havana Chelsea** • 190 Eighth Ave
- **La Luncheonette** • 130 Tenth Ave
- **La Taza de Oro** • 96 Eighth Ave
- **Le Gamin** • 183 Ninth Ave
- **Moonstruck Diner** • 400 W 23rd St
- **Pepe Giallo** • 253 Tenth Ave
- **The Red Cat** • 227 Tenth Ave
- **Salon Mexico** • 509 Ninth Ave
- **Sandwich Planet** • 534 Ninth Ave
- **Skylight Diner** • 402 W 34th St
- **Spice** • 199 Eighth Ave
- **Tick Tock Diner** • 481 Eighth Ave
- **Viceroy** • 160 Eighth Ave

Shopping

- **B&H Photo** • 420 Ninth Ave
- **Buon Italia** • 75 Ninth Ave
- **Chelsea Garden Center** • 455 W 16th St
- **Chelsea Wholesale Flower Market** • 75 Ninth Ave
- **Fat Witch Bakery** • 75 Ninth Ave
- **Kitchen Market** • 218 Eighth Ave
- **Portico** • 75 Ninth Ave

Video Rental

- **Alan's Alley Video** • 207A Ninth Ave
- **Rina** • 364 W 23rd St

Lincoln Tunnel
to NJ
Hudson River Park
Jacob K Javits Convention Center
PAGE 194
W 40th St
W 39th St
W 38th St
W 37th St
W 36th St
W 35th St
W 34th St
W 33rd St
W 31st St
W 30th St
W 29th St
W 28th St
W 27th St
W 26th St
W 25th St
W 24th St
W 23rd St
W 22nd St
W 21st St
W 20th St
W 19th St
W 18th St
W 17th St
W 16th St
W 15th St
W 14th St
Dyer Ave
34th Street Penn Station
PAGE 245
J A Farley Post Office
Penn Station/ MSG
PAGE 219
Chelsea Park
Penn Station South Houses
Hudson River
West Side Hwy
9a
Eleventh Ave
Tenth Ave
Ninth Ave
Eighth Ave
Chelsea Waterside Park
23rd Street
Chelsea Piers
PAGE 212
Hudson River Park
14th Street
8th Avenue

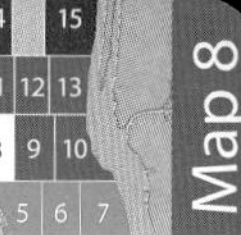

Parking and driving in this area are quite bad during the day and quite good at night, although there just aren't many spots at all above 30th Street. Games at Madison Square Garden and the Lincoln Tunnel are major sources of traffic. Tragically, there are no subway lines west of Eighth Avenue, although they're finally studying the feasibility of running a line out to the Javits (duh!).

Subways

A C E .... 34 St-Penn Station
A C E .... 14th St/Eighth Ave
C E .... 23rd St

Bus Lines

10 20 .. Seventh Ave/Eighth Ave/Central Park W
11 ....Ninth Ave/Tenth Ave
14 .... 14th St Crosstown
16 .... 34th St Crosstown
23 .... 23rd St Crosstown
34 .... 34th St Crosstown

Car Rental

- **Bermuda Limousine** • 537 W 20th St
- **New York Rent-A-Car** • 325 W 34th St
- **U-Haul** • 562 W 23rd St
- **U-Save Auto Rental** • 333 Tenth Ave

Car Washes

- **235 10th Ave Car Wash** • 235 Tenth Ave
- **Steve's Detailing & Tires** • 516 W 27th St
- **Tenth Avenue Car Wash** • 450 W 15th St

Gas Stations

- **Amoco** • 110 Eighth Ave
- **BP** • W 34th St & Tenth Ave
- **Exxon** • 215 Tenth Ave
- **Getty** • 239 Tenth Ave
- **Mobil** • 309 Eleventh Ave
- **Mobil** • 70 Tenth Ave

Parking

W 39th St
W 38th St
W 37th St
W 36th St
W 35th St
Macy's
Herald Square
Herald Square
W 34th St
Empire State Building
Morgan Library
Park Ave S
PAGE 245
PAGE 219
PAGE 192
J A Farley Post Office
Madison Square Garden
Penn Station
W 33rd St
W 32nd St
W 31st St
Garment District
W 30th St
W 29th St
Flower District
W 28th St
W 27th St
W 26th St
W 25th St
W 24th St
W 23rd St
W 22nd St
W 21st St
W 20th St
W 19th St
W 18th St
W 17th St
W 16th St
W 15th St
W 14th St
Eighth Ave
Seventh Ave (Fashion Ave)
Sixth Ave (Ave of the Americas)
Broadway
Fifth Ave
Madison Ave
Madison Sq Plz
Madison Square Park
Metropolitan Life Insurance Company
Chelsea Hotel
Flatiron Building
Theodore Roosevelt Birthplace
Union Square
12
10
8
5
6
1
2

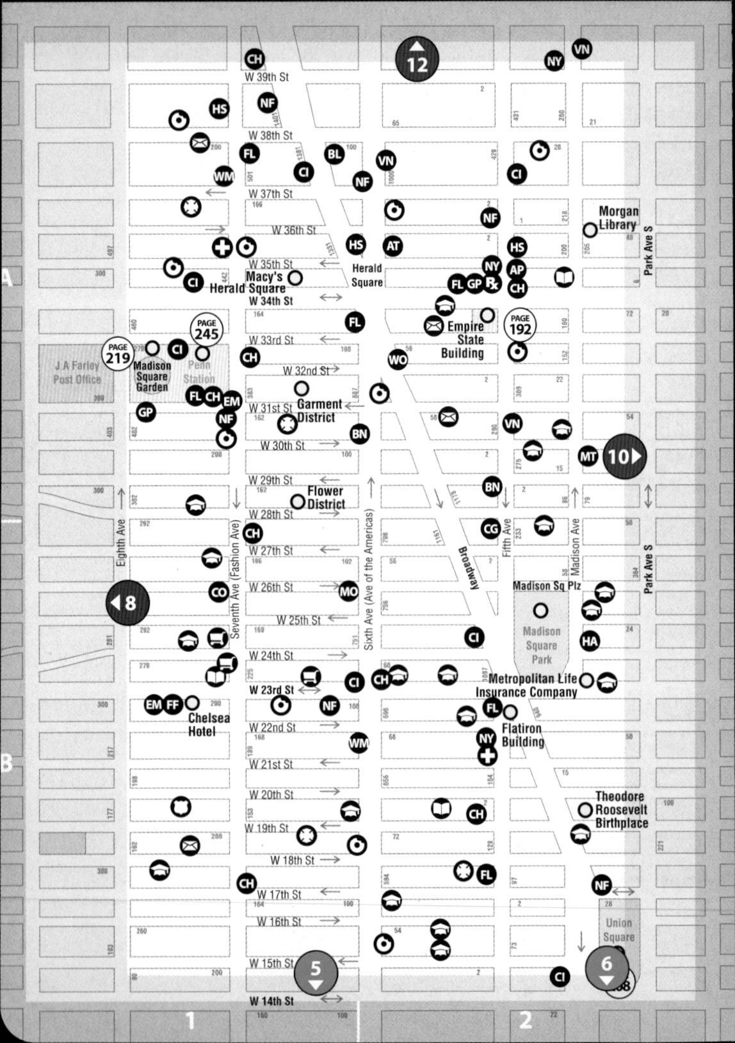

If you stand in the middle of traffic at the junction of Broadway, Fifth Avenue, and 24th Street and turn slowly around, you'll see the Flatiron Building, the Met Life Building, the New York Life Building, and the Empire State Building. It's perhaps the single most awe-inspiring spot in all of Manhattan—if you don't get run over.

ATMs

AM • Amalgamated • 11 Union Sq W
AP • Apple • 350 Fifth Ave
AT • Atlantic • 960 Sixth Ave
BL • Bank Leumi • 1400 Broadway
NY • Bank of New York • 162 Fifth Ave
NY • Bank of New York • 260 Madison Ave
NY • Bank of New York • 350 Fifth Ave
BN • Broadway National • 250 Fifth Ave
BN • Broadway National • 855 Sixth Ave
CH • Chase • 127 Seventh Ave
CH • Chase • 1411 Broadway
CH • Chase • 2 Penn Plz
CH • Chase • 305 Seventh Ave
CH • Chase • 349 Fifth Ave
CH • Chase • 399 Seventh Ave
CH • Chase • 5 W 19th St
CH • Chase • 71 W 23rd St
CG • Cho Hung • 241 Fifth Ave
CI • Citibank • 1107 Broadway
CI • Citibank • 1384 Broadway
CI • Citibank • 201 W 34th St
CI • Citibank • 411 Fifth Ave
CI • Citibank • 717 Sixth Ave
CI • Citibank • 79 Fifth Ave
CO • Commerce Bank • 200 W 26th St
EM • Emigrant • 250 W 23rd St
EM • Emigrant • 371 Seventh Ave
FL • Fleet • 116 Fifth Ave
FL • Fleet • 1293 Broadway
FL • Fleet • 186 Fifth Ave
FL • Fleet • 350 Fifth Ave
FL • Fleet • 4 Penn Plz
FL • Fleet • 515 Seventh Ave
FF • Fourth Federal Savings • 242 W 23rd St
GP • Greenpoint Bank • 1 Penn Plz
GP • Greenpoint Bank • 10 E 34th St
HA • Habib American Bank • 99 Madison Ave
HS • HSBC • 1350 Broadway
HS • HSBC • 550 Seventh Ave
MT • Manufacturers and Traders Trust • 95 Madison Ave
CU • Montauk Credit Union • 111 W 26th St
NF • North Fork Bank • 1001 Sixth Ave
NF • North Fork Bank • 120 W 23rd St
NF • North Fork Bank • 1407 Broadway
NF • North Fork Bank • 31 E 17th St
NF • North Fork Bank • 370 Seventh Ave
NF • North Fork Bank • 404 Fifth Ave
VN • Valley National Bank • 1040 Sixth Ave
VN • Valley National Bank • 275 Madison Ave
VN • Valley National Bank • 295 Fifth Ave
WM • Washington Mutual • 498 Seventh Ave
WM • Washington Mutual • 700 Sixth Ave
WO • Woori America Bank • 1250 Broadway

Bagels

- **23rd St Bagel** • 170 W 23rd St
- **Bagel Maven** • 370 Seventh Ave
- **Bagels & Co** • 243 W 38th St
- **Bagels Off Fifth** • 4 E 38th St
- **Bread Factory Café** • 470 Seventh Ave
- **Brooklyn Bagel Bakery** • 319 Fifth Ave
- **Chelsea Bagel Bakery** • 544 Sixth Ave
- **Le Bon Bagel** • 980 Sixth Ave
- **Liberty Bagel** • 876 Sixth Ave
- **Mom's Bagels** • 240 W 35th St
- **Pick-a-Bagel** • 601 Sixth Ave

Fire Departments

- **Engine 1, Ladder 24** • 142 W 31st St
- **Engine 14** • 14 E 18th St
- **Engine 26** • 220 W 37th St
- **Engine 3, Ladder 12** • 146 W 19th St

Hospitals

- **American Association for Bikur Cholim Hospital** • 156 Fifth Ave
- **National Jewish Center For Immunology** • 450 Seventh Ave

Landmarks

- **Chelsea Hotel** • 23rd St btwn Seventh & Eighth Aves
- **Empire State Building** • 34th St & Fifth Ave
- **Flatiron Building** • 175 Fifth Ave
- **Flower District** • 28th St btwn Sixth & Seventh Aves
- **Garment District** • West 30's south of Herald Sq
- **Macy's Herald Square** • 151 W 34th St
- **Madison Square Garden** • 4 Penn Plz
- **Madison Square Park** • 23rd St & Broadway
- **Metropolitan Life Insurance Co** • 1 Madison Ave
- **Morgan Library** • 29 E 36th St
- **Penn Station** • 31st St & Eighth Ave
- **Theodore Roosevelt Birthplace** • 28 E 20th St
- **Union Square** • 14th St-Union Sq

Libraries

- **Andrew Heiskell Library for the Blind** • 40 W 20th St
- **Muhlenberg** • 209 W 23rd St
- **Science, Industry, and Business Library** • 188 Madison Ave

24-Hour Pharmacies

- **Duane Reade** • 358 Fifth Ave

Police

- **10th Precinct** • 230 W 20th St

Post Offices

- **Empire State** • 19 W 33rd St
- **Greeley Square** • 39 W 31st St
- **Midtown** • 223 W 38th St
- **Old Chelsea** • 217 W 18th St

Schools

- **All Saints School** • 52 E 30th St
- **American Academy of Dramatic Arts** • 120 Madison Ave
- **Apex Technical School** • 635 Sixth Ave
- **Ballet Tech / NYC PS for Dance** • 890 Broadway
- **Baruch College** • 46 E 26th St
- **Bourel Technical** • 50 W 34th St
- **East Manhattan School** • 35 W 15th St
- **Fashion Institute of Technology** • 227 W 27th St
- **High School for Fashion Industries** • 225 W 24th St
- **Institute for Culinary Education** • 50 E 23rd St
- **John A Coleman School** • 590 Sixth Ave
- **Liberty High School** • 250 W 18th St
- **Manhattan Village Academy** • 43 W 22nd St
- **NY Institute of Credit** • 71 W 23rd St
- **Physical City High School** • 55 E 25th St
- **PS 723 Manhattan Transition Center** • 22 E 28th St
- **Studio Semester** • 229 W 28th St
- **Touro College** • 27 W 23rd St
- **Xavier High School** • 30 W 16th St

Supermarkets

- **Associated** • 244 Seventh Ave
- **Garden of Eden Gourmet** • 162 W 23rd St
- **Whole Foods Market** • 250 Seventh Ave

Map 9 • Flatiron / Lower Midtown

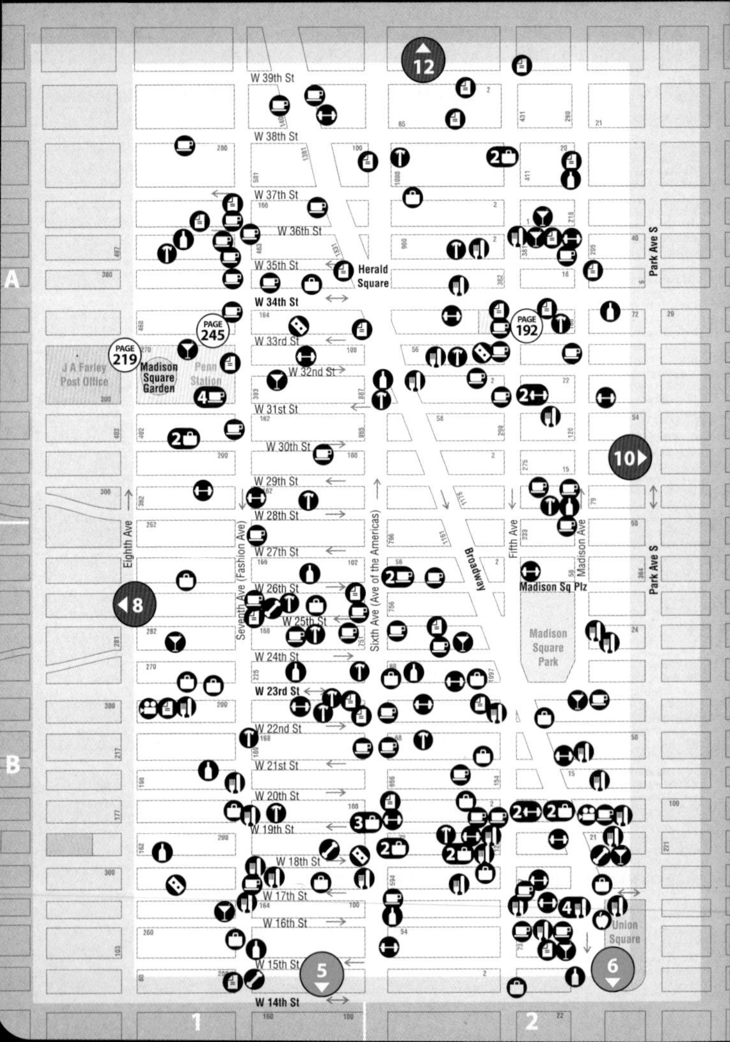

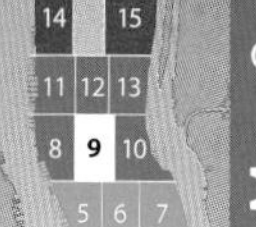

The Flatiron/Lower Midtown area contains two of New York's most famous business districts, the Garment District (in the west 30s south of Herald Square) and the Flower District (28th Street between Sixth and Seventh Avenues). Kang Suh is one of several great Korean restaurants—they're all located in the low 30s and they're all worth trying.

Bars

- **Blarney Stone** • 106 W 32nd St
- **Cutting Room** • 19 W 24th St
- **Dusk of Miami** • 147 W 24th St
- **Ginger Man** • 11 E 36th St
- **Heartland Brewery** • 35 Union Sq W
- **Live Bait** • 14 E 23rd St
- **Merchants** • 112 Seventh Ave
- **Old Town Bar & Restaurant** • 45 E 18th St
- **Tir Na Nog** • 5 Penn Plz
- **Under The Volcano** • 12 E 36th St

Coffee

- **Aleem's Coffee Shop** • 46 W 21st St
- **Andrew's Coffee Shop:**
  - 136 Fifth Ave
  - 1410 Broadway
  - 246 W 38th St
  - 463 Seventh Ave
- **Au Bon Pain** • 350 Fifth Ave
- **Big Apple Coffee Shop** • 350 Fifth Ave
- **Caffe Rafaella** • 134 Seventh Ave S
- **Coffee Shop** • 29 Union Sq W
- **Cosi:**
  - 202 W 36th St
  - 3 E 17th St
  - 498 Seventh Ave
  - 700 Sixth Ave
- **Dunkin' Donuts:**
  - 1 Penn Plz
  - 150 W 30th St
  - 24 E 23rd St
  - 289 Seventh Ave
  - 302 Fifth Ave
  - 80 Madison Ave
- **Emack & Bolio's** • 151 W 34th St
- **Guy & Gallard** • 475 Park Ave S
- **Harrie's Coffee Shop** • 1407 Broadway
- **Hollywood Coffee Shop** • 574 Sixth Ave
- **Jamie's** • 164 Madison Ave
- **Jazz N Java** • 868 Broadway
- **Kavehaz** • 37 W 26th St
- **Kostas & Angelo Coffee Shop** • 44 E 32nd St
- **Mama Cassie's Coffee House** • 765 Sixth Ave
- **Milanese Coffee Shop** • 168 W 25th St
- **Minx Coffee Shop** • 307 Seventh Ave
- **New Big Apple Coffeeshop** • 76 Madison Ave
- **New Spirit Cafe** • 43 W 24th St
- **New World Coffee** • 125 Seventh Ave
- **News Bar** • 2 W 19th St
- **Oren's Daily Roast** • Penn Station LIRR Concourse Level
- **Seattle Coffee Roasters** • 202 W 34th St
- **Starbucks:**
  - 1 Penn Plz
  - 1372 Broadway
  - 200 Madison Ave
  - 261 Fifth Ave
  - 334 Fifth Ave
  - 370 Seventh Ave
  - 41 Union Sq W
  - 450 Seventh Ave
  - 462 Seventh Ave
  - 525 Seventh Ave
  - 675 Sixth Ave
  - 684 Sixth Ave
  - 750 Sixth Ave
  - 776 Sixth Ave
- **West Front Store** • 28 W 32nd St

Copy Shops

- **A-A-D United Reprographic Services (8:30 am-5:15 pm)** • 40 W 25th St
- **AAA Wonder Copy & Printing (9 am-5:30 pm)** • 16 W 23rd St
- **Acu-Copy (8:30 am-midnight)** • 26 W 39th St
- **ADS Copying (8 am-6 pm)** • 29 W 38th St
- **Century Copy Center (8:30 am-7 pm)** • 70 Seventh Ave
- **Chelsea Quality Copy & Printing (9 am-6 pm)** • 255 W 23rd St
- **Comzone (8:30 am-10 pm)** • 21 E 15th St
- **Copy Door Corp (8 am-7:30 pm)** • 1011 Sixth Ave
- **Kasray (7 am-6:30 pm)** • 122 W 26th St
- **Kinko's:**
  - 191 Madison Ave
  - 245 Seventh Ave
  - 500 Seventh Ave
  - 650 Sixth Ave
  - 350 Fifth Ave (7-11)
- **Longacre Copy Center (9 am-6 pm)** • 235 W 36th St
- **Mail Boxes Etc (8:30 am-6:30 pm)** • 244 Madison Ave
- **Parrot Color Copy Center (9 am-5 pm)** • 1328 Broadway
- **Staples:**
  - 1293 Broadway (7 am-7 pm)
  - 16 E 34th St (7 am-7 pm)
  - 699 Sixth Ave (7 am-8 pm)
  - Penn Station (7 am-8 pm)
- **Swift Copy Printing (9 am-6 pm)** • 10 E 36th St
- **The UPS Store (8:30 am-7 pm)** • 101 W 23rd St
- **The Village Copier** • 10 E 39th St

Farmer's Markets

- **Union Square Greenmarket** • Broadway & 17th St

Gyms

- **19th St Gym** • 22 W 19th St
- **Bally Sports Club** • 139 W 32nd St
- **Bally Total Fitness** • 641 Sixth Ave
- **David Barton Gym** • 552 Sixth Ave
- **Definitions** • 139 Fifth Ave
- **Duomo** • 11 E 26th St
- **Equinox Fitness Club** • 897 Broadway
- **Fitness Results** • 137 Fifth Ave
- **Kyokushin USA** • 284 Fifth Ave
- **Middletown Health Club** • 290 Fifth Ave
- **New York Health & Racquet Club** • 60 W 23rd St
- **New York Sports Clubs** • 1372 Broadway
- **New York Sports Clubs** • 200 Madison Ave
- **New York Sports Clubs** • 50 W 34th St
- **Pex Personalized Exercise** • 924 Broadway
- **Pierre Romain** • 208 W 29th St
- **Steel Gym** • 146 W 23rd St
- **Synergy Fitness Clubs** • 43 W 23rd St
- **YMCA** • 333 Seventh Ave
- **Zone Studios 121** • 31 E 31st St

Hardware Stores

- **727 Hardware** • 727 Sixth Ave
- **A&M 28th St Hardware** • 15 E 28th St
- **Adco Hardware** • 23 W 35th St
- **Admore Hardware & Lock** • 11 E 33rd St
- **B&N Hardware** • 12 W 19th St
- **Central Hardware & Electric** • 1055 Sixth Ave
- **Elm Electric & Hardware** • 884 Sixth Ave
- **Halmor Hardware and Supply** • 48 W 22nd St
- **Harris Hardware** • 151 W 19th St
- **Jamali Hardware & Garden Supplies** • 149 W 28th St
- **KDM Hardware** • 150 W 26th St
- **Kove Brothers Hardware** • 189 Seventh Ave
- **Simon Greenspan Hardware** • 261 W 35th St
- **Spacesaver Hardware** • 132 W 23rd St
- **Whitey's Hardware** • 37 W 32nd St

Liquor Stores

- **A&J Kessler Liquors** • 23 E 28th St
- **Burgundy Wine Co** • 143 W 26th St
- **Chelsea Wine Cellar** • 200 W 21st St
- **Harry's Liquors** • 270 W 36th St
- **Honig's Wines and Liquors** • 61 W 23rd St
- **House of Cheers** • 261 W 18th St
- **Landmark Wine & Spirit** • 167 W 23rd St
- **Lewis-Kaye Wines & Liquors** • 60 E 34th St
- **Madison Ave Liquors** • 244 Madison Ave
- **Old Chelsea Wine & Liquor Store** • 86 Seventh Ave
- **Sonest Liquors** • 878 Sixth Ave
- **Union Square Wine & Spirits** • 33 Union Sq W
- **Wine Gallery** • 576 Sixth Ave

Movie Theaters

- **Clearview's Chelsea** • 260 W 23rd St
- **Loews 19th St East** • 890 Broadway

Pet Shops

- **Doggone Purrrty** • 151 W 25th St
- **New York Pet Spa and Hotel** • 145 W 18th St
- **Petco** • 860 Broadway
- **Spot Pets Inc** • 78 Seventh Ave

Restaurants

- **Basta Pasta** • 37 W 17th St
- **Blue Water Grill** • 31 Union Sq W
- **Burritoville** • 264 W 23rd St
- **Cafeteria** • 119 Seventh Ave
- **Chat 'n Chew** • 10 E 16th St
- **City Bakery** • 3 W 18th St
- **Coffee Shop** • Union Sq W
- **Craft** • 43 E 19th St
- **Eisenberg Sandwich Shop** • 174 Fifth Ave
- **Eleven Madison Park** • 11 Madison Ave
- **Elmo** • 156 Seventh Ave
- **Francisco's Centro Vasco** • 159 W 23rd St
- **Gramercy Tavern** • 42 E 20th St
- **Hangawi** • 12 E 32nd St
- **Kang Suh** • 1250 Broadway
- **Kum Gang San** • 49 W 32nd St
- **Le Madri** • 168 W 18th St
- **Le Pain Quotidien** • 38 E 19th St
- **Le Zie 2000** • 172 Seventh Ave
- **Luna Park** • 50 E 17th St
- **Mesa Grill** • 102 Fifth Ave
- **Periyali** • 35 W 20th St
- **Petite Abeille** • 107 W 18th St
- **Republic** • 37 Union Sq W
- **Silver Swan** • 41 E 20th St
- **Tabla** • 11 Madison Ave
- **Toledo** • 6 E 36th St
- **Uncle Moe's** • 14 W 19th St
- **Union Square Cafe** • 21 E 16th St
- **Woo Chon** • 8 W 36th St

Shopping

- **17 at 17 Thrift Shop** • 17 W 17th St
- **30th St Guitars** • 236 W 30th St
- **ABC Carpet & Home** • 888 Broadway
- **Abracadabra** • 19 W 21st St
- **Academy Records & CDs** • 12 W 18th St
- **Adorama Camera** • 42 W 18th St
- **Ariston** • 69 Fifth Ave
- **Bed Bath & Beyond** • 620 Sixth Ave
- **Capitol Fishing Tackle** • 218 W 23rd St
- **City Quilter, The** • 133 W 25th St
- **CompUSA** • 420 Fifth Ave
- **Container Store, The** • 629 Sixth Ave
- **Fish's Eddy** • 889 Broadway
- **Housing Works Thrift Shop** • 143 W 17th St
- **Jam Paper & Envelope** • 611 Sixth Ave
- **Jazz Record Center** • 236 W 26th St
- **Just Bulbs** • 936 Broadway
- **Krups Kitchen and Bath** • 11 W 18th St
- **Loehmann's** • 101 Seventh Ave
- **Lord & Taylor** • 424 Fifth Ave
- **Macy's** • 151 W 34th St
- **Midnight Records** • 263 W 23rd St
- **Paper Access** • 23 W 18th St
- **Paragon Sporting Goods** • 867 Broadway
- **Phoenix** • 64 W 37th St
- **Pleasure Chest** • 156 Seventh Ave
- **Radio Shack** • 36 E 23rd St
- **Rogue Music** • 251 W 30th St
- **Sam Flax** • 12 W 20th St
- **Sports Authority** • 636 Sixth Ave
- **Tekserve** • 119 W 23rd St

Video Rental

- **155 Video Center** • 155 W 33rd St
- **603 Video Store** • 603 Sixth Ave
- **Koryo Video** • 7 W 32nd St
- **Video Blitz** • 267 W 17th St

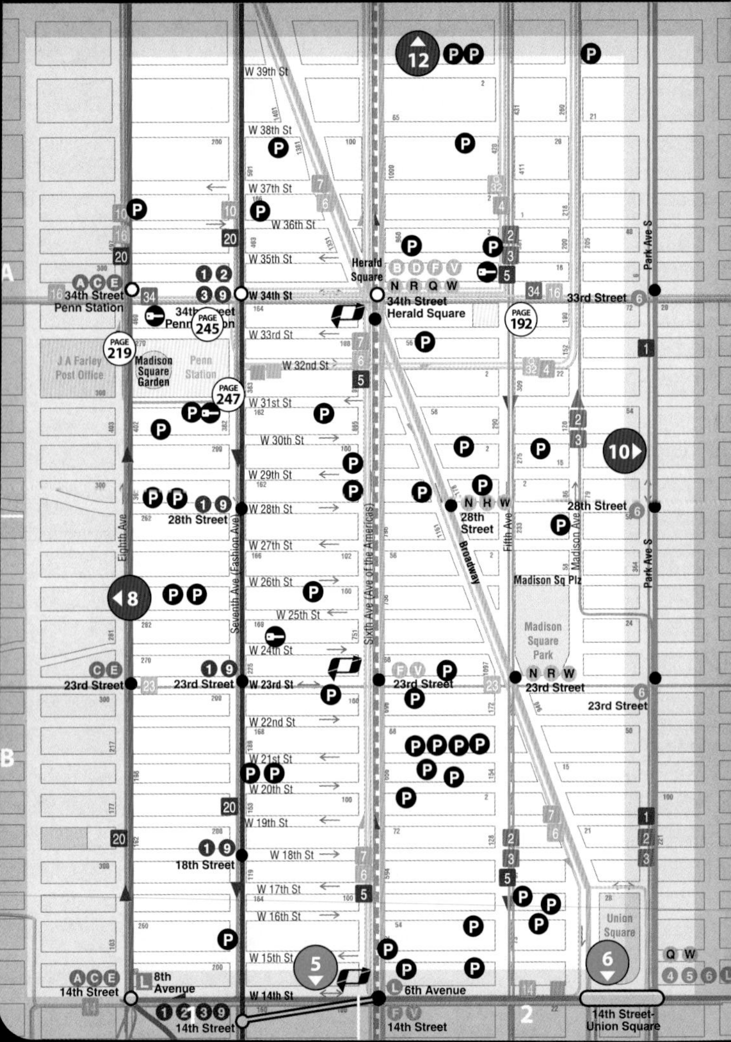

Map 9 • Flatiron / Lower Midtown

W 39th St
W 38th St
W 37th St
W 36th St
W 35th St
W 34th St
W 33rd St
W 32nd St
W 31st St
W 30th St
W 29th St
W 28th St
W 27th St
W 26th St
W 25th St
W 24th St
W 23rd St
W 22nd St
W 21st St
W 20th St
W 19th St
W 18th St
W 17th St
W 16th St
W 15th St
W 14th St
Herald Square
34th Street Herald Square
34th Street Penn Station
34th Street Penn Station
33rd Street
28th Street
23rd Street
18th Street
14th Street
8th Avenue
6th Avenue
14th Street-Union Square
J A Farley Post Office
Madison Square Garden
Penn Station
Madison Square Park
Madison Sq Plz
Union Square
Eighth Ave
Seventh Ave (Fashion Ave)
Sixth Ave (Ave of the Americas)
Broadway
Fifth Ave
Madison Ave
Park Ave S
PAGE 219
PAGE 245
PAGE 247
PAGE 192

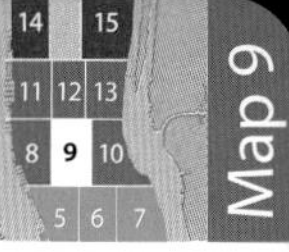

Parking during the day and on weekends is extremely difficult in this area, due to the number of business districts and commercial enterprises that are here. Driving isn't much better, since Lincoln Tunnel traffic has far-ranging repercussions.

Subways

1 2 3 9 .... 34 St-Penn Station
1 9 .... 18 St
1 9 .... 23 St
1 9 .... 28 St
B D F V N Q R W 34 St-Herald Sq
F V .... 23rd St
R W .... 23 St
R W .... 28 St

Bus Lines

10 20 .... Seventh Ave/Eighth Ave (Central Park West)/Frederick Douglass Blvd
16 .... 34th St Crosstown
2 3 .... Fifth Ave/Madison Ave
23 .... 23rd St Crosstown
4 .... Fifth Ave/Madison Ave/Broadway
5 .... Fifth Ave/Sixth Ave/Riverdale Dr
6 .... Seventh Ave/Broadway/Sixth Ave
7 ....Columbus Ave/Amsterdam Ave/ Lenox Ave/Sixth Ave/Seventh Ave/Broadway
Q32 .... Penn Station/Jackson Heights, Queens

PATH

- **23 St** • 23rd St & Sixth Ave
- **33 St** • 33rd St & Sixth Ave

Car Rental

- **Avis** • 220 W 31st St
- **Eldan Rent-A-Car** • 350 Fifth Ave
- **Enterprise** • 106 W 24th St
- **Hertz** • 250 W 34th St

Parking

Map 10 • Murray Hill / Gramercy

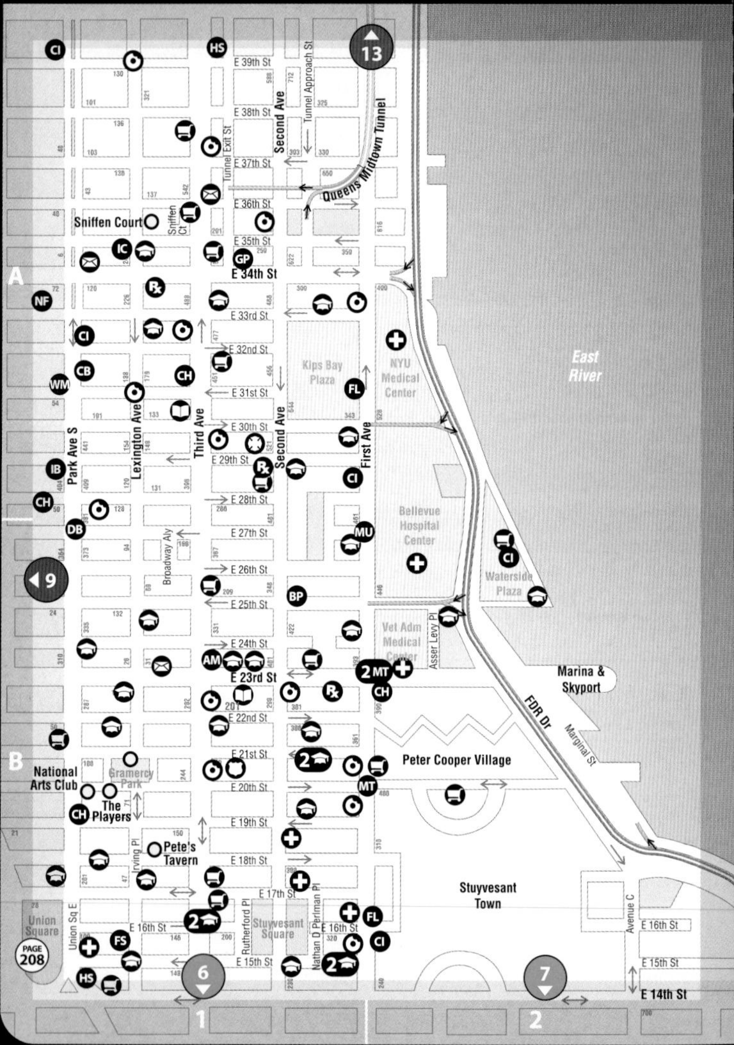

E 39th St
E 38th St
E 37th St
E 36th St
E 35th St
E 34th St
E 33rd St
E 32nd St
E 31st St
E 30th St
E 29th St
E 28th St
E 27th St
E 26th St
E 25th St
E 24th St
E 23rd St
E 22nd St
E 21st St
E 20th St
E 19th St
E 18th St
E 17th St
E 16th St
E 15th St
E 14th St
Tunnel Approach St
Tunnel Exit St
Queens Midtown Tunnel
Second Ave
Third Ave
Lexington Ave
Park Ave S
First Ave
Sniffen Court
Sniffen Ct
Kips Bay Plaza
NYU Medical Center
East River
Bellevue Hospital Center
Waterside Plaza
Broadway Aly
Vet Adm Medical Center
Asser Levy Pl
Marina & Skyport
FDR Dr
Marginal St
Peter Cooper Village
National Arts Club
Gramercy Park
The Players
Irving Pl
Pete's Tavern
Rutherford Pl
Stuyvesant Square
Nathan D Perlman Pl
Stuyvesant Town
Avenue C
Union Sq E
Union Square
PAGE 208
A
B
1
2
6
7
9
13

This area is home to one of Manhattan's most pastoral and beautiful settings, Gramercy Park. It also contains two humongous and drab residential communities, Stuyvesant Town and Peter Cooper Village, plus huge Eastern Bloc-style apartment buildings like Kips Bay Towers. For juxtaposition, check out charming little Sniffen Court.

ATMs

AM • Amalgamated • 301 Third Ave
BP • Banco Popular • 441 Second Ave
CH • Chase • 225 Park Ave S
CH • Chase • 386 Park Ave S
CH • Chase • 390 Park Ave S
CH • Chase • 400 E 23rd St
CH • Chase • 450 Third Ave
CI • Citibank • 1 Park Ave
CI • Citibank • 25 Waterside Plz
CI • Citibank • 262 First Ave
CI • Citibank • 481 First Ave
CI • Citibank • 90 Park Ave
CO • Commerce Bank • 475 Park Ave S
DB • Doral Bank • 387 Park Ave S
FL • Fleet • 550 First Ave
FL • Fleet • First Ave & E 16th St
FS • Flushing Savings Bank • 33 Irving Pl
GP • Greenpoint Bank • 254 E 34th St
HS • HSBC • 10 Union Sq E
HS • HSBC • 605 Third Ave
IC • Independence Community • 250 Lexington Ave
IB • Interbank • 420 Park Ave S
MT • Manufacturers and Traders Trust • 385 First Ave
MT • Manufacturers and Traders Trust • 397 First Ave
MT • Manufacturers and Traders Trust • 401 E 20th St
CU • Municipal Credit Union • 462 First Ave
NF • North Fork Bank • 2 Park Ave
WM • Washington Mutual • 460 Park Ave S

Bagels

- **Bagel du Jour** • 478 Third Ave
- **Bagel & Schmear** • 116 E 28th St
- **Bagelry** • 429 Third Ave
- **Bagels Around the Clock** • 637 Second Ave
- **Bagels & More** • 331 Lexington Ave
- **Daniel's Bagels** • 569 Third Ave
- **David's Bagels** • 331 First Ave
- **Eastbridge Bagels** • 587 First Ave
- **Ess-A-Bagel** • 359 First Ave
- **Gramercy Park Bagel** • 244 Third Ave
- **La Bagel** • 263 First Ave
- **Pick-a-Bagel** • 297 Third Ave
- **Shaun's Bagel Café** • 178 Lexington Ave
- **Tony Bagels** • 310 E 23rd St

Fire Departments

- **Engine 16, Ladder 7** • 234 E 29th St

Hospitals

- **Bellevue Hospital Center** • 462 First Ave
- **Beth Israel Medical Center** • 281 First Ave
- **Beth Israel Medical Center: Phillips Ambulatory/Cancer Center** • 10 Union Sq E
- **Cabrini Medical Center** • 227 E 19th St
- **Hospital for Joint Diseases** • 301 E 17th St
- **NYU Medical Center: Tisch Hospital** • 560 First Ave
- **VA Hospital** • 423 E 23rd St

Landmarks

- **Gramercy Park** • Irving Pl & 20th St
- **National Arts Club** • 15 Gramercy Park S
- **Pete's Tavern** • 129 E 18th St
- **Sniffen Court** • 36th St & Third Ave
- **The Players** • 16 Gramercy Park S

Libraries

- **Epiphany** • 228 E 23rd St
- **Kips Bay** • 446 Third Ave

24-Hour Pharmacies

- **CVS Pharmacy** • 342 E 23rd St
- **Duane Reade** • 155 E 34th St
- **Rite Aid** • 542 Second Ave

Police

- **13th Precinct** • 230 E 21st St

Post Offices

- **Madison Square** • 149 E 23rd St
- **Murray Hill** • 205 E 36th St
- **Murray Hill Finance** • 115 E 34th St

Schools

- **Baruch College** • 151 E 25th St
- **Baruch College Campus High School** • 111 E 18th St
- **Baruch College Campus High School** • 17 Lexington Ave
- **The Child School** • 317 E 33rd St
- **Churchill School** • 301 E 29th St
- **Epiphany Elementary School** • 234 E 22nd St
- **Friends Seminary** • 222 E 16th St
- **Health Prof & Human Svcs High School** • 345 E 15th St
- **HS 431 School of the Future** • 127 E 22nd St
- **Jack & Jill School** • 209 E 16th St
- **The Lee Strasberg Theater Institiute** • 115 E 15th St
- **Manhattan Night Comprehensive High School** • 240 Second Ave
- **MS 104 Simon Baruch** • 330 E 21st St
- **New York College of Optometry** • 100 E 24th St
- **Norman Thomas High School** • 111 E 33rd St
- **NYU Dental School** • First Ave & 24th St
- **NYU Medical Center** • 30th St & First Ave
- **Phillips Beth Israel School of Nursing** • 310 E 22nd St
- **PS 040 Augustus St Gaudens & MS 255 Salk** • 319 E 19th St
- **PS 106 Bellevue Hospital** • 27th St & First Ave
- **PS 116 Mary L Murray School** • 210 E 33rd St
- **PS 226 & Institute for Collaborative Education** • 345 E 15th St
- **PS-JHS 047 School for the Deaf** • 225 E 23rd St
- **School of Visual Arts** • 209 E 23rd St
- **Stern College for Women of Yeshiva U** • 245 Lexington Ave
- **United Nations International School** • 24 FDR Dr
- **Washington Irving High** • 40 Irving Pl

Supermarkets

- **Associated** • 278 Park Ave S
- **Associated** • 311 E 23rd St
- **D'Agostino** • 341 Third Ave
- **D'Agostino** • 528 Third Ave
- **D'Agostino** • 532 E 20th St
- **D'Agostino** • 578 Third Ave
- **Food Emporium** • 10 Union Sq E
- **Food Emporium** • 200 E 32nd St
- **Gristede's** • 25 Waterside Plz
- **Gristede's** • 355 First Ave
- **Gristede's** • 460 Third Ave
- **Gristede's** • 512 Second Ave
- **Gristede's** • 549 Third Ave
- **Met Food** • 180 Third Ave

Map 10 • Murray Hill / Gramercy

E 39th St
E 38th St
E 37th St
E 36th St
E 35th St
E 34th St
E 33rd St
E 32nd St
E 31st St
E 30th St
E 29th St
E 28th St
E 27th St
E 26th St
E 25th St
E 24th St
E 23rd St
E 22nd St
E 21st St
E 20th St
E 19th St
E 18th St
E 17th St
E 16th St
E 15th St
E 14th St
Park Ave S
Lexington Ave
Third Ave
Second Ave
First Ave
Tunnel Exit St
Tunnel Approach St
Queens Midtown Tunnel
Sniffen Ct
Broadway Aly
Irving Pl
Union Sq E
Rutherford Pl
Nathan D Perlman Pl
Asser Levy Pl
Avenue C
FDR Dr
Marginal St
Kips Bay Plaza
NYU Medical Center
Bellevue Hospital Center
Waterside Plaza
Vet Adm Medical Center
Marina & Skyport
Peter Cooper Village
Stuyvesant Town
Gramercy Park
Stuyvesant Square
Union Square
East River
A
B
1
2
13
9
6
7
PAGE 208

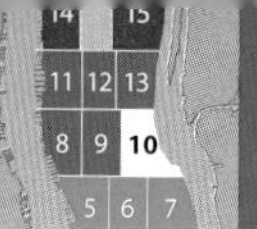

This area is a study in contrast—great ethnic Indian food on Lexington, including an NFT favorite (Pongal), but an equal number of drab eateries, especially on First Avenue. And one of the city's best bars, Pete's Tavern, balanced by ungodly "meat market" bars throughout the neighborhood. Choose wisely.

Bars

- **Abbey Tavern** • 354 Third Ave
- **Bar 515** • 515 Third Ave
- **Galaxy** • 15 Irving Pl
- **High Bar @ Gramercy Park Hotel** • 2 Lexington Ave
- **Joshua Tree** • 513 Third Ave
- **Mercury Bar** • 493 Third Ave
- **Molly's** • 287 Third Ave
- **Revival** • 129 E 15th St
- **Waterfront Ale House** • 540 Second Ave

Coffee

- **Aristotle Coffee Shop** • 350 Park Ave S
- **Breadsoul Café** • 200 Lexington Ave
- **Cosi** • 257 Park Ave S
- **Cosi** • 461 Park Ave S
- **Dunkin' Donuts** • 152 W 34th St
- **Dunkin' Donuts** • 266 First Ave
- **Dunkin' Donuts** • 421 Third Ave
- **Dunkin' Donuts** • 601 Second Ave
- **Espresso Coffee Roaster** • 157 E 18th St
- **Guy & Gallard** • 230 Lexington Ave
- **Oren's Daily Roast** • 434 Third Ave
- **Starbucks** • 10 Union Sq E
- **Starbucks** • 145 Third Ave
- **Starbucks** • 296 Third Ave
- **Starbucks** • 304 Park Ave S
- **Starbucks** • 395 Third Ave
- **Starbucks** • 424 Park Ave S
- **Starbucks** • 585 Second Ave
- **Trevi Coffee Shop** • 48 Union Sq E
- **Uncommon Grounds** • 533 Third Ave

Copy Shops

- **Columbia Enterprises Inc (8:30 am-5:30 pm)** • 116 E 16th St
- **Ever Ready Blue Print (8 am-5:30 pm)** • 200 Park Ave S
- **Mail Boxes Etc (8 am-7:30 pm)** • 350 Third Ave
- **Mail Boxes Etc (8:30 am-7 pm)** • 163 Third Ave
- **Mail Boxes Etc (8:30 am-7 pm)** • 527 Third Ave
- **On-Site Sourcing** • 443 Park Ave S
- **Staples (7 am-7 pm)** • 345 Park Ave S
- **Tower Copy East(9 am-6 pm)** • 427 Third Ave

Gyms

- **Club 29** • 155 E 29th St
- **Crunch Fitness** • 554 Second Ave
- **LUYE Aquafit** • 310 E 23rd St
- **Manhattan Place Condominium Health Club** • 630 First Ave
- **New York Sports Clubs** • 10 Irving Pl
- **New York Sports Clubs** • 113 E 23rd St
- **New York Sports Clubs** • 131 E 31st St
- **New York Sports Clubs** • 3 Park Ave
- **New York Sports Clubs** • 614 Second Ave
- **Park Avenue Executive Fitness** • 90 Park Ave
- **Peak Performance Sport & Fitness Center** • 106 E 19th St
- **Rivergate Fitness Center** • 401 E 34th St
- **Synergy Fitness Clubs** • 201 E 23rd St
- **Synergy Fitness Clubs** • 4 Park Ave

Hardware Stores

- **Gurell Hardware** • 132 E 28th St
- **Homefront Hardware & Lumber** • 202 E 29th St
- **J&M Hardware & Locksmiths** • 238 Park Ave S
- **Lumber Boys** • 698 Second Ave
- **Lumberland Hardware** • 400 Third Ave
- **Simon's Hardware & Bath** • 421 Third Ave
- **Town & Village Hardware** • 345 E 18th St
- **Vercesi Hardware** • 152 E 23rd St
- **Warshaw Hardware & Electrical** • 248 Third Ave

Liquor Stores

- **Buy Rite Discount Liquors** • 398 Third Ave
- **First Ave Wine & Spirits** • 383 First Ave
- **First Avenue Wine & Spirits Supermarket** • 383 First Ave
- **Flynn Winfield Liquor Ltd** • 558 Third Ave
- **Frank's Liquor Shop** • 46 Union Sq E
- **Gramercy Park Wines & Spirits** • 121 E 23rd St
- **HS Wine & Liquor** • 161 Third Ave
- **House of Wine & Liquor** • 250 E 34th St
- **Italian Wine Merchants** • 108 E 16th St
- **LP Wines & Spirits Limited** • 474 Third Ave
- **New Gramercy Liquors** • 279 Third Ave
- **Quality House** • 2 Park Ave
- **Royal Wine Merchants Ltd** • 25 Waterside Plz
- **Sky Spirits** • 381 Park Ave S
- **Stuyvesant Square Liquors** • 333 Second Ave
- **Thomas J Mc Adam Liquor** • 398 Third Ave
- **Wine Shop** • 345 Lexington Ave
- **Zeichner Wine & Liquor** • 279 First Ave

Movie Theaters

- **Loews Kips Bay** • 550 Second Ave
- **MoMA Film at the Gramercy Theater** • 127 E 23rd St
- **Scandinavia House** • 58 Park Ave

Pet Shops

- **All Paws** • 120 E 34th St
- **Doggie-Do & Pussycats Too** • 567 Third Ave
- **Furry Paws** • 120 E 34th St
- **Furry Paws 5** • 310 E 23rd St
- **Natural Pet** • 238 Third Ave
- **New World Aquarium** • 204 E 38th St
- **Petco** • 550 Second Ave
- **Petland Discounts** • 404 Third Ave
- **Thirty-Third & Bird** • 40 E 33rd St

Restaurants

- **Angelo & Maxie's** • 233 Park Ave S
- **Artisanal** • 2 Park Ave
- **Blockheads Burritos** • 499 Third Ave
- **Coppola's** • 378 Third Ave
- **El Parador Cafe** • 325 E 34th St
- **Gemini Restaurant** • 641 Second Ave
- **Gramercy Restaurant** • 184 Third Ave
- **Haandi** • 113 Lexington Ave
- **I Trulli** • 122 E 27th St
- **Jackson Hole** • 521 Third Ave
- **Jaiya Thai** • 396 Third Ave
- **L'Express** • 249 Park Ave S
- **Park Avenue Country Club** • 381 Park Ave S
- **Patria** • 250 Park Ave S
- **Patsy's Pizza** • 509 Third Ave
- **Pete's Tavern** • 129 E 18th St
- **Pongal** • 110 Lexington Ave
- **Pongsri Thai** • 311 Second Ave
- **Sarge's Deli** • 548 Third Ave
- **Tatany** • 380 Third Ave
- **Union Pacific** • 111 E 22nd St
- **Verbena** • 54 Irving Pl
- **Via Emilia** • 240 Park Ave S
- **Water Club** • 500 E 30th St
- **Yama** • 122 E 17th St
- **Zen Palate** • 34 Union Sq E

Shopping

- **Alkit Pro Camera** • 222 Park Ave S
- **City Opera Thrift Shop** • 222 E 23rd St
- **Housing Works Thrift Shop** • 157 E 23rd St
- **Nemo Tile Company** • 48 E 21st St
- **Pearl Paint** • 207 E 23rd St
- **Poggenpohl US** • 230 Park Ave
- **Quark Spy** • 537 Third Ave
- **Radio Shack** • 270 Park Ave S
- **Speedo Authentic Fitness** • 90 Park Ave
- **Urban Angler** • 206 Fifth Ave

Video Rental

- **Blockbuster Video** • 151 Third Ave
- **Blockbuster Video** • 155 E 34th St
- **Blockbuster Video** • 312 First Ave
- **Blockbuster Video** • 344 Third Ave
- **Video Maven** • 715 Second Ave
- **Video Stop** • 367 Third Ave

Map 10 • Murray Hill / Gramercy

E 39th St
E 38th St
E 37th St
E 36th St
E 35th St
E 34th St
E 33rd St
E 32nd St
E 31st St
E 30th St
E 29th St
E 28th St
E 27th St
E 26th St
E 25th St
E 24th St
E 23rd St
E 22nd St
E 21st St
E 20th St
E 19th St
E 18th St
E 17th St
E 16th St
E 15th St
E 14th St

Tunnel Approach St
Tunnel Exit St
Queens Midtown Tunnel
Second Ave
Third Ave
Lexington Ave
Park Ave S
First Ave
Sniffen Ct
Broadway Aly
Irving Pl
Union Sq E
Rutherford Pl
Nathan D Perlman Pl
Asser Levy Pl
Avenue C
FDR Dr
Marginal St

33rd Street
28th Street
23rd Street
14th Street-Union Square
3rd Avenue
1st Avenue

Kips Bay Plaza
NYU Medical Center
Bellevue Hospital Center
Waterside Plaza
Vet Adm Medical Center
Marina & Skyport
Peter Cooper Village
Stuyvesant Town
Gramercy Park
Stuyvesant Square
Union Square
East River

PAGE 208

Transportation

Overnight parking is difficult, but there are many meter spots to be had, especially on the avenues. We're very excited by the prospect of the Second Avenue subway line, even if it won't be open until after we've retired to Fort Lauderdale.

Subways

6 .... 23rd St
6 .... 28rd St
6 .... 33rd St
4 5 6 L N Q R W .... 14th St
L .... First Ave
L .... Third Ave

Bus Lines

1 2 3 .... Fifth Ave/Madison Ave
101 ....Third Ave/Lexington Ave
102 .... Third Ave/Lexington Ave
103 ....Third Ave/Lexington Ave
9 ....Avenue B/East Broadway
14 .... 14th St Crosstown
34 .... 34th St Crosstown
15 .... First Ave/Second Ave
16 .... 34th St Crosstown
21 .... Houston St Crosstown
23 .... 23rd St Crosstown
98 ....Third Ave/Lexington Ave

Car Rental

- **Dollar** • 329 E 22nd St
- **Hertz** • 150 E 24th St
- **National** • 142 E 31st St

Gas

- **Gulf** • E 23rd St

Parking

Map 11 • Hell's Kitchen

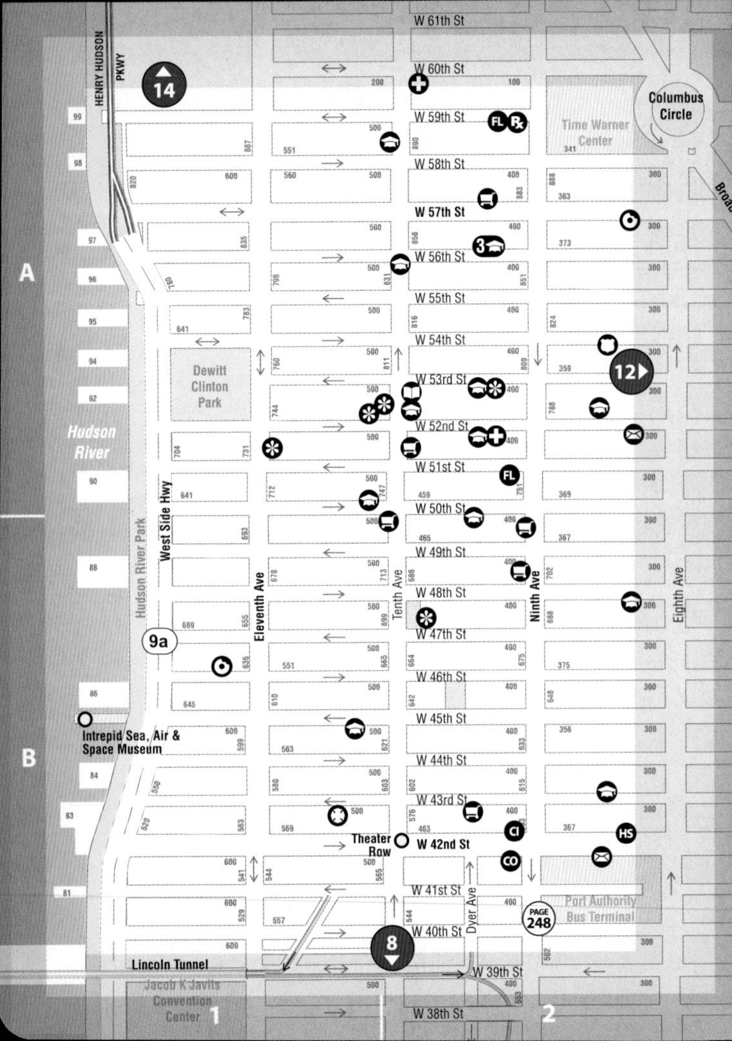

W 61st St
W 60th St
W 59th St
W 58th St
W 57th St
W 56th St
W 55th St
W 54th St
W 53rd St
W 52nd St
W 51st St
W 50th St
W 49th St
W 48th St
W 47th St
W 46th St
W 45th St
W 44th St
W 43rd St
W 42nd St
W 41st St
W 40th St
W 39th St
W 38th St
HENRY HUDSON PKWY
Columbus Circle
Time Warner Center
Broad
Dewitt Clinton Park
Hudson River
Hudson River Park
West Side Hwy
Eleventh Ave
Tenth Ave
Ninth Ave
Eighth Ave
Dyer Ave
Intrepid Sea, Air & Space Museum
Theater Row
Port Authority Bus Terminal
Lincoln Tunnel
Jacob K Javits Convention Center
PAGE 248
14
12
8
9a
A
B
1
2

The continuing gentrification of Hell's Kitchen (and name change to "Clinton") will doubtlessly increase the number of essential services, for instance, the number of banks. The area around the Port Authority Bus Terminal is still one of the most authentically seedy places in Manhattan.

ATMs

CI • Citibank • 401 W 42nd St
CO • Commerce Bank • 582 Ninth Ave
FL • Fleet • 415 W 51st St
FL • Fleet • 428 W 59th St
HS • HSBC • 330 W 42nd St

Bagels

• **Bagel Baron of 57th** • 315 W 57th St
• **H&H Bagels** • 639 W 46th St

Community Gardens

Fire Departments

• **Rescue 1** • 530 W 43rd St

Hospitals

• **St Clare's Hospital & Health Center** • 426 W 52nd St
• **St Luke's Roosevelt Hospital Center** • 1000 Tenth Ave

Landmarks

• **Intrepid Sea, Air & Space Museum** • Twelfth Ave & 45th St
• **Theater Row** • 42nd St between Ninth & Tenth Aves

Libraries

• **Columbus** • 742 Tenth Ave

24-Hour Pharmacies

• **CVS Pharmacy** • 400 W 59th St

Police

• **Mid-Town North** • 306 W 54th St

Post Offices

• **Radio City** • 322 W 52nd St
• **Times Square** • 340 W 42nd St

Schools

• **American Academy McAllister Institute** • 450 W 56th St
• **Borough Academies** • 850 Tenth Ave
• **Career Education Center** • 448 W 56th St
• **High School for Environmental Studies** • 444 W 56th St
• **High School of Graphic Communication Arts** • 439 W 49th St
• **Holy Cross School** • 332 W 43rd St
• **John Jay College** • 899 Tenth Ave
• **Park West High School** • 525 W 50th St
• **PS 051 Elias Howe School** • 520 W 45th St
• **PS 111 Adolph S Ochs School** • 440 W 53rd St
• **PS 212 & Professional Performing Arts High School** • 328 W 48th St
• **PS 35 Manhattan School** • 317 W 52nd St
• **Sacred Heart of Jesus School** • 456 W 52nd St

Supermarkets

• **Amish Manhattan Farmers Market** • 731 Ninth Ave
• **D'Agostino** • 353 W 57th St
• **D'Agostino** • 815 Tenth Ave
• **Food Emporium** • 452 W 43rd St
• **Key Foods** • 725 Ninth Ave

W 61st St
W 60th St
W 59th St
W 58th St
W 57th St
W 56th St
W 55th St
W 54th St
W 53rd St
W 52nd St
W 51st St
W 50th St
W 49th St
W 48th St
W 47th St
W 46th St
W 45th St
W 44th St
W 43rd St
W 42nd St
W 41st St
W 40th St
W 39th St
W 38th St
Henry Hudson Pkwy
West Side Hwy
Hudson River Park
Hudson River
Eleventh Ave
Tenth Ave
Ninth Ave
Eighth Ave
Dyer Ave
Broadway
Columbus Circle
Time Warner Center
Dewitt Clinton Park
Port Authority Bus Terminal
Lincoln Tunnel
Jacob K Javits Convention Center
14
12
8
9a
A
B
1
2

PAGE 248

For food, try the Afghan Kebab House, Island Burgers 'N Shakes, and Hallo Berlin ("The Best Wurst" in the city). The Bull Moose and Otis are reliably good for a drink or two, and Rudy's is a quintessential New York bar. Only order the hot dogs when extremely drunk.

Bars

- **Bellevue Bar** • 538 Ninth Ave
- **Bull Moose Saloon** • 354 W 44th St
- **Hudson Hotel Library** • 356 W 58th St
- **Landmark Tavern** • 626 Eleventh Ave
- **Otis** • 754 Ninth Ave
- **Rudy's Bar & Grill** • 627 Ninth Ave
- **Siberia Bar** • 356 W 40th St
- **Xth** • 642 Tenth Ave

Coffee

- **The Coffee Beanery Ltd** • 601 W 54th St
- **The Coffee Pot** • 350 W 49th St
- **Dunkin' Donuts** • 580 Ninth Ave
- **Felix Coffee Shop** • 630 Tenth Ave
- **Flame Coffee House** • 893 Ninth Ave
- **Starbucks** • 322 W 57th St
- **Starbucks** • 325 W 49th St
- **Starbucks** • 682 Ninth Ave
- **Studio Coffee Shop** • 630 Ninth Ave
- **Tom's Coffee** • 360 W 55th St

Copy Shops

- **Mail Boxes Etc (8:30 am-7 pm)** • 331 W 57th St
- **Mail Boxes Etc (8:30 am-7 pm)** • 676A Ninth Ave

Farmer's Markets

- **57th Street/Balsley Park Greenmarket** • Ninth Ave & 57th St

Gyms

- **Bally Sports Club** • 350 W 50th St
- **Crunch Fitness** • 555 W 42nd St
- **Equinox** • 59th St & Columbus Cir
- **Manhattan Plaza Health Club** • 482 W 43rd St
- **New York Underground Fitness** • 440 W 57th St
- **Strand Health Club** • 500 W 43rd St

Hardware Stores

- **Columbus Hardware** • 852 Ninth Ave
- **Lopez Sentry Hardware** • 691 Ninth Ave
- **Metropolitan Lumber & Hardware** • 617 Eleventh Ave
- **New Era Industrial Hardware** • 359 W 54th St
- **Straight Hardware & Supply** • 613 Ninth Ave
- **True Value** • 718 Tenth Ave

Liquor Stores

- **54 Wine & Spirits** • 840 Ninth Ave
- **860 Ninth Liquors** • 860 W 9th St
- **B&G Wine & Liquor Store** • 507 W 42nd St
- **Manhattan Plaza Winery** • 589 Ninth Ave
- **Ninth Avenue Vintner** • 669 Ninth Ave
- **Ninth Avenue Wine & Liquor** • 474 Ninth Ave
- **Ray & Frank Liquor Store** • 706 Ninth Ave
- **Vintage Wine Warehouse** • 665 Eleventh Ave
- **West 57th St Wine & Spirit** • 340 W 57th St

Pet Shops

- **Canine Castle** • 410 W 56th St
- **Metropets** • 594 Ninth Ave
- **Petland Discounts** • 734 Ninth Ave
- **Spoiled Brats** • 340 W 49th St

Restaurants

- **Afghan Kebab House** • 764 Ninth Ave
- **Ariana Afghan Kebab** • 787 Ninth Ave
- **Burritoville** • 625 Ninth Ave
- **Churruscaria Plataforma** • 316 W 49th St
- **Grand Sichuan Int'l** • 745 Ninth Ave
- **Hallo Berlin** • 402 W 51st St
- **Island Burgers 'N Shakes** • 766 Ninth Ave
- **Jezebel** • 630 Ninth Ave
- **Joe Allen** • 326 W 46th St
- **Les Sans Culottes** • 347 W 46th St
- **Meskerem** • 468 W 47th St
- **Old San Juan** • 765 Ninth Ave
- **Orso** • 322 W 46th St
- **Ralph's** • 862 Ninth Ave
- **Soul Cafe** • 444 W 42nd St
- **Uncle Nick's** • 747 Ninth Ave
- **Zen Palate** • 663 Ninth Ave

Shopping

- **Just Pickles** • 569 Ninth Ave
- **Little Pie Company** • 424 W 43rd St
- **Metro Bicycles** • 360 W 47th St
- **Ninth Avenue International** • 543 Ninth Ave
- **Pan Aqua Diving** • 460 W 43rd St
- **Poseidon Bakery** • 629 Ninth Ave
- **Radio Shack** • 333 W 57th St
- **Sea Breeze** • 541 Ninth Ave

Video Rental

- **57th St Video & Photo** • 332 W 57th St

Map 11 • Hell's Kitchen

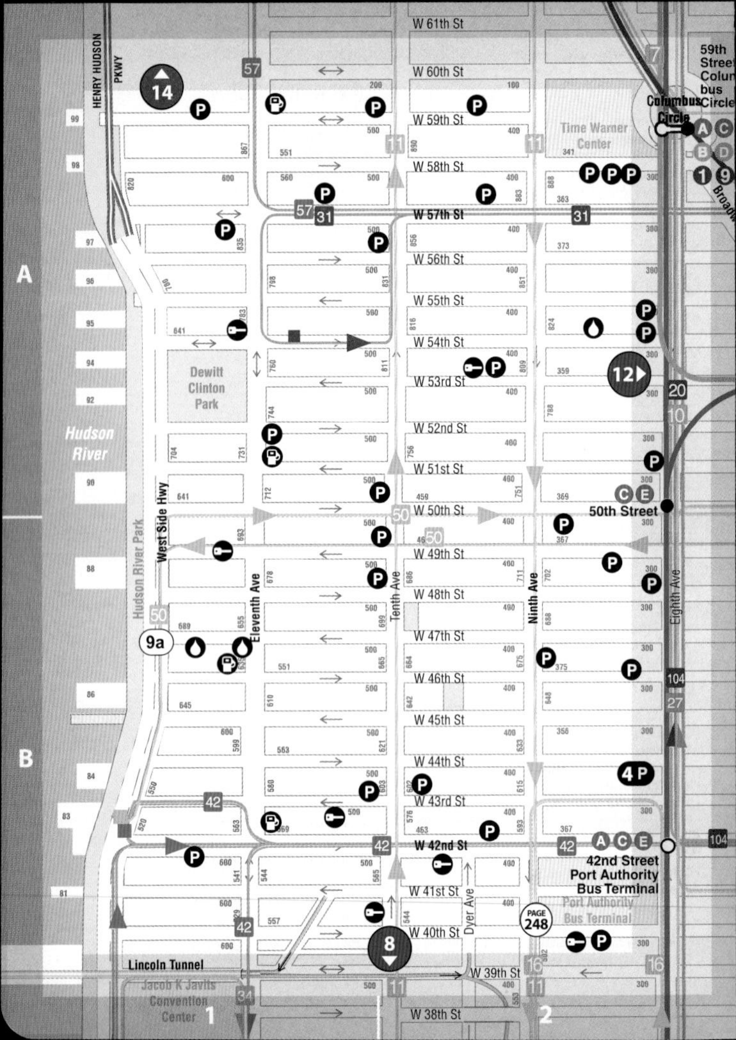

W 61st St
W 60th St
W 59th St
W 58th St
W 57th St
W 56th St
W 55th St
W 54th St
W 53rd St
W 52nd St
W 51st St
W 50th St
W 49th St
W 48th St
W 47th St
W 46th St
W 45th St
W 44th St
W 43rd St
W 42nd St
W 41st St
W 40th St
W 39th St
W 38th St
HENRY HUDSON PKWY
West Side Hwy
Hudson River Park
Hudson River
Eleventh Ave
Tenth Ave
Ninth Ave
Eighth Ave
Dyer Ave
Broadway
Dewitt Clinton Park
Time Warner Center
Columbus Circle
59th Street Columbus Circle
50th Street
42nd Street Port Authority Bus Terminal
Port Authority Bus Terminal
Lincoln Tunnel
Jacob K Javits Convention Center
PAGE 248
A
B
1
2
14
12
8
9a

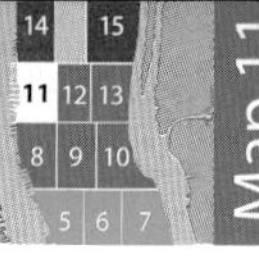

The Lincoln Tunnel jams this area up during the day. If you're coming from downtown, try taking the Tenth Avenue approach. If you're coming from uptown, you're screwed. (The mishmash of Columbus Circle also doesn't help matters.) This is also where the West Side "Highway" begins to have traffic lights and becomes a parking lot for most of the day (try taking Eleventh Avenue downtown if you can). Enjoy.

Subways

C E .... 50th St
A C E 42nd St/Port Authority Bus Terminal
A C B D 1 9 ..59th St/Columbus Cir

Bus Lines

11 .... Ninth Ave/Tenth Ave
16 .... 34th St Crosstown
27 .... 49th St/50th St Crosstown
31 .... 57th St Crosstown
42 .... 42nd St Crosstown
50 .... 49th St/50th St Crosstown
57 .... 57th St Crosstown
104 .... Broadway/42nd St

Car Rental

- **All-State Auto Rental** • 540 W 43rd St
- **Avis** • 460 W 42nd St
- **Courier Car Rental** • 537 Tenth Ave
- **Enterprise** • 455 W 53rd St
- **Enterprise** • 653 Eleventh Ave
- **Hertz** • 346 W 40th St
- **Value Rent-A-Car** • 641 W 49th St

Car Washes

- **JL Custom Car Cleaner** • 349 W 54th St
- **Kenny Car Wash System** • 625 Eleventh Ave
- **Westside Highway Car Wash** • 638 W 47th St

Gas Stations

- **BP** • 59th St & Eleventh Ave
- **Mobil** • 561 Eleventh Ave
- **Mobil** • 718 Eleventh Ave
- **Sunoco** • 639 Eleventh Ave

Parking

Map 12 • Midtown

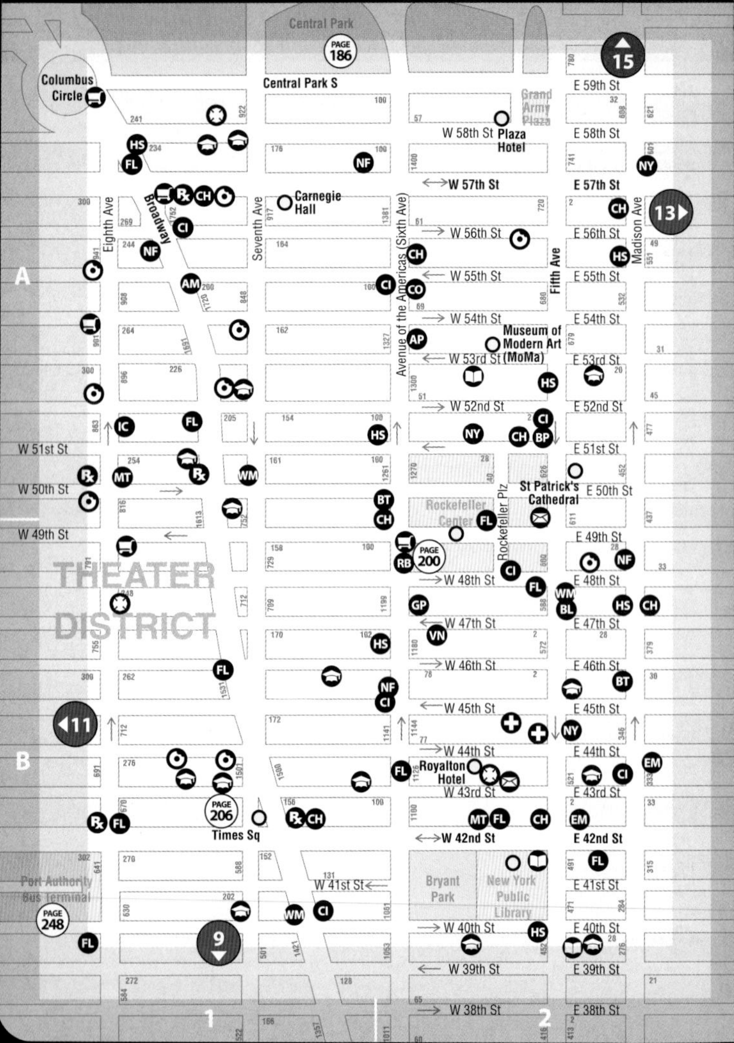

Central Park

PAGE 186

15

Columbus Circle

Central Park S

E 59th St

Grand Army Plaza

W 58th St

Plaza Hotel

E 58th St

W 57th St

E 57th St

Carnegie Hall

Eighth Ave

Broadway

Seventh Ave

13

W 56th St

E 56th St

Avenue of the Americas (Sixth Ave)

Fifth Ave

Madison Ave

A

W 55th St

E 55th St

W 54th St

E 54th St

Museum of Modern Art (MoMa)

W 53rd St

E 53rd St

W 52nd St

E 52nd St

W 51st St

E 51st St

W 50th St

St Patrick's Cathedral

E 50th St

W 49th St

Rockefeller Center

Rockefeller Plz

E 49th St

PAGE 200

THEATER DISTRICT

W 48th St

E 48th St

W 47th St

E 47th St

W 46th St

E 46th St

W 45th St

E 45th St

11

B

W 44th St

E 44th St

Royalton Hotel

W 43rd St

E 43rd St

PAGE 206

Times Sq

W 42nd St

E 42nd St

Port Authority Bus Terminal

Bryant Park

New York Public Library

W 41st St

E 41st St

PAGE 248

W 40th St

E 40th St

9

W 39th St

E 39th St

W 38th St

E 38th St

1

2

For all intents and purposes, this is the heart of New York. However, Times Square, the Theater District, and Rockefeller Center are all areas that many New Yorkers avoid. Instead, try the beautifully reconstructed Bryant Park, the classy Oak Bar at the Plaza Hotel, and Phillipe Starck's utterly cool Royalton Hotel.

$ ATMs

AM • Amalgamated • 1745 Broadway
AP • Apple • 1320 Sixth Ave
BP • Banco Popular • 7 W 51st St
BL • Bank Leumi • 579 Fifth Ave
NY • Bank of New York • 51 W 51st St
NY • Bank of New York • 530 Fifth Ave
NY • Bank of New York • 575 Madison Ave
BT • Bank of Tokyo • 1251 Sixth Ave
BT • Bank of Tokyo • 360 Madison Ave
CH • Chase • 11 W 51st St
CH • Chase • 1251 Sixth Ave
CH • Chase • 1370 Sixth Ave
CH • Chase • 250 W 57th St
CH • Chase • 3 Times Sq
CH • Chase • 401 Madison Ave
CH • Chase • 510 Fifth Ave
CH • Chase • 600 Madison Ave
CI • Citibank • 1 Rockefeller Plz
CI • Citibank • 1155 Sixth Ave
CI • Citibank • 1345 Sixth Ave
CI • Citibank • 1440 Broadway
CI • Citibank • 1748 Broadway
CI • Citibank • 330 Madison Ave
CI • Citibank • 640 Fifth Ave
CO • Commerce Bank • 1350 Sixth Ave
EM • Emigrant • 335 Madison Ave
EM • Emigrant • 5 E 42nd St
RB • First Republic Bank • 1230 Sixth Ave
FL • Fleet • 1140 Sixth Ave
FL • Fleet • 1535 Broadway
FL • Fleet • 1675 Broadway
FL • Fleet • 1775 Broadway
FL • Fleet • 30 Rockefeller Plz
FL • Fleet • 42nd & Eighth Ave
FL • Fleet • 55 W 42nd St
FL • Fleet • 56 E 42nd St
FL • Fleet • 592 Fifth Ave
FL • Fleet • 625 Eighth Ave
GP • Greenpoint Bank • 1200 Sixth Ave
HS • HSBC • 1185 Sixth Ave
HS • HSBC • 1271 Sixth Ave
HS • HSBC • 1790 Broadway
HS • HSBC • 415 Madison Ave
HS • HSBC • 452 Fifth Ave
HS • HSBC • 555 Madison Ave
HS • HSBC • 666 Fifth Ave
IC • Independence Community • 864 Eighth Ave
MT • Manufacturers and Traders Trust • 41 W 42nd St
MT • Manufacturers and Traders Trust • 830 Eighth Ave
NF • North Fork Bank • 101 W 57th St
NF • North Fork Bank • 1166 Sixth Ave
NF • North Fork Bank • 1745 Broadway
NF • North Fork Bank • 424 Madison Ave
VN • Valley National Bank • 62 W 47th St
WM • Washington Mutual • 1431 Broadway
WM • Washington Mutual • 589 Fifth Ave
WM • Washington Mutual • 787 Seventh Ave

Bagels

- **Bagel House** • 308 W 50th St
- **Bagel-N-Bean** • 828 Seventh Ave
- **Bread Factory Café** • 935 Eighth Ave
- **Fraiche** • 6 E 48th St
- **New York Bagel** • 1674 Broadway
- **Pick-a-Bagel** • 200 W 57th St
- **Pick-a-Bagel** • 891 Eighth Ave
- **Pinnacle Bagel Corp** • 22 W 56th St
- **Strathmore Bagel Franchise** • 240 W 44th St
- **Times Square Bagels** • 200 W 44th St

Fire Departments

- **Engine 23** • 215 W 58th St
- **Engine 54, Ladder 4** • 782 Eighth Ave
- **Engine 65** • 33 W 43rd St

Hospitals

- **American Friends of Laniado Hospital** • 18 W 45th St
- **National Jewish Center for Immunology & Respiratory** • 535 Fifth Ave

O Landmarks

- **Carnegie Hall** • 154 W 57th St
- **Museum of Modern Art (MoMA)** • 11 W 53rd St
- **New York Public Library** • Fifth Ave & 42nd St
- **Plaza Hotel** • 768 Fifth Ave
- **Rockefeller Center** • 600 Fifth Ave
- **Royalton Hotel** • 44th St between Fifth Ave & Sixth Ave
- **St Patrick's Cathedral** • Fifth Ave & 50th St
- **Times Square** • 42nd St-Times Sq

Libraries

- **Donnell Library Center** • 20 W 53rd St
- **Humanities & Social Sciences Library** • 42nd St & Fifth Ave
- **Mid-Manhattan Library** • 455 Fifth Ave

24-Hour Pharmacies

- **Duane Reade** • 1633 Broadway
- **Duane Reade** • 224 W 57th St
- **Duane Reade** • 4 Times Sq
- **Duane Reade** • 661 Eighth Ave
- **Rite Aid** • 303 W 50th St

Post Offices

- **Bryant** • 23 W 43rd St
- **Rockefeller Center** • 610 Fifth Ave

Schools

- **Berkeley College** • 3 E 43rd St
- **Circle in the Square Theater School** • 1633 Broadway
- **Coalition School for Social Change & Landmark High School** • 220 W 58th St
- **Daytop Village Secondary School** • 54 W 40th St
- **Jacqueline Kennedy Onassis High School** • 120 W 46th St
- **Katharine Gibbs School** • 50 W 40th St
- **Laboratory Institute of Merchandising** • 12 E 53rd St
- **Lyceum Kennedey French School** • 225 W 43rd St
- **New York Academy of Comedic Arts** • 1626 Broadway
- **Pace University** • 551 Fifth Ave
- **Parsons School of Design, Midtown** • 560 Seventh Ave
- **Practicing Law Institute** • 810 Seventh Ave
- **Repertory School** • 123 W 43rd St
- **Spanish-American Institute** • 215 W 43rd St
- **St Thomas Choir School** • 202 W 58th St
- **Wood Tobe-Coburn School** • 8 E 40th St

Supermarkets

- **Associated** • 225 W 57th St
- **Citarella** • 1250 Sixth Ave
- **Food Emporium** • 810 Eighth Ave
- **Gristede's** • 907 Eighth Ave
- **Whole Foods Market** • 59th St & Columbus Cir

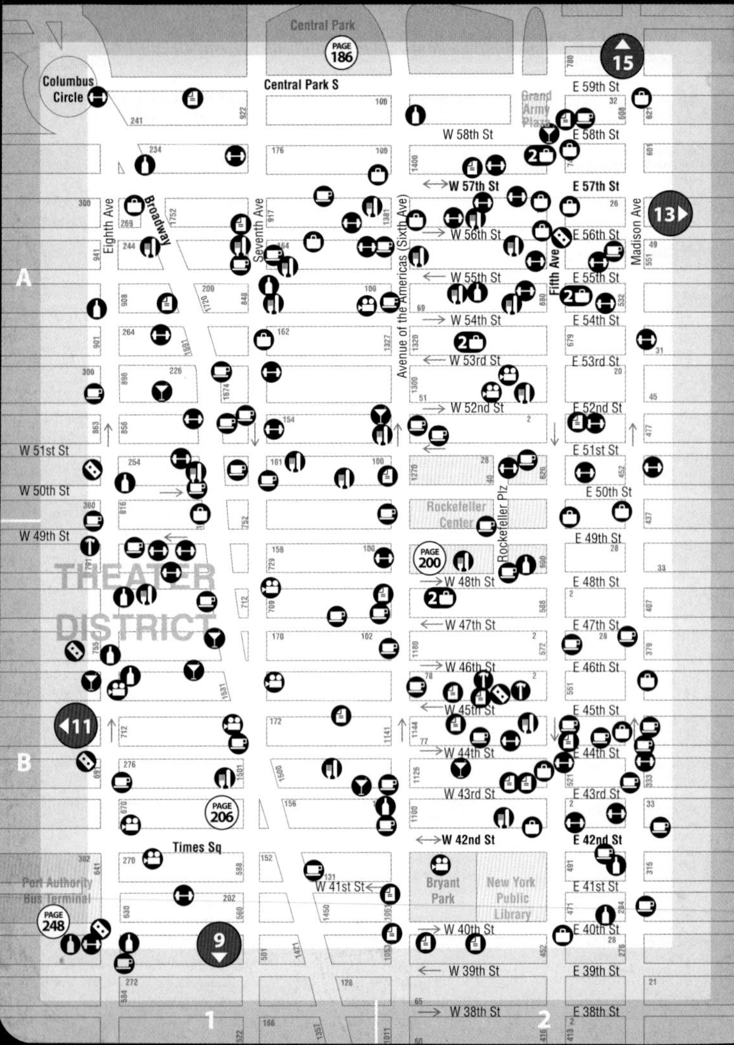

Map 12 • Midtown

Central Park

PAGE 186

Columbus Circle

Central Park S

Grand Army Plaza

15

E 59th St

W 58th St

E 58th St

W 57th St

E 57th St

13

Eighth Ave

Broadway

Seventh Ave

Avenue of the Americas (Sixth Ave)

Fifth Ave

Madison Ave

W 56th St

E 56th St

W 55th St

E 55th St

A

W 54th St

E 54th St

W 53rd St

E 53rd St

W 52nd St

E 52nd St

W 51st St

E 51st St

W 50th St

E 50th St

Rockefeller Center

Rockefeller Plz

W 49th St

E 49th St

PAGE 200

THEATER DISTRICT

W 48th St

E 48th St

W 47th St

E 47th St

W 46th St

E 46th St

W 45th St

E 45th St

11

W 44th St

E 44th St

B

W 43rd St

E 43rd St

PAGE 206

W 42nd St

E 42nd St

Times Sq

Port Authority Bus Terminal

Bryant Park

New York Public Library

W 41st St

E 41st St

PAGE 248

9

W 40th St

E 40th St

W 39th St

E 39th St

W 38th St

E 38th St

1

2

You can find almost anything here, but it's probably going to be less of a pain in the butt to find it somewhere else in the city. Midtown has three of the best places to see a movie—the huge Ziegfeld, the classy Paris, and outdoors at Bryant Park. Oh, and don't forget Show World.

Bars

- **Heartland Brewery** • 127 W 43rd St
- **Heartland Brewery** • 1285 Sixth Ave
- **Howard Johnson's** • 1551 Broadway
- **Oak Bar @ the Plaza Hotel** • 768 Fifth Ave
- **Paramount Bar** • 235 W 46th St
- **The Royalton** • 44 W 44th St
- **Russian Vodka Room** • 265 W 52nd St
- **Scruffy Duffy's** • 743 Eighth Ave

Coffee

- **Au Bon Pain** • 1211 Sixth Ave
- **Au Bon Pain** • 1251 Sixth Ave
- **Au Bon Pain** • 16 E 44th St
- **Cafe Metro** • 625 Eighth Ave
- **Cosi** • 11 W 42nd St
- **Cosi** • 1633 Broadway
- **Cosi** • 61 W 48th St
- **Cyber Cafe** • 250 W 49th St
- **Dunkin' Donuts:**
  - 1115 Sixth Ave
  - 1515 Broadway
  - 1680 Broadway
  - 761 Seventh Ave
- **Evergreen Coffee Shop Restaurant** • 145 W 47th St
- **Fluffy's Café & Bakery** • 855 Seventh Ave
- **La Parisienne Coffee House** • 910 Seventh Ave
- **Oren's Daily Roast** • 33 E 58th St
- **Red Flame Coffee Shop** • 67 W 44th St
- **Starbucks**:
  - 1100 Sixth Ave
  - 1166 Sixth Ave
  - 1185 Sixth Ave
  - 120 W 56th St
  - 1290 Sixth Ave
  - 1345 Sixth Ave
  - 1460 Broadway
  - 156 W 52nd St
  - 1585 Broadway
  - 1656 Broadway
  - 295 Madison Ave
  - 30 Rockefeller Plz
  - 330 Madison Ave
  - 335 Madison Ave
  - 400 Madison Ave
  - 545 Fifth Ave
  - 550 Madison Ave
  - 575 Fifth Ave
  - 600 Eighth Ave
  - 684 Eighth Ave
  - 750 Seventh Ave
  - 821 Eighth Ave
  - 871 Eighth Ave
- **Teresa's Gourmet Coffee Bar** • 51 W 51st St
- **The Greeks Coffee Shop** • 347 Madison Ave

Copy Shops

- **Accurate Copy Services (8:30 am-5 pm)** • 888 Seventh Ave
- **Copy Door II Inc (8:30 am-7 pm)** • Sixth Ave & 40th St
- **Deanco Press (9 am-5 pm)** • 767 Fifth Ave
- **Discovery Copy Services (24 hrs)** • 45 W 45th St
- **Document Technologies Inc (24 hrs)** • 145 W 45th St
- **Genie Instant Printing Center (8 am-5 pm)** • 37 W 43rd St
- **Kinko's** • 1211 Sixth Ave
- **Kinko's** • 16 E 52nd St
- **Kinko's** • 233 W 54th St
- **Kinko's** • 240 Central Park S
- **Kinko's** • 60 W 40th St
- **Longacre Copy Center (8 am-6 pm)** • 80 W 40th St
- **National Reproductions** • 25 W 45th St
- **Servco (8 am-8:30 pm)** • 56 W 45th St
- **Staples (7 am-8 pm)** • 535 Fifth Ave
- **Staples (7 am-8 pm)** • 57 W 57th St
- **Staples (7 am-9 pm)** • 1065 Sixth Ave
- **The Complete Copy Center (8:30 am-5 pm)** • 1271 Sixth Ave
- **The Village Copier** • 25 W 43rd St

Gyms

- **Athletic and Swim Club at Equitable Center** • 787 Seventh Ave
- **Bally Sports Club** • 335 Madison Ave
- **Bally Total Fitness** • 45 E 55th St
- **Definitions** • 712 Fifth Ave
- **Drago's Gymnasium** • 50 W 57th St
- **Equinox Fitness Club** • 1633 Broadway
- **Equinox Fitness Club** • 521 Fifth Ave
- **Exude Fitness** • 16 E 52nd St
- **Fitness Center at the New York Palace** • 455 Madison Ave
- **Gravity** • 119 W 56th St
- **Lucille Roberts Health Club** • 300 W 40th St
- **Mid City Gym** • 244 W 49th St
- **Midtown's Fitness By Design** • 39 W 56th St
- **New York Health & Racquet Club:**
  - 110 W 56th St
  - 20 E 50th St
- **New York Sports Clubs:**
  - 1221 Sixth Ave
  - 1601 Broadway
  - 1657 Broadway
  - 19 W 44th St
  - 230 W 41st St
  - Rockefeller Center
- **Pilates on Fifth** • 501 Fifth Ave
- **Prescriptive Fitness** • 250 W 54th St
- **Radu's Physical Culture Studio** • 24 W 57th St
- **Ritz Plaza Health Club** • 235 W 48th St
- **Sheraton New York & Manhattan Health Clubs** • 811 Seventh Ave
- **Sports Club/LA** • 45 Rockefeller Plz
- **Town Sports International** • 888 Seventh Ave
- **Ultimate Training Center** • 532 Madison Ave
- **US Athletic Training Center** • 515 Madison Ave

Hardware Stores

- **AAA Locksmiths** • 44 W 46th St
- **Garden Hardware & Supply** • 785 Eighth Ave
- **New Hippodrome Hardware,** • 23 W 45th St

Liquor Stores

- **Acorn Wine & Liquor** • 268 W 46th St
- **Athens Wine & Liquor** • 302 W 40th St
- **Cambridge Wine & Liquors** • 594 Eighth Ave
- **Carnegie Spirits & Wine** • 849 Seventh Ave
- **Columbus Circle Wine & Liquor** • 1780 Broadway
- **Fifty Fifth St Liqour Shop** • 40 W 55th St
- **Morrell & Co Wine & Spirits** • 1 Rockefeller Plz
- **O'Ryan Package Store,** • 1424 Sixth Ave
- **Park Ave Liquor Shop** • 15 E 40th St
- **Park Ave Liquor Shop** • 292 Madison Ave
- **Reidy Wine & Liquor** • 768 Eighth Ave
- **Royal Bee** • 1119 Sixth Ave
- **Shon 45 Liquors** • 840 Eighth Ave
- **Westerly Liquors** • 921 Eighth Ave

Movie Theaters

- **AMC Empire 25** • 234 W 42nd St
- **Bryant Park Summer Film Festival (outdoors)** • Bryant Park, between 40th & 42nd Sts
- **Cine One & Two** • 711 Seventh Ave
- **Clearview's Ziegfeld** • 141 W 54th St
- **Common Basis Theater** • 750 Eighth Ave
- **Loews 42nd Street E Walk** • 247 W 42nd St
- **Loews Astor Plaza** • 1515 Broadway
- **Loews State** • 1540 Broadway
- **Museum of TV and Radio** • 25 W 52nd St
- **New York Public Library-Donnell Library Center** • 20 W 53rd St
- **Paris Theatre** • 4 W 58th St

Restaurants

- **'21' Club** • 21 W 52nd St
- **Angelo & Maxie's** • 1285 Sixth Ave
- **Aquavit** • 13 W 54th St
- **Baluchi's** • 240 W 56th St
- **Carnegie Deli** • 854 Seventh Ave
- **Cosi Sandwich Bar** • 11 W 42nd St
- **Cosi Sandwich Bar** • 1633 Broadway
- **Cosi Sandwich Bar** • 61 W 48th St
- **Haru** • 205 W 43rd St
- **Joe's Shanghai** • 24 W 56th St
- **Le Bernardin** • 155 W 51st St
- **Molyvos** • 871 Seventh Ave
- **Nation Restaurant & Bar** • 12 W 45th St
- **Norma's** • 118 W 57th St
- **Pongsri Thai** • 244 W 48th St
- **Pret a Manger** • 1350 Sixth Ave\
- **The Pump Energy Food** • 40 W 55th St
- **Redeye Grill** • 890 Seventh Ave
- **Virgil's Real BBQ** • 152 W 44th St

Shopping

- **Alkit Pro Camera** • 830 Seventh Ave
- **Baccarat** • 625 Madison Ave
- **Bergdorf Goodman** • 754 Fifth Ave
- **Brooks Brothers** • 346 Madison Ave
- **Bruno Magli** • 677 Fifth Ave
- **Burberry** • 9 E 57th St
- **Carnegie Card & Gifts** • 56 W 57th St
- **CCS Counter Spy Shop** • 444 Madison Ave
- **Colony Music** • 1619 Broadway
- **CompUSA** • 1775 Broadway
- **Ermenegildo Zegna** • 743 Fifth Ave
- **Felissimo** • 10 W 56th St
- **Henri Bendel** • 712 Fifth Ave
- **International Cutlery** • 367 Madison Ave
- **Joseph Patelson Music House** • 160 W 56th St
- **Kate's Paperie** • 140 W 57th St
- **Manny's Music** • 156 W 48th St
- **Manon, Le Chocolatier** • 754 Fifth Ave
- **Mets Clubhouse Shop** • 11 W 42nd St
- **MoMA Design Store** • 44 W 53rd St
- **Museum of Arts and Design Shop** • 40 W 53rd St
- **Orvis Company** • 522 Fifth Ave
- **Radio Shack** • 1134 Sixth Ave
- **Saks Fifth Avenue** • 611 Fifth Ave
- **Sam Ash** • 160 W 48th St
- **Smythson of Bond Street** • 4 W 57th St
- **Steinway and Sons** • 109 W 57th St
- **Takashimaya** • 693 Fifth Ave
- **Tiffany & Co** • 727 Fifth Ave

Video Rental

- **300 Book Center** • 300 W 40th St
- **691 Video Center** • 691 Eighth Ave
- **Blockbuster Video** • 835 Eighth Ave
- **High Quality Video (Japanese only)** • 21 W 45th St
- **Rec Video** • 301 W 46th St
- **Tower Records** • 721 Fifth Ave

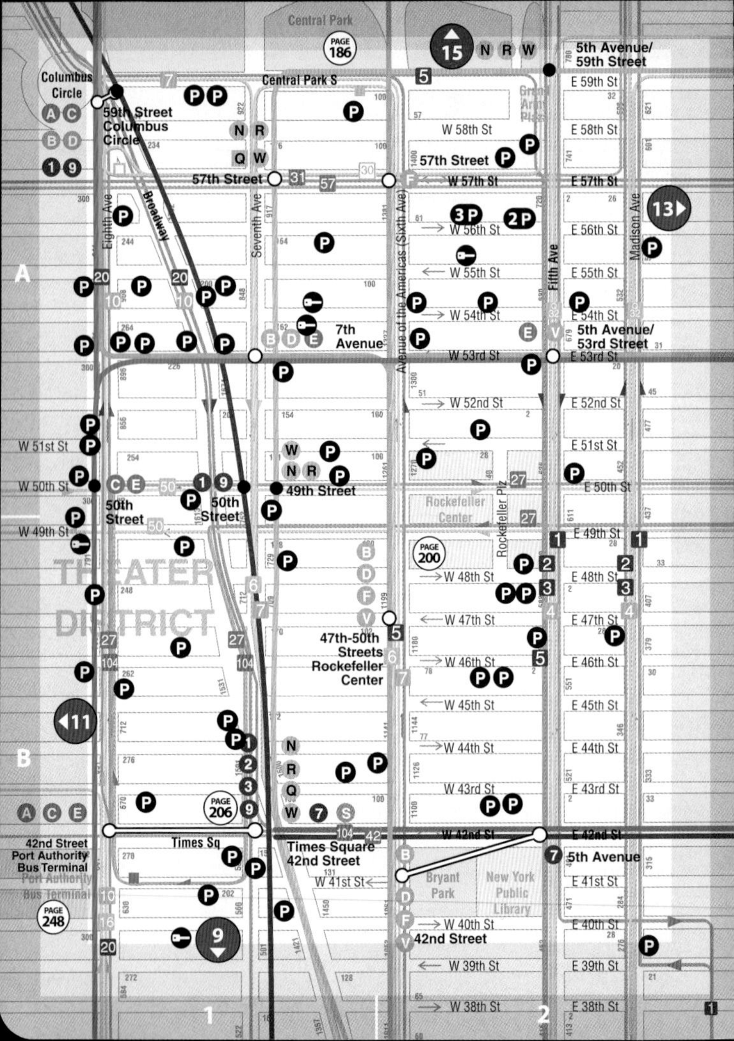

Map 12 • Midtown

Central Park
PAGE 186
15 N R W
5th Avenue/ 59th Street
Columbus Circle
A C B D 1 9
59th Street Columbus Circle
Central Park S
N R Q W
57th Street
W 58th St
E 59th St
E 58th St
Grand Army Plaza
57th Street
W 57th St
E 57th St
Eighth Ave
Broadway
Seventh Ave
Avenue of the Americas (Sixth Ave)
Fifth Ave
Madison Ave
W 56th St
E 56th St
W 55th St
E 55th St
W 54th St
E 54th St
7th Avenue
B D E
E V
5th Avenue/ 53rd Street
W 53rd St
E 53rd St
W 52nd St
E 52nd St
W 51st St
E 51st St
W 50th St
E 50th St
C E
50th Street
1 9
50th Street
W N R
49th Street
Rockefeller Center
Rockefeller Plz
W 49th St
E 49th St
PAGE 200
THEATER DISTRICT
B D F V
W 48th St
E 48th St
W 47th St
E 47th St
47th-50th Streets Rockefeller Center
W 46th St
E 46th St
W 45th St
E 45th St
W 44th St
E 44th St
W 43rd St
E 43rd St
A C E
PAGE 206
1 2 3 9
N R Q W 7 S
42nd Street Port Authority Bus Terminal
Port Authority Bus Terminal
Times Sq
Times Square 42nd Street
W 42nd St
E 42nd St
7 5th Avenue
W 41st St
E 41st St
Bryant Park
New York Public Library
B D F V
42nd Street
W 40th St
E 40th St
PAGE 248
W 39th St
E 39th St
W 38th St
E 38th St
A
B
1
2

Driving in midtown has now turned into a fate worse than post-apocalyptic, with the addition of the new "through streets" and "no-turn avenues," which now means you'll have to drive fully crosstown to make a turn somewhere. We expect a boycott by the delivery folks shortly.

Subways

1 9 .... 50th St
1 9 A C B D .... 59th St-Columbus Cir
A C E .... 42th St/Port Authority
B D E ....Seventh Ave
B D F V ... 47th St-50th St/Rockefeller Ctr
7 B D F V .... 42th St/Fifth Ave
C E .... 50th St
E V ....Fifth Ave/53th St
F .... 57th St
1 2 3 9 7 N Q R W S .... Times Sq/42th St
N R Q W .... 57th St
N R W .... 49th St
N R W ....Fifth Ave/59th St

Bus Lines

1 2 3 4 .... Fifth Ave/Madison Ave
10 20 .... Seventh Ave/Eighth Ave (Central Park West)/Frederick Douglass Blvd
104 .... Broadway/42nd St
16 .... 34th St Crosstown
27 .... 49th St/50th St Crosstown
30 .... 57th St /72nd St Crosstown
31 .... York Ave/57th St
42 .... 42nd St Crosstown
5 .... Fifth Ave/Sixth Ave/Riverside Dr
50 .... 49th St/50th St Crosstown
57 .... 57th St Crosstown
6 ....Seventh Ave/Broadway/Sixth Ave
7 .... Columbus Ave/Amsterdam Ave/ Lenox Ave/Sixth Ave/Seventh Ave/Broadway
Q32 .... Penn Station/Jackson Heights, Queens

- **Avis** • 153 W 54th St
- **Budget** • 304 W 49th St
- **Dollar** • 156 W 54th St
- **Hertz** • 126 W 55th St
- **National** • 252 W 40th St

Parking

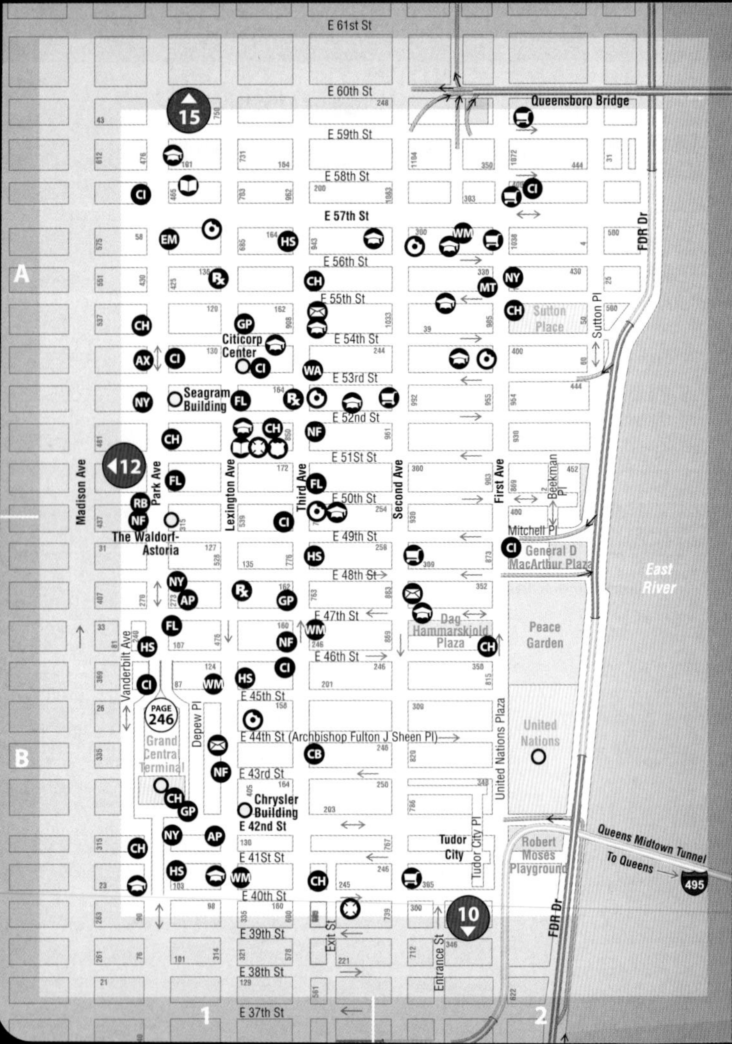

E 61st St
E 60th St
Queensboro Bridge
E 59th St
E 58th St
E 57th St
E 56th St
E 55th St
E 54th St
E 53rd St
E 52nd St
E 51St St
E 50th St
E 49th St
E 48th St
E 47th St
E 46th St
E 45th St
E 44th St (Archbishop Fulton J Sheen Pl)
E 43rd St
E 42nd St
E 41St St
E 40th St
E 39th St
E 38th St
E 37th St
Madison Ave
Park Ave
Vanderbilt Ave
Lexington Ave
Third Ave
Second Ave
First Ave
Sutton Pl
Beekman Pl
Mitchell Pl
Depew Pl
United Nations Plaza
Tudor City Pl
Exit St
Entrance St
FDR Dr
Citicorp Center
Seagram Building
The Waldorf-Astoria
Grand Central Terminal
Chrysler Building
Sutton Place
General D MacArthur Plaza
Dag Hammarskjold Plaza
Peace Garden
United Nations
Tudor City
Robert Moses Playground
East River
Queens Midtown Tunnel
To Queens
495
15
12
10
A
B
1
2

PAGE 246

This is a busy and diverse part of town, packed with consulates, hotels, Grand Central Terminal, the United Nations, the Queensboro Bridge, and two exclusive housing enclaves—Tudor City and Sutton Place. Park Avenue between 40th and 60th Streets contains some of the finest examples, if not the finest example, of every major architectural style from the past 100 years.

ATMs

AX • AmEx Travel-Related Services • 374 Park Ave
AP • Apple • 122 E 42nd St
AP • Apple • 277 Park Ave
NY • Bank of New York • 100 E 42nd St
NY • Bank of New York • 1006 First Ave
NY • Bank of New York • 277 Park Ave
NY • Bank of New York • 360 Park Ave
CH • Chase • 345 Park Ave
CH • Chase • 410 Park Ave
CH • Chase • 60 E 42nd St
CH • Chase • 633 Third Ave
CH • Chase • 825 United Nations Plz
CH • Chase • 850 Third Ave
CH • Chase • 919 Third Ave
CH • Chase • 994 First Ave
CH • Chase • Grand Central lobby
CI • Citibank • 1044 First Ave
CI • Citibank • 153 E 53rd St
CI • Citibank • 200 Park Ave
CI • Citibank • 399 Park Ave
CI • Citibank • 460 Park Ave
CI • Citibank • 734 Third Ave
CI • Citibank • 800 Third Ave
CI • Citibank • 866 United Nations Plz
CO • Commerce Bank • 685 Third Ave
EM • Emigrant • 445 Park Ave
RB • First Republic Bank • 320 Park Ave
FL • Fleet • 200 Park Ave
FL • Fleet • 345 Park Ave
FL • Fleet • 599 Lexington Ave
FL • Fleet • 825 Third Ave
GP • Greenpoint Bank • 109 E 42nd St
GP • Greenpoint Bank • 643 Lexington Ave
GP • Greenpoint Bank • 770 Third Ave
HS • HSBC • 101 Park Ave
HS • HSBC • 250 Park Ave
HS • HSBC • 441 Lexington Ave
HS • HSBC • 777 Third Ave
HS • HSBC • 950 Third Ave
MT • Manufacturers and Traders Trust • 401 E 55th St
NF • North Fork Bank • 320 Park Ave
NF • North Fork Bank • 420 Lexington Ave
NF • North Fork Bank • 750 Third Ave
NF • North Fork Bank • 845 Third Ave
WM • Washington Mutual • 355 Lexington Ave
WM • Washington Mutual • 360 E 57th St
WM • Washington Mutual • 466 Lexington Ave
WM • Washington Mutual • 875 Third Ave

Bagels

- **Bagel the Bagel** • 875 Third Ave
- **Ess-A-Bagel** • 831 Third Ave
- **Everything Bagel** • 141 E 44th St
- **Jumbo Bagels & Bialys** • 1070 Second Ave
- **Tal Bagels** • 977 First Ave
- **Zanett Inc** • 135 E 57th St

Fire Departments

- **Engine 21** • 238 E 40th St
- **Engine 8, Ladder 2** • 165 E 51st St

Landmarks

- **Chrysler Building** • 405 Lexington Ave
- **Citicorp Center** • 153 E 53rd St
- **Grand Central Terminal** • 42nd St
- **Seagram Building** • 375 Park Ave
- **United Nations** • First Ave between 42nd & 48th Sts
- **Waldorf-Astoria** • 301 Park Ave

Libraries

- **58th St** • 127 E 58th St
- **Terence Cardinal Cooke-Cathedral** • 560 Lexington Ave

24-Hour Pharmacies

- **CVS Pharmacy** • 630 Lexington Ave
- **Duane Reade** • 485 Lexington Ave
- **Duane Reade** • 866 Third Ave

Police

- **17th Precinct** • 167 E 51st St

Post Offices

- **Dag Hammarskjold** • 884 Second Ave
- **Franklin D Roosevelt** • 909 Third Ave
- **Grand Central Station** • 450 Lexington Ave

Schools

- **The Beekman School** • 220 E 50th St
- **Beginning with Children Charter School** • 900 Third Ave
- **Cathedral High School** • 350 E 56th St
- **Family School** • 323 E 47th St
- **High School of Art & Design** • 1075 Second Ave
- **Manhattan Borough Academy** • 40 E 40th St
- **Montessori School of New York** • 347 E 55th St
- **Neighborhood Playhouse School** • 340 E 54th St
- **New York School of Astrology** • 350 Lexington Ave
- **PS 59 Beekman Hill School** • 228 E 57th St
- **SCS Business & Technical School** • 575 Lexington Ave
- **The Sonia Moore Studio** • 485 Park Ave
- **Turtle Bay Music School** • 244 E 52nd St

Supermarkets

- **Associated** • 908 Second Ave
- **D'Agostino** • 1031 First Ave
- **Food Emporium** • 405 E 59th St
- **Food Emporium** • 969 Second Ave
- **Gristede's** • 1052 First Ave
- **Gristede's** • 748 Second Ave

Map 13 • East Midtown

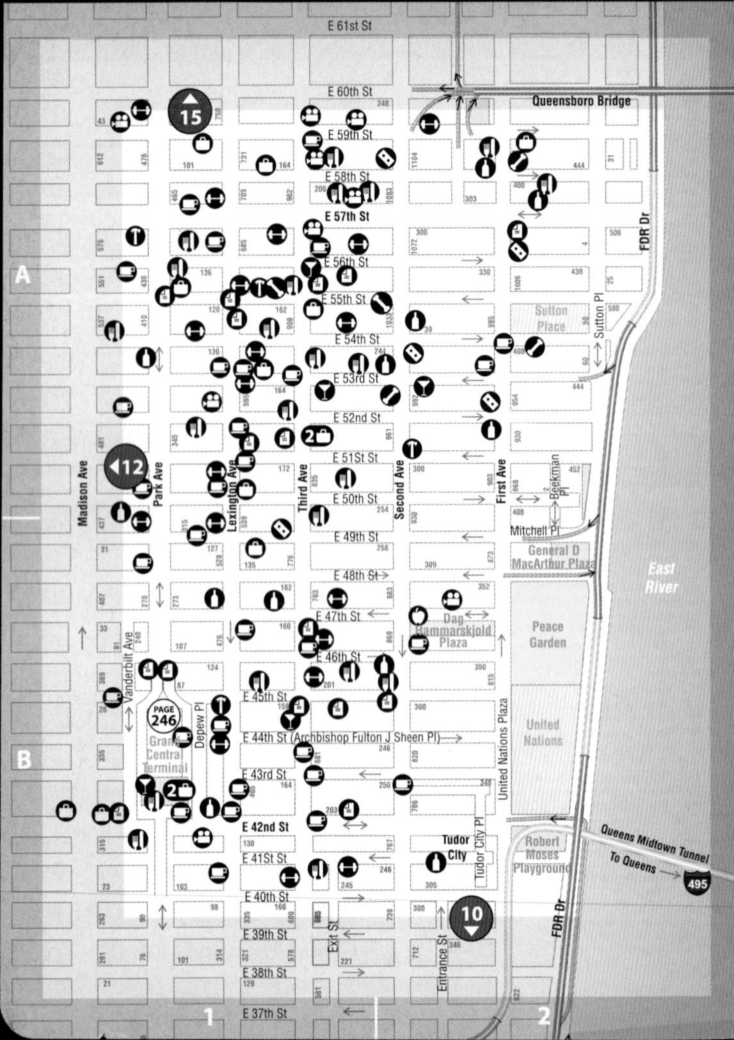

E 61st St
E 60th St
Queensboro Bridge
E 59th St
E 58th St
E 57th St
E 56th St
E 55th St
E 54th St
E 53rd St
E 52nd St
E 51St St
E 50th St
E 49th St
E 48th St
E 47th St
E 46th St
E 45th St
E 44th St (Archbishop Fulton J Sheen Pl)
E 43rd St
E 42nd St
E 41St St
E 40th St
E 39th St
E 38th St
E 37th St
Madison Ave
Park Ave
Lexington Ave
Third Ave
Second Ave
First Ave
Vanderbilt Ave
Depew Pl
Sutton Pl
Sutton Place
Beekman Pl
Mitchell Pl
General D MacArthur Plaza
Dag Hammarskjold Plaza
Peace Garden
United Nations
United Nations Plaza
Tudor City
Tudor City Pl
Robert Moses Playground
Grand Central Terminal
PAGE 246
Exit St
Entrance St
FDR Dr
East River
Queens Midtown Tunnel
To Queens
495
15
12
10
A
B
1
2

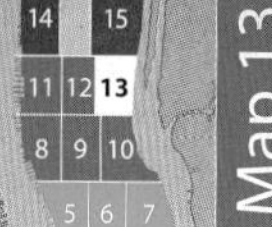

Some of New York's top eateries are in this grid—including Vong, Smith & Wollensky, Dawat, March, and Lutece. Check out the cool stores under the Queensboro Bridge—including Bridge Kitchenware and the Terence Conran Shop.

Bars

- **Blarney Stone** • 710 Third Ave
- **The Campbell Apartment** • Grand Central Terminal
- **Metro 53** • 307 E 53rd St
- **PJ Clarke's** • 915 Third Ave
- **Tammany Hall** • 218 E 53rd St

Coffee

- **Andrew's Coffee Shop** • 138 E 43rd St
- **Au Bon Pain** • 875 Third Ave
- **The Coffee Beanery Ltd** • 569 Lexington Ave
- **Columbus Bakery** • 957 First Ave
- **Cosi** • 165 E 52nd St
- **Cosi** • 320 Park Ave
- **Cosi** • 369 Lexington Ave
- **Cosi** • 38 E 45th St
- **Cosi** • 60 E 56th St
- **Cosi** • 685 Third Ave
- **Dunkin' Donuts** • 203 E 59th St
- **Dunkin' Donuts** • 47 E 42nd St
- **Dunkin' Donuts** • 801 Second Ave
- **Friars Coffee Shop** • 303 E 46th St
- **Manhattan Espresso HD** • 146 E 49th St
- **New World Coffee** • 830 Third Ave
- **Oren's Daily Roast** • 105 E 42nd St
- **Oren's Daily Roast** • Grand Central Market
- **Palace Restaurant Coffee House** • 122 E 57th St
- **Starbucks** • 107 E 43rd St
- **Starbucks** • 135 E 57th St
- **Starbucks** • 150 E 42nd St
- **Starbucks** • 280 Park Ave
- **Starbucks** • 400 E 54th St
- **Starbucks** • 450 Lexington Ave
- **Starbucks** • 55 E 52nd St
- **Starbucks** • 560 Lexington Ave
- **Starbucks** • 599 Lexington Ave
- **Starbucks** • 630 Lexington Ave
- **Starbucks** • 639 Third Ave
- **Starbucks** • 685 Third Ave
- **Starbucks** • 757 Third Ave
- **Starbucks** • Grand Central Terminal

Copy Shops

- **Caps Copy Print Corp(9 am-6:30 am)** • 209 E 56th St
- **Copy Right Reprographics (9 am-6 pm)** • 133 E 55th St
- **Copy Room Inc** • 850 Third Ave
- **Copycats** • 216 E 45th St
- **Insti Copy (8 am- 8 pm)** • 249 E 55th St
- **Kinko's** • 230 Park Ave
- **Kinko's** • 641 Lexington Ave
- **Kinko's** • 747 Third Ave
- **Lightining Copy Center (8 am-6 pm)** • 60 E 42nd St
- **Mail Boxes Etc(8:30 am-6 pm)** • 1040 First Ave
- **Mail Boxes Etc(8:30 am- 7 pm)** • 847 Second Ave
- **Staples (7 am-7 pm)** • 205 E 42nd St
- **Staples (7 am-7 pm)** • 425 Park Ave
- **Staples (7 am-7 pm)** • 575 Lexington Ave
- **Staples (7 am-7 pm)** • 730 Third Ave

Farmer's Markets

- **Dag Hammerskjold Plaza Greenmarket** • Second Ave & 47th St

Gyms

- **Away Spa-Gym** • 541 Lexington Ave
- **Body Perfection** • 123 E 54th St
- **Dag Hammarskjold Tower** • 240 E 47th St
- **Dolphin Fitness Clubs** • 330 E 59th St
- **Dolphin Fitness Clubs** • 50 E 42nd St
- **Equinox Fitness Club** • 250 E 54th St
- **Equinox Fitness Club** • 420 Lexington Ave
- **Excelsior Athletic Club** • 301 E 57th St
- **Lift Gym** • 139 E 57th St
- **New York Health & Racquet Club** • 115 E 57th St
- **New York Health & Racquet Club** • 132 E 45th St
- **New York Sports Clubs** • 502 Park Ave
- **New York Sports Clubs** • 575 Lexington Ave
- **New York Sports Clubs** • 633 Third Ave
- **Plus One Fitness Clinic** • 301 Park Ave
- **Sparta Strength and Conditioning** • 133 E 55th St
- **Upper Body** • 343 Lexington Ave
- **Vanderbilt Health Club** • 240 E 41st St
- **YMCA Vanderbilt** • 224 E 47th St
- **YWCA** • 610 Lexington Ave

Hardware Stores

- **55th St Hardware** • 155 E 55th St
- **Kramer's** • 952 Second Ave
- **Midtown Hardware** • 155 E 45th St
- **Sherle Wagner International** • 60 E 57th St

Liquor Stores

- **Ambassador Wines & Spirits** • 1020 Second Ave
- **American First Liquors** • 1059 First Ave
- **Beekman Liquors** • 500 Lexington Ave
- **Diplomat Wine & Spirits** • 939 Second Ave
- **Divine Wines & Spirits** • 764 Third Ave
- **Grand Harvest Wines** • 107 E 42nd St
- **Jeffrey Wine & Liquors** • 939 First Ave
- **Midtown Wine & Liquor Shop** • 44 E 50th St
- **Schumer's Wine & Liquors** • 59 E 54th St
- **Sussex Liquor Store** • 300 E 41st St
- **Sutton Wine Shop** • 403 E 57th St
- **Turtle Bay Liquors** • 855 Second Ave

Movie Theaters

- **Cineplex Odeon: Coronet Cinemas** • 993 Third Ave
- **City Cinemas 1, 2, 3** • 1001 Third Ave
- **City Cinemas: Eastside Playhouse** • 919 Third Ave
- **City Cinemas: Sutton 1 & 2** • 205 E 57th St
- **Clearview's 59th St East** • 239 E 59th St
- **French Institute** • 55 E 59th St
- **Instituto Cervantes** • 122 E 42nd St
- **Japan Society** • 333 E 47th St
- **YWCA** • 610 Lexington Ave

Pet Shops

- **Chic Doggie by Corey** • 400 E 54th St
- **Finishing Touches by Stephanie** • 414 E 58th St
- **Furry Paws** • 1039 Second Ave
- **Petland Discounts** • 976 Second Ave
- **Sherpa's Pet Trading Co** • 135 E 55th St

Restaurants

- **Cosi Sandwich Bar** • 165 E 52nd St
- **Cosi Sandwich Bar** • 60 E 56th St
- **Dawat** • 210 E 58th St
- **Docks Oyster Bar** • 633 Third Ave
- **Felidia** • 243 E 58th St
- **Four Seasons** • 99 E 52nd St
- **Lutece** • 249 E 50th St
- **March** • 405 E 58th St
- **Menchanko-tei** • 131 E 45th St
- **Oceana** • 55 E 54th St
- **Organic Harvest Café** • 235 E 53rd St
- **Oyster Bar** • Grand Central, Lower Level
- **Palm** • 837 Second Ave
- **Pershing Square** • 90 E 42nd St
- **PJ Clarke's** • 915 Third Ave
- **Rosa Mexicano** • 1063 First Ave
- **Shun Lee Palace** • 155 E 55th St
- **Smith & Wollensky** • 797 Third Ave
- **Sparks Steak House** • 210 E 46th St
- **Vong** • 200 E 54th St

Shopping

- **Adriana's Caravan** • Grand Central Station
- **Bridge Kitchenware** • 214 E 52nd St
- **Godiva Chocolatier** • 560 Lexington Ave
- **Innovative Audio** • 150 E 58th St
- **Mets Clubhouse Shop** • 143 E 54th St
- **Modell's** • 51 E 42nd St
- **New York Transit Museum** • Grand Central, Main Concourse
- **Radio Shack** • 940 Third Ave
- **Sam Flax** • 425 Park Ave
- **Sports Authority** • 845 Third Ave
- **Terence Conran Shop** • 407 E 59th St
- **World of Golf** • 147 E 47th St
- **Yankee Clubhouse Shop** • 110 E 59th St
- **Zaro's Bread Basket** • 89 E 42nd St

Video Rental

- **American Video** • 780 Third Ave
- **Blockbuster Video** • 1023 First Ave
- **Flick's Video To Go Eastside** • 1093 Second Ave
- **International Video** • 962 Second Ave
- **New York Video** • 949 First Ave

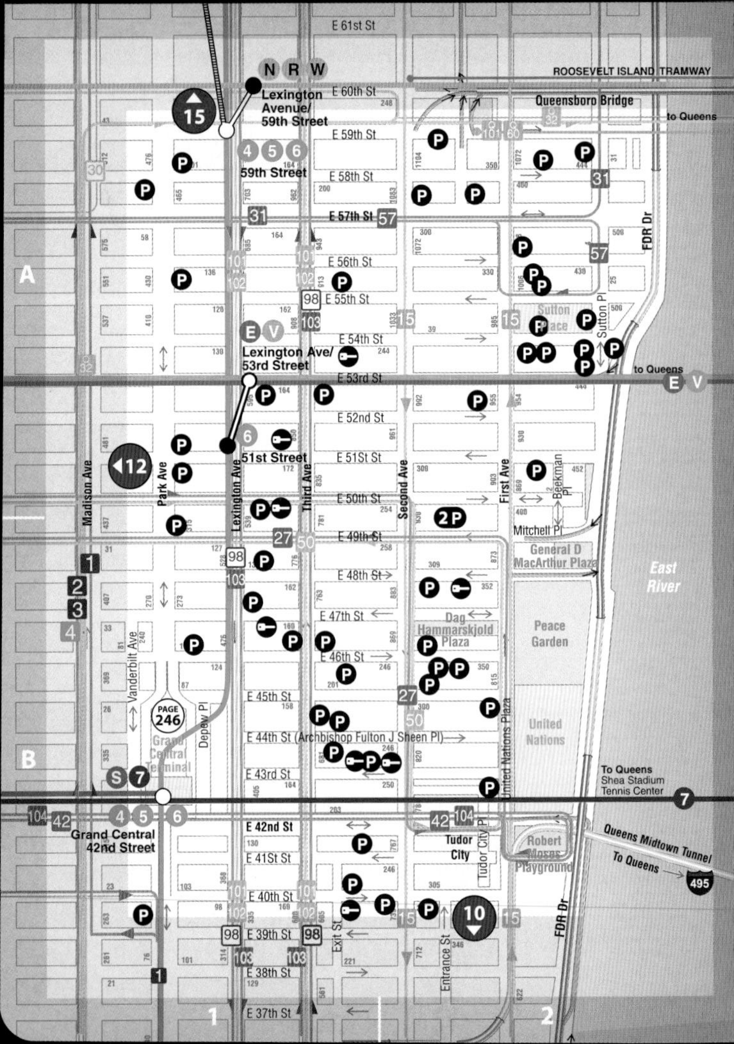
E 61st St
N R W
Lexington Avenue/ 59th Street
E 60th St
ROOSEVELT ISLAND TRAMWAY
Queensboro Bridge
to Queens
15
E 59th St
4 5 6
59th Street
E 58th St
E 57th St
E 56th St
E 55th St
E 54th St
E V
Lexington Ave/ 53rd Street
E 53rd St
to Queens
E 52nd St
6
51st Street
E 51St St
E 50th St
E 49th St
E 48th St
E 47th St
E 46th St
E 45th St
E 44th St (Archbishop Fulton J Sheen Pl)
E 43rd St
E 42nd St
E 41St St
E 40th St
E 39th St
E 38th St
E 37th St
12
10
A
B
1
2
Madison Ave
Park Ave
Lexington Ave
Third Ave
Second Ave
First Ave
FDR Dr
Sutton Pl
Sutton Place
Beekman Pl
Mitchell Pl
General D MacArthur Plaza
East River
Dag Hammarskjold Plaza
Peace Garden
United Nations
United Nations Plaza
Vanderbilt Ave
Depew Pl
PAGE 246
Grand Central Terminal
S 7
Grand Central 42nd Street
To Queens
Shea Stadium
Tennis Center
Queens Midtown Tunnel
To Queens
495
Tudor City
Tudor City Pl
Robert Moses Playground
Exit St
Entrance St
FDR Dr

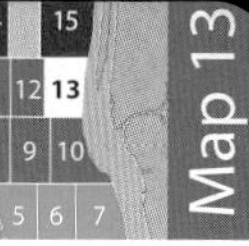

Other than the quirky ramps running around Grand Central and the snarl around the Queensboro Bridge, traffic in this area could be far worse than it is. However, it's always wise to pay attention to when the President or some other major dignitary is at the U.N., because you'll want to use mass transit that day. Some of the midtown "through street" nightmares do spill over to this area, unfortunately.

Subways

4 5 6 N R W ... Lexington Ave-59th St
6 E V .... 51st St-Lexington Ave-53rd St
4 5 6 7 S .... Grand Central-42nd St

Bus Lines

104 .... Broadway
15 .... First Ave/Second Ave
27 50 .... 49th St/50th St Crosstown
30 .... 72nd St/57th St Crosstown
31 .... York Ave/57th St
42 .... 42nd St Crosstown
57 .... 57th St Crosstown
57 .... Washington Heights/Midtown Limited
98 101 102 103 .... Third Ave/Lexington Ave
Q32 .... Queens-to-Midtown

Car Rental

- **Avis** • 217 E 43rd St
- **Avis** • 240 E 54th St
- **Budget** • 225 E 43rd St
- **Enterprise** • 135 E 47th St
- **Hertz** • 222 E 40th St
- **Hertz** • 310 E 48th St
- **National** • 138 E 50th St
- **New York Rent-A-Car** • 151 E 51st St

Parking

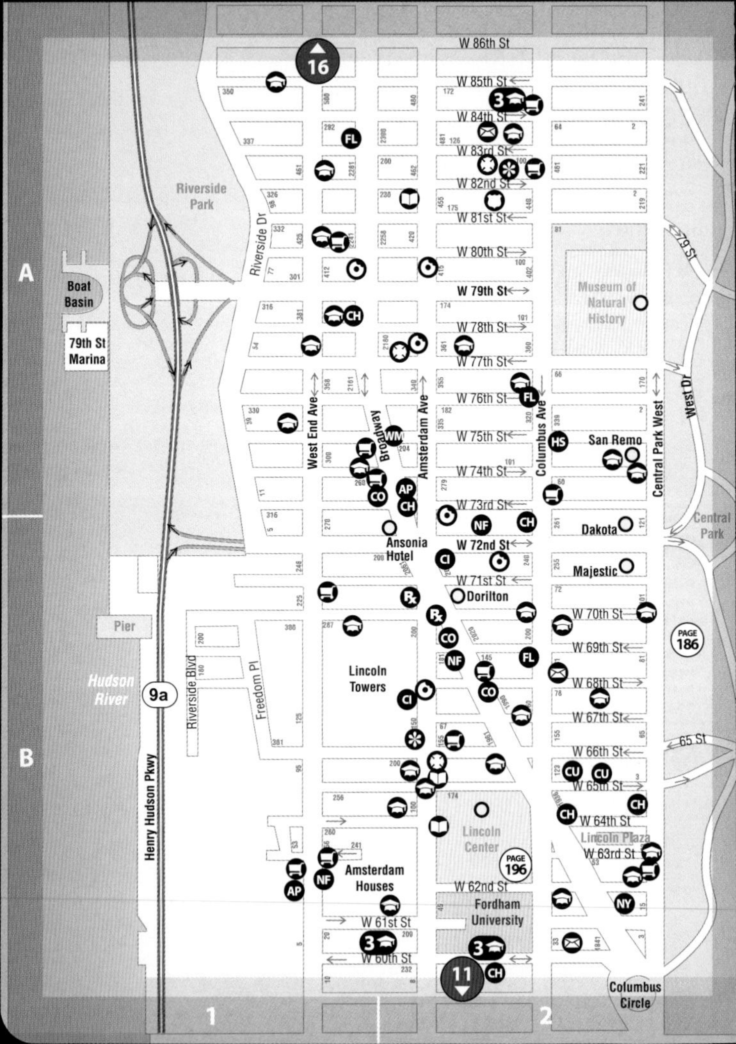

Map 14 • Upper West Side (Lower)

W 86th St
W 85th St
W 84th St
W 83rd St
W 82nd St
W 81st St
W 80th St
W 79th St
W 78th St
W 77th St
W 76th St
W 75th St
W 74th St
W 73rd St
W 72nd St
W 71st St
W 70th St
W 69th St
W 68th St
W 67th St
W 66th St
W 65th St
W 64th St
W 63rd St
W 62nd St
W 61st St
W 60th St
W 79 St
65 St
Riverside Park
Riverside Dr
Boat Basin
79th St Marina
West End Ave
Broadway
Amsterdam Ave
Columbus Ave
Central Park West
West Dr
Central Park
Museum of Natural History
San Remo
Dakota
Majestic
Dorilton
Ansonia Hotel
Lincoln Towers
Lincoln Center
Lincoln Plaza
Amsterdam Houses
Fordham University
Columbus Circle
Pier
Hudson River
Henry Hudson Pkwy
Riverside Blvd
Freedom Pl
9a
16
11
PAGE 186
PAGE 196
A
B
1
2

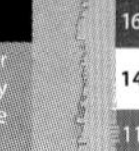

The presence of Lincoln Center and the Museum of Natural History gives the southern half of the Upper West Side more than its share of the major cultural hotspots in Manhattan. And you can stop by several truly remarkable apartment buildings (the Ansonia, the Apthorp, the Dorilton, the Dakota, the Majestic, and the San Remo) on your way to Strawberry Fields to pay respect to Mr. Lennon.

ATMs

CU • **ABC Employees Federal** • 30 W 66th St
CU • **ABC Employees Federal** • 77 W 66th St
AP • **Apple** • 2100 Broadway
AP • **Apple** • 45 West End Ave
NY • **Bank of New York** • 47 W 62nd St
CH • **Chase** • 1 Lincoln Plz
CH • **Chase** • 124 W 60th St
CH • **Chase** • 2099 Broadway
CH • **Chase** • 2219 Broadway
CH • **Chase** • 260 Columbus Ave
CI • **Citibank** • 162 Amsterdam Ave
CI • **Citibank** • 170 W 72nd St
CO • **Commerce Bank** • 1995 Broadway
CO • **Commerce Bank** • 2109 Broadway
CO • **Commercial Bank** • 2025 Broadway
FL • **Fleet** • 192 Columbus Ave
FL • **Fleet** • 2301 Broadway
FL • **Fleet** • 334 Columbus Ave
HS • **HSBC** • 301 Columbus Ave
NF • **North Fork Bank** • 175 W 72nd St
NF • **North Fork Bank** • 2025 Broadway
NF • **North Fork Bank** • 75 West End Ave
WM • **Washington Mutual** • 2139 Broadway

Bagels

• **Bagel Talk** • 368 Amsterdam Ave
• **Bagels & Co** • 393 Amsterdam Ave
• **Bagels on Amsterdam** • 164 Amsterdam Ave
• **Bread Factory Café** • 2079 Broadway
• **H&H Bagels** • 2239 Broadway
• **Pick-a-Bagel** • 130 W 72nd St

Community Gardens

Fire Departments

• **Engine 40, Ladder 35** • 133 Amsterdam Ave
• **Engine 74** • 120 W 83rd St
• **Ladder 25** • 205 W 77th St

Landmarks

• **Ansonia Hotel** • 2109 Broadway & 73rd St
• **Dakota** • Central Park West & 72nd St
• **Dorilton** • Broadway & 71st St
• **Lincoln Center** • Broadway & 64th St
• **Majestic** • 115 Central Park W
• **Museum of Natural History** • Central Park W & 79th St
• **San Remo** • Central Park W & 74th St

Libraries

• **New York Public Library for the Performing Arts** • 40 Lincoln Center Plz
• **Riverside** • 127 Amsterdam Ave
• **St Agnes** • 444 Amsterdam Ave

24-Hour Pharmacies

• **Duane Reade** • 2025 Broadway
• **Rite Aid** • 210 Amsterdam Ave

Police

• **20th Precinct** • 120 W 82nd St

Post Offices

• **Ansonia** • 178 Columbus Ave
• **Columbus Circle** • 27 W 60th St
• **Planetarium** • 127 W 83rd St

Schools

• **Alvin Ailey American Dance Center** • 211 W 61st St
• **American Musical and Drama Academy** • 2109 Broadway
• **Beacon High School** • 227 W 61st St
• **Beit Rabban Day School** • 8 W 70th St
• **Blessed Sacrement School** • 147 W 70th St
• **The Calhoun School** • 433 West End Ave
• **Collegiate School** • 260 W 78th St
• **Collegiate School** • 370 West End Ave
• **Ethical Culture-Fieldston School** • 33 Central Park W
• **Fiorello H LaGuardia High School** • 100 Amsterdam Ave
• **Fordham University** • 113 W 60th St
• **Institute of Allied Medical Professionals** • 106 Central Park S
• **IS 044 William J O'Shea School** • 100 W 77th St
• **Louis D Brandeis High School** • 145 W 84th St
• **Lucy Moses School For Music & Dance** • 129 W 67th St
• **Manhattan Day School** • 310 W 75th St
• **Mannes College of Music** • 150 W 85th St
• **Martin Luther King Jr High School** • 122 Amsterdam Ave
• **Metropolitan Montessori School** • 325 W 85th St
• **New York Academy of Sciences** • 2 E 63rd St
• **New York Institute of Technology Metropolitan Center** • 1855 Broadway
• **Parkside School** • 48 W 74th St
• **Professional Children's School** • 132 W 60th St
• **PS 009 Renaissance School** • 100 W 84th St
• **PS 087 William Sherman** • 160 W 78th St
• **PS 191 Amsterdam School** • 210 W 61st St
• **PS 199 Jesse Straus School** • 270 W 70th St
• **PS 252** • 20 West End Ave
• **PS 811** • 466 West End Ave
• **Stephen Gaynor School** • 22 W 74th St
• **York Prep** • 40 W 68th St

Supermarkets

• **Associated** • 466 Columbus Ave
• **Balducci's** • 155 W 66th St
• **Citarella East** • 2135 Broadway
• **Fairway Market** • 2127 Broadway
• **Food Emporium** • 2008 Broadway
• **Food Emporium** • 228 West End Ave
• **Gristede's** • 2109 Broadway
• **Gristede's** • 25 Central Park W
• **Gristede's** • 504 Columbus Ave
• **Gristede's** • 80 West End Ave
• **Pioneer** • 289 Columbus Ave
• **Western Beef** • 75 West End Ave
• **Zabar's** • 249 W 80th St

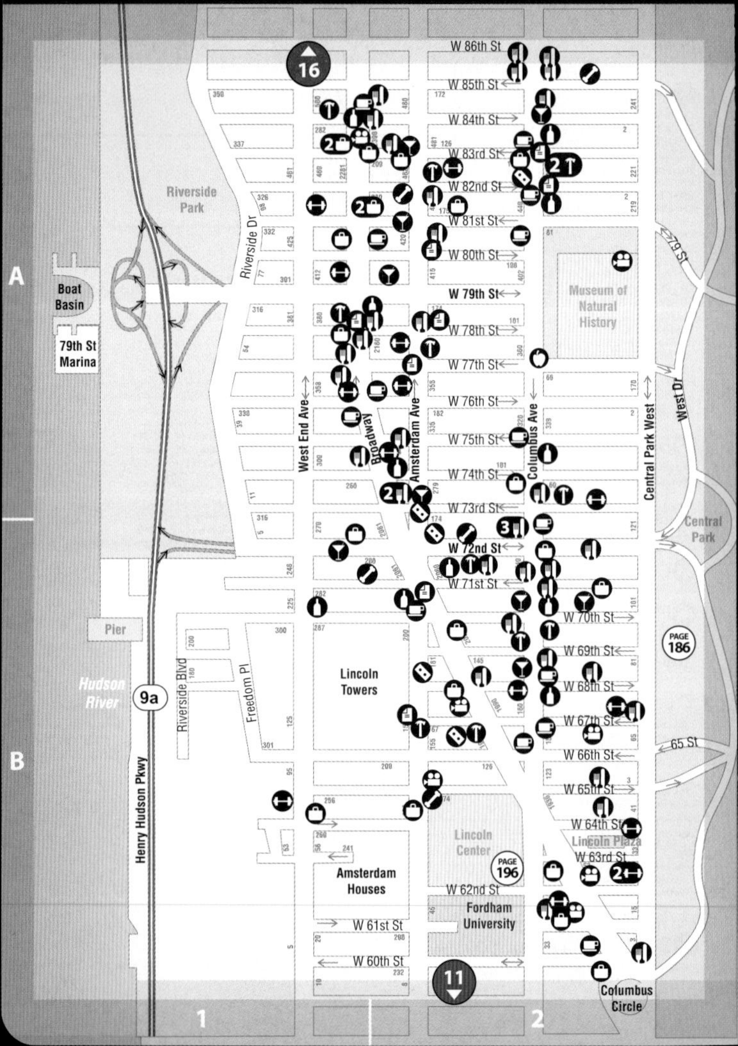

Map 14 • Upper West Side (Lower)

W 86th St
W 85th St
W 84th St
W 83rd St
W 82nd St
W 81st St
W 80th St
W 79th St
W 78th St
W 77th St
W 76th St
W 75th St
W 74th St
W 73rd St
W 72nd St
W 71st St
W 70th St
W 69th St
W 68th St
W 67th St
W 66th St
W 65th St
W 64th St
W 63rd St
W 62nd St
W 61st St
W 60th St
Riverside Park
Riverside Dr
West End Ave
Broadway
Amsterdam Ave
Columbus Ave
Central Park West
West Dr
79 St
65 St
Museum of Natural History
Central Park
Boat Basin
79th St Marina
Pier
Hudson River
9a
Henry Hudson Pkwy
Riverside Blvd
Freedom Pl
Lincoln Towers
Lincoln Center
Lincoln Plaza
Amsterdam Houses
Fordham University
Columbus Circle
PAGE 186
PAGE 196
16
11
A
B
1
2

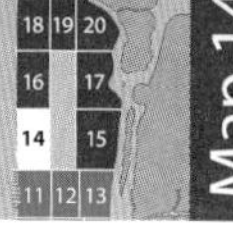

Home to the famous Zabar's, several quality watering holes (such as the Dublin House and the All-State Café), and the viciously tasty and unhealthy Big Nick's Burger Joint (at 2175 Broadway), this part of the Upper West Side has more character than people suspect at first glance. The new Riverside South Park on the Hudson is quite nice, though we still think Trump is, well...Trump. Best place to eat at the new Time Warner Center? Answer: Whole Foods in the basement.

Bars

- **All-State Café** • 250 W 72nd St
- **Dead Poet** • 450 Amsterdam Ave
- **Dublin House** • 225 W 79th St
- **Emerald Inn** • 220 Columbus Ave
- **Jake's Dilemma** • 430 Amsterdam Ave
- **P&G** • 279 Amsterdam Ave
- **Prohibition** • 503 Columbus Ave
- **Raccoon Lodge** • 480 Amsterdam Ave
- **Shalel Lounge** • 65 W 70th St

Coffee

- **Columbus Bakery** • 474 Columbus Ave
- **Cosi** • 2160 Broadway
- **Edgar's Cafe** • 255 W 84th St
- **New World Coffee** • 159 Columbus Ave
- **New World Coffee** • 2151 Broadway
- **New World Coffee** • 416 Columbus Ave
- **Starbucks** • 152 Columbus Ave
- **Starbucks** • 1841 Broadway
- **Starbucks** • 2 Columbus Ave
- **Starbucks** • 2045 Broadway
- **Starbucks** • 2252 Broadway
- **Starbucks** • 267 Columbus Ave
- **Starbucks** • 338 Columbus Ave
- **Starbucks** • 444 Columbus Ave

Copy Shops

- **Gavin Printing (9 am-6 pm)** • 387 Amsterdam Ave
- **Kinko's** • 221 W 72nd St
- **Mail Boxes Etc (8:30 am-7 pm)** • 459 Columbus Ave
- **Mail Boxes Etc (9:30 am-7:30 pm)** • 163 Amsterdam Ave
- **New 77 Copy Center (8 am-10 pm)** • 225 W 77th St
- **Panda Copy (9 am-8:20 pm)** • 2202 Broadway
- **Printing Express and Speed Copy Center (9:15 am-7 pm)** • 104 W 83rd St
- **Staples (7 am-9 pm)** • 2248 Broadway
- **Upper Westside Copy Center (8 am-11 pm)** • 2054 Broadway

Farmer's Markets

- **77th Street/IS 44 Greenmarket** • Columbus Ave & 77th St

Gyms

- **All Star Fitness Center** • 75 West End Ave
- **Club 30** • 30 W 63rd St
- **Crunch Fitness** • 160 W 83rd St
- **Equinox Fitness Club** • 344 Amsterdam Ave
- **La Palestra** • 11 W 67th St
- **New York Sports Clubs** • 2162 Broadway
- **New York Sports Clubs** • 23 W 73rd St
- **New York Sports Clubs** • 248 W 80th St
- **New York Sports Clubs** • 61 W 62nd St
- **Reebok Sports Club NY** • 160 Columbus Ave
- **Synergy Fitness Clubs** • 2130 Broadway
- **Top of the One Club** • 1 Lincoln Plz
- **West River Racquet Ball** • 424 West End Ave
- **YMCA West Side** • 5 W 63rd St

Hardware Stores

- **A&I Hardware** • 207 Columbus Ave
- **AJA Decorative Hardware** • 381 Amsterdam Ave
- **Amsterdam Hardware** • 147 Amsterdam Ave
- **Beacon Paint & Wallpaper** • 371 Amsterdam Ave
- **Ben Franklin Paints** • 2193 Broadway
- **Gartner's Hardware** • 134 W 72nd St
- **Gracious Home** • 1992 Broadway
- **Klosty Hardware** • 471 Amsterdam Ave
- **Ronnie's Hardware** • 208 Columbus Ave
- **Roxy Hardware and Paint** • 469 Columbus Ave
- **Supreme Hardware & Supply** • 65 W 73rd St
- **True Value Hardware** • 466 Columbus Ave

Liquor Stores

- **67 Wine & Spirits** • 179 Columbus Ave
- **79th Street Wine & Spirits** • 230 W 79th St
- **Acker Merrall** • 160 W 72nd St
- **Bacchus Wine Made Simple** • 2056 Broadway
- **Beacon Wines & Spirits** • 2120 Broadway
- **Central Wine & Liquor Store** • 227 Columbus Ave
- **Dix Broadway Liquors** • 2315 Broadway
- **Ehrlich Liquor Store** • 222 Amsterdam Ave
- **Nancy's Wines** • 313 Columbus Ave
- **Rose Wine & Liquor** • 449 Columbus Ave
- **West End Wine** • 204 West End Ave
- **West Side Wine & Spirits Shop** • 481 Columbus Ave

Movie Theaters

- **American Museum of Natural History IMAX** • Central Park W & 79th St
- **Clearview's 62nd & Broadway** • 1871 Broadway
- **Lincoln Plaza Cinemas** • 30 Lincoln Plz
- **Loew's 84th St** • 2310 Broadway
- **Loews Lincoln Square & IMAX Theatre** • 1992 Broadway
- **Makor** • 35 W 67th St
- **Walter Reade Theater** • 70 Lincoln Plz

Pet Shops

- **Furry Paws 4** • 141 Amsterdam Ave
- **Pet Health Store** • 440 Amsterdam Ave
- **Pet Market** • 210 W 72nd St
- **Petland Discounts** • 137 W 72nd St
- **Red Rover International** • 77 W 85th St

Restaurants

- **All-State Cafe** • 250 W 72nd St
- **Avenue** • 520 Columbus Ave
- **Baluchi's** • 283 Columbus Ave
- **Big Nick's** • 2175 Broadway
- **Cafe Des Artistes** • 1 W 67th St
- **Cafe Lalo** • 201 W 83rd St
- **Cafe Luxembourg** • 200 W 70th St
- **Caprice** • 199 Columbus Ave
- **China Fun** • 246 Columbus Ave
- **Edgar's Cafe** • 255 W 84th St
- **EJ's Luncheonette** • 447 Amsterdam Ave
- **Fairway Cafe** • 2127 Broadway
- **The Firehouse** • 522 Columbus Ave
- **French Roast** • 2340 Broadway
- **Gray's Papaya** • 2090 Broadway
- **Harry's Burrito Junction** • 241 Columbus Ave
- **Hunan Park** • 235 Columbus Ave
- **Jackson Hole** • 517 Columbus Ave
- **Jean Georges** • 1 Central Park W
- **Jean-Luc** • 507 Columbus Ave
- **Josie's** • 300 Amsterdam Ave
- **Krispy Kreme** • 141 W 72nd St
- **La Caridad 78** • 2197 Broadway
- **La Fenice** • 2014 Broadway
- **Le Pain Quotidien** • 50 W 72nd St
- **Lenge** • 200 Columbus Ave
- **Manhattan Diner** • 2180 Broadway
- **Penang** • 240 Columbus Ave
- **Picholine** • 35 W 64th St
- **Planet Sushi** • 380 Amsterdam Ave
- **Rosa Mexicano** • 51 Columbus Ave
- **Ruby Foo's Dim Sum & Sushi Palace** • 2182 Broadway
- **Santa Fe** • 72 W 69th St
- **Sarabeth's** • 423 Amsterdam Ave
- **Shun Lee** • 43 W 65th St
- **Taco Grill** • 146 W 72nd St
- **Vince and Eddie's** • 70 W 68th St
- **Vinnie's Pizza** • 285 Amsterdam Ave

Shopping

- **Alphabets** • 2284 Broadway
- **Assets London** • 464 Columbus Ave
- **Balducci's** • 155 W 66th St
- **Bed Bath & Beyond** • Broadway between W 64th St & W 65th St
- **Bruce Frank** • 215 W 83rd St
- **Bruno the King of Ravioli** • 2204 Broadway
- **Claire's Accessories** • 2267 Broadway
- **Country Rooster Flowers** • 70 W 71st St
- **EMS** • 20 W 61st St
- **Ethan Allen** • 103 West End Ave
- **Fish's Eddy** • 2176 Broadway
- **Godiva Chocolatier** • 245 Columbus Ave
- **Gracious Home** • 1992 Broadway
- **Gryphon Record Shop** • 233 W 72nd St
- **Harry's Shoes** • 2299 Broadway
- **Housing Works Thrift Shop** • 306 Columbus Ave
- **Lincoln Stationers** • 1889 Broadway
- **NYCD** • 173 W 81st St
- **Paper Access** • 2030 Broadway
- **Tumi** • 10 Columbus Cir
- **Yarn Co** • 2274 Broadway
- **Zabar's** • 2245 Broadway

Video Rental

- **Amsterdam Video** • 287 Amsterdam Ave
- **Blockbuster Video** • 197 Amsterdam Ave
- **Channel Video** • 472 Columbus Ave
- **Flik's Video 2 Go** • 175 W 72nd St
- **Tower Records-Video-Books** • 1961 Broadway

Map 14 • Upper West Side (Lower)

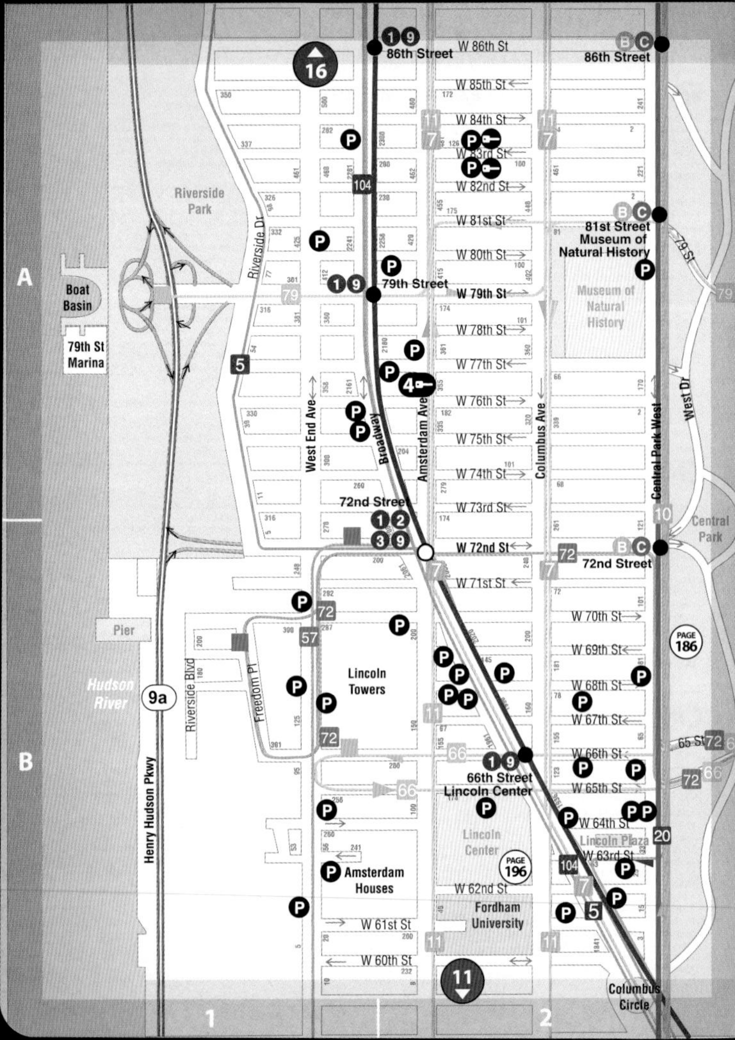

16
86th Street
W 86th St
86th Street
W 85th St
W 84th St
W 83rd St
W 82nd St
104
Riverside Park
W 81st St
81st Street
Museum of Natural History
W 80th St
Riverside Dr
79th Street
W 79th St
79 St
Boat Basin
79th St Marina
Museum of Natural History
W 78th St
W 77th St
5
W 76th St
West End Ave
Broadway
Amsterdam Ave
Columbus Ave
Central Park West
West Dr
W 75th St
W 74th St
72nd Street
W 73rd St
Central Park
W 72nd St
72nd Street
W 71st St
W 70th St
Pier
Lincoln Towers
PAGE 186
W 69th St
Hudson River
9a
Riverside Blvd
Freedom Pl
W 68th St
W 67th St
65 St
W 66th St
66th Street
Lincoln Center
W 65th St
Henry Hudson Pkwy
W 64th St
Lincoln Center
Lincoln Plaza
W 63rd St
PAGE 196
Amsterdam Houses
W 62nd St
Fordham University
W 61st St
W 60th St
11
Columbus Circle
A
B
1
2

Parking and driving are both actually doable in this area, with most of the available spots on or near Riverside Drive. We recommend the 79th Street Transverse for crossing Central Park to the east side. The Lincoln Center area is by far the messiest traffic problem here—you can avoid it by taking West End Avenue.

Subways

- 1 2 3 9 .... 72 St
- 1 9 .... 66 St-Lincoln Center
- 1 9 .... 79 St
- B C .... 72 St
- B C .... 81 St-Museum of Natural History

Bus Lines

- 10 20 ... Seventh Ave/Eighth Ave/Douglass Blvd
- 104 .... Broadway/42nd St
- 11 .... Ninth Ave/Tenth Ave
- 5 ....Fifth Ave/Sixth Ave/Riverside Dr
- 57 .... 57th St Crosstown
- 66 .... 66th St/67th St Crosstown
- 7 ....Columbus Ave/Amsterdam Ave/ Lenox Ave/Sixth Ave/Broadway
- 72 ....72nd St Crosstown
- 79 .... 79th St Crosstown

Car Rental

- **Avis** • 216 W 76th St
- **Budget** • 207 W 76th St
- **Enterprise** • 147 W 83rd St
- **Hertz** • 210 W 77th St
- **National** • 219 W 77th St
- **New York Rent-A-Car** • 146 W 83rd St

Parking

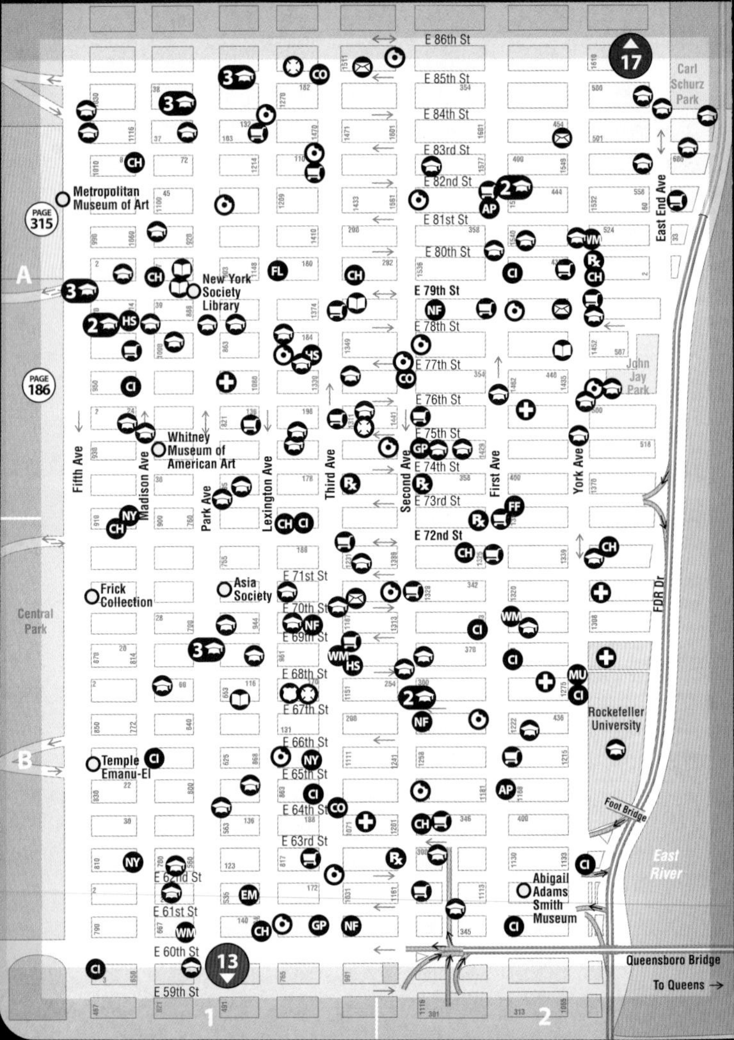

E 86th St
E 85th St
E 84th St
E 83rd St
E 82nd St
E 81st St
E 80th St
E 79th St
E 78th St
E 77th St
E 76th St
E 75th St
E 74th St
E 73rd St
E 72nd St
E 71st St
E 70th St
E 69th St
E 68th St
E 67th St
E 66th St
E 65th St
E 64th St
E 63rd St
E 62nd St
E 61st St
E 60th St
E 59th St

Fifth Ave
Madison Ave
Park Ave
Lexington Ave
Third Ave
Second Ave
First Ave
York Ave
East End Ave
FDR Dr

Metropolitan Museum of Art
New York Society Library
Whitney Museum of American Art
Frick Collection
Asia Society
Temple Emanu-El
Abigail Adams Smith Museum
Rockefeller University
Carl Schurz Park
John Jay Park
Central Park
East River
Foot Bridge
Queensboro Bridge
To Queens →

PAGE 315
PAGE 186
17
13

A
B
1
2

The southern half of the Upper East Side is a hotbed of culture, research, and education, containing one of the world's top museums (the Metropolitan Museum of Art); several top schools, including Cornell University Medical Center and Rockefeller University; and perhaps the foremost cancer hospital in the world, Memorial Sloan-Kettering Cancer Center.

ATMs

AP • Apple • 1168 First Ave
AP • Apple • 1555 First Ave
NY • Bank of New York • 1100 Third Ave
NY • Bank of New York • 706 Madison Ave
NY • Bank of New York • 909 Madison Ave
CH • Chase • 1003 Lexington Ave
CH • Chase • 1025 Madison Ave
CH • Chase • 1121 Madison Ave
CH • Chase • 201 E 79th St
CH • Chase • 300 E 64th St
CH • Chase • 35 E 72nd St
CH • Chase • 360 E 72nd St
CH • Chase • 501 E 79th St
CH • Chase • 770 Lexington Ave
CI • Citibank • 1078 Third Ave
CI • Citibank • 1266 First Ave
CI • Citibank • 1275 York Ave
CI • Citibank • 1285 First Ave
CI • Citibank • 1512 First Ave
CI • Citibank • 171 E 72nd St
CI • Citibank • 501 E 62nd St
CI • Citibank • 757 Madison Ave
CI • Citibank • 785 Fifth Ave
CI • Citibank • 976 Madison Ave
CO • Commerce Bank • 1091 Third Ave
CO • Commerce Bank • 1470 Second Ave
CO • Commerce Bank • 1504 Third Ave
EM • Emigrant • 812 Lexington Ave
FL • Fleet • 1143 Lexington Ave
FF • Fourth Federal Savings • 1355 First Ave
GP • Greenpoint Bank • 1010 Third Ave
GP • Greenpoint Bank • 1432 Second Ave
HS • HSBC • 1002 Madison Ave
HS • HSBC • 1165 Third Ave
HS • HSBC • 1340 Third Ave
CU • Municipal Credit Union • 525 E 68th St
NF • North Fork Bank • 1011 Third Ave
NF • North Fork Bank • 1180 Third Ave
NF • North Fork Bank • 1258 Second Ave
NF • North Fork Bank • 300 E 79th St
WM • Washington Mutual • 1191 Third Ave
WM • Washington Mutual • 1308 First Ave
WM • Washington Mutual • 1520 York Ave
WM • Washington Mutual • 510 Park Ave

Bagels

- **Bagel Mill Café** • 1461 Third Ave
- **Bagel Shoppe** • 1421 Second Ave
- **Bagelry** • 1228 Lexington Ave
- **Bagels & Co** • 500 E 76th St
- **Bagelworks** • 1229 First Ave
- **Bread Factory Cafe** • 785 Lexington Ave
- **Eastside Bagel** • 1496 First Ave
- **Elaine's Bagel** • 941 Park Ave
- **H&H Bagels East** • 1551 Second Ave
- **Healthy Bagel & Things** • 1355 Second Ave
- **Hot & Tasty Bagels** • 1323 Second Ave
- **Monsieur Bagel** • 874 Lexington Ave
- **New World Coffee** • 1046 Third Ave
- **New World Coffee** • 1246 Lexington Ave
- **NYC Bagels** • 1228 Second Ave
- **Pick-a-Bagel** • 1101 Lexington Ave
- **Pick-a-Bagel** • 1475 Second Ave

Fire Departments

- **Engine 22, Ladder 13** • 159 E 85th St
- **Engine 39, Ladder 16** • 157 E 67th St
- **Engine 44** • 221 E 75th St

Hospitals

- **Gracie Square Hospital** • 420 E 76th St
- **Hospital for Special Surgery** • 535 E 70th St
- **Lenox Hill Hospital** • 100 E 77th St
- **Manhattan Eye, Ear & Throat Hospital** • 210 E 64th St
- **Memorial Sloan-Kettering Cancer Center** • 1275 York Ave
- **New York Hospital - Cornell Medical Center** • 525 E 68th St

Landmarks

- **Abigail Adams Smith Museum** • 421 E 61st St
- **Asia Society** • 725 Park Ave
- **Frick Collection** • 1 E 70th St
- **Metropolitan Museum of Art** • 1000 Fifth Ave
- **New York Society Library** • 53 E 79th St
- **Temple Emanu-El** • 1 E 65th St
- **Whitney Museum of American Art** • 945 Madison Ave

Libraries

- **67th Street** • 328 E 67th St
- **New York Society Library** • 53 E 79th St
- **Webster** • 1465 York Ave
- **Yorkville** • 222 E 79th St

24-Hour Pharmacies

- **CVS Pharmacy** • 1396 Second Ave
- **Duane Reade** • 1191 Second Ave
- **Duane Reade** • 1279 Third Ave
- **Duane Reade** • 1345 First Ave
- **Duane Reade** • 1498 York Ave

Police

- **19th Precinct** • 153 E 67th St

Post Offices

- **Cherokee** • 1483 York Ave
- **Filmfest Contract Postal Unit** • 1594 York Ave
- **Gracie** • 229 E 85th St
- **Lenox Hill** • 217 E 70th St

Schools

- **Abraham Lincoln School** • 12 E 79th St
- **Allen-Stevenson School** • 132 E 78th St
- **Birch Wathen Lenox School** • 210 E 77th St
- **Brearly School** • 610 E 83rd St
- **Browning School** • 52 E 62nd St
- **Buckley School** • 113 E 73rd St
- **Caedmon School** • 416 E 80th St
- **Cathedral School** • 319 E 74th St
- **Chapin School** • 100 East End Ave
- **Children's All Day School** • 109 E 60th St
- **Cornell University Medical College** • 445 E 69th St
- **Dominican Academy** • 44 E 68th St
- **Eleanor Roosevelt High School** • 411 E 76th St
- **Ella Baker School** • 317 E 67th St
- **Episcopal School** • 35 E 69th St
- **Garden House School** • 593 Park Ave
- **Hewitt School** • 45 E 75th St
- **Hunter College** • 695 Park Ave
- **JHS 167 Robert F Wagner School** • 220 E 76th St
- **Lower Rudolf Steiner School** • 15 E 79th St
- **Loyola School** • 980 Park Ave
- **Lycée Français de New York** • 505 E 75th St
- **Manhattan High School for Girls** • 154 E 70th St
- **Martha Graham School** • 316 E 63rd St
- **Marymount Manhattan College** • 221 E 71st St
- **Marymount School** • 1026 Fifth Ave
- **New York School of Interior Design** • 170 E 70th St
- **PS 006 Lillie D Blake School** • 45 E 81st St
- **PS 158 Bayard Taylor School** • 1458 York Ave
- **PS 183 R L Stevenson School** • 419 E 66th St
- **PS 290 Manhattan New School** • 311 E 82nd St
- **Rabbi Arthur Schneier Park East Day** • 164 E 68th St
- **Ramaz Lower School** • 125 E 85th St
- **Ramaz Middle School** • 114 E 85th St
- **Ramaz Upper School** • 60 E 78th St
- **Regis High School** • 55 E 84th St
- **Renanim Pre-School** • 336 E 61st St
- **Rockefeller University** • 1230 York Ave
- **Rudolf Steiner Lower School** • 15 E 79th St
- **Rudolf Steiner Upper School** • 15 E 78th St
- **Sotheby's Educational Studies** • 1334 York Ave
- **Spanish Institute** • 684 Park Ave
- **St Ignatius Loyola School** • 50 E 84th St
- **St Jean Baptiste High School** • 173 E 75th St
- **St Stephan of Hungary School** • 408 E 82nd St
- **St Vincent Ferrer High School** • 151 E 65th St
- **Talent Unlimited High School** • 300 E 68th St
- **Temple Israel Early Childhood Learning Center** • 112 E 75th St
- **Town School** • 540 E 76th St
- **Ukrainian Institute of America** • 2 E 79th St
- **Urban Academy Lab High School** • 317 E 67th St
- **York Avenue Preschool** • 1520 York Ave

Supermarkets

- **Agata & Valentina** • 1505 First Ave
- **Associated** • 1565 First Ave
- **Citarella** • 1313 Third Ave
- **D'Agostino** • 1074 Lexington Ave
- **D'Agostino** • 1233 Lexington Ave
- **D'Agostino** • 1507 York Ave
- **Eli's Manhattan** • 1411 Third Ave
- **Food Emporium** • 1066 Third Ave
- **Food Emporium** • 1175 Third Ave
- **Food Emporium** • 1328 Second Ave
- **Food Emporium** • 1331 First Ave
- **Food Emporium** • 1450 Third Ave
- **Food Emporium** • 1498 York Ave
- **Gourmet Garage East** • 301 E 64th St
- **Grace's Marketplace** • 1237 Third Ave
- **Gristede's** • 1180 Second Ave
- **Gristede's** • 1208 First Ave
- **Gristede's** • 1350 First Ave
- **Gristede's** • 1365 Third Ave
- **Gristede's** • 1446 Second Ave
- **Gristede's** • 40 East End Ave

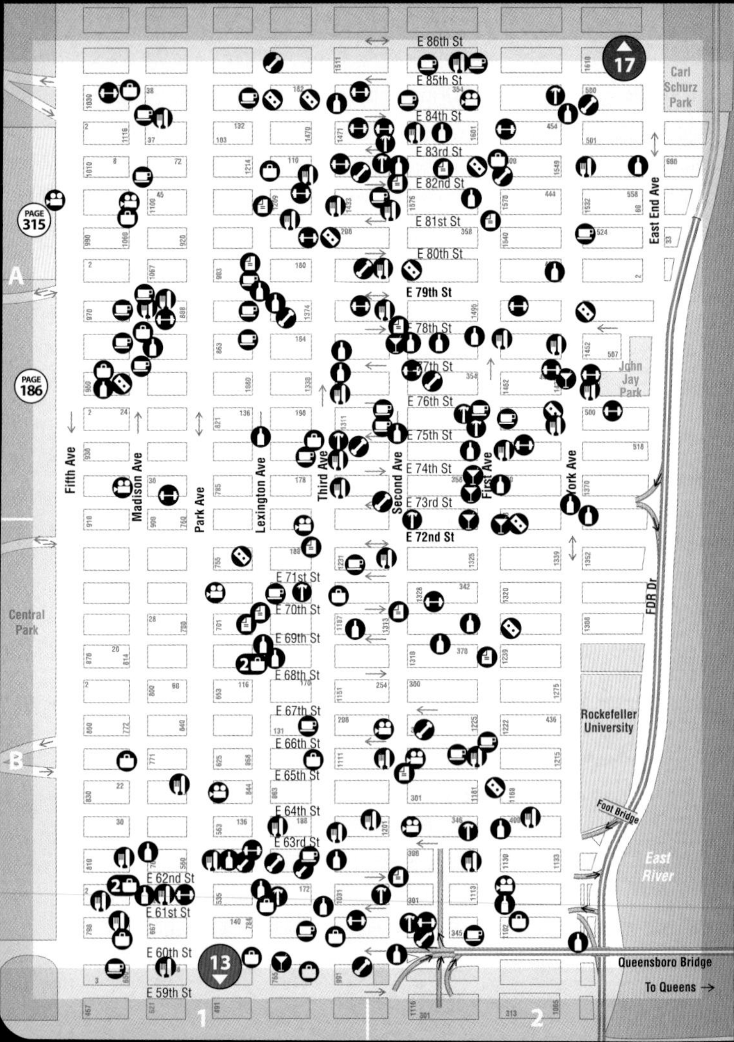

Map 15 • Upper East Side (Lower)

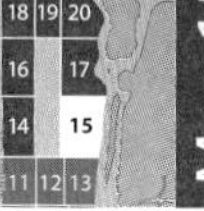

The Upper East Side has itself covered pretty well here, and it also has another of New York's classic movie theaters, the Beekman. Maya may well serve the best Mexican food in the city. If you want to go slumming, the Subway Inn is the place.

Bars

- **Banshee Pub** • 1373 First Ave
- **Brother Jimmy's** • 1485 Second Ave
- **Finnegan's Wake** • 1361 First Ave
- **Hi-Life** • 1340 First Ave
- **Raccoon Lodge** • 1439 York Ave
- **Session 73** • 1359 First Ave
- **Subway Inn** • 143 E 60th St

Coffee

- **Caffe Bacio** • 1223 Third Ave
- **Caffe Bianco** • 1486 Second Ave
- **DT * UT** • 1626 Second Ave
- **Dunkin' Donuts** • 1225 First Ave
- **First Avenue Coffee Shop** • 1433 First Ave
- **Genes Coffee Shop** • 26 E 60th St
- **Java Girl** • 348 E 66th St
- **Le Pain Quotidien** • 1131 Madison Ave
- **Mr Chip's Coffee Shop** • 1530 York Ave
- **Nectar Coffee Shop** • 1022 Madison Ave
- **Nectar Coffee Shop** • 1090 Madison Ave
- **Neil's Coffee Shop** • 961 Lexington Ave
- **New World Coffee** • 1046 Third Ave
- **New World Coffee** • 1246 Lexington Ave
- **Oren's Daily Roast:** • 1144 Lexington Ave • 1574 First Ave • 985 Lexington Ave
- **Rohrs M** • 303 E 85th St
- **Sant Ambroeus** • 1000 Madison Ave
- **Starbucks**: • 1102 First Ave • 1117 Lexington Ave • 1128 Third Ave • 1290 Third Ave • 1445 First Ave • 1449 Second Ave • 1559 Second Ave • 1631 First Ave
- **Tramway Coffee Shop** • 1143 Second Ave
- **Viand Coffee Shop** • 1011 Madison Ave

Copy Shops

- **Complete Copy Center (8 am-9 pm)** • 349 E 82nd St
- **Copyland Center (8 am-10 pm)** • 335 E 65th St
- **Copyland Center (8 am-11 pm)** • 1579 Second Ave
- **Kinko's** • 1122 Lexington Ave
- **Mail Boxes Etc (8:30 am-7 pm)** • 1173A Second Ave
- **Mail Boxes Etc (9 am-7 pm)** • 1202 Lexington Ave
- **Mail Boxes Etc (9 am-7 pm)** • 954 Lexington Ave
- **Mail Boxes Etc (9 am-7:30 pm)** • 1275 First Ave
- **The UPS Store (9 am-7 pm)** • 1562 First Ave
- **Universal Copy Inc (8 am-10 pm)** • 1343 Second Ave

Gyms

- **Casa at the Regency** • 540 Park Ave
- **Casa Fitness Club** • 48 E 73rd St
- **Curves for Women** • 1460 Second Ave
- **David Barton Gyms** • 30 E 85th St
- **Definitions** • 39 E 78th St
- **Eastside Sports Physical Therapy** • 244 E 84th St
- **Elissa's Personal Best Gym** • 334 E 79th St
- **Equinox Fitness** • 205 E 85th St
- **Equinox Fitness Club** • 140 E 63rd St
- **Hampton House Health Club** • 404 E 79th St
- **Lenox Hill Neighborhood House** • 331 E 70th St
- **Liberty Fitness Center** • 244 E 84th St
- **New York Health & Racquet Club** • 1433 York Ave
- **New York Sports Clubs** • 349 E 76th St
- **Pavilion Personal Fitness Center** • 500 E 77th St
- **Promenade Health Club** • 530 E 76th St
- **Savoy Spa** • 200 E 61st St
- **Sports Club/LA** • 330 E 61st St
- **Strathmore Swim & Health Club** • 400 E 84th St
- **Synergy Fitness Clubs** • 1438 Third Ave
- **Trainers Place** • 1421 Third Ave
- **Training Floor** • 428 E 75th St

Hardware Stores

- **72nd Street Hardware** • 1398 Second Ave
- **ATB Locksmith & Hardware** • 1603 York Ave
- **Gracious Home** • 1220 Third Ave
- **Kraft Hardware** • 315 E 62nd St
- **Lexington Hardware & Electric** • 797 Lexington Ave
- **New York Paint & Hardware** • 1593 Second Ave
- **Queensboro Hardware** • 1157 Second Ave
- **Rainbow Ace Hardware** • 1449 First Ave
- **S&V General Supply** • 1450 First Ave
- **Sutton Hardware & Home Center** • 1153 First Ave
- **Thalco Maintenance Supply** • 1462 Second Ave
- **Third Ave Supply** • 1301 Third Ave

Liquor Stores

- **1375 First Liquors** • 1375 First Ave
- **76 Liquors** • 1473 First Ave
- **Aulden Cellars** • 334 York Ave
- **Big Apple Wine & Spirits** • 1408 Second Ave
- **Carlyle Wines** • 997 Madison Ave
- **City Liquor** • 1145 Second Ave
- **Columbus Circle Liquor Store** • 1780 Broadway
- **Cork and Bottle Liquor Store** • 1158 First Ave
- **Crown Wine & Liquor** • 1587 Second Ave
- **East End Wines & Spirits** • 1599 York Ave
- **East River Liquors** • 1364 York Ave
- **Embassy Liquors** • 796 Lexington Ave
- **Garnet Wines & Liquors** • 929 Lexington Ave
- **Headington Wines & Liquors** • 1135 Lexington Ave
- **In Vino Veritas** • 1375 First Ave
- **Jamil Liquor Store** • 1364 York Ave
- **Kris & Bill Wine & Liquor** • 1587 Second Ave
- **Lumers Fine Wines & Spirits** • 1479 Third Ave
- **Mc Cabe's Wines & Spirits** • 1347 Third Ave
- **Milli Liquors** • 300 E 78th St
- **Monro Wines & Liquors** • 68 East End Ave
- **Rosenthal Wine Merchant** • 318 E 84th St
- **Sherry Wine & Spirits** • 677 Madison Ave
- **Sherry-Lehman** • 679 Madison Ave
- **Stuart's Wines & Spirits** • 1043 Third Ave
- **Towers Liquor Store** • 1043 Third Ave
- **Viski Wines** • 1050 Lexington Ave
- **Waldorf Liquor Shop** • 1495 York Ave
- **Windsor Wine Shop** • 1114 First Ave
- **The Wine Cart** • 235 E 69th St
- **Woody Liquor 7 Wine** • 1450 Second Ave
- **York Wines & Spirits** • 1291 First Ave

Movie Theaters

- **Asia Society** • 725 Park Ave
- **Cineplex Odeon: Beekman Theater** • 1254 Second Ave
- **Clearview's First & 62nd St** • 400 E 62nd St
- **Crown Theatre** • 1271 Second Ave
- **Czech Center** • 1109 Madison Ave
- **Loews 72nd St East** • 1230 Third Ave
- **Metropolitan Museum of Art** • 1000 Fifth Ave
- **New York Youth Theater** • 593 Park Ave
- **Regal/UA** • 1210 Second Ave
- **Regal/UA** • 1629 First Ave
- **Whitney Museum** • 945 Madison Ave

Pet Shops

- **American Kennels** • 798 Lexington Ave
- **Animal Attractions** • 343 E 66th St
- **Calling All Pets** • 1590 York Ave
- **Calling All Pets** • 301 E 76th St
- **Canine Styles** • 830 Lexington Ave
- **Dogs Cats & Co** • 208 E 82nd St
- **Just Cats** • 244 E 60th St
- **Karen's for People Plus Pets** • 1195 Lexington Ave
- **Le Chien Pet Salon** • 1044 Third Ave
- **Lolly's Pet Salon** • 228 E 80th St
- **Pet Market** • 1570 First Ave
- **Pet Market Inc** • 1400 Second Ave
- **Pet Necessities** • 236 E 75th St
- **Pets on Lex** • 1271 Lexington Ave
- **Sutton Dog Parlour Kennel & Daycare Center** • 311 E 60th St

Restaurants

- **Afghan Kebab House** • 1345 Second Ave
- **Atlantic Grill** • 1341 Third Ave
- **Aureole** • 34 E 61st St
- **Baluchi's** • 1149 First Ave
- **Baluchi's** • 1565 Second Ave
- **Barking Dog Luncheonette** • 1453 York Ave
- **Brunelli** • 1409 York Ave
- **Canyon Road** • 1470 First Ave
- **Daniel** • 60 E 65th St
- **EJ's Luncheonette** • 1271 Third Ave
- **Haru** • 1329 Third Ave
- **Jackson Hole** • 1611 Second Ave
- **Jackson Hole** • 232 E 64th St
- **JG Melon** • 1291 Third Ave
- **Jo Jo** • 160 E 64th St
- **John's Pizzeria** • 408 E 64th St
- **Le Pain Quotidien:** • 1131 Madison Ave • 1336 First Ave • 833 Lexington Ave
- **Mary Ann's** • 1503 Second Ave
- **Maya** • 1191 First Ave
- **Our Place** • 1444 Third Ave
- **Park Avenue Cafe** • 100 E 63rd St
- **Pearson's Texas Barbecue** • 170 E 81st St
- **Penang** • 1596 Second Ave
- **Pintaile's Pizza:** • 1237 Second Ave • 1443 York Ave • 1577 York Ave
- **Post House** • 28 E 63rd St
- **Rain** • 1059 Third Ave
- **RM** • 33 E 60th St
- **Serafina Fabulous Grill** • 29 E 61st St
- **Spada** • 1431 Third Ave
- **Totonno Pizzeria Napolitano** • 1544 Second Ave
- **Viand** • 1011 Madison Ave
- **Viand** • 673 Madison Ave

Shopping

- **A Bear's Place** • 789 Lexington Ave
- **Aveda Environmental Lifestyle Store** • 1122 Third Ave
- **Baldwin Fish Market** • 1584 First Ave
- **Bang & Olufsen** • 952 Madison Ave
- **Barneys New York** • 660 Madison Ave
- **Bed Bath & Beyond** • 410 E 61st St
- **Bloomingdale's** • 1000 Third Ave
- **Dempsey & Carroll** • 1058 Madison Ave
- **Diesel** • 770 Lexington Ave
- **Dylan's Candy Bar** • 1011 Third Ave
- **Garnet Wines & Liquors** • 929 Lexington Ave
- **Giorgio Armani** • 760 Madison Ave
- **Gracious Home** • 1217 Third Ave
- **Hermes** • 691 Madison Ave
- **Housing Works Thrift Shop** • 202 E 77th St
- **Kate's Paperie** • 1282 Third Ave
- **Lyric Hi-Fi** • 1221 Lexington Ave
- **Radio Shack** • 925 Lexington Ave
- **Steuben** • 667 Madison Ave
- **Venture Stationers** • 1156 Madison Ave

Video Rental

- **Blockbuster Video** • 1251 Lexington Ave
- **Blockbuster Video** • 1270 First Ave
- **Champagne Video** • 1194 First Ave
- **Champagne Video** • 1416 Third Ave
- **Champagne Video** • 1577 First Ave
- **Couch Potato Video** • 1456 Second Ave
- **Express Video** • 421 E 72nd St
- **Fifth Dimension Video** • 1427 York Ave
- **Filmfest Video** • 1594 York Ave
- **Video Vogue** • 976 Lexington Ave
- **Videoroom** • 1487 Third Ave
- **York Video** • 1472 York Ave
- **Zitomer Department Store & Electronics** • 969 Madison Ave

Transportation

Parking is extremely difficult during the day due to the number of schools in this area. It gets a bit better (but not much) at night, especially in the upper 70s and lower 80s near the FDR. (You'll never find legal street parking near Bloomingdale's, however.) Park Avenue is the best street to travel downtown during rush hour.

Subways

6 .... 68 St-Hunter College
6 .... 77 St
4 5 6 .... 86 St
F .... Lexington Ave/63 St
N R W .... 5 Ave/59 St
4 5 6 N R W .... Lexington Ave/59 St

Bus Lines

1 2 3 .... Fifth Ave/Madison Ave
101 102 103 Q32 .... Third Ave/Lexington Ave
15 .... First Ave/Second Ave
30 .... 72nd St/57th St Crosstown
31 .... York Ave/57th St Crosstown
4 .... Fifth Ave/Madison Ave/Broadway
66 .... 67th St/68th St Crosstown
72 .... 72nd St Crosstown
79 .... 79th St Crosstown
98 .... Washington Heights/Midtown
Q101 .... Astoria
Q60 .... Jamaica

Car Rental

- **Avis** • 310 E 64th St
- **Dollar** • 157 E 84th St
- **Enterprise** • 425 E 61st St
- **Hertz** • 327 E 64th St
- **Hertz** • 355 E 76th St
- **National** • 305 E 80th St

Gas Stations

- **Mobil** • 1132 York Ave

Parking

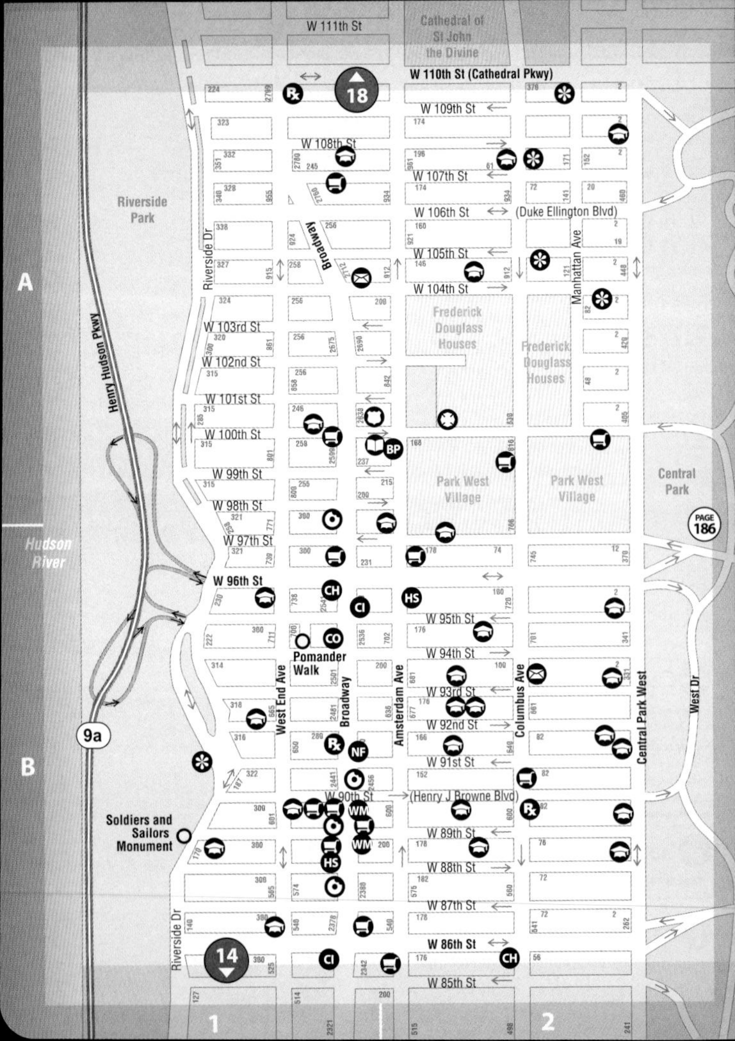

W 111th St
Cathedral of St John the Divine
W 110th St (Cathedral Pkwy)
W 109th St
W 108th St
W 107th St
W 106th St (Duke Ellington Blvd)
W 105th St
W 104th St
W 103rd St
W 102nd St
W 101st St
W 100th St
W 99th St
W 98th St
W 97th St
W 96th St
W 95th St
W 94th St
W 93rd St
W 92nd St
W 91st St
W 90th St (Henry J Browne Blvd)
W 89th St
W 88th St
W 87th St
W 86th St
W 85th St
Riverside Park
Riverside Dr
Broadway
West End Ave
Amsterdam Ave
Columbus Ave
Manhattan Ave
Central Park West
West Dr
Central Park
Henry Hudson Pkwy
Hudson River
9a
Frederick Douglass Houses
Park West Village
Pomander Walk
Soldiers and Sailors Monument
A
B
1
2
18
14
PAGE 186

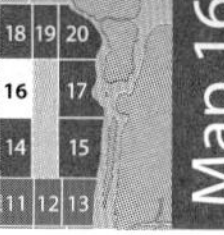

This part of the Upper West Side is extremely residential. Riverside Drive, West End Avenue, and Central Park West are all highly desirable addresses—if you can afford them. Gentrification continues to creep up past 96th Street towards Columbia, especially towards the west. Check out Riverside Park for all sorts of amusements.

ATMs

BP · Banco Popular · 799 Amsterdam Ave
CH · Chase · 2551 Broadway
CH · Chase · 59 W 86th St
CI · Citibank · 2350 Broadway
CI · Citibank · 2560 Broadway
CO · Commerce Bank · 2521 Broadway
HS · HSBC · 2401 Broadway
HS · HSBC · 739 Amsterdam Ave
NF · North Fork Bank · 2460 Broadway
WM · Washington Mutual · 2438 Broadway
WM · Washington Mutual · 2554 Broadway

Bagels

- **Bagel Basket** · 2415 Broadway
- **Hot & Crusty Bagel Cafe** · 2387 Broadway
- **Lenny's Bagels** · 2601 Broadway
- **Tal Bagels** · 2446 Broadway

Community Gardens

Fire Departments

- **Engine 76, Ladder 22** · 145 W 100th St

Landmarks

- **Pomander Walk** · 261 W 94th St
- **Soldiers and Sailors Monument** · Riverside Dr & 89th St

Libraries

- **Bloomingdale** · 150 W 100th St

24-Hour Pharmacies

- **Duane Reade** · 2465 Broadway
- **Duane Reade** · 609 Columbus Ave
- **Rite Aid** · 2833 Broadway

Police

- **24th Precinct** · 151 W 100th St

Post Offices

- **Cathedral** · 215 W 104th St
- **Park West** · 693 Columbus Ave

Schools

- **Abraham Joshua Heschel School** · 270 W 89th St
- **Alexander Robertson School** · 3 W 95th St
- **Ascension School** · 224 W 108th St
- **Columbia Grammar and Prepatory School** · 5 W 93rd St
- **Dwight School** · 291 Central Park W
- **Holy Name School & De La Salle Academy** · 202 W 97th St
- **JHS 054 B Washington School** · 103 W 107th St
- **Morningside Montessori School** · 251 W 100th St
- **MS 258 Community Action School** · 154 W 93rd St
- **PS 075 Emily Dickinson School/MS 250 Collaborative** · 735 West End Ave
- **PS 084 Lillian Weber School/MS 247 Dual Language** · 32 W 92nd St
- **PS 145 Bloomingdale School** · 150 W 105th St
- **PS 163 Alfred E Smith School** · 163 W 97th St
- **PS 165 Robert E Simon School/MS 246 Crossroads** · 234 W 109th St
- **PS 166 Arts & Sciences School** · 132 W 89th St
- **PS 333 Manhattan School for Children** · 154 W 93rd St
- **PS 38 Roberto Clemente School** · 232 E 103rd St
- **Solomon Schechter High School** · 1 W 91st St
- **St Agnes Boys School** · 555 West End Ave
- **St Gregory the Great School** · 138 W 90th St
- **Studio Elementary School** · 124 W 95th St
- **Trinity School** · 139 W 91st St
- **Upper Trevor Day School** · 1 W 88th St
- **West Side Montessori School** · 309 W 92nd St
- **Yeshiva Ketana of Manhattan** · 346 W 89th St

Supermarkets

- **Associated** · 13 W 100th St
- **Associated** · 755 Amsterdam Ave
- **C-Town** · 818 Columbus Ave
- **D'Agostino** · 633 Columbus Ave
- **Food Emporium** · 2415 Broadway
- **Gourmet Garage West** · 2567 Broadway
- **Gristede's** · 251 W 86th St
- **Gristede's** · 2633 Broadway
- **Gristede's** · 2780 Broadway
- **Gristede's Mega Store** · 262 W 96th St
- **Kosher Marketplace** · 2442 Broadway
- **Met Food** · 530 Amsterdam Ave
- **Whole Foods Market** · 2421 Broadway

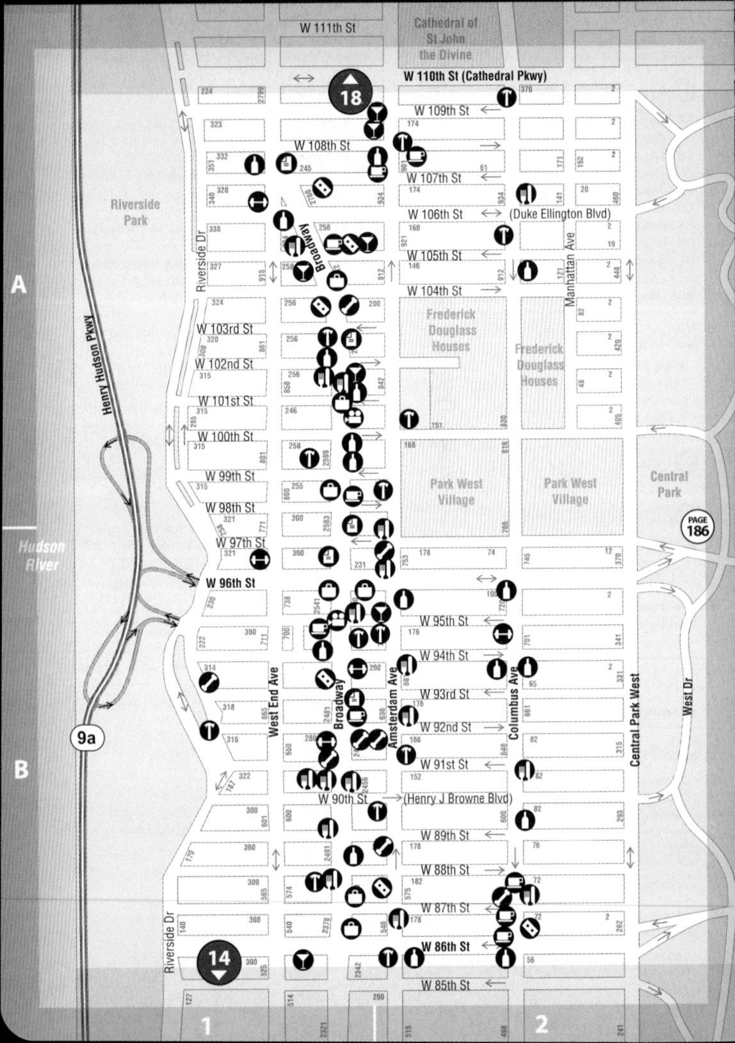

Cathedral of St John the Divine

W 111th St

W 110th St (Cathedral Pkwy)

18

W 109th St

W 108th St

W 107th St

W 106th St (Duke Ellington Blvd)

W 105th St

W 104th St

W 103rd St

W 102nd St

W 101st St

W 100th St

W 99th St

W 98th St

W 97th St

W 96th St

W 95th St

W 94th St

W 93rd St

W 92nd St

W 91st St

W 90th St (Henry J Browne Blvd)

W 89th St

W 88th St

W 87th St

W 86th St

W 85th St

14

Riverside Park

Riverside Dr

Henry Hudson Pkwy

9a

Hudson River

Broadway

West End Ave

Amsterdam Ave

Columbus Ave

Manhattan Ave

Central Park West

West Dr

Central Park

Frederick Douglass Houses

Frederick Douglass Houses

Park West Village

Park West Village

PAGE 186

A

B

1

2

This area is saved from being totally bland by the proliferation of excellent and cheap Latin American cuisine, as well as by the Broadway Dive. For something more upscale, hit Docks Oyster Bar on Broadway.

Bars

- **Abbey Pub** • 237 W 105th St
- **Broadway Dive** • 2662 Broadway
- **Dive Bar** • 732 Amsterdam Ave
- **The Parlour** • 250 W 86th St
- **Sip** • 998 Amsterdam Ave
- **Smoke** • 2751 Broadway
- **SOHA** • 988 Amsterdam Ave

Coffee

- **108 Mini Cafe** • 196 W 108th St
- **964 Jumbo Pizza Coffee Shop** • 964 Amsterdam Ave
- **Columbus Cafe** • 556 Columbus Ave
- **Silver Moon Bakery** • 2740 Broadway
- **Starbucks** • 2498 Broadway
- **Starbucks** • 2521 Broadway
- **Starbucks** • 2600 Broadway
- **Starbucks** • 2681 Broadway
- **Starbucks** • 540 Columbus Ave
- **Three Star Coffee Shop** • 541 Columbus Ave

Copy Shops

- **Columbia Copy Center (8 am-11 pm)** • 2790 Broadway
- **Copy Concept (8 am-9 pm)** • 216 W 103rd st
- **Global Copy (8 am-9 pm)** • 2578 Broadway
- **Mail Boxes Etc (8:30 am-7 pm)** • 2472 Broadway
- **Mail Boxes Etc (8:30 am-7 pm)** • 2565 Broadway

Gyms

- **Equinox Fitness Club** • 2465 Broadway
- **New York Sports Clubs** • 2527 Broadway
- **Paris Health Club** • 752 West End Ave
- **Synergy Fitness Clubs** • 700 Columbus Ave

Hardware Stores

- **Ace Hardware** • 817 Amsterdam Ave
- **Altman Hardware** • 641 Amsterdam Ave
- **Aquarius Hardware & Houseware** • 601 Amsterdam Ave
- **B Cohen & Son** • 969 Amsterdam Ave
- **Broadway Home Center** • 2672 Broadway
- **C&S Hardware** • 788 Amsterdam Ave
- **Garcia Hardware Store** • 995 Columbus Ave
- **Grand Metro Home Centers** • 2524 Broadway
- **Jimmy's Hardware** • 914 Columbus Ave
- **Leo Hardware** • 716 Amsterdam Ave
- **Mike's Lumber Store** • 254 W 88th St
- **Quintessentials** • 532 Amsterdam Ave
- **SW Tool** • 200 Riverside Dr
- **World Houseware** • 2617 Broadway

Liquor Stores

- **86th Corner Wine & Liquor** • 536 Columbus Ave
- **Adel Wine & Liquor** • 925 Columbus Ave
- **Best Liquor & Wine** • 2648 Broadway
- **Columbus Ave Wine & Spirits** • 700 Columbus Ave
- **Columbus Ave Wine & Spirits** • 730 Columbus Ave
- **Gotham Wines And Liquors** • 2517 Broadway
- **H&H Broadway Wine Center Ltd** • 2669 Broadway
- **Hong Liquor Store** • 2616 Broadway
- **Martin Brothers Liquor Store** • 2781 Broadway
- **Mitchell's Wine & Liquor Store** • 200 W 86th St
- **Polanco Liquor Store** • 948 Amsterdam Ave
- **Retail Wine & Liquors** • 2373 Broadway
- **Riverside Liquor** • 2746 Broadway
- **Roma Discount Wine & Liquor** • 737 Amsterdam Ave
- **Turin Wines & Liquors** • 609 Columbus Ave
- **Vintage New York** • 2492 Broadway
- **Westlane Wines & Liquor** • 689 Columbus Ave
- **Wine Place** • 2406 Broadway

Movie Theaters

- **Clearview's Metro Twin** • 2626 Broadway
- **Leonard Nimoy Thalia** • 2537 Broadway

Pet Shops

- **Amazing Pet Products** • 564 Columbus Ave
- **Amsterdog Groomers** • 586 Amsterdam Ave
- **Aquarius Aquarium Installation** • 214 Riverside Dr
- **Little Creatures** • 770 Amsterdam Ave
- **Pet Market** • 2459 Broadway
- **Pet Stop** • 564 Columbus Ave
- **Petland Discounts** • 2708 Broadway

Restaurants

- **A** • 947 Columbus Ave
- **Afghan Kebob House** • 2680 Broadway
- **Bella Luna** • 584 Columbus Ave
- **Cafe Con Leche** • 726 Amsterdam Ave
- **Carmine's** • 2450 Broadway
- **City Diner** • 2441 Broadway
- **Docks Oyster Bar** • 2427 Broadway
- **Flor de Mayo** • 2651 Broadway
- **Gabriela's** • 685 Amsterdam Ave
- **Gennaro** • 665 Amsterdam Ave
- **Henry's** • 2745 Broadway
- **Lemongrass Grill** • 2534 Broadway
- **Mary Ann's** • 2452 Broadway
- **Pampa** • 768 Amsterdam Ave
- **Popover Cafe** • 551 Amsterdam Ave
- **Saigon Grill** • 2381 Broadway
- **Trattoria Pesce Pasta** • 625 Columbus Ave

Shopping

- **Ann Taylor** • 2380 Broadway
- **Banana Republic** • 2360 Broadway
- **Ben & Jerry's** • 2722 Broadway
- **Gothic Cabinet Craft** • 2652 Broadway
- **Gourmet Garage** • 2567 Broadway
- **Health Nuts** • 2611 Broadway
- **Metro Bicycles** • 231 W 96th St

Video Rental

- **Blockbuster Video** • 2510 Broadway
- **Blockbuster Video** • 2689 Broadway
- **Books, Videos, & More** • 580 Amsterdam Ave
- **Hollywood Video** • 535 Columbus Ave
- **Khan Video Entertainment Center** • 2768 Broadway
- **Movie Place** • 237 W 105th St

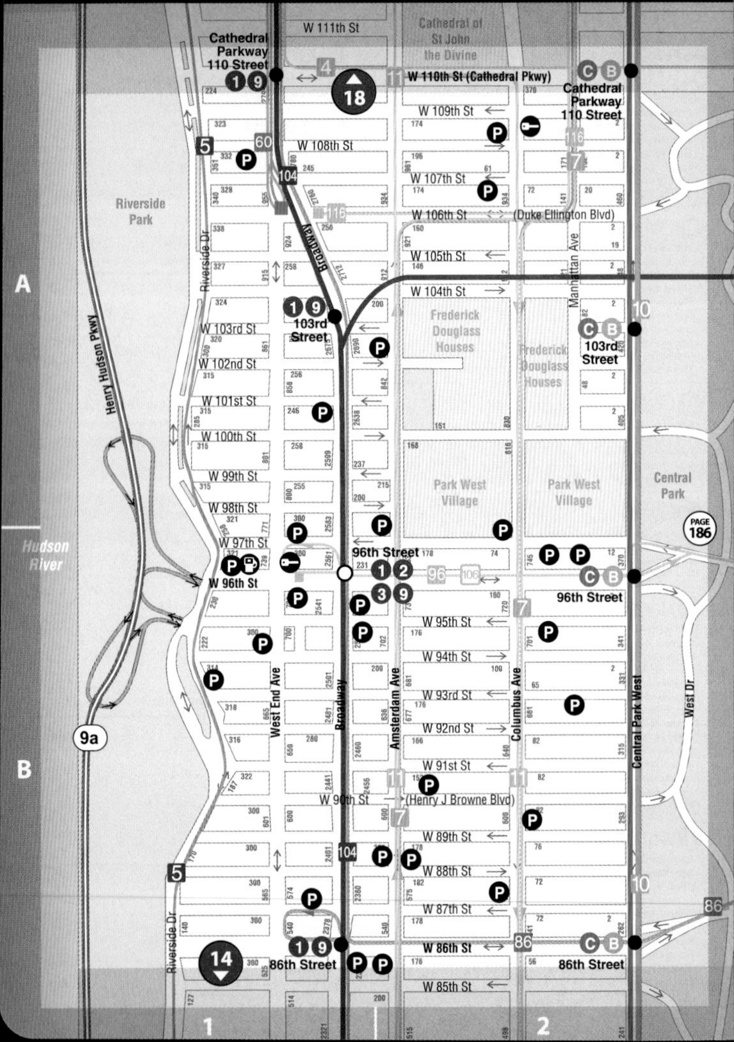

Cathedral Parkway 110 Street
W 111th St
Cathedral of St John the Divine
W 110th St (Cathedral Pkwy)
Cathedral Parkway 110 Street
W 109th St
W 108th St
W 107th St
W 106th St (Duke Ellington Blvd)
W 105th St
W 104th St
Riverside Park
Riverside Dr
Broadway
Manhattan Ave
103rd Street
Frederick Douglass Houses
Frederick Douglass Houses
103rd Street
W 103rd St
W 102nd St
W 101st St
W 100th St
W 99th St
W 98th St
W 97th St
W 96th St
Park West Village
Park West Village
Central Park
Henry Hudson Pkwy
Hudson River
96th Street
96th Street
W 95th St
W 94th St
W 93rd St
W 92nd St
W 91st St
W 90th St (Henry J Browne Blvd)
W 89th St
W 88th St
W 87th St
W 86th St
W 85th St
West End Ave
Amsterdam Ave
Columbus Ave
Central Park West
West Dr
86th Street
86th Street
PAGE 186
18
14

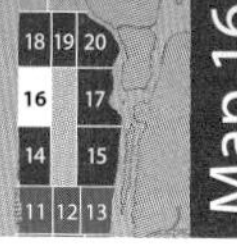

The 96th Street Transverse is by far the best way to cross Central Park. And isn't it nice that the Upper West Side has two separate subway lines?

Subways

1 2 3 9 .... 96 St
1 9 .... 103 St
1 9 .... 86 St
B C .... 103 St
B C .... 86 St
B C .... 96 St

Bus Lines

10 ....Seventh Ave/Central Park W
104 .... Broadway
106 ....106th St Crosstown
11 ....Columbus Ave/Amsterdam Ave
116 .... 116th St Crosstown
5 .... Fifth Ave/Sixth Ave/Riverside Dr
60 .... LaGuardia Airport
7 ....Columbus Ave/Amsterdam Ave
86 ....86th St Crosstown
96 ....96th St Crosstown

Car Rental

- **AAMCAR** • 303 W 96th St
- **New York Rent-A-Car** • 963 Columbus Ave

Gas Stations

- **Exxon** • 303 W 96th St

Parking

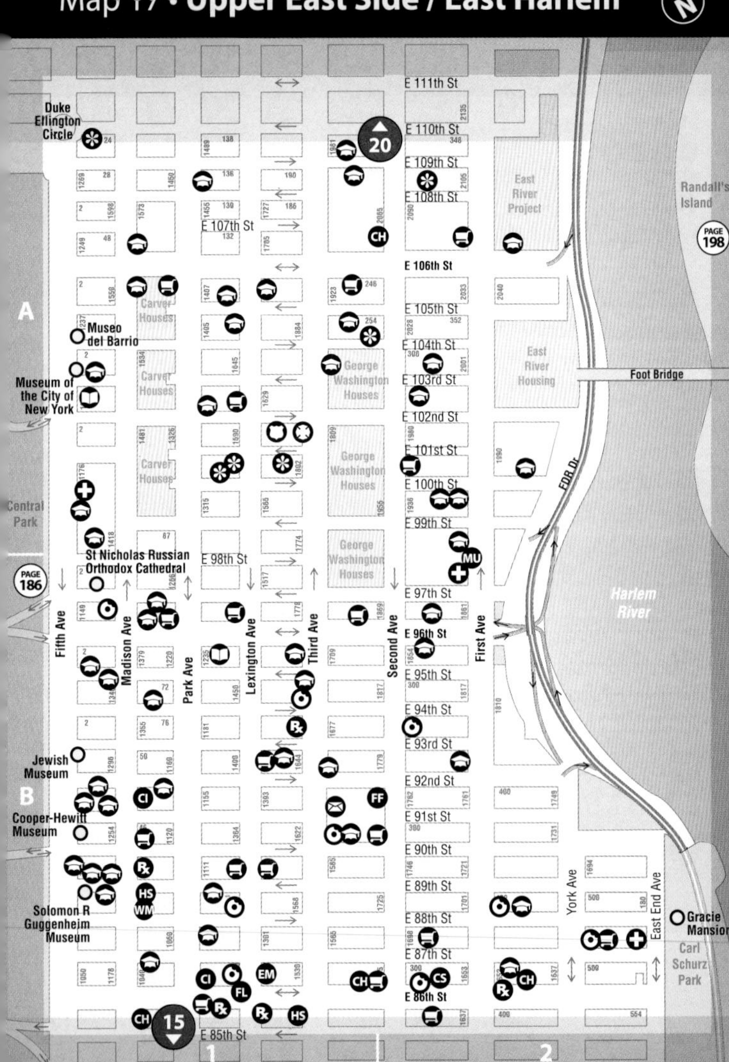

Duke Ellington Circle
Museo del Barrio
Museum of the City of New York
Carver Houses
George Washington Houses
East River Project
East River Housing
Foot Bridge
Randall's Island
PAGE 198
Central Park
St Nicholas Russian Orthodox Cathedral
PAGE 186
Harlem River
FDR Dr
Jewish Museum
Cooper-Hewitt Museum
Solomon R Guggenheim Museum
Gracie Mansion
Carl Schurz Park
Fifth Ave
Madison Ave
Park Ave
Lexington Ave
Third Ave
Second Ave
First Ave
York Ave
East End Ave
E 111th St
E 110th St
E 109th St
E 108th St
E 107th St
E 106th St
E 105th St
E 104th St
E 103rd St
E 102nd St
E 101st St
E 100th St
E 99th St
E 98th St
E 97th St
E 96th St
E 95th St
E 94th St
E 93rd St
E 92nd St
E 91st St
E 90th St
E 89th St
E 88th St
E 87th St
E 86th St
E 85th St
20
15
A
B
1
2

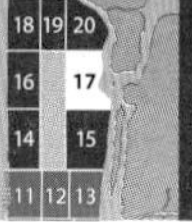

If you were unsure as to whether or not New York had enough cultural institutions, Museum Mile should convince you. The Guggenheim is one of the greatest architectural tours de force in Manhattan, notwithstanding its rapaciously high admission fees. Note the strange icon dispersal between everything north of 96th Street and everything south of 96th Street.

ATMs

CH • Chase • 126 E 86th St
CH • Chase • 2065 Second Ave
CH • Chase • 255 E 86th St
CH • Chase • 453 E 86th St
CI • Citibank • 123 E 86th St
CI • Citibank • 1275 Madison Ave
CS • City and Suburban FSB • 345 E 86th St
EM • Emigrant • 1270 Lexington Ave
FL • Fleet • 1276 Lexington Ave
FF • Fourth Federal Savings • 1751 Second Ave
HS • HSBC • 186 E 86th St
HS • HSBC • 45 E 89th St
CU • Municipal Credit Union • 1901 First Ave
WM • Washington Mutual • 1221 Madison Ave

Bagels

• **Bagel Bob's** • 1638 York Ave
• **Bagel Express** • 1804 Second Ave
• **Bagel Mill** • 1700 First Ave
• **Bagelry** • 1324 Lexington Ave
• **Bagelry** • 1380 Madison Ave
• **Einstein Bros** • 1695 Third Ave
• **New York Hot Bagel** • 1585 Third Ave
• **Tal Bagels** • 333 E 86th St

Community Gardens

Fire Departments

• **Engine 53, Ladder 43** • 1836 Third Ave

Hospitals

• **Beth Israel Medical Center: Singer Division** • 170 East End Ave
• **Metropolitan Hospital** • 1901 First Ave
• **Mt Sinai Medical Center** • 1190 Fifth Ave

Landmarks

• **Cooper-Hewitt Museum** • 2 E 91st St
• **Gracie Mansion** • Carl Schulz Park & 88th St
• **Jewish Museum** • 1109 Fifth Ave
• **Museo del Barrio** • Fifth Ave & 104th St
• **Museum of the City of New York** • Fifth Ave & 103rd St
• **Solomon R Guggenheim Museum** • 1071 Fifth Ave
• **St Nicholas Russian Orthodox Cathedral** • 15 E 97th St

Libraries

• **96th Street** • 112 E 96th St
• **New York Academy of Medicine Library** • 1216 Fifth Ave

24-Hour Pharmacies

• **CVS Pharmacy** • 1622 Third Ave
• **Duane Reade** • 1231 Madison Ave
• **Duane Reade** • 125 E 86th St
• **Duane Reade** • 401 E 86th St
• **Rite Aid** • 146 E 86th St

Police

• **23rd Precinct** • 162 E 102nd St

Post Offices

• **Yorkville** • 1617 Third Ave

Schools

• **Amber Charter School** • 220 E 106th St
• **Ballet Academy East** • 1651 Third Ave
• **Brick Church School** • 62 E 92nd St
• **Churchill School** • 22 E 95th St
• **Convent of the Sacred Heart** • 1 E 91st St
• **Dalton School** • 108 E 89th St
• **East Harlem School at Exodus House** • 309 E 103rd St
• **Heritage School** • 1680 Lexington Ave
• **HS 580 Richard Green High School of Teaching** • 421 E 88th St
• **Hunter College Elementary School** • 71 E 94th St
• **JHS 013 Jackie Robinson** • 1573 Madison Ave
• **JHS 099 Julio De Burgos School & Environmental Science** • 410 E 100th St
• **JHS 117 Jefferson Park School** • 240 E 109th St
• **Life Sciences Secondary School** • 320 E 96th St
• **Lower Trevor Day School** • 11 E 89th St
• **Lycée Français de New York** • 3 E 95th St
• **Manhattan Country School** • 7 E 96th St
• **Mount Sinai School of Medicine** • 1 Gustave Levy Pl
• **MS 224 Manhattan East Center for Arts & Academics** • 410 E 100th St
• **National Academy School of Fine Arts** • 1083 Fifth Ave
• **Nightingale-Bamford School** • 20 E 92nd St
• **Our Lady of Good Counsel School** • 323 E 91st St
• **Park East High School** • 234 E 105th St
• **PS 072** • 131 E 104th St
• **PS 083 Luis Munoz Rivera School** • 219 E 109th St
• **PS 108 Peter Minuit School** • 1615 Madison Ave
• **PS 109 Century** • 433 E 100th St
• **PS 146 Anna M Short School** • 421 E 106th St
• **PS 151 Eleanor Roosevelt School** • 1763 First Ave
• **PS 169 Robert F Kennedy School** • 110 E 88th St
• **PS 171 Patrick Henry School** • 19 E 103rd St
• **PS 38 Galileo School** • 232 E 103rd St
• **PS 77 Lower Lab School** • 1700 Third Ave
• **Reece School** • 180 E 93rd St
• **Richard Green High School** • 421 E 88th St
• **School of Cooperative Technical Education** • 321 E 96th St
• **Solomon Schechter School** • 50 E 87th St
• **Spence School** • 22 E 91st St
• **St Bernard's School** • 4 E 98th St
• **St David's School** • 12 E 89th St
• **St Francis de Sales School** • 116 E 97th St
• **St Joseph School Yorkville** • 420 E 87th St
• **St Lucy's Academy** • 340 E 104th St
• **Young Women's Leadership High School** • 105 E 106th St

Supermarkets

• **Associated** • 1486 Lexington Ave
• **Associated** • 1490 Madison Ave
• **Associated** • 1635 Lexington Ave
• **Associated** • 1968 Second Ave
• **Food Emporium** • 1211 Madison Ave
• **Food Emporium** • 1660 Second Ave
• **Gristede's** • 120 E 86th St
• **Gristede's** • 1343 Lexington Ave
• **Gristede's** • 1356 Lexington Ave
• **Gristede's** • 1644 York Ave
• **Gristede's** • 202 E 96th St
• **Gristede's Mega Store** • 350 E 86th St
• **Key Food** • 1769 Second Ave
• **Met Food** • 235 E 106th St
• **Pioneer** • 1407 Lexington Ave
• **Pioneer** • 2076 First Ave

PAGE 198
PAGE 186

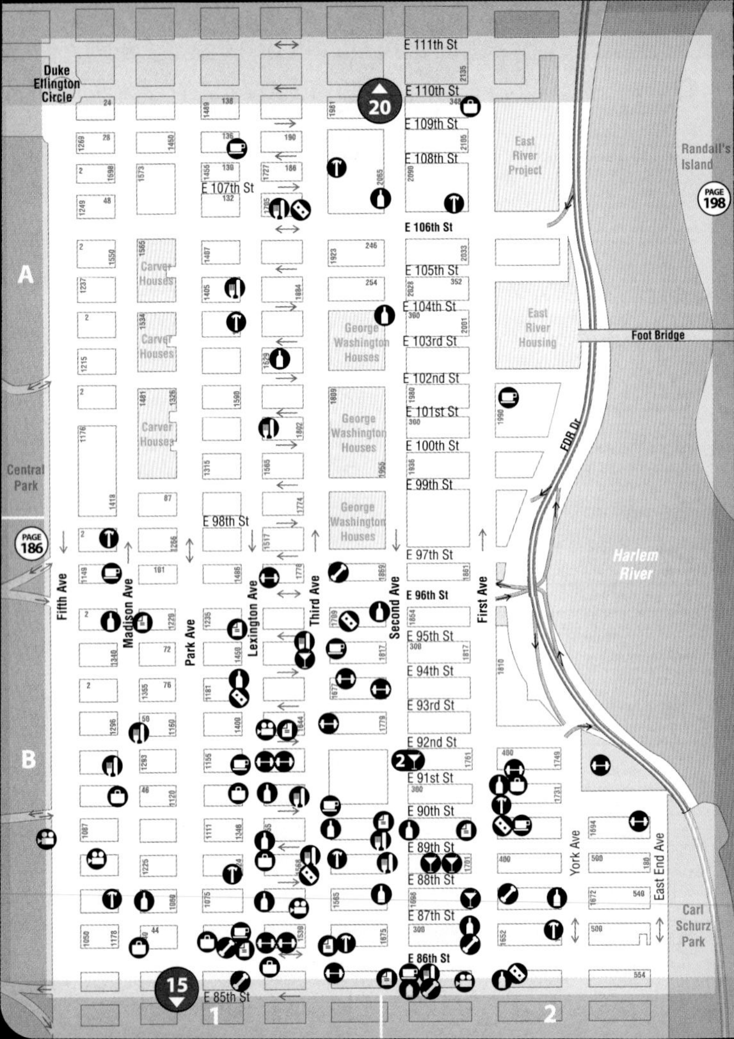

There's a dramatic change in the number of services north of 96th Street, much of which is due to several large housing projects. However, a few new building projects on 97th and 98th Streets illustrate the creep of gentrification north of 96th Street.

Bars

- **Auction House** • 300 E 89th St
- **Big Easy** • 1768 Second Ave
- **Kinsale Tavern** • 1672 Third Ave
- **Rathbones Pub** • 1702 Second Ave
- **Ruby's Tap House** • 1754 Second Ave
- **Who's on First?** • 1683 First Ave

Coffee

- **Good Coffee Shop** • 1735 Lexington Ave
- **Juliano Gourmet Coffee** • 1378 Lexington Ave
- **New World Coffee** • 1595 Third Ave
- **Starbucks** • 120 E 87th St
- **Starbucks** • 1378 Madison Ave
- **Starbucks** • 1642 Third Ave
- **Starbucks** • 400 E 90th St
- **Viand Coffee Shop** • 300 E 86th St

Copy Shops

- **Copy Quest First Avenue (8 am-6 pm)** • 1749 First Ave
- **Copy Quest (8 am-6 pm)** • 159 E 92nd St
- **Desktop USA** • 1476 Lexington Ave
- **Mail Boxes Etc (8 am-6:30 pm)** • 1369 Madison Ave
- **Staples (7 am-9 pm)** • 1280 Lexington Ave
- **The UPS Store (8:30 am-7 pm)** • 217 E 86th St

Gyms

- **92nd St Y- May Center** • 1395 Lexington Ave
- **Asphalt Green** • 555 E 90th St
- **Bally Total Fitness** • 144 E 86th St
- **Carnegie Park Swim & Health Club** • 200 E 94th St
- **Dolphin Fitness Clubs** • 1781 Second Ave
- **Monterey Sports Club** • 175 E 96th St
- **New York Sports Clubs** • 151 E 86th St
- **New York Sports Clubs** • 1637 Third Ave
- **Pumping Iron Gym** • 403 E 91st St
- **Synergy Fitness Clubs** • 1781 Second Ave

Hardware Stores

- **El Barrio Hardware** • 1876 Third Ave
- **Feldmans IV** • 1190 Madison Ave
- **Johnny's Hardware** • 1708 Lexington Ave
- **K&G Hardware & Supply** • 401 E 90th St
- **M&E Madison Hardware** • 1396 Madison Ave
- **Morales Brothers Hardware** • 1959 Third Ave
- **Service Hardware** • 1338 Lexington Ave
- **Wankel's Hardware & Paint** • 1573 Third Ave

Liquor Stores

- **86th St Wine & Liquor** • 306 E 86th St
- **American Spirits** • 1744 Second Ave
- **Best Cellars** • 1291 Lexington Ave
- **Braun Julius Wines & Liquors** • 1361 Lexington Ave
- **East 87th St Wine Traders** • 1693 Second Ave
- **Edwin's Wines & Liquors** • 176 E 103rd St
- **Harmony Liquors** • 2073 Second Ave
- **K&D Wines & Spirits** • 1366 Madison Ave
- **Mister Wright** • 1593 Third Ave
- **Normandie Wines** • 1857 Second Ave
- **Park East Liquors** • 1657 York Ave
- **Pet Wines & Spirits** • 415 E 91st St
- **Rivera Liquor Store** • 2025 First Ave
- **Shoprite Wines & Liquors** • 2073 Second Ave
- **Uptown Wine Shop** • 1361 Lexington Ave
- **West Coast Wine & Liquor** • 1440 Lexington Ave
- **Yorkshire Wines & Spirits** • 1646 First Ave

Movie Theaters

- **92nd St Y** • Lexington Ave & 92nd St
- **City Cinemas: East 86th St** • 210 E 86th St
- **Goethe Institute** • 1014 Fifth Ave
- **Loews Cineplex Orpheum** • 1538 Third Ave
- **Solomon R Guggenheim Museum** • 1071 Fifth Ave

Pet Shops

- **Furry Paws** • 1705 Third Ave
- **Petco** • 147 E 86th St
- **Petland Discounts** • 304 E 86th St
- **Shaggy Dog** • 400 E 88th St
- **World Wide Kennel** • 1661 First Ave

Restaurants

- **Barking Dog Luncheonette** • 1678 Third Ave
- **Blue Grotto** • 1576 Third Ave
- **Burritoville** • 1606 Third Ave
- **Dinerbar** • 1569 Lexington Ave
- **El Paso Taqueria** • 1642 Lexington Ave
- **Elaine's** • 1703 Second Ave
- **Jackson Hole** • 1270 Madison Ave
- **La Fonda Boricua** • 169 E 106th St
- **Saigon Grill** • 1700 Second Ave
- **Sarabeth's** • 1295 Madison Ave
- **Viand** • 300 E 86th St

Shopping

- **Best Buy** • 1280 Lexington Ave
- **Blades Board & Skate** • 120 W 72nd St
- **Eli's Vinegar Factory** • 431 E 91st St
- **FACE Stockholm** • 1263 Madison Ave
- **La Tropezienne** • 2131 First Ave
- **Piece of Cake Bakery** • 1370 Lexington Ave
- **Steve Madden** • 150 E 86th St
- **Super Runners Shop** • 1337 Lexington Ave
- **Williams-Sonoma** • 1175 Madison Ave

Video Rental

- **Blockbuster Video** • 1646 First Ave
- **Blockbuster Video** • 1707 Third Ave
- **Blockbuster Video** • 1924 Third Ave
- **We Deliver Videos** • 1716 First Ave
- **York Video** • 1428 Lexington Ave

Map 17 • Upper East Side / East Harlem

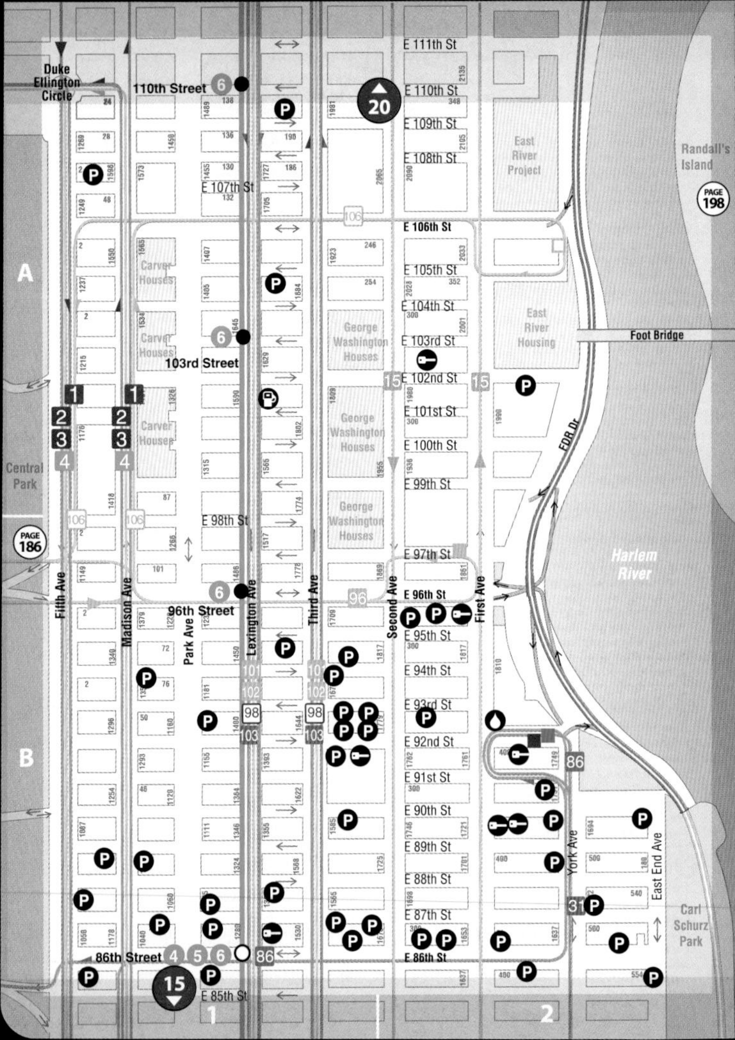

PAGE 198
PAGE 186
20
15

Transportation

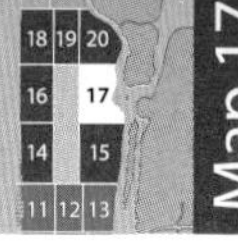

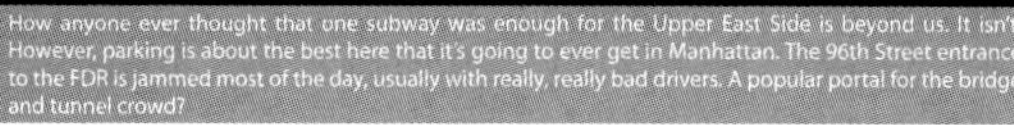
How anyone ever thought that one subway was enough for the Upper East Side is beyond us. It isn't. However, parking is about the best here that it's going to ever get in Manhattan. The 96th Street entrance to the FDR is jammed most of the day, usually with really, really bad drivers. A popular portal for the bridge and tunnel crowd?

Subways

- 4 5 6 .... 86 St
- 6 .... 103 St
- 6 .... 96 St

Bus Lines

- 1 2 3 .... Fifth Ave/Madison Ave
- 101 .... Third Ave/Lexington Ave
- 102 .... Third Ave/Lexington Ave
- 103 .... Third Ave/Lexington Ave
- 106 .... 96th St/106th St Crosstown
- 15 .... First Ave/Second Ave
- 31 .... York Ave/57th St
- 4 .... Fifth Ave/Madison Ave/Broadway
- 86 .... 86th St Crosstown
- 96 .... 96th St Crosstown
- 98 .... Washington Heights/Midtown

Car Rental

- **A-Value Rent-A-Car** • 1989 First Ave
- **Avis** • 420 E 90th St
- **Enterprise** • 1833 First Ave
- **Farrell's Limousine Service** • 430 E 92nd St
- **Hertz** • 412 E 90th St
- **New York Rent-A-Car** • 154 E 87th St

Car Washes

- **Eastside Car Wash** • 1770 First Ave

Gas Stations

- **Amoco** • 1599 Lexington Ave

Parking

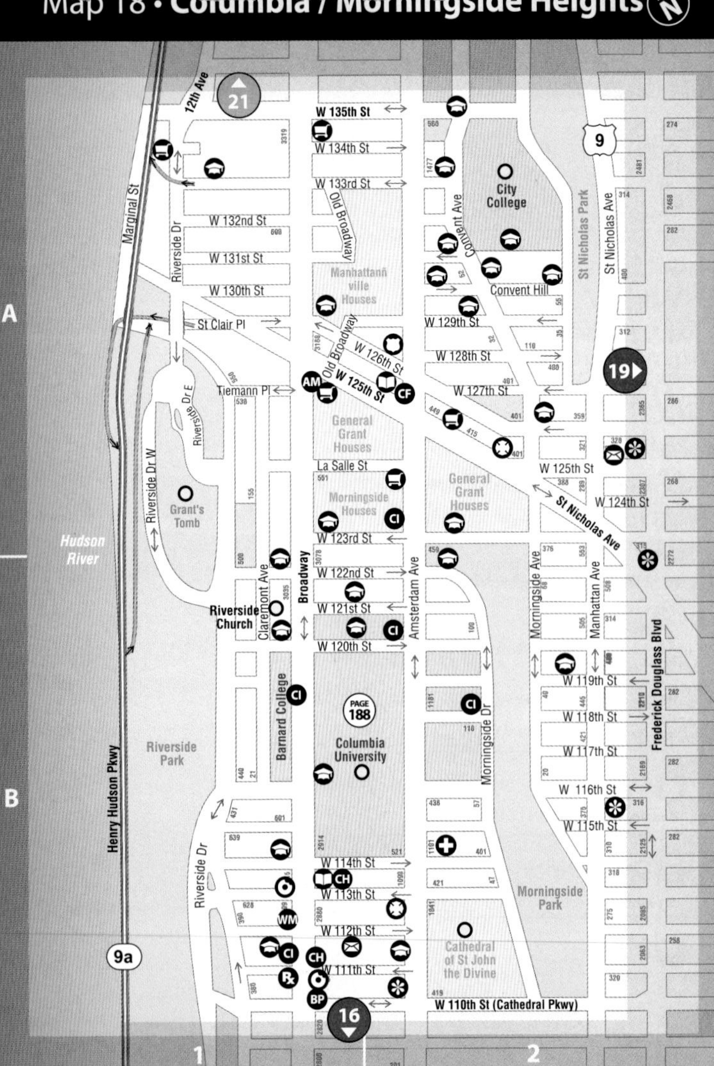

Hudson River
Henry Hudson Pkwy
Marginal St
12th Ave
Riverside Dr
W 135th St
W 134th St
W 133rd St
W 132nd St
W 131st St
W 130th St
St Clair Pl
Tiemann Pl
Old Broadway
Manhattanville Houses
W 126th St
W 125th St
La Salle St
General Grant Houses
Morningside Houses
W 123rd St
W 122nd St
W 121st St
W 120th St
Broadway
Claremont Ave
Riverside Church
Grant's Tomb
Riverside Dr E
Riverside Dr W
Riverside Park
Barnard College
Columbia University
PAGE 188
W 114th St
W 113th St
W 112th St
W 111th St
W 110th St (Cathedral Pkwy)
Amsterdam Ave
Morningside Dr
Morningside Park
Cathedral of St John the Divine
Convent Ave
City College
Convent Hill
W 129th St
W 128th St
W 127th St
W 125th St
St Nicholas Ave
St Nicholas Park
W 124th St
Morningside Ave
Manhattan Ave
Frederick Douglass Blvd
W 119th St
W 118th St
W 117th St
W 116th St
W 115th St
21
19
16
9
9a
A
B
1
2

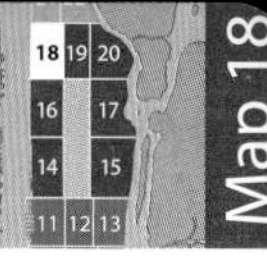

This is perhaps one of the most truly economically diverse parts of the city, with tons of Columbia students mixing with high-, middle-, and low-income professionals and families. The Cathedral of St. John the Divin e is the most eclectic and astounding building in Manhattan.

ATMs

AM • Amalgamated • 564 W 125th St
BP • Banco Popular • 2852 Broadway
CF • Carver Federal Savings • 503 W 125th St
CH • Chase • 2824 Broadway
CH • Chase • 2898 Broadway
CI • Citibank • 1310 Amsterdam Ave
CI • Citibank • 2861 Broadway
CI • Citibank • 3009 Broadway
CI • Citibank • 420 W 118th St
CI • Citibank • 525 W 120th St
WM • Washington Mutual • 2875 Broadway

Bagels

- **Columbia Bagels** • 2836 Broadway
- **Nussbaum & Wu** • 2897 Broadway

Community Gardens

Fire Departments

- **Cathedral of St John the Divine** • 112th St & Amsterdam Ave
- **City College** • 138th St & Convent Ave
- **Columbia University** • 116th St & Broadway
- **Grant's Tomb** • 122nd St & Riverside Drive
- **Riverside Church** • 490 Riverside Dr

Hospitals

- **St Luke's Hospital Center** • 1111 Amsterdam Ave

Landmarks

- **Cathedral of St John the Divine** • 112th St & Amsterdam Ave
- **City College** • 135th St & Convent Ave
- **Columbia University** • 2960 Broadway
- **Grant's Tomb** • 122nd St & Riverside Dr
- **Riverside Church** • 490 Riverside Dr

Libraries

- **George Bruce** • 518 W 125th St
- **Morningside Heights Library** • 2900 Broadway

24-Hour Pharmacies

- **Duane Reade** • 2864 Broadway

Police

- **26th Precinct** • 520 W 126th St

Post Offices

- **Columbia University** • 534 W 112th St
- **Manhattanville** • 365 W 125th St

Schools

- **A Philip Randolph Campus High School** • 443 W 135th St
- **Annunciation School** • 461 W 131st St
- **Bank Street College of Education** • 610 W 112th St
- **Barnard College** • 3009 Broadway
- **Cathedral School** • 1047 Amsterdam Ave
- **City College** • 138th St & Convent Ave
- **Columbia University** • 2960 Broadway
- **Corpus Christi** • 535 W 121st St
- **IS 195 Roberto Clemente School** • 625 W 133rd St
- **IS 223 Mott Hall** • 71 Convent Ave
- **IS 286 Renaissance Military** • 509 W 129th St
- **Jewish Theological Seminary of America** • 3080 Broadway
- **JHS 043 Adam C Powell School** • 509 W 129th St
- **Manhattan School of Music** • 120 Claremont Ave
- **PS 036 Margaret Douglas School** • 123 Morningside Dr
- **PS 125 Ralph Bunche School** • 425 W 123rd St
- **PS 129 John H Finley School** • 425 W 130th St
- **PS 161 Pedro A Campos School** • 499 W 133rd St
- **PS 180 Hugo Newman School** • 370 W 120th St
- **PS-IS 223 Mott Hall School** • W 131st St & Convent Ave
- **St Hilda and Hugh School** • 619 W 114th St
- **St Joseph's School** • 168 Morningside Ave
- **Teachers College, Columbia University** • 525 W 120th St

Supermarkets

- **C-Town** • 3320 Broadway
- **C-Town** • 560 W 125th St
- **Citarella** • 461 W 125th St
- **Fairway Market** • 2328 Twelfth Ave
- **Met Food** • 1316 Amsterdam Ave

A
B
1
2
21
19
16
9
9a
PAGE 188
12th Ave
Marginal St
Henry Hudson Pkwy
Hudson River
Riverside Dr
Riverside Dr E
Riverside Dr W
Riverside Park
Grant's Tomb
Riverside Church
Claremont Ave
Barnard College
Broadway
Old Broadway
Amsterdam Ave
Convent Ave
Convent Hill
City College
St Nicholas Park
St Nicholas Ave
Morningside Ave
Morningside Dr
Morningside Park
Manhattan Ave
Frederick Douglass Blvd
Manhattanville Houses
General Grant Houses
Morningside Houses
Columbia University
Cathedral of St John the Divine
W 135th St
W 134th St
W 133rd St
W 132nd St
W 131st St
W 130th St
St Clair Pl
W 129th St
W 128th St
W 127th St
W 126th St
W 125th St
Tiemann Pl
La Salle St
W 124th St
W 123rd St
W 122nd St
W 121st St
W 120th St
W 119th St
W 118th St
W 117th St
W 116th St
W 115th St
W 114th St
W 113th St
W 112th St
W 111th St
W 110th St (Cathedral Pkwy)

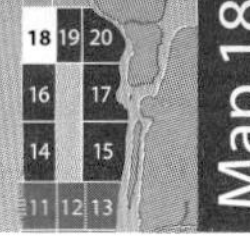

Many services can be found near Columbia University on Broadway. Labyrinth Books is a great place to blow some money. Columbia plans to expand its campus north and westward towards the river, which will no doubt spur development of services. And community meetings. For some decent grub, check out Toast on Broadway.

Bars

- **1020 Amsterdam** • 1020 Amsterdam Ave
- **Cotton Club** • 666 W 125th St
- **Heights Bar & Grill** • 2867 Broadway
- **Nacho Mama's Kitchen Bar** • 2893 Broadway
- **West End** • 2911 Broadway

Coffee

- **Jimbo's Coffee Shop** • 1345 Amsterdam Ave
- **Oren's Daily Roast** • 2882 Broadway
- **Starbucks** • 2853 Broadway
- **Starbucks** • 2929 Broadway

Copy Shops

- **Broadway Copy Center(9 am-6 pm)** • 3062 Broadway
- **Mail Boxes Etc (8:30 am-7 pm)** • 2840 Broadway
- **The Village Copier** • 2872 Broadway

Gyms

- **Lucille Roberts Health Club** • 505 W 125th St

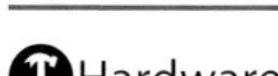

Hardware Stores

- **Academy Hardware & Supply** • 2869 Broadway
- **Clinton Supply** • 1256 Amsterdam Ave
- **Columbia Hardware** • 2905 Broadway
- **Philip Glick Supply** • 421 W 125th St
- **Scotty Boys Hardware** • 3147 Broadway
- **TriBoro Hardware** • 433 W 125th St

Liquor Stores

- **Amsterdam Liquor Mart** • 1356 Amsterdam Ave
- **Caro Wines & Liquor** • 3139 Broadway
- **International Wines and Spirits** • 2903 Broadway

Movie Theaters

- **Italian Academy** • 1161 Amsterdam Ave

Pet Shops

- **NYC Pet Place** • 431 W 125th St

Restaurants

- **Bistro Ten 18** • 1018 Amsterdam Ave
- **Hungarian Pastry Shop** • 1030 Amsterdam Ave
- **Kitchenette Uptown** • 1272 Amsterdam Ave
- **Le Monde** • 2885 Broadway
- **M & G Soul Food Diner** • 383 W 125th St
- **Massawa** • 1239 Amsterdam Ave
- **Max SoHa** • 1274 Amsterdam Ave
- **Ollie's** • 2957 Broadway
- **Pisticci** • 125 La Salle St
- **Symposium** • 544 W 113th St
- **Terrace in the Sky** • 400 W 119th St
- **The Mill Korean Restaurant** • 2895 Broadway
- **Toast** • 3157 Broadway

Shopping

- **JAS Mart** • 2847 Broadway
- **Kim's Mediapolis** • 2906 Broadway
- **Labyrinth Books** • 536 W 112th St
- **Nine West Outlet Store** • 282 St Nicholas St

Video Rental

- **Blockbuster Video** • 1280 Amsterdam Ave
- **Films & Games** • 243 W 125th St
- **Kim's Mediapolis** • 2906 Broadway

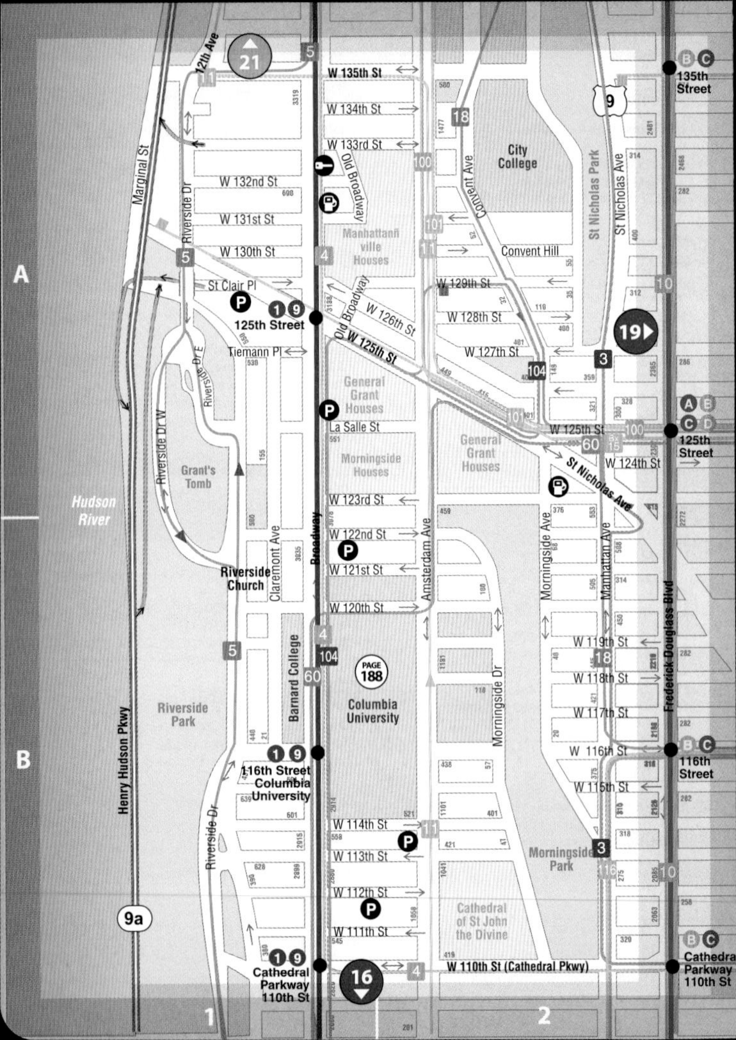

W 135th St
W 134th St
W 133rd St
W 132nd St
W 131st St
W 130th St
St Clair Pl
W 129th St
W 128th St
W 127th St
W 126th St
W 125th St
Tiemann Pl
La Salle St
W 124th St
W 123rd St
W 122nd St
W 121st St
W 120th St
W 119th St
W 118th St
W 117th St
W 116th St
W 115th St
W 114th St
W 113th St
W 112th St
W 111th St
W 110th St (Cathedral Pkwy)

12th Ave
Marginal St
Riverside Dr
Riverside Dr E
Riverside Dr W
Henry Hudson Pkwy
Claremont Ave
Broadway
Old Broadway
Amsterdam Ave
Convent Ave
Convent Hill
St Nicholas Park
St Nicholas Ave
Morningside Ave
Morningside Dr
Manhattan Ave
Frederick Douglass Blvd

Hudson River
Grant's Tomb
Riverside Church
Riverside Park
Barnard College
Columbia University
Manhattanville Houses
General Grant Houses
Morningside Houses
City College
Morningside Park
Cathedral of St John the Divine

135th Street
125th Street
116th Street
116th Street Columbia University
Cathedral Parkway 110th St

PAGE 188
21
19
16

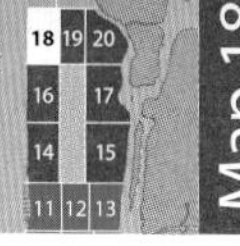

Driving and parking are both pretty decent around here, and the area is also served well by subway. We wish we could say that about the rest of the city.

Subways

- 1 9 .... 116th St Columbia University
- 1 9 .... 125th St
- 1 9 .... Cathedral Pkwy (110th St)
- B C .... 135th St
- A C B D .... 125th St

Bus Lines

- 100 .... 86th St Crosstown
- 101 .... 96th St Crosstown
- 104 .... 106th St Crosstown
- 11 .... Columbus Ave/Amsterdam Ave
- 18 .... Convent Ave
- 3 .... Fifth Ave/Madison Ave
- 4 .... Fifth Ave/Sixth Ave/Riverside Dr
- 5 .... Columbus Ave/Amsterdam Ave
- Bx 15 .... 116th St Crosstown

Car Rental

- **U-Haul** • 3270 Broadway

Gas Stations

- **BP** • 619 W 125th St
- **Mobil** • 3260 Broadway

Parking

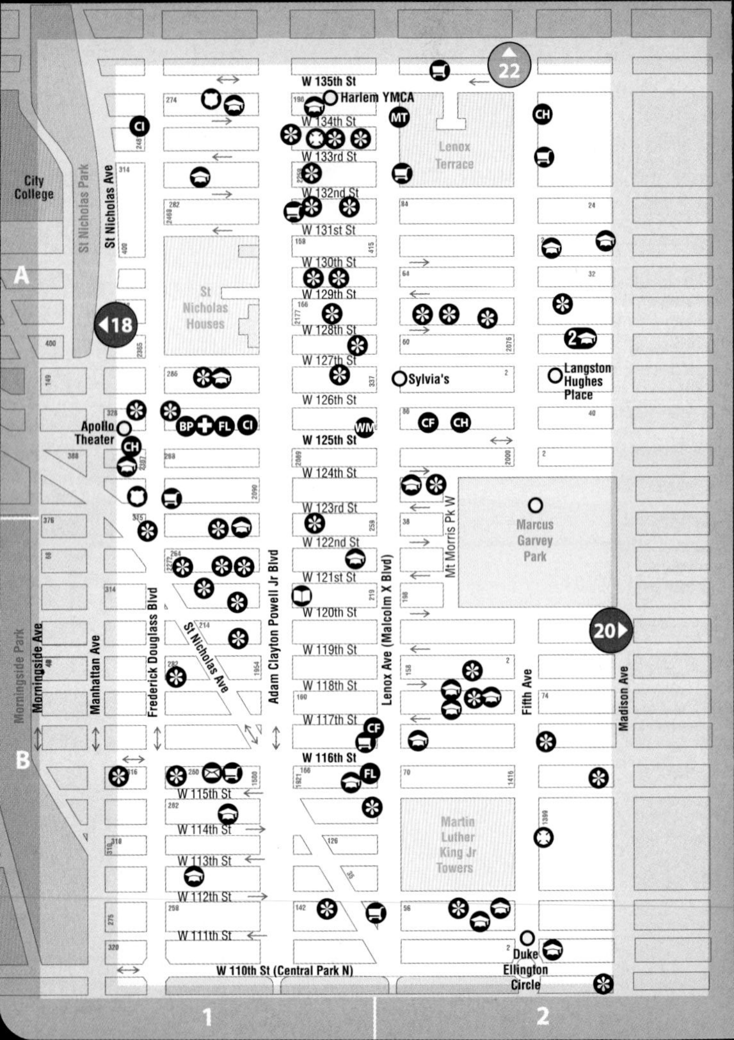

W 135th St
Harlem YMCA
W 134th St
W 133rd St
W 132nd St
W 131st St
W 130th St
W 129th St
W 128th St
W 127th St
W 126th St
W 125th St
W 124th St
W 123rd St
W 122nd St
W 121st St
W 120th St
W 119th St
W 118th St
W 117th St
W 116th St
W 115th St
W 114th St
W 113th St
W 112th St
W 111th St
W 110th St (Central Park N)
City College
St Nicholas Park
St Nicholas Ave
St Nicholas Houses
Lenox Terrace
Sylvia's
Langston Hughes Place
Apollo Theater
Marcus Garvey Park
Mt Morris Pk W
Martin Luther King Jr Towers
Duke Ellington Circle
Morningside Park
Morningside Ave
Manhattan Ave
Frederick Douglass Blvd
Adam Clayton Powell Jr Blvd
Lenox Ave (Malcolm X Blvd)
Fifth Ave
Madison Ave
18
20
22
A
B
1
2

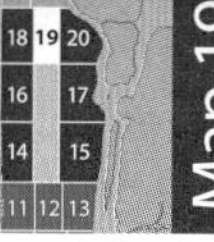

This neighborhood revolves around all the shops and services on 125th Street—also the location of the famous Apollo Theater. And don't forget to stop by and say hello to Mr. Clinton.

ATMs

BP • Banco Popular • 231 W 125th St
CF • Carver Federal Savings • 142 Malcolm X Blvd
CF • Carver Federal Savings • 75 W 125th St
CH • Chase • 2218 Fifth Ave
CH • Chase • 322 W 125th St
CH • Chase • 55 W 125th St
CI • Citibank • 201 W 125th St
CI • Citibank • 2518 Frederick Douglass Blvd
FL • Fleet • 102 W 116th St
FL • Fleet • 215 W 125th St
MT • Manufacturers and Traders Trust • 498 Lenox Ave
WM • Washington Mutual • 105 W 125th St

Community Gardens

Fire Departments

- **Engine 58, Ladder 26** • 1367 Fifth Ave
- **Engine 59, Ladder 30** • 111 W 133rd St

Hospitals

- **Renaissance Health Care Network** • 215 W 125th St

Landmarks

- **Apollo Theater** • 253 W 125th St
- **Duke Ellington Circle** • 110th St & Fifth Ave
- **Harlem YMCA** • 180 W 135th St
- **Langston Hughes Place** • 20 E 127th St
- **Marcus Garvey Park** • E 120-124th Sts & Madison Ave
- **Sylvia's** • 328 Lenox Ave

Libraries

- **Harlem** • 2011 Adam Clayton Powell Jr Blvd

Police

- **28th Precinct** • 2271 Eighth Ave
- **32nd Precinct** • 250 W 135th St

Post Offices

- **Morningside** • 232 W 116th St

Schools

- **Center for Continuing Education** • 22 E 128th St
- **Christ Crusader Academy** • 302 W 124th St
- **College of New Rochelle Rosa Parks Campus** • 144 W 125th St
- **Eight Plus Academy** • 212 W 120th St
- **JHS 088 Wadleigh** • 215 W 114th St
- **Northside Center Day School** • 1301 Fifth Ave
- **Pregnant and Parenting Students School** • 22 E 128th St
- **PS 076 A Philip Randolph School** • 220 W 121st St
- **PS 092 Mary M Bethune School** • 222 W 134th St
- **PS 133 Fred R Moore School** • 2121 Fifth Ave
- **PS 144 Hans C Anderson School** • 134 W 122nd St
- **PS 149 Sojourner Truth School** • 34 W 118th St
- **PS 154 Harriet Tubman** • 250 W 127th St
- **PS 175-IS Henry Highland** • 175 W 134th St
- **PS 185 John M Langston School** • 20 W 112th St
- **PS 207 Norbert Rillieux School** • 41 W 117th St
- **PS 208 Alain L Locke School** • 21 W 111th St
- **PS 41 Family Academy** • 240 W 113th St
- **Rice High School** • 74 W 124th St
- **Sister Clara Mohammed School** • 102 W 116th St
- **Sisulu Children's Charter School** • 125 W 115th St
- **St Aloysius School** • 223 W 132nd St
- **Wadleigh High School** • 215 W 114th St

Supermarkets

- **Associated** • 2170 Fifth Ave
- **Associated** • 2296 Eighth Ave
- **Associated** • 448 Lenox Ave
- **C-Town** • 2217 Adam Clayton Powell Jr Blvd
- **C-Town** • 24 W 135th St
- **Met Food** • 101 W 116th St
- **Met Food** • 238 W 116th St
- **Met Food** • 37 Lenox Ave
- **Pioneer Supermarket** • 134 Lenox Ave

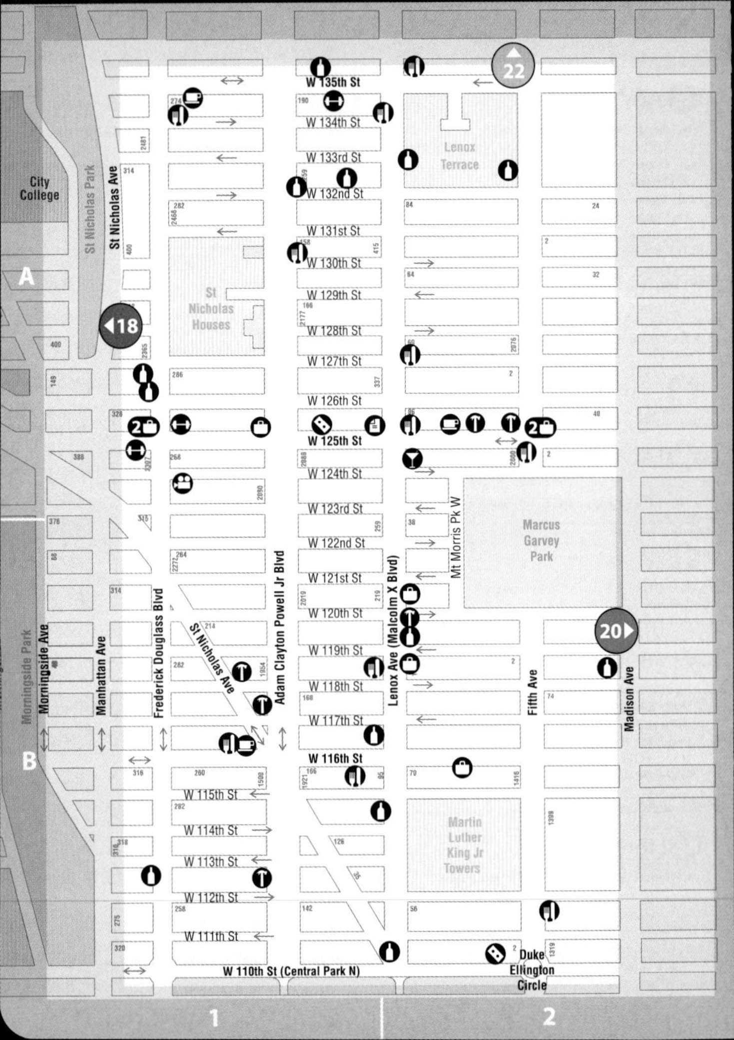

Map 19 • Harlem (Lower)

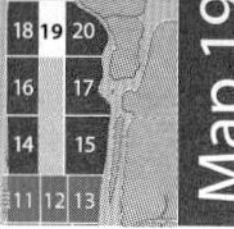

The Magic Johnson Multiplex on 124th Street is a great thing for the neighborhood. Sylvia's really is as good as everyone says it is, but it's definitely not the only great place for food anymore.

Bars

- **Lenox Lounge** • 288 Lenox Ave

Coffee

- **Farafena Coffee Shop** • 219 W 116th St
- **Starbucks** • 77 W 125th St

Copy Shops

- **Staples (7am-8pm)** • 105 W 125th St

Gyms

- **Dolphin Fitness Clubs** • 209 W 125th St
- **New York Sports Clubs** • 2311 Frederick Douglass Blvd
- **YMCA: Harlem** • 180 W 135th St

Hardware Stores

- **Bill's Hardware & Paints** • 1 W 125th St
- **Citi General Hardware** • 100 St Nicholas Ave
- **Concordia Electrical & Plumbing** • 2297 Adam Clayton Powell Jr Blvd
- **Harlem Locksmith** • 106 Malcolm X Blvd
- **Manhattan Paint Fair** • 17 W 125th St
- **StaLoc Lock & Hardware** • 1958 Adam Clayton Powell Jr Blvd

Liquor Stores

- **115th St Liquor Store** • 5 E 115th St
- **2341** • 2366 Frederick Douglass Blvd
- **458 Lenox Liquors** • 458 Lenox Ave
- **A&D Liquor** • 23 Lenox Ave
- **Conrad Spirits** • 178 Lenox Ave
- **DRM Liquors** • 2178 Fifth Ave
- **Fred's Wine & Liquors** • 77 Lenox Ave
- **Grand Liquors** • 2049 Frederick Douglass Blvd
- **Harlem Retail Wine & Liquor** • 1902 Adam Clayton Powell Jr Blvd
- **Harlem USA Wine & Liquor Store** • 101 W 132nd St
- **Just In Liquors** • 2178 Fifth Ave
- **Palace Liquors** • 2215 Adam Clayton Powell Jr Blvd

Movie Theaters

- **Magic Johnson Harlem USA** • 124th St & Frederick Douglass Blvd

Restaurants

- **Amy Ruth's** • 113 W 116th St
- **Bayou** • 308 Lenox Ave
- **Fifth Ave Seafood** • 2014 Fifth Ave
- **Home Sweet Harlem Café** • 270 W 135th St
- **Jimmy's Uptown** • 2207 Seventh Ave
- **Keur Sokhna** • 225 W 116th St
- **Manna's Too** • 486 Lenox Ave
- **Native** • 161 Lenox Ave
- **Sylvia's** • 328 Lenox Ave
- **Yvonne Yvonne** • 301 W 135th St

Shopping

- **Champs** • 208 W 125th St
- **Dr Jays Harlem NYC** • 256 125th Street
- **H&M** • 125 W 125th St
- **Harlem Underground Clothing Co** • 2027 Fifth Ave
- **Harlemade** • 174 Lenox Ave
- **Malcolm Shabazz Harlem Market** • 58 W 116th St
- **Sette Pani** • 196 Lenox Ave
- **The Body Shop** • 1 E 125th St

Video Rental

- **Blockbuster Video** • 121 W 125th St
- **Bus Stop Video** • 9 W 110th St

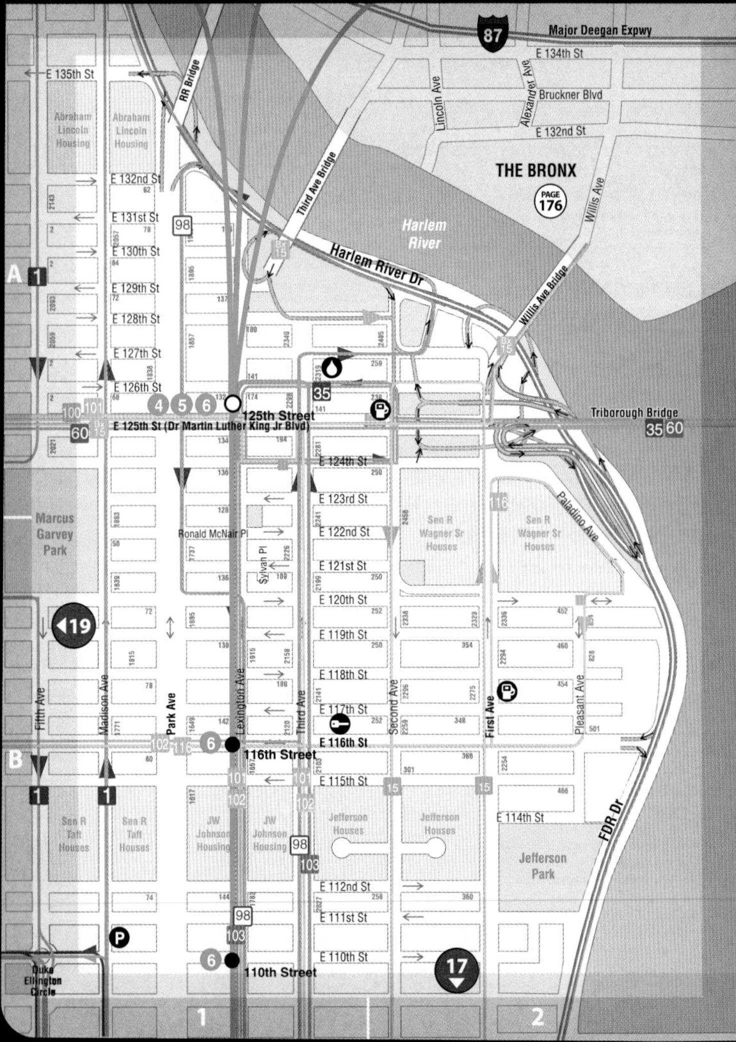

Major Deegan Expwy
87
E 134th St
E 135th St
RR Bridge
Abraham Lincoln Housing
Abraham Lincoln Housing
Lincoln Ave
Alexander Ave
Bruckner Blvd
E 132nd St
THE BRONX
PAGE 176
Willis Ave
Third Ave Bridge
Harlem River
Harlem River Dr
Willis Ave Bridge
E 132nd St
E 131st St
E 130th St
E 129th St
E 128th St
E 127th St
E 126th St
98
35
4 5 6
125th Street
Triborough Bridge
35 60
100 101
60
E 125th St (Dr Martin Luther King Jr Blvd)
E 124th St
E 123rd St
Ronald McNair Pl
E 122nd St
Sylvan Pl
E 121st St
E 120th St
E 119th St
E 118th St
E 117th St
E 116th St
116th Street
E 115th St
E 114th St
E 112nd St
E 111st St
E 110th St
110th Street
Marcus Garvey Park
Sen R Wagner Sr Houses
Sen R Wagner Sr Houses
Paladino Ave
116
19
Fifth Ave
Madison Ave
Park Ave
Lexington Ave
Third Ave
Second Ave
First Ave
Pleasant Ave
FDR Dr
102 116
6
101
102
15
Sen R Taft Houses
Sen R Taft Houses
JW Johnson Housing
JW Johnson Housing
Jefferson Houses
Jefferson Houses
Jefferson Park
98
103
P
Duke Ellington Circle
17
A
B
1
2

Transportation

Driving across 110th Street should be good, but it's usually a pain. 116th Street is much better. Parking is pretty good, even on the major avenues. There's a bike lane on St. Nicholas Avenue.

Subways

2 3 .... 116 St
2 3 .... 125 St
2 3 .... 135 St
2 3 .... Central Park N (110 St)
B C .... 116 St
B C .... Cathedral Pkwy (110 St)

Bus Lines

1 .... Fifth Ave/Madison Ave
10 .... Seventh Ave/Eighth Ave/ Frederick Douglass Blvd
100 .... Amsterdam Ave/Broadway/125th St
101 ..... Third Ave/Lexington Ave/Amsterdam Ave
102 ..... Third Ave/Lexington Ave/Malcolm X Blvd
116 .... 116th St Crosstown
2 .... Fifth Ave/Madison Ave/Powell Blvd
4 .... Fifth Ave/Madison Ave/Broadway
60 .... LaGuardia Airport via 125th St
7 .... Columbus Ave/Amsterdam Ave/ Lenox Ave/Sixth Ave/Seventh Ave/Broadway
BX 15 .... 125th St Crosstown
BX 33 .... 135th St Crosstown

Gas Stations

- **Exxon** • 2040 Frederick Douglass Blvd
- **Shell** • 235 St Nicholas Ave

Parking

Major Deegan Expwy
87
E 134th St
E 135th St
RR Bridge
Lincoln Ave
Alexander Ave
Bruckner Blvd
E 132nd St
Abraham Lincoln Housing
Abraham Lincoln Housing
THE BRONX
PAGE 176
Third Ave Bridge
Willis Ave
E 132nd St
E 131st St
E 130th St
Harlem River
Harlem River Dr
E 129th St
Willis Ave Bridge
Keith Haring "Crack is Wack" Mural
E 128th St
E 127th St
E 126th St
Triborough Bridge
E 125th St (Dr Martin Luther King Jr Blvd)
E 124th St
Harlem Fire Watch Tower
E 123rd St
Paladino Ave
Marcus Garvey Park
Ronald McNair Pl
E 122nd St
Sen R Wagner Sr Houses
Sen R Wagner Sr Houses
Sylvan Pl
E 121st St
Harlem Courthouse
E 120th St
19
E 119th St
E 118th St
Fifth Ave
Madison Ave
Park Ave
Lexington Ave
Third Ave
E 117th St
Second Ave
First Ave
Pleasant Ave
E 116th St
Church of Our Lady of Mt Carmel
E 115th St
E 114th St
Sen R Taft Houses
Sen R Taft Houses
JW Johnson Housing
JW Johnson Housing
Jefferson Houses
Jefferson Houses
Jefferson Park
FDR Dr
E 112nd St
E 111st St
E 110th St
17
Duke Ellington Circle
A
B
1
2

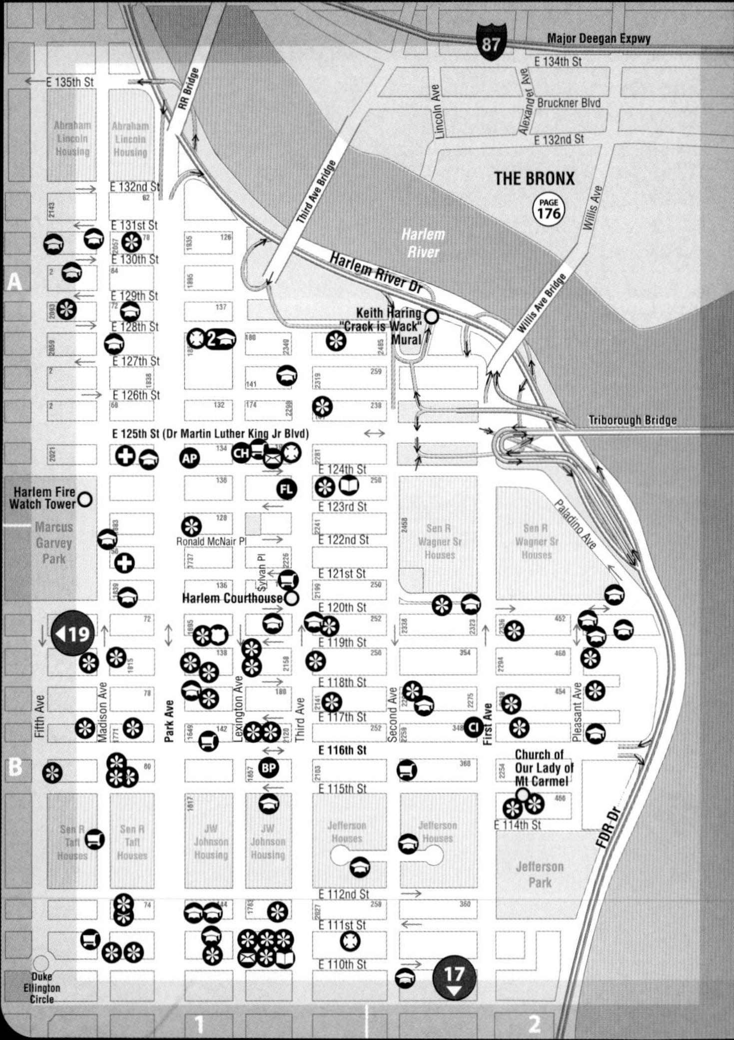

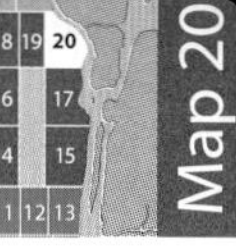

Rich and vibrant in history and culture, exploring El Barrio is highly recommended. Both Marcus Garvey and Jefferson Parks are excellent places to take a break, too.

ATMs

AP • Apple • 124 E 125th St
BP • Banco Popular • 164 E 116th St
CH • Chase • 160 E 125th St
CI • Citibank • 2261 First Ave
FL • Fleet • 2250 Third Ave

Community Gardens

Fire Departments

- **Engine 35, Ladder 14** • 2282 Third Ave
- **Engine 36** • 120 E 125th St
- **Engine 91** • 242 E 111th St

Hospitals

- **Manhattan Eye, Ear & Throat Hospital** • 55 E 124th St
- **North General Hospital** • 1879 Madison Ave

Landmarks

- **Church of Our Lady of Mt Carmel** • 448 E 115th St
- **Harlem Courthouse** • 170 E 121st St
- **Harlem Fire Watchtower** • Marcus Garvey Park
- **Keith Haring "Crack is Wack" Mural** • Second Ave & 127th St

Libraries

- **125th St** • 224 E 125th St
- **Aguilar** • 174 E 110th St

Police

- **25th Precinct** • 120 E 119th St

Post Offices

- **Hell Gate** • 153 E 110th St
- **Triborough** • 167 E 124th St

Schools

- **All Saints School** • 52 E 130th St
- **Children's Storefront School** • 70 E 129th St
- **The Choir Academy of Harlem** • 2005 Madison Ave
- **Helene Fuld School of Nursing North** • 1879 Madison Ave
- **Highway Christian Academy** • 132 E 111th St
- **JHS 045 J C Roberts School** • 2351 First Ave
- **King's Academy** • 2341 Third Ave
- **Manhattan Center for Science & Math** • 260 Pleasant Ave
- **Mount Carmel-Holy Rosary School** • 371 Pleasant Ave
- **NY College of Podiatric Medicine** • 1800 Park Ave
- **Our Lady Queen of Angels** • 232 E 113th St
- **PS 007 Samuel Stern** • 160 E 120th St
- **PS 057 James W Johnson School** • 176 E 115th St
- **PS 079 Horan School** • 55 E 120th St
- **PS 096 Joseph Lanzetta School** • 216 E 120th St
- **PS 101 Draper School** • 141 E 111th St
- **PS 102 Cartier School** • 315 E 113th St
- **PS 112 Jose Celso Barbasa School** • 535 E 119th St
- **PS 138** • 144 E 128th St
- **PS 155 William Paca School** • 319 E 117th St
- **PS 206 Jose Celso Babosa School** • 508 E 120th St
- **St Ann School** • 314 E 110th St
- **St Paul School** • 114 E 118th St

Supermarkets

- **Associated** • 125 E 116th St
- **Associated** • 2212 Third Ave
- **C-Town** • 1718 Madison Ave
- **C-Town** • 309 E 115th St
- **Pathmark** • 160 E 125th St
- **Pioneer** • 1666 Madison Ave

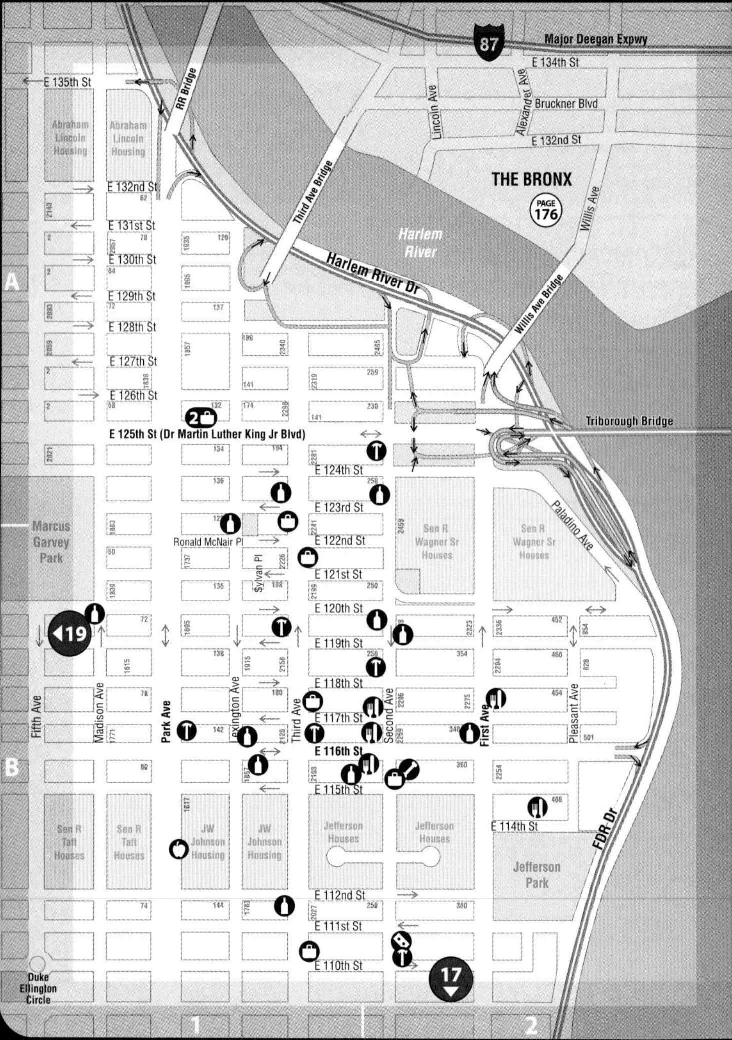

Map 20 • El Barrio

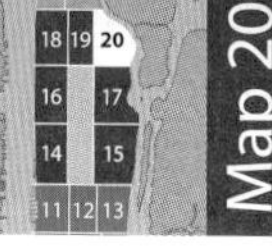

Patsy's Pizza really is the "original" New York thin-crust pizza, and Rao's is another New York landmark restaurant.

Farmer's Markets

- **La Marqueta** • E 115th St & Park Ave

Hardware Stores

- **A Vanderline Hardware** • 323 E 110th St
- **B&B Supply & Hardware** • 2338 Second Ave
- **N&J Locksmith & Hardware** • 1637 Park Ave
- **Novelle** • 218 E 125th St
- **SM Hardware** • 2139 Third Ave
- **Third Ave Home Center** • 2196 Third Ave

Liquor Stores

- **249 E 115th Liquor** • 249 E 115th St
- **Baez Liquor** • 2030 Third Ave
- **IC Liquors** • 2255 First Ave
- **Jebke Liquor Store** • 2010 Lexington Ave
- **Jesiry Liquor** • 1861 Lexington Ave
- **JM Liquor** • 1861 Lexington Ave
- **New York Beverage** • 207 E 123rd St
- **RA Landrau Liquors & Wines** • 2334 Second Ave
- **Ramos Liquor Store** • 1814 Madison Ave
- **Third Ave Liquors** • 2030 Third Ave

Pet Shops

- **Ideal Pet Warehouse** • 356 E 116th St

Restaurants

- **La Hacienda** • 219 E 116th St
- **Mi Mundo Bar & Restaurant** • 2259 Second Ave
- **Patsy's Pizza** • 2287 First Ave
- **Rao's** • 455 E 114th St
- **Sandy's Restaurant** • 2261 Second Ave

Shopping

- **The Children's Place** • 163 E 125th St
- **Gothic Cabinet Craft** • 2268 Third Ave
- **Mario's Italian Deli** • 2246 Second Ave
- **Motherhood Maternity** • 163 E 125th St
- **Payless Shoe Source** • 2143 Third Ave
- **R&S Strauss Auto** • 2005 Third Ave
- **VIM** • 2239 Third Ave

Video Rental

- **First Run Video** • 1147 1/2 Second Ave

Major Deegan Expwy
E 134th St
E 135th St
Bruckner Blvd
Lincoln Ave
Alexander Ave
E 132nd St
RR Bridge
Abraham Lincoln Housing
Abraham Lincoln Housing
THE BRONX
PAGE 176
Willis Ave
Third Ave Bridge
Harlem River
Harlem River Dr
Willis Ave Bridge
E 132nd St
E 131st St
E 130th St
E 129th St
E 128th St
E 127th St
E 126th St
125th Street
E 125th St (Dr Martin Luther King Jr Blvd)
Triborough Bridge
E 124th St
E 123rd St
E 122nd St
Ronald McNair Pl
Sylvan Pl
E 121st St
E 120th St
E 119th St
E 118th St
E 117th St
E 116th St
116th Street
E 115th St
E 114th St
E 112nd St
E 111st St
E 110th St
110th Street
Marcus Garvey Park
Sen R Wagner Sr Houses
Sen R Wagner Sr Houses
Paladino Ave
Fifth Ave
Madison Ave
Park Ave
Lexington Ave
Third Ave
Second Ave
First Ave
Pleasant Ave
FDR Dr
Sen R Taft Houses
Sen R Taft Houses
JW Johnson Housing
JW Johnson Housing
Jefferson Houses
Jefferson Houses
Jefferson Park
Duke Ellington Circle

The best route to the Triborough is to go up Third Avenue and make a right on 124th Street, especially when the FDR is jammed. We feel for the folks who live over on Pleasant Avenue and have to hike five miles to the nearest subway (or worse yet, wait for the bus).

Subways

4 5 6 .... 125 St
6 .... 110 St
6 .... 116 St

Bus Lines

1 .... Fifth/Madison Aves
101 ..... Third Ave/Lexington Ave/Amsterdam Ave
102 ..... Third Ave/Lexington Ave/Malcolm X Blvd
103 .... Third/Lexington Aves
116 .... 116th St Crosstown
15 .... First Ave/Second Ave
35 .... Randall's Island/Ward Island
60 .... LaGuardia Airport
98 .... Washington Heights/Midtown
Bx 15 .... 125th St Crosstown

Car Rental

- **Autorent Car Rental** • 220 E 117th St

Car Washes

- **JRP Carwash** • 247 E 127th St

Gas Stations

- **Amoco** • 125th St & Second Ave
- **Getty** • 2276 First Ave

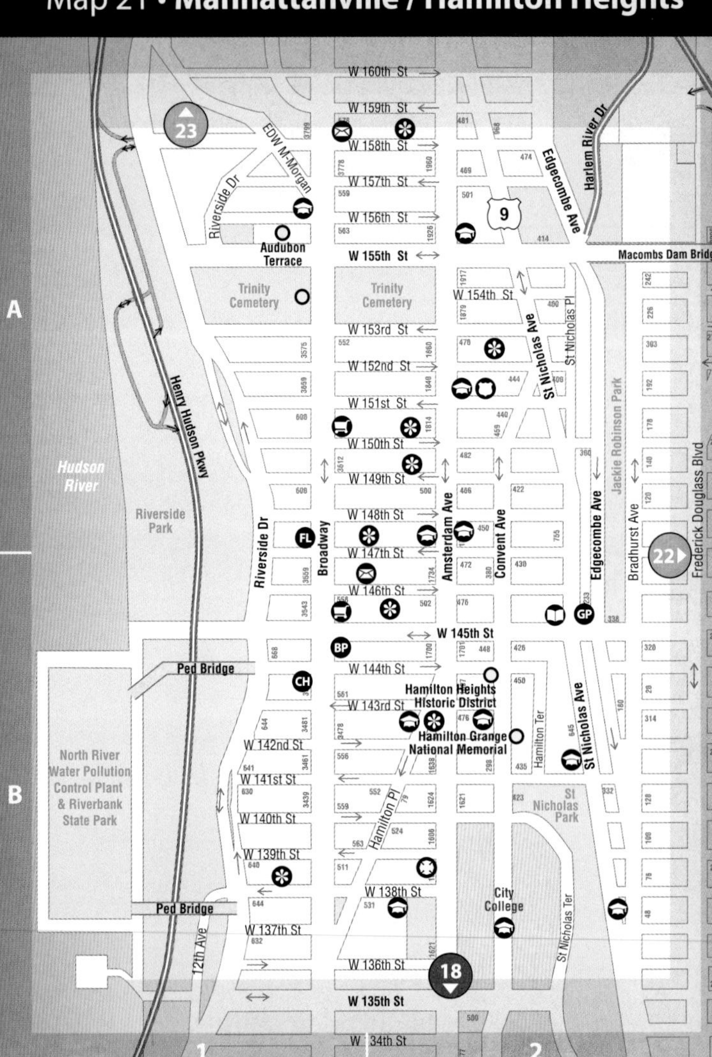
W 160th St
W 159th St
W 158th St
W 157th St
W 156th St
W 155th St
W 154th St
W 153rd St
W 152nd St
W 151st St
W 150th St
W 149th St
W 148th St
W 147th St
W 146th St
W 145th St
W 144th St
W 143rd St
W 142nd St
W 141st St
W 140th St
W 139th St
W 138th St
W 137th St
W 136th St
W 135th St
W 134th St
23
22
18
EDW M-Morgan
Riverside Dr
Audubon Terrace
Trinity Cemetery
Trinity Cemetery
Harlem River Dr
Edgecombe Ave
Macombs Dam Bridge
St Nicholas Ave
St Nicholas Pl
Jackie Robinson Park
Henry Hudson Pkwy
Hudson River
Riverside Park
Broadway
Amsterdam Ave
Convent Ave
Bradhurst Ave
Frederick Douglass Blvd
Ped Bridge
Hamilton Heights Historic District
Hamilton Grange National Memorial
Hamilton Ter
St Nicholas Park
North River Water Pollution Control Plant & Riverbank State Park
Hamilton Pl
City College
St Nicholas Ter
12th Ave
A
B
1
2

Essentials

This neighborhood is quite varied, both in its extremely hilly topography and in the side-by-side existence of run down areas with overlooked Manhattan landmarks such as Trinity Cemetery, Audubon Terrace and Sugar Hill. Convent Avenue and Hamilton Terrace are two of the prettiest streets in Manhattan—we (still) await "gentrification". Riverbank State Park should be the dictionary definition of the phrase "only in New York"—a park built over a sewage treatment plant.

ATMs

BP • Banco Popular • 3540 Broadway
CH • Chase • 3515 Broadway
FL • Fleet • 3579B Broadway
GP • Greenpoint Bank • 700 St Nicholas Ave

Community Gardens

Fire Departments

- **Engine 80, Ladder 23** • 503 W 139th St

Landmarks

- **Audubon Terrace** • Broadway & W 155th St
- **Hamilton Grange National Memorial** • 287 Convent Ave
- **Hamilton Heights Historic District** • W 141st- W 145th Sts & Convent Ave
- **Trinity Church Cemetery's Graveyard of Heroes** • 3699 Broadway

Libraries

- **Hamilton Grange** • 704 St Nicholas Ave

Police

- **30th Precinct** • 451 W 151st St

Post Offices

- **Fort Washington** • 556 W 158th St
- **Hamilton Grange** • 521 W 146th St

Schools

- **Boricua College** • 3755 Broadway
- **Childs' Memorial Christian Academy** • 1763 Amsterdam Ave
- **Dance Theatre of Harlem** • 466 W 152nd St
- **Harlem School of the Arts** • 645 St Nicholas Ave
- **Our Lady of Lourdes School** • 468 W 143rd St
- **PS 028 Wright Brothers School** • 475 W 155th St
- **PS 153 Adam C Powell School** • 1750 Amsterdam Ave
- **PS 192 Jacob H Schiff School** • 500 W 138th St
- **Thurgood Marshall Academy** • 6 Edgecombe Ave

Supermarkets

- **C-Town** • 3550 Broadway
- **C-Town** • 3632 Broadway

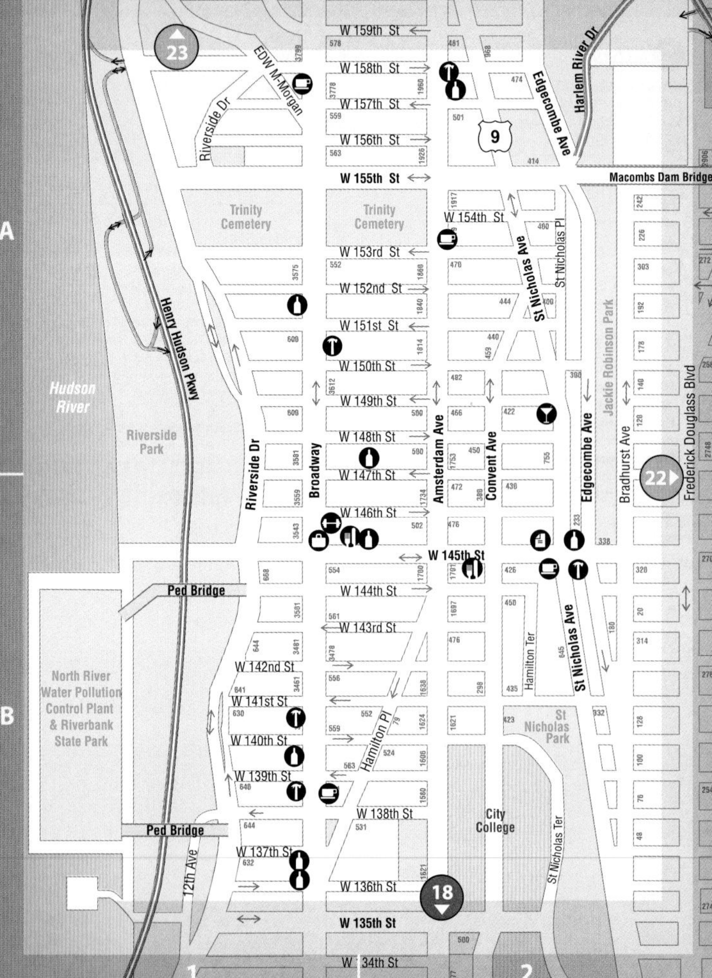

W 160th St
W 159th St
W 158th St
W 157th St
W 156th St
W 155th St
Macombs Dam Bridge
W 154th St
W 153rd St
W 152nd St
W 151st St
W 150th St
W 149th St
W 148th St
W 147th St
W 146th St
W 145th St
W 144th St
W 143rd St
W 142nd St
W 141st St
W 140th St
W 139th St
W 138th St
W 137th St
W 136th St
W 135th St
W 134th St
EDW M-Morgan
Riverside Dr
Harlem River Dr
Edgecombe Ave
Trinity Cemetery
Trinity Cemetery
St Nicholas Ave
St Nicholas Pl
Jackie Robinson Park
Henry Hudson Pkwy
Hudson River
Riverside Park
Broadway
Amsterdam Ave
Convent Ave
Bradhurst Ave
Frederick Douglass Blvd
Ped Bridge
Ped Bridge
North River Water Pollution Control Plant & Riverbank State Park
Hamilton Ter
Hamilton Pl
St Nicholas Park
City College
St Nicholas Ter
12th Ave
A
B
1
2
23
22
18
9

Sundries / Entertainment

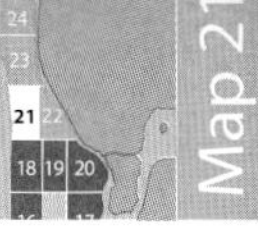

Sugar Hill Bistro is a fine example of how this neighborhood can improve over the next several years. Services, however, are still few and far between. In fact, this may be the first neighborhood ever that fought to get a Starbucks to stay.

Bars

- **St Nick's Pub** • 773 St Nicholas Ave

Coffee

- **Astron Coffee Shop** • 3795 Broadway
- **Coffee Shop** • 398 W 145th St
- **Fernando Coffee Shop** • 1875 Amsterdam Ave
- **Starbucks** • 3410 Broadway

Copy Shops

- **Our Community Copy Center (8 am-5:45 pm)** • 402 W 145th St

Gyms

- **NYC Fitness** • 3552 Broadway

Hardware Stores

- **Cohen & Cohen** • 1982 Amsterdam Ave
- **Felix Supply** • 3650 Broadway
- **Fred's Locksmith and Hardware** • 708 St Nicholas Ave
- **O&J Hardware** • 3405 Broadway
- **Westside Home Center** • 3447 Broadway

Liquor Stores

- **2001 Liquor** • 3671 Broadway
- **Brand's Liquor** • 550 W 145th St
- **HLK Liquors** • 3375 Broadway
- **JOCL Liquor Store** • 561 W 147th St
- **Jumasol Liquors** • 1963 Amsterdam Ave
- **La Alta Gracia Liquor Store** • 3435 Broadway
- **Reliable Wine & Liquor Shop** • 3375 Broadway
- **Unity Liquors** • 708 St Nicholas Ave

Restaurants

- **Copeland's** • 547 W 145th St
- **Sugar Hill Bistro** • 458 W 145th St

Shopping

- **VIM** • 508 W 145th St

Map 21 • Manhattanville / Hamilton Heights

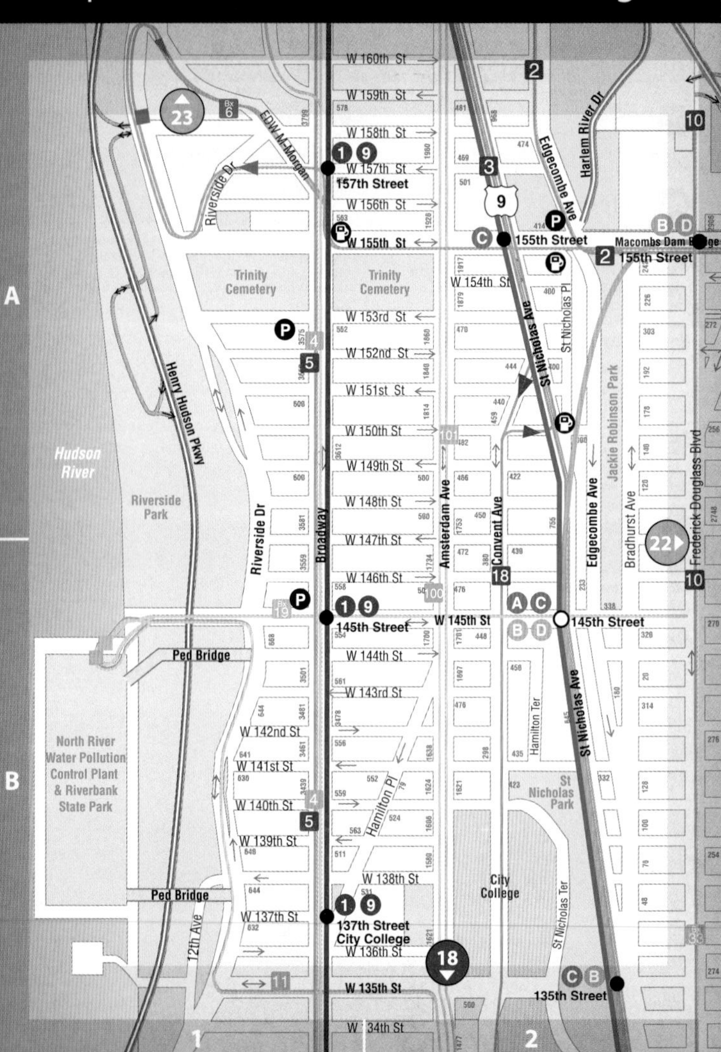

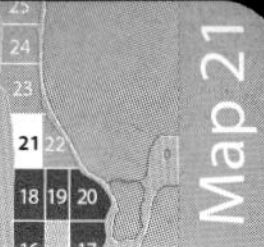

Despite the fact that the signs outside the 135th and 155th Street stations list the A and C trains, the A train stops at them only during late nights, when it runs local. Riverside Drive can be an intriguing alternative to traffic on during rush hour as one moves closer to the George Washington Bridge.

Subways

1 9 .... 137 St-City College
1 9 .... 145 St
1 9 .... 157 St
A C B D .... 145 St
C .... 155 St

Bus Lines

100 .... Amsterdam Ave/Broadway/125th St
101 .. Third Ave/Lexington Ave/Broadway/125th St
11 .... Ninth (Columbus)/Tenth (Amsterdam Ave)/Convent Ave
18 .... Convent Ave
2 .... Fifth Ave/Madison Ave/Powell Blvd
3 .... Fifth Ave/Madison Ave/St Nicholas Blvd
4 .... Fifth Ave/Madison Ave/Broadway
5 .... Fifth Ave/Sixth Ave/Riverside Dr
Bx 19 .... 145th St Crosstown
Bx 6 .... E 161st St/E 163rd St

Gas Stations

- **Getty** • 156 St Nicholas Pl
- **Mobil** • 3740 Broadway
- **Mobil** • 800 St Nicholas Ave

Parking

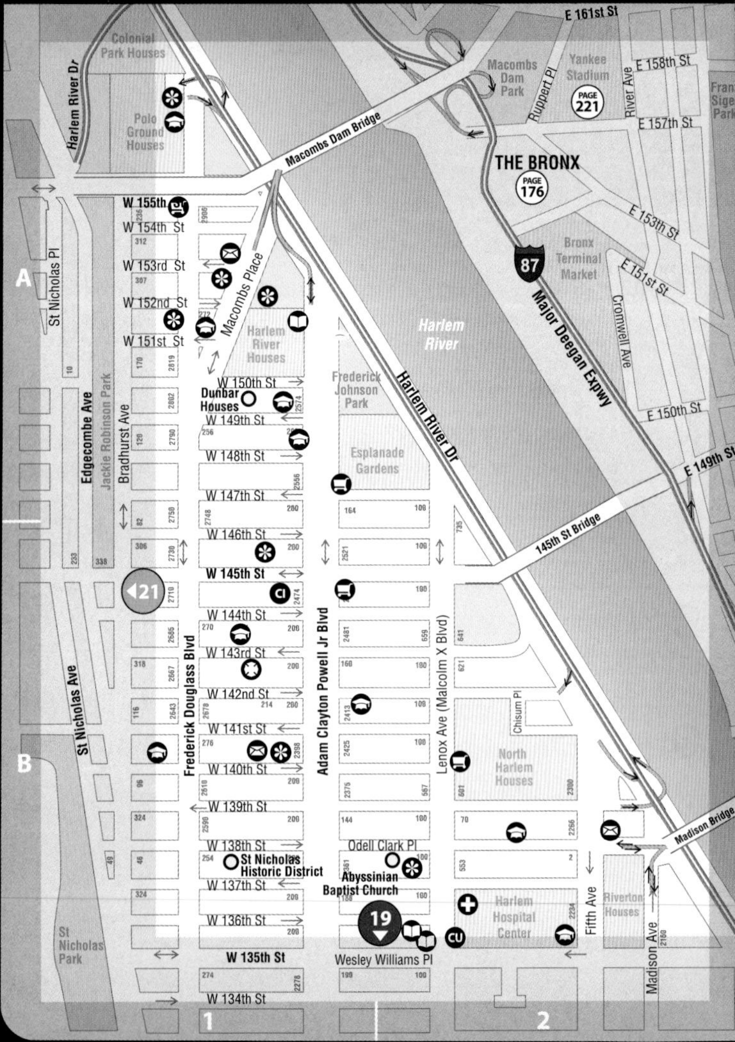

Map 22 • Harlem (Upper)

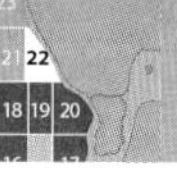

As much as people who live in the Polo Grounds Houses need housing, we really wish the Polo Grounds itself was still there.

ATMs

CI • Citibank • 2481 Adam Clayton Powell Jr Blvd
CU • Municipal Credit Union • 506 Lenox Ave

Community Gardens

Fire Departments

• **Engine 69, Ladder 28** • 248 W 143rd St

Hospitals

• **Harlem Hospital Center** • 506 Lenox Ave

Landmarks

• **Abyssinian Baptist Church** • 132 Odell Clark Pl
• **Dunbar Houses** • Frederick Douglass Blvd & W 149th St
• **St Nicholas Historic District** • 202 W 138th St

Libraries

• **Countee Cullen** • 104 W 136th St
• **Macomb's Bridge** • 2650 Adam Clayton Powell Jr Blvd
• **Schomburg Center for Research in Black Culture** • 515 Malcolm X Blvd

Post Offices

• **College Station** • 217 W 140th St
• **Colonial Park** • 99 Macombs Pl
• **Lincolnton** • 2266 Fifth Ave

Schools

• **Fredrick Douglas Secondary School** • 2581 Seventh Ave
• **PS 046 Tappan School** • 2987 Frederick Douglass Blvd
• **PS 123 Mahalia Jackson School** • 301 W 140th St
• **PS 194 Countee Cullen School** • 244 W 144th St
• **PS 197 John Russwurm School** • 2230 Fifth Ave
• **PS 200 James Smith School** • 2589 Seventh Ave
• **Resurrection School** • 282 W 151st St
• **St Charles Borromeo School** • 214 W 142nd St
• **St Mark the Evangelist School** • 55 W 138th St

Supermarkets

• **Associated** • 2927 Eighth Ave
• **Met Food** • 2541 Adam Clayton Powell Jr Blvd
• **Met Food** • 592 Lenox Ave
• **Pioneer** • 2497 Adam Clayton Powell Jr Blvd

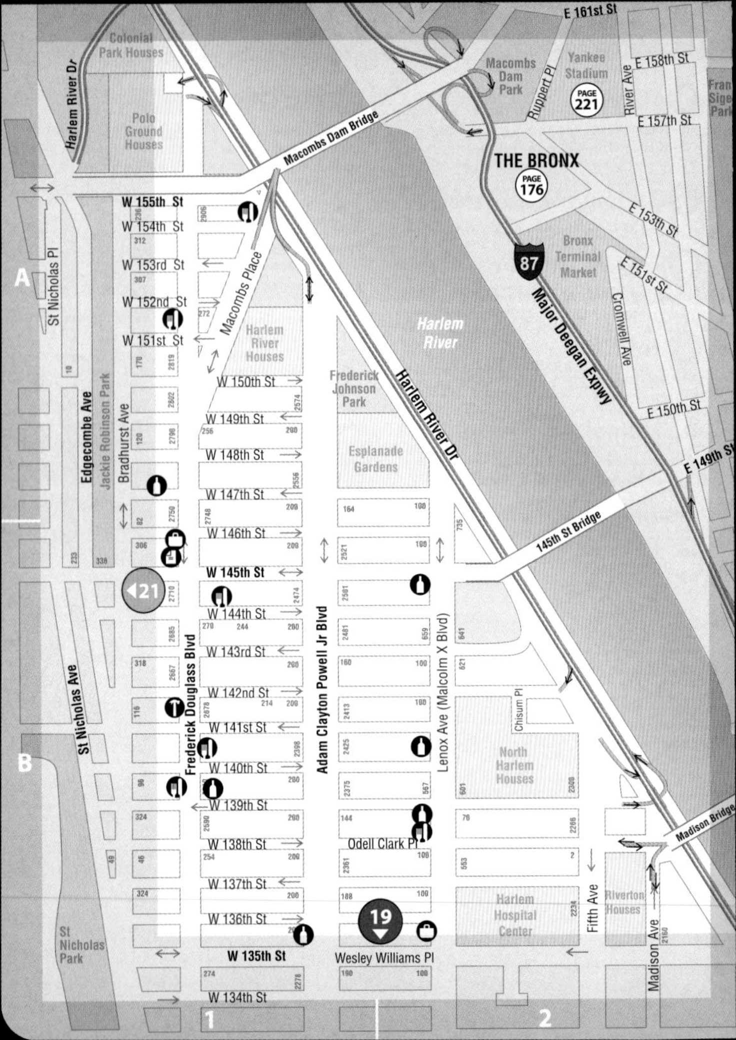

E 161st St
Colonial Park Houses
Macombs Dam Park
Ruppert Pl
Yankee Stadium
PAGE 221
River Ave
E 158th St
E 157th St
Harlem River Dr
Polo Ground Houses
Macombs Dam Bridge
THE BRONX
PAGE 176
W 155th St
W 154th St
W 153rd St
W 152nd St
W 151st St
W 150th St
W 149th St
W 148th St
W 147th St
W 146th St
W 145th St
W 144th St
W 143rd St
W 142nd St
W 141st St
W 140th St
W 139th St
W 138th St
W 137th St
W 136th St
W 135th St
W 134th St
E 153th St
E 151st St
Bronx Terminal Market
87
Major Deegan Expwy
Cromwell Ave
Macombs Place
Harlem River Houses
Harlem River
St Nicholas Pl
Frederick Johnson Park
Esplanade Gardens
E 150th St
E 149th St
Edgecombe Ave
Jackie Robinson Park
Bradhurst Ave
145th St Bridge
21
Frederick Douglass Blvd
Adam Clayton Powell Jr Blvd
Lenox Ave (Malcolm X Blvd)
St Nicholas Ave
Chisum Pl
North Harlem Houses
Madison Bridge
Odell Clark Pl
Fifth Ave
Harlem Hospital Center
Riverton Houses
Madison Ave
19
St Nicholas Park
Wesley Williams Pl
A
B
1
2

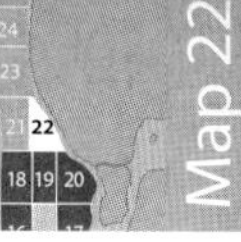

Charles' Southern-Style Chicken doesn't look very impressive, but the fried chicken is better, and way cheaper, than any 10 downtown faux-southern hipster restaurants. For a classic Italian throwback, hit the oddly-named Flash Inn, which sounds more like a strip club in LA.

Copy Shops

- **Kev's Copy Center (8:30 am-8 pm)** • 2730 Eighth Ave

Hardware Stores

- **B&E Hardware & Lockshop** • 2647 Frederick Douglass Blvd

Liquor Stores

- **All-Rite Liquors** • 2651 Frederick Douglass Blvd
- **Dorden Liquors** • 555 Lenox Ave
- **F&J Liquors** • 361 W 147th St
- **Friedland Wine & Liquor Store** • 605 Lenox Ave
- **Harlem Discount Liquors** • 2302 Adam Clayton Powell Jr Blvd
- **Luis Liquor** • 108 W 145th St

Restaurants

- **Charles's Southern-Style Chicken** • 2841 Eighth Ave
- **Flash Inn** • 107 Macombs Pl
- **Londel's Supper Club** • 2620 Frederick Douglass Blvd
- **Margie's Red Rose** • 267 W 144th St
- **Miss Mamie's/Miss Maude's** • 547 Lenox Ave
- **Sugar Shack** • 2611 Eighth Ave

Shopping

- **Baskin-Robbins** • 2730 Frederick Douglass Blvd
- **New York Public Library Shop** • 515 Malcolm X Blvd, Schomburg Ctr

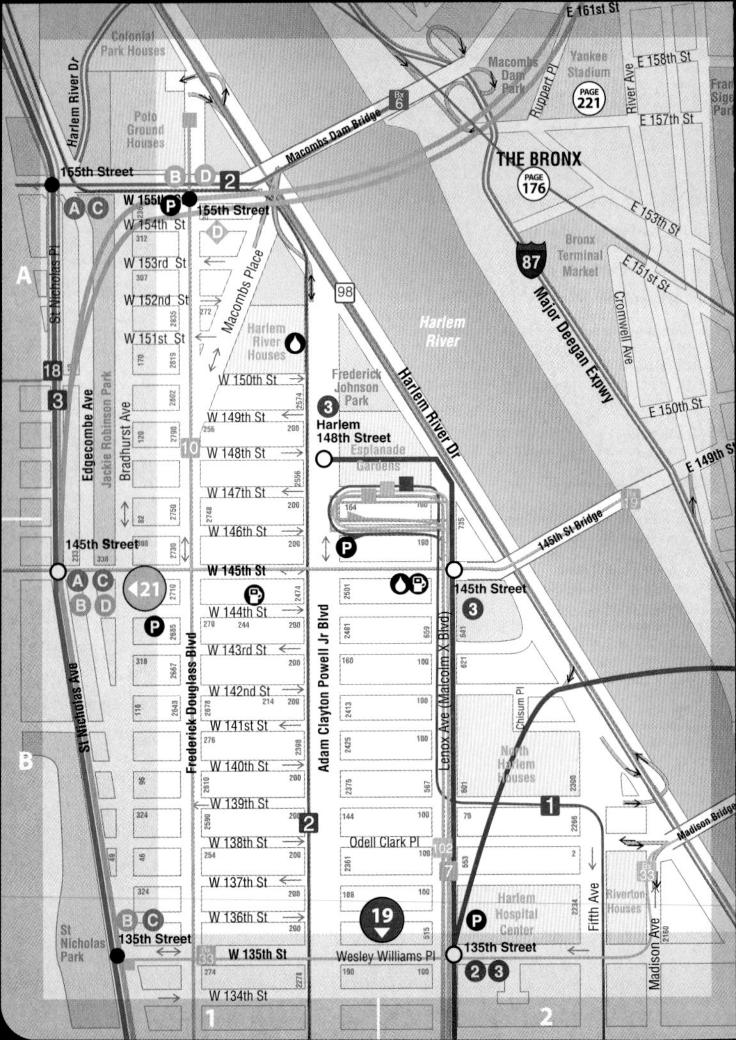

Colonial Park Houses
Polo Ground Houses
Harlem River Dr
155th Street
W 155th St
155th Street
Macombs Dam Bridge
Macombs Dam Park
Ruppert Pl
Yankee Stadium
River Ave
E 161st St
E 158th St
E 157th St
THE BRONX
E 153th St
E 151st St
E 150th St
E 149th St
Bronx Terminal Market
Major Deegan Expwy
Cromwell Ave
Harlem River
Macombs Place
Harlem River Houses
Frederick Johnson Park
Harlem 148th Street
Esplanade Gardens
Harlem River Dr
145th St Bridge
W 154th St
W 153rd St
W 152nd St
W 151st St
W 150th St
W 149th St
W 148th St
W 147th St
W 146th St
W 145th St
W 144th St
W 143rd St
W 142nd St
W 141st St
W 140th St
W 139th St
W 138th St
W 137th St
W 136th St
W 135th St
W 134th St
St Nicholas Pl
Edgecombe Ave
Jackie Robinson Park
Bradhurst Ave
145th Street
145th Street
St Nicholas Ave
Frederick Douglass Blvd
Adam Clayton Powell Jr Blvd
Lenox Ave (Malcolm X Blvd)
Chisum Pl
North Harlem Houses
Odell Clark Pl
Wesley Williams Pl
Harlem Hospital Center
Fifth Ave
Riverton Houses
Madison Ave
Madison Bridge
St Nicholas Park
135th Street
135th Street

PAGE 221
PAGE 176
21
19

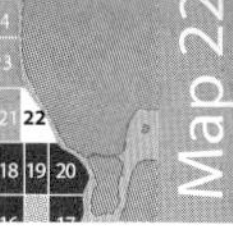

If the FDR Drive is jammed, feel free to drive up Frederick Douglass Boulevard, grab some fried chicken, and jump back on the FDR at 155th Street before heading out to the shopping paradise that is New Jersey.

Subways

3 .... 145 St
3 .... Harlem-148 St
B D .... 155 St

Bus Lines

1 .... Fifth Ave/Madison Ave
10 .... Seventh Ave/Eighth Ave (Central Park West)/Frederick Douglass Blvd
102 ..... Third Ave/Lexington Ave/Malcolm X Blvd
2 .... Fifth Ave/Madison Ave/Powell Blvd
7 .... Columbus Ave/Amsterdam Ave/ Sixth Ave/Seventh Ave/Broadway
98 .... Washington Heights/Midtown
Bx 19 .... 145th St Crosstown
Bx 33 .... 135th St Crosstown
Bx 6 .... E 161st St/E 163rd St

Car Washes

- **Harlem Hand Car Wash** • 2600 Adam Clayton Powell Jr Blvd
- **Los Amigos** • 119 W 145th St

Gas Stations

- **Amoco** • 232 W 145th St
- **Hess** • 128 W 145th St

Parking

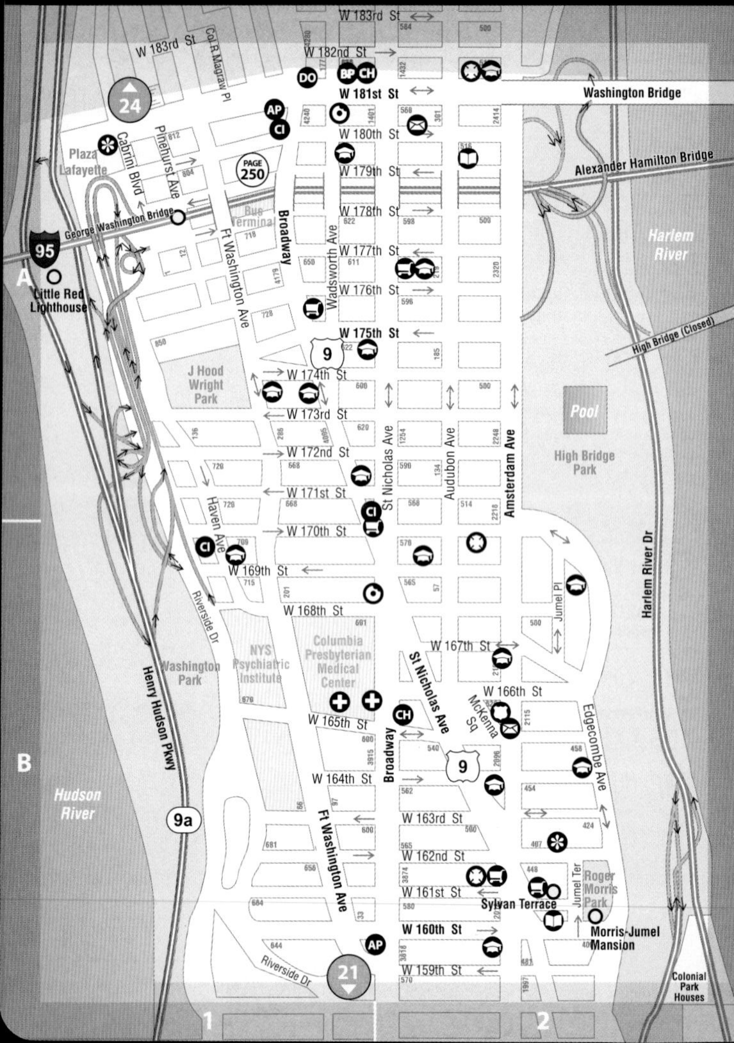

W 183rd St
W 182nd St
W 181st St
W 180th St
W 179th St
W 178th St
W 177th St
W 176th St
W 175th St
W 174th St
W 173rd St
W 172nd St
W 171st St
W 170th St
W 169th St
W 168th St
W 167th St
W 166th St
W 165th St
W 164th St
W 163rd St
W 162nd St
W 161st St
W 160th St
W 159th St

Col R Magraw Pl
Cabrini Blvd
Pinehurst Ave
Ft Washington Ave
Broadway
Wadsworth Ave
St Nicholas Ave
Audubon Ave
Amsterdam Ave
Haven Ave
Riverside Dr
Henry Hudson Pkwy
Edgecombe Ave
Jumel Pl
Jumel Ter
Sylvan Terrace
Harlem River Dr
McKenna Sq

Washington Bridge
Alexander Hamilton Bridge
George Washington Bridge
High Bridge (Closed)
Bus Terminal

Plaza Lafayette
Little Red Lighthouse
J Hood Wright Park
High Bridge Park
Pool
Washington Park
NYS Psychiatric Institute
Columbia Presbyterian Medical Center
Roger Morris Park
Morris-Jumel Mansion
Colonial Park Houses

Hudson River
Harlem River

95
9
9a

24
PAGE 250
21

A
B
1
2

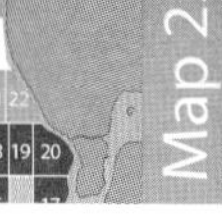

One of New York's more notorious neighborhoods of the last 20 years, Washington Heights has improved quite a bit since its days as the one-stop drug shop for Jersey, though it still has some problems. Sylvan Terrace is the most un-Manhattan-looking place in Manhattan—it's way cool.

ATMs

AP • **Apple** • 3815 Broadway
AP • **Apple** • 706 W 181st St
BP • **Banco Popular** • 615 W 181st St
CH • **Chase** • 1421 St Nicholas Ave
CH • **Chase** • 3940 Broadway
CI • **Citibank** • 4058 Broadway
CI • **Citibank** • 4249 Broadway
CI • **Citibank** • 60 Haven Ave
DO • **Doral Bank** • 4246 Broadway

Bagels

- **Bagel Cafe** • 657 W 181st St
- **Mike's Bagels** • 4003 Broadway

Community Gardens

Fire Departments

- **Engine 67** • 518 W 170th St
- **Engine 84, Ladder 34** • 515 W 161st St
- **Engine 93, Ladder 45** • 515 W 181st St

Hospitals

- **Columbia-Presbyterian Medical Center** • 622 W 168th St
- **Morgan Stanley Children's Hospital** • 3959 Broadway

Landmarks

- **George Washington Bridge** • W 178th St
- **Little Red Lighthouse** • under the George Washington Bridge
- **Morris-Jumel Mansion** • Edgecombe Ave & 161st St
- **Sylvan Terrace** • between Jumel Ter & St Nicholas Ave

Libraries

- **Fort Washington** • 535 W 179th St
- **Washington Heights** • 1000 St Nicholas Ave

Police

- **33rd Precinct** • 2120 Amsterdam Ave

Post Offices

- **Audubon** • 511 W 165th St
- **Washington Bridge** • 555 W 180th St

Schools

- **HS 552 Gregorio Luperon** • 516 W 181st St
- **Incarnation Elementary School** • 570 W 175th St
- **IS 164 Edward W Stitt School** • 401 W 164th St
- **IS 90** • 21 Jumel Pl
- **PS 004 Duke Ellington** • 500 W 160th St
- **PS 008 Luis Belliard** • 465 W 167th St
- **PS 115 Humboldt School** • 586 W 177th St
- **PS 128 Audubon School** • 560 W 169th St
- **PS 173** • 306 Ft Washington Ave
- **PS 210 21st Century Academy** • 4111 Broadway
- **St Rose of Lima** • 517 W 164th St
- **St Spyridon Parochial School** • 120 Wadsworth Ave

Supermarkets

- **Associated** • 2050 Amsterdam Ave
- **C-Town** • 1016 St Nicholas Ave
- **C-Town** • 1314 St Nicholas Ave
- **Gristede's** • 4037 Broadway

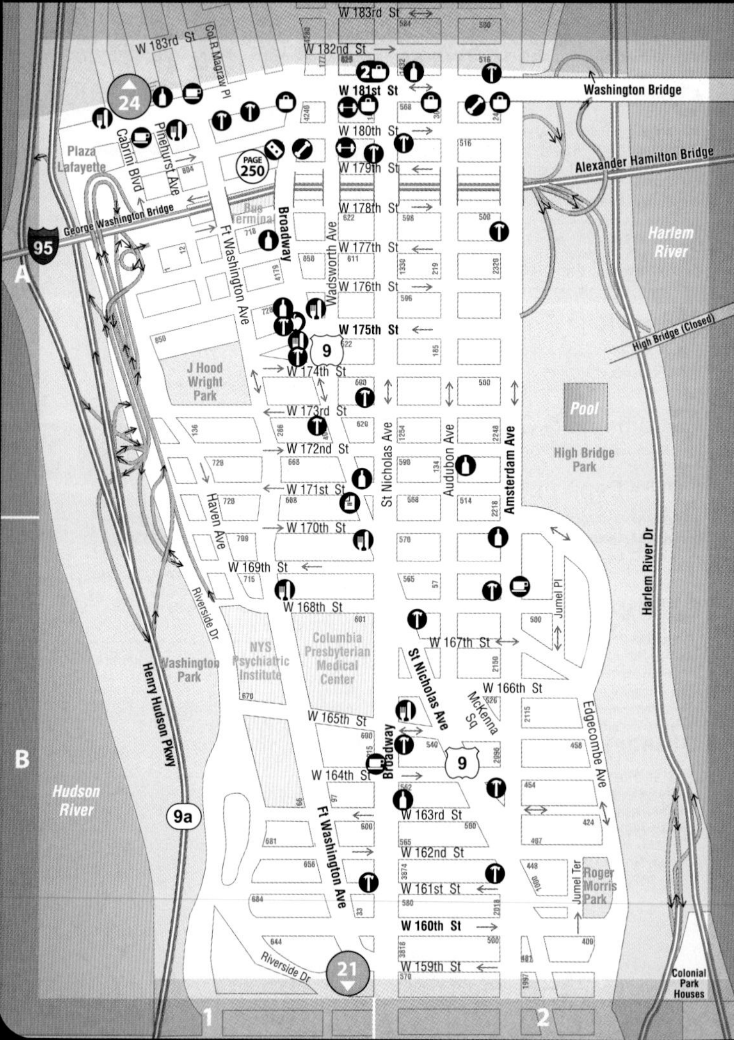

W 183rd St
W 182nd St
W 181st St
W 180th St
W 179th St
W 178th St
W 177th St
W 176th St
W 175th St
W 174th St
W 173rd St
W 172nd St
W 171st St
W 170th St
W 169th St
W 168th St
W 167th St
W 166th St
W 165th St
W 164th St
W 163rd St
W 162nd St
W 161st St
W 160th St
W 159th St
Col R Magraw Pl
Cabrini Blvd
Pinehurst Ave
Ft Washington Ave
Broadway
Wadsworth Ave
St Nicholas Ave
Audubon Ave
Amsterdam Ave
Haven Ave
Riverside Dr
Jumel Pl
Jumel Ter
Edgecombe Ave
McKenna Sq
Harlem River Dr
Henry Hudson Pkwy
Washington Bridge
Alexander Hamilton Bridge
High Bridge (Closed)
George Washington Bridge
Bus Terminal
Plaza Lafayette
J Hood Wright Park
High Bridge Park
Pool
Harlem River
Hudson River
Washington Park
NYS Psychiatric Institute
Columbia Presbyterian Medical Center
Roger Morris Park
Colonial Park Houses
PAGE 250
24
21
95
9
9a
A
B
1
2

Sundries / Entertainment

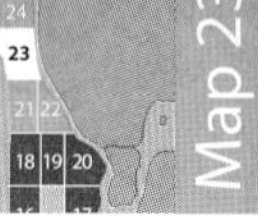

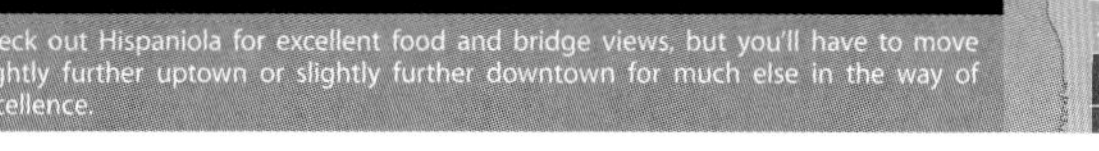
Check out Hispaniola for excellent food and bridge views, but you'll have to move slightly further uptown or slightly further downtown for much else in the way of excellence.

Coffee

- **Cafe Emilou** • 829 W 181st St
- **Chris Coffee Shop** • 500 W 168th St
- **Hathie's Coffee Shop** • 3915 Broadway
- **Starbucks** • 803 W 181st St

Copy Shops

- **The UPS Store (8:30 am-7 pm)** • 4049 Broadway

Farmer's Markets

- **Washington Heights Greenmarket** • Broadway & 175th St

Gyms

- **Big Gym** • 625 W 181st St
- **Lucille Roberts Health Club** • 1387 St Nicholas Ave

Hardware Stores

- **3841 Hardware** • 3841 Broadway
- **756 Hardware** • 756 W 181st St
- **AT Mini Hardware** • 1388 St Nicholas Ave
- **AHS Hardware** • 2416 Amsterdam Ave
- **Blue Bell Lumber** • 2360 Amsterdam Ave
- **Bridge Hardware** • 4193 Broadway
- **Chavin Hardware** • 1348 St Nicholas Ave
- **Cibao Hardware** • 1041 St Nicholas Ave
- **E&T Hardware** • 4087 Broadway
- **Ernesto's Hardware Store** • 2180 Amsterdam Ave
- **EZ Open Hardware** • 2304 Amsterdam Ave
- **Fort Washington Hardware** • 3918 Broadway
- **Martinez Hardware** • 1269 St Nicholas Ave
- **Nunez Hardware** • 4147 Broadway
- **Taveras Hardware** • 2029 Amsterdam Ave
- **Washington Heights Hardware** • 736 W 181st St

Liquor Stores

- **All-Star Spirits** • 4189 Broadway
- **Cabrina Wines & Liquors** • 831 W 181st St
- **Galicia Liquors** • 3906 Broadway
- **Guadalupe Barbara** • 4084 Broadway
- **Heights Liquor Supermarket** • 547 W 181st St
- **In Good Spirits** • 3819 Broadway
- **McLiquor Store** • 2208 Amsterdam Ave
- **Vargas Liquor Store** • 114 Audubon Ave

Pet Shops

- **Pet Place** • 518 W 181st St

Restaurants

- **Dallas BBQ** • 3956 Broadway
- **El Malecon** • 4141 Broadway
- **El Ranchito** • 4129 Broadway
- **Empire Szechuan** • 4041 Broadway
- **Hispaniola** • 839 W 181st St
- **Jessie's Place** • 812 W 181st St
- **Kismat** • 187 Ft Washington Ave

Shopping

- **The Children's Place** • 600 W 181st St
- **Baskin-Robbins** • 728 W 181st St
- **Goodwill Industries** • 512 W 181st St
- **Modell's** • 606 W 181st St
- **Payless Shoe Source** • 617 W 181st St
- **VIM** • 561 W 181st St

Video Rental

- **Blockbuster Video** • 4211 Broadway

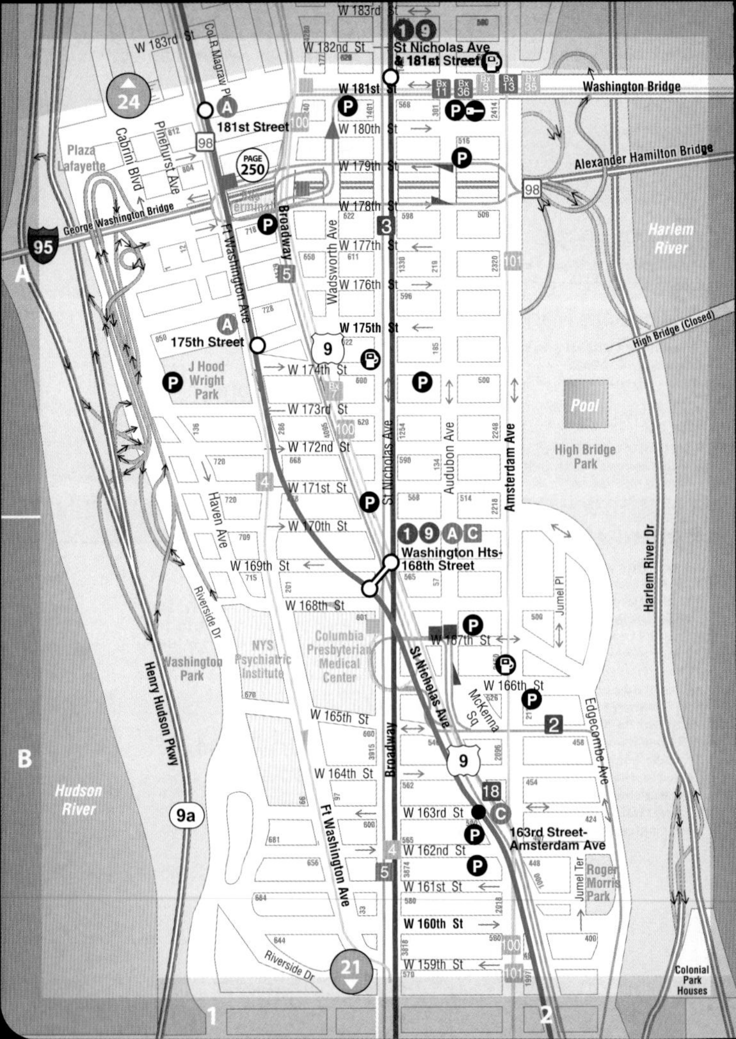

PAGE 250
24
21

Pay close attention when you cross over into Manhattan from New Jersey on the George Washington Bridge, because if you miss the "Harlem River Drive–Last Exit in Manhattan" exit, you'll be crossing over into the Bronx and sitting in traffic on what is categorically the most miserable highway in all the world, the Cross Bronx Expressway.

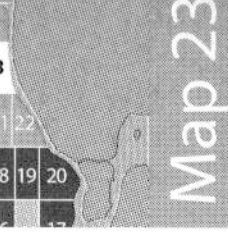

Subways

- 1 9 .... 181 St
- A .... 175 St
- A .... 181 St
- 1 9 A C .... 168 St-Washington Hts
- C .... 163 St-Amsterdam Ave

Bus Lines

- 100 .... Amsterdam Ave/Broadway/125th St
- 101 .... Third and Lexington Aves/Malcolm X Blvd
- 18 .... Convent Ave
- 2 .... Fifth and Madison Aves/ Adam Clayton Powell Jr Blvd
- 3 .... Fifth and Madison Aves/St Nicholas Ave
- 4 .... Fifth and Madison Aves/Broadway
- 5 .... Fifth Ave/Sixth Ave/Riverside Dr
- 98 .... Washington Heights/Midtown
- Bx 11 .... to Southern Blvd via 170th St
- Bx 13 .... to Yankee Stadium via Ogden Ave
- Bx 3 .... to Riverdale, 238th St-Broadway
- Bx 35 .... to West Farms Rd via 167th St
- Bx 36 .... to Olmstead Ave/Randall Ave via 180th St
- Bx 7 .... Riverdale Ave/Broadway

Car Rental

- **Discount Car Rental** • 506 W 181St St

Gas Stations

- **Getty** • 4116 Broadway
- **Shell** • 2157 Amsterdam Ave
- **Shell** • 2420 Amsterdam Ave

Parking

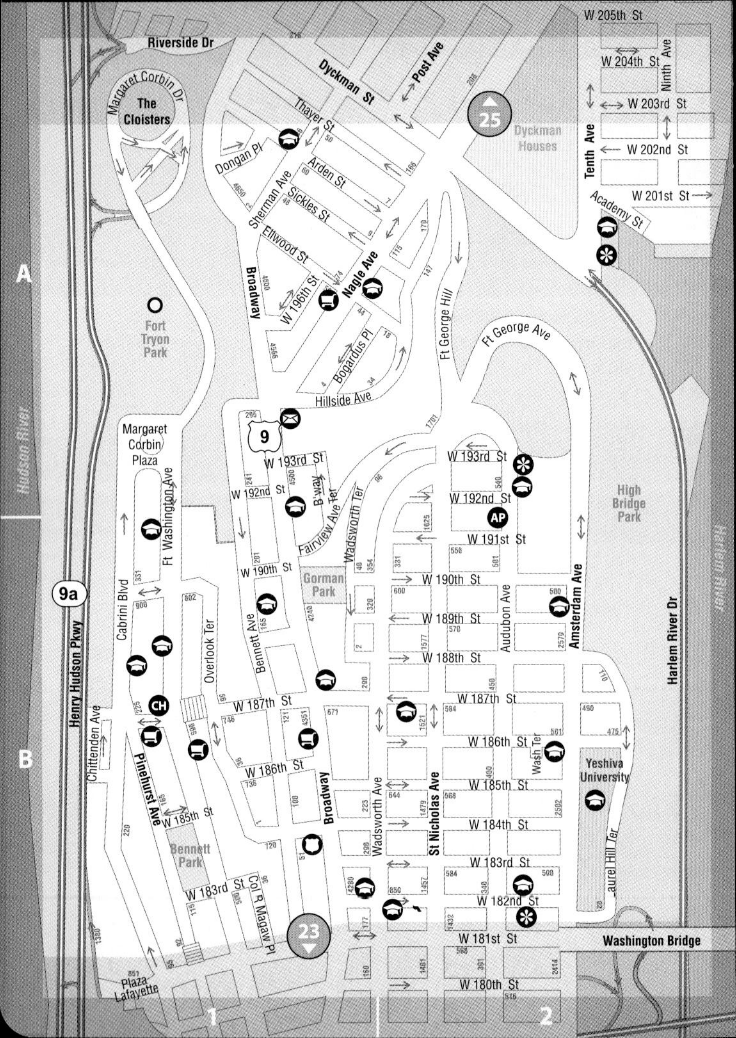

Map 24 • Fort George / Fort Tyron

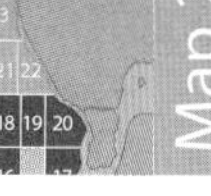

You'll get a workout walking up and down all the hills and stairs in this neighborhood. Fort Tryon Park, including the Cloisters Museum, is a treasure that allows visitors to gaze over the Hudson and go for a hike right in the city.

ATMs

AP • **Apple** • 515 Audubon Ave
CH • **Chase** • 596 Ft Washington Ave

Community Gardens

Landmarks

• **Fort Tyron Park** • Ft Washington Ave

Police

• **34th Precinct** • 4295 Broadway

Post Offices

• **Fort George** • 4558 Broadway

Schools

• **George Washington High School Complex: George Washington High, Health Careers & Sciences High, Business & Finance High, Law & Public Service High, and Media & Communications High** • 549 Audubon Ave
• **IS 143 Eleanor Roosevelt School** • 511 W 182nd St
• **IS 218 Salome Ukena School** • 4600 Broadway
• **Mestiva Rabbi Samson Raphael** • 220 Bennett Ave
• **Mother Cabrini High School** • 701 Ft Washington Ave
• **Our Lady Queen of Martyrs** • 71 Arden St
• **PS 005 Ellen Lurie School** • 3703 Tenth Ave
• **PS 048 Officer Buczek School** • 4360 Broadway
• **PS 132 Juan Pablo Duarte School** • 185 Wadsworth Ave
• **PS 152 Dyckman Valley School** • 93 Nagle Ave
• **PS 187/IS 287 Hudson Cliffs School** • 349 Cabrini Blvd
• **PS 189** • 2580 Amsterdam Ave
• **PS 528 Bea Fuller Rodgers School** • 180 Wadsworth Ave
• **St Elizabeth School** • 612 W 187th St
• **Yeshiva University** • 500 W 185th St
• **Yeshiva University High School** • 2540 Amsterdam Ave

Supermarkets

• **Associated** • 592 Ft Washington Ave
• **Frank's Meat Market** • 811 W 187th St
• **Key Food** • 4365 Broadway
• **Pioneer** • 72 Nagle Ave

Riverside Dr
Margaret Corbin Dr
The Cloisters
Dyckman St
Post Ave
Thayer St
Dongan Pl
Arden St
Sherman Ave
Sickles St
Ellwood St
Nagle Ave
Broadway
W 196th St
Bogardus Pl
Hillside Ave
Fort Tryon Park
Ft George Hill
Ft George Ave
Dyckman Houses
W 205th St
W 204th St
Ninth Ave
W 203rd St
Tenth Ave
W 202nd St
W 201st St
Academy St
Hudson River
Harlem River
High Bridge Park
Margaret Corbin Plaza
Ft Washington Ave
Cabrini Blvd
W 193rd St
W 192nd St
B'way
Fairview Ave
Wadsworth Ter
W 191st St
W 190th St
Gorman Park
W 189th St
W 188th St
Bennett Ave
Overlook Ter
Audubon Ave
Amsterdam Ave
Harlem River Dr
W 187th St
W 186th St
Wash Ter
Yeshiva University
W 185th St
W 184th St
St Nicholas Ave
Wadsworth Ave
Henry Hudson Pkwy
Chittenden Ave
Pinehurst Ave
Bennett Park
W 183rd St
Col R Magaw Pl
Laurel Hill Ter
W 182nd St
W 181st St
Washington Bridge
W 180th St
Plaza Lafayette
9a
9
23
25
A
B
1
2

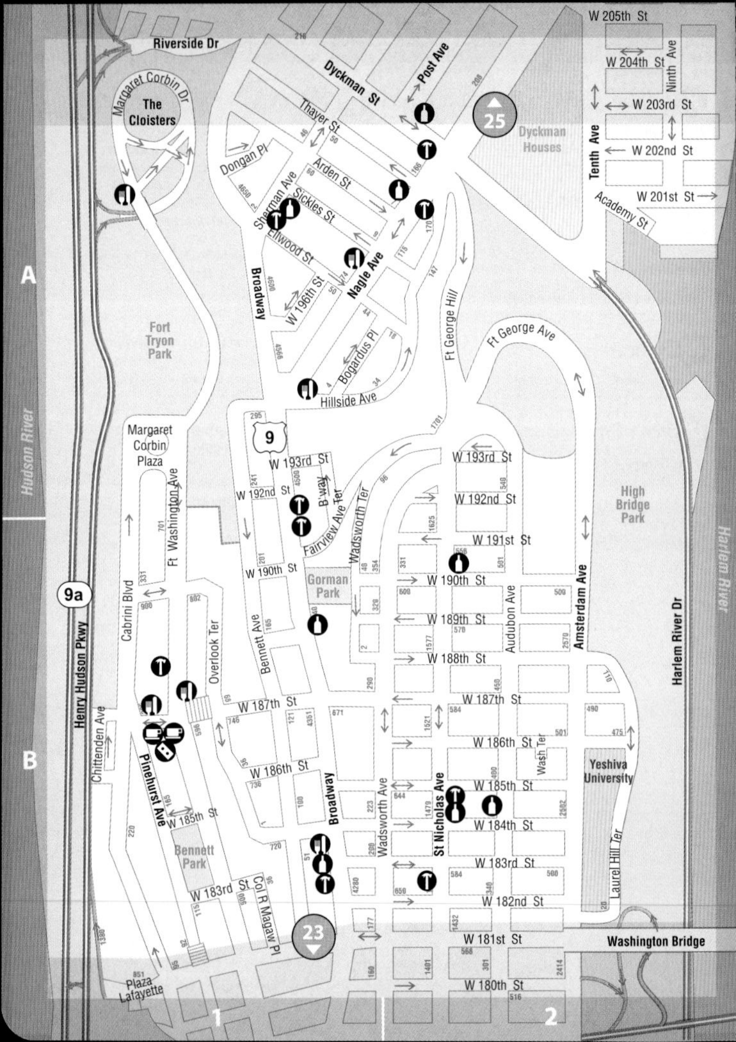

Sundries / Entertainment

Anyone who says northern Manhattan has nothing cool to do hasn't been here. Lots of small independent restaurants combine downtown ambience with small-town feel and uptown prices—check out Bleu Evolution and the rest of W 187th near Ft Washington.

Coffee

- **Angela's Coffee Shop** • 805 W 187th St
- **The Monkey Room** • 189 Ft Washington Ave

Hardware Stores

- **Apex Supply** • 4580 Broadway
- **Castillo Hardware** • 1449 St Nicholas Ave
- **Century Hardware** • 4309 Broadway
- **Geomart Hardware** • 607 Ft Washington Ave
- **Nagle Hardware Store** • 145 Nagle Ave
- **St Nicholas Hardware** • 1488 St Nicholas Ave
- **Supreme Hardware** • 106 Dyckman St
- **Victor Hardware Store** • 25 Sherman Ave
- **VNJ Hardware** • 4476 Broadway

Liquor Stores

- **185 Street Liquor Store** • 4329 Broadway
- **Alex's Liquor Store** • 1598 St Nicholas Ave
- **Dyckman Liquors** • 121 Dyckman St
- **J&P Discount Liquors** • 377 Audubon Ave
- **Las Vegas Wine & Liquor** • 154 Nagle Ave
- **Sanchez Liquors** • 4500 Broadway
- **Sherman Liquor** • 25 Sherman Ave
- **Yuan & Yuan Wine & Liquors** • 1492 St Nicholas Ave

Restaurants

- **107 West** • 811 W 187th St
- **Bleu Evolution** • 808 W 187th St
- **Caridad Restaurant** • 4311 Broadway
- **Frank's Pizzeria** • 94 Nagle Ave
- **New Leaf Cafe** • 1 Margaret Corbin Dr
- **Rancho Jubilee** • 1 Nagle Ave

Video Rental

- **Ft Washington Video** • 805 W 187th St

Map 24 • Fort George / Fort Tyron

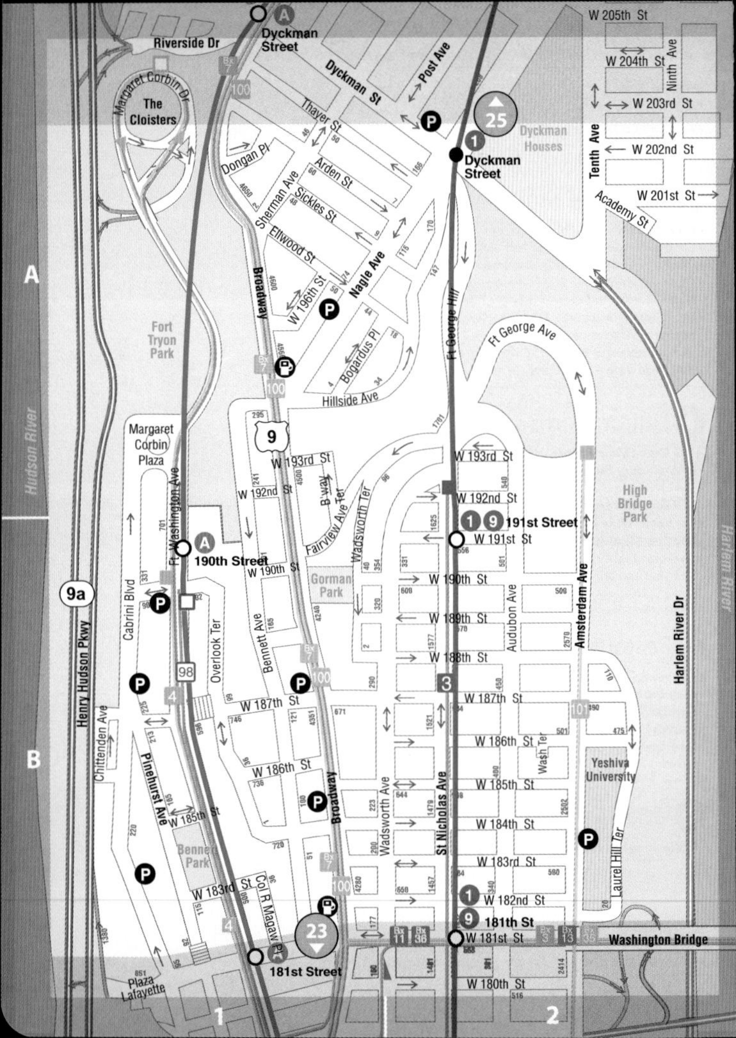

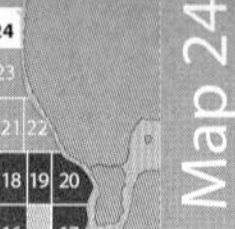

Living on the A line is a blessing before 11 pm, when it runs express, but beware at night when you'll have to sit through every stop between 59th and 125th and beyond. Tight streets, double parking, and bad drivers always makes driving in this area interesting.

Subways

1 .... Dyckman St
1 9 .... 191 St
A .... 190 St

Bus Lines

100 .... Broadway
100 .... Amsterdam Ave
3 .... St Nicholas Ave
4 .... Ft Washington Ave
98 .... Ft Washington Ave

Bx 7 .... Broadway

Gas Stations

- **Rammco Service Station** • 4275 Broadway
- **Sunoco** • 4469 Broadway

Parking

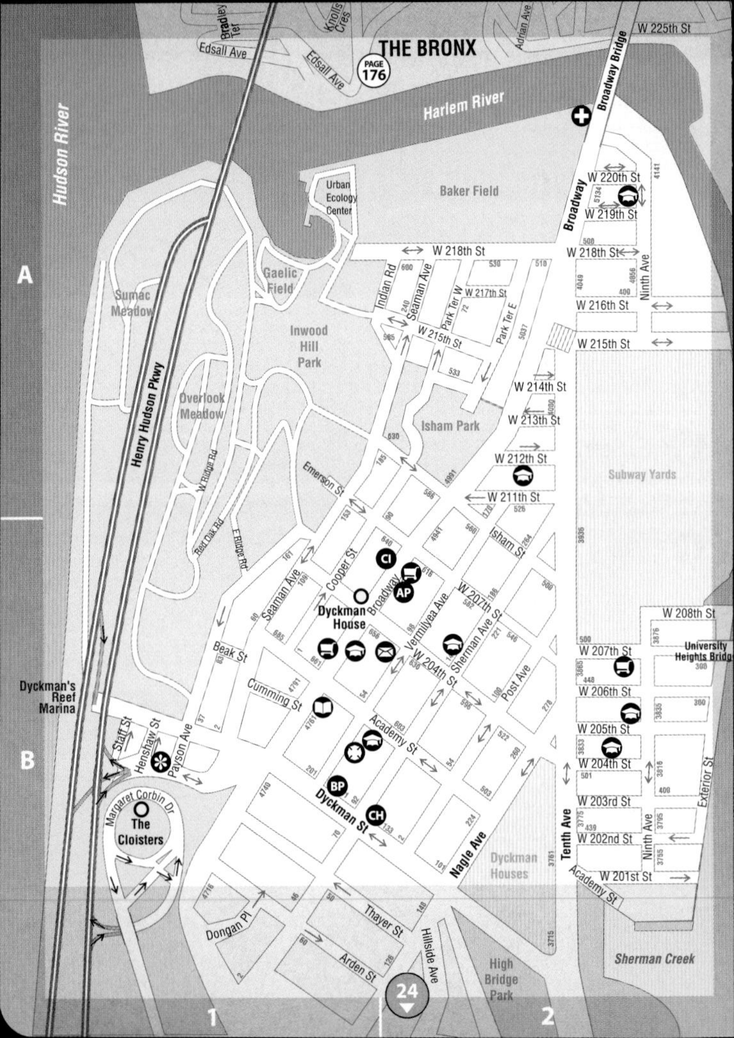

THE BRONX
PAGE 176
Hudson River
Harlem River
Bradley Ter
Knolls Cres
Adrian Ave
Edsall Ave
W 225th St
Broadway Bridge
Broadway
Baker Field
Urban Ecology Center
W 220th St
W 219th St
W 218th St
Gaelic Field
Sumac Meadow
Inwood Hill Park
Indian Rd
Seaman Ave
Park Ter W
Park Ter E
W 217th St
W 216th St
Ninth Ave
W 215th St
W 214th St
W 213th St
Isham Park
W 212th St
W 211th St
Subway Yards
Overlook Meadow
Henry Hudson Pkwy
W Ridge Rd
Red Oak Rd
E Ridge Rd
Emerson St
Isham St
Cooper St
Dyckman House
Vermilyea Ave
W 207th St
Sherman Ave
W 204th St
Post Ave
Beak St
Cumming St
Academy St
Dyckman St
Nagle Ave
W 208th St
University Heights Bridge
W 207th St
W 206th St
W 205th St
W 204th St
W 203rd St
W 202nd St
W 201st St
Tenth Ave
Exterior St
Dyckman Houses
Academy St
Dyckman's Reef Marina
Staff St
Henshaw St
Payson Ave
Margaret Corbin Dr
The Cloisters
Dongan Pl
Thayer St
Arden St
Hillside Ave
High Bridge Park
Sherman Creek

24

A
B
1
2

Inwood is definitely Manhattan's best-kept housing secret—the houses along Payson Avenue and Seaman Avenue are very nice. Inwood Hill Park is a shady, overgrown, semi-wild park with a killer view of the Cloisters and Fort Tryon Park. Inwood also contains one of Manhattan's oldest buildings, the Dyckman House (it looks it!).

AP • Apple • 4950 Broadway
BP • Banco Popular • 175 Dyckman St
CH • Chase • 161 Dyckman St
CI • Citibank • 4949 Broadway

- **Engine 95, Ladder 36** • 29 Vermilyea Ave

- **Columbia-Presbyterian Allen Pavilion** • 5141 Broadway

Landmarks

- **The Cloisters** • Ft Tryon Park
- **Dyckman House** • 4881 Broadway

Libraries

- **Inwood** • 4790 Broadway

Post Offices

- **Inwood Post Office** • 90 Vermilyea Ave

Schools

- **IS 052 Inwood School** • 650 Academy St
- **Manhattan Christian Academy** • 401 W 205th St
- **PS 018** • 4124 Ninth Ave
- **PS 098 Shorac Kappock School** • 512 W 212nd St
- **PS 176** • 4862 Broadway
- **St Jude School** • 433 W 204th St
- **St Matthew Lutheran School** • 200 Sherman Ave

Supermarkets

- **C-Town** • 4918 Broadway
- **Fine Fare Supermarket** • 4776 Broadway
- **Pathmark** • 410 W 207th St

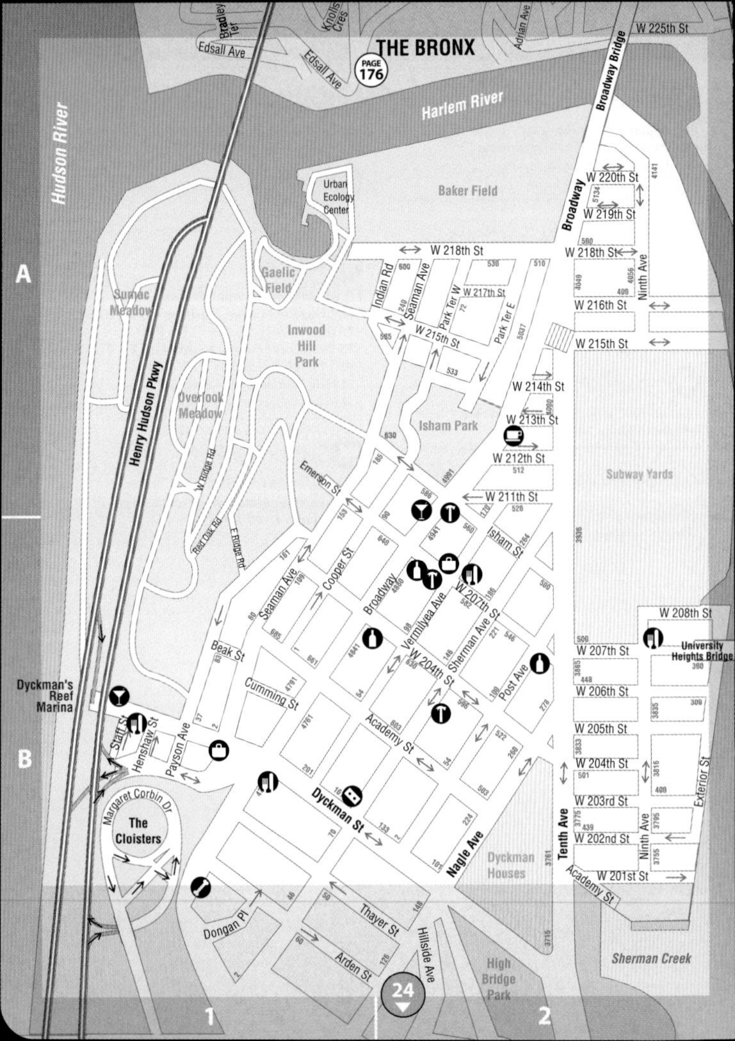

THE BRONX

PAGE 176

Harlem River

Hudson River

Baker Field

Urban Ecology Center

Gaelic Field

Sumac Meadow

Inwood Hill Park

Overlook Meadow

Isham Park

Subway Yards

Henry Hudson Pkwy

Broadway Bridge

University Heights Bridge

Dyckman's Reef Marina

The Cloisters

Dyckman Houses

High Bridge Park

Sherman Creek

A

B

1

2

24

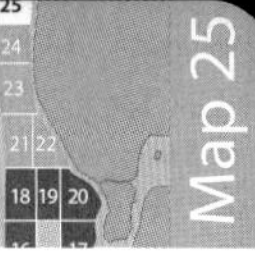

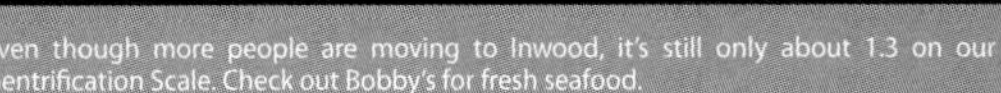

Even though more people are moving to Inwood, it's still only about 1.3 on our Gentrification Scale. Check out Bobby's for fresh seafood.

Bars

- **Piper's Kilt** • 4944 Broadway
- **Tubby Hook Cafe** • 348 Dyckman St

Coffee

- **JCT Coffee Shop** • 5009 Broadway

Hardware Stores

- **Dick's Hardware** • 4947 Broadway
- **Inwood Paint & Hardware** • 165 Sherman Ave
- **J&A Hardware** • 132 Vermilyea Ave

Liquor Stores

- **Esposito Wines & Liquors** • 608 W 207th St
- **PJ Liquor Warehouse** • 4898 Broadway
- **Q Royal** • 529 W 207th St

Pet Shops

- **Pic a Pet** • 4701 Broadway

Restaurants

- **Bobby's Fish and Seafood Market and Restaurant** • 3842 Ninth Ave
- **Cloisters Restaurant Pizza** • 4754 Broadway
- **Hoppin' Jalapenos Bar & Grill** • 597 W 207th St

Shopping

- **Payless Shoe Source** • 560 W 207th St
- **Tread Bicycles** • 225 Dyckman St
- **VIM** • 565 W 207th St

Video Rental

- **Blockbuster Video** • 165 Dyckman St

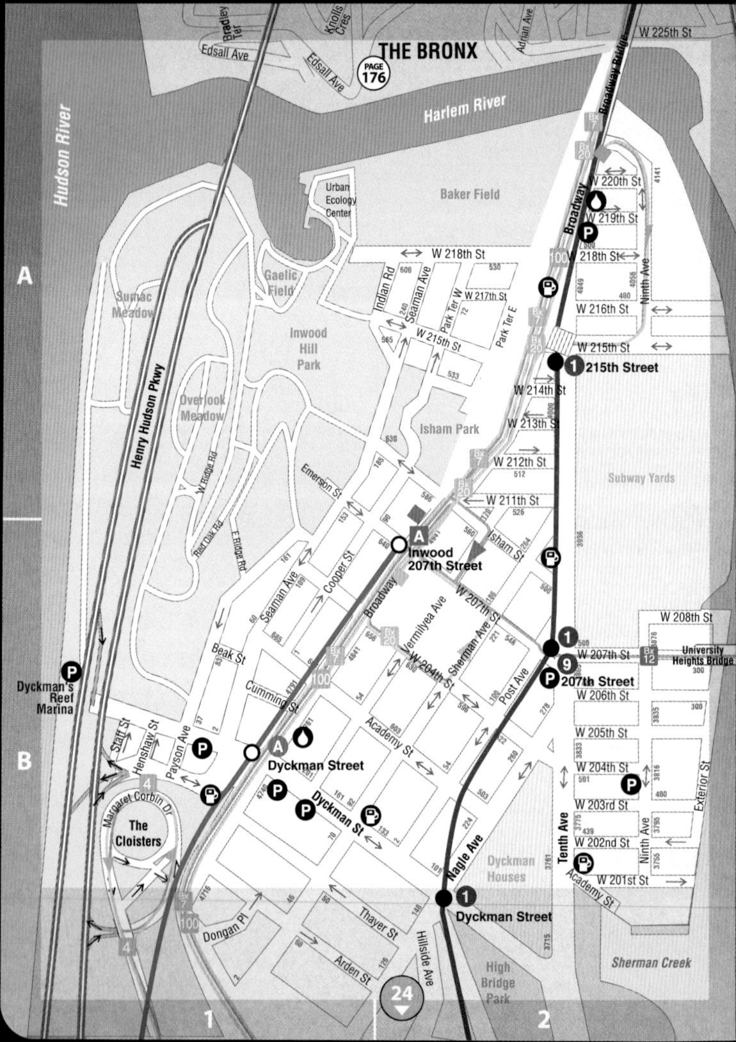

Map 25 • Inwood

THE BRONX
PAGE 176
Bradley Ter
Knolls Cres
Adrian Ave
W 225th St
Edsall Ave
Broadway Bridge
Harlem River
Hudson River
Urban Ecology Center
Baker Field
W 220th St
W 219th St
W 218th St
W 217th St
W 216th St
W 215th St
Broadway
Ninth Ave
Indian Rd
Seaman Ave
Park Ter W
Park Ter E
Gaelic Field
Sumac Meadow
Inwood Hill Park
215th Street
W 214th St
W 213th St
W 212th St
W 211th St
Henry Hudson Pkwy
Overlook Meadow
Isham Park
Subway Yards
W Ridge Rd
Red Oak Rd
E Bridge Rd
Emerson St
Inwood 207th Street
Isham St
Cooper St
W 207th St
W 208th St
University Heights Bridge
Vermilyea Ave
Sherman Ave
W 204th St
Post Ave
207th Street
W 206th St
W 205th St
W 204th St
W 203rd St
W 202nd St
W 201st St
Beak St
Cumming St
Academy St
Dyckman's Reef Marina
Staff St
Henshaw St
Payson Ave
Dyckman Street
Dyckman St
Margaret Corbin Dr
The Cloisters
Nagle Ave
Dyckman Houses
Tenth Ave
Exterior St
Academy St
Dyckman Street
Dongan Pl
Thayer St
Arden St
Hillside Ave
High Bridge Park
Sherman Creek

24

A
B
1
2

The stupid toll plaza at the tip of the Henry Hudson is only one of many reasons why driving in New York is nothing short of a nightmare. You might as well be getting your car washed at one of Inwood's many fine establishments. Parking is usually not too much of a problem, even close to Inwood Hill Park.

Subways

- 1 .... 215 St
- 1 9 .... 207 St
- A .... Dyckman St
- A .... Inwood-207 St

Bus Lines

- 100 .... Amsterdam Ave/Broadway/125th St
- 4 .... Fifth/Madison Aves/Broadway
- Bx12 .... Riverdale/263rd St via Riverdale Ave
- Bx20 .... Riverdale/246th St via Henry Hudson Pky
- Bx7 .... Riverdale Ave/Broadway

Car Washes

- **Broadway Bridge Car Wash** • 5134 Broadway
- **Broadway Hand Car Wash** • 4778 Broadway

Gas Stations

- **BP** • 204th St & Tenth Ave
- **Getty** • 242 Dyckman St
- **Getty** • 4880 Broadway
- **Shell** • 3761 Tenth Ave
- **Sunoco** • 3936 Tenth Ave

Parking

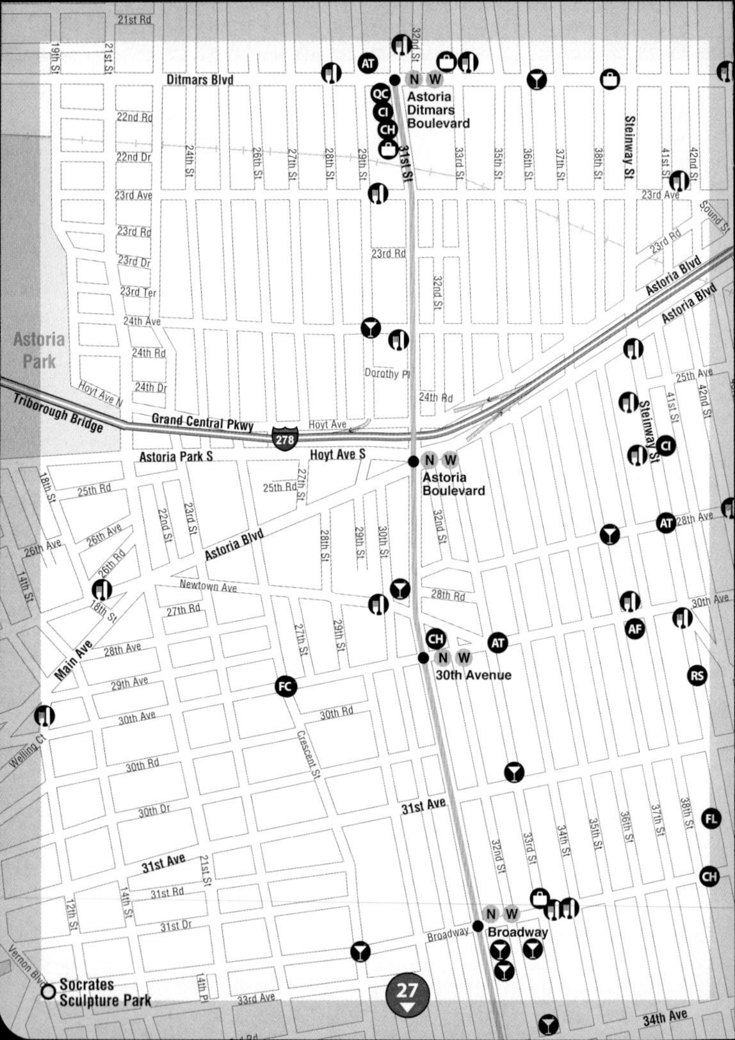

Map 26 • Astoria

21st Rd
19th St
21st St
32nd St
Ditmars Blvd
N W
Astoria Ditmars Boulevard
22nd Rd
22nd Dr
24th St
26th St
27th St
28th St
29th St
31st St
33rd St
35th St
36th St
37th St
38th St
Steinway St
41st St
42nd St
23rd Ave
Sound St
23rd Rd
23rd Dr
23rd Ter
24th Ave
24th Rd
24th Dr
Astoria Park
Astoria Blvd
25th Ave
Dorothy Pl
Hoyt Ave N
Triborough Bridge
Grand Central Pkwy
278
Hoyt Ave
24th Rd
Astoria Park S
Hoyt Ave S
N W
Astoria Boulevard
18th St
25th Rd
22nd St
23rd St
27th St
26th Ave
26th Rd
14th St
28th St
29th St
30th St
28th Ave
Newtown Ave
27th Rd
28th Rd
30th Ave
Main Ave
18th St
27th St
29th St
N W
30th Avenue
29th Ave
30th Rd
Crescent St
Welling Ct
30th Dr
31st Ave
21st St
31st Rd
31st Dr
12th St
14th St
32nd St
33rd St
34th St
35th St
36th St
37th St
38th St
N W
Broadway
Vernon Blvd
Socrates Sculpture Park
14th Pl
33rd Ave
34th Ave

27

Centuries after Peter Minuet claimed it as a part of his famous $24 purchase of the island we know and love, Astoria is still considered a "mini-Manhattan" and a haven for city-dwellers in search of lower rents. On a half-hour stroll through Astoria, one can discover hundreds of ethnic shops, dozens of magnificent sculptures, and a fabulous view of Manhattan across the East River. Anything and everything can be found on Astoria's Steinway Street. You'll find a fabulous beer garden at Bohemian Hall, a Greek cafe on nearly every block, a handful of Irish pubs, an Egyptian coffee shop or two, and a few spots that are just plain trendy (like Café Bar). Great restaurants are plentiful, also—check out Piccola Venezia for fantastic Italian, Christos and S'Agapo for Greek, and Ubol's Kitchen for Thai. The brand-new all-weather track and miles of trails at Astoria Park are suitable for burning the calories gained from such fine dining.

$ ATMs

AF • Astoria Federal • 3716 30th Ave
AT • Atlantic • 28-07 Steinway St
AT • Atlantic • 29-10 Ditmars Blvd
AT • Atlantic • 33-12 30th Ave
CH • Chase • 22-45 31st St
CH • Chase • 31-05 30th Ave
CH • Chase • 38-18 Broadway
CI • Citibank • 22-16 31st St
CI • Citibank • 25-91 Steinway St
FC • First Central Savings • 35-01 30th Ave
FL • Fleet • 31-81 Steinway St
QC • Queens County Savings • 31-09 Ditmars Blvd
RS • Roslyn Savings • 30-75 Steinway St

O Landmarks

- **Socrates Sculpture Park** • Broadway & Vernon Blvd

Bars

- **Amnesia** • 3203 Broadway
- **Bohemian Hall** • 29-19 24th Ave
- **Brick Café** • 30-95 33rd St
- **Byzantio** • 28-31 31st St
- **Café Bar** • 32-90 34th Ave
- **Gibney's** • 32-01 Broadway
- **McCann's Pub & Grill** • 3615 Ditmars Blvd
- **McLoughlin's Bar** • 31-06 Broadway

Restaurants

- **Amici Amore I** • 29-35 Newtown Ave
- **Christos Hasapo-Taverna** • 41-08 23rd Ave
- **Elias Corner** • 24-02 31st St
- **Esperides** • 37-01 30th Ave
- **Kabab Café** • 25-12 Steinway St
- **Lorusso Foods** • 18-01 26th Rd
- **Piccola Venezia** • 42-01 28th Ave
- **Ponticello** • 46-11 Broadway
- **Porto Bello** • 43-18 Ditmars Blvd
- **Rizzo's Pizza** • 30-13 Steinway St
- **S'Agapo** • 34-21 34th St
- **Stamatis** • 29-12 23rd Ave
- **Taverna Kyclades** • 33-07 Ditmars Blvd
- **Tierras Colombianas** • 33-01 Broadway
- **Tierras Colombianas** • 82-18 Roosevelt Ave
- **Ubol's Kitchen** • 24-42 Steinway St
- **Uncle George's** • 33-19 Broadway

Shopping

- **Bagel House** • 3811 Ditmars Blvd
- **Book Value** • 3318 Broadway
- **Mediterranean Foods** • 23-18 31st St
- **Top Tomato** • 33-15 Ditmars Blvd

Map 27 • Long Island City

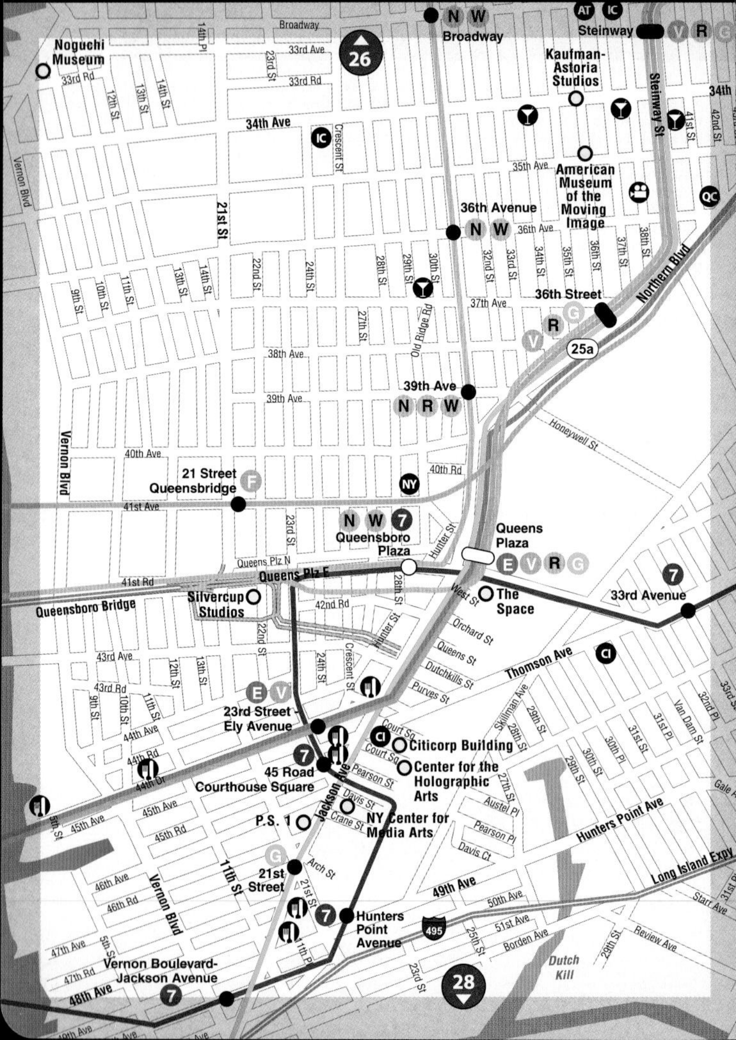

Unfortunately, the island of Manhattan cannot grow in tandem with its population. Akin to that in Brooklyn, a yuppie invasion of Long Island City has made it acceptable, even trendy, for Manhattanites to set foot into their neighbor to the east. Gentrification of this former industrial town has led to small battles between the natives and those who began the renaissance. In the case of P.S.1's solid concrete wall, good fences do not make good neighbors. Long Island City is the place to be if you want to check out great modern art. P.S.1 thankfully kept its reasonable entrance price tag even when MoMA temporarily moved in next door. Near Queens Plaza, The Space provides decorative public art that makes a statement, sometimes political, often puzzling. Although not as romantic as the Brooklyn Bridge or the Staten Island Ferry, a walk over the Pulaski Bridge provides a great view of midtown Manhattan's skyline. In contrast to the rest of the borough, public transportation serves people in this area of Queens well. A special treat is a newly implemented Hunters Point Ferry that travels to E 34th Street or Pier 11 near Wall Street.

ATMs

AT • Atlantic • 36-10 Broadway
NY • Bank of NY • 29-37 41st Ave
CH • Chase • 10-51 Jackson Ave
CI • Citibank • 31-10 Thompson AvE
CI • Citibank • One Court Sq
GP • Greenpoint • 40-20 Queens Blvd
IC • Independence Community • 22-59 31st St
IC • Independence Community • 24-28 34th St
IC • Independence Community • 37-10 Broadway
IN • Interbank of NY • 31-01 Broadway
QC • Queens County Savings • 4202 Northern Blvd

Landmarks

- **American Museum of the Moving Image** • 35th Ave & 36th St
- **Center for the Holographic Arts** • 45-10 Court Sq
- **Citicorp Building** • 1 Court Sq
- **Isamu Noguchi Museum** • 32-37 Vernon Blvd
- **Kaufman-Astoria Studios** • 34-12 36th St
- **NY Center for Media Arts** • 45-12 Davis St
- **P.S. 1** • 22-25 Jackson Ave
- **Silvercup Studios** • 42-22 22nd St
- **The Space** • 42-16 West St

Bars

- **Café Athens** • 32-07 30th St
- **Club XL** • 25-22 34th Ave
- **Krash** • 34-48 Steinway St
- **Tupelo** • 34-18 34th Ave

Movie Theaters

- **Regal/UA** • 35-30 38th St

Restaurants

- **Brooks 1890 Restaurant** • 24-28 Jackson Ave
- **Court Square Diner** • 45-30 23rd St
- **Dazies** • 3941 Queens Blvd
- **Jackson Avenue Steakhouse** • 12-23 Jackson Ave
- **La Vuelta** • 10-43 44th Dr
- **Manducatis** • 13-27 Jackson Ave
- **Manetta's** • 10-76 Jackson Ave
- **Sage American Kitchen** • 26-21 Jackson Ave
- **Tournesol** • 50-12 Vernon Blvd
- **Water's Edge** • 44th Dr & East River

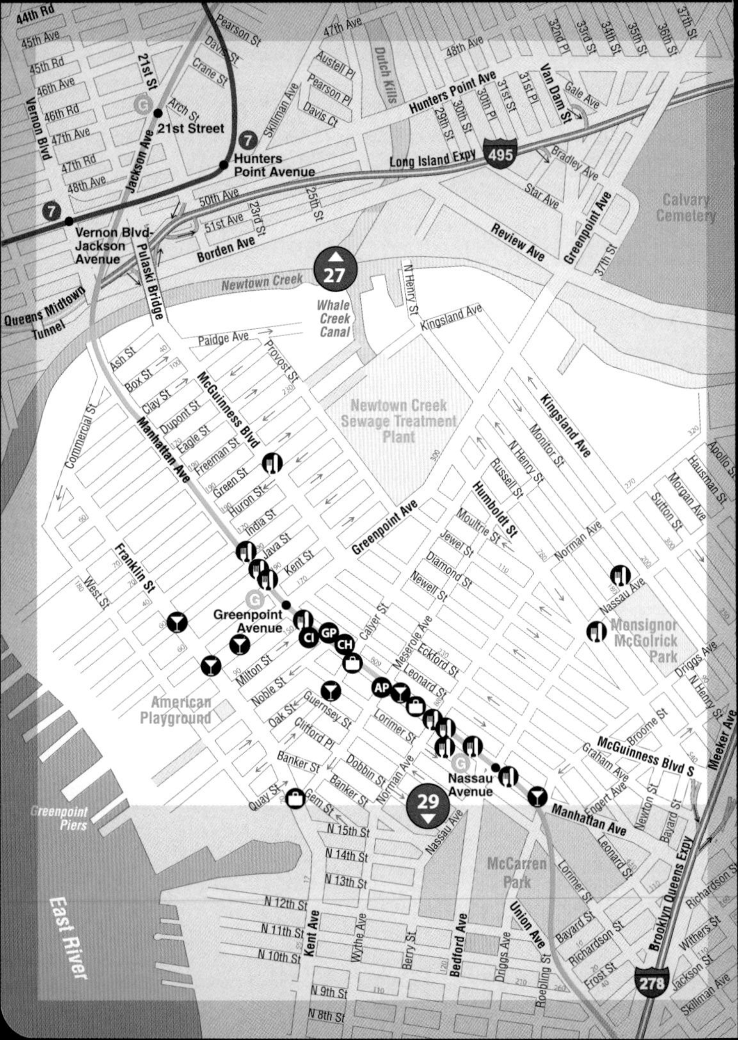
44th Rd
45th Ave
45th Rd
46th Ave
46th Rd
47th Ave
47th Rd
48th Ave
Vernon Blvd
21st St
Jackson Ave
21st Street
Hunters Point Avenue
Vernon Blvd-Jackson Avenue
Pearson St
Davis St
Crane St
Arch St
47th Ave
Austell Pl
Pearson Pl
Davis Ct
Skillman Ave
Dutch Kills
48th Ave
Hunters Point Ave
29th St
30th St
30th Pl
31st St
31st Pl
Van Dam St
32nd Pl
33rd St
34th St
35th St
36th St
37th St
Gale Ave
Long Island Expy
495
Bradley Ave
Star Ave
Review Ave
Greenpoint Ave
37th St
Calvary Cemetery
50th Ave
51st Ave
23rd St
25th St
Borden Ave
Pulaski Bridge
Queens Midtown Tunnel
Newtown Creek
27
Whale Creek Canal
N Henry St
Kingsland Ave
Paidge Ave
Provost St
Ash St
Box St
Clay St
Dupont St
Eagle St
Freeman St
Green St
Huron St
India St
Java St
Kent St
McGuinness Blvd
Manhattan Ave
Commercial St
Newtown Creek Sewage Treatment Plant
Kingsland Ave
Monitor St
N Henry St
Russell St
Humboldt St
Moultrie St
Jewel St
Diamond St
Newell St
Greenpoint Ave
Norman Ave
Apollo St
Hausman St
Morgan Ave
Sutton St
Nassau Ave
Monsignor McGolrick Park
Driggs Ave
N Henry St
Franklin St
West St
Greenpoint Avenue
CI
GP
CH
Calyer St
Meserole Ave
Eckford St
Leonard St
AP
Milton St
Noble St
Oak St
Guernsey St
Clifford Pl
Lorimer St
American Playground
Banker St
Dobbin St
Norman Ave
Quay St
Gem St
Banker St
Nassau Avenue
29
Broome St
Graham Ave
McGuinness Blvd S
Meeker Ave
Engert Ave
Newton St
Bayard St
Manhattan Ave
Greenpoint Piers
N 15th St
N 14th St
N 13th St
N 12th St
N 11th St
N 10th St
N 9th St
N 8th St
Nassau Ave
McCarren Park
Leonard St
Lorimer St
Union Ave
Brooklyn Queens Expy
Richardson St
Withers St
Jackson St
Skillman Ave
Bayard St
Richardson St
Frost St
278
East River
Kent Ave
Wythe Ave
Berry St
Bedford Ave
Driggs Ave
Roebling St

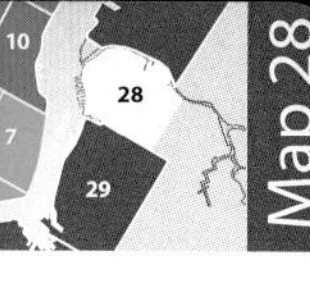

Whole lotta Polish but not for much longer. In search of lower rents in a close proximity to their mecca, Williamsburg, the hipsters are making it less possible for Greenpoint to keep its 'Little Warsaw' distinction. Great second-hand clothing, especially jeans, can be found at Pop's. The Warsaw on Driggs has great live music and here's a tip for wine drinkers—Z&J Liquor gives a 20% discount when you buy three bottles at a time.

ATMs

AP • **Apple Bank** • 776 Manhattan Ave
CH • **Chase** • 798 Manhattan Ave
CI • **Citibank** • 836 Manhattan Ave
GP • **Greenpoint Bank** • 807 Manhattan Ave

Bars

- **Enid's** • 560 Manhattan Ave
- **Europa** • 765 Manhattan Ave
- **Pencil Factory** • 142 Franklin St
- **Splendid** • 132 Greenpoint Ave

Restaurants

- **Amarin Café** • 617 Manhattan Ave
- **Casanova** • 338 McGuinness Blvd
- **Christina's** • 853 Manhattan Ave
- **Divine Follie Café** • 929 Manhattan Ave
- **Greenpoint #1 Tex-Mex Express** • 681 Manhattan Ave
- **Manhattan 3 Decker Restaurant** • 695 Manhattan Ave
- **Old Poland Bakery and Restaurant** • 192 Nassau Ave
- **OTT** • 970 Manhattan Ave
- **SunView Luncheonette** • 221 Nassau Ave
- **Thai Café** • 925 Manhattan Ave
- **Valdiano** • 659 Manhattan Ave
- **Wasabi** • 638 Manhattan Ave

Shopping

- **Dee & Dee** • 777 Manhattan Ave
- **Pop's Popular Clothing** • 7 Franklin St
- **Z &J Liquor** • 761 Manhattan Ave

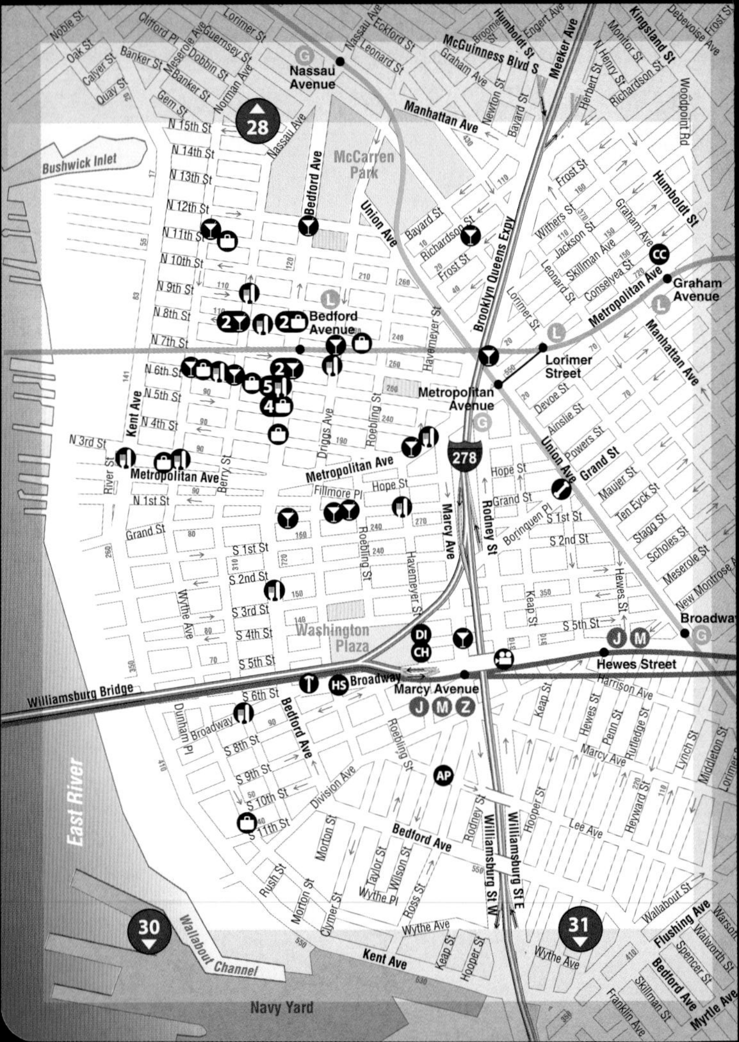

Map 29 • Williamsburg

Nassau Avenue
McCarren Park
Bedford Avenue
Metropolitan Avenue
Lorimer Street
Graham Avenue
Marcy Avenue
Hewes Street
Broadway
Bushwick Inlet
East River
Williamsburg Bridge
Washington Plaza
Wallabout Channel
Navy Yard
Brooklyn Queens Expy
McGuinness Blvd S
Meeker Ave
Manhattan Ave
Metropolitan Ave
Union Ave
Bedford Ave
Kent Ave
Wythe Ave
Berry St
Driggs Ave
Roebling St
Havemeyer St
Marcy Ave
Rodney St
Grand St
Division Ave
Williamsburg St W
Williamsburg St E
Flushing Ave
Myrtle Ave
28
29
30
31
278

Essentials / Sundries

As far as food and fun go, you don't have to leave Williamsburg to find tasty eats, cheap beer, and a night on the town. A self-contained little community one stop from Manhattan, this 'hood continues to lure Manhattanites in search of trends. Check out great stores such as Spoonbill and Sugartown (books), Earwax Records (music), and Beacon's Closet for resale items.

ATMs

AP • Apple • 44 Lee Avenue
CH • Chase • 225 Havemeyer St
CC • Cross County • 731 Metropolitan Ave
DI • Dime • Havemeyer St
HS • HSBC • 175 Broadway

Bars

- **The Abbey** • 536 Driggs Ave
- **Black Betty** • 366 Metropolitan Ave
- **Boogaloo** • 168 Marcy Ave
- **BQE** • 300 N 6th St
- **Brooklyn Ale House** • 103 Berry St
- **Brooklyn Brewery** • 79 N 11th St
- **Charleston** • 174 Bedford Ave
- **Galapagos** • 70 N 6th St
- **Greenpoint Tavern** • 188 Bedford Ave
- **Iona** • 180 Grand St
- **Pete's Candy Store** • 709 Lorimer St
- **Stinger Club** • 241 Grand St
- **Sweetwater Tavern** • 105 N 6th St
- **Toybox** • 256 Grand St
- **Turkey's Nest** • 94 Bedford Ave
- **Union Pool** • 484 Union Ave

Restaurants

- **Acqua Santa** • 556 Driggs Ave
- **Allioli** • 291 Grand St
- **Anna Maria Pizza** • 179 Bedford Ave
- **Anytime** • 93 N 6th St
- **Bliss** • 191 Bedford Ave
- **Bonita** • 338 Bedford Ave
- **Ciao Bella** • 138 N 8th St
- **Diner** • 85 Broadway
- **Miss Williamsburg Diner** • 206 Kent Ave
- **Oznot's Dish** • 79 Berry St
- **Planet Thailand** • 133 N 7th St
- **Relish** • 225 Wythe St
- **Siam Orchid** • 378 Metropolitan Ave
- **Teddy's Bar and Grill** • 96 Berry St
- **Vera Cruz** • 195 Bedford Ave

Shopping

- **Artist & Craftsman** • 221 N 8th St
- **Beacon's Closet** • 88 N 11th St
- **Brooklyn Industries** • 154 Bedford Ave
- **Crypto** • 152 Bedford Ave
- **Domsey's Warehouse** • 496 Wythe Ave
- **Earwax** • 218 Bedford Ave
- **Isa** • 88 N 6th St
- **The Mini-Market** • 218 Bedford Ave
- **Otte** • 218 Bedford Ave
- **Spacial Etc.** • 149 N 6th St
- **Spoonbill and Sugartown** • 218 Bedford Av
- **Wythe Studios** • 240 Wythe Ave
- **Yarn Tree** • 347 Bedford Ave

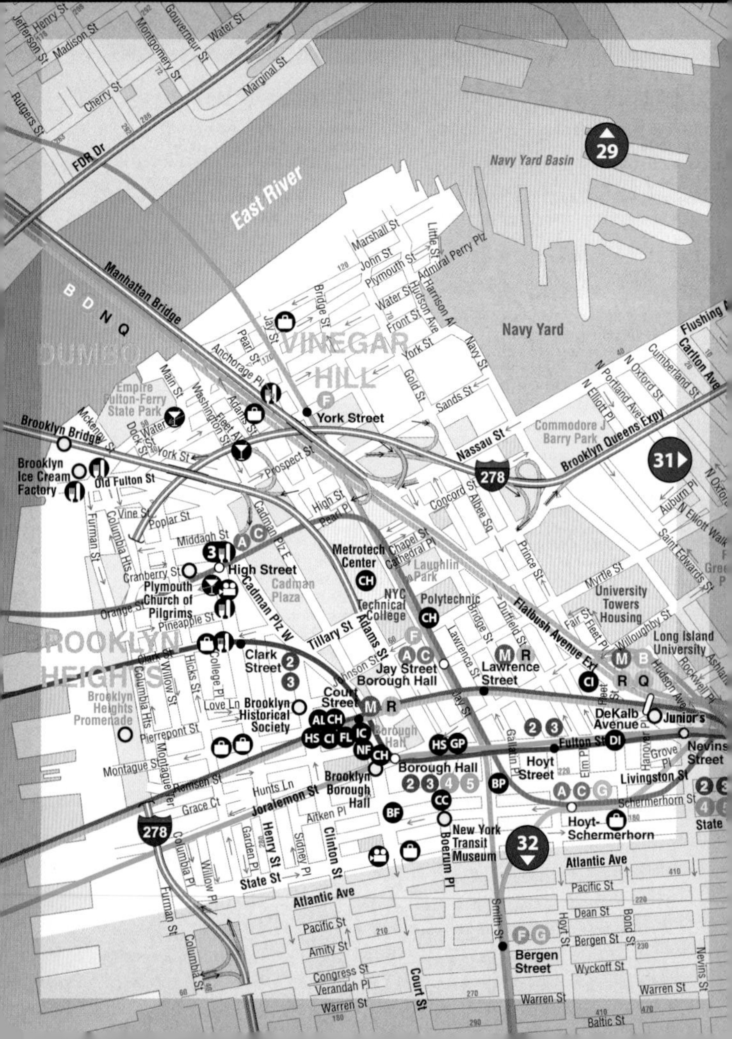

East River
Navy Yard Basin
Navy Yard
29
31
32
VINEGAR HILL
DUMBO
BROOKLYN HEIGHTS
Manhattan Bridge
Brooklyn Bridge
Brooklyn Queens Expy
Flatbush Avenue Ext
FDR Dr
278
Empire Fulton-Ferry State Park
Brooklyn Ice Cream Factory
Commodore J Barry Park
Cadman Plaza
Laughlin Park
Metrotech Center
NYC Technical College
Polytechnic
University Towers Housing
Long Island University
Plymouth Church of Pilgrims
Brooklyn Historical Society
Brooklyn Heights Promenade
Brooklyn Borough Hall
New York Transit Museum
Junior's
York Street
High Street
Clark Street
Court Street
Borough Hall
Jay Street Borough Hall
Lawrence Street
DeKalb Avenue
Nevins Street
Hoyt Street
Hoyt-Schermerhorn
Bergen Street
Jefferson St
Henry St
Madison St
Rutgers St
Cherry St
Montgomery St
Gouverneur St
Water St
Marginal St
Marshall St
John St
Plymouth St
Little St
Admiral Perry Plz
Bridge St
Jay St
Pearl St
Anchorage Pl
Front St
Hudson Ave
Harrison Al
York St
Gold St
Navy St
Sands St
Nassau St
Main St
Washington St
Adams St
Fleet Al
Water St
Dock St
Mckenney St
Prospect St
Old Fulton St
Vine St
Poplar St
Furman St
Columbia Hts
Middagh St
Cadman Plz E
Cadman Plz W
High St
Pearl Pl
Chapel St
Cathedral Pl
Concord St
Albee Sq
Prince St
Cranberry St
Orange St
Pineapple St
Tillary St
Clark St
Willow St
Hicks St
College Pl
Johnson St
Lawrence St
Duffield St
Myrtle St
Fair St
Fleet Pl
Willoughby St
Hudson Ave
Rockwell Pl
Ashland Pl
N Portland Ave
N Oxford St
N Elliott Pl
Cumberland St
Carlton Ave
Flushing Ave
Auburn Pl
N Elliott Walk
Saint Edwards St
Love Ln
Pierrepont St
Montague St
Montague Ter
Remsen St
Grace Ct
Hunts Ln
Joralemon St
Aitken Pl
Fulton St
Gallatin Pl
Elm Pl
Hanover Pl
Grove Pl
Livingston St
Schermerhorn St
Boerum Pl
Smith St
Columbia Pl
Willow Pl
Garden Pl
Henry St
Sidney Pl
Clinton St
State St
Atlantic Ave
Pacific St
Amity St
Congress St
Verandah Pl
Warren St
Court St
Dean St
Bergen St
Wyckoff St
Hoyt St
Bond St
Nevins St
Baltic St
State

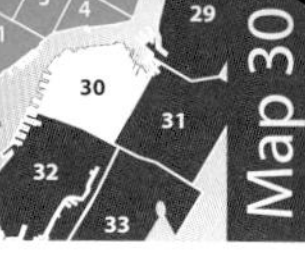

A rather dizzying mix of fast food, hipster joints, and neighborhood stalwarts show the difference in these neighborhoods. Some institutions, however, include Junior's, Grimaldi's, and Henry's End. A new Barnes & Noble and googol-plex has changed the tenor of Court Street north of Atlantic, though not enough—it's still somewhat seedy. For more indie viewing fare, try the Heights Cinema.

ATMs

AL • **Atlantic Liberty** • 186 Montague St
BP • **Banco Popular** • 166 Livingston St
BF • **Brooklyn Federal** • 81 Court St
CH • **Chase** • 177 Montague St
CH • **Chase** • 4 Metrotech Ctr
CH • **Chase** • 1 MetroTech Center
CH • **Chase** • 16 Court St
CI • **Citibank** • 1 University Plaza
CI • **Citibank** • 181 Montague St
CC • **Community Capital** • 111 Livingston St
DI • **Dime** • 9 DeK alb Ave
FL • **Fleet Bank** • 205 Montague St
GP • **Greenpoint Bank** • 356 Fulton St
HS • **HSBC** • 200 Montague St
HS • **HSBC** • 342 Fulton St
IC • **Independence Community** • 195 Montague St
NF • **North Fork Bank** • 50 Court St

Bars

• **Henry Street Ale House** • 62 Henry St
• **Water Street Bar** • 66 Water St

Landmarks

• **Brooklyn Borough Hall** • 209 Joralemon St
• **Brooklyn Bridge** • Adams St & East River
• **Brooklyn Heights Promenade** •
• **Brooklyn Historical Society** • 128 Pierrepoint St
• **Brooklyn Ice Cream Factory** • Fulton Ferry Pier
• **Junior's Cheesecakes** • 386 Flatbush Ave
• **New York Transit Museum** • Boerum Pl & Schermerhorn St
• **Plymouth Church of Pilgrims** • 56 Cranberry St

Movie Theaters

• **Pavilion Brooklyn Heights** • 70 Henry St
• **Regal/UA Court Street** • 108 Court St

Restaurants

• **Fascati Pizzeria** • 80 Henry St
• **Grimaldi's** • 19 Old Fulton St
• **Henry's End** • 44 Henry St
• **Noodle Pudding** • 38 Henry St
• **River Café** • 1 Water St
• **Superfine** • 126 Front St
• **Yokohama** • 71 Clark St

Shopping

• **ABC Carpet & Home** • 20 Jay St
• **Barnes & Noble** • 106 Court St
• **Gourd Chips** • 113A Court St
• **Heights Prime Meats** • 59 Clark St
• **Lassen & Hennigs** • 114 Montague St
• **Soft Skull Press** • 71 Bond St
• **Soho Art Materials** • 111 Front St
• **Tapestry the Salon** • 107 Montague St

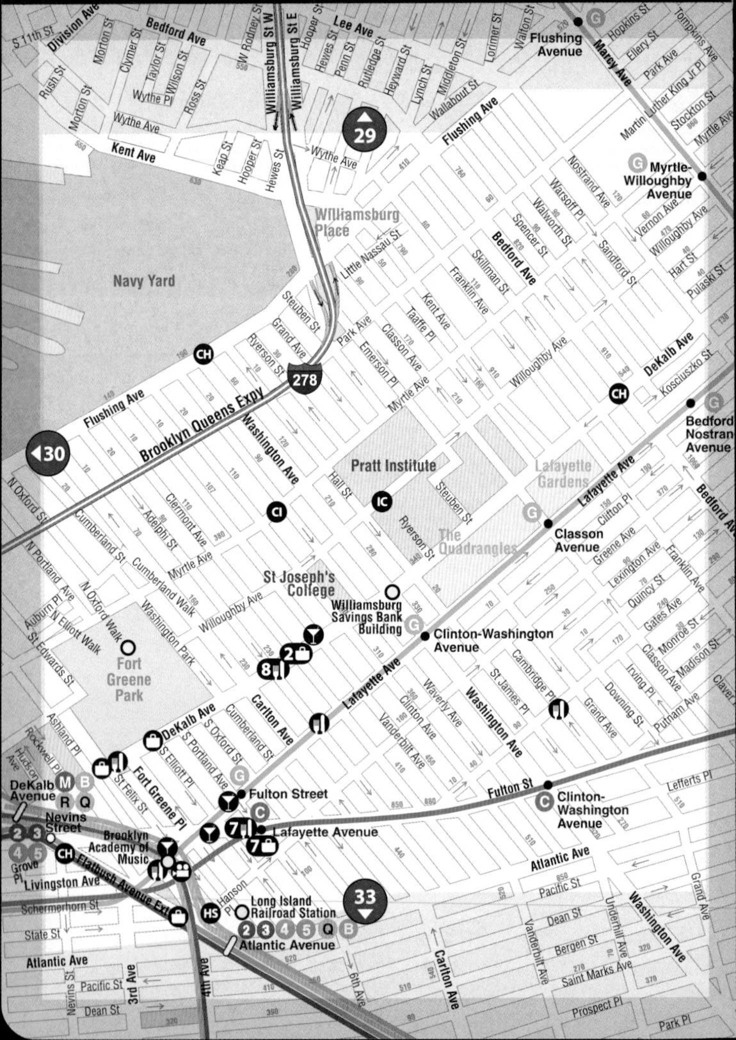

Navy Yard

Pratt Institute

St Joseph's College

Williamsburg Savings Bank Building

Fort Greene Park

Lafayette Gardens

The Quadrangles

Williamsburg Place

Brooklyn Academy of Music

Long Island Railroad Station

Flushing Avenue

Myrtle-Willoughby Avenue

Bedford Nostrand Avenue

Classon Avenue

Clinton-Washington Avenue

Fulton Street

Lafayette Avenue

DeKalb Avenue

Nevins Street

Atlantic Avenue

Brooklyn Queens Expy

Flatbush Avenue Ext

29
30
33

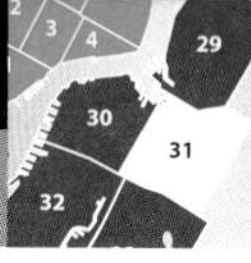

Today, this up and coming neighborhood is one of Brooklyn's finest, being not only close to Manhattan (just two subway stops away), but home to the Brooklyn Academy of Music (BAM), Madiba and Cambodian Cuisine (the only South African and Cambodian restaurants in the city, respectively), and Frank's Lounge. A good green grocer is sorely need, however.

ATMs

CH • Chase • 20 Flatbush Ave
CH • Chase • 210 Flushing Ave
CH • Chase • 975 Bedford Ave
CI • Citibank • 430 Myrtle Ave
HS • HSBC Bank • 1 Hanson Pl
IC • Independence Community • 200 Willoughby Ave

Bars

- **BAM Café** • 30 Lafayette Ave
- **Frank's Lounge** • 660 Fulton St
- **Moe's** • 80 Lafayette Ave

Landmarks

- **Brooklyn Academy of Music** • 30 Lafayette Ave
- **Fort Greene Park** • Dekalb Ave & Washington Park
- **Long Island Railroad Station** • Hanson Pl & Flatbush Ave
- **Williamsburg Savings Bank Building** • 1 Hanson Pl

Movie Theaters

- **BAM Rose Cinemas** • 30 Lafayette Ave

Restaurants

- **1 Greene Sushi and Sashimi** • 1 Greene Ave
- **À Table** • 171 Lafayette Ave
- **Academy Restaurant** • 69 Lafayette Ave
- **BAM Café** • 30 Lafayette Ave
- **Black Iris** • 228 DeKalb Ave
- **Café Lafayette** • 99 S Portland Ave
- **Cambodian Cuisine** • 87 S Elliot Pl
- **Chez Oskar** • 211 DeKalb Ave
- **Good Joy Chinese Takeout** • 216 DeKalb Ave
- **Keur N' Deye Restaurant** • 737 Fulton St
- **Liquors** • 219 DeKalb Ave
- **Locanda Vini & Olii** • 129 Gates Ave
- **Loulou** • 222 DeKalb Ave
- **Madiba** • 195 DeKalb Ave
- **Mario's Pizzeria** • 224 DeKalb Ave
- **Mo-Bay** • 112 DeKalb Ave
- **Night of the Cookers** • 767 Fulton St
- **Pequena** • 86 S Portland Ave
- **Sol** • 229 DeKalb Ave

Shopping

- **Cake Man Raven Confectionary** • 708 Fulton St
- **Carol's Daughter** • 1 S Elliot Pl
- **Exodus Industrial** • 771 Fulton St
- **Indigo Café and Books** • 672 Fulton St
- **Jacob Eyes** • 114 Dekalb Ave
- **L'Epicerie** • 270 Vanderbilt Ave
- **Malchijah Hats** • 225 DeKalb Ave
- **Marquet** • 680 Fulton St
- **Midtown Greenhouse Garden Center** • 115 Flatbush Ave
- **My Little India** • 96 S Elliot Pl
- **Myrna's Natural Shoppe** • 713 Fulton St
- **Yu Interiors** • 15 Greene Ave

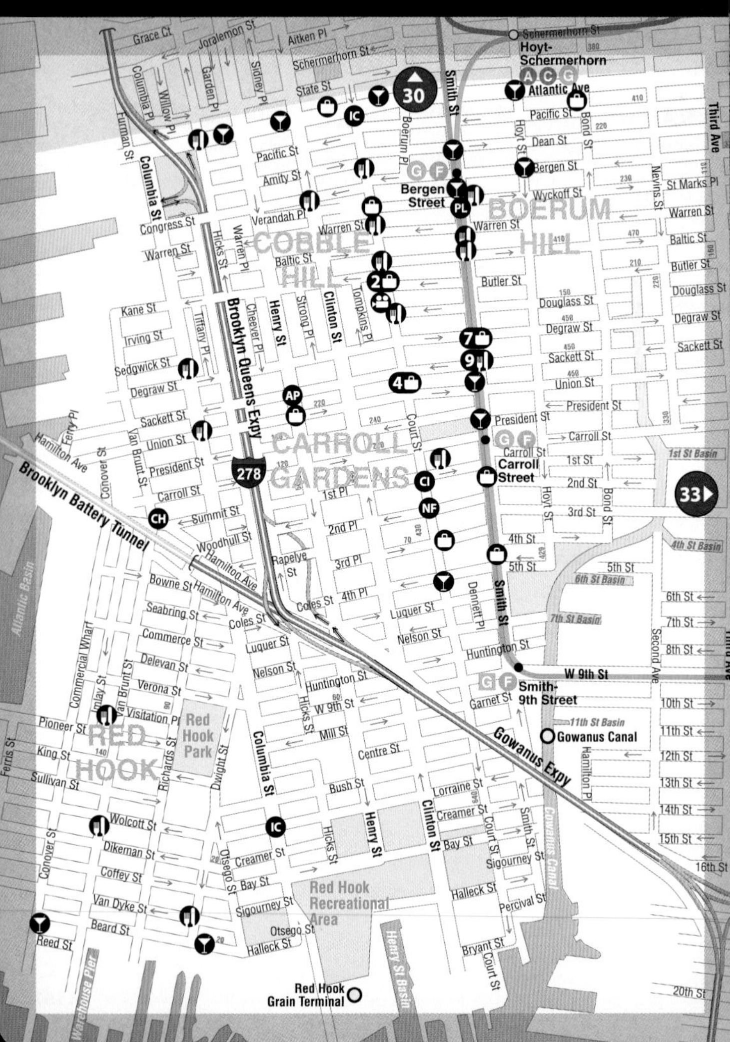

Cobble Hill
Boerum Hill
Carroll Gardens
Red Hook
Hoyt-Schermerhorn
Bergen Street
Carroll Street
Smith-9th Street
Gowanus Canal
Red Hook Grain Terminal
Red Hook Park
Red Hook Recreational Area
Brooklyn Queens Expy
Brooklyn Battery Tunnel
Gowanus Expy
Atlantic Basin
Warehouse Pier
Henry St Basin
1st St Basin
4th St Basin
6th St Basin
7th St Basin
11th St Basin
Gowanus Canal
Smith St
Court St
Clinton St
Henry St
Hicks St
Columbia St
Hoyt St
Bond St
Nevins St
Third Ave
Second Ave
Atlantic Ave
Pacific St
Dean St
Bergen St
Wyckoff St
Warren St
Baltic St
Butler St
Douglass St
Degraw St
Sackett St
Union St
President St
Carroll St
1st St
2nd St
3rd St
W 9th St
30
33
278

Five years ago, Smith Street was bodegas, dollar stores and junk shoes. Today, over 20 furniture/design/clothing/hipster shops line it from First Place up to Pacific Street, as well as over a dozen restaurants and several bars. Most of it's quite good and there's tons more to explore on Court Street if you get bored. For peace and quiet, stroll Henry and Clinton Streets and the surrounding blocks.

ATMs

AP • Apple • 518 Henry St
AP • Apple • 326 Court St
CH • Chase • 79 Hamilton Ave
CI • Citibank • 375 Court St
IC • Independence Community • 130 Court St
IC • Independence Community • 498 Columbia St
NF • North Fork • 420 Court St
PL • Ponce De Leon • 169 Smith St

Bars

- **Boat** • 175 Smith St
- **Brazen Head** • 228 Atlantic Ave
- **Brooklyn Inn** • 148 Hoyt St
- **Gowanus Yacht Club** • 323 Smith St
- **Kili** • 81 Hoyt St
- **Last Exit** • 136 Atlantic Ave
- **Magnetic Field** • 97 Atlantic Ave
- **PJ Hanely's** • 449 Court St
- **Quench** • 282 Smith St
- **Sunny's** • 253 Conover St
- **Waterfront Ale House** • 155 Atlantic Ave
- **Zombie Hut** • 263 Smith St

Landmarks

- **Gowanus Canal**
- **Red Hook Grain Terminal**

Movie Theaters

- **Cobble Hill Cinema** • 265 Court St

Restaurants

- **Alma** • 187 Columbia St
- **Banania Café** • 241 Smith St
- **Cafe Luluc** • 214 Smith St
- **Delicatessen** • 264 Clinton St
- **El Portal** • 217 Smith St
- **Faan** • 209 Smith St
- **Fatoosh** • 330 Hicks St
- **Ferdinando's** • 151 Union St
- **The Grocery** • 288 Smith St
- **Hope & Anchor** • 347 Van Brunt St
- **Joya** • 215 Court St
- **Leonardo's Brick Oven Pizza** • 383 Court St
- **Liberty Heights Tap Room** • 34 Van Dyke St
- **Margaret Palca Bakes** • 191 Columbia St
- **Osaka** • 272 Court St
- **Patois** • 255 Smith St
- **Sal's Pizzeria** • 305 Court St
- **Sam's Restaurant** • 238 Court St
- **Savoia** • 277 Smith St
- **Schnack** • 122 Union St
- **Sherwood Café/Robin des Bois** • 195 Smith St
- **Siam Garden** • 172 Court St
- **Zaytoons** • 283 Smith St

Shopping

- **American Beer Distributors** • 256 Court St
- **Apple Tree (24-hour deli)** • 312 Court St
- **Astro Turf** • 290 Smith St
- **Caputo's Bake Shop** • 329 Court St
- **Caputo's Fine Foods** • 460 Court St
- **College Bakery** • 239 Court St
- **Frida's Closet** • 296 Smith St
- **Granny's Attic** • 305 Smith St
- **The Green Onion** • 274 Smith St
- **KC Art Supplies** • 252 Court St
- **Kimera** • 366 Atlantic Ave
- **Mazzola Bakery** • 192 Union St
- **Monte Leone's Pasticceria** • 355 Court St
- **Olive's** • 434 Court St
- **Park Natural Foods** • 274 Union St
- **Refinery** • 254 Smith St
- **Stacia** • 267 Smith St
- **Staubitz Meat Market** • 222 Court St
- **Swallow** • 361 Smith St

Atlantic Avenue
Pacific Street
7th Avenue
Bergen Street
Brooklyn Tabernacle
Grand Army Plaza
PROSPECT HEIGHTS
Brooklyn Museum of Art
Brooklyn Botanic Garden
Prospect Park Wildlife Center
Union Street
PARK SLOPE
The Old Stone House
4th Avenue-9th Street
7th Avenue
Park Slope Food Co-op
15th Street-Prospect Park
Prospect Park
Prospect Avenue
Prospect Expy
Flatbush Ave
Atlantic Ave
Pacific St
Dean St
Bergen St
St Mark's Ave
Prospect Pl
Park Pl
Sterling Pl
St Johns Pl
Lincoln Pl
Washington Ave
Carlton Ave
Vanderbilt Ave
Underhill Ave
Plaza St E
Third Ave
Fourth Ave
Fifth Ave
Sixth Ave
Seventh Ave
Eighth Ave
Prospect Park W
Prospect Park SW
Tenth Ave
Eleventh Ave
Windsor Pl
Prospect Ave
17th St
18th St
19th St

Blue Ribbon's arrival was a big deal for the neighborhood, which has seen an influx of incredible restaurants in the past few years. The Food Co-Op on Union Street is the largest member- owned and operated co-op in the nation. Prospect Heights has much to call its own and for a great (but pricey) night out, check out the cats at up Over Jazz Café

$ ATMs

AF • **Astoria Federal** • 110 7th Ave
AF • **Astoria Federal** • 451 5th Ave
CFS • **CFS** • 137 12th St
CH • **Chase** • 127 7th Ave
CH • **Chase** • 401 Flatbush Ave
CH • **Chase** • 444 5th Ave
CI • **Citibank** • 114 7th Ave
CF • **Columbia Federal** • 625 Atlantic Ave
FL • **Fleet** • Flatbush Ave & Atlantic Ave
GP • **Greenpoint** • 516 5th Ave
HS • **HSBC** • 325 9th St
IC • **Independence Community** • 234 Prospect Park W
MT • **M & T Bank** • 354 Flatbush Ave

Bars

- **Bar 4** • 444 7th Ave
- **Barbes** • 376 9th St
- **Freddy's** • 485 Dean St
- **The Gate** • 321 5th Ave
- **Ginger's** • 363 5th Ave
- **Great Lakes** • 284 5th Ave
- **Loki Lounge** • 304 5th Ave
- **Mooney's Pub** • 353 Flatbush Ave
- **O'Connor's** • 39 5th Ave
- **Park Slope Ale House** • 356 6th Ave
- **Up Over Jazz Café** • 351 Flatbush Ave

Landmarks

- **Brooklyn Botanic Garden** • 900 Washington Ave
- **Brooklyn Museum of Art** • 200 Eastern Pkwy
- **Brooklyn Tabernacle** • 290 Flatbush Ave
- **Grand Army Plaza** • Flatbush Ave & Plaza St
- **The Old Stone House** • 336 3rd St
- **Park Slope Food Co-Op** • 782 Union St
- **Prospect Park Wildlife Center** • 450 Flatbush Ave

Movie Theaters

- **Pavilion Flatbush** • 314 Flatbush Ave
- **Pavilion Movie Theatres** • 188 Prospect Park W

Restaurants

- **12th Street Bar and Grill** • 1123 8th Ave
- **2nd Street Café** • 189 7th Ave
- **Al Di La Trattoria** • 248 5th Ave
- **Beso** • 210 5th Ave
- **Blue Ribbon Brooklyn** • 280 Fifth Ave
- **Café Steinhof** • 422 7th Ave
- **Chip Shop** • 383 5th Ave
- **Convivium Osteria** • 68 5th Ave
- **Cousin John's Café and Bakery** • 70 7th Ave
- **Cucina** • 256 5th Ave
- **El Castillo de Jagua** • 302 Flatbush Ave
- **Garden Café** • 620 Vanderbilt Ave
- **Geido** • 331 Flatbush Ave
- **Junior's** • 386 Flatbush Ave
- **La Taqueria** • 72 7th Ave
- **Lemongrass Grill** • 61A Seventh Ave
- **Long Tan** • 196 5th Ave
- **Luce** • 411 11th St
- **Mamma Duke** • 243 Flatbush Ave
- **Mitchell's Soul Food** • 617 Vanderbilt Ave
- **New Prospect Café** • 393 Flatbush Ave
- **Olive Vine Café** • 362 15th St
- **Olive Vine Pizza** • 131 6th Ave
- **Olive Vine Pizza** • 81 7th Ave
- **Parkside Restaurant** • 355 Flatbush Ave
- **Rose Water** • 787 Union St
- **Santa Fe Grill** • 60 7th Ave
- **Sweets Village** • 702 Washington Ave
- **Tavern on Dean** • 755 Dean St
- **Tom's** • 782 Washington Ave
- **Tutta Pasta** • 160 7th Ave
- **Two Boots** • 514 2nd St

Shopping

- **Barnes & Noble** • 267 7th Ave
- **The Bicycle Station** • 560 Vanderbilt Ave
- **Bird** • 430 7th Ave
- **Bob and Judi's Collectibles** • 217 5th Ave
- **The Brainy Bunch** • 397 Flatbush Ave
- **Castor & Pollux** • 76 6th Ave
- **Clay Pot** • 162 7th Ave
- **Community Book Store** • 143 7th Ave
- **Eco-mat Cleaners** • 837 Union St
- **Eidolon** • 233 5th Ave
- **Hibiscus** • 564A Vandebilt Ave
- **Hooti Couture** • 321 Flatbush Ave
- **Kimera** • 274 5th Ave
- **Leaf and Bean** • 83 7th Ave
- **McSweeney's Store** • 429 7th Ave
- **Nancy Nancy** • 244 Fifth Ave
- **Pieces** • 671 Vanderbilt Ave
- **Red Lipstick** • 64 6th Ave
- **Sound Track** • 119 7th Ave
- **Uncle Louie G's** • 741 Union St
- **Uprising Bread Bakery** • 138 7th Ave
- **Uprising Bread Bakery** • 328 7th Ave

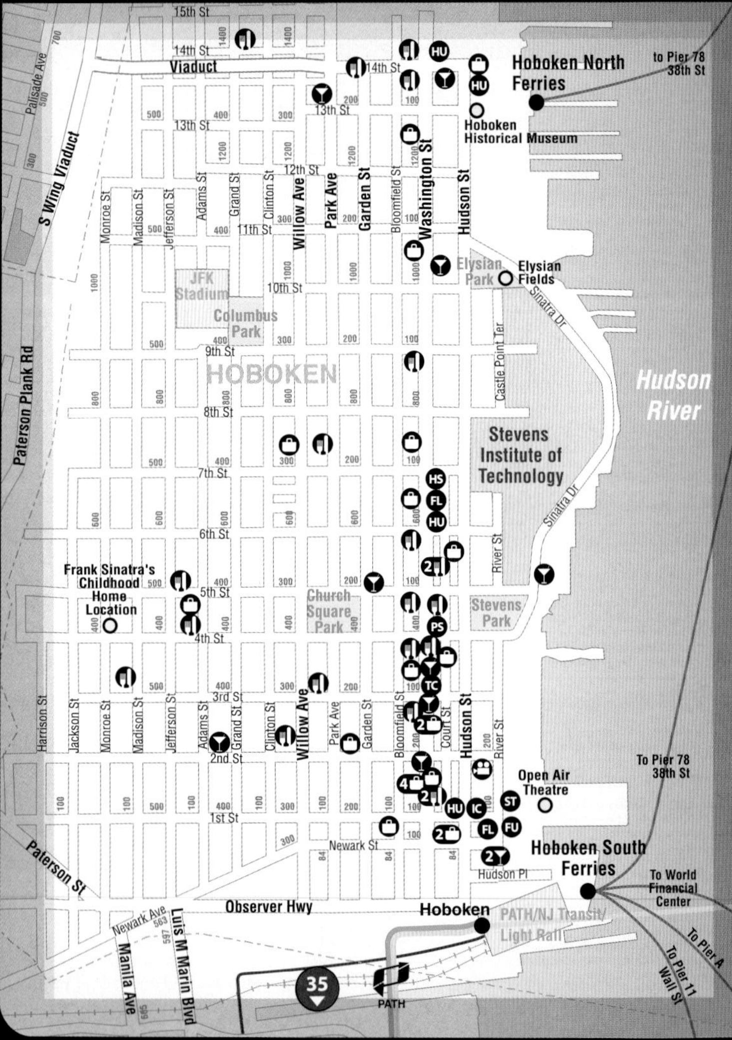
15th St
14th St
Viaduct
14th St
13th St
13th St
12th St
11th St
10th St
9th St
8th St
7th St
6th St
5th St
4th St
3rd St
2nd St
1st St
Newark St
Observer Hwy
Palisade Ave
S Wing Viaduct
Paterson Plank Rd
Paterson St
Newark Ave
Manila Ave
Luis M Marin Blvd
Monroe St
Madison St
Jefferson St
Adams St
Grand St
Clinton St
Willow Ave
Park Ave
Garden St
Bloomfield St
Washington St
Hudson St
Harrison St
Jackson St
Court St
River St
Castle Point Ter
Sinatra Dr
Hudson Pl
JFK Stadium
Columbus Park
HOBOKEN
Church Square Park
Stevens Park
Elysian Park
Elysian Fields
Stevens Institute of Technology
Hoboken North Ferries
Hoboken Historical Museum
to Pier 78 38th St
Hudson River
Frank Sinatra's Childhood Home Location
Open Air Theatre
To Pier 78 38th St
Hoboken South Ferries
To World Financial Center
To Pier A
To Pier 11 Wall St
Hoboken
PATH/NJ Transit/ Light Rail
PATH
35

Just 9 minutes away from Manhattan by PATH train or 10 minutes by ferry, Hoboken is almost another borough of New York City. Wall Street types have driven the dizzying gentrification of this once gritty longshoreman town. Sinatra denied his Hoboken heritage because of the seedy reputation, but this "city on the waterfront" seems to be morphing before our eyes into one of the most desirable locales in the area; it has the new condos, high rises, day spas, trendy boutiques, and sushi restaurants to prove it. Every weekend, recent grads pour in from all over NJ for pub-crawls and good-time college partying, but the old-time Italian roots still show in the brick-oven bread, fresh mozzarella, Feast of St. Ann street festival, and house-dressed ladies sitting on front porches.

ATMs

FU · First Union National · 95 River St
FL · Fleet · 615 Washington St
FL · Fleet · 1 Firehouse Plz
HS · Haven Savings · 621 Washington St
HU · Hudson United · 101 Washington St
HU · Hudson United · 60 14th St
HU · Hudson United · 1325 Hudson St
HU · Hudson United · 609 Washington St
IC · Independence Community · 86 River St
PS · Pamrapo Savings · 401 Washington St
ST · Sumitomo Trust · 111 River St
TC · Trust Co · 301 Washington St

Landmarks

- **Elysian Fields** (site of first recorded baseball game)
- **Frank Sinatra's Childhood Home Location** · 415 Monroe St
- **Hoboken Historical Museum** · 1301 Hudson St
- **Open Air Theatre** (summer)

Bars

- **Black Bear** · 205 Washington St
- **City Bistro** · 56 14th St
- **Leo's Grandezvous** · 200 Grand St
- **Louise & Jerry's** · 329 Washington St
- **Martini Blue** · 1300 Park Ave
- **Maxwell's** · 1039 Washington St
- **Mile Square** · 221 Washington St
- **Moran's** · 501 Garden St
- **Oddfellows** · 80 River St
- **Sinatra Park Café** · 529 Sinatra Dr
- **Texas Arizona** · 76 River St

Movie Theaters

- **Hudson Street Cinemas** · 5 Marineview Plz

Restaurants

- **Amanda's** · 908 Washington St
- **Arthur's Tavern** · 237 Washington St
- **Baja** · 104 14th St (b/w Bloomfield & Washington)
- **Bangkok City** · 335 Washington St
- **Biggies Clam Bar** · 318 Madison St
- **Brass Rail** · 135 Washington St
- **Delfino's** · 500 Jefferson St
- **East LA** · 508 Washington St
- **Far Side Bar & Grill** · 531 Washington St
- **Frankie & Johnnie's** · 14th St & Garden St
- **Gas Light** · 400 Adams St
- **Gobi Grill** · 746 Park Ave
- **Hoboken Gourmet Company** · 423 Washington St
- **Karma Kafe** · 505 Washington St
- **La Isla** · 104 Washington St
- **La Scala** · 159 14th St
- **La Tartuferia** · 1405 Grand St
- **Robongi** · 520 Washington St
- **Trattoria Saporito** · 328 Washington St
- **Zack's Oak Bar and Grill** · 232 Willow Ave
- **Zafra** · 301 Willow Ave

Shopping

- **Air Studio** · 55 First St
- **Arts on Sixth** · 155 Sixth St
- **Basic Foods** · 204 Washington St
- **Battaglia's** · 319 Washington St
- **Big Fun Toys** · 602 Washington St
- **City Paint & Hardware** · 130 Washington St
- **Gallatea** · 1224 Washington St
- **Hand Mad** · 116 Washington St
- **Hoboken Farmboy** · 127 Washington St
- **Makeovers** · 302 Washington St
- **Peper** · 1030 Washington St
- **Sobsey's Produce** · 92 Bloomfield St
- **Sparrow Wine and Liquor** · 1224 Shipyard Ln
- **Sparrow Wine and Liquor** · 126 Washington St
- **Tunes New & Used CDs** · 225 Washington St
- **Yes I Do** · 312 Washington St

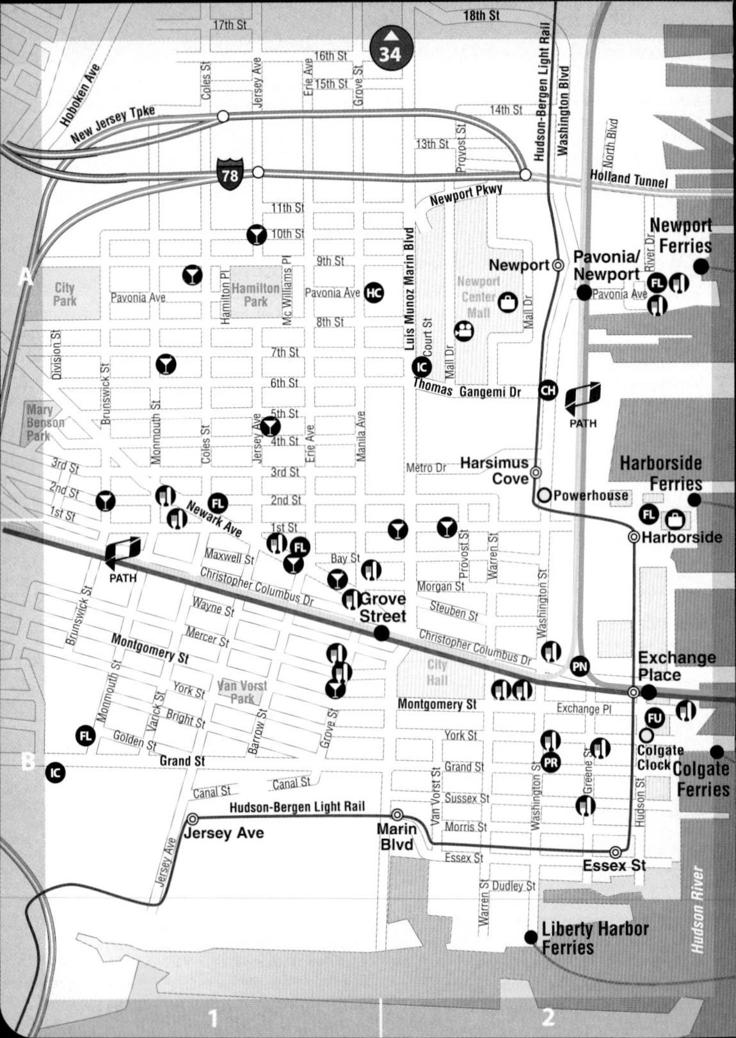

Map 35 • Jersey City

N

18th St
17th St
16th St
15th St
34
Hoboken Ave
Coles St
Jersey Ave
Erie Ave
Grove St
Hudson-Bergen Light Rail
Washington Blvd
New Jersey Tpke
14th St
13th St
Provost St
North Blvd
78
Holland Tunnel
Newport Pkwy
11th St
10th St
9th St
Luis Munoz Marin Blvd
Newport Ferries
A
City Park
Pavonia Ave
Hamilton Pl
Hamilton Park
Mc Williams Pl
Pavonia Ave
HC
Newport
Pavonia/ Newport
River Dr
FL
Pavonia Ave
Newport Center Mall
Mall Dr
8th St
Court St
Division St
7th St
Mall Dr
IC
Brunswick St
6th St
Thomas Gangemi Dr
CH
PATH
Mary Benson Park
Monmouth St
5th St
Jersey Ave
4th St
Coles St
Erie Ave
Manila Ave
3rd St
3rd St
Metro Dr
Harsimus Cove
Harborside Ferries
2nd St
2nd St
Powerhouse
1st St
Newark Ave
FL
1st St
Provost St
Warren St
FL
Harborside
PATH
Maxwell St
Bay St
Christopher Columbus Dr
Grove Street
Morgan St
Brunswick St
Wayne St
Steuben St
Washington St
Mercer St
Montgomery St
Christopher Columbus Dr
City Hall
PN
Exchange Place
York St
Van Vorst Park
Monmouth St
Varick St
Bright St
Montgomery St
Exchange Pl
FU
Barrow St
Grove St
York St
FL
Golden St
Colgate Clock
Colgate Ferries
B
Grand St
Grand St
Washington St
PR
Greene St
IC
Van Vorst St
Canal St
Canal St
Sussex St
Hudson St
Hudson-Bergen Light Rail
Jersey Ave
Marin Blvd
Morris St
Jersey Ave
Essex St
Essex St
Warren St
Dudley St
Hudson River
Liberty Harbor Ferries
1
2

If you are taking the ferry from Manhattan, you will quickly notice that the entire waterfront of Jersey City is under construction. (You'll see at least ten new buildings going up.) Is Jersey City the "Sixth Borough" of New York? Not yet, but when all of the building is complete, it will be interesting to see what has evolved. With many fine restaurants and an increasing number of after-work hangouts popping up, Jersey City is growing as a neighborhood that is well worth checking out.

ATMs

CH • Chase • 575 Washington St
FU • First Union National • 10 Exchange Pl
FL • Fleet • 123 Harborside Financial Center
FL • Fleet • 125 Pavonia Ave
FL • Fleet • 186 Newark Ave
FL • Fleet • 235 Monmouth St
FL • Fleet • 420 Grand St
HC • Hudson City Savings • 495 Grove St
IC • Independence Community • 224 Newark Ave
IC • Independence Community • 400 Marin Blvd
PN • PNC • 95 Christopher Columbus Dr
PR • Provident Savings • 239 Washington St

Landmarks

• **Colgate Clock** • 105 Hudson St
• **Powerhouse** • 344 Washington Blvd

Bars

• **Coles Street Café** • 174 Coles St
• **Dennis and Maria's Bar** • 322 1/2 7th St
• **Hamilton Park Ale House** • 708 Jersey Ave
• **LITM** • 140 Newark Ave
• **Lamp Post Bar and Grille** • 382 2nd St
• **Markers** • Harborside Financial Ctr, Plz II
• **The Merchant** • 279 Grove St
• **PJ Ryan's** • 172 First St
• **White Star** • 230 Brunswick St

Coffee

• **Dunkin' Donuts** • 116 Newark Ave
• **Dunkin' Donuts** • 402 Grand St
• **Eleni's Coffee Shop** • 626 Newark Ave
• **Ground** • 530 Jersey Ave
• **Starbucks** • 97 Pavonia Ave

Movie Theaters

• **Loews Cineplex Newport Center 11** • 30 Mall Dr W

Restaurants

• **Casablanca Coffee Shop** • 354 Grove St
• **Ibby's Falafel** • 303 Grove St
• **Iron Monkey** • 97 Greene St
• **Kitchen Cafe** • 60 Sussex St
• **Komegashi** • 103 Montgomery St
• **Komegashi Too** • 99 Pavonia Ave
• **Madame Claude Cafe** • 364 4th St
• **Marco and Pepe** • 289 Grove St
• **Miss Saigon** • 249 Newark Ave
• **Nicco's Restaurant** • 247 Washington St
• **Oddfellows Restaurant** • 111 Montgomery St
• **Rosie Radigans** • 10 Exchange Pl (Lobby Floor)
• **Saigon Café** • 188 Newark Ave
• **Tania's** • 348 Grove St
• **Unlimited Pizza Café & Diner** • 116 Newark Ave
• **Uno Chicago Bar & Grill** • 286 Washington St
• **ZZ's Brick Oven Pizza** • 118 Pavonia Ave

Shopping

• **Harborside Shopping Complex** • Exchange Pl
• **Newport Center Mall** • 30 Mall Dr W

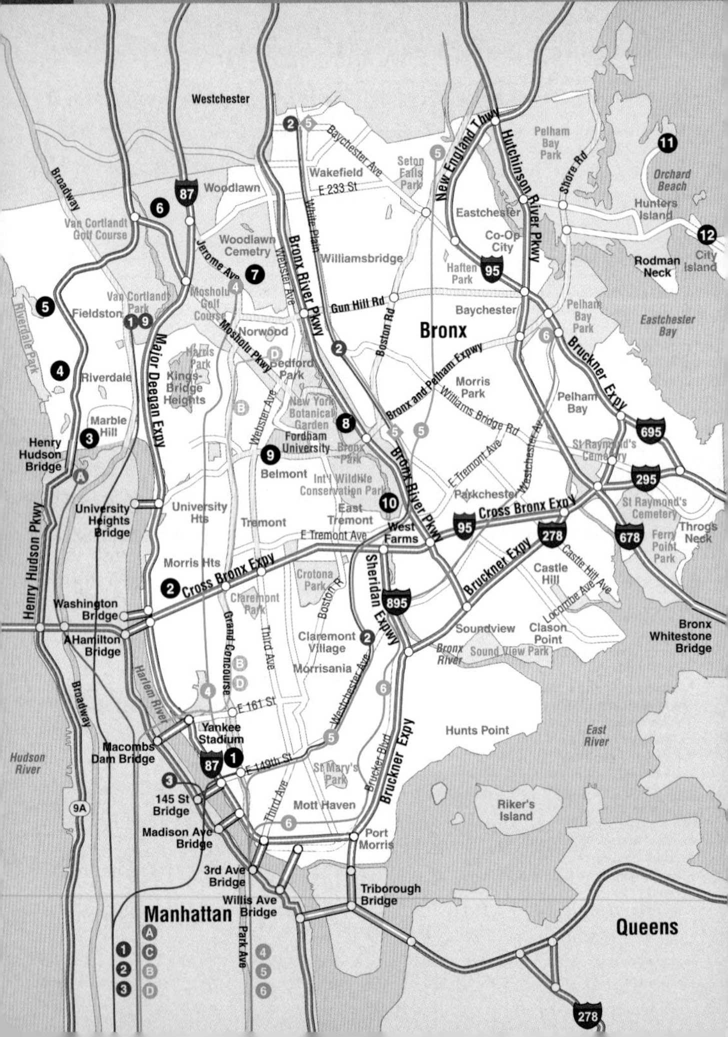

N

Westchester
Woodlawn
Wakefield
E 233 St
Seton Falls Park
Pelham Bay Park
Orchard Beach
Hunters Island
City Island
Rodman Neck
Van Cortlandt Golf Course
Woodlawn Cemetery
Williamsbridge
Eastchester
Co-Op City
Haften Park
Van Cortlandt Park
Mosholu Golf Course
Fieldston
Riverdale Park
Norwood
Gun Hill Rd
Baychester
Bronx
Pelham Bay Park
Eastchester Bay
Harris Park
Kings-Bridge Heights
Bedford Park
Riverdale
Morris Park
Pelham Bay
New York Botanical Garden
Marble Hill
Fordham University
Bronx Park
Henry Hudson Bridge
Belmont
Int'l Wildlife Conservation Park
St Raymond's Cemetery
University Heights Bridge
University Hts
East Tremont
Parkchester
Tremont
E Tremont Ave
West Farms
Throgs Neck
Ferry Point Park
Morris Hts
Crotona Park
Castle Hill
Claremont Park
Washington Bridge
Hamilton Bridge
Claremont Village
Soundview
Clason Point
Bronx Whitestone Bridge
Morrisania
Bronx River
Sound View Park
Yankee Stadium
E 161 St
Hunts Point
East River
Hudson River
Macombs Dam Bridge
E 149th St
St Mary's Park
145 St Bridge
Mott Haven
Riker's Island
Madison Ave Bridge
Port Morris
3rd Ave Bridge
Triborough Bridge
Willis Ave Bridge
Manhattan
Queens
Broadway
Jerome Ave
Mosholu Pkwy
Major Deegan Expy
Henry Hudson Pkwy
Harlem River
Webster Ave
Bronx River Pkwy
White Plain
Boston Rd
Baychester Ave
New England Thwy
Hutchinson River Pkwy
Shore Rd
Bronx and Pelham Expwy
Williams Bridge Rd
Bruckner Expy
E Tremont Ave
Westchester Av
Cross Bronx Expy
Castle Hill Ave
Locombe Ave
Sheridan Expy
Grand Concourse
Third Ave
Westchester Ave
Bruckner Blvd
Park Ave
87
95
695
295
678
278
895
9A
1 2 3 4 5 6 7 8 9 10 11 12

The Bronx gets probably the worst rap of any of the five boroughs, but it's really not deserved. And since part of the Bronx's problems were caused by Robert Moses, you really can't blame it. However, while there are many nice sections of the Bronx, it still feels as though they're the exceptions and not the rule.

Communities

The Bronx has perhaps the largest dichotomy between communities—the private, wooded mansions of Riverdale **4** versus the problematic South Bronx, a general name for the area near Yankee Stadium. The Bronx also contains a huge co-op complex (named "Co-Op City"), quiet streets around Pelham Parkway, several waterfront communities including City Island **12** (one of those rare, interesting places that feel totally un-New York), and one of New York's major universities, Fordham **9**. Finally, although the community of Marble Hill **3** is physically in the Bronx, it's actually part of New York County.

Culture

Some of the Bronx's most interesting cultural spots are actually vestiges of long-gone institutions (or people). For instance, beautiful Woodlawn Cemetery **7** has the remains of Mayor Fiorello LaGuardia, Duke Ellington, and Herman Melville. The bizarre and interesting "Hall of Fame" at Bronx Community College **2** is actually leftover from New York University's dismantled University Heights campus. And Wave Hill **5**, formerly a private estate, is now a wonderful park and occasional concert venue.

Sports

Yankee Stadium **1**, perhaps the Bronx's best-known landmark, has been a fixture on the Harlem River for over seventy years. Since opening, it's seen over 20 Yankee World Series championships. Another major Bronx sports institution is one of America's oldest golf courses, Van Cortlandt Golf Course **6**, or "Vanny" to regulars. You walk past a beautiful lily pond with ducks before dealing with dry, brown fairways, and garbage-strewn roughs. Ah, New York.

Nature

Besides an excellent and underrated system of parks—including Pelham Bay Park, Soundview Park, Van Cortlandt Park, and Ferry Point Park—the Bronx has its well-known Botanical Gardens **8** and zoo, now called the International Wildlife Conservation Park **10**. It also has the extremely popular Orchard Beach **11**.

Food

Belmont: Dominick's, 2335 Arthur Ave, 718-733-2807—Quintessential Italian eatery.
City Island: The Lobster Box, 34 City Island Ave, 718-885-1952—When in Rome, eat seafood.
Riverdale: Bellavista, 554 W 235th St, 718-548-2354—Good, standard Italian food.
University Heights: Jimmy's Bronx Café, 281 W Fordham Rd, 718-329-2000—A Bronx institution.

Landmarks

1 Yankee Stadium
2 The Hall of Fame at Bronx Community College
3 Marble Hill
4 Riverdale
5 Wave Hill
6 Van Cortlandt Golf Course
7 Woodlawn Cemetery
8 Botanical Garden
9 Fordham University
10 Int'l Wildlife Conservation Park
11 Orchard Beach
12 City Island

Manhattan
Hudson River
East River
Holland Tunnel
West Side Expy
Williamsburg Bridge
Manhattan Bridge
Brooklyn Bridge
Brooklyn Battery Tunnel
Governors Island
Greenpoint
Northside
Williamsburg
Sunnyside
Maspeth
Queens
Bushwick
Metropolitan Ave
Grand Ave
Long Island Expy
Broadway
Brooklyn-Queens Expy
Flushing Ave
Myrtle Ave
Fort Greene
Brooklyn Heights
Atlantic Ave
Cobble Hill
Boerum Hill
Carroll Gardens
Red Hook
Park Slope
Prospect Park
Bedford-Stuyvesant
Crown Heights
Eastern Pkwy
Kings Hwy
Brownsville
East New York
Linden Blvd
Empire Blvd
Wingate
Green-Wood Cemetery
Gowanus Expy
Prospect Expy
4th Ave
Sunset Park
Bay Ridge
Fort Hamilton Pkwy
Borough Park
Dyker Heights
Bay Ridge Pkwy
Washington Cemetery
Bensonhurst
Fort Hamilton
Verrazano-Narrows Bridge
Bath Beach
Lower Bay
Ocean Pkwy
Coney Island Ave
Flatbush
Flatbush Ave
Midwood
Flatlands
Rockaway Pkwy
Starrett City
Canarsie
Spring Creek
Carnasie Island
Jamaica Bay
Marine Park
Mill Basin
Bergen Beach
Ruffle Bar
Floyd Bennett Field
Belt Pkwy
Sheepshead Bay
Gravesend
Shore Pkwy
Manhattan Beach
Brighton Beach
Sea Gate
Coney Island
Rockaway Inlet
Rockaway

Until 1898, Brooklyn was its own city. Looking at it objectively today, it could still be a damn fine city all on its own. Of course, with glittering Manhattan just across the water, Brooklyn gets second billing, if it's not ignored altogether. This, of course, makes Brooklynites seethe with justifiable anger, for they believe their borough is just as beautiful and interesting as Manhattan. But since Manhattan rents are skyrocketing, more and more hipsters, yuppies, and just plain folks are moving to Brooklyn—which might make long-time residents start wishing they hadn't been bragging so much for the last 100 years. C'est la vie.

Communities

Brooklyn has 2.5 million people, which makes it one of the largest cities in the US. It has every single type of community you could wish for, and, of course, some you really wouldn't wish for. And many of these communities are in transition, including—but not limited to—Park Slope, Boerum Hill, Carroll Gardens, Bushwick, Red Hook, Williamsburg, Greenpoint, and Fort Greene (the communities all closest to Manhattan!).

However, if you've never explored further out into Brooklyn than the obligatory trip to Coney Island, you're missing some very interesting, and very different, neighborhoods. For instance, Bay Ridge **4** has beautiful single-family homes along its western edge, a killer view of the Verrazano Bridge, and excellent shops and restaurants. Dyker Heights **6** is almost all single-family homes, many of which go all-out with Christmas light displays during the holiday season. Brighton Beach **8** continues to be a haven to many Russian expatriates. And both Ocean Parkway **10** and Midwood **11** have quiet, tree-lined streets that can make one forget all about the hustle and bustle of downtown Brooklyn, or downtown anywhere else for that matter. Finally, while Bedford-Stuyvesant **12** does have its problems, it also has a host of cool public buildings, fun eateries, and beautiful brownstones.

Sports

Brooklyn can't wait for the San Andreas Fault Line to give its final heave and toss all of California into the Pacific Ocean. Why? Because deep down, its residents know that it's the only way the Dodgers will ever come back to Brooklyn. But in the interim, you can check out the Brooklyn Cyclones, the Mets' Class A affiliate, at 1904 Surf Avenue in Coney Island.

Attractions

There are many reasons to dislike Coney Island **7**, but they're simply not good enough when you stack it up against the Cyclone, the ferris wheel, Nathan's, Totonno's, the beach, the freaks, and *The Warriors*. Close by is the Aquarium **13**. Nature trails, parked blimps, views of the water, and scenic marinas all combine to make historical Floyd Bennet Field **9** a very interesting trip. For more beautiful views, you can check out Owl's Point Park **3** in Bay Ridge or the parking lot underneath the Verrazano-Narrows Bridge **5** (located right off the Shore Parkway). It might not be New York's most beautiful bridge, but the Verrazano is hands-down the most awe-inspiring. Both Greenwood Cemetery **2** and Prospect Park **1** can provide enough greenery to keep you happy until you can get to Yosemite. Finally, Brooklyn Heights **14** is the most beautiful residential neighborhood in all of New York. Don't believe us? Go stand on the corner of Willow & Orange Streets.

Food

Here are some restaurants in some of the outlying areas of Brooklyn:
Bay Ridge: Tuscany Grill, 8620 Third Ave—The gorgonzola steak is a must.
Coney Island: Totonno Pizzeria Napolitano,1524 Neptune Ave—Killer pizza, paper-thin. Bizarre hours.
Midwood: DiFara's Pizzeria, 1424 Ave J—Dirty, cheap, disgusting, awesome!
Sunset Park: Nyonya, 5223 Eighth Ave—Good quality Malaysian.

Landmarks

1 Prospect Park
2 Greenwood Cemetery
3 Owl's Point Park
4 Bay Ridge
5 Verrazano-Narrows Bridge
6 Dyker Heights
7 Coney Island
8 Brighton Beach
9 Floyd Bennett Field
10 Ocean Parkway
11 Midwood
12 Bedford-Stuyvesant
13 New York Aquarium
14 Brooklyn Heights

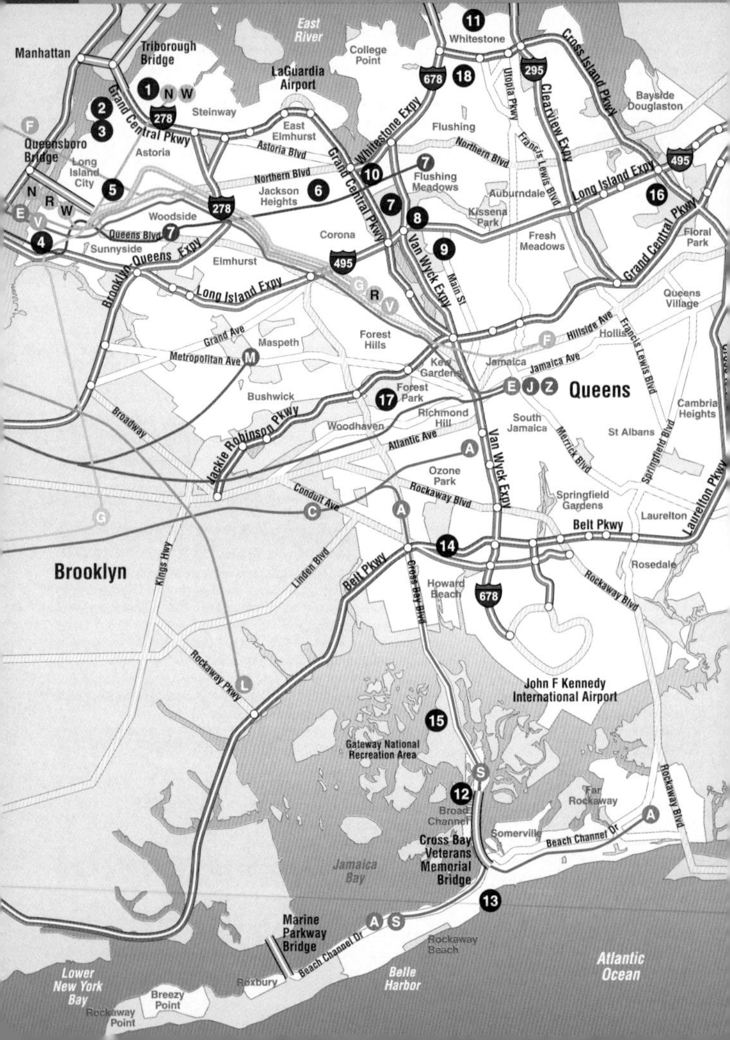

N

East River
Manhattan
Triborough Bridge
LaGuardia Airport
College Point
Whitestone
Queensboro Bridge
Long Island City
Astoria
Steinway
East Elmhurst
Flushing
Bayside
Douglaston
Jackson Heights
Flushing Meadows
Auburndale
Kissena Park
Woodside
Sunnyside
Corona
Fresh Meadows
Floral Park
Elmhurst
Queens Village
Maspeth
Forest Hills
Kew Gardens
Jamaica
Hollis
Bushwick
Forest Park
Richmond Hill
Woodhaven
Queens
South Jamaica
Cambria Heights
St Albans
Ozone Park
Springfield Gardens
Laurelton
Rosedale
Brooklyn
Howard Beach
John F Kennedy International Airport
Gateway National Recreation Area
Broad Channel
Far Rockaway
Somerville
Cross Bay Veterans Memorial Bridge
Jamaica Bay
Marine Parkway Bridge
Rockaway Beach
Atlantic Ocean
Lower New York Bay
Roxbury
Belle Harbor
Breezy Point
Rockaway Point

Grand Central Pkwy
Astoria Blvd
Northern Blvd
Whitestone Expy
Utopia Pkwy
Francis Lewis Blvd
Clearview Expy
Cross Island Pkwy
Long Island Expy
Queens Blvd
Brooklyn-Queens Expy
Van Wyck Expy
Main St
Grand Ave
Metropolitan Ave
Hillside Ave
Jamaica Ave
Jackie Robinson Pkwy
Broadway
Atlantic Ave
Merrick Blvd
Springfield Blvd
Rockaway Blvd
Conduit Ave
Belt Pkwy
Laurelton Pkwy
Kings Hwy
Linden Blvd
Cross Bay Blvd
Rockaway Pkwy
Beach Channel Dr

278
678
295
495

1 2 3 4 5 6 7 8 9 10 11 12 13 14 15 16 17 18

N W R E V F G M J Z A C L S

Queens has everything you'd expect of a big city—great art, great food, ethnic diversity, beautiful parks, sporting events, etc. However, since Queens is New York's largest borough, this is all spread out over 100 square miles. And as Mets fans have discovered long ago, it's more than a hop, skip, and a jump to Flushing—and then there's another 5 miles of Queens east of Flushing that's not even serviced by subway. But if you've got wheels or large, unfinished Thomas Pynchon novels for the subway, exploring Queens can be a blast.

Communities

Queens has almost 2 million people, and they are far from similar to each other. Astoria **1** has the largest concentration of Greek people outside of Greece, Jackson Heights **6** has a vibrant Indian and Pakistani community, and that's just for starters. Mix in the relatively upscale communities of Whitestone **11** and Forest Hills, working-class Howard Beach, industrial Maspeth, sprawling Jamaica, and sleepy Broad Channel **12**, and you've got endless diversity.

Culture

We can't say enough about how cool Socrates Sculpture Park **2** is. Located on the waterfront (next to founder Mark Di Suvero's sculpture studio) at the end of Broadway (take the N train to the Broadway stop and walk west), this park has had some of New York's best outdoor sculpture for the last ten years. Right down the street is the excellent Noguchi Museum **3** (currently under renovation). Astoria is also home to the American Museum of the Moving Image **5**, located in the Kaufman-Astoria Studios district. In Hunter's Point, the expanded and brilliant P.S. 1 Art Museum **4** is a must-see. In Flushing Meadows-Corona Park, check out the gigantic Hall of Science **8**. Finally, if you've never seen the scale model of New York City at the Queens Museum **9** in Corona Park, you should.

Sports

Home to the lovable New York Mets, Shea Stadium **10** is right off the 7 train and the Port Washington branch of the LIRR. Aqueduct Racetrack **14** has its own A train stop (open 11 am-7 pm on racing days). Rockaway Beach **13** is great for swimming (especially mid-week!), and, if there doesn't happen to be anything you want to do at 3 am in Manhattan, drive out to Whitestone Lanes **18**, off the Linden Place exit of the Whitestone Expressway, for your 24-hour bowling pleasure. Every Labor Day, the popular U.S. Open is held at the National Tennis Center **7**.

Nature

Queens is home to the vast Gateway National Recreation Area, which has some excellent trails at its Jamaica Bay Wildlife Refuge **15** facility. Alley Pond Park **16** also has several sections of interest, including the quiet "Upper Alley" area. Finally, the 165 wooded acres of Forest Park **17** provide excellent walks, ponds, and stands of trees.

Food

Below is an insanely short list of Queens eateries, but at least we can say that what's listed is great:
Astoria: Stamatis, 29-12 23rd Ave, 718-932-8596—Really great, unpretentious Greek food.
Corona: Park Side, 107-01 Corona Ave, 718-271-9274—Great neighborhood Italian.
Forest Hills: Nick's Pizza, 108-26 Ascan Ave, 718-263-1126—Queens' best pizza.
Jackson Heights: Jackson Diner, 37-47 74th St, 718-672-1232—Excellent, cheap Indian in a busy neighborhood.
Sunnyside: Hemsin, 39-17 Queens Blvd, 718-937-1715—Turkish. Recommended.
Whitestone: Cooking With Jazz, 1201 154th St, 718-767-6979—Good Cajun food, many miles from Louisiana.

Landmarks

1 Astoria
2 Socrates Sculpture Park
3 Noguchi Museum
4 P.S. 1 Art Museum
5 American Museum of the Moving Image
6 Jackson Heights
7 U.S. Open/National Tennis Center
8 Hall of Science
9 Queens Museum
10 Shea Stadium
11 Whitestone
12 Broad Channel
13 Rockaway Beach
14 Aqueduct Racetrack
15 Jamaica Bay Wildlife Refuge
16 Alley Pond Park
17 Forest Park
18 Whitestone Lanes

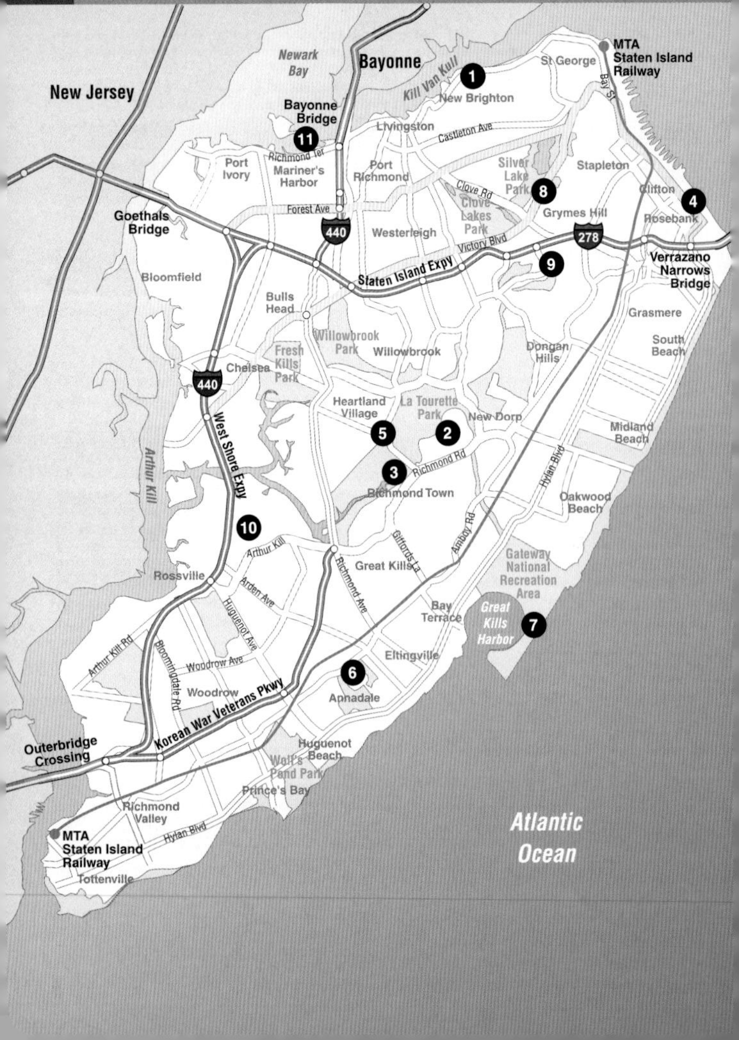

New Jersey
Newark Bay
Bayonne
Kill Van Kull
Bayonne Bridge
11
1
St George
MTA Staten Island Railway
Bay St
New Brighton
Livingston
Castleton Ave
Richmond Ter
Port Ivory
Mariner's Harbor
Port Richmond
Silver Lake Park
Stapleton
Clove Rd
Clove Lakes Park
8
Clifton
4
Goethals Bridge
Forest Ave
440
Westerleigh
Grymes Hill
Rosebank
Victory Blvd
278
Staten Island Expy
9
Verrazano Narrows Bridge
Bloomfield
Bulls Head
Grasmere
Willowbrook Park
Willowbrook
Dongan Hills
South Beach
Fresh Kills Park
Chelsea
440
Heartland Village
La Tourette Park
New Dorp
5
2
Midland Beach
West Shore Expy
Arthur Kill
Richmond Rd
3
Hylan Blvd
Richmond Town
Oakwood Beach
10
Arthur Kill
Giffords La
Amboy Rd
Gateway National Recreation Area
Great Kills
Rossville
Arden Ave
Richmond Ave
Bay Terrace
Great Kills Harbor
7
Huguenot Ave
Arthur Kill Rd
Bloomingdale Rd
Woodrow Ave
Eltingville
6
Woodrow
Korean War Veterans Pkwy
Annadale
Outerbridge Crossing
Huguenot Beach
Wolf's Pond Park
Prince's Bay
Richmond Valley
Atlantic Ocean
Hylan Blvd
MTA Staten Island Railway
Tottenville

Staten Island. Night. The moon rises over the Fresh Kills Landfill. A dog howls in the distance. You take the last bite of your philly cheesesteak and wait for your quarry to emerge from the bushes. A rustle of leaves, and—well, okay, maybe it's not that exciting. But Staten Island, like bagels, the MoMA, and Sonic Youth, is a New York institution. And even though many of its residents would like to secede from NYC, and many other NYC residents would like them to, everyone has to admit that it just wouldn't be the same. And anyway, who would take over the management of the Verrazano-Narrows Bridge?

But Staten Island, while perhaps not the most terribly exciting place, has its share of excellent cultural institutions, history, parks, quirks, and (of course) jerks. Here are some high(low)lights:

Culture

1 **Snug Harbor Cultural Center**, 1000 Richmond Ter, 718-448-2500 Staten Island's premiere cultural hotspot. This interesting complex of buildings was once a maritime hospital and home for retired sailors. Now it hosts excellent art exhibits and concerts, as well as providing gardens, a children's museum, Greek Revival architecture, and walking paths in its 83-acre setting.

2 **Jacques Marchais Museum of Tibetan Art**, 338 Lighthouse Ave, 718-987-3500 An excellent collection of Tibetan art, courtesy of a former New York art dealer.

3 **Historic Richmondtown**, 441 Clark Ave, 718-351-1611 A 30-acre complex of historic buildings on the site of an early Dutch settlement—the oldest building is from 1695.

4 **Alice Austen House**, 2 Hylan Blvd, 718-816-4506 Alice Austen was an early 20th century amateur photographer and a contemporary of Jacob Riis. Some of her 8,000 images are always on view at her house, which also has a great view of lower New York Harbor.

Nature

5 **The Staten Island Greenbelt**, 200 Nevada Ave, 718-667-2165 Although this 2,500-acre swath of land (comprising several different parks) in the center of the island houses a golf course, a hospital, a scout camp, and several graveyards, there is still plenty of real forest to explore on many different trails. Excellent views and nature-walking. A good starting point is High Rock Park, accessible from Nevada Avenue.

6 **Blue Heron Park**, 222 Poillon Ave, 718-967-3542 Accessible from Poillon Avenue in southwestern Staten Island, this quiet 147-acre park has a unique serenity to it. Good ponds, bird-watching, wetlands, streams, etc.

7 **Great Kills Park**, 718-987-6790 This is part of the Gateway National Recreation Area and houses some excellent beaches, a marina, and a nature preserve. It's right off Hylan Boulevard.

8 **Wagner College**, 1 Campus Rd, 718-390-3100 Wagner sits atop a hill commanding beautiful views and has very serene, pleasant surroundings. Worth the winding drive up the hill. Accessible from Howard Avenue.

Other

9 **110/120 Longfellow Road** The estate owned by the Corleone family in *The Godfather*. You might have to wait a while for Johnny Fontaine to show up and sing, though.

10 **The Fresh Kills Landfill**, right off Route 440. Excellent hiking, backcountry camping, and scavenging. Bring the whole family.

11 **Ship Graveyard**, off of Richmond Terrace just west of the Bayonne Bridge. Excellent views of rotting ships, the Bayonne Bridge, and other industrial wonders. Recommended.

Food

Snug Harbor:

R.H. Tugs, 1115 Richmond Ter, 718-447-6369 Overlooks Kill Van Kull so there's a lot of tug and tanker action.

Rosebank:

Aesop's Tables, 1233 Bay St & Maryland Ave, 718-720-2005 Seasonal dishes and a lush outdoor garden for the warmer months.
Marina Café, 154 Mansion Ave & Hillside Ter, 718-967-3077 Pricey seafood joint where the best feature is the view!

Richmondtown:

Parsonage, 74 Arthur Kill Rd & Clarke Ave, 718-351-7879 Charming atmosphere offering reasonable food at reasonable prices.

Driving In/Through Staten Island

At certain times, it can be a very quick trip from Brooklyn to New Jersey via Staten Island. You take the Verrazano to the Staten Island Expressway (Route 278) to Route 440 to the Outerbridge Crossing, and you're almost halfway to Princeton or the Jersey shore. However...the Staten Island Expressway can many times be jammed. Two scenic, though not really quicker, alternatives: one, you can take Hylan Boulevard all the way south to almost the southwest tip of Staten Island, and then cut up to the Outerbridge Crossing; two, you can take Richmond Terrace around the north shore and cross to New Jersey at the Goethals Bridge. Remember, neither is really faster, but at least you'll be moving.

Battery Park Parks Conservancy: 212-267-9700

Battery Park City is a 92-acre planned community on Manhattan's southwest tip. Built on landfill from the construction of the World Trade Center, it was also among the hardest hit by the events of September 11th, but it is well on its way to recovery. This is not a surprise, since the neighborhood has some distinct advantages—its views of the harbor, its plentiful green space, and the overall good planning that has gone into the community (mostly sparing it from the shortcomings of Roosevelt Island). The Battery Park City Authority keeps track of changes to the area on their interesting and informative website at www.batteryparkcity.org.

BPC has gone through many stages of urban planning over the course of its history, but the latest plan—42% residential, 30% open space, 19% streets, and 9% commercial—does seem to include something for everyone. A total of 14,000 living units are planned, with a potential occupancy of 25,000 residents. There are big plans for "green" apartment buildings—all future projects will have water- and power- saving features, and the first building, Solaire, opened its doors in July 2003 to rave reviews. BPC's network of parks—Robert F. Wagner, Jr., South Cove, Rector, North Cove, the Esplanade, and Governor Nelson A. Rockefeller—is swiftly becoming known for beautiful views, excellent outdoor sculptures (by Louise Bourgeois, Tom Otterness, Martin Puryear, Jim Dine, and Brian Tolle), and as great places to just chill out. And the presence of Stuyvesant High School, Siah Armajani's Tribeca Bridge, Kevin Roche's Museum of Jewish Heritage, and Caesar Pelli's Winter Garden and World Financial Center make the architecture of Battery Park City nothing to sneeze at. Despite all this, BPC is still a bit un-NY—too planned and too boring (there's no nightlife). A nice place to visit, but, unless you have a family, not a great place to live.

For more information, you can check out www.lowermanhattan.info, www.batteryparkcityonline.com, www.bpcparks.org, and www.bpcdogs.org.

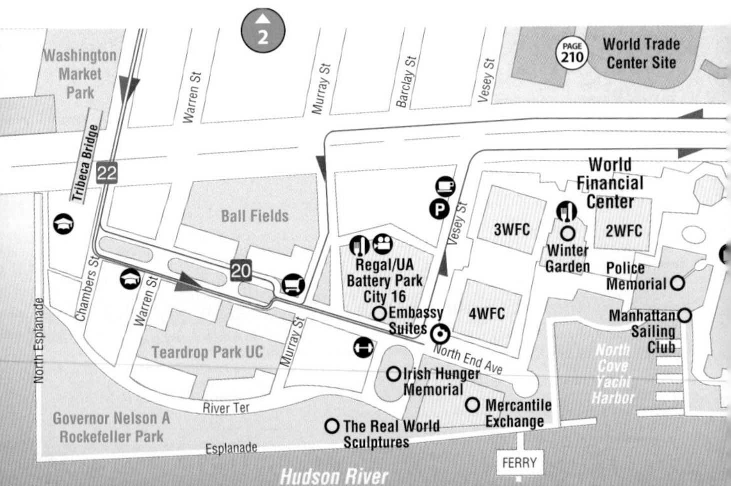

ATMs

CH • **Chase** • 331 South End Ave

Landmarks

- **Embassy Suites**
- **Irish Hunger Memorial**
- **Municipal Credit Union**
- **Manhattan Sailing Club**
- **Mercantile Exchange**
- **Police Memorial**
- **The Real World Sculptures**
- **Ritz-Carlton**
- **Winter Garden**

Schools

- **IS 289 & PS 89** • 201 Warren St
- **Stuyvesant High School** • 345 Chambers St

Coffee

- **Starbucks** • 250 Vesey St

Gyms

- **Liberty Club MCB** • 200 Rector Pl
- **New York Sports Clubs** • 102 North End Ave

Liquor Stores

- **Bulls & Bears Winery** • 309 South End Ave

Movie Theaters

- **Regal Battery Park City 16** • 102 North End Ave

Restaurants

- **Cove Restaurant** • 2 South End Ave
- **Foxhounds** • 320 South End Ave
- **The Grill Room** • Winter Garden, World Financial Center
- **Picasso Pizza** • 303 South End Ave
- **Samantha's Fine Foods** • 235 South End Ave
- **Steamer's Landing** • 375 South End Ave
- **Wave Japanese Restaurant** • 21 South End Ave
- **Zen** • 311 South End Ave

Video Rental

- **Video Room** • 300 Rector Pl

Shopping

- **Battery Park Pharmacy** • 327 South End Ave

Car Rental

- **Avis** • 345 South End Ave

Parking

Bus Lines

9 20 22

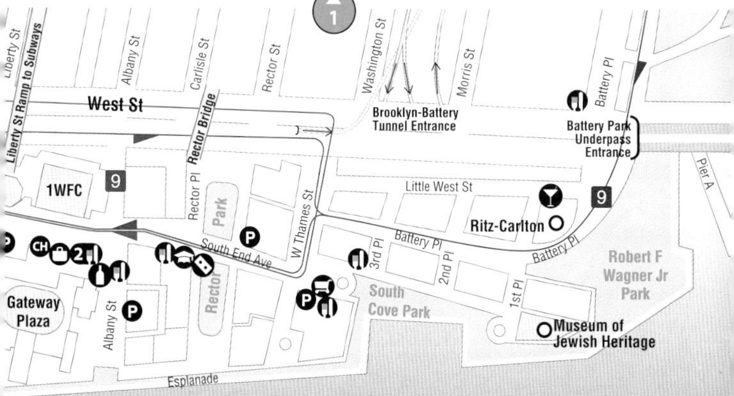

General Information

www.centralpark.org
Central Park Conservancy: 212-310-6600
Shakespeare in the Park: 212-539-8750

Overview

Central Park, designed by Frederick Law Olmsted (with help from Calvert Vaux) in the 1850s, is an 843-acre haven to many New Yorkers. On a summer Saturday, one can walk through the park and see jugglers, magicians, disco roller-skater-bladers, Hungarian folk dancing, skateboarders, joggers, operas, rock concerts, ball players, *Troilus and Cressida*, boaters, art, turtles, frogs, birds, and…oh, yes, billions of people. However, the park is big enough so that there are many, many quiet spots (including official "quiet zones" such as the Shakespeare Gardens **17** for reading, picnicking, and napping.

Practicalities

Central Park is easily accessible by subway, since the A C B D N R W 1 2 3 9 trains all ring the park (odd, though, that there are no stations within the park). Parking along Central Park West is usually pretty good—if you go in the mornings, you'll have an even easier time of it since most New Yorkers are "late to bed, late to rise" types. Unless you're there for a big concert, a softball game, or for Shakespeare in the Park, walking around Central Park (especially alone!) at night is not recommended.

Attractions

Like the city itself, Central Park is an eclectic mix of many different types of attractions. Just when you think that Central Park is nothing more than an overcrowded noisy place crawling with roller bladers banging into each other, you'll stumble upon a quiet glade that houses a small sculpture and three people reading books.

Nature

There are an amazing number of both plant and animal species that inhabit the park (separate from the creatures housed in its two zoos **4** & **8**). A good source of information on all the flora and fauna is schoolteacher Leslie Day's web site, at www.nysite.com/nature/index.htm.

Architecture & Sculpture

Architecturally, Central Park is known for several structures. Emma Stebbins designed the beautiful Bethesda Fountain and Terrace **11** that has become the "center" of the park for many people. The view of Turtle Pond from Belvedere Castle **16** (home of the Central Park Learning Center) is also not to be missed. The Arsenal **5** is a wonderful ivy-clad building that houses several Parks Department offices. There are tons of sculptures in the park, although two of the most notable are perhaps Alice in Wonderland **15** and the Obelisk **19**. Oh…The Metropolitan Museum of Art also happens to be in the park.

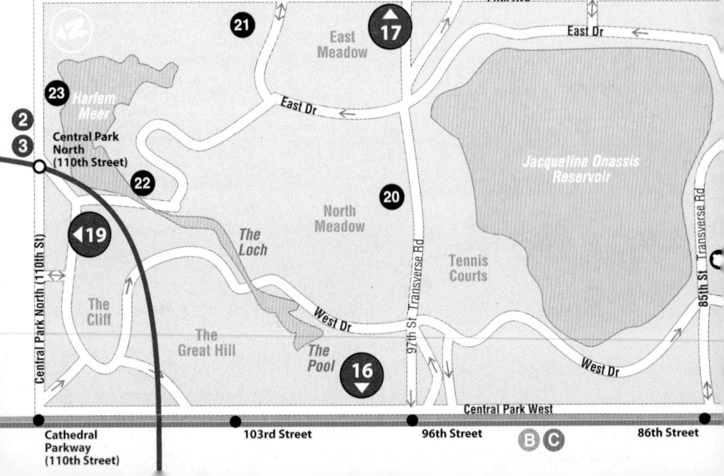

Open Spaces

Perhaps the attractions most loved by New Yorkers are Central Park's "spaces." Space being at a premium in the average New Yorker's apartment probably has a lot to do with this, but nonetheless, places such as Strawberry Fields **10**, the Great Lawn, the Ramble, and Sheep's Meadow are prime hang-outs for many New Yorkers.

Performance

Central Park is a microcosm of the great cultural attractions New York has to offer. The Delacorte Theater **18** is the home of Shakespeare in the Park, a New York tradition begun by famous director Joseph Papp. Summerstage **9** is now an extremely popular summer concert venue for all types of music, including the occasional killer rock concert. Opera companies and classical philharmonics also show up in the park frequently, as does the odd mega-star (Garth Brooks, Diana Ross, etc.).

Sports

Roller blading and roller skating are very popular (not just at the Roller Skating Rink **7**—see www.centralparkskate.com, www.cpdsa.org, and www.skatecity.com), as is jogging, especially around the Reservoir (1.57 mi) and the loop (about 6 mi). The Great Lawn, since its reconstruction, has beautiful softball fields. There are also softball fields at Heckscher Playground. There are 30 tennis courts in Central Park (usually with a long waiting list), fishing at Harlem Meer, gondola rides and boat rentals at the Loeb Boathouse, model boat rentals at the Conservatory Water, chess and checkers at the Chess and Checkers House **25**, and rock-climbing lessons at the North Meadow Rec Center. There is also volleyball, basketball, skateboarding, bicycling, and an infinite number of pick-up soccer, frisbee, football, and kill-the-carrier games being played. If horseback riding is more your speed, you can rent a steed from Claremont Riding Academy (212-724-5100) on W 89th Street at Amsterdam Avenue and ride into the park. Finally, Central Park is where the NYC Marathon ends each year, in case you're still not tired.

Landmarks

1 Wollman Rink
2 Carousel
3 The Dairy
4 The Zoo
5 The Arsenal
6 Tavern on the Green
7 Roller Skating Rink
8 Children's Zoo
9 Summerstage
10 Strawberry Fields
11 Bethesda Fountain
12 Bow Bridge
13 Loeb Boathouse
14 Model Boat Racing
15 Alice in Wonderland
16 Belvedere Castle
17 Shakespeare Gardens
18 Delacorte Theater
19 The Obelisk
20 North Meadow Recreation Center
21 Conservatory Garden
22 Lasker Rink
23 Dana Discovery Center
24 Metropolitan Museum of Art
25 Chess & Checkers House

Police Precinct
86th St & Transverse Rd

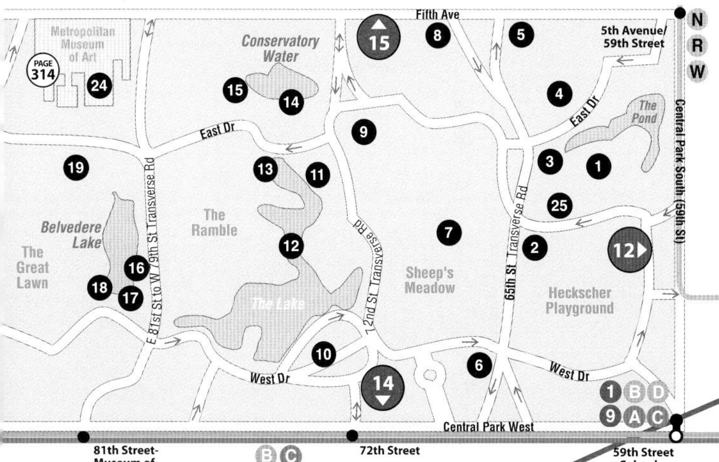

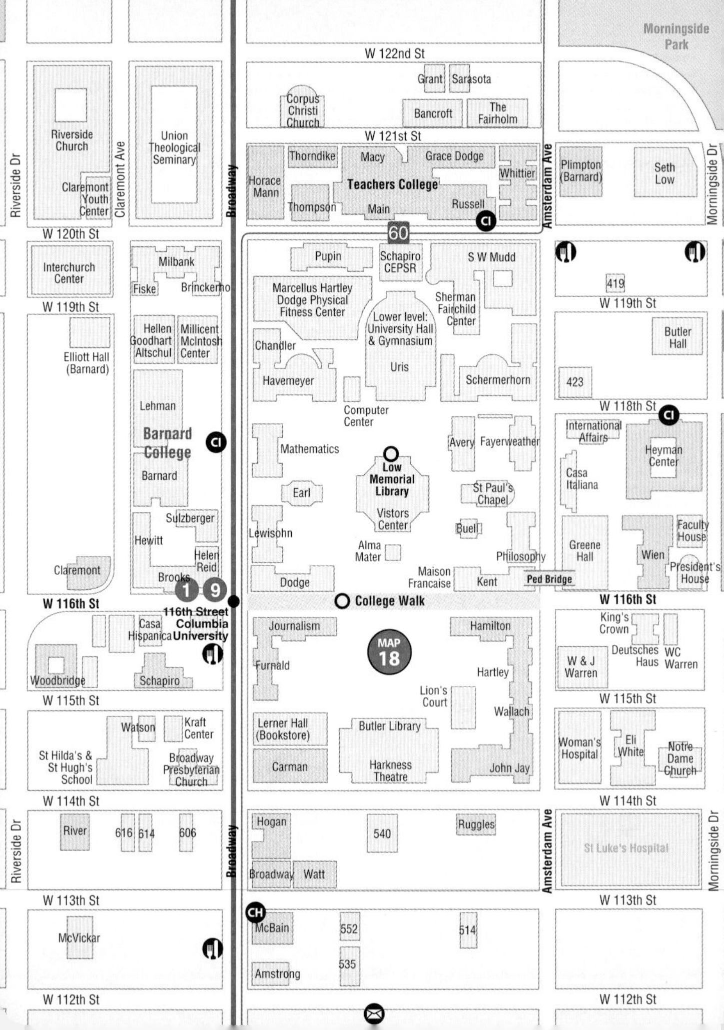
Morningside Park
W 122nd St
Grant
Sarasota
Corpus Christi Church
Bancroft
The Fairholm
W 121st St
Riverside Church
Union Theological Seminary
Claremont Youth Center
Riverside Dr
Claremont Ave
Broadway
Horace Mann
Thorndike
Macy
Grace Dodge
Whittier
Teachers College
Thompson
Main
Russell
Amsterdam Ave
Plimpton (Barnard)
Seth Low
Morningside Dr
W 120th St
60
Interchurch Center
Milbank
Fiske
Brinckerhoff
Pupin
Schapiro CEPSR
S W Mudd
419
W 119th St
Marcellus Hartley Dodge Physical Fitness Center
Sherman Fairchild Center
Lower level: University Hall & Gymnasium
Elliott Hall (Barnard)
Hellen Goodhart Altschul
Millicent McIntosh Center
Chandler
Uris
Butler Hall
Havemeyer
Schermerhorn
423
Computer Center
W 118th St
Lehman
Barnard College
International Affairs
Mathematics
Avery
Fayerweather
Heyman Center
Low Memorial Library
Barnard
Casa Italiana
Earl
St Paul's Chapel
Sulzberger
Vistors Center
Buell
Faculty House
Hewitt
Lewisohn
Greene Hall
Helen Reid
Alma Mater
Wien
Claremont
Philosophy
President's House
Brooks
Dodge
Maison Francaise
Kent
Ped Bridge
1
9
W 116th St
College Walk
W 116th St
116th Street Columbia University
Casa Hispanica
Journalism
Hamilton
King's Crown
MAP 18
Deutsches Haus
WC Warren
W & J Warren
Furnald
Hartley
Woodbridge
Schapiro
W 115th St
Lion's Court
W 115th St
Wallach
Watson
Kraft Center
Lerner Hall (Bookstore)
Butler Library
Woman's Hospital
Eli White
Notre Dame Church
St Hilda's & St Hugh's School
Broadway Presbyterian Church
Carman
Harkness Theatre
John Jay
W 114th St
W 114th St
Hogan
River
616
614
606
540
Ruggles
St Luke's Hospital
Broadway
Watt
W 113th St
W 113th St
CH
McBain
552
514
McVickar
535
Amstrong
W 112th St
W 112th St

Overview

Founded in 1754 and originally known as King's College, Columbia University is among the country's most famous and prestigious universities. Columbia moved to its present campus, designed by McKim, Mead, and White, in 1897. Back then, the surrounding area was quite sparsely occupied, but in the hundred-plus years since, the neighborhood of Morningside Heights has been built up considerably. The relationship between the University and the Morningside Heights neighborhood is a complicated one. On the one hand, Columbia is a focal point for the neighborhood and provides it with students quite ready to dispose of money in its stores and restaurants (and all that intellectual stuff, too). At times though, community members have put up opposition to the school's policies, and there's certainly some resentment for what some perceive as heavy- handedness by Columbia. The most famous of these struggles came in response to Columbia's plans to build a gymnasium in Morningside Park. Thankfully, the park was saved, so that today people can continue to avoid walking through it.

Phone Numbers

Morningside Campus	212-854-1754
Health Services Campus	212-305-2500
Visitors Center	212-854-4900
Public Affairs	212-854-5573
University Development and Alumni Relations	212-870-3100
Library Information	212-854-2271

General Info

Columbia University
NFT Map Number: 18
2960 Broadway
www.columbia.edu

Student Enrollment (Fall 2002):
Undergraduate: 7,054
Graduate: 5,638
Professional: 6,130
Health Sciences: 2,382
Special Programs & Non-degree Students: 2,218
University Total: 23,422

Endowment: Market Value as of June 30, 2002
$4.238 billion

ATMs

CI • Citibank • 3009 Broadway
CI • Citibank • 420 W 118th St
CI • Citibank • 525 W 120th St
CH • Chase • 2898 Broadway

* Generic ATMs are located in the entrance to John Jay Hall, the lobby of Dodge Physical Fitness Center and in the copy center in the International Affairs Building. John Jay is accessible 24-Hours.

Landmarks

• **College Walk**
• **Low Memorial Library**

Post Office

• **Columbia University** • 534 W 112th St

Restaurants

• **Le Monde** • 2885 Broadway • 212-531-3939
• **Massawa** • 1239 Amsterdam Ave • 212-663-0505
• **Ollie's** • 2957 Broadway • 212-932-3300
• **Terrace in the Sky** • 400 W 119th St • 212-666-9490

Popular to residents of the East Village and the Lower East Side, East River Park is a long, thin slice of land sandwiched between FDR Drive and the East River that runs from Jackson Street up to 14th Street. East River Park was built in the early '40s as part of FDR Drive (a.k.a. another Robert Moses project). With the Park's recent refurbishments, its sporting facilities are some of the best in Manhattan. We eagerly await the completion of construction along the East River Esplanade with its inclusion as an eastern leg of the East Coast Greenway through Manhattan, which is sure to make it one of the best spots for walking on the island!

How to Get There

Two FDR Drive exits will get you very close to East River Park—the Houston Street exit and the Grand Street exit. Technically, however, there are no cars allowed in the park. There is some parking available at the extreme south end of the park by Jackson Street off the access road, but it's hard to get to and not well marked. Plan to find street parking just west of the FDR and cross over on a footbridge.

If you are taking the subway, you'd better have your hiking boots on—the fact that the closest subway (the F train at Delancey/Essex Street) is so far away (at least 4 avenue blocks) is one of the reasons East River Park has stayed mainly a neighborhood park. Fortunately, if you're into buses, the 14 and the 8 get you pretty close. Regardless of the bus or subway lines, you will have to cross one of the 5 pedestrian bridges that traverse FDR Drive. Of course, the most scenic way of getting to the park is by using the East River Esplanade that runs from Battery Park (these paths are still being worked on, so they aren't perfect yet) up to the Upper East Side.

Attractions

The usually quiet park comes alive in the summer and on weekends. Hundreds of families barbeque in the areas between the athletic fields, blaring music and eating to their hearts' content. Others take leisurely strolls or jogs along the East River Esplanade, which offers some of the most dramatic and pretty views of the East River and Brooklyn. Many have turned empty areas of the park into unofficial dog runs, places for pick-up games of ultimate frisbee or soccer, and spaces to simply

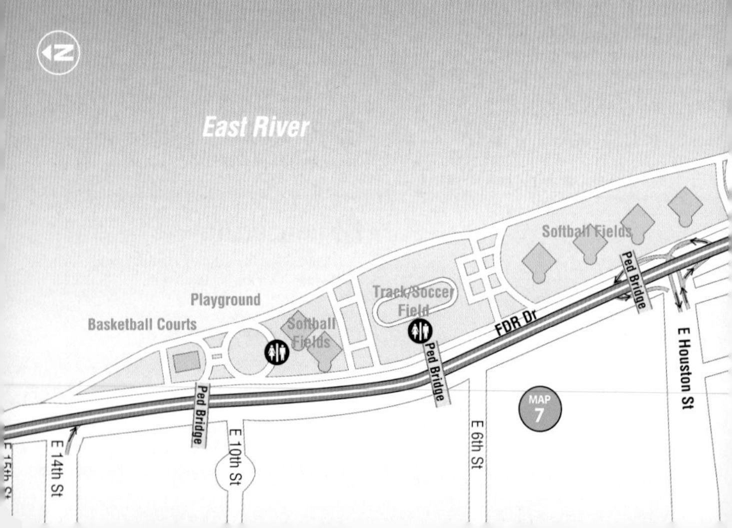

sunbathe. It's common to see fishermen along the water trying to catch fish—believe it or not, people actually catch fish—bluefish and striped bass even. Unsurprisingly, nothing caught in the East River should be eaten—while the water quality has improved dramatically, it's still full of pollutants.

Sports

The sports facilities at East River Park have gone through a heavy reconstruction project. The park now includes facilities for football, softball, basketball, cricket, soccer, and tennis. You can call 212-387-7678 for information on reserving a field or court. Thankfully, many of the fields have been re-surfaced with a resilient synthetic turf. This was a smart move given the amount of use the park gets by all the different sports leagues.

Facilities

There are three bathroom facilities located in the park; one at the tennis courts, one at the soccer/track field, and one up in the northern part of the park by a children's playground. The reconstruction has provided the park with new benches, game tables, a harbor seals spray sprinkler with animal art, and new drinking fountains. Aside from the occasional guy with a grocery cart full of cold drinks or pushcart with flavored ice, there aren't any food or drink facilities close by. Your best bet is to arrive to the park with any supplies you might need—if that's too difficult, try a bodega on Avenue D.

Safety

The park is relatively safe, especially during the daytime, but we would not recommend hanging out after dark, even if you are just passing through.

Esoterica

The fancy $3.5 million ampitheater/restaurant that was to replace the sad-looking, abandoned, graffiti-covered, crumbling Corlears Hook Pavilion band-shell is not happening. Built in 1941, and closed since 1971, this amphitheater was actually the original home of Joseph Papp's Shakespeare in the Park. A less ambitious reconstruction took place in 2001 and with new seating, a renovated bandshell and a good scrubbing, the facility is currently available for use.

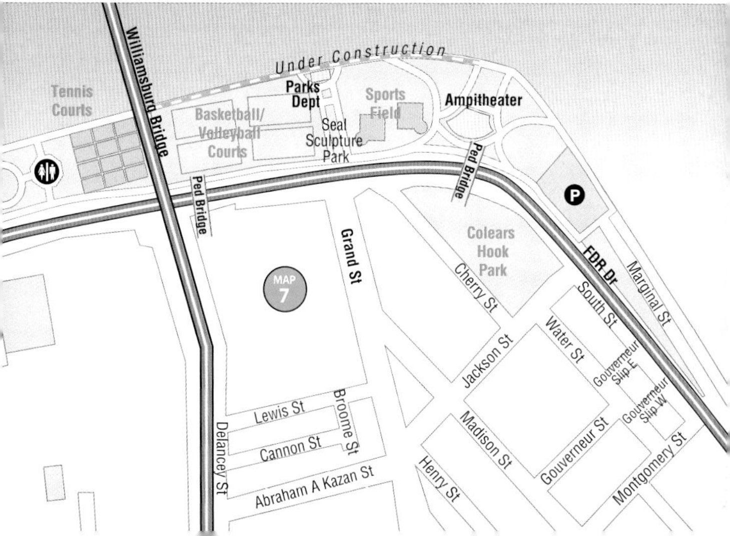

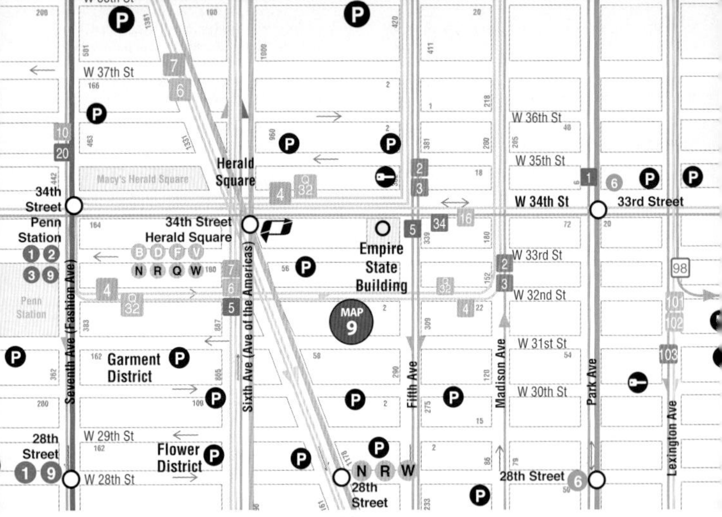

General Information

Location: 350 Fifth Ave at 34th St
NFT Map Number: 9
General Information: 212-736-3100 or info@esbnyc.com
Website: www.esbnyc.com
Observatory Hours: 9:30 am to midnight, last elevator to top is at 11:15 pm.
Holiday Observatory Hours: New Year's Eve 9 am-7 pm, last elevator goes up at 6:15 pm. New Year's Day 11 am to midnight, last elevator leaves at 11:15 pm.
Observatory Admission: $11 for adults, $10 for children aged 12-17 and seniors, $9 for military, and $6 for children aged 6-11. Toddlers (under 5) accompanied by an adult and military personnel in uniform get in free.

Overview

The Empire State Building, designed by the firm of Schreve, Lamb & Harmon Associates, was built in about 14 months by a lot of very determined individuals. Its framework was constructed in an unprecedented two-month span. Much of the building was prefabricated, and assembly took place at an average rate of four-and-a-half stories per week. It's no wonder, then, that the mayor gets frustrated when it takes four years to re-do a mile-long stretch of the FDR Drive.

The ESB is a natural lightning conductor and is struck up to 100 times a year. On Valentine's Day, the chapel on the 80th floor houses a giant group wedding for all who show up. The NYC Roadrunners Club hosts an annual Run-Up, where the fastest runners have to bound up all 1,860 steps in under 11 minutes. The Mezzanine is now the scene of New York Skyride, a giant "thrill ride" simulation of a rooftop helicopter flight. There are two observation areas—the open terrace on the 86th floor and the glass-enclosed 102nd floor. Unfortunately, due to limited capacity and long waiting lines, the 102nd floor has been closed to the general public.

The ESB also has an excellent, info-packed website (www.esbnyc.com) that includes history, trivia, and a complete schedule of events.

The Lights

The top 30 floors of the ESB have automated color fluorescent lighting that is lit for holidays and other days of recognition, celebration, and memoriam. Between holidays and events, white lighting is used. The following semi-official lighting schedule lists colors from bottom to top as they appear from the street.

Lighting Schedule (for updates/changes, check www.esbnyc.com)

January • Martin Luther King, Jr Day
January • March of Dimes
January/Febuary • Lunar New Year
February 14 • Valentine's Day
February • President's Day
February • Westminster Kennel Club
February • Swisspeaks Festival for Switzerland
February • World Cup Archery Championship
March 17 • St Patrick's Day
March • Greek Independence Day
March • Equal Parents Day/ Childrens' Rights
March • Wales/St David's Day
March • Oscar Week in NYC
March • Colon Cancer Awareness
March • Red Cross Month
March–April • Spring/Easter Week
April • Earth Day
April • Child Abuse Prevention
April • National Osteoporosis Society
April • Rain Forest Day
April • Israel Independence Day
April • Dutch Queen's Day
April • Tartan Day
May • Muscular Dystrophy
May • Armed Forces Day
May • Memorial Day
May • Police Memorial Day
May • Fire Department Memorial Day
May • Haitian Culture Awareness
June 14 • Flag Day
June • Portugal Day
June • NYC Triathlon
June • Stonewall Anniversary/Gay Pride
July 4 • Independence Day
July • Bahamas Independence Day
July • Bastille Day
July • Peru Independence
July • Columbia Heritage & Independence
August • US Open
August • Jamaica Independence Day
August • India Independence Day
August • Pakistan Independence Day
September • Mexico Independence Day
September • Labor Day
September • Brazil Independence Day
September • Pulaski Day
September • Race for the Cure
September • Switzerland admitted to the UN
September • Qatar Independence
September • Fleet Week/Support our Servicemen and Servicewomen/ Memorial for 9/11
September • Feast of San Gennaro
October • Breast Cancer Awareness
October • German Reunification Day
October • Columbus Day
October 24 • United Nations Day
October • Big Apple Circus
October • Pennant/World Series win for the Yankees
October • Pennant/World Series win for the Mets [Ha!]
October • NY Knicks Opening Day
October–November • Autumn
October • Walk to End Domestic Violence
November • NYC Marathon
November • Veterans' Day
November • Alzheimer's Awareness
December • First night of Hannukah
December • "Day Without Art/Night Without Lights"/AIDS Awareness
December-January 7 (with interruptions) • Holiday Season

Hudson River Park
West Side Hwy
Jacob K Javits Convention Center
Eleventh Ave
Tenth Ave
Dyer Ave
Ninth Ave
Eighth Ave
W 38th St
W 37th St
W 36th St
W 35th St
W 34th St
W 33rd St
MAP 8
34th Street Penn Station

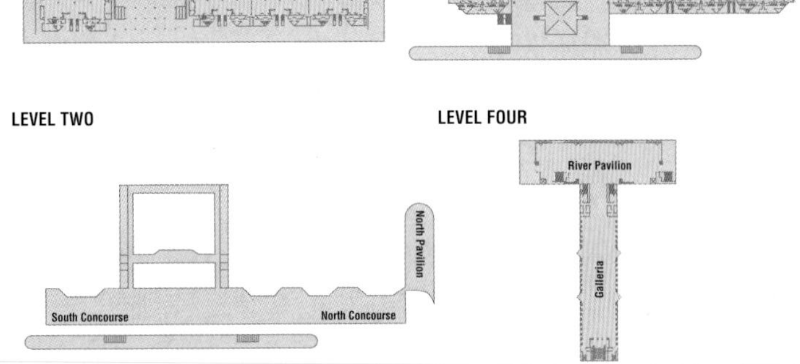
LEVEL ONE
1E
1D
1C
1B
1A
LEVEL THREE
3E
3D
3B
3A
LEVEL TWO
South Concourse
North Concourse
North Pavilion
LEVEL FOUR
River Pavilion
Galleria

General Information

NFT Map Number: 8
Website: www.javitscenter.com
Phone Number: 212-216-2000
Fax Number: 212-216-2588

Location:
Jacob K. Javits Convention Center
655 W 34th St

Overview

The Jacob K. Javits Center, designed by the firm I.M. Pei & Partners and completed in 1986, is a massive glass-and-steel behemoth of a convention hall next to the Hudson River between 34th and 40th Streets. It was built with the purpose of providing a place for big trade shows, conventions, and expositions, but its true purpose is clearly to annoy anyone who has to go there, since it's in the middle of nowhere with no subway link. If you do get there, you might find that the glass walls and ceiling are impressive, as is the center's capacity and flexibility, but as far as convention centers go, it's definitely not up to the standards of other big cities (it now ranks about 14th in terms of its size). Still, it replaced the Coliseum, which somehow managed to be worse than the Javits.

There's been talk of expanding it, along with building an on-site hotel and a stadium for the Jets nearby, but, as of now, there is no groundbreaking ceremony in sight.

Usually a massive build-up of expensive buildings in a small-scale neighborhood is a bad idea, but in this case it might be an okay compromise, since the surrounding area is currently quite bleak and sketchy. Exactly why nice restaurants and hotels didn't spring up around the city's biggest meeting place for business travelers is a mystery, but as it is, Eleventh Avenue and the surrounding streets offer little in eating options and accommodations.

How to Get There—Mass Transit

Until they extend that 7 train, there's no direct subway access to the center. The closest subway stop is at 34th Street/Penn Station 1 2 3 9 A C E, but even that's a good 4- to 5-block hike away. You can also take the buses from the 42nd Street 42 and 34th Street 34 subway stops which will both drop you off right outside the center.

There are also numerous shuttle buses that run to various participating hotels and other locales free of charge for convention goers. Schedules and routes vary for each convention, so ask at the information desk on the first floor.

From New Jersey, the NY Waterway operates a ferry from Weehawken, NJ that ships you across the Hudson River to 39th Street and Twelfth Avenue in 4 minutes, dropping you just one block from the Javits Center. The ferry leaves every 10-15 minutes during peak hours. Call 1-800-53-FERRY for a schedule and more information

ATMs

CH • Chase • Level One
CH • Chase • Level Three

Services

Coat Check
Concierge Services
First Aid
Hudson News
Information
Lost and Found
Mailboxes Etc
My New York Office
Shoeshine

Food

The food at the Javits Center is, of course, rapaciously expensive, and, if you're exhibiting, usually sold out by 2:30 in the afternoon. Our suggestion is to look for people handing out Chinese food menus and have them deliver to your booth. (And yes, they take credit cards. And yes, it's bad Chinese food.)

Asian Star
The Bakery
Boar's Head Deli
Caliente Cab Company
Carvel Ice Cream Bakery
Cocktail Lounge
Dai Kichi Sushi
The Dining Car
Feast of the Dragon
Gourmet Coffee Bar
The Grille
Korean Market
Kosher Food and Sushi
Nathan's
Panini
Villa Cucina Italiana
Villa Pizza

Lincoln Center / Columbus Circle

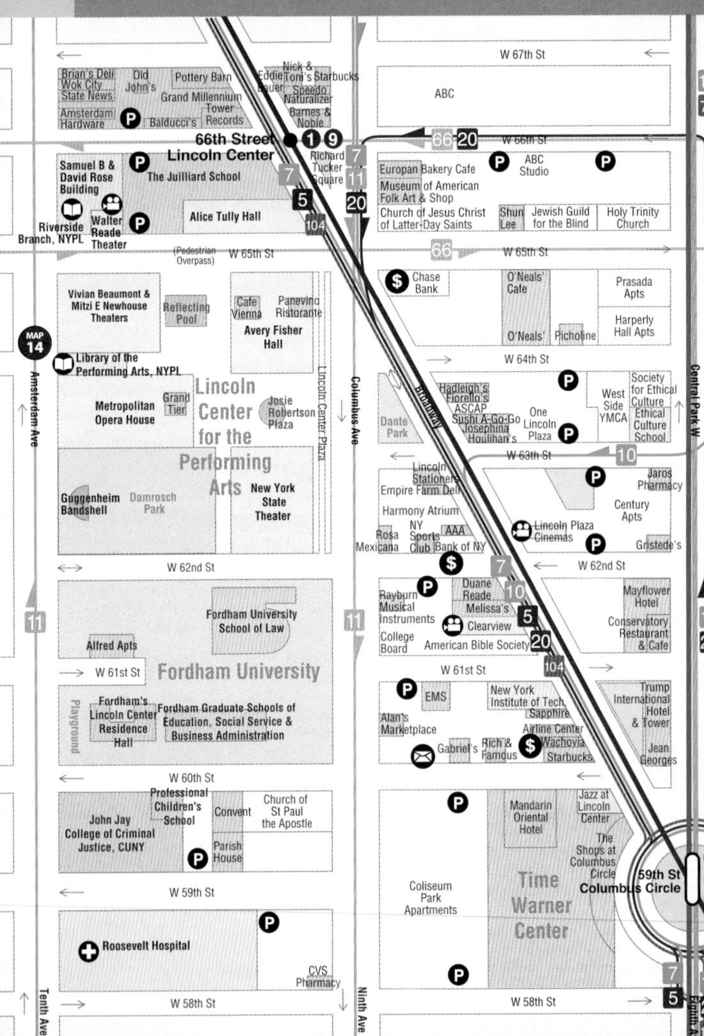

General Information

Website: www.lincolncenter.org
General Information 212-546-2656 (212-LINCOLN)
Customer Service 212-875-5456
Alice Tully Hall 212-875-5050
Avery Fisher Hall 212-875-5030
The Chamber Music Society 212-875-5775
Film Society of Lincoln Center 212-875-5600
Guided Tours 212-875-5350
Jazz at Lincoln Center 212-258-9800
The Julliard School 212-799-5000
Lincoln Center Theater 212-362-7600
The Metropolitan Opera House 212-362-6000
New York City Ballet and Opera 212-870-5500
New York Philharmonic 212-875-5700
New York State Theater 212-870-5570
Parking Garage 212-874-9021
Walter Reade Theater 212-875-5601

Ticket Purchase Phone Numbers

Center Charge, Alice Tully and Avery Fisher Halls . 212-721-6500
Film Society of Lincoln Center 212-496-3809
MovieFone, Walter Reade Theater: 212-777-FILM
TeleCharge, Lincoln Center Theater 212-239-6200
Ticketmaster, New York State Theater 212-307-4100
Ticketmaster, Met & Ballet 212-307-4100

Overview

Lincoln Center is easily one of Manhattan's most vibrant and romantic spots. It's almost obscene how much culture is packed into this four-square-block area—Lincoln Center has one of the world's most famous opera houses, three beautiful theaters, an acoustically designed music hall, an outdoor bandshell, a movie theater, a performing arts library, a ballet school, and an association with one of the best music schools in the country. Not bad for what was once a terrible, poverty-ridden section of New York. Even Robert Moses got some things right.

Lincoln Center, besides all its performance spaces, also boasts some of the city's signature art and architectural gems. Henry Moore's Reclining Figure is the centerpiece of the reflecting pool, and Mark Chagall's murals grace the foyer of the Metropolitan Opera House. Philip Johnson's plaza fountain holds the entire center together, creating an intimate space where New Yorkers can go to forget about their appallingly high rents and their unpaid parking tickets.

Who Lives Where

Lincoln Center is home to so many different companies, groups, and troupes that we figured we'd provide a list of who is where. Perhaps the most confusing thing about Lincoln Center is that the "Lincoln Center Theater" is actually two theaters—the Vivian Beaumont and the Mitzi E. Newhouse Theaters. The newest building at Lincoln Center, the Samuel B. and David Rose Building, contains the Stanley Kaplan penthouse performance space, the School of American Ballet, the administrative offices of the Film Society and the Chamber Music Society, the Walter Reade Theater, dorms for the Julliard School, the Riverside Branch of the New York Public Library, and a fire house. (Take a breath!) Jazz at Lincoln Center has now moved into the new AOL/Time Warner Center located nearby at Frederick P. Rose Hall, the first space in the world designed specifically for jazz education, performance, and broadcast.

American Ballet Theater — Metropolitan Opera House
Chamber Music Society — Alice Tully Hall
Film Society of Lincoln Center — Samuel B. and David Rose Building
Jazz at Lincoln Center — Frederick P. Rose Hall
Julliard Orchestra — Alice Tully Hall
Julliard Symphony — Alice Tully Hall
Metropolitan Opera Company — Metropolitan Opera House
Mitzi E. Newhouse Theater — Lincoln Center Theater
Mostly Mozart Festival — Avery Fisher Hall
New York City Ballet — New York State Theater
New York City Opera — New York State Theater
New York Philharmonic — Avery Fisher Hall
School of American Ballet — Samuel B. and David Rose Building
Vivian Beaumont Theater — Lincoln Center Theater

Practical Information

Lincoln Center is right off Broadway and only a few blocks north of Columbus Circle, so getting there is pretty easy. The closest subway is the 66th Street 1 9, which has an exit right on the edge of the center. It's also only a five-minute walk from the plethora of trains that roll into Columbus Circle 1 9 A C B D. If you are more inclined towards above-ground transportation, the 5 7 10 11 66 104 bus lines all stop within one block of Lincoln Center. There is also a parking lot underneath Lincoln Center for those bent on driving.

Columbus Circle

Columbus Circle has seen a major overhaul in the past several years, with the addition of an always understated Trump International Hotel and Tower, the destruction of the New York Coliseum, and the battles about what would replace it. The recently opened AOL/Time Warner Center was the eventual winner, and with offices, jazz, movies, the Mandarin Oriental hotel, and condominiums making it the largest mixed-use complex ever constructed in New York history, it should prove to be a virtual epicenter in the city that's already considered "The Center of the Universe."

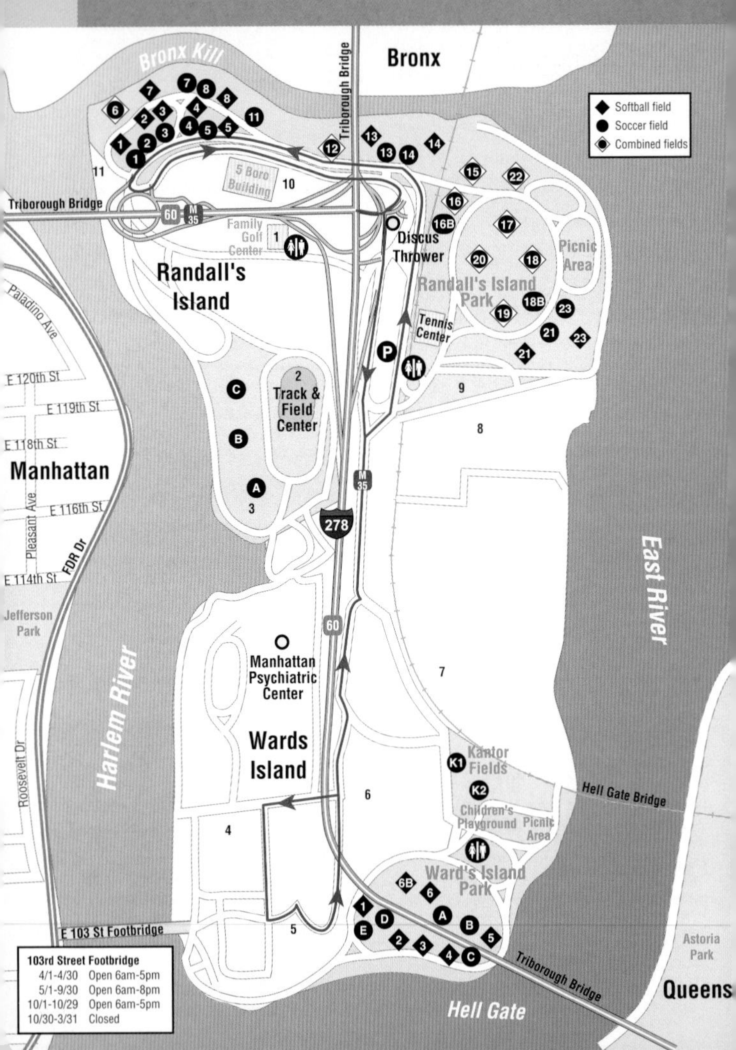

Bronx Kill
Bronx
Triborough Bridge
Softball field
Soccer field
Combined fields
5 Boro Building
Family Golf Center
Discus Thrower
Randall's Island
Picnic Area
Randall's Island Park
Tennis Center
Track & Field Center
Paladino Ave
E 120th St
E 119th St
E 118th St
Manhattan
E 116th St
Pleasant Ave
FDR Dr
E 114th St
Jefferson Park
East River
Manhattan Psychiatric Center
Harlem River
Wards Island
Roosevelt Dr
Kantor Fields
Hell Gate Bridge
Children's Playground
Picnic Area
Ward's Island Park
E 103 St Footbridge
Astoria Park
Queens
Hell Gate
103rd Street Footbridge
4/1-4/30 Open 6am-5pm
5/1-9/30 Open 6am-8pm
10/1-10/29 Open 6am-5pm
10/30-3/31 Closed

General Information

Randall's Island Sports Foundation: 212-830-7722
www.risf.citysearch.com

Overview

Most New Yorkers associate Randall's Island solely with the Triborough Bridge, not realizing the island (Randall's and Wards Islands were connected together by landfill) has 440 acres of parkland for public use. In fact, Randall's & Wards Island is host to some of the best athletic fields and parkland in Manhattan. Originally conceived of and built by the infamous Robert Moses, Randall's and Wards Island Park is now administered by the Randall's Island Sports Foundation—the same way the Central Park Conservancy works. Their mission is to continue to improve and upgrade the park for the families of New York City. Phase I of their very big plan includes replacing Downing Stadium with a state-of-the-art track-and-field center to be completed in the summer of 2004 and an amphitheater for concerts slated to open in 2005. They are improving all the bike and pedestrian trails and renovating the soccer and softball fields. Future phases include adding a cricket field and ferry service—there's even talk of a water park opening in 2006. Hopefully part of their plan will include some food facilities. As it is, the only food available is the snack bar in the golf center, and the lunch trucks scattered around the former Downing Stadium and the Fire Training Center.

Getting there

By Car — Take the Triborough bridge, exit Randall's Island. There's a $3.50 toll to get on the island with your car. It's free to leave!

By Subway/Bus — From Manhattan: take the 4 5 6 train to 125th Street, then transfer on the corner of 125th Street and Lexington Avenue for the 35 bus to Randall's Island. There's a bus about every 40 minutes during the day. From Queens: take the from 61st Street-Woodside.

By Foot — A pedestrian footbridge at 103rd Street was built by Robert Moses in the '50s to provide Harlem residents access to the recreational facilities of the parks after the then-city council president Newbold Morris criticized the lack of facilities in Harlem. Its hours are seasonal and limited. Please see the chart on the map.

1 **Family Golf Center @ Randall's Island** • 212-427-5689 • Family Golf Center is a national chain of 92 golf centers. The golf center on Randall's Island was opened in 1994 by American Golf Center and was taken over 5 years ago by Family Golf Center. The driving range is open year-round and has 80 heated stalls. There is a snack bar, bathrooms, 2 18-hole mini-golf courses, and 9 batting cages. A shuttle service is available every hour on the hour from Manhattan (86th and Third Avenue) with a $10 round-trip fee. Summer hours are 6 am–11 pm Tues–Sun and 11 am–11 pm on Mondays with off-season hours from 7 am-9 pm daily.

2 A new **Track & Field Center** will replace the large crater in the ground that was once Downing Stadium in the summer of 2004. The sprinters of the city can't wait.

3 The New York City Rodeo & Riding Academy has now been replaced with the abundantly apparent blue-and-yellow tent of the **Cirque Du Soleil**. Hopefully this will be a permanent fixture as New Yorkers are always in need of more entertainment options.

4 **Project H.E.L.P. Employment Center** • 212-534-3866

5 **Charles H. Gay Shelter for Men** —Volunteers of America - Greater New York • 212-369-8900 • www.voa-gny.org

6 **Odyssey House Drug Rehab Center**—Mabon Building • 212-426-6677

7 **DEP Water Pollution Control Plant** • 718-595-6600 • www.ci.nyc.ny.us/html/dep/html/drainage.html

8 **Fire Department Training Center** • The NYC Fire Academy is located on 27 acres of landfill on the east side of Randall's Island. In an effort to keep the city's "bravest" in shape, the academy utilizes the easily accessible 68 acres of parkland for physical fitness programs. The ultra-cool training facility includes eleven Universal Studios-like buildings for simulations training, a 200,000-gallon water supply tank, gasoline and diesel fuel pumps, and a 300-car parking lot. In addition, the New York Transit Authority installed tracks and subway cars for learning and developing techniques to battle subway fires and other emergencies. It's really too bad they don't sell tickets and offer tours!

9 **Tennis Courts** • 212-534-4845 • 11 outdoor courts. Indoor courts heated for winter use.

10 **Robert Moses Building** • We're sure many an urban planning student has made a pilgrimage here.

11 **NYPD** • They launch cool-looking police boats from here.

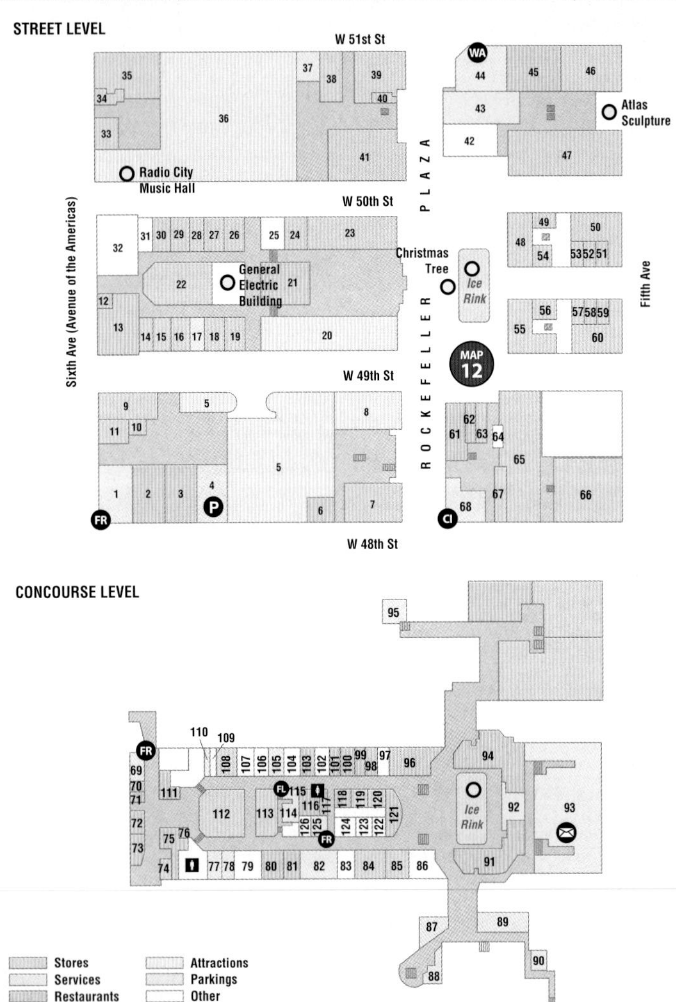
STREET LEVEL
W 51st St
W 50th St
W 49th St
W 48th St
Sixth Ave (Avenue of the Americas)
Fifth Ave
PLAZA
ROCKEFELLER
Radio City Music Hall
General Electric Building
Christmas Tree
Ice Rink
Atlas Sculpture
MAP 12
WA
FR
P
CI
CONCOURSE LEVEL
Ice Rink
FL
FR
Stores
Services
Restaurants
Attractions
Parkings
Other

Rockefeller Center is a 3-square-block complex of business, retail, entertainment, and dining. Architect Hugh Hardy put it best when he said that "it invented Midtown," and it remains one of the focal points of Midtown to this day. Like the Empire State Building, Rockefeller Center is made more impressive by the fact that it was built during the Depression, which of course is why that it possesses beautiful Art Deco flourishes on its exteriors and interiors.

Among the prominent businesses that operate out of "Rock Center" are the Associated Press, General Electric, and NBC (the Today Show studio overlooks the main plaza of the Center). Quite a few television shows tape at "30 Rock" as well, including *Saturday Night Live* and *Late Night with Conan O'Brien*.

Rockefeller Center is perhaps most associated with Christmas, from the famous tree to the ice-skating rink to St. Patrick's to the Rockettes in Radio City Music Hall. And of course, all the stores in the Center and on Fifth Avenue. What all this means is that most New Yorkers never go to Rockefeller Center. Such is life.

Stores, Services & Restaurants

Key: S: Street level; C: Concourse level; B: Both levels

#	Name	Level
1	FR • First Republic Bank	S
2	Cosi Sandwich Shop	S
3	Shaan of India	S
4	Central Parking	S
5	Christie's	S
6	Daikichi Sushi	S
7	Pokémon Center NY	S
8	Today Show Studio	S
9	Tristan & AMERICA	S
10	RA Newsstand	B
11	Nine West	S
12	Citarella To Go	S
13	Citarella The Restaurant	S
14	Statesman Shoes	S
15	Pants And	S
16	Crane & Co Paper Makers	S
17	Studio Optix	S
18	Tumi	S
19	La Maison Du Chocolat	S
20	NBC Experience Store	S
20	NBC Studios	S
21	Rainbow Room & Grill	S
22	Wella Studio, The	S
23	J. Crew	S
24	Origins	S
26	Godiva Chocolatier	S
27	Louis Martin Jewelers	S
28	Delfino	S
29	An American Craftsman	S
30	Erwin Pearl	S
33	Radio City Gift Shop	S
34	Body Shop	S
35	French Connection	S
36	Radio City Music Hall	S
37	Berlitz Language School	S
38	Fire Zone Store & Museum	S
39	Sharper Image	S
40	RA Newsstand	B
41	Nautica	S
43	Pulse Restaurant & Bar	S
43	Sports Club/LA, The	S
44	WA • Wachovia	S
45	Tuscan Square	B
46	Facconable	B
47	Banana Republic	B
48	Brookstone	S
49	Coach	S
50	Cole Haan	S
51	Teuscher Chocolates	S
52	Crabtree & Evelyn	S
53	Botticelli	S
54	Watch World	S
55	Metropolitan Museum Store	S
56	Movado	S
57	Sunglass Hut	S
58	Librairie De France	S
59	Anne Fontaine	S
60	Kenneth Cole	S
61	Dean & Deluca	S
62	Morrell Wine Bar & Restaurant	S
63	Morrell & Company Wine Store	S
65	Kinokuniya Bookstore	S
66	Barnes & Noble	S
67	Irene Hayes Wadley & Smythe	S
68	CI • Citibank	S
69	FR • First Republic ATM	C
70	Central Market	C
71	Subway	C
72	Krispy Kreme	C
73	Hot & Crusty	C
74	RA Newsstand	B
75	Sbarro	C
76	Dahlia	C
77	Eddie's Shoe Repair	C
78	Franco Hair Salon Colorgroup	C
80	Pret A Manger	C
81	Hale & Hearty	C
82	Value Drugs	C
84	Electronics Boutique	C
85	RA Newsstand	B
87	Perfection Blueprints	C
88	Salon Vijin	C
89	UPS Store	C
90	Gary's Top Shoe	C
91	Sea Grill	C
92	Ice Skate House	C
93	United States Postal Service	C
94	Rock Center Café	C
95	Jerry's Hair Styling	C
96	Cucina & Co	C
98	Mendy's Kosher Deli	C
99	Tossed	C
100	Two Boots	C
101	Emerald Planet, The	C
103	Manchu WOK	C
105	Kodak/Alpha Photo	C
108	GNC	C
110	Splendid Dry Cleaners	C
111	Starbucks	C
112	Hallmark	C
113	Waldenbooks	C
114	Its Easy	C
115	FL • Fleet ATM	C
116	Ben & Jerry's	C
117	Auntie Anne's Pretzels	C
118	Yummy Sushi	C
119	NR Wireless	C
120	Godiva Chocolatier	C
121	Starbucks Coffee	C
125	FR • First Republic ATM	C

Overview

Roosevelt Island could be one of the coolest places in New York—imagine, a 147-acre island in the middle of the East River, connected to Manhattan by tramway and subway, and connected to Queens by roadway and subway. Unfortunately, though, it's not one of the coolest places in New York. Digitalcity.com calling it "New York's Island Getaway" is the overstatement of the century. All services are conveniently located on "Main Street" (wherever did they come up with that name?!?), which makes the rest of the island feel deserted. Two hospitals, several abandoned buildings, and the lack of comforting city sights such as taxis, hot dog vendors, and crazy people make Roosevelt Island feel, well…creepy.

However, Roosevelt Island's creepiness is part of its charm. The ivy-covered remains of the Smallpox Hospital, the looming Octagon Tower (formerly the site of a 19th-century mental hospital), and the solitary house and church on West Road make a jaunt to Roosevelt Island interesting, to say the least. A trip to the island is best done on the Tramway (costing $1.50 and forever immortalized in the movies *Nighthawks*, and, more recently, *Spiderman*). Other attractions include the Chapel of the Good Shepherd, the Blackwell House, the western and eastern promenades, and the island's several parks.

For more information, the Roosevelt Island Operating Corporation has a very informative website at www.rioc.com. This site discusses several interesting proposals for further development of the island, as well as providing practical information and demographics on the Roosevelt Island community.

How to Get There

Roosevelt Island can be reached via the F subway line, and by the extremely quick but not totally reliable tramway at 60th Street and Second Avenue in Manhattan. To get there by car, take the Queensboro Bridge and follow signs for the "21st Street-North" exit. Go north on 21st Street and make a left on 36th Avenue. Go west on 36th Avenue and cross over the red Roosevelt Island Bridge. The only legal parking is at Motorgate Plaza at the end of the bridge, but it's more fun to drive around and harass the Roosevelt Island police by parking illegally and stopping in front of all the really creepy stuff.

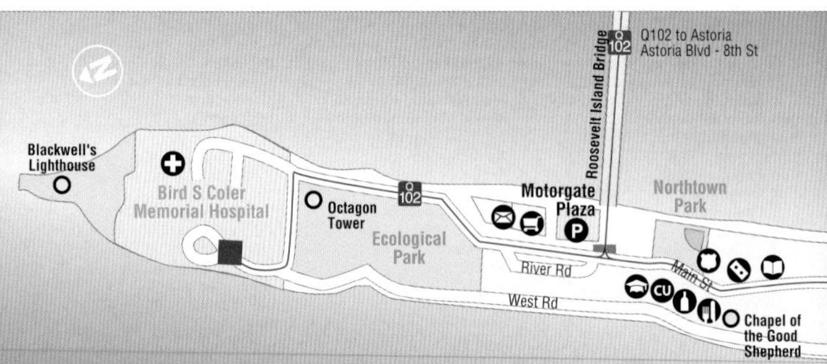

ATMs

CU • Credit Union • 559 Main St

Hospitals

- **Bird S Coler Memorial Hospital** • 900 Main St
- **Goldwater Memorial Hospital** • 1 Main St

Landmarks

- **Blackwell House** • 591 Main St
- **Blackwell's Lighthouse**
- **Chapel of the Good Shepherd**
- **Octagon Tower**
- **Smallpox Hospital**
- **Tramway** • Tramway Plz

Libraries

- **Roosevelt Island Library** • 524 Main St

Post Offices

- **Roosevelt Island Post Office** • 694 Main St

Schools

- **PS-IS 217** • 645 Main St

Gyms

- **Sportspark** • Main St

Liquor Store

- **Grog Shop** • 605 Main St

Supermarkets

- **Gristedes** • 686 Main St

Video Rentals

- **KIO Enterprise** • 544 Main St

Subway

F .... Roosevelt Island

Bus Lines

Q102 .... Main St/East and West Rds

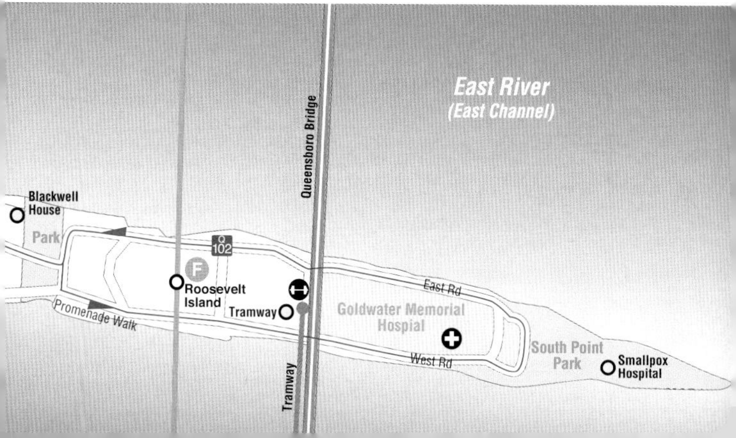

East River
(East Channel)
Queensboro Bridge
Blackwell House
Park
Q102
F
Roosevelt Island
Tramway
Promenade Walk
East Rd
Goldwater Memorial Hospial
West Rd
South Point Park
Smallpox Hospital
Tramway

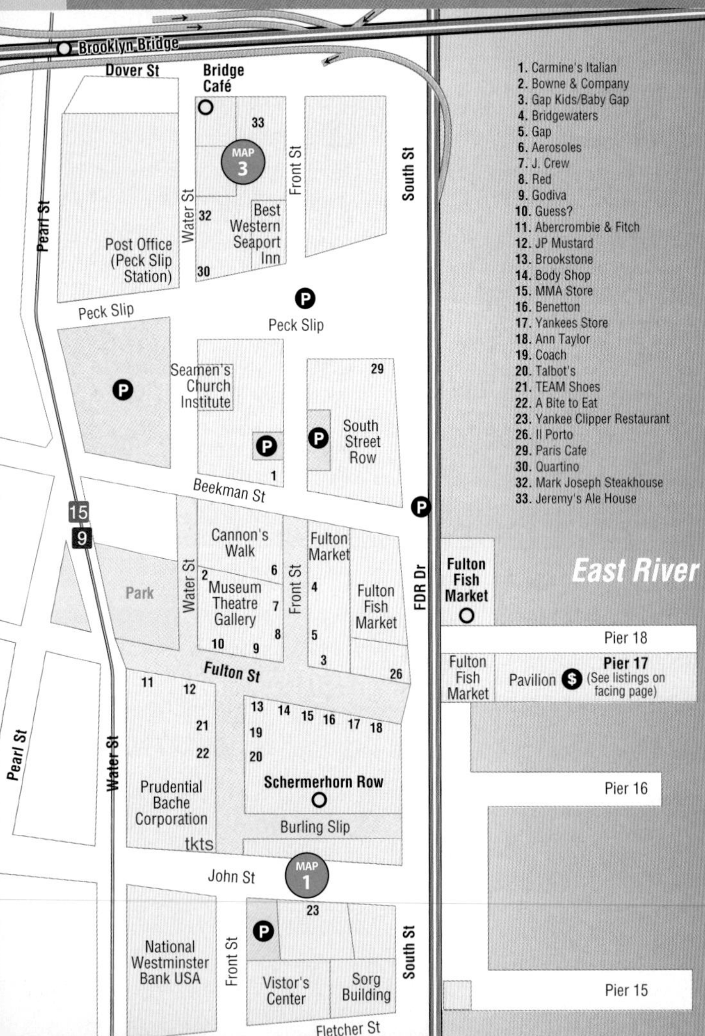
Brooklyn Bridge
Dover St
Bridge Café
MAP 3
Front St
South St
Water St
Pearl St
Best Western Seaport Inn
Post Office (Peck Slip Station)
Peck Slip
Peck Slip
Seamen's Church Institute
South Street Row
Beekman St
Cannon's Walk
Fulton Market
Museum Theatre Gallery
Fulton Fish Market
FDR Dr
Park
Fulton St
Fulton Fish Market
East River
Pier 18
Fulton Fish Market
Pavilion
Pier 17 (See listings on facing page)
Schermerhorn Row
Burling Slip
Pier 16
Prudential Bache Corporation
tkts
John St
MAP 1
National Westminster Bank USA
Vistor's Center
Sorg Building
Pier 15
Fletcher St
1. Carmine's Italian
2. Bowne & Company
3. Gap Kids/Baby Gap
4. Bridgewaters
5. Gap
6. Aerosoles
7. J. Crew
8. Red
9. Godiva
10. Guess?
11. Abercrombie & Fitch
12. JP Mustard
13. Brookstone
14. Body Shop
15. MMA Store
16. Benetton
17. Yankees Store
18. Ann Taylor
19. Coach
20. Talbot's
21. TEAM Shoes
22. A Bite to Eat
23. Yankee Clipper Restaurant
26. Il Porto
29. Paris Cafe
30. Quartino
32. Mark Joseph Steakhouse
33. Jeremy's Ale House

In some ways, South Street Seaport is the most blatant tourist site in New York, with its museums and malls—certainly the stores in the Pier 17 pavilion are not at all "New York." Yet there is quite a lot of interesting history to be found here if one looks for it. Most obvious are the large ships docked in the harbor, including the Peking, Wavertree, and Ambrose. There are some finely preserved and renovated 19th-century buildings in the area as well, not just on Fulton Street, but also on Beekman, Peck Slip, and Dover Street. The Seaport itself houses about twenty-five restaurants, but we recommend the Bridge Café, Mark Joseph Steakhouse, or Quartino, all of which are located north of the Seaport and just south of the Brooklyn Bridge.

The Bridge looms over the whole area—the back decks of the pavilion have a great view, as does the East Side Promenade, which passes underneath it. Sadly, the most authentic part of the neighborhood, the Fulton Fish Market, will be moving to the Bronx soon. We suggest going down to South Street and having a drink at the bar in the Paris Café one night at 2 am to mourn its passing...

If you're downtown and looking for discounted theater tickets, the tkts booth that was formerly located in the World Trade Center is now at the corner of Front Street and John Street. Check the electronic board for show times and discounts, then go inside and book. For matinee shows, you need to book tickets the day before from this downtown location.

General Information

NFT Map Number: 1
Phone: 212-SEA-PORT
Phone (museum): 212-748-8600
Museum:
www.southstseaport.org
Retail:
www.southstreetseaport.com

Landmarks

Schermerhorn Row
Fulton Fish Market (South St)
Bridge Café
Brooklyn Bridge

Subway

2 3 4 5 J M Z .... Fulton Street
A C ..... Broadway-Nassau
Walk east on Fulton Street to Water Street

Bus Lines

15 ..... First and Second Aves
9 ...... Ave B/East Broadway

ATMs

PNC Bank, ground floor of Pier 17 Pavilion

Pier 17 Pavilion

ABCDE
Alamo Flags
American Eagle Outfitters
Art A La Cart
Bath & Body Works
Beyond The Wall
Broadway Beat
Christmas Dove
City Streets
Claire's Accessories
EB Games
Express
Express Men
Filmline Gallery
Harbour Lights
Jewelry Mine
Lids
Mariposa The Butterfly Gallery
The New York Shell Shop
New York: A View of the World
9000 Perfumery Inc
Nutcracker Sweets
Purple-icious
Seaport Leather
Seaport News
Seaport Watch Co
The Sharper Image
Steps
Sunglass Hut & Watch Station
Taqueria Mexicali
Teazeria
Victoria's Secret
Waxology

Food

Athenian Express
Bergin's Wine & Beer Garden
Cabana
Cajun Café
China Max Asian Cuisine
Cyber Cigar and Coffee Bar
Daikichi Sushi
Haagen Dazs
Harbour Lights
Heartland Brewery & Beer Hall
Heavenly Soup & Smoothie
Il Porto
JP Mustard
MacMenamin's Irish Pub
Murph's
Nathan's Famous
Pizza on the Pier
Pizzeria Uno
Red
Salad Mania
Seaport café
Sedutto Ice Cream
Sequoia
Simply Seafood
Skipper's Pierside Café
Subway
Taqueria Mexicali
Yorkville Burger

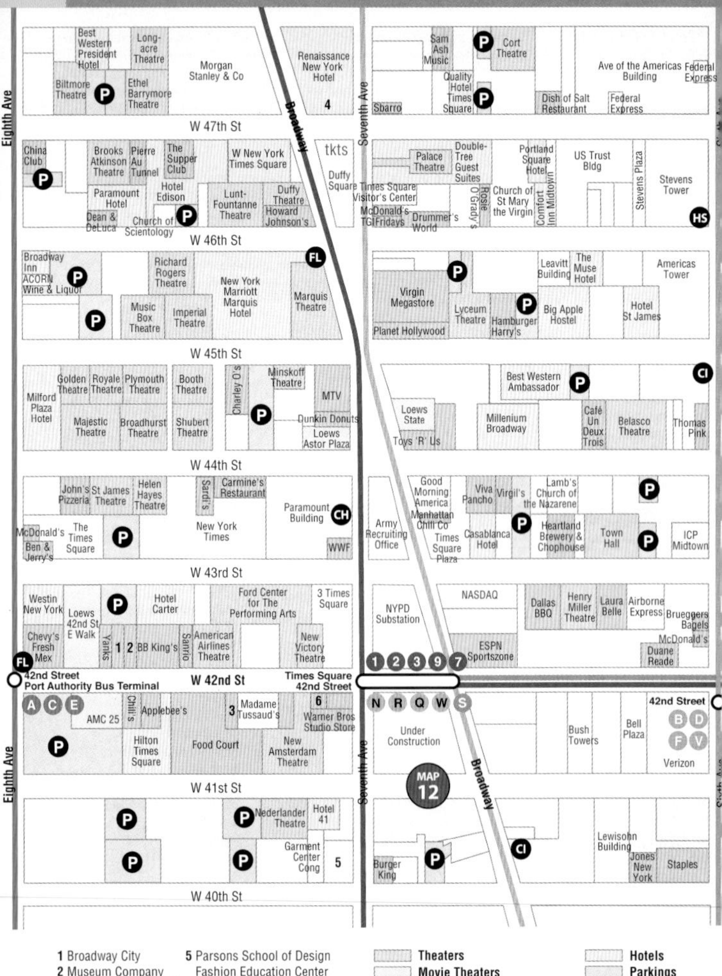

1 Broadway City
2 Museum Company
3 Easy Everything
4 Olive Garden
5 Parsons School of Design Fashion Education Center
6 McDonald's

Theaters
Movie Theaters
Theme Restaurants/Stores
Hotels
Parkings
Other

For an area named after a high-brow newspaper, Times Square has seen mostly middle- and low-brow entertainment over the last one hundred years, from Vaudeville to the golden age of Broadway to the "golden age" of porn and finally to the current "Disney-fication." Of all the neighborhoods in New York for a New Yorker to avoid, this has to be at the top, but inevitably your cousin from out of town is going to want to see it, so...

Helpful Website

www.timessquare.com

Transit

Take the 1 2 3 9 7 N R Q W and S trains to get to the center of everything at the 42nd Street/Times Square stop.

ATMs

CH • Chase • 3 Times Sq
CI • Citibank • 1440 Broadway
CI • Citibank • Sixth Ave & 45th St
FL • Fleet • 1535 Broadway
FL • Fleet • 42nd St & Eighth Ave
HS • HSBC • 1185 Sixth Ave

Hotels

- **Best Western President Hotel** • 234 W 48th St
- **Best Western Ambassador** • 132 W 45th St
- **Big Apple Hostel** • 119 W 45th St
- **Broadway Inn** • 264 W 46th St
- **Casablanca Hotel** • 147 W 43rd St
- **Comfort Inn Midtown** • 129 W 46th St
- **Doubletree Guest Suites** • 1568 Broadway
- **Hilton Times Square** • 234 W 42nd St
- **Hotel 41** • 206 W 41st St
- **Hotel Carter** • 250 W 43rd St
- **Hotel St James** • 109 W 45th St
- **Milford Plaza Hotel** • 270 W 45th St
- **Millennium Broadway** • 145 W 44th St
- **The Muse Hotel** • 130 W 46th St
- **New York Marriott Marquis Hotel** • 1535 Broadway
- **Paramount Hotel** • 235 W 46th St
- **Portland Square Hotel** • 132 W 47th St
- **Hotel Edison** • 228 W 47th St
- **Quality Hotel Times Square** • 157 W 47th St
- **Renaissance New York Hotel** • 714 Seventh Ave
- **W New York Times Square** • 1567 Broadway
- **Westin New York** • 270 W 43rd St

Movie Theaters

- **AMC Empire 25** • 234 W 42nd St
- **Loews Astor Plaza** • 1515 Broadway
- **Loews State** • 1540 Broadway
- **Loews 42nd St E-Walk** • 247 W 42nd St

Theme Restaurants/ Stores

- **Applebee's** • 234 W 42nd St
- **Pierre Au Tunnel** • 250 W 47th St
- **BB King's Blues Club** • 237 W 42nd St
- **Ben & Jerry's** • 680 Eighth Ave
- **Broadway City** • 241 W 42nd St
- **Bruegger's Bagels Bakery** • 1115 Sixth Ave
- **Burger King** • 561 Seventh Ave
- **Café Un Deux Trois** • 123 W 44th St
- **Carmine's Restaurant** • 200 W 44thSt
- **Charley O's** • 218 W 45th St
- **Chevy's Fresh Mex** • 243 W 42nd St
- **Chili's Grill & Bar** • 234 W 42nd St
- **China Club** 268 W 47th St
- **Dallas BBQ** • 132 W 43rd St
- **Dean & DeLuca** • 235 W 46th St
- **Dish of Salt Restaurant** • 133 W 47th St
- **Drummers World** • 151 W 46th St
- **Duane Reade Pharmacy** • 115 W 42nd St
- **Dunkin' Donuts** • 1515 Broadway
- **Easy Everything** • 234 W 42nd St
- **ESPN Sportszone** • 4 Times Sq
- **Food Court** • 234 W 42nd St
- **Hamburger Harry's** • 145 W 45th St
- **Heartland Brewery** • 127 W 43rd St
- **Howard Johnson's** • 1551 Broadway
- **John's Brick Oven Pizzeria** • 260 W 44th St
- **Jones New York** • 119 W 40th St
- **Laura Belle** • 120 W 43rd St
- **Manhattan Chili Co** • 1500 Broadway
- **McDonald's** • 220 W 42nd St
- **McDonald's** • 688 8th Ave
- **McDonald's** • 1109 Sixth Ave
- **McDonald's** • 1560 Broadway
- **MTV** • 1515 Broadway
- **Museum Company** • 239 W 42nd St
- **Olive Garden** • 2 Times Square
- **Planet Hollywood** • 1540 Broadway
- **Rosie O'Grady's** • 149 W 46th St
- **Sam Ash Music** • 160 W 48th St
- **Sanrio** • 233 W 42nd St
- **Sardi's** • 234 W 44th St
- **Sbarro** • 701 Seventh Ave
- **Staples** • 1065 Sixth Ave
- **The Supper Club** • 240 W 47th St
- **TGI Friday's** • 1552 Broadway
- **Thomas Pink** • 1155 Sixth Ave
- **Toys 'R' Us** • 1514-1530 Broadway
- **Virgil's Real Barbecue** • 152 W 44th St
- **Virgin Megastore** • 1540 Broadway
- **Viva Pancho** • 156 W 44th St
- **WWF New York** • 1501 Broadway
- **Warner Bros Studio Store** • 1 Times Square Plz
- **Yankee Clubhouse Shop** • 245 W 42nd St

Theaters

- **American Airlines Theater** • 227 W 42nd St
- **Belasco Theatre** • 111 W 44th St
- **Biltmore Theatre** • 261 W 47th St
- **Booth Theatre** • 222 W 45th St
- **Broadhurst Theatre** • 235 W 44th St
- **Brooks Atkinson Theatre** • 256 W 47th St
- **Cort Theatre** • 138 W 48th St
- **Duffy Theatre** • 1553 Broadway
- **Ethel Barrymore Theatre** • 243 W 47th St
- **Ford Center for the Performing Arts** • 213 W 42nd St
- **John Golden Theatre** • 252 W 45th St
- **Helen Hayes Theatre** • 240 W 44th St
- **Henry Miller Theatre** • 124 W 43rd St
- **Imperial Theatre** • 249 W 45th St
- **Longacre Theatre** • 220 W 48th St
- **Lunt-Fontanne Theatre** • 205 W 46th St
- **Lyceum Theatre** • 149 W 45th St
- **Majestic Theatre** • 274 W 44th St
- **Marquis Theatre** • 1535 Broadway
- **Minskoff Theatre** • 200 W 45th St
- **Music Box Theatre** • 239 W 45th St
- **Nederlander Theatre**• 208 W 41st St
- **New Amsterdam Theatre** • 214 W 42nd St
- **New Victory Theatre** • 209 W 42nd St
- **Palace Theatre** • 1564 Broadway
- **Plymouth Theatre** • 236 W 45th St
- **Richard Rogers Theatre** • 226 W 46th St
- **Royale Theatre** • 242 W 45th St
- **Shubert Theatre** • 225 W 44th St
- **St James Theatre** • 246 W 44th St
- **Town Hall** • 123 W 43rd St

* Here's a tip: You can win $20 "Rent" tickets in the random drawing if you line up at the Nederlander by 6:30 pm, just in case that cousin wants to see "a show."

Other

- **Army Recruiting Office** • *Want to join the Army?* Opened in 1946, more people have done it here than at any other recruiting station. (43rd St & Broadway)
- **tkts** • Discount theater tickets.

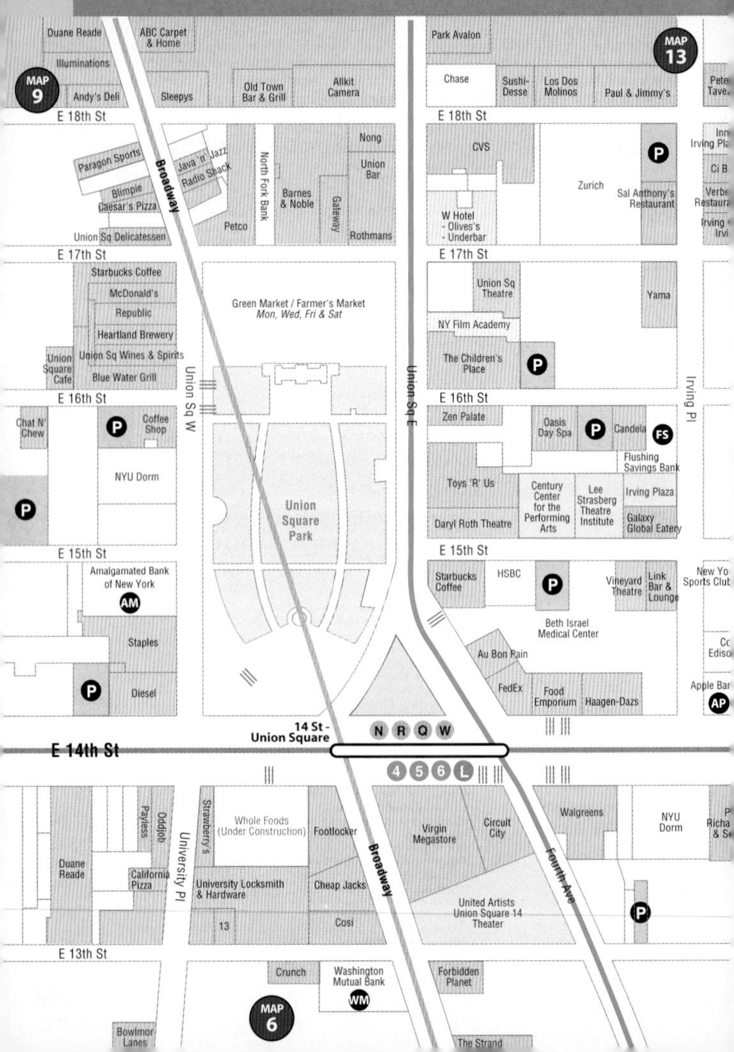
MAP 9
MAP 13
MAP 6
Duane Reade
ABC Carpet & Home
Illuminations
Andy's Deli
Sleepys
Old Town Bar & Grill
Allkit Camera
Park Avalon
Chase
Sushi-Desse
Los Dos Molinos
Paul & Jimmy's
E 18th St
Paragon Sports
Broadway
Java 'n' Jazz
Radio Shack
Blimpie
Caesar's Pizza
Union Sq Delicatessen
Petco
North Fork Bank
Barnes & Noble
Gateway
Nong
Union Bar
Rothmans
CVS
W Hotel - Olives's - Underbar
Zurich
Sal Anthony's Restaurant
Irving Pl
E 17th St
Starbucks Coffee
McDonald's
Republic
Heartland Brewery
Union Sq Wines & Spirits
Union Square Cafe
Blue Water Grill
Union Sq W
Green Market / Farmer's Market
Mon, Wed, Fri & Sat
Union Sq E
Union Sq Theatre
Yama
NY Film Academy
The Children's Place
E 16th St
Chat N' Chew
Coffee Shop
NYU Dorm
Union Square Park
Zen Palate
Oasis Day Spa
Candela
FS
Flushing Savings Bank
Toys 'R' Us
Century Center for the Performing Arts
Lee Strasberg Theatre Institute
Irving Plaza
Daryl Roth Theatre
Galaxy Global Eatery
E 15th St
Amalgamated Bank of New York
AM
Staples
Diesel
Starbucks Coffee
HSBC
Vineyard Theatre
Link Bar & Lounge
Beth Israel Medical Center
Au Bon Pain
FedEx
Food Emporium
Haagen-Dazs
Apple Bar
AP
14 St - Union Square
N R Q W
E 14th St
4 5 6 L
Payless
Oddjob
Duane Reade
California Pizza
University Pl
Strawberry's
Whole Foods (Under Construction)
Footlocker
University Locksmith & Hardware
Cheap Jacks
13
Cosi
Virgin Megastore
Circuit City
United Artists Union Square 14 Theater
Fourth Ave
Walgreens
NYU Dorm
E 13th St
Crunch
Washington Mutual Bank
WM
Forbidden Planet
Bowlmor Lanes
The Strand

The large square at the union of Broadway and Fourth Avenue (originally Bloomingdale and Bowery, New York's most important streets) has been many things to many New Yorkers over the years—posh residential neighborhood, center of retail, center of Vaudeville, center of depravity, center of chain stores—but it retains a vitality not found in many other open spaces of New York, as the place where downtown's grunginess meets midtown sophistication. The large crowds of people gathered there on any particularly sunny afternoon could just as likely be protesters, hipsters, office workers eating lunch outside, or NYU students.

The domain of the rich in the early 19th century, the square gradually became a commercial area, with theaters moving in once retail moved farther uptown. In the early 20th century, it was a major focal point for labor activity and leftist political rallies in general, which in turn led to the art scene in the '50s and '60s centered around Andy Warhol's Factory. By 1983, the area had been declining for years, and a Business Improvement District was created to bring the area back from the brink. These days, it has become quite safe and mainstream (to its detriment, some would say). One thing that remains, though, is its role as a locus for political rallies, protests, and other events. In the past few years, it has been the center of September 11th remembrances, as well as protests against the war in Iraq.

Quite a few of New York's best restaurants are near Union Square, including Blue Water Grill, Mesa Grill, and Union Square Café. For less extravagant food, the frequent Farmer's Market on the northwest side of the park sells fresh fruit, home baked cakes, and the most delicious hard sourdough pretzels you'll ever taste!

ATMs

AM • Amalgamated Bank of NY • 15 Union Sq
AP • Apple • 4 Irving Pl
CH • Chase • 225 Park Ave S
FS • Flushing Savings • 33 Irving Pl
HS • HSBC • 10 Union Sq E
WM • Washington Mutual • 835 Broadway

Hotels

Chelsea Inn • 46 West 17th St
Inn at Irving Place • 56 Irving Pl
W Hotel • 201 Park Avenue S

Stores/Restaurants

13 • 35 E 13th St
ABC Carpet & Home • 888 Broadway
Alkit Camera • 222 Park Ave S
Andy's Deli • 873 Broadway
Ann Saks Tile & Stone • 5 E 16th St
Au Bon Pain • 6 Union Sq E
Barnes & Noble • 33 E 17th St
Blimpie • 863 Broadway
Blue Water Grill • 31 Union Sq W
Caesar's Pizza • 861 Broadway
California Pizza • 122 University Pl
Candela • 116 E 16th St
Cheap Jack's • 841 Broadway
Children's Place • 36 Union Sq E
Circuit City • 52-64 E 14th St
Coffee Shop • 29 Union Sq W
Cosi • 841 Broadway
CVS • 215 Park Ave S (not 24 hours)
Diesel • 1 Union Sq W
Duane Reade • 873 Broadway
Fed Ex • 4 Union Sq E
Food Emporium • 10 Union Sq E
Foot Locker • 853 Broadway
Forbidden Planet • 840 Broadway
Galaxy Global Eatery • 15 Irving Pl
Garden of Eden • 7 E 14th Street
Gateway • 200 Park Ave S
Heartland Brewery • 35 Union Sq W
Illuminations • 873 Broadway
Irving on Irving • 52 Irving Pl
Java 'N' Jazz • 868 Broadway
Link Bar & Lounge • 120 E 15th St
Los Dos Molinos • 119 E 18th St
McDonald's • 39 Union Sq W
Mesa Grill • 102 Fifth Ave
Nong • 220 Park Ave S
Oasis Day Spa • 108 E 16th St
Oddjob • 36 E 14th St
Old Town Bar & Grill • 45 E 18th St
Paragon Sports • 867 Broadway
Park Avalon • 225 Park Ave S
Paul & Jimmy's • 123 E 18th St
Payless • 34 E 14th St
PC Richard & Son • 120 E 14th St
Petco • 860 Broadway
Pete's Tavern • 129 E 18th St
Radio Shack • 866 Broadway
Republic • 37 Union Sq W
Rothman's • 200 Park Ave S
Sal Anthony's Restaurant • 55 Irving Pl
Sleepy's • 874 Broadway
Staples • 5-9 Union Sq W
Starbucks • 10 Union Sq E
Starbucks • 41 Union Sq W
Strawberry's • 38 E 14th St
Sushi-Desse • 113 E 18th St
The Strand • 828 Broadway
Toys R Us • 24 Union Sq E
Union Bar • 204 Park Ave S
Union Square Café • 21 E 16th St
Union Square Delicatessen • 857 Broadway
Union Square Wines & Spirits • 33 Union Sq W
University Locksmith & Hardware • 121 University Pl
Verbena Restaurant • 54 Irving Pl
Virgin Megastore • 52 E 14th St
Walgreens • 145 Fourth Ave
Wiz • 17 Union Sq W
Yama • 122 E 17th St
Zen Palate • 34 Union Sq E

Entertainment

Century Center for the Performing Arts • 111 E 15th St
Classic Stage Company • 136 East 13th St
Dance Forum • 20 East 17th St
Daryl Roth Theatre • 20 Union Sq E
Djoniba Dance and Drum Centre • 37 E 18th St
Irving Plaza • 17 Irving Pl
Lee Strasberg Theatre Institute • 115 E 15th St
Union Square Theatre • 100 E 17th St
Regal/United Artists Union Square 14 Theater • 850 Broadway
Vineyard Theatre • 108 E 15th St

24 Hour Services

Duane Reade • 24 E 14th Street

Other

Amalgamated Bank of New York • 11 Union Sq W
Beth Israel Medical Center • 10 Union Sq E
Bowlmor Lanes • 110 University Pl
Carlyle Court • 25 Union Sq W
Con Edison • 4 Irving Pl
Crunch • 54 E 13th St
New York Sports Clubs • 10 Irving Pl
NY Film Academy • 100 E 17th St
The Palladium • 140 E 14th St
Peridance Center • 132 Fourth Ave
Zurich • 105 E 17th St

PHASE ONE

URBAN AND LANDSCAPE DEVELOPMENT:
Connect Greenwich Street, connect Fulton Street, establish wedge of light and Heroes Park.

GROUND ZERO MEMORIAL SITE:
Ground Zero Memorial site, museum.

LOT C STATION DEVELOPMENT:
Lower Manhattan station; underground access, public concourse retail and access to subway and PATH (mezz/-1/-2), loading-dock (-3), bus parking (-3/-4), car parking (-4).

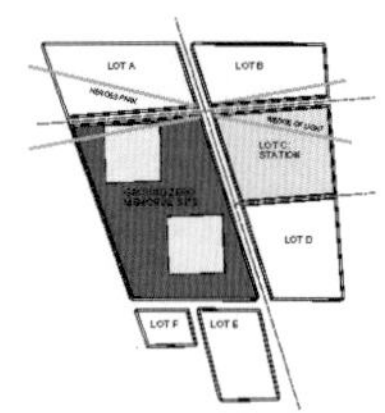

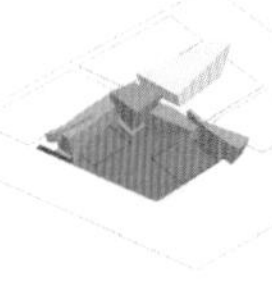

PHASE TWO

LOT A:
Antenna tower with gardens and office tower; retail on Fulton Street, Greenwich Street and Vesey Street; Performing Arts Center.

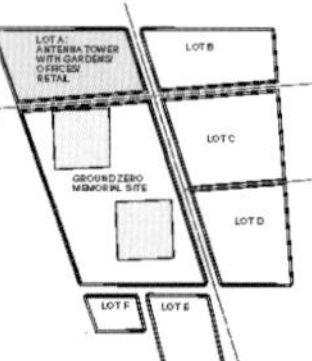

PHASE THREE

LOT C:
Offices; retail on Greenwich Street, Fulton Street, Church Street; retail on Cortlandt Street (0 to +3).

LOT D:
Offices; retail on Greenwich Street, Church Street and Liberty Street; retail on Cortlandt Street (0 to +3).

PHASE FOUR

LOT B:
Hotel, offices; retail on Greenwich Street, Fulton Street, Church Street and Vesey Street.

LOT E:
Offices; retail on Greenwich Street and Liberty Street.

LOT F:
Offices

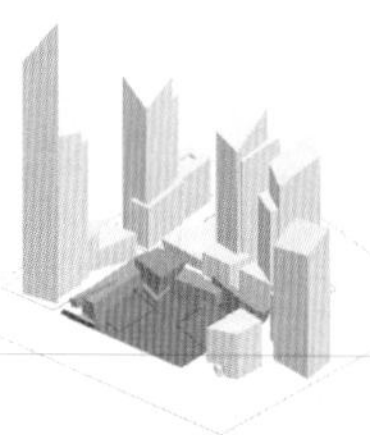

The rebuilding of the World Trade Center site has proven extremely complicated because of the numerous groups competing to see that their vision for the project is fulfilled. The Port Authority originally built the buildings and owned them when they were destroyed. However, just before September 11th, the buildings had been leased to Larry Silverstein, and as leaseholder he had the rights to collect insurance on it and redevelop the site. Into this mix was added the Lower Manhattan Development Corporation, created by Governor Pataki, which was given the task of overseeing the development of the site. Finally, the families of victims and the rest of the public have had their say, voicing their support and (often) their lack of support for various plans, with some even expressing the sentiment that the original towers should be rebuilt.

In the fall of 2002, a single design was selected from over 400 submissions to the LMDC. Studio Daniel Libeskind's proposal, "Memory Foundations," achieved the nearly impossible task of getting the approval of the LMDC, Port Authority, city, and state of New York. The Libeskind design included a 4.5-acre memorial garden, an Interpretive Museum, and most striking, a 1,776-foot tall spire-like building (expected to be the tallest building in the world). A piece of the original Slurry Wall, constructed on bedrock foundations and designed to hold back the Hudson River, will be preserved as a symbol of resilience. Despite this being accepted as the official master plan, the final result after construction may or may not resemble the original plan.

Though Libeskind created a master plan for the site, he didn't actually design any of the buildings. Silverstein decided to have architect Larry Childs complete the designs because of his extensive experience in designing office buildings. Under pressure from the LMDC, Childs collaborated with Libeskind on building designs based on the master plan. Throughout late 2003, local papers suggested that the two were feuding over designs. However, late in the year, Libeskind and Childs surprisingly emerged with an amicable compromise plan, changing the arrangement of the buildings and parks on the ground and altering the look of the Freedom Tower. The current plan for the tower includes a clear top section with energy-generating wind turbines and a large broadcast antenna. In early 2004, revised plans were released for a memorial at the site called "Reflecting Absence." The memorial was designed by architect Michael Arad and will incorporate waterfalls flowing into sunken "footprints" of the twin towers, cascading onto the names etched in stone of those who died at the site.

Despite these considered designs, debate still rages regarding many aspects of the project, from the height and look of the other towers (Silverman hired three other architects to design the remaining buildings in Libeskind's plan) to the design of a memorial space, to how many streets will be allowed to run through the site (they were demapped when the WTC was originally built).

In the meantime, transit has been restored to its pre-September 11th condition, with all the subway lines resuming their service to the area, along with the return of PATH service through a newly constructed PATH station. By 2009, a large station designed by Spanish architect Santiago Calatrav, connecting the subway, PATH, and trains to JFK airport, will be completed on the site.

Useful Websites

- "New York New Visions," is a coalition of several groups looking at different options for rebuilding the area: http://nynv.aiga.org

- The New York Skyscraper Museum continues to add information about the WTC and downtown NYC in general; they also contributed to the historical panels placed on the viewing wall around the site: http://www.skyscraper.org/

- The Lower Manhattan Development Corporation has the most up-to-date information concerning the rebuilding project: www.renew.nyc.com

- New York Newsday's compendium of articles and plans about the WTC site: www.nynewsday.com/news/local/manhattan/wtc/

- Website of the largest Sept. 11 advocacy group, representing the WTC memorial position of over 4,000 Sept. 11 family members, survivors, rescue workers, and others: www.coalitionof911families.org/

- The World Trade Center Health Registry will track the health survey of thousands of people most directly exposed to the events of 9/11: www.nyc.gov/html/doh/html/wtc/index.html

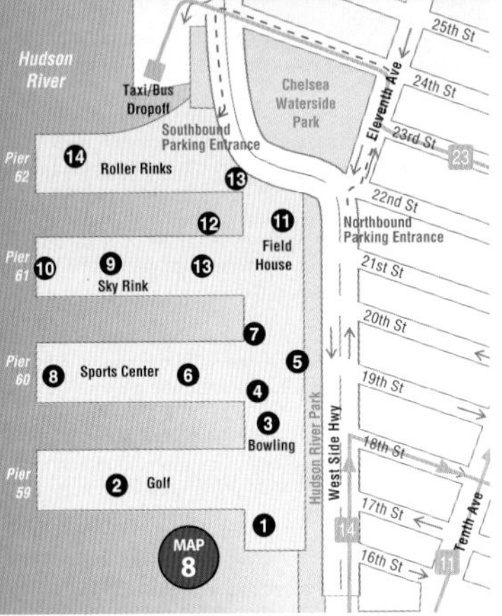

Overview

Website: www.chelseapiers.com

First opened in 1910 as a very popular port for trans-Atlantic ships, Chelsea Piers found itself abandoned, neglected, and deteriorating by the '60s. In 1992, Roland W. Betts began the plan to renovate and refurbish the piers as a shiny, huge 30-acre sports and entertainment center. In 1995, Chelsea Piers re-opened its doors to the public. The cost of renovating the piers was an estimated $120 million when all was said and done—all private money. The only help from the state was a very generous 49-year lease. By 1998, Chelsea Piers was the third-most visited attraction in New York City.

How to Get There

Unless you live in Chelsea, it's a real pain to get to. The closest subway is the C E to 23rd Street and Eighth Avenue and then it's a three-avenue block hike across to the river. If you're lucky, a 23 bus will come trundling along 23rd Street and you can expedite the last leg of your journey by using your free MetroCard transfer. If you're into taking the crosstown bus, you can also take the 1 9 to 23rd Street (and Seventh Avenue) or the B D F V to 23rd Street (and Sixth Avenue). L train commuters should get off at the Eighth Avenue stop and take the 14 bus across to the West Side Highway. Although, it's a 14 bus, it actually makes its final stop on 18th Street, just off the West Side Highway and right across the street from Chelsea Piers—a good option if you're planning on hanging out at the south end for some golf or a few ales at the brewery.

If you drive, entering from the south can be a little tricky. It's pretty well signed so keep your eyes peeled. Basically you're going to exit right at Eleventh Avenue and 22nd Street, turn left onto 24th Street and then make a left onto the West Side Highway, at which point you will enter Chelsea Piers the same way you would if you were approaching from the north. Parking starts at $9 for the first hour and $12 for up to 2 hours. Street parking in the west 20s is an excellent alternative in the evenings after 6 pm.

Facilities

Chelsea Piers is amazing. It's got swimming pools, ice skating rinks, a bowling alley, spa, restaurants, shops, batting cages... you name it. So, what's the catch? Well, it's gonna cost ya. Like Manhattan rents, only investment bankers can afford this place.

1 **Chelsea Brewing Company** — 212-336-6440. Microbrewery and restaurant. Try the amber ale—it's delicious! The wings, nachos, spinach dip, and cheesy fries are all excellent.

2 **Golf Club** — 212-336-6400. Aside from potentially long wait times, the 200-yard driving range with 52 heated stalls is pretty awesome. There is an automated ball-feed—no buckets or bending over. It's $25/100 balls (peak) and $20/100 balls (off-peak). Club hire is $4 for one club, $5 for 2, $6 for 3, or you can take your own. Before 5 pm on weekdays, you can whack balls for an hour for $20—as many as you can hit and one club is included in the price.

3 **AMF Chelsea Piers** — 212-835-BOWL. A very schmancy 40-lane bowling alley equipped with video games and bar. $7.50 per game plus $4.50 shoe rental.

4 **Ruthy's Bakery & Café** — 212-336-6333. Pastries and sandwiches.

5 **New York Presbyterian Sports Medicine Center** — 212-366-5100

6 **The Spa at Chelsea Piers** — 212-336-6780. It's not Canyon Ranch. A basic 50-minute massage is $100, a basic 50-minute facial is $80. They also have a range of scrubs, wraps, polishes, manicures, pedicures, and waxes.

7 **College Sports Television** — New street-level broadcast center accessible to the public, with interactive events and activities for college sports fans.

8 **The Sports Center** — 212-336-6000. A very expensive, monster health club with a 10,000-sq.-ft. climbing wall, a quarter-mile track, swimming pool, and enough fitness equipment for a small army in training. If you have to ask how much the membership is, you can't afford it.

9 **Sky Rink** — 212-336-6100. Two 24/7 ice rinks that are mainly used for classes, training, and Bar Mitzvahs.

10 **The Lighthouse** — 212-336-6144. 10,000-sq.-ft. event space for private gatherings, with food catered by Abigail Kirsch.

10 **The Field House** — 212-336-6500. The Field House is an 80,000 sq.-ft-building that has a 30-ft climbing wall, a gymnastics training center, 4 batting cages, 2 basketball courts, and 2 indoor soccer fields. To give you an idea of prices for adults, a season (10 games plus playoffs) of soccer is $220 per person, basketball is $150 per person, yoga is $16 per one-hour session, rock-climbing is $15 per 2-hour session, and gymnastics is $25 per 90-minute session.

11 **Spirit Cruise** — 212-727-2789. www.spiritofnewyork.com. Ships run out of Chelsea Piers and also Weehawken, NJ. Dinner cruises are approximately $88 per person, and if you're having a big function, you can rent the entire boat!

12 **Blades Board & Skate Shop** — 212-336-6299 @roller rinks, 212-336-6199 @sky rink. A cool, hip supplier of skating gear.

13 **Roller Rink** — 212-336-6200. Two regulation-size outdoor skating rinks and an "extreme" skate park. If you're a member, the Skate Park costs $10 each day, otherwise each session is $14 (on weekends, sessions are only 3-hours long).

Unfortunately, but not surprisingly, there are no golf courses on the island of Manhattan. Thankfully, there are two driving ranges where you can at least smack the ball around until you can get to a real course, as well as a golf simulator at Chelsea Piers that lets you play a full round "at" various popular courses (Pebble Beach, St. Andrews, etc.). NYC has a number of private and public courses throughout the outer boroughs and Westchester; however, they by no means satisfy the area's huge demand for courses.

Golf Courses

Golf Courses	*Borough*	*Address*	*Par*	*Phone*
Mosholu Golf Course (9-hole)	Bronx	3700 Jerome Ave	35	718-655-9164
Pelham/Split Rock Golf Course	Bronx	870 Shore Rd (in Pelham Bay Park)	71	718-885-1258
Van Cortlandt Golf Course	Bronx	Van Cortlandt Pk S & Bailey Ave	70	718-543-4595
Dyker Beach Golf Course	Brooklyn	86th St at 7th Ave	71	718-836-9722
Marine Park Golf Club	Brooklyn	2880 Flatbush Ave	72	718-338-7113
Breezy Point Pitch & Putt	Queens	155th St & Boardwalk	55	718-474-1623
Clearview Golf Course	Queens	20212 Willets Point Blvd	70	718-229-2570
Douglaston Golf Course	Queens	6320 Marathon Pkwy	67	718-428-1617
Flushing Meadows Pitch & Putt	Queens	Flushing Meadows–Corona Park	54	718-271-8182
Forest Park Golf Course	Queens	101 Forest Park Dr	70	718-296-0999
Kissena Park Golf Course	Queens	164-15 Booth Memorial Ave	64	718-939-4594
LaTourette Golf Course	Staten Island	1001 Richmond Hill Rd	72	718-351-1889
Silver Lake Golf Course	Staten Island	915 Victory Blvd	69	718-447-5686
South Shore Golf Course	Staten Island	200 Huguenot Ave	72	718-984-0101

Fees are generally as follows (reservations are a must, and usually cost an extra $2):

Weekdays before 1 pm—$22 Weekends before 1 pm—$25
Weekdays after 1 pm—$19 Weekends after 1 pm—$21
Carts $13.75 per person

Golf Simulator – Chelsea Piers Golf Club (see page 212): $35 per hour, $315 for a 10-hour package

Driving Ranges in Manhattan

Driving Ranges in Manhattan		*Fees*	*Phone*
Chelsea Piers: Pier 59	59, Chelsea Piers (at 23rd St) Golf Club Pier	$20/80 balls (peak), $20/100 balls (off-peak) Clubs: 1 for $4, 2 for $5, 3 for $6, 10 for $12 Till 5 pm: $20 an hour, all you can hit, one club rental included.	212-336-6400
Randall's Island Golf Center	1 Randalls Rd	$6.00/small bucket, $10.00/large bucket	212-427-5689

Bowling Alleys

Bowling Alleys	*Address*	*Phone*	*Fees*
Bowlmor Lanes	110 University Pl b/w 12th &13th Sts	212-255-8188	$6.45-$8.95 per person per game $5 for shoes
AMF Chelsea Piers Bowl	Pier 60	212-835-2695	$7.50-$8.25 per person per game $4.50 for shoes
Leisure Time	625 Eighth Ave/Port Authority Bus Terminal	212-268-6909	$7.50 per person per game $4 for shoes

Pools

Pools	Address	Phone	Type — Fees	Map
All Star Fitness Club	75 West End Ave	212-265-8200	Indoor — $25 per day	14
Asphalt Green	555 E 90th St	212-369-8890	Indoor — $20 per day	17
Asser Levy	E 23rd St & Asser Levy Pl	212-447-2020	Indoor — $75 per year (not open during summer) / Outdoor — Free*	10
Athletic and Swim Club at the Equitable Center	787 Seventh Ave	212-265-3490	Indoor — call for membership fees	12
Bally's Sports Club	335 Madison Ave	212-983-5320	Indoor — $25	12
Bally's Sports Club	139 W 32nd St	212-465-1750	Indoor — $25	9
Bally's Sports Club	350 W 50th St	212-265-9400	Indoor — $25	11
Battery Park Swim & Fitness Center	375 South End Ave	212-321-1117	Indoor/Outdoor — call for membership fees $26 per day	BPC
Carmine Recreation Center	1 Clarkson St	212-242-5228	Indoor — $725 per year Outdoor — Free*	5
Chelsea Piers Sports Center	Pier 60	212-336-6000	Indoor — $50 per day	8
Coles Sports and Recreation Center	181 Mercer St	212-998-2020	Indoor -- call for membership fees	6
Crowne Plaza	1601 Broadway	212-977-4000	Indoor — $25 per day	12
East 54th Street	348 E 54th St	212-397-3154	Indoor — $25 per year	13
Emanu-el Midtown YM-YWHA Alliance	344 E 14th St	212-780-0800	Indoor — $15 per day	13
Excelsior Athletic Club	301 E 57th St	212-688-5280	Indoor — $25 per day	7
New York Sports Club	1637 Third Ave	212-987-7200	Indoor — $25 per day	19
Gravity Fitness and Spa	119 W 56th St	212-245-1144	Indoor — $50 per day	12
Hamilton Fish Recreation Center	128 Pitt St	212-387-7687	Outdoor — Free*	23
Hansborough Recreation Center	35 W 134th St	212-234-9603	Indoor — $75 per year	11
Highbridge	173rd St & Amsterdam	212-927-2400	Outdoor — Free	21
Holiday Inn	440 W 57th St	212-581-8100	Outdoor — $30 per day	11
Jackie Robinson Pool	146 St & 89 Bradhurst Ave	212-234-9606	Outdoor — Free*	21
John Jay	E 77th St & Cherokee Pl	212-794-6566	Outdoor — Free*	15
Lasker Pool	110 Lenox Ave	212-534-7639	Outdoor — Free*	19
Lenox Hill Neighborhood House	331 E 70th St	212-744-5022	Indoor — $10 per day	15
Manhattan Plaza Health Club	482 W 43rd St, 2nd Fl	212-563-7001	Indoor — $25.03 per day (no day pass during summer)	11
Marcus Garvey Swimming Pool	13 E 124th St	212-410-2818	Outdoor — Free*	20
Monterey Sports Club	175 E 96th St	212-996-8200	Indoor — $5695 per year	17
New York Health & Racquet Club	132 E 45th St	212-986-3100	Indoor -- $50	13
New York Health & Racquet Club	110 W 56th St	212 541-7200	Indoor -- $50	12
New York Sports Club	1635 E 91st St	212-987-7200	Indoor -- $25	17
New York Sports Club	1614 Second Ave	212-213-5999	Indoor -- $25	15
Paris Health Club	752 West End Ave	212-749-3500	Indoor — $7745 per year	16
Reebok Sports Club	160 Columbus Ave	212-362-6800	Indoor — $35 with a member, or call for membership fees $1200 to become a member, $188 per month	14
Riverbank State Park	679 Riverside Dr	212-694-3600	Indoor/Outdoor — $2 per day	21
Sheltering Arms Park W	129th St & Amsterdam Ave	212-662-6191	Outdoor — Free*	18
Sheraton New York Health Club	811 Seventh Ave	212-621-8591	Indoor — $40 per day	12
Dry Dock Swimming Pool	408 E 10th St	212-677-4481	Outdoor — Free*	7
Thomas Jefferson Swimming Pool	2180 First Ave	212-860-1372	Outdoor — Free*	20
Tompkins Square Mini Pool	500 E 9th St	212-387-7685	Outdoor — Free*	7
UN Plaza Health Club	1 UN Plz	212-702-5016	Indoor — $35 per day	13
West 59th Street Swimming Pool	533 W 59th St	212-397-3159	Indoor — $725 per year	11
Mayor Robert F Wagner	E 124th St b/w First & Second Aves	212-534-4238	Outdoor — Free*	6
YMCA	1810 W 135th St	212-281-4100	Indoor — $7 per day	19
YMCA	1395 Lexington Ave	212-415-5700	Indoor — $30 per day	17
YMCA	224 E 47th St	212-756-9600	Indoor — $25 per day	13
YWCA	610 Lexington Ave	212-755-4500	Indoor — $20 per day	13

* summer only (Fourth of July–Labor Day)

There are more tennis courts on the island of Manhattan than you might think, although getting to them may be a bit more than you've bargained for. Most of the public courts in Manhattan are either smack in the middle of Central Park or are on the edges of the city—East River Park, for instance, and Riverside Park. These courts in particular can make for some pretty windy playing conditions.

Public Courts—Outdoor	*Address*	*# of Cts.*	*Type*	*Phone*
Central Park Tennis Center	93rd St & Central Park W	30	Clay/Hard	212-280-0205
East River Park Tennis Courts	FDR Dr & Broome St	12	Hard	212-387-7678
Fort Washington Park	H Hudson Pkwy & 170th St	10	Hard	212-304-2322
F Johnson Playground	51st St & Seventh Ave	8	Hard	212-234-9609
Inwood Hill Park	207th St & Seaman Ave	9	Hard	212-304-2381
Octagon Park*	Main St, Roosevelt Island	6	Hard	N/A
Randall's Island Sunken Meadow	East and Harlem Rivers	11	Hard	212-860-1827
Riverbank State Park	W 145th St & Riverside Dr	4	Hard	212-694-3600
Riverside Park	96th St & Riverside Dr	10	Clay	212-469-2006
Riverside Park	119th-122nd St & Riverside Dr	10	Hard	212-496-2006

*Check www.rioc.com for permit rates on Roosevelt Island

Public Courts—Indoor	*Address*	*# of Cts.*	*Type*	*Phone*
Randall's Island Indoor Tennis*	Randall's Island Park	4	Hard	212-534-4845
Sutton East Tennis Club*	York Ave and 60th St	8	Clay	212-751-3452
Village Tennis Courts	110 University Pl	3	Hard	212-989-2300

*Courts are only available October through April. Please call for more information.

Private Clubs	*Address*	*# of Cts.*	*Type*	*Phone*
Columbia Tennis Center	575 W 218th St	6	Hard	212-942-7100
Manhattan Plz Racquet Club	450 W 43rd St	5	Hard	212-594-0554
Midtown Tennis Club	341 Eighth Ave	8	Har-Tru	212-989-8572
River Club	447 E 52th St	2	Clay	212-751-0100
Roosevelt Island Racquet Club	281 Main St	11	Clay	212-935-0250
The Tennis Club	15 Vanderbilt Ave	2	Hard	212-687-3841
Tower Tennis Courts	1725 York Ave	2	Hard	212-860-2464
Town Tennis Club	430 E 56th St	3	Hard/Clay	212-752-4059
UN Plz/Park Hyatt Hotel	1 UN Plz	1	Hard	212-702-5016
Wall St Racquet Club	South St, Piers 13 and 14	8	Clay	212-422-9300

Schools	*Address*	*# of Cts.*	*Type*	*Phone*
Coles Center, NYU	181 Mercer St	6	Clay	212-998-2020
JHS 167 YTC	E 75th St (b/w 2nd & 3rd)	4	Hard	212-879-7562
PS 125	425 W 123rd St	3	Hard	N/A
PS 137	327 Cherry St	5	Hard	N/A
PS 144	134 W 122nd St	4	Hard	N/A
PS 146	421 E 106th St	3	Hard	N/A
PS 187	349 Cabrini Blvd	4	Hard	N/A
Rockefeller University	1230 York Ave	1	Hard	212-327-8000

Getting a Permit

The tennis season, according to the NYC Parks Department, lasts from April 3 to November 23. Permits are good for use until the end of the season at all public courts, and are good for one hour of singles or two hours of doubles play. Fees are:

Juniors (18 yrs and under) $10
Adults (19-61 yrs) $100
Senior Citizen (62 yrs and over) $20
Single-play tickets $5

General Information

Manhattan Parks Dept: 212-360-8131
website: www.nycgovparks.org
Permit Locations: The Arsenal, 830 5th Ave @ 64th St; Paragon Sporting Goods, Broadway @ 18th St

Yoga

Finding a Class

Looking for a venue to perfect your downward-facing dog can be somewhat overwhelming in NYC with all of the schools and studios available. Whether you're seeking to relieve some stress or to improve your bodily and spiritual well-being, you're bound to find something to appeal to your inner pretzel. Once you've familiarized yourself with the different branches of yoga, you're going to want to find a studio that best suits your needs. Check out the Yellow Pages for a long list of all the studios in town, or if that catalog proves too vast and vague, ask a friend to recommend a teacher. If all else fails, here's a short list of places to try. You should contact the studio in advance to find out their approach to classes, what branches they focus on, class size, appropriate attire, cost, a class schedule, and whether or not you should bring your own mat.

Word to the wise: You may want to begin with an introductory class wherever you land. Even if you consider yourself a seasoned yogi, different studios follow different methods, so you'll want to familiarize yourself with the facilities before jumping in head-stand first.

Recommended Studios in Manhattan...

Jivamukti Yoga Center • 404 Lafayette St • 212-353-0214 • www.jivamuktiyoga.com
Karma Yoga • 37 W 65th St, 4th Fl • 212-769-YOGA • www.karmayoganyc.com
OM Yoga Center • 826 Broadway, 6th Fl • 212-254-YOGA • www.omyoga.com
exhale • 980 Madison Ave • 212-249-3000 • www.exhalespa.com
Sonic Yoga • 754 Ninth Ave • 212-397-6344 • www.sonicyoga.com
Bikram Yoga NYC • 182 Fifth Ave • 212-245-2525 • www.bikramyoganyc.com
Laughing Lotus • 59 W 19th St, 3rd Fl • 212-414-2903 • www.laughinglotus.com
Virayoga • 580 Broadway, Rm 1109 • 212-334-9960 • www.virayoga.com
Himalayan Institute - Yoga Science • 78 Fifth Ave, Ste 2 • 212-243-5995 • www.hinyc.org
Be Yoga • 160 E 56th St, 12th Fl • 212-935-9642 • www.beyoga.com
Integral Yoga Institute • 227 W 13th St • 212-929-0586 • www.integralyogany.org
Ashtanga Yoga Shala • 295 E 8th St • 212-614-9537 • www.ashtangayogashala.net
Kula Yoga Project • 28 Warren St, 4th Fl • 212-945-4460 • www.kulayoga.com

And Some for Brooklyn...

Yoga People • 157 Remsen St, Brooklyn Heights • 718-522-9642
Hot Yoga People • (offers Hot and Vinyasa style classes) 659 Fulton St, Fort Greene • 718-237-2300
Park Slope Yoga Center • 792 Union St, 2nd Fl (above Dixon's Bike Shop) • 718- 789-2288
DEVI • 837 Union St, Park Slope • 718-789-2288
Go Yoga • 218 Bedford Ave, Williamsburg • 718-486-5602

Billiards

Billiards	Address	Phone	Fee	Hours
128 Billiards	128 Elizabeth St	212-925-8219	$6 per hour	Until 3 am
Amsterdam Billiard Club	344 Amsterdam Ave	212-496-8180	$24 cover charge	12-3 pm weekdays 11 am-4 pm weekends
Amsterdam Billiard Club	210 E 86th St	212-570-4545	$24 cover charge	12-3 pm weekdays 11 am-4 pm weekends
Billiard Club	220 W 19th St	212-206-7665	$25 cover charge, $30 on Sun	12 pm-2 am weekdays, 3 pm-4 pm weekends
Broadway Billiard Café	10 E 21st St	212-388-1582	$4 per person/hour	9 am-6 pm Mon-Fri
Chelsea Bar & Billiards	54 W 21st St	212-989-0096	$15 per hour, $17 per hour weekends	11 am-2 am Sun-Wed, 11 am-4 am Thur-Sat
Corner Billiards	85 Fourth Ave	212-995-1314	$9 per hour, $12 per hour after 6 pm	12 am-2 am
East Side Billiard Club	163 E 86th St	212-831-7665	$4 per person/hour, $7 weekends	11 pm-2 am
Fat Cat Billiards	75 Christopher St	212-675-6056	$4 per hour	2 pm-2 am
Grand Billiard & Café	90 Eldridge St	212-431-9232		
Guys & Gals Billiard Parlor	500 W 207th St	212-567-9279	$5 per hour	1 pm-dawn
Mammoth Billiards	558 Eighth Ave	212-535-0331	$3-$4 per person/hour	24 hours
Post Billiards Café	154 Post Ave	212-569-1840	$6 per hour, $10 per hour weekends	12 pm-dawn
Pressure	110 University Pl	212-352-1161	$21 per hour $24 per hour weekends	Thur 7 pm-2 am Fri-Sat 9 pm-4 am
Q Lounge	220 W 19th St	212-206-7665		Mon-Thur 11 am-1 am, Fri 11 am-4 am, Sat 12 pm-3:30 am, Sun 1 pm-1 am
Slate Restaurant Bar Billiards	54 W 21st St	212-989-0096	$15 per hour Sun-Wed $17 per hour	Sun-Wed 11 pm-2 am, Thur-Sat 11 am-4 am
Soho Billiard Sport Ctr	298 Mulberry St	212-925-3753	$10 per hour	11 am-3 am

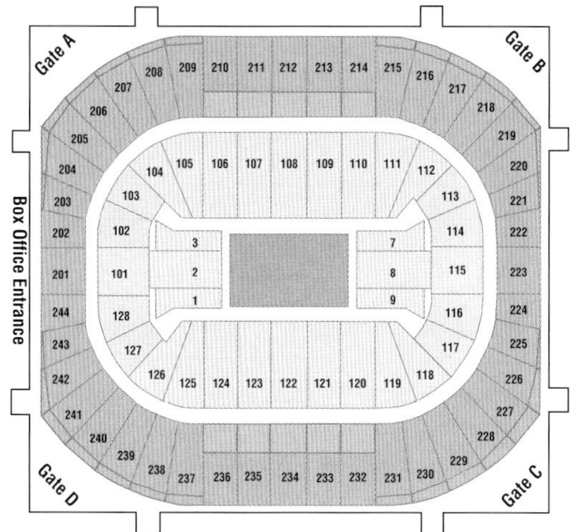

General Information

Ticketmaster: 212-307-7171, www.ticketmaster.com
Website: www.meadowlands.com/coarenafaq.asp
Devils: www.newjerseydevils.com
Nets: www.nba.com/nets
Gladiators: www.allsports.com/arena/gladiators

Overview

Once upon a time, this was called Brendan Byrne Arena, and was the home of two very bad pro teams, the New Jersey Nets and the New Jersey Devils. Now, it's called the Continental Airlines Arena and is the home of two suddenly very good teams. Though things seem to be going well game-wise for the Nets, financially they've been having troubles for quite sometime. Currently the NJ Nets are in talks to sell and move the team to Brooklyn for over $300 million dollars. Developer Bruce Ratner hopes to move the team to a proposed $435 million arena as a part of a residential, shopping, and office complex development to be built in the Prospect Heights area within the next five years. The NJ Storm lacrosse team up and relocated to Anaheim, CA as well. And then there were two.

How to Get There—Driving

Continental Airlines is only 5 miles from the Lincoln Tunnel. Luckily, since the fan base for the teams that play there is primarily in New Jersey, you won't have to deal with the same New York City and Long Island traffic that Giants Stadium games get. Additionally, the number of people attending is much smaller than for football, even on the rare occasion when the Nets or Devils (or the, uh, New Jersey Gladiators arena football team) sell out. You can take the Lincoln Tunnel to Route 3 West to Route 120 North to get there, or you can try either the Holland Tunnel to the New Jersey Turnpike (North) to exit 16W, or the George Washington Bridge to the New Jersey Turnpike (South) to exit 16W. Accessing the stadium from exit 16W allows direct access to the parking areas.

How to Get There–Mass Transit

A less stressful way to get to Continental Airlines Arena than driving is to take a bus from the Port Authority Bus Terminal directly to the arena. It costs $7 round trip when you buy in advance ($4 each way on the bus, exact change only!), and buses usually start running two hours before the start of the game.

How to Get Tickets

The box office is open Monday–Saturday from 11:00 am to 6:00 pm and is closed Sunday, unless there is an event. The phone number for ticket information only is 201-935-3900. To get tickets without going to the box office, you have to call Ticketmaster or visit their website.

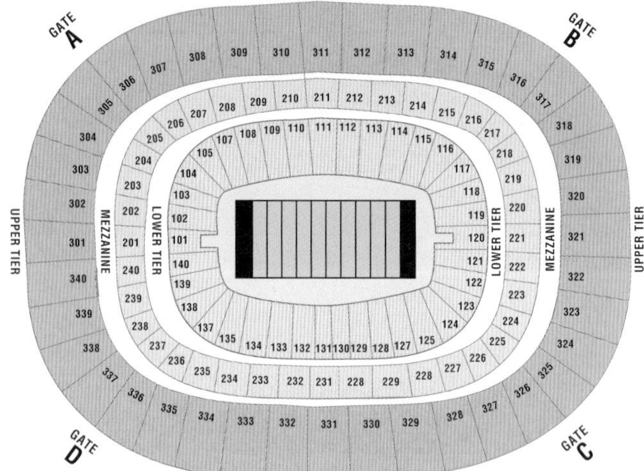

General Information

Ticketmaster: 212-307-7171, www.ticketmaster.com
Website: www.giantsstadium.com
New York Giants: www.giants.com
New York Jets: www.newyorkjets.com
New York Metrostars: www.metrostars.com
Giants Stadium Information: 201-935-3900

Overview

Giants Stadium, located in the scenic and smelly Meadowlands Sports Complex of New Jersey, is the home of both the New York Giants and New York Jets football teams (it's the only stadium to host two professional football teams). They play here on alternating Sundays throughout the fall, and the only way to get regular-priced tickets is to inherit them, since both teams are sold out through the next ice age. Giants Stadium also houses Major League Soccer's Metrostars (for which many, many tickets are available) and is the site of several concerts and other sporting and religious events throughout the year. The stadium's field has seen a few changes recently: astroturf was replaced by a removable grass field in 2000, which in turn was replaced by the synthetic FieldTurf after the grass proved almost unplayable.

How to Get There—Driving

Giants Stadium is only 5 miles from the Lincoln Tunnel (closer to midtown than Shea Stadium, even) but leave early if you want to get to the game on time—remember that the Giants and the Jets are a) sold out for every game and b) have tons of fans from both Long Island and the five boroughs. You can take the Lincoln Tunnel to Route 3 West to Route 120 North to get there, or you can try either the Holland Tunnel to the New Jersey Turnpike (North) to exit 16W, or the George Washington Bridge to the New Jersey Turnpike (South) to exit 16W. Accessing the stadium from exit 16W allows direct access to the parking areas.

How to Get There–Mass Transit

A less stressful way to get to Giants Stadium than driving is to take a bus from the Port Authority Bus Terminal directly to the stadium. It costs $7 round trip ($4 each way when purchased on the bus), and buses usually start running two hours before kickoff.

How to Get Tickets

For the Jets and the Giants, scalpers and friends are the only options. For the MetroStars and for concerts, you can call Ticketmaster or visit Ticketmaster's website.

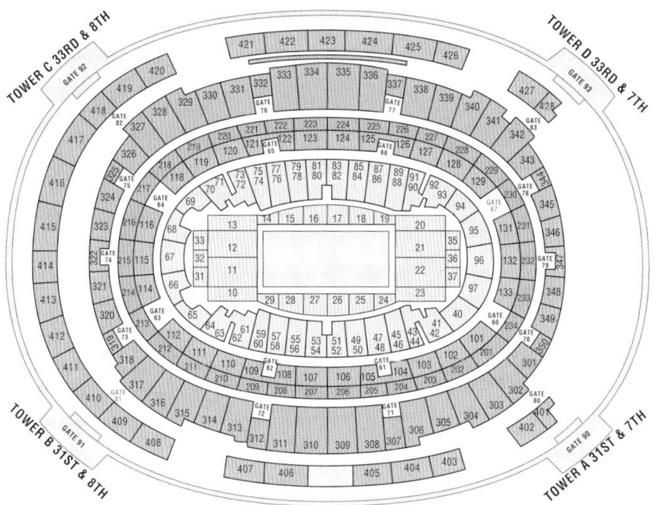

General Information

Ticketmaster: 212-307-7171, www.ticketmaster.com
Knicks: www.nyknicks.com
Liberty: www.nyliberty.com
Rangers: www.newyorkrangers.com
General Information: 212-465-6741
Website: www.thegarden.com

Overview

Madison Square Garden is home to the Knicks, the Rangers, and the Liberty. If you don't know which sports these teams play, then we can't help you. Either way, we probably can't help you get tickets for the Knicks or the Rangers. Don't worry, though—the Liberty games are the most fun, anyway—especially now that Jeff Van Gundy isn't coaching the Knicks anymore. MSG also hosts a ton of other events throughout the year, including rock concerts, tennis tournaments, political conventions, and, for those of you with 2+ years of graduate school, monster truck rallies and "professional" wrestling. Check out MSG's website for the full calendar of events.

How to Get There–Mass Transit

MSG is right next to Penn Station, so it's extremely convenient to get there. You can take the A C E and 1 2 3 9 lines to 34th Street and Penn Station, or the N R Q W, B D F V, and PATH lines to 34th Street and 6th Avenue

How to Get Tickets

You can try Ticketmaster for single seats for the Knicks and the Rangers, but a better bet would be to try the "standby" line for these teams (show up a half-hour before game time). There are also the ubiquitous ticket scalpers ringing the Garden for when your rich out-of-town friends breeze in to see a game. You can usually get Liberty tickets (and tickets for other events) through Ticketmaster.

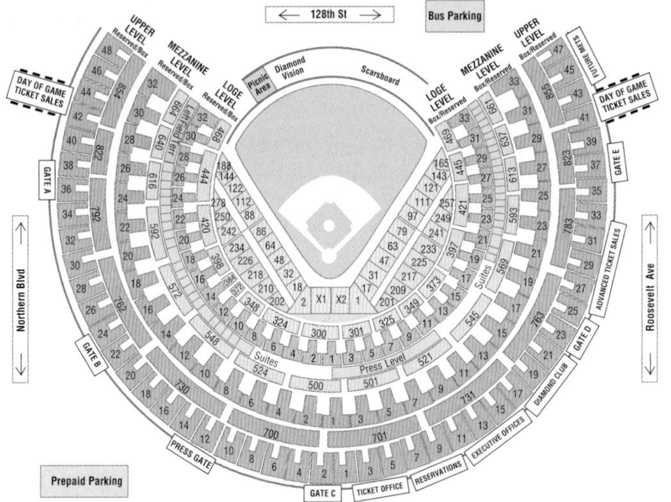

General Information

Mets Clubhouse Shops: 143 E 54th St & 11 W 42nd St
Shea Stadium Box Office: 718-507-TIXX
Website: www.mets.com
Location: 126th St and Roosevelt Ave, Flushing, Queens
Ferry: 800-53-FERRY

Overview

Shea Stadium is the home of the New York Mets. It's painted in those lovely garish colors of Dodger Blue and Giant Orange (homage to the two baseball teams that deserted New York City for the west coast) and is located in Flushing Meadows in Queens. Although the Mets had one of the most abysmal starts in baseball history in 1962 (going 40-120), since that time, they've won two World Series (in 1969 and 1986), appeared in two others, and have been competitive in at least some portion of every decade. With off-season additions of some classic fan-favorites (namely Tom Glavine and David Cone), slightly better food than Yankee Stadium, and slightly cheaper tickets, the Mets are doing their best to keep people coming to Flushing.

How To Get There—Driving

Driving to Shea Stadium is easy, although commuter traffic during the week can cause tie-ups. You can take the Triborough Bridge to the Grand Central Parkway; the Mid-Town Tunnel to the Long Island Expressway to the Grand Central; or the Brooklyn-Queens Expressway to the LIE to the Grand Central. If you want to try and avoid the highways, get yourself over to Astoria Boulevard in Queens, make a right on 108th Street, then a left onto Roosevelt Avenue.

How To Get There–Mass Transit

The good news is that the 7 train runs straight to Shea Stadium. The bad news is: 1) it's the 7 train, usually rated the worst among all train lines; and 2) it's the only train that goes there. However, it will get you there and back (eventually), and the 7 is accessible from almost all the other train lines in Manhattan. Alternately, you can take the E to Roosevelt Avenue and pick up the 7 there, saving about 30 minutes. Also New York Waterway runs a ferry service (the "Mets Express") to Shea from the South Street Seaport, E 34th Street, and E 94th Street. The other option is the Port Washington LIRR from Penn Station, which stops at Shea on game days.

How To Get Tickets

You can order Mets tickets by phone through the Mets' box office, on the internet through the Mets' website, or at the Mets Clubhouse Shops.

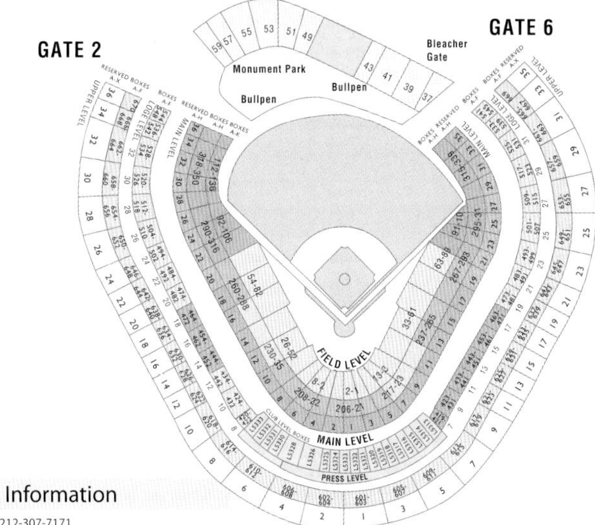

General Information

Ticketmaster: 212-307-7171
Yankee Stadium Box Office: 718-293-6000 (group sales)
Yankee Store: 393 5th Ave
Website: www.yankees.com
Ferry: 800-53-FERRY
Location: 161st St & River Ave, The Bronx

Overview

Hellish ticket prices and extremely mediocre food won't stop us from going to Yankee Stadium, the Bronx's most famous landmark since the 1920s. Since moving in, the Yankees have won more than a quarter of the World Series that have been played (26 of 100), making them one of the most successful sports franchises in history. Last fall's disappointing loss to the Florida Marlins in Game 6 has been pushed out of our minds for now. We expect the Yanks back in the playoffs this fall (mainly due to the aquisition of Mr. A-Rod), just like everyone else does…

How To Get There—Driving

Driving to Yankee Stadium from Manhattan usually isn't that bad, although with weeknight games now starting at 7:05, leaving at around 6:45 from midtown will no longer get you in your seats in time. It's best to take the Willis Avenue Bridge from either First Avenue or FDR Drive and get on the Major Deegan for about one mile until you see the stadium exit. From the upper west side, you can try taking Broadway up to 155th Street and using the Macombs Dam Bridge to cross over to the stadium (avoiding lots of crosstown traffic). Parking (as compared to ticket prices) is usually pretty cheap, especially at those lots that are a few blocks from the stadium.

How To Get There–Mass Transit

Getting to the stadium by subway is easy. The 4, D, and the B (on weekdays) all run express to the stadium, and you can easily hook up with either train at several junctions in Manhattan. It should take you no longer than 45 minutes from any point in Manhattan, less from midtown. Also, New York Waterway runs a wonderful ferry (the "Yankee Clipper") from South Street Seaport, E 34th Street, and E 94th Street.

How To Get Tickets

You can order tickets by phone through Ticketmaster, buy tickets at the box office or at the Yankee store, or buy tickets over the web through either Ticketmaster or the Yankee web site.

Airline	*Phone*	*JFK*	*EWR*	*LGA*
Aer Lingus	888-474-7424	■		
Aeroflot	800-340-6400	■		
Aerolineas Argentinas	800-333-0276	■		
Aeromar	877-237-6627	■		
Aeromexico	800-237-6639	■		
Aerosvit Ukranian	212-661-1620	■		
Air Canada	888-247-2262	■	■	■
Air France	800-237-2747	■	■	
Air India	212-751-6200	■	■	
Air Jamaica	800-523-5585	■	■	
Air Malta	800-756-2582	■		
Air Plus Comet	877-999-7587	■		
Air Tran	800-247-8726		■	■
Air Ukraine	212-230-1001	■		
Alaska Airlines	800-426-0333		■	
Alitalia	800-223-5730	■	■	
All Nippon	800-235-9262	■		
America West (domestic)	800-235-9292	■	■	
America West (international)	800-363-2597	■		
American (domestic)	800-433-7300	■	■	■
American (international)	800-433-7300	■	■	
American Eagle	800-433-7300	■		
Asiana	800-227-4262	■		
ATA	800-435-9282		■	
Austrian Airlines	800-843-0002	■		
Avianca	800-284-2622	■		
Biman Bangladesh	212-808-4477	■		
British Airways	800-247-9297	■	■	
BWIA	800-538-2942	■		
Casino Express	775-738-6040		■	
Cathay Pacific	800-233-2742	■		
China Airlines	800-227-5118	■		
Colgan	800-428-4322			■
Comair	800-354-9822			■
Continental (domestic)	800-525-0280	■	■	■
Continental (international)	800-231-0856		■	
Corsair (seasonal)	800-677-0720	■		
Czech Airlines	212-765-6545	■		
Delta (domestic)	800-221-1212	■	■	■
Delta (international)	800-241-4141	■	■	
Delta Express	800-235-9359	■	■	■
Egyptair	212-315-0900	■		
El Al	800-223-6700	■	■	
Ethiopian Airlines	212-867-0095		■	
Eva Airways	800-695-1188		■	
Finnair	800-950-5000	■		
Frontier Airlines	800-432-1359			■
Guyana Airways	718-523-2300	■		
Hooters Air	888-359-4668		■	
Iberia	800-772-4642	■		
Icelandair	800-223-5500	■		

Airline	*Phone*	*JFK*	*EWR*	*LGA*
Japan Airlines	800-525-3663	■		
Jet Blue	800-538-2583	■		
KLM	800-374-7747	■		
Korean Air	800-438-5000	■		
Kuwait Airways	800-458-9248	■		
Lacsa	800-225-2272	■		
Lan Chile	800-735-5526	■		
Lan Peru	800-735-5590	■		
LOT Polish	800-223-0593	■	■	
Lufthansa	800-645-3880	■	■	
Malaysia	800-582-9264		■	
Malev Hungarian	800-223-6884	■		
Mexicana	800-531-7921		■	
Miami Air (charter)	305-871-3300	■	■	
Midwest Express	800-452-2022		■	■
National Airlines	888-757-5387		■	
Nigeria Airlines	212-972-4565	■		
North American	718-656-2650	■	■	
Northwest (domestic)	800-225-2525	■	■	■
Northwest (international)	800-447-4747	■		
Olympic	800-223-1226	■		
Pakistan Int'l Airlines	212-370-9157	■		
Pan American Airways	800-FLY-PANAM		■	
Qantas	800-227-4500	■	■	
Royal Air Maroc	800-344-6726	■		
Royal Jordanian	212-949-0050	■		
SAS	800-221-2350		■	
Saudi Arabian Airlines	800-472-8342	■		
Singapore Airlines	800-742-3333	■	■	
Song	800-359-7664	■		
South African Airways	800-722-9675	■		
Southeast	800-359-7325		■	
Spirit	800-772-7117			■
Swiss Airlines	800-221-4750	■	■	
TACA	800-535-8780	■		
TACV Cabo Verde	617-472-2431	■		
Tap Air Portugal	800-221-7370		■	
Tarom Romanian	212-560-0840	■		
Thai Airways	800-560-0840	■		
Turkish	800-874-8875	■		
United Airlines (domestic)	800-241-6522	■	■	■
United Airlines (international)	800-241-6522		■	
Universal	718-441-4900	■		
US Airways	800-428-4322		■	■
USA3000	800-577-3000		■	
Uzbekistan	212-245-1005	■		
Varig	800-468-2744	■		
Virgin Atlantic	800-862-8621	■	■	
World Airways	770-632-8000	■		

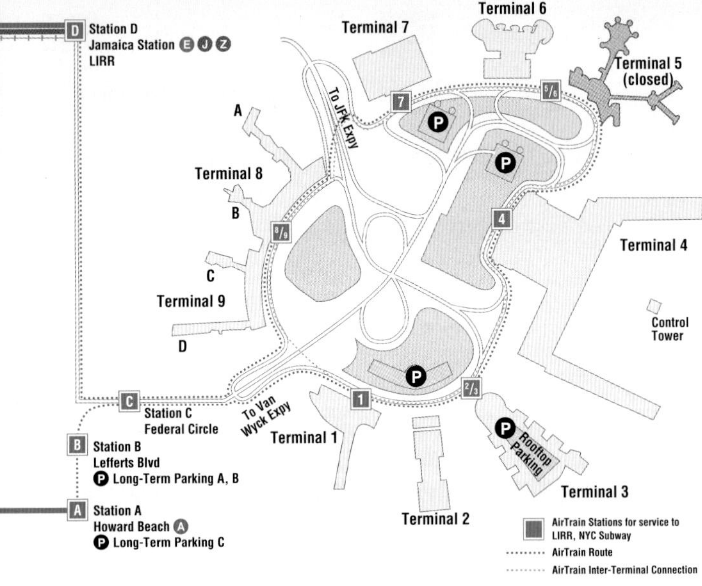

Airline	Terminal
Aer Lingus	4
Aero Mexico	3
Aeroflot	3
Aerolineas Argentinas	4
Aeromar	1
Aerosvit Ukrainian	4
Air Canada	7
Air China	1
Air France	1
Air India	4
Air Jamaica	2
Air Malta	4
Air Plus Comet	4
Air Ukraine	4
Alitalia	1
All Nippon Airways	3
America West	7
American (dom/ San Juan)	9
American (intl/Carib)	8
Asiana	4
Austrian Airlines	1
Avianca	3
Biman Bangladesh	4
British Airways	7
BWIA	4
Cathay Pacific	7
China Airlines	3
Continental Airlines	4
Czech Airlines	3
Delta	3
Egypt Air	4
El Al	4
Finnair	8
Ghana Airways	4
Iberia	8
Icelandair	7
Japan	1
JetBlue Airways	6
KLM	4
Korean	1
Kuwait	4
Lacsa	4
Lan Chile	4
Lan Peru	4
LOT Polish	8
Lufthansa	1
Malev	4
Miami Air	4
National	4
Nigeria Airways	4
North American	4
Northwest	4
Olympic	1
PACE Airlines	4
Pakistan	4
Qantas	7
Royal Air Maroc	1
Royal Jordanian	3
Saudi Arabian Airlines	2
Singapore	1
Song	2
South African	3
Swiss International	4
TACA International	4
TACV Cabo Verde	4
TAP Air Portugal	4
Tarom Romanian	4
Turkish	1
United	7
Universal	4
Uzbekistan Airlines	4
Varig	4
Virgin Atlantic	4
World Airways	4

General Information

Address:	JFK Expressway, Jamaica, NY
Phone:	718-244-4444
Lost and Found:	718-244-4225
Website:	www.kennedyairport.com
AirTrain:	www.airtrainjfk.com
AirTrain Phone:	718-570-1048
Long Island Rail Road:	www.mta.info/lirr

Overview

Ah, JFK. It's long been a nemesis to Manhattanites due to the fact that it's the furthest of the three airports from Manhattan. Nonetheless, 32 million people used JFK in 2003. A $9.5 billion expansion and modernization program is well underway, including the recently completed AirTrain (a new direct rail link to the Jamaica LIRR Station), as well as the addition of some chi-chi retail options (Hermes, Bulgari, H. Stern) but all we can say is, if you live in Manhattan, try Newark instead.

However, if you're already at JFK, have some time to kill, and want to give the AirTrain a whirl, all terminal-to-terminal connections are free. Terminals 1 and 4 have far-and-away the best shops and food, and architecture buffs can catch a nice glimpse of Eero Saarinen's masterful Terminal 5 (now unoccupied).

How to Get There–Driving

You can take the lovely and scenic Belt Parkway straight to JFK as long as it's not rush hour. This is about a 30-mile trip, even though JFK is only 15 or so miles from Manhattan. You can access the Belt by taking the Brooklyn-Battery Tunnel to the Gowanus (the best route) or by taking the Brooklyn, Manhattan, or Williamsburg Bridges to the Brooklyn-Queens Expressway to the Gowanus. If you're sick of stop and go highway traffic, an alternate route using local roads is to take Atlantic Avenue in Brooklyn and drive east until you hit Conduit Avenue. You can take this straight to JFK. It's direct and fairly simple. You can get to Atlantic Avenue from any of the three downtown bridges (look at a map first, though!) From midtown, you can take the Queens Midtown Tunnel to the Long Island Expressway to the Van Wyck Expressway South (there's never much traffic on the LIE, of course...). From uptown, you can take the Triboro Bridge to the Grand Central Parkway to the Van Wyck Expressway South.

How to Get There–Mass Transit

This is your chance to finish War and Peace. The new AirTrain will make your journey marginally smoother, but it will also make your wallet a little lighter. Where once there was a free shuttle bus service from the Howard Beach/JFK Airport stop on the A subway line, the AirTrain will now whisk you across for a mere 5 bucks. Depending on where you're traveling from in Manhattan, Queens or Brooklyn, the E, J, and M subway lines to Jamaica Station (end of the line) also connect with the AirTrain.

All subway-AirTrain combos will set you back a total of $7. If you're anywhere near Penn Station and your time is valuable, the LIRR to Jamaica will cost you $4.75 off-peak and $6.75 during peak times and the journey takes roughly 20 minutes. The AirTrain will be an additional $5.

If you want to give your Metrocard a workout, you can take the Turnpike/Kew Gardens stop, and transfer to the 3. Another possibility is the [illegible] to New Lots Avenue, where you transfer to the B15 to JFK. The easiest and most direct option is to take a bus from either Grand Central, Penn Station or the Port Authority on either Olympia or New York Airport Service buses ($10–13). Since they travel on service roads, Friday afternoon is not an advisable time to try them out. Taxis from the airport to Manhattan are a flat $45 + tolls. Fares to the airport are metered + tolls. The SuperShuttle will drop you anywhere between Battery Park and 227th, including all hotels, for $17-$19 but it could end up taking a while, depending on where your fellow passengers are going—a good option if you want door-to-door service, have a lot of time to kill, but not a lot of cash.

Parking

Rates for the Central Terminal Area lots are $3 for the first half-hour, $6 for up to 1 hour, $3 for every hour after that, and $24 per day. Long-term parking is $10 per day, for a maximum of 30 days. Be warned, though—many of the ongoing construction projects at JFK affect both their short-term and long-term lots, so be sure to allow extra time for any unpleasant surprises.

Rental Cars (On-Airport)

1 • **Avis** • 718-244-5406 or 800-230-4898
2 • **Budget** • 718-656-6010 or 800-527-0700
3 • **Dollar** • 718-656-2400 or 800-800-4000
4 • **Hertz** • 718-656-7600 or 800-654-3131
5 • **National** • 718-632-8300 or 800-227-7368

Hotels

Four Points Sheraton • 151-20 Baisley Blvd • 718-489-1000
Hilton JFK Airport • 138-10 135th Ave • 718-322-8700
Holiday Inn JFK Airport • 144-02 135th Ave • 718-659-0200
Pan American Hotel • 79-00 Queens Blvd • 718-446-7676
Radisson Hotel at JFK • 135-40 140th St • 718-322-2300

Car Services

Airport Limousine Service • 973-961-3220
Classic Limousine • 631-567-5100
Precept Transportation Service • 800-910-5466 or 201-997-7268
Super Saver by Carmel • 800-924-9954 or 212-666-6666
Tel Aviv Limo Service • 800-222-9888 or 212-777-7777

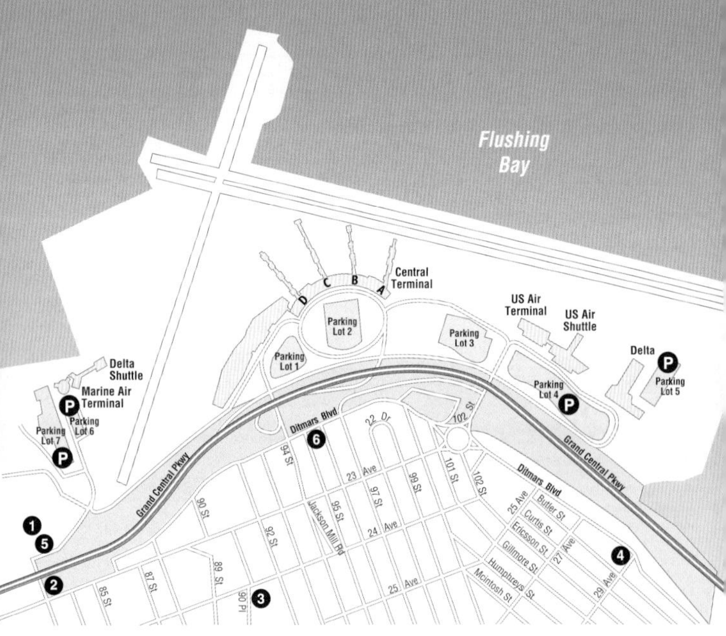

Airline	*Terminal*
Air Canada	A
Air Tran	B
American	D
American Eagle	C
ATA	B
Colgan	US Airways
Comair	Delta
Continental	A
Continental Express	A
Delta	Delta
Delta Connection	Delta

Airline	*Terminal*
Delta Shuttle	Marine
Frontier Airlines	B
Midwest Express	B & C
Northwest	Delta
Spirit	B
United	B
United (to DCA & BOS)	US Air Shuttle
United Express	C
US Airways	US Airways
US Airways Express	US Airways
US Airways Shuttle	US Air Shuttle

General Information

Address:	LaGuardia Airport, Flushing, NY 11371
Recorded Info:	718-533-3400
Lost and Found:	718-533-3988
Police:	718-533-3900
Website:	www.laguardiaairport.com

Overview

The best thing we can say about LaGuardia Airport is that it is named for a most excellent (and, unfortunately, dead) New York City mayor, Fiorello LaGuardia. Although LaGuardia has improved over recent years, there is still a way to go before it catches up to the nation's other airports. However, a number of new food and beverage stands and retail stores have opened up, particularly in the Central Terminal and US Airways Terminal, including fancy-schmancy places like Godiva, Brooks Brothers, and the Metropolitan Museum of Art store. There are also two bookstores in the airport: Barbara's Bestsellers in Central Terminal and Benjamin Books in US Airways Terminal. LaGuardia is inconvenient to public transportation, since the nearest subway station is miles away. But it's closer to the city than either Kennedy or Newark, especially from the Upper West or Upper East Sides.

How to Get There—Driving

LaGuardia is mere inches away from the Grand Central Parkway, which can be reached from both the Brooklyn-Queens Expressway (BQE) or from the Triboro Bridge. From lower Manhattan, take the Brooklyn, Manhattan, or Williamsburg bridges to the BQE to the Grand Central Parkway East. From midtown Manhattan, take the FDR Drive to the Triboro to the Grand Central. A potential alternate route (and money-saver) would be to take the 59th Street Bridge to 21st Street north in Queens. Once you're heading north on 21st Street, you can make a right on Astoria Boulevard and follow it all the way to 94th Street, where you can make a left and go straight into LaGuardia. This can be used if the FDR and/or the BQE is jammed, though that probably means that the 59th Street Bridge won't be much better.

How to Get There—Mass Transit

Alas, no subway line goes to LaGuardia (although there should be one that runs across 96th Street in Manhattan, through Astoria, and ending at LaGuardia—but that's another story). The closest the subway gets is the 7 E F G R Jackson Heights/Roosevelt Avenue/74th Street stop in Queens, where you can then transfer to the Q33 or Q47 bus that goes to LaGuardia. Sound exciting? It stinks, actually. The better bus to take is the M60, which runs across 125th Street and goes right to the airport. A better bet would be to pay the extra few bucks and take the New York Airport Service Express Bus ($8-12, 718-875-8200) from Grand Central Station. It runs every 15-30 minutes, only takes half an hour, and doesn't stop anywhere else. You can get it on Park Avenue between 41st and 42nd Streets. It also runs from Penn Station and the Port Authority Bus Terminal. A taxi will cost you at least $20. There's also the improbably named SuperShuttle Manhattan, which is a shared mini-bus that picks you up ($15-$22, 800-358-5826).

How to Get There—Really

Two words: car service. Call them, they'll pick you up at your door, drop you at the terminal, and you're done.

Some car services are: Allstate Car and Limousine: 212-333-3333 ($30 in the am & $38 in the pm + tolls from Union Square); Tri-State: 212-777-7171 ($30 + tolls from Union Square; best to call in the morning); Tel Aviv: 212-777-7777 ($30 in the am & $40 in the pm + tolls from Union Square)

Parking

Typically usurious, parking rates at LaGuardia are $3 for the first half-hour, $6 for up to 1 hour, $3 for every hour after that, and $24 per day. Long-term parking is $24 maximum for the first day and then $10 per day thereafter, only in Lot 3.

Another parking option is independent parking lots, such as Satellite Parking Systems (23-28 89th Street, 718-478-2200), Clarion Airport Parking (Ditmars Boulevard & 94th Street, 718-335-6713), and AviStar (23rd Avenue and 90th Street, 800-621-PARK). They run their own shuttle buses from their lots, and they usually charge $14-$17 per day. If all the parking garages onsite are full, follow the "P" signs to the airport exit and park in one of the off-airport locations.

Rental Cars

1 Avis • LGA 800-230-4898 or 718-507-3600
2 Budget •83-34 23rd Ave 800-527-0700 or 718-639-6400
3 Dollar • 90-05 25th Ave 718-779-5600 or 800-800-4000
4 Enterprise • 104-04 Ditmars Blvd 718-457-2900
5 Hertz • LGA 800-654-3131 or 718-478-5300
6 National • Ditmars Blvd & 95th St 800-227-7368 or 718-429-5893

Hotels

Clarion Hotel • 94-00 Ditmars Blvd • 718-335-1200
Courtyard La Guardia • 718-446-4800
Crowne Plaza • 104-04 Ditmars Blvd • 718-457-6300 or 800-692-5429
Eden Park Hotel • 113-10 Corona Ave • 718-699-4500
Garden Hotel LGA • 136-36 39th Ave • 718-359-8383
LaGuardia Marriott Hotel • 102-05 Ditmars Blvd • 718-565-8900
Paris Suites Hotel • 109-17 Horace Harding Expy • 718-760-2820
Sheraton LaGuardia East • 135-20 39 Ave • 718-460-6666
Wyndham Garden Hotel – LaGuardia • 100-15 Ditmars Blvd • 718-426-8900

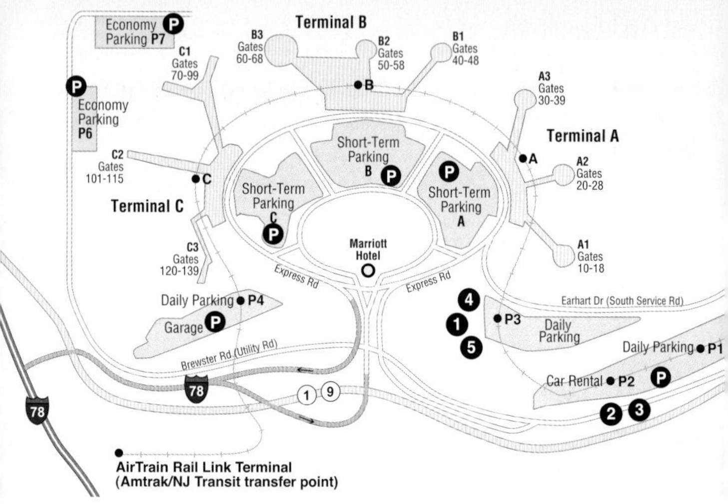

Airline	*Terminal*
Air Canada	A
Air France	B
Air India	B
Air Jamaica	B
Air Tran	A
Alaska Airlines	A
Alitalia	B
America West	A
American (domestic)	A
American (international)	A/B*
ATA (domestic)	A
ATA (international)	A/B*
British Airways	B
Casino Express	A
Continental	C
Continental (Chicago/Atlanta/Dallas)	A
Continental Express	C
Delta	B
El Al	B
Ethiopian Airlines	B
Eva Airways	B
Hooters Air	B
LOT Polish	B

Airline	*Terminal*
Lufthansa	B
Malaysia	B
Martinair (seasonal)	B
Mexicana	B
Miami Air	B
Midwest Express	B
National Airlines	A
North American	B
Northwest	B
Pan American Airways	A
Qantas	A
SAS	B
Singapore Airlines	B
Southeast	A
Swiss International Air Lines	B
TAP Air Portugal	B
United (domestic)	A
United (international)	A/B*
United Express	A
USA3000	B
US Airways	A
US Airways Express	A
Virgin Atlantic	B

* Departs Terminal A, arrives Terminal B.

General Information

Address:	10 Toler Pl, Newark, NJ
Phone:	888-EWR-INFO
Police/Lost and Found:	201-961-6230
Transportation Info:	800-AIR-RIDE (247-7533)
Radio Station:	530 AM (traffic reports near airport)
Website:	www.newarkairport.com

Overview

Newark Airport is easily the nicest of the three major metropolitan airports. The monorail and the AirTrain link from Penn Station, as well as a diverse food court, make it immensely preferable to its New York neighbors. And Newark's burgeoning international connections are increasing its popularity, although you might be languishing in the Holland Tunnel trying to get there long after your plane has left the ground.

If your flight gets delayed or you find yourself with time on your hands, check out the new d-parture spa in Terminal C, Gate 92 (also one opening soon in Terminal B). They offer everything from massage and facials to haircuts and make-up! The friendly staff watches the clock so you don't have to. www.departurespa.com, 973-242-3444.

How to Get There–Driving

By car, the route to Newark Airport is easy—just take either the Holland Tunnel or the Lincoln Tunnel to the New Jersey Turnpike South. You can use either Exit 14 or Exit 13A. If you want a cheaper and slightly more scenic (from an industrial standpoint) drive, follow signs for the Pulaski Skyway once you exit the Holland Tunnel. It's free, it's one of the coolest bridges in America, and it leads you to the airport just fine. If possible, check a traffic report before leaving Manhattan—sometimes there are viciously long tie-ups, especially at the Holland Tunnel. It's always worth it to see which outbound tunnel has the shortest wait.

How to Get There–Mass Transit

If you're allergic to traffic, try taking the new (but pricey) AirTrain service from Penn Station. It's jointly run by Amtrak ($26-$27 one-way) and NJ Transit ($11.55 one-way), which run alternating trains to Newark Airport's monorail two-to-three times per hour. If you use NJ Transit, choose a train that runs on the Northeast Corridor or North Jersey Coast Line with a scheduled stop for Newark Airport. If you use Amtrak, choose a train that runs on the Northeast Corridor Line with a scheduled stop for Newark Airport. You can also take direct buses from Port Authority Bus Terminal (which has the advantage of a bus-only lane running right out of it into the Lincoln Tunnel), Grand Central Terminal, and Penn Station (the New York version) on Olympia (for $12). The SuperShuttle will set you back $15-$19 and a taxi into Manhattan will cost you around $50.

How to Get There–Car Services

Car services are always the simplest option, although they're a bit more expensive for Newark Airport than they are for LaGuardia. Some car services are: Allstate Car and Limousine: 212-333-3333 ($44 in the am & $52 in the pm + tolls from Union Square); Tri-State: 212-777-7171 ($43 + tolls from Union Square; best to call in the morning); Tel Aviv: 212-777-7777 ($44 in the am & $54 in the pm + tolls from Union Square).

Parking

Regular parking rates are $3 for the first half-hour, $6 for up to 1 hour, $3 for every hour after that, and now a disgusting $20 per day for the P1, P3, and P4 monorail-serviced lots (one-year price hike from $12). Parking lots P6 and P7 are a lot farther away, are only serviced by a shuttle bus, and are $10 per day. Valet parking is $28 per day.

Rental Cars

1 • **Avis**	800-230-4898
2 • **Budget**	800-527-0700
3 • **Dollar**	973-824-2002
4 • **Hertz**	800-654-3131
5 • **National**	800-227-7368
6 • **Alamo** (Off-Airport)	800-327-9633
7 • **Enterprise** (Off-Airport)	800-325-8007

Hotels

Marriott Hotel (On-Airport) • 973-623-0006
Courtyard Newark Marriott • 600 Rte 1 & 9 South • 973-643-8500
Hilton Newark Airport • 1170 Spring St • 908-351-3900
Howard Johnson Hotel • 50 Port St • 201-344-1500
Sheraton Newark Airport Hotel • 128 Frontage Rd • 973-690-5500
Hampton Inn Newark Airport • 1128-38 Spring St • 908-355-0500
Best Western • 101 International Wy • 973-621-6200
Holiday Inn North • 160 Frontage Rd • 973-589-1000
Newark-Days Inn Airport • 450 Rte 1 South • 973-242-0900
Ramada Inn • US Hwy 1 and 9 & Haynes Ave • 973-824-4000
Four Points Sheraton Newark International Airport • 901 Spring St • 908-527-1600

Transit • **Bridges & Tunnels**

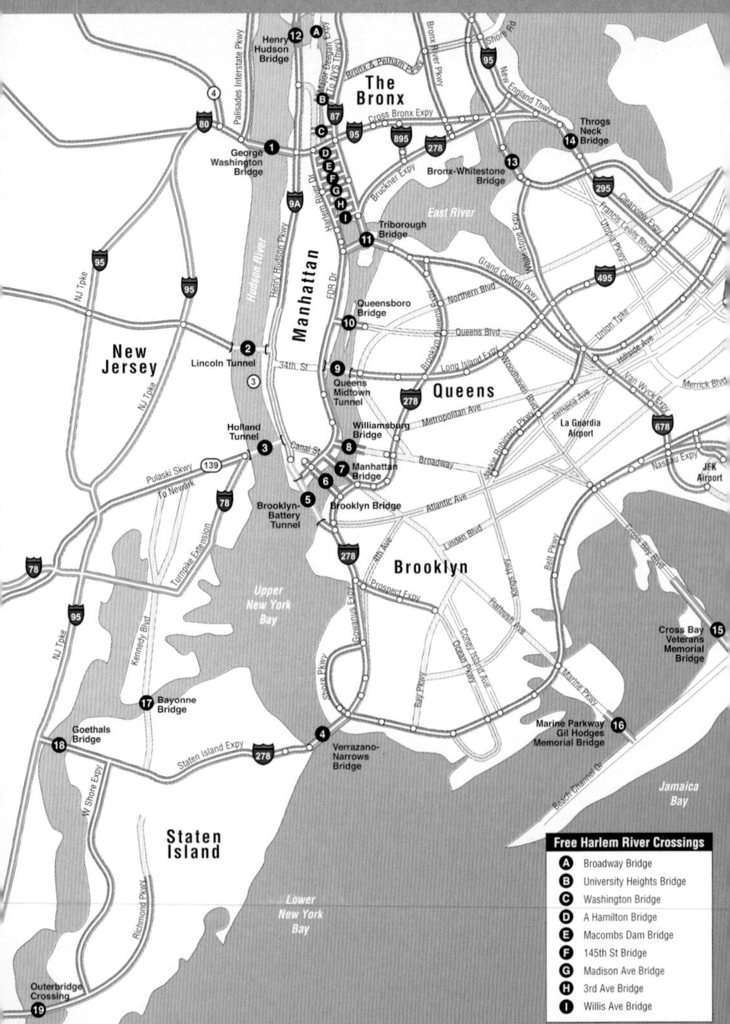

Overview

Since NYC is an archipelago, it's no wonder that there are so many bridges and 4 major tunnels. Most of the bridges listed in the chart below have broken records or are considered landmarks. The world's first vehicular tunnel ever built was the Holland Tunnel in 1927. New York City's first bridge, King's Bridge, built between Manhattan and the Bronx, was built in 1693, but, sadly, demolished in 1917. Highbridge, the oldest existing bridge in NYC, was built in 1843, but is not open to vehicles or pedestrians. Brooklyn Bridge, built in 1883, is the oldest NYC bridge open to vehicles and pedestrians and is still considered one of the most beautiful bridges ever built.

Unfortunately, there was severe neglect in the preservation of many of the bridges during the '70s. Inspections in the '80s and huge maintenance and refurbishment plans in the '90s/'00s will make the bridges stronger and safer than ever before. On certain holidays when the weather permits it, the world's largest free-flying American flag flies from the upper arch of the New Jersey tower on the George Washington Bridge.

General Information

Port Authority of NY and NJ: www.panynj.gov
DOT: www.ci.nyc.ny.us/html/dot/home.html • 212 or 718-CALLDOT
MTA: www.mta.nyc.ny.us
EZPass: www.e-zpassny.com • 1-800-333-TOLL
Transportation Alternatives: www.transalt.org
Best overall site: www.nycroads.com

		Toll/EZPass peak/EZPass off-peak	# of lanes	Pedestrians/bicyclists?	# of vehicles/day (in thousands)	Original cost (in millions)	Engineer	Main span/length	Operated by	Opened to traffic
1	Geo. Washington Bridge	6.00/5.00/4.00 (inbound only)	14	yes	300	59	Othmar H. Ammann	4,760'	PANYNJ	10/25/31
2	Lincoln Tunnel	6.00/5.00/4.00 (inbound only)	6	no	120	75	Othmar H. Ammann Ole Singstad	8,216'	PANYNJ	12/22/37
3	Holland Tunnel	6.00/5.00/4.00 (inbound only)	4	no	100	48	Clifford Holland/ Ole Singstad	8,558'	PANYNJ	11/13/27
4	Verrazano-Narrows Bridge	*	12	no	190	320	Othmar H. Ammann	4,260'	MTA	11/21/64
5	Brooklyn-Battery Tunnel	4.00/3.50	4	no	60	90	Ole Singstad	9,117'	MTA	5/25/50
6	Brooklyn Bridge	free	6	yes	140	15	John Roebling/ Washington Roebling	1,595.5'	DOT	5/24/1883
7	Manhattan Bridge	free	6	yes	78	25	Leon Moisseiff	1,470'	DOT	12/31/09
8	Williamsburg Bridge	free	8	yes	140	30	Leffert L. Buck	1,600'	DOT	12/19/03
9	Queens-Midtown Tunnel	4.00/3.50	4	no	80	52	Ole Singstad	6,414'	MTA	11/15/40
10	Queensboro Bridge	free	10	yes	155	20	Gustav Lindenthal	1,182'	DOT	3/30/09
11	Triborough Bridge	4.00/3.50	8/ 6/8	yes	200	60	Othmar H. Ammann	1,380'/ 310'/383'	MTA	7/11/36
12	Henry Hudson Bridge	2.00/1.50	7	yes	75	5	David Steinman	800'	MTA	12/12/36
13	Whitestone Bridge	4.00/3.50	6	no	110	20	Othmar H. Ammann	2300'	MTA	4/29/39
14	Throgs Neck Bridge	4.00/3.50	6	no	100	92	Othmar H. Ammann	1800'	MTA	1/11/61
15	Cross Bay Veterans Memorial Bridge	2.00/1.33	6	yes	20	29	N/A	3000'	MTA	5/28/70
16	Marine Parkway Gil Hodges Memorial Bridge	2.00/1.33	4	no	25	12	Madigan and Hyland	540'	MTA	7/3/37
17	Bayonne Bridge	6.00/5.00/4.00	4	yes	21	13	Othmar H. Ammann	5,780'	PANY/NJ	11/13/31
18	Geothals Bridge	6.00/5.00/4.00	4	no	80	7	Othmar H. Ammann	7,100'	PANY/NJ	6/29/28
19	Outerbridge Crossing	6.00/5.00/4.00	4	no	86	9	Othmar H. Ammann	8,800'	PANY/NJ	6/29/28

* $8.00/$7.00 with EZPass to Staten Island ($5.60/4.00 for registered Staten Island residents with EZPass) , $1.75 with three or more occupants—cash only). Free to Brooklyn.

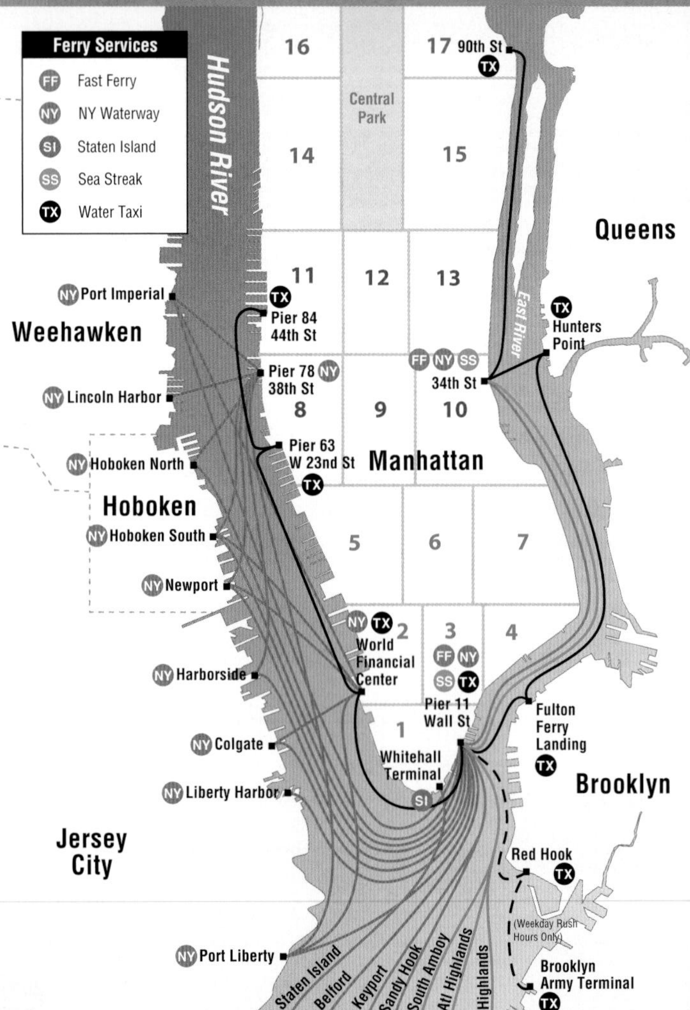
Ferry Services
FF Fast Ferry
NY NY Waterway
SI Staten Island
SS Sea Streak
TX Water Taxi
Hudson River
East River
Central Park
16
17
14
15
11
12
13
8
9
10
5
6
7
2
3
4
1
90th St
Queens
Port Imperial
Weehawken
Pier 84
44th St
Pier 78
38th St
Lincoln Harbor
Hunters Point
34th St
Pier 63
W 23nd St
Manhattan
Hoboken North
Hoboken
Hoboken South
Newport
World Financial Center
Harborside
Pier 11
Wall St
Fulton Ferry Landing
Colgate
Whitehall Terminal
Liberty Harbor
Brooklyn
Jersey City
Red Hook
(Weekday Rush Hours Only)
Port Liberty
Brooklyn Army Terminal
Staten Island
Belford
Keyport
Sandy Hook
South Amboy
Atl Highlands
Highlands

Ferries/Boat Tours, Rentals, & Charters

Name	Contact Info	Map
Staten Island Ferry	718-815-2628 • www.home.nyc.gov/html/dot/html/get_around/ferry/statfery.html This free ferry goes from Battery Park to Staten Island. On weekdays it leaves every 15-20 minutes from 6:30 am-9 am and 4 pm-8 pm. On weekends, it leaves every hour from 12:30 am–7:30 am. All other times it's every half hour.	1
NY Waterway	800-53-FERRY • www.nywaterway.com This is the largest ferry service in NY. They offer many commuter routes (mostly from New Jersey), sightseeing tours, and very popular shuttles to Yankees and Mets games.	1, 10, 15
Sea Streak	1-800-BOAT-RIDE • www.seastreakusa.com Catamarans that go pretty fast from the Highlands in NJ to Wall Street, E 34th Street, and the Brooklyn Army Terminal.	1,10
NY Fast Ferry	1-800-NYF-NYFF • www.nyff.com This ferry goes between Highlands, NJ and Pier 11 (Wall Street) or E 34th Street, Manhattan	1,10
Circle Line	212-563-3200 • http://www.circleline.com Circle Line offers many sightseeing tours including the full island cruise (departs from Pier 83 at 42nd Street - $25, no reservations needed) and the visit to Ellis Island (departs from Pier 16 at South Street Seaport - $13)	1, 11
Spirit of New York	212-727-2789 • www.spiritcruises.com Offers lunch and dinner cruises. Prices start at $43. Leaves from Pier 61 at Chelsea Piers. Make a reservation at least one week in advance, but the earlier the better.	8
Loeb Boathouse	212-517-2233 • www.centralparknyc.org/virtualpark/thegreatlawn/loebboathouse/ You can rent rowboats from March through October at The Lake, seven days a week weather permitting, in Central Park. It's $10 for the first hour and $2.50 for each additional 15 minutes ($30 cash deposit). It's open 10 am-5 pm, but the last boat goes out at 4:30 pm. Up to five people per boat. No reservations needed.	Central Park
World Yacht Cruises	212-630-8100 • www.worldyacht.com These very fancy, three-hour dinner cruises start at $69.95 per person. They leave from Pier 81 (41st Street) and you need a reservation. The cruise boards at 6pm, sails at 7pm, and returns at 10pm. There's also a Sunday brunch cruise April–December that is $41.90 per person.	11

Marinas/Passenger Ship Terminal

Name	Contact Info	Map
Surfside III	212-336-7873 • www.surfside3.com Dockage at Chelsea Piers. They have daily, weekly, and seasonal (there is a waiting list) per foot rates.	8
NY Skyports Inc	212-686-4547 Located on the East River at 23rd Street. Transient dockage is $3 per foot.	10
79th St Marina	212-496-2105 This dock has lots of long-term houseboat residents. It's located at 79th Street and the Hudson River. Open from May to October.	14
Dyckman Marina	212-567-5120 Transient dockage on the Hudson River at Dyckman Street	25
Passenger Ship Terminal	212-246-5451 • www.nypst.com If Love Boat re-runs aren't enough, and you decide to go on a cruise, you'll leave from the Passenger Ship Terminal. W 55th Street at 12th Avenue Take the West Side Highway to Piers 88-92.	11

Helicopter Services

Name	Contact Info	Map
Helicopter Flight Services	212-355-0801 • www.heliny.com For a minimum of $109, you can hop on a helicopter at the Downtown Manhattan Heliport at South Street Seaport on weekdays or at the W 30th Street Heliport on weekends and spend 15 minutes gazing down on Manhattan. Make sure to call in advance.	3, 8
Liberty Helicopter Tours	212-967-6464 • www.libertyhelicopters.com Leaves from the heliport at W 30th Street and 12th Avenue (9 am-9 pm) or the Downtown Manhattan Heliport at South Street Seaport (9 am-6 pm). Prices start at $56 and you only need a reservation when boarding at the Seaport. Flights depart every 5-10 minutes once there is a minimum of four passengers.	3, 8
Wall Street Helicopter	212-943-5959 • www.wallstreetheli.qpg.com Leaves from any heliport in Manhattan. Executive/corporate helicopter and twin engine aircraft charters. No sightseeing.	3

General Information

EZ-Pass Information: 800-333-TOLL
Radio Station Traffic Updates: 1010 WINS
DOT Website: www.ci.nyc.ny.us/html/dot/html/motorist/motorist.html
Real-Time Web Traffic Information: www.metrocommute.com

Driving in Manhattan

Hardware requirements: Small, durable car with big, wide tires. New York plates. Plenty of dents and scratches. Loud, obnoxious horn. Stick shift. Semi-automatic tripod-mounted tommy gun.
Software requirements: NFT™. Hagstrom 5-Borough Atlas. EZ-Pass. Sweet'N Low. Fix-A-Flat can.

Basic rules: Never look in your rear-view mirror.
Always assume that the cab that looks like it's about to cut you off, will.
Always assume that the bus that looks like it's about to cut you off, will.
Never, ever pull into an intersection unless you're SURE you can make it all the way through before the light turns red.
Never let them see the whites of your eyes.

But seriously, driving in Manhattan is not for the timid, clueless, or otherwise emotionally fragile. The following are some tips that we've encountered over the years:

Hudson River Crossings

The George Washington Bridge is by far the best Hudson River crossing. It's got more lanes and better access than the two crappy tunnels. If you're going anywhere in the country that's north of central New Jersey, take it. The Lincoln Tunnel is pretty good inbound, but check 1010 AM (WINS) if you have the chance—even though they can be horribly inaccurate and frustrating. If you have to take the Holland Tunnel, try the Broome Street approach.

East River Crossings

Brooklyn - Pearl Street to the Brooklyn Bridge is the least-known approach to the Brooklyn Bridge. Only the Williamsburg Bridge has direct access (i.e. no traffic lights) to the northbound BQE in Brooklyn, and only the Brooklyn Bridge has direct access to the FDR Drive in Manhattan. Again, listen to the radio if you can, but all three bridges can suck hard simultaneously, especially since all are perpetually being worked on. Now that construction on the Williamsburg is complete, it is by far the best route into Brooklyn and is much better than the Manhattan Bridge back into Manhattan. Your best option to go anywhere in Brooklyn is usually the Brooklyn-Battery Tunnel, which can be reached from the FDR. It's not free ($4.00), but you've got EZ-Pass anyway ($3.50) (if you're not a schmuck).

Queens - There are three options for crossing into Queens by car. The Queens Midtown Tunnel is usually miserable, since it feeds directly onto the always-busy Long Island Expressway. The 59th Street bridge is the only free crossing to Queens. The best approach to it is First Avenue to 57th Street. If you're in Queens and want to go downtown in Manhattan, you can take the lower level of the 59th Street Bridge since it will feed directly onto Second Avenue, which of course goes downtown. The Triborough Bridge is usually the best option (especially if you're going to LaGuardia, Shea, or Astoria for Greek food). The FDR to the Triborough is good except for rush hour—then try Third Avenue to 124th Street.

Harlem River Crossings

The Triborough ($4.00) will get you to the Bronx in pretty good shape, especially if you are heading east on the Bruckner towards 95 or the Hutchinson (which will take you to eastern Westchester and Connecticut). To get to Yankee Stadium, take the Willis or the Macomb's Dam (which are both free). The Henry Hudson Bridge will take you up to western Westchester along the Hudson, and, except for the antiquated and completely unnecessary toll plaza, is pretty good. (The booth attendants there win the "most disarmingly nice in NY" award.) Always attempt to avoid the Cross-Bronx Expressway.

Manhattan's "Highways"

There are two so-called highways in Manhattan, the Harlem River Drive/FDR Drive (which prohibits commercial vehicles) and the Henry Hudson Parkway/West Side Highway. The main advantage of the FDR is that it has no traffic lights, while the West Side Highway has lights from Battery Park up through 57th Street. If there's been a lot of rain, both highways will flood, so you're out of luck. We also think that FDR Drive drivers are one percent better than West Side Highway drivers.

Driving Uptown

The 96th Street transverse across Central Park is usually the best one. If you're driving on the west side, Riverside Drive is the best route, followed next by West End Avenue. People drive like morons on Broadway, and Columbus jams up at Columbus Circle. Amsterdam is a good uptown route if you can get to it. For the east side, you can take Fifth Avenue downtown to about 65th Street, whereupon you should bail out and cut over to Park Avenue for the rest of the trip. The 96th Street entrance to the FDR screws up First and Third Avenues going north and the 59th Street Bridge screws up Lexington and Second Avenues going downtown. Getting stuck in 59th Street Bridge traffic is one of the most frustrating things in the universe because there is absolutely no way out of it.

Driving in Midtown

Good luck! Sometimes Broadway is best because everyone's trying to get out of Manhattan, jamming up the west side (via the Lincoln Tunnel) and the east side (via the 59th Street Bridge and the Queens Midtown Tunnel). The "interior" city is the last place to get jammed up—it's surprisingly quiet at 8 am. At 10 am, however, it's a parking lot.

The city's latest "innovation" in Midtown is the demarcation of several "Thru Streets" east-west, which somtimes don't allow you to turn left or right for several avenues. Joy.

Driving in the Village

If you're coming into the Village from the northwest, 14th Street is the safest crosstown route heading east. However, going west, take 13th Street. Houston Street is usually okay in both directions and has the great benefit of having direct access to FDR Drive, both getting onto it and coming off of it. If you want to get to Houston Street from the Holland Tunnel, take Hudson Street to King Street to the Avenue of the Americas to Houston Street (this is the **only** efficient way to get to the Village from the Holland Tunnel). First Avenue is good going north and Fifth Avenue is good going south. Washington Street is the only way to make any headway in the West Village.

Driving Downtown

Don't do it unless you have to. Western Tribeca is okay and so is the Lower East Side—try not to "turn in" to SoHo, Chinatown, or City Center. Canal Street is a complete mess during the day (avoid it at all costs), since on its western end everyone is trying to get to the Holland Tunnel, and on its eastern end everyone is mistakenly driving over the Manhattan Bridge (your only other option when heading east on Canal is to turn **right** on the Bowery!).

DMV Locations in Manhattan

If you're going to the DMV to get your first NY license (including drivers with other states' licenses), you'll need extensive documentation of your identity. The offices have a long list of accepted documents, but your best bet is a U.S. Passport and a Social Security card. If you don't have these things, birth certificates from the U.S., foreign passports, and various INS documents will be ok under certain conditions.

Greenwich Street Office
11 Greenwich St
New York, NY 10004
(Cross Streets Battery Park Pl & Morris St)
M - F 8:30 am - 4:00 pm
212-645-5550 or 718-966-6155

Harlem Office
159 E 125th St, 3rd Fl
New York, NY 10035
(Lexington and Third)
M, T, W & F 8:30 am - 4:00 pm, Thursday 8:30 am - 6:00 pm
212-645-5550 or 718-966-6155

Herald Square Office
1293-1311 Broadway, 8th Fl
New York, NY 10001
(Between W 33 & W 34 Sts)
M - F 8:30 am - 4:00 pm
212-645-5550 or 718-966-6155

Manhattan
License X-Press Office*
300 W 34th St
New York, NY 10001
(Between Eighth & Ninth Ave)
*Service Limited: You can't renew your boat or snowmobile license here, only stuff for cars and trucks.
M, T, W 8:00 am - 5:30 pm, Thursday 8:00 am - 7:00 pm, Closed Fridays; 212-645-5550 or 718-966-6155

Information

Department of Transportation (DOT): 212-225-5368 (24 hours)
TTY Deaf or Hearing-Impaired: 212-442-9488
Website: www.ci.nyc.ny.us/html/dot/
Parking Violations Help Line: 718-422-7800
TTY Automated Information for the Hearing Impaired: 718-802-3555
Website: www.ci.nyc.ny.us/finance (parking ticket info)

Parking Meter Zones

All No Parking signs in meter zones are suspended on ASP (alternate side parking) and MLH (major legal holidays) days; however, coins must be deposited during posted hours.

Meters

At a broken meter, parking is allowed **only** up to one hour (60 minutes). Where a meter is missing, parking is still allowed for the maximum time on the posted sign. (An hour for a one-hour meter, 2 hours for a two-hour meter, etc.).

Signs

New York City Traffic Rules state that one sign per block is sufficient. Check the entire block and read all signs carefully before you park. Then read them again.

If there is more than one sign posted for the same area, the more restrictive one is the one in effect (of course). If a sign is missing on a block, the remaining posted regulations are the ones that are in effect.

The Blue Zone

The Blue Zone is a "No Parking" (Mon–Fri 7 am–7 pm) area in lower Manhattan. Its perimeter has been designated with blue paint; however, there are no individual "Blue Zone" signs posted. Any other signs posted in that area supersede Blue Zone regulations. Confused yet??

General

- All of NYC was designated a Tow Away Zone under the State's Vehicle & Traffic Law and the NYC Traffic Rules. This means that any vehicle parked or operated illegally, or with missing or expired registration or inspection stickers, may and probably will be towed.

- On major legal holidays, stopping, standing, and parking, are permitted except in areas where stopping, standing, and parking rules are in effect seven days a week (for example, "No Standing Anytime").

- Double-parking of passenger vehicles is illegal at all times, including street-cleaning days, regardless of location, purpose, or duration. Everyone, of course, does this anyway.

- It is illegal to park within 15 feet of either side of a fire hydrant. The painted curbs at hydrant locations do not indicate where you can park. Isn't New York great?

- If you think you're parked legally in Manhattan, you're probably not, so go and read the signs again.

- There is now clearly an all-out effort to harass everyone who is insane enough to drive and/or park during the day in downtown Manhattan. Beware.

Alternate Side Parking Suspension Calendar 2005 (estimated*)

Holiday	Date	Day	Rules
New Year's Day	Jan 1	Sat	MHL
Martin Luther King Jr's Birthday	Jan 17	Mon	ASP
Idul Adha	Jan 21-23	Fri-Sun	ASP
Asian Lunar New York	Feb 9	Wed	ASP
Ash Wednesday	Feb 9	Wed	ASP
Lincoln's Birthday	Feb 12	Sat	ASP
President's Day	Feb 21	Mon	ASP
Holy Thursday	Mar 24	Thurs	ASP
Good Friday	Mar 25	Fri	ASP
Purim	Mar 25	Fri	ASP
Passover, 1st/2nd Day	April 24-25	Sun-Mon	ASP
Passover, 7th/8th Day	April 30-May 1	Sat-Sun	ASP
Memorial Day	May 30	Mon	MHL
Solemnity of Ascension	June 9	Thurs	ASP
Shavout, 1st/2nd Day	June 13-14	Mon-Tues	ASP
Independence Day	July 4	Mon	MHL
Assumption of the Blessed Virgin	Aug 15	Mon	ASP
Labor Day	Sept 5	Mon	MHL
Rosh Hashanah, 1st/2nd Day	Oct 4-5	Tues-Wed	ASP
Columbus Day	Oct 10	Mon	ASP
Yom Kippur	Oct 13	Thurs	ASP
Succoth, 1st/2nd Day	Oct 18-19	Tues-Wed	ASP
Shemini Atzereth	Oct 25	Tues	ASP
Simchat Torah	Oct 26	Wed	ASP
All Saints Day	Nov 1	Tues	ASP
Idul-Fitr, 1st/2nd/3rd Day	Nov 3-5	Thurs-Sat	ASP
Veterans Day	Nov 11	Wed	ASP
Thanksgiving Day	Nov 24	Thurs	MHL
Immaculate Conception	Dec 8	Thurs	ASP
Christmas Eve	Dec 24	Sat	MHL
Christmas Day	Dec 25	Sun	MHL
New Year's Eve	Dec 31	Sat	MHL

** Note: We go to press before the DOT issues its official calendar. However, using various techniques, among them a Ouija Board, a chainsaw, and repeated phone calls to said DOT, we think it's pretty accurate. Nonetheless, caveat* parkor.

- **Street Cleaning Rules** (SCR)
  Most SCR signs are clearly marked with the "P" symbol with the broom through it. Some SCR signs are the traditional 3-hour ones ("8 am to 11 am" etc.) but many others vary considerably. Check the times before you park. Then check them again.
- **Alternate Side Parking Suspended** (ASP)
  No Parking signs in effect one day a week or on alternate days are suspended on days designated ASP; however, all No Stopping and No Standing signs remain in effect.
- **Major Legal Holiday Rules in Effect** (MLH)
  No Parking and No Standing signs that are in effect fewer than 7 days a week are suspended on days designated MLH in the above calendar.
- If the city finds that a neighborhood keeps its streets clean enough, it may lessen or eliminate street cleaning days. So listen to your mother and don't litter.

Tow Pounds

Manhattan
Pier 76 at W 38th St & Twelfth Ave
Monday: 7 am–11 pm, Tuesday–Saturday: 7 am, open 24 hours through Sunday: 6 am
212-971-0771 or 212-971-0772

Bronx
745 E 141st St between Bruckner Expressway & East River
Mon-Fri: 8 am–9 pm, Saturday: 8 am–3 pm, Sunday: Closed
718-585-1385 or 718-585-1391

Brooklyn
Brooklyn Navy Yard; entrance is at corner of Sands St & Navy St
Mon-Fri: 8 am–9 pm, Saturday: 8 am–4 pm, Sunday: 12 pm–8 pm, 718-694-0696

Queens
Under the Kosciusko Bridge at 56th Rd & Laurel Hill Blvd
Mon-Fri: 8 am–6 pm, Saturday: 7 am–3 pm, Sunday: 12 pm–8 pm, 718-786-7122, 718-786-7123 or 718-786-7136

Find out if your car was towed (and not stolen or disintegrated): 718-422-7800 or 718-802-3555
www.nyc.gov/html/dof/html/nycserv_epayment.html

Another fine trick is—once you've discovered that your car has indeed been towed—to find out which borough it's been towed to. This is dependent on who exactly towed your car—the DOT, the Marshal, etc. Don't assume that since your car was parked in Manhattan that they will tow it to Manhattan—always call first.

General Information

New York City	718-217-LIRR
Nassau County	516-822-LIRR
Suffolk County	631-231-LIRR
TDD (Hearing Impaired)	718-558-3022
Group Travel and Tours (M–F 8 pm–4 pm)	718-558-7498
Mail and Ride (Toll Free)	800-649-NYNY
MTA Police Eastern Region	718-558-3300
	or 516-733-3900
Lost & Found (M-F 7:20 am–7:20 pm)	212-643-5228
Ticket Refunds	718-558-3488
Ticket Vending Machine Assistance	877-LIRR-TSM
Hamptons Reserve Service	718-558-8070
Website	www.lirr.org/lirr/

Overview

The Long Island Railroad is the busiest railroad in North America. It has nine lines with 124 stations stretching from Penn Station in midtown Manhattan, to the eastern tip of Long Island, Montauk Point. An estimated 84 million people ride the LIRR every year. If you enjoy traveling on overcrowded, smelly trains with intermittent air-conditioning, then the LIRR is for you.

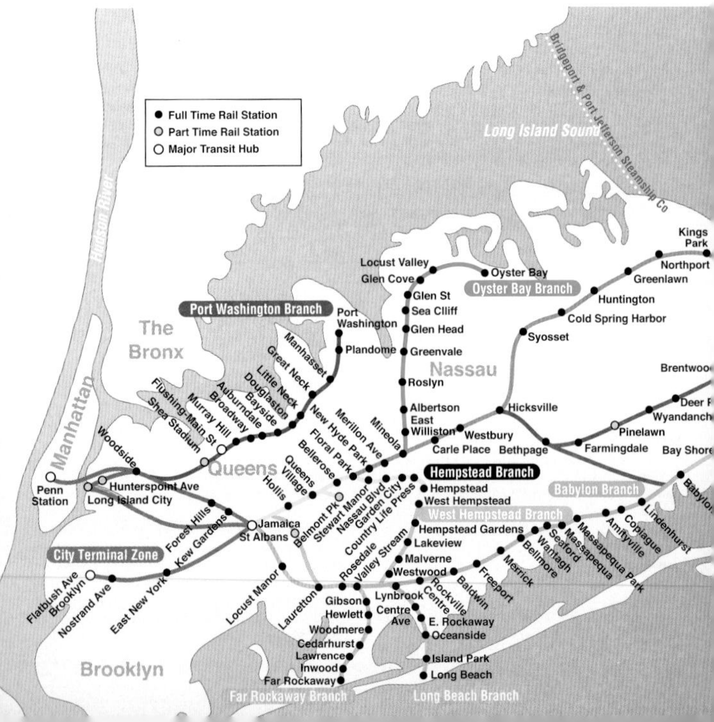

Fares and Schedules

Fares and schedules can be obtained by calling one of the general information lines, depending on your area. They can also be found on the LIRR website. Make sure to buy your ticket before you get on the train at a ticket window or at one of the ticket vending machines in the station. Otherwise it'll cost you an extra two to three dollars, depending on your destination. As it is a commuter railroad, the LIRR offers weekly and monthly passes, as well as ten-trip packages for on- or off-peak hours.

Pets on the LIRR

Trained service animals accompanying passengers with disabilities are permitted on LIRR trains. Other small pets are allowed on trains, but they must be confined to closed, ventilated containers.

Bikes on the LIRR

You need a permit ($5) to bring your bicycle onto the Long Island Railroad. Pick one up at a ticket window, or online at the LIRR web site.

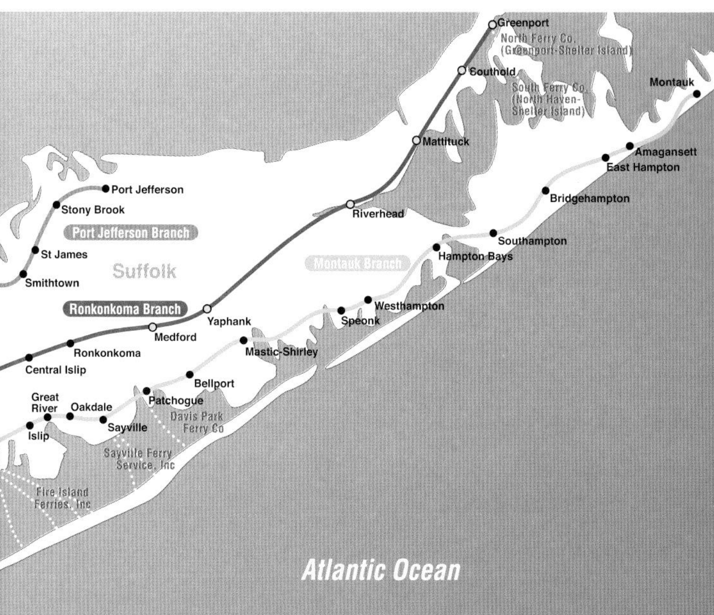

Transit • Metro North Railroad

Metro North is an extremely accessible and efficient railroad that originates from Grand Central Station in Manhattan. Its three main lines (Hudson, Harlem, and New Haven) form one of the largest commuter railroads in the U.S. There are over 100 stations in its system, and each of the main lines travels more than 70 miles from New York City.

Fares and Schedules

Fares and schedules can be easily obtained on Metro North's website or at Grand Central Station. If you wait until you're on the train to pay, it'll cost you an extra two bucks. Since Metro North is a commuter rail line, there are monthly and weekly rail passes available. For more information, use Metro North's extraordinarily detailed website, which offers in-depth information on each station, full timetables, and excellent maps.

Pets

Only seeing-eye dogs and small pets, if restrained or confined, are allowed.

General Information

In NYC: 212-532-4900
All other areas: 800-METRO-INFO
Lost and Found (Grand Central): 212-712-4500
MTA Inspector General Hotline: 800-MTA-IG4U
Website: www.mta.info

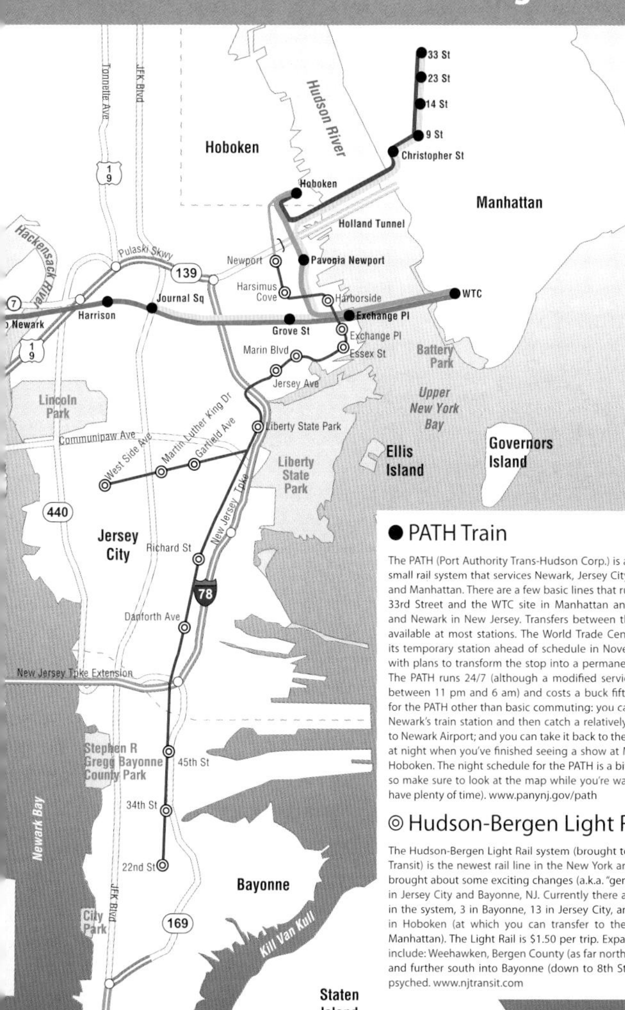

● PATH Train

The PATH (Port Authority Trans-Hudson Corp.) is an excellent small rail system that services Newark, Jersey City, Hoboken, and Manhattan. There are a few basic lines that run between 33rd Street and the WTC site in Manhattan and Hoboken and Newark in New Jersey. Transfers between the lines are available at most stations. The World Trade Center opened its temporary station ahead of schedule in November 2003 with plans to transform the stop into a permanent location. The PATH runs 24/7 (although a modified service operates between 11 pm and 6 am) and costs a buck fifty. Two uses for the PATH other than basic commuting: you can take it to Newark's train station and then catch a relatively cheap cab to Newark Airport; and you can take it back to the Village late at night when you've finished seeing a show at Maxwell's in Hoboken. The night schedule for the PATH is a bit confusing, so make sure to look at the map while you're waiting (you'll have plenty of time). www.panynj.gov/path

◎ Hudson-Bergen Light Rail

The Hudson-Bergen Light Rail system (brought to you by NJ Transit) is the newest rail line in the New York area, and has brought about some exciting changes (a.k.a. "gentrification") in Jersey City and Bayonne, NJ. Currently there are 17 stops in the system, 3 in Bayonne, 13 in Jersey City, and a station in Hoboken (at which you can transfer to the PATH into Manhattan). The Light Rail is $1.50 per trip. Expansion plans include: Weehawken, Bergen County (as far north as Tenafly), and further south into Bayonne (down to 8th Street). We're psyched. www.njtransit.com

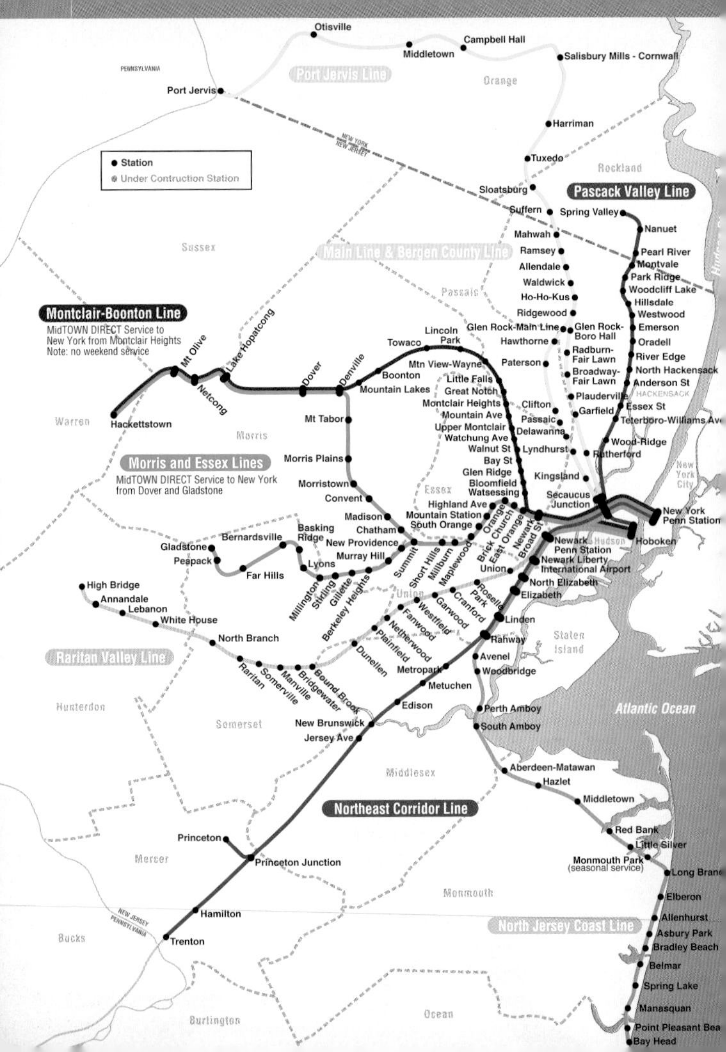
Otisville
Middletown
Campbell Hall
Salisbury Mills - Cornwall
PENNSYLVANIA
Port Jervis Line
Orange
Port Jervis
NEW YORK
NEW JERSEY
Harriman
Station
Under Contruction Station
Tuxedo
Rockland
Sloatsburg
Pascack Valley Line
Suffern
Spring Valley
Nanuet
Mahwah
Sussex
Main Line & Bergen County Line
Ramsey
Pearl River
Allendale
Montvale
Park Ridge
Waldwick
Woodcliff Lake
Passaic
Ho-Ho-Kus
Hillsdale
Ridgewood
Westwood
Montclair-Boonton Line
MidTOWN DIRECT Service to New York from Montclair Heights
Note: no weekend service
Lincoln Park
Glen Rock-Main Line
Glen Rock-Boro Hall
Emerson
Towaco
Hawthorne
Oradell
Radburn-Fair Lawn
River Edge
Mt Olive
Lake Hopatcong
Mtn View-Wayne
Paterson
North Hackensack
Boonton
Broadway-Fair Lawn
Dover
Denville
Little Falls
Anderson St
Netcong
Mountain Lakes
Great Notch
Plauderville
HACKENSACK
Montclair Heights
Clifton
Essex St
Garfield
Mountain Ave
Passaic
Teterboro-Williams Ave
Hackettstown
Mt Tabor
Upper Montclair
Delawanna
Warren
Morris
Watchung Ave
Wood-Ridge
Walnut St
Lyndhurst
Rutherford
Morris and Essex Lines
MidTOWN DIRECT Service to New York from Dover and Gladstone
Morris Plains
Bay St
New York City
Glen Ridge
Kingsland
Morristown
Bloomfield
Essex
Watsessing
Secaucus Junction
Convent
Highland Ave
New York Penn Station
Madison
Mountain Station
Orange
Chatham
South Orange
Brick Church
East Orange
Newark Broad St
Basking Ridge
Bernardsville
New Providence
Hoboken
Gladstone
Newark Penn Station
Hudson
Murray Hill
Peapack
Lyons
Summit
Newark Liberty International Airport
Far Hills
Short Hills
Millburn
Maplewood
Union
High Bridge
Millington
Stirling
Gillette
Berkeley Heights
North Elizabeth
Roselle Park
Elizabeth
Annandale
Union
Cranford
Lebanon
Garwood
Westfield
White House
Fanwood
Linden
Netherwood
Staten Island
North Branch
Plainfield
Rahway
Raritan Valley Line
Avenel
Dunellen
Metropark
Woodbridge
Raritan
Somerville
Manville
Bridgewater
Bound Brook
Metuchen
Hunterdon
Edison
Perth Amboy
Atlantic Ocean
Somerset
New Brunswick
South Amboy
Jersey Ave
Middlesex
Aberdeen-Matawan
Hazlet
Northeast Corridor Line
Middletown
Red Bank
Princeton
Little Silver
Mercer
Princeton Junction
Monmouth Park (seasonal service)
Long Branch
Monmouth
Elberon
Hamilton
Allenhurst
NEW JERSEY
PENNSYLVANIA
North Jersey Coast Line
Asbury Park
Bucks
Trenton
Bradley Beach
Belmar
Spring Lake
Ocean
Burlington
Manasquan
Point Pleasant Beach
Bay Head

General Information

Phone: 973-762-5100 or 800-772-3606
Address: NJ Transit Headquarters, 1 Penn Plaza East, Newark, NJ 07105
Website: www.njtransit.com
Mail Tik (monthly passes): 973-491-8491
Emergency Hotline: 973-491-7400
Newark Lost and Found: 973-491-8792
Hoboken Lost and Found: 201-714-2739
New York Lost and Found: 212-630-7389
Newark International Airport Station & AirTrain: 973-961-6230
Atlantic City Terminal (5:45 am–10:45 pm daily): 609-343-7174

Overview

NJ Transit carries hundreds of thousands of New Jersey commuters to New York every morning—well, almost. While the trains are usually clean (and immune to the weirdness that plagues the LIRR), some lines (such as the Pascack Valley Line) just seem to creep along—and then you have to transfer. However, they've added new stations, such as a large transfer station at Secaucus, and are expanding the light rail system (see PATH page). There's also the AirTrain link to Newark Airport. While NJ Transit isn't going to compete with Japanese rail systems any time soon, it still beats waiting in traffic at the three measly Hudson River automobile crossings. NJ Transit also offers bus lines to Hoboken and Newark for areas not served by train lines.

Secaucus Transfer Station

The new, three-level train hub at Secaucus cost around $450 million and took 14 years to complete—the project was initially drawn up in 1989 and construction began in spring 1995.

The building has been dedicated as the Frank R. Lautenberg Rail Station (former NJ Democratic senator) for his role in securing the federal funds necessary to construct the station. The former Secaucus Transfer Station is now officially known as the Frank R Lautenberg Station at Secaucus Junction. We're certain that most commuters will adopt this new name whenever referring to the station.

By far the biggest advantage of the new station is that riders can now avoid going out of their way to Hoboken in order to get to Penn Station (an 8-minute ride from Secaucus). The Secaucus hub connects 10 of NJ Transit's 11 rail lines and also offers service to Newark Airport, downtown Newark, Trenton, and the Jersey Shore.

Fares and Schedules

Fares and schedules can be obtained at Hoboken, at Newark, at Penn Station, on NJ Transit's website, or by calling NJ Transit. If you wait to pay until you're on the train, you'll pay extra for the privilege. NJ Transit does have monthly, weekly, weekend, and ten-trip tickets available for regular commuters.

Pets

Only seeing-eye dogs and small pets in carry-on containers are allowed.

Bikes

You can take your bicycle onboard a NJ Transit train only during off-peak hours (weekdays from 9:30 am to 4 pm, and from 7 pm to 5 am) and all day Saturday and Sunday. Bikes are banned on most holidays. A folding frame bicycle can be taken onboard at any time. Most NJ Transit buses offer the "Rack 'n Roll" program, where you can load your bike right on to the front of the bus.

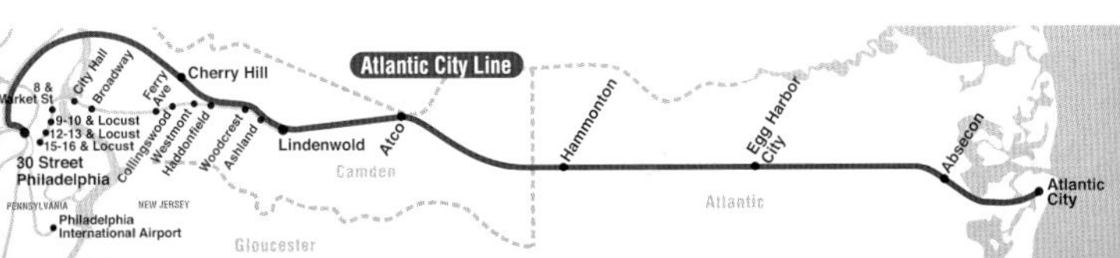

Overview

Phone: 800-USA-RAIL
Website: www.amtrak.com

General Information

Amtrak is the United States version of a national train system, and while it's not very good, it can at least get you to many major northeastern cities in half a day or less. Unless you manage to get a promotional discount, prices are unreasonably expensive, making it more attractive to fly to cities such as Boston or Washington, DC. However, if you're doing things at the last minute and have missed requisite advances on buying your airline tickets, you might want to at least shop Amtrak's fares.

Amtrak was created by the federal government in 1971. Currently, Amtrak services 500+ stations in 46 states (no service in Alaska, Hawaii, South Dakota, and Wyoming—Maine finally got service a couple of years ago). Amtrak serves over 24 million passengers a year, employs 22,000 people, and provides "contract-commuter services" for several state and regional rail lines. Amtrak has 351 diesel locomotives and 74 electric locomotives, 1,100 passenger cars, and 1,000 freight cars in its fleet.

Amtrak in New York

In New York City, Amtrak runs out of Pennsylvania Station, which is currently located in a rat's maze underneath Madison Square Garden at Seventh Avenue and 33rd Street. However, don't despair—chances are, the city you'll wind up in will have a very nice station, and, if all goes well, so will we, once the front half of the Farley Post Office is converted to a "new" Penn Station.

Popular Destinations

Many New Yorkers use Amtrak to get to Boston, Philadelphia, or Washington, DC. Amtrak also runs a line up to Montreal and another one which goes through most of the major cities in western New York state (Buffalo, Rochester, Albany, etc.) You can get a complete listing of all stations on Amtrak's web site.

Going to Boston

Amtrak usually runs 18 trains daily to Boston, MA. The one-way fare is $64; it takes about four-and-a-half hours to get to South Station in downtown Boston. For $99 one-way you can take the high speed Acela ("acceleration" and "excellence" combined into one word, though perhaps "expensive" would have been more appropriate) and complete the journey in three to three-and-a-half-hours.

Going to Philadelphia

You can get on 40 or so different Amtrak trains on any given day that will pass through Philadelphia. It will cost you about $52 one-way on a regular Amtrak train; if you're really in a hurry, you can take the special "Metroliner" service for $87 which will get you there in an hour and fifteen minutes, or the Acela, $95 and about one hour station-to-station. The cheapest rail option to Philly is actually to take NJ Transit to Trenton and then hook up with Eastern Pennsylvania's excellent SEPTA service—this will take longer, but will cost you under $25.

Going to Washington, DC

(Subtitle: *How Much is Your Time Worth?*)
Amtrak runs over 40 trains daily to DC and the prices vary dramatically. The cheapest trains cost $89 one-way and take a bit less than 4 hours. However, the Acela service costs almost double at $147 one-way, and delivers you there in just under 3 hours. Worth it? It's your call.

A Note About Fares

While the prices quoted above for Boston, Philly, and DC destinations tend to stay fairly consistent, fare rates to other destinations, such as Cleveland, Chicago, etc., can vary depending on how far in advance you book your seat. For instance, if you want to take a train to Chicago tomorrow, you might pay $85 one-way; booking 2 months in advance would only be a small difference at $72. Again, check www.amtrak.com's database and "rail sales" for particulars.

Baggage Check (Amtrak Passengers)

A maximum of three items may be checked up to thirty minutes prior to departure. Up to three additional bags may be checked for a fee of $10 (two carry-on items allowed). No electronic equipment, plastic bags, or paper bags may be checked. See the "Amtrak Policies" section of their website for details.

Overview

Penn Station, designed by McKim, Mead & White (New York's greatest architects), is a Beaux Arts treasure, filled with light and...oh, that's the one they tore down. Penn Station today is essentially a basement, only without the bowling trophies and the Johnny Walker Black.

BUT...good news seems to be coming from around the corner, in the form of a plan to convert the eastern half of the Farley Post Office (also designed by McKim, Mead, & White) to a new, above-ground (a novel concept), light-filled station, set for completion in 2007. We can't wait. Until then, Penn Station will just go on being an ugly, crappy underground terminal (citysearch.com says it has "all the charm of a salt mine") under Madison Square Garden, a terminal which services over 600,000 people per day—making it the busiest railway station in the United States.

Penn Station services Amtrak, the LIRR, and NJ Transit trains, which is admittedly a lot of responsibility. Amtrak (800-872-7245), which is surely the worst national train system of any country above the poverty line, administers the station. Although we're hoping the new station proposal will go through, we still won't be able to afford the ridiculously high fares that Amtrak charges to go to places like DC, Philly, and Boston.

General Information

NFT Map Number: 8
Address: 7th Ave and 33rd St
General Information (Amtrak): 800-872-7245
MTA Subway Stops: 1 2 3 9 A C E
MTA Bus Lines: 4 10 16 34
Train Lines: LIRR, Amtrak, NJ Transit
Newark Airport Bus Service: Olympia (212-964-6233, $12)
LaGuardia Airport Bus Service: NY Airport Service (718-706-9658, $10)
JFK Airport Bus Service: NY Airport Service (718-706-9658, $13)
Passengers per day: 600,000
Year Opened:1968

Terminal Shops

On the LIRR Level

Food & Drink

Auntie Anne's Pretzels
Caruso's Pizza
Central Market
Dunkin' Donuts
Haagen Dazs
Hot and Crusty
Island Dine
Java Shop
KFC
Knot Just Pretzels
Le Bon Café
McDonald's
Nedick's
NY City's Famous 5 Star Grill
Rosa's Pizza and Pasta
Seattle Coffee Roasters
Sedutto
Smoothie King
Starbucks
TGI Friday's
Tracks Raw Bar & Grill

Other

Carlton Cards
Dreyfus Financial Center
GNC
Hallmark
Hudson News
K-Mart
Penn Books
Perfumania
Soleman—Shoe repair, locksmith
The Petal Pusher
T-Mobile

On the Amtrak Level

Food & Drink

Baskin Robbins
Dipsy Dog
Don Pepi Pizza
Don Pepi's Delicatessen
Gyro II
Houlihan's Restaurant and Bar
Kabooz's Bar and Grille
Krispy Kreme Doughnuts
Primo Cappuccino
Zaro's Breadbasket

Other

Book Corner
Duane Reade
Elegance
Gifts and Electronics
New York New York
Shoetrician—Shoe repair and shine
Tiecoon
Tourist Information Center

On Both Levels

Nathan's
Pizza Hut
Roy Rogers

There is a Chase 24-hour ATM located on the Amtrak level and a Fleet 24-hour ATM located on the LIRR level, in addition to the generic (money-thieving) ATMs located in several stores throughout the station.

Temporary Parcel/Baggage Check

The only facility for storing parcels and baggage in Penn Station is at the Baggage Check on the Amtrak level (to the left of the ticket counter). There are no locker facilities at Penn Station. The Baggage Check is open from 5 am until midnight and costs $4.50 per item for each 24-hour period.

Main Concourse

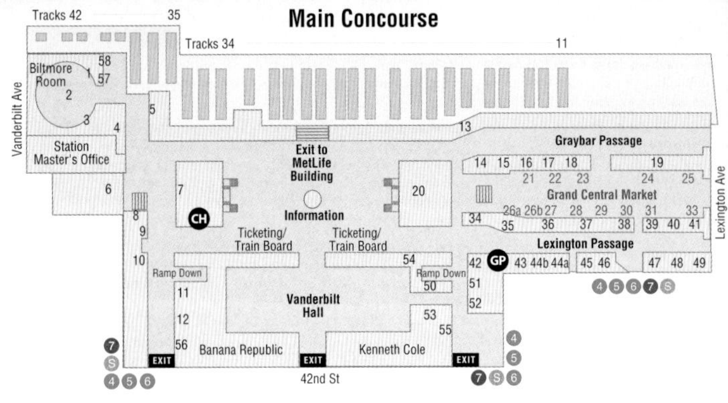

Balcony

Dining Concourse

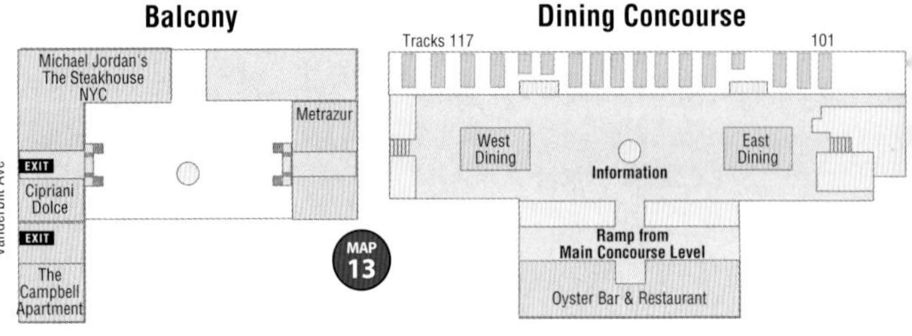

MAP 13

Stores

1. Eddie's Shoe Repair
2. Eastern News
3. Dahlia
4. Junior's
5. Starbucks
6. New York Transit Museum
7. Zaro's Bread Basket
8. Discovery Channel Store
9. Posman Books
10. Rite Aid
11. Central Market
12. Hot & Crusty
13. Zaro's Bread Basket
14. Olivers & Co
15. Grande Harvest Wines
16. Cobbler & Shine
17. Stop'N Go Wireless
18. O' Henry's Film Works
19. GNC
20. Hudson News
21. Greenwich Produce
22. Koglin German Hams
23. Murray's Cheese
24. Ceriello Fine Foods
25. Greenwich Produce
26a. Pescatore Seafood Company
26b. Dishes at Home
27. Li-Lac Chocolates
28. Oren's Daily Roast
29. Adriana's Caravan
30. Zaro's Bread Basket
31. Wild Edibles
33. Corrado Bread & Pastry
34. Flowers on Lexington
35. Grand Central Optical
36. Tumi
37. L'Occitane
38. Michael Eigen Jewelers
39. Our Name is Mud
40. Watch Station
41. Starbucks
42. Matt Hunter & Cov
43. Origins
44a. Children's General Store
44b. Leeper Kids
45. Train Tunes
46. Pink Slip
47. TOTO
48. LaCrasia Gloves & Creative Accessories
49. Godiva Chocolatier
50. Super Runners Shop
51. Papyrus
52. Oren's Daily Roast
53. Douglas Cosmetics
54. Joon Stationary
55. Super Runners Shop
56. Neuhaus Boutique
57. Grand Central Raquet
58. Central Watch Band Stand

General Information

NFT Map Number:	13
Address:	42nd St and Park Ave
General Information:	212-340-2210
Lost and Found:	212-712-4500
Website:	www.grandcentralterminal.com
MTA Subway Stops:	4 5 6 7 S
MTA Bus Lines:	1 2 3 4 42 98 101 102 104 [illegible]
Other Rail Lines:	Metro North
Newark Airport Bus Service:	Olympia (212-964-6233, $12)
LaGuardia Airport Bus Service:	NY Airport Express (718-875-8200, $10)
JFK Airport Bus Service:	NY Airport Express (718-875-8200, $13)
Year Opened:	1913

Overview

Grand Central Terminal, designed in the Beaux Arts style by Warren & Wetmore, is by far the most beautiful of Manhattan's major terminals; indeed, it ranks as one of the most beautiful terminals in the world. What's also nice about it is that it's convenient (located right in the heart of Midtown), newly refurbished, and utterly cool. The only bad thing is that it only services Metro North—you have to go to Penn Station for LIRR and NJ Transit trains.

Grand Central's refurbishment is now complete. If you ever find yourself taking that renovation for granted, just look up at the ceiling towards the Vanderbilt Avenue side—there's a small patch of black there showing how dirty the ceiling was previously. And it was really dirty...

If you've got extra time for a drink, check out the exceptionally cool and snotty (no sneakers!) bar, The Campbell Apartment, near the Vanderbilt Street entrance. Or snag some seafood at the Oyster Bar & Restaurant, then go right outside its entrance to hear a strange audio anomaly: if you and a friend stand in opposite corners and whisper, you can hear each other clearly.

There are THREE separate tours of Grand Central: the hour-long LaSalle Tour (212-340-2347), the Municipal Arts Society Tour (212-935-3960), and the Grand Central Partnership Tour (212-697-1245). The last two tours are **free**!

ATMs

Chase
Greenpoint
Numerous generic (money-thieving) ATMs at stores throughout the station.

East Dining

Café Spice
Central Market Grill
Golden Krust Patties
Little Pie Company
Two Boots
Zaro's Bread Basket
Zócalo Bar and Restaurant

West Dining

Dishes
Eata Pita
Feng Shui
Hale and Hearty Soups
Junior's
Masa Sushi
Mendy's Kosher Delicatessen
New York Pretzel
Paninoteca Italiana
Pepe Rosso
T's Louisiana to Geaux

General Information

NFT Map Number: 11 • Address: 41st St & 8th Ave
General Information: 212-564-8484
Kinney System P.A. Garage: 212-502-2341
Lost and Found: Are you kidding?
Website: www.panynj.gov/tbt/pabframe.HTM
Subway: A C E ....Port Authority
1 2 3 9 7 N R Q W S Times Square
MTA Bus Lines: 10 11 16 20 27 42 104
Other Bus Lines: See right-hand page

Newark Airport Bus Service: Olympia (212-964-6233, $10)
LaGuardia Airport Bus Service: NY Airport Express (718-875-8200, $10)
JFK Airport Bus Service: NY Airport Express (718-875-8200, $13)
Passengers per day: 200,000
Passengers since opening: over 3 billion

Overview

In 1939, eight separate bus terminals scattered throughout the city were increasing traffic congestion. Although a consolidated, larger central terminal seemed like the obvious solution, many of the smaller terminals refused to merge. At that point Mayor Fiorello LaGuardia asked the Port Authority of New York and New Jersey to take over the project and develop one central terminal. On January 27, 1949, construction began at the site bordered by Eighth Avenue, 40th Street, Ninth Avenue, and 41st Street On December 15, 1950, after an investment of $24 million, the Port Authority Bus Terminal opened.

That investment has now grown to $443 million, and although the terminal is located in perhaps the last genuinely shady neighborhood in Manhattan, the dozens of terminal shops and amenities (including a post office, bank, refurbished bathrooms, a blood bank, subway access, and even a bowling alley) make Port Authority a convenient departure and arrival point. The last remaining grungy area of the terminal is the lower bus level, which is a dirty, exhaust-filled space, best visited just a few minutes before you need to board your bus. The chart on the right shows which bus companies run out of the Port Authority and a basic description of their destinations.

On Easter Sunday, Christmas Eve, or Thanksgiving, one can see all the angst-ridden sons and daughters of suburban New Jersey parents joyfully waiting in cramped, disgusting corridors for that nauseating bus ride back to Leonia or Morristown or Plainfield or wherever. A fascinating sight.

Terminal Shops

South Wing—Lower Bus Level
Green Trees
Hudson News

South Wing—Subway Mezzanine
Au Bon Pain
Hudson News
Music Explosion

South Wing—Main Concourse
Au Bon Pain
California Burrito
Casa Java
Deli Plus
Duane Reade
First Stop-Last Stop Cafe
GNC
Hudson News
Hudson News Book Corner
Marrella Men's Hair Stylist
NY Blood Center
Radio Shack
Ruthie's Hallmark
Stop 'n Go Wireless
Villa Pizza
World's Fare Restaurant Bar
Zaro's Bakery

South Wing—Second Floor
Café Metro
Drago Shoe Repair
Fleet Bank
Hudson News Book Corner
Kelly Film Express
Leisure Time Bowling Center & Cocktail Lounge
McAnn's Pub
Mrs Fields Bakery Café
Munchy's Gourmet
Sak's Florist
Sweet Factory

South Wing—Fourth Floor
First Stop-Last Stop Café
Hudson News

North Wing-Lower Bus Level
Snacks-N-Wheels

North Wing—Subway Mezzanine
Fleet Bank (ATM)
Green Trees
Hudson News

North Wing—Main Concourse
Continental Airlines
Hudson News
Mrs Fields Cookies

North Wing—on 42nd Street
Big Apple Café

North Wing—Second Floor
Fleet Bank (ATM)
Hudson News
Jay's Hallmark Bookstore
Tropica Juice Bar
USO
US Postal Service

North Wing—Third Floor
Hudson News
Tropica Juice Bar

Bus Company	*Phone*	*Area Served*
Academy Bus Transportation	800-242-1339	Serves New York City, including Staten Island, Wall Street and Port Authority, and New Jersey, including Hoboken.
Adirondack Trailways	800-858-8555	Serves all of New York State with coach connections throughout the U.S.
Bonanza Bus	800-556-3815	Serves many points between New York and New England, including Cape Cod and the Berkshires.
Capitol Trailways	800-333-8444	Service between Pennsylvania, Virginia, New York State, and New York City.
Carl Bieber Bus	800-243-2374	Service to and from Port Authority and Wall Street in New York and Reading, Kutztown, Wescosville, Hellertown, and Easton in Pennsylvania.
Community Coach	800-522-4514	Service between New York City and W. Orange, Livingston, Morristown, E. Hanover, Whippany, and Floram Park, New Jersey.
DeCamp Bus	800-631-1281	Service between New York City and New Jersey, including the Meadowlands.
Greyhound Bus	800-231-2222	Serves most of the U.S. and Canada.
Gray Line Bus	212-397-2620	Service offered throughout the U.S. and Canada.
Hudson Bus	201-653-2222	Serves 48 states.
Lakeland Bus	201-366-0600	Service between New York and New Jersey.
Martz Group	800-233-8604	Service between New York and Pennsylvania.
New Jersey Transit	800-772-2222 (NJ) 973-762-5100 (all other)	Serves New York, New Jersey, and Philadelphia.
NY Airport Service	212-8758200	Service between Port Authority and Kennedy and LaGuardia Airports.
Olympia Trails	212-964-6233	Provides express bus service between Manhattan and Newark Airport. Makes stops all over New York City, including Penn Station, Grand Central, and many connections with hotel shuttles.
Peter Pan Lines	800-343-9999	Serves the East, including New Hampshire, Maine, Philly, DC. Also goes to Canada.
Pine Hill-Kingston	800-858-8555	Services New York state area.
Rockland Coaches/ Red and Tan Services	201-384-2400	Services New York's Port Authority, GW bridge, and 44th and 8th Streets to and from most of Bergen County and upstate New York.
ShortLine Bus	800-631-8405	Serves the New York City airports, Atlantic City, and the Hudson Valley.
Suburban Trails	732-249-1100	Offers commuter service from Central New Jersey to and from Port Authority and Wall Street. Also services between the Route 9 Corridor and New York City.
Susquehanna Trailways	800-692-6314	Service to and from New York City and Newark (Greyhound Terminal) and Summerville, New Jersey and many stops in Central Pennsylvania, ending in Williamsport and Lock Haven.
Trans-Bridge Lines	610-868-6001 800-962-9135	Offers service between New York, Pennsylvania, and New Jersey, including Newark and Kennedy airports.
Trans-Hudson Express	800-772-3689	Serves New York City and Hudson County, New Jersey.

George Washington Bridge Bus Terminal

NFT Map Number: 23
Address: 4211 Broadway, New York, NY 10033
Phone: 800-221-9903
Website: www.panynj.gov/tbt/gwbframe.HTM
Subway: A (175th St), A 1 9 (181st St)
Buses: 100 98 5 4 3 Bx
Passengers in 2001: 5.5 million
Year opened: 1963

Overview

Completed in 1963, the George Washington Bridge Bus Terminal, located between 178th and 179th Streets on Fort Washington Avenue, is a bit like the bastard sibling of the 42nd Street terminal. It's fairly reminiscent of its downtown brother, but for the wrong reasons: the omnipresent smell of gasoline, assorted strange people hanging around, and a slightly seedy aura. To be fair, it's been getting better over the last few years, and they've been renovating it, but any place where one of the centerpiece establishments is OTB has a way to go.

Stores

Concourse:
Bridge Opticians—Edward Friedman, OD
Bridge Stop Newsstand
Dentists—Howard Bloom, DDS; Steve Kaufman DDS
E-Z Visions Travel
Food Plus Café
GW Books and Electronics
Joseph's Leather Designs
Neighborhood Trust Federal Credit Union
New York National Bank
Off Track Betting
Pizza Palace
Terminal Barber Shop

Street Level:
Blockbuster Video
Rite-Aid Pharmacy
Urban Pathways—Homeless Outreach Office
Port Authority Business Outreach Center (179th St underpass)

Bus Companies

Astro-Eastern Bus Company • 201-865-2230 • www.easternbus.com. Florida (purchase tickets on upper level).

Coach USA • 800-877-1888 • Atlantic City.

New Jersey Transit • www.njtransit.com/sf_bus.shtm Various routes through Bergen County.

Red & Tan Lines/Coach USA • www.redandtanlines.com Various routes through Bergen County.

Shortline/Coach USA • 800-631-8405 • www.shortlinebus.com. Various routes to Bergen, Rockland Counties.

Express Bus Service • 973-881-9122 • www.spanishtransportation.com. Frequent service to points in Bergen County, including Garden State Plaza and Willowbrook Malls.

Vanessa Express • 201-583-0999. Frequent Bergen County routes to towns near the Hudson, south of the bridge.

Chinatown Buses

NFT Map Number: 3

There are several inexpensive bus lines running from Chinatown in NY to the respective Chinatowns in Boston, Philadelphia, and Washington, DC. Tickets can be purchased online or in person at the pick-up locations and can typically run you about $10-20 each way. There may even be an in-bus kung-fu movie if you're lucky. Passengers are urged to arrive at least 30 minutes prior to take-off and, as always, schedules and prices are subject to change, so call or consult the company's website before planning your trip. However, if you walk down East Broadway under the Manhattan Bridge, chances are you'll be solicited without even having to ask.

Fung Wah Bus Transportation • 212-925-8889 • www.fungwahbus.com. To Boston every hour 7 am–11 pm, 139 Canal Street to 68 Beach Street in Boston. One-way $10.

Lucky Star Bus Transportation • 888-881-0887 • www.luckystarbus.com. To Boston every hour 7 am–8 pm, and 10 pm. Corner of Chrystie and Hester Streets to 2B Harrison Avenue in Boston. One-way $10.

Boston Deluxe • 617-354-2101 • www.ivymedia.com/bostondeluxe. Several daily departures from 88 East Broadway to Boston, Hartford, Baltimore, Washington, DC, Albany and the Woodbury Common Outlets, tickets cost $15-20.

Dragon Coach • 617-354-2101 • www.ivymedia.com/dragoncoach/. From 2 Mott Street to destinations in Albany, Washington DC, Baltimore, and the Woodbury Common Outlets. Tickets are $20.

Eastern Travel • 617-354-2101 • www.ivymedia.com/eastern. Departs 88 East Broadway at 8 am, 11 am, noon, 5 pm, and 6 pm for 715 H Street NW Washington, DC or 430 Hungerford Drive in Rockville, MD. One-way $20.

New Century Travel • 215-627-2666 • www.2000coach.com. A bus service for $12 to Philadelphia and $20 to DC takes off several times throughout the day from 88 East Broadway.

Today's Bus • 617-354-2101 • www.ivymedia.com/todaysbus. From 88 & 109 East Broadway with destinations to Washington, DC ($12 one-way) and Philadelphia ($20 one-way) leaving several times per day.

General Information

Department of City Planning website: www.ci.nyc.ny.us/html/dcp/html/bike/home.html
Transportation Alternatives website: www.transalt.org   Phone: 212-629-8080
New York Cycle Club: www.nycc.org • Empire Skate Club: www.empireskate.org

While not for the faint of heart, biking and skating around Manhattan can be one of the most efficient and exhilarating forms of transportation (insight into the abundance of bike messengers careening around town). The terrain of Manhattan is pretty flat (for the most part), and the fitness and environmental advantages of using people power are immense. However, there are also some downsides, including, but not limited to: psychotic cab drivers, buses, traffic, pedestrians, pavement with potholes, glass and debris, and poor air quality. In 1994, the Bicycle Network Development Program was created to increase bicycle usage in the NYC area. Since then, many bike lanes have been created on streets and in parks. These tend to be the safest places to ride, though they sometimes get blocked by parked or standing cars (to get a listing of lanes, go to the websites listed above). Central Park is a great place to ride, as are the newly developed paths from Battery Park to Chelsea Piers that run along the Hudson River. You'll also find East River Park to be nice for recreational riding and skating—just not after dark! In addition to bicycle rentals, Pedal Pusher Bike Shop (1306 Second Ave, 212-288-5592) offers recorded tours of Central Park, so you can learn about the park and exercise at the same time.

Recreational skating venues in Manhattan include Wollmann and Lasker Rinks in Central Park, Chelsea Piers, The Roxy (515 W 18th Street), Riverbank State Park (Riverside Drive at 145th Street), and Rivergate Ice Rink (401 E 34th Street). For more information about where to skate in the boroughs, check out www.skatecity.com. For organized events, see Empire Skate Club at www.empireskate.org.

Bikes are less convenient than skates, and are always at risk of being stolen (always lock them to immovable objects with the best lock you can afford), but can be a much faster, less demanding form of transport. An advantage of skating is that you can easily put your skates in a bag and carry them with you anywhere—subways, indoors, on buses—which also eliminates the possibility of theft.

Bike Rentals (and Sales)

all phone numbers are 212 area code unless otherwise noted

Metro Bicycle Stores:
- 88th St at Lexington • 427-4450 • Map 17
- 360 W 47th St at 9th • 581-4500 • Map 11
- 96th St at Broadway • 663-7531 • Map 16
- 14th St between First & Second • 228-4344 • Map 6
- Sixth Ave at W 15th St • 255-5100 • Map 9
- Sixth Ave b/w Canal & Grand • 334-8000 • Map 2

Anewgen Bicycles • 832 Ninth Ave • 757-2418 • Map 11
Toga Bike Shop • 110 West End Ave at 64th • 799-9625 • Map 14
Gotham Bikes • 112 W Broadway b/w Duane & Reade • 732-2453 • Map 2
Bicycle Habitat • 244 Lafayette b/w Spring & Prince • 431-3315 • Map 6
Bike Works • 106 Ridge St • 388-1077 • Map 7
Bicycle Heaven • 348 E 62 St • 230-1919 • Map 15
City Bicycles • 315 W 38th St• 563-3373 • Map 11
Eddie's Bicycles Shop • 490 Amsterdam Ave • 580-2011 • Map 14
Larry and Jeff's Bicycles Plus • 1690 Second Ave between 87th & 88th • 722-2201 • Map 17
Pedal Pusher Bike Shop • 1306 Second Ave • 288-5592 • Map 15
Manhattan Bicycles • 791 Ninth Ave • 262-0111 • Map 11
New York Cyclist • 301 Cathedral Pkwy • 864-4449 • Map16

Bikes and Mass Transit

Surprisingly, you can take your bike on trains and some buses—just make sure it's not during rush hour and you are courteous to other passengers. The subway requires you to carry your bike down staircases, use the service gate instead of the turnstile, and board at the very front or back end of the train. The commuter railroads require you to purchase a bike permit. See transportation pages (232-250) for contact information.

Amtrak: Train with baggage car required.
LIRR: $5 permit required.
Metro-North: $5 permit required.
New Jersey Transit: Free permit required.
PATH: No permit required.
NY Waterway: $1 extra fee.
Staten Island Ferry: Enter at lower level.
Bus companies: Call individual companies.

January

Event	Location	Description
• Winter Antiques Show	Park Ave at 67th St	Selections from all over the country.
• Three Kings Day Parade	El Museo del Barrio	Features a cast of hundreds from all over the city dressed as kings or animals–camels, sheep, and donkeys. (Early Jan)
• Outsider Art Fair	Corner of Lafayette & Houston	Art in many forms of media.
• National Boat Show	Jacob Javits Convention Center	Don't go expecting a test drive.
• Chinese New Year	Chinatown	Features dragons, performers, and parades.

February

Event	Location	Description
• Empire State Building Run-Up	Empire State Building	Run until the 86th floor, or heart seizure.
• The Art Show	Park Ave at 67th St	A very large art fair.
• Westminster Dog Show	Madison Square Garden	Canines.
• International Cat Show	Madison Square Garden	Fine felines.

March

Event	Location	Description
• St Patrick's Day Parade	Fifth Avenue	Irish pride. (March 17)
• Ringling Bros and Barnum & Bailey Circus	Madison Square Garden	Greatest Show on Earth. (March–May)
• Whitney Biennial	Whitney Museum	Whitney's most important American art. (March–June)
• Greek Independence Day Parade	Fifth Avenue	Floats and bands representing area Greek Orthodox churches and Greek federations and organizations. (Late March)
• Small Press Book Fair	Small Press Center	Sometimes-interesting fair of small publishers and self-published authors.

April

Event	Location	Description
• Easter Parade	Fifth Avenue	Starts at 11 am, get there early. (Easter Sunday)
• New York Antiquarian Book Fair	Park Ave at 67th St	170 international booksellers exhibition.
• New York International Auto Show	Jacob Javits Convention Center	Traffic jam.
• Spring Spectacular	Radio City Music Hall	The Rockettes in bunny costumes? (Easter week)
• Macy's Spring Flower Parade	Broadway and 34th St	Flowers.
• New York City Ballet Spring Season	Lincoln Center	Features new and classical ballet. (April–June)

May

Event	Location	Description
• Tribeca Film Festival	Various locations including Regal 16 at BPC, BMCC Chambers St, Battery Park	Festival includes film screenings, panels, lectures, discussion groups, and concerts. (Early May)
• The Great Five Boro Bike Tour	Battery Park to Staten Island	Tour de NYC.
• Ninth Avenue International Food Festival	Ninth Ave from 37th to 57th Sts	A truly fabulous experience!
• Fleet Week	USS Intrepid	Boats and sailors from many navies. (Last week in May)
• Lower East Side Festival of the Arts	Theater for the New City ,155 First Ave	Celebrating Beatniks and Pop Art. (Last weekend in May)
• Spring Flower Exhibition	NY Botanical Garden, Bronx	More flowers.
• Cherry Blossom Festival	Brooklyn Botanic Garden	Flowering trees.
• Martin Luther King, Jr Parade	Fifth Avenue	Celebration of equal rights. (Third Sunday in May)
• Thursday Night Concert Series	South Street Seaport	Free varied concerts. (May–September)

June

Event	Location	Description
• Toyota Comedy Festival	Various locations	Japan's dullest cars, America's funniest comics.
• Puerto Rican Day Parade	Fifth Avenue	Puerto Rican pride. (First Sunday in June)
• Metropolitan Opera Parks Concerts	Various locations	Free performances.
• Museum Mile Festival	Fifth Avenue	Museum open-house. (Second Tuesday in June)
• Gay and Lesbian Pride Parade	Columbus Circle, Fifth Ave & Christopher St	Commemorates the 1969 Stonewall riots.
• New York Jazz Festival	Various locations	All kinds of jazz.
• JVC Jazz Festival	Various locations	Descends from the Newport Jazz Festival.
• Mermaid Parade	Coney Island	Showcase of sea-creatures, freaks.
• Feast of St Anthony of Padua	Little Italy	Patron saint of expectant mothers, mail, Portugal, seekers of lost articles, shipwrecks, Tigua Indians, and travel hostesses, among other things. (Saturday before summer solstice)
• Roses, Roses, Roses	NY Botanical Garden, Bronx	We won't spoil the surprise and tell you what you'll see…
• Central Park SummerStage	Central Park	Free concerts. (June–August)
• New York Shakespeare Festival	Delacorte Theater in Central Park	2 free plays every summer. (June–August)
• Bryant Park Free Summer Season	Sixth Ave at 42nd St	Free music, dance, and film. (June–August)
• Midsummer Night Swing	Lincoln Center	Performances with free dance lessons. (June–July)

July

Event	Location	Description
• Macy's Fireworks Display	East River	Independence Day's literal highlight. (July 4)
• American Crafts Festival	Lincoln Center	Celebrating quilts and such. (First 2 weekends in July)
• Washington Square Music Festival	W 4th St at LaGuardia Pl	Open-air concert. (July–August)

• New York Philharmonic Concerts	Various locations	Varied programs. (July–August)
• Summergarden	MoMA	Free classical concerts. (July–August)
• Celebrate Brooklyn! Performing Arts Festival	Prospect Park Bandshell	9 weeks of free outdoor events. (July–August)
• Mostly Mozart	Lincoln Center	The name says it all. (July–August)
• Music on the Boardwalk	Coney Island	"Under the Boardwalk" not on the setlist, presumably… (July–August)

August

• Harlem Week	Harlem	Black and Latino culture.
• Hong Kong Dragon Boat Festival	Flushing-Meadows Park Lake, Queens	39-foot boats race.
• Greenwich Village Jazz Festival	Greenwich Village	10-day festival ends with a free concert in Washington Square Park.
• The Fringe Festival	Various locations, Lower East Side	Avant garde theatre.
• US Open	USTA National Tennis Center, Flushing	Final Grand Slam event of the year. (August–September)
• Howl Festival	Tompkins Square Park	Jazz, East Village merchants, art, etc. Recommended.

September

• West Indian Day Carnival	Eastern Parkway from Utica—Grand Army Plaza, Brooklyn	Children's parade on Saturday, adult's parade on Labor Day. (Labor Day Weekend)
• Richmond County Fair	441 Clarke Ave, Staten Island	Best agricultural competitions. (Labor Day)
• Wigstock	Pier 54 b/w 12th–13th Sts, west side	Celebration of drag, glamour, and artificial hair. (Labor Day Weekend)
• Feast of San Gennaro	Little Italy	Plenty of greasy street food. (Third week in September)
• Downtown Arts Festival	Various locations, SoHo	Mammoth art exhibitions.
• Broadway on Broadway	Times Square	Sneak peak at old and new plays.
• Brooklyn BeerFest	N 11th St between Berry and Wythe, Brooklyn	Taste test of over 100 beers.
• Atlantic Antic	Brooklyn Heights	Multicultural street fair. (Last Sunday in September)
• New York Is Book Country	Fifth Avenue	Publishers and bookstores from around NYC. (Third Sunday in September)
• Race for the Mayor's Cup	NY Harbor	And the winner gets to find out what he's been drinking! (September–November)
• New York City Opera Season	Lincoln Center	Popular and classical operas.

October

• New York Film Festival	Lincoln Center	Features film premieres. (Early October)
• Fall Crafts Park Avenue	Seventh Regiment Armory on Park Avenue, b/w 66th and 67th Sts	Display and sale of contemporary American crafts by 175 of the nation's finest craft artists.
• Columbus Day Parade	Fifth Avenue	Celebrating the second person to discover America. (Columbus Day)
• Halloween Parade	West Village	Brings a new meaning to costumed event. (October 31)
• Fall Antique Show	Pier 92	Look at old things you can't afford.
• Chrysanthemum and Bonsai Festival	NY Botanical Garden, Bronx	Even more flowers.
• Blessing of the Animals	St John the Divine, Morningside Heights	Where to take your gecko.
• Big Apple Circus	Lincoln Center	Step right up! (October–January)
• Hispanic Day Parade	Fifth Ave b/w 44th and 86th Sts	A celebration of Latin America's rich heritage. (Mid-October)

November

• New York City Marathon	Verazanno to Central Park	26 miles of NYC air. (First Sunday of November)
• Veteran's Day Parade	Fifth Ave from 42nd St to 79th St	Service at Eternal Light Memorial in Madison Square Park following the parade.
• Macy's Thanksgiving Day Parade	Central Park West at 79th St to Macy's	Santa starts the holiday season.
• Chase Championships, Corel WTA Tour	Madison Square Garden	Women's tennis.
• The Nutcracker Suite	Lincoln Center	Christmas tradition. (November–December)
• Singing Christmas Tree	South Street Seaport	Warning: might scare small children, family pets, and stoners. (November–December)
• Christmas Spectacular	Radio City Music Hall	Rockettes star. (November–January)
• A Christmas Carol	Madison Square Garden	Dickens a la New York City. (Nov–Jan)
• Origami Christmas Tree	Museum of Natural History	Hopefully not decorated with candles. (Nov–Jan)

December

• Christmas Tree Lighting Ceremony	Rockefeller Center	Most enchanting spot in the city during the holidays.
• Messiah Sing-In	Call 212-333-5333	Handel would be proud.
• New Year's Eve Fireworks	Central Park	Hot cider and food available. (December 31)
• New Year's Eve Ball Drop	Times Square	Welcome the new year with a freezing mob. (Dec 31)
• Blessing of the Animals	Central Presbyterian Church	Where to take your other gecko. (December 24)
• Menorah Lighting	Fifth Avenue	Yarmulka required.
• Kwanzaa Holiday Expo	Jacob Javits Convention Center	Black pride retail.
• Midnight Run	Central Park	For the brave.

"New York is the concentrate of art and commerce and sport and religion and entertainment and finance, bringing to a single compact arena the gladiator, the evangelist, the promoter, the actor, the trader and the merchant."—E.B. White

Useful Phone Numbers

See also Essential Numbers on back inside cover.

Emergencies	911
General Info	311
City Board of Elections	866-868-3692
Con-Ed	800-75 CON ED
Time Warner Cable	212-674-9100
Verizon	212-890-1550
City Hall	212-788-9600
Police Headquarters	212-374-5000
Public Advocate	212-669-7250

Websites

www.notfortourists.com/web.html • The ultimate NYC web directory.

www.newyork.citysearch.com • Still a good overview to businesses, landmarks, and attractions in the city, though it's gotten increasing less useful the past few years because of too many paid listings, pop-up ads, and the like.

www.allny.com • The most detailed and varied site about anything you can imagine that relates to NY.

www.fieldtrip.com/ny/index_ny.htm • Hundreds of suggestions for places to visit in the city.

www.forgotten-ny.com • Fascinating look at the relics of New York's past.

www.ny1.com • Local news about the city; weather.

www.newyork.craigslist.com • Classifieds in almost every area, including personals, apartments for rent, musicians, and more.

www.nyc.gov • New York City government resources.

www.gothamist.com • Blog detailing various daily news and goings-on in the city.

www.nycsubway.org • Complete history and overview of the subways.

www.lowermanhattanmap.com
www.downtowninfocenter.org
www.lowermanhattan.info • All excellent resources for maps and information on Lower Manhattan.

www.nycvisit.com • The official NYC tourism site.

Bathrooms

When nature calls, New York can make your life excruciatingly difficult. The city sponsored public bathroom offerings, including dodgy subway restrooms and the sporadic trying out of self-cleaning super porta-potties, leave a lot to be desired. Your best bet, especially in an emergency, remains bathrooms in stores and other buildings that are open to the public.

The three most popular bathroom choices for needy New Yorkers (and visitors) are Barnes and Noble, Starbucks, and any kind of fast food chain. Barnes and Noble bathrooms are essentially open to everyone (as long as you are willing to walk past countless shelves of books during your navigation to the restrooms). They're usually clean enough, but sometimes you'll find yourself waiting in line during the evening and weekends. Although Starbucks bathrooms are more prevalent, they tend to be more closely guarded (in most places you have to ask for a key) and not as clean as you'd like. Fast food restrooms are similarly unhygienic but easy to use inconspicuously without needing to purchase anything.

For a comprehensive listing of bathrooms in NY (including hours and even ratings), try allny.com (and select "NYC Bathroom Guide") and the Bathroom Diaries at www.thebathroomdiaries.com/usa/new+york/.

If you're busting to go and you can't find a Barnes and Noble, Starbucks, or fast food chain, consider the following options:

- **Public buildings**—including train stations (Grand Central, Penn Station), and malls (South Street Seaport, World Financial Center, Manhattan Mall).
- **Government buildings**—government offices, courthouses, police stations.
- **Department stores**—Macy's, Bloomingdales, Saks, K-Mart, etc.
- **Other stores**—Old Navy, Bed Bath and Beyond, FAO Schwartz, NBA store, The Strand, etc.
- **Food stores**—McDonald's, Burger King, Starbucks, etc.
- **Supermarkets**—Pathmark, Food Emporium, D'Agostino, Gristede's, Key Food, etc. You'll probably have to ask, because the restrooms in supermarkets are usually way in the back amongst the employee lockers.
- **Bars**—a good choice at night when most other places are closed. Try to choose a busy one so as not to arouse suspicion. Most bars have those intimidating signs that warn you that the restrooms are for customers only!
- **Museums**—most are closed at night and most require an entry fee during the day. How desperate are you?
- **Colleges**—better if you're young enough to look like a student.
- **Parks**—great during the day, closed at night.
- **Hotels**—you might have to sneak past the desk though.
- **Times Square visitors centers**—1560 Broadway and 810 Seventh Avenue.
- **Places of worship**—unpredictable hours and not all have public restrooms.
- **Subways**—how bad do you have to go? Your best bets are express stops on the IND lines, for example, 34th Street and 6th Avenue. Some stations have locked bathrooms, with keys available at the booths.
- **Gyms**—i.e. places you have a membership with.
- **Outdoor public bathrooms**—they try these once in a while (if you can find one)—apparently the city signed on for 20 of them in 2004.

We're Number One!

World's Largest Station: Grand Central Terminal
World's Greatest Number of Subway Stations
World's Largest Museum: Museum of Natural History
World's Largest Cathedral: St John the Divine
World's Largest St Patrick's Day Parade
World's Largest Store: Macy's
World's Largest Hostel: Hostelling International, 891 Amsterdam Ave
World's Largest Bell Carillon: Riverside Church

27 Essential New York Movies

The Crowd (1928)
42nd Street (1933)
King Kong (1933)
On the Town (1949)
The Blackboard Jungle (1955)
The Apartment (1960)
Breakfast at Tiffany's (1961)
West Side Story (1961)
Midnight Cowboy (1969)
French Connection (1970)
Shaft (1971)
Mean Streets (1973)
Godfather II (1974)
The Taking of Pelham One Two Three (1974)
Taxi Driver (1976)
Saturday Night Fever (1977)
Manhattan (1979)
The Warriors (1979)
Escape From New York (1981)
Nighthawks (1981)
Ghostbusters (1984)
The Muppets Take Manhattan (1984)
Wall Street (1987)
Do the Right Thing (1989)
When Harry Met Sally (1989)
A Bronx Tale (1993)
Men in Black (1997)

25 Essential New York Songs

"Sidewalks of New York" — Various, written by James Blake and Charles Lawlor, 1894
"Give My Regards to Broadway" — Various, written by George Cohan, 1904
"I'll Take Manhattan" — Various, written by Rodgers and Hart, 1925
"Puttin' on the Ritz" — Various, written by Irving Berlin, 1929
"42nd Street" — Various, written by Al Dubin and Harry Warren, 1932
"Take the A Train" — Duke Ellington, 1940
"Autumn in New York" — Frank Sinatra, 1947
"Spanish Harlem" — Ben E. King, 1961
"Car 54 Where Are You?" — Nat Hiken and John Strauss, 1961
"On Broadway" — Various, written by Weil/Mann/Leiber/Stoller, 1962
"Talkin' New York" — Bob Dylan, 1962
"Up on the Roof" — The Drifters, 1963
"59th Street Bridge Song" — Simon and Garfunkel, 1966
"I'm Waiting for My Man" — Velvet Underground, 1967
"Crosstown Traffic" — Jimi Hendrix, 1969
"Personality Crisis"— The New York Dolls, 1973
"New York State of Mind" — Billy Joel, 1976
"53rd and 3rd" — The Ramones, 1977
"Shattered" — Rolling Stones, 1978
"New York, New York" — Frank Sinatra, 1979
"Life During Wartime" — Talking Heads, 1979
"New York New York" — Grandmaster Flash and the Furious 5, 1984
"No Sleep Til Brooklyn" — Beastie Boys, 1987
"Christmas in Hollis" — Run-DMC, 1987
"New York" — U2, 2000

New York Timeline — a timeline of significant events in New York history (by no means complete)

1524: Giovanni de Verrazano enters the New York harbor.
1609: Henry Hudson explores what is now called the Hudson River.
1625: The Dutch purchase Manhattan and New Amsterdam is founded.
1647: Peter Stuyvesant becomes Director General of New Amsterdam.
1664: The British capture the colony and rename it New York.
1754: King's College/Columbia founded.
1776: British drive colonial army from New York and hold it for the duration of the war.
1776: Fire destroys a third of the city.
1788: Washington takes the Oath of Office as the first President of the United States
1811: The Commissioners Plan dictates a grid plan for the streets of New York.
1812: City Hall completed.
1835: Great Fire destroys 300 buildings and kills 30 New Yorkers.
1859: Central Park opens.
1863: The Draft Riots terrorize New York for three days.
1868: Prospect Park opens.
1880: The population of Manhattan is over 1 million for the first time.
1883: Brooklyn Bridge opens.
1886: The Statue of Liberty is dedicated, inspires first ticker tape parade.
1888: The Blizzard of '88 incapacitates the city for two weeks.
1892: Ellis Island opens; 16 million immigrants will pass through in the next 32 years.
1897: Steeplechase Park open, first large amusement park in Coney Island.
1898: The City of Greater New York is founded when the five boroughs are merged.
1904: The subway opens.
1906: First New Year's celebration in Times Square.
1911: Triangle Shirtwaist Fire kills 146, impels work safety movement.
1920: A TNT-packed horse cart explodes on Wall Street, killing 30; the crime goes unsolved.
1923: The Yankees win their first World Championship.
1929: Stock market crashes, signaling the beginning of the Great Depression.
1929: The Chrysler Building is completed.
1930: The Empire State Building is built, then tallest in the world.
1927: The Holland Tunnel opens, making it the world's longest underwater tunnel.
1931: The George Washington Bridge is completed.
1933: Fiorello LaGuardia elected mayor.
1934: Robert Moses becomes Parks Commissioner.
1939: The city's first airport, LaGuardia, opens.
1950: United Nations opens.
1955: Dodgers win the World Series; they move to LA two years later.
1964: The Verrazano-Narrows Bridge is built, at the time the world's longest suspension bridge.
1965: Malcolm X assassinated in the Audubon Ballroom.
1965: Pennsylvania Station is demolished, to the dismay of many; preservation efforts gain steam.
1965: Blackout strands hundreds of thousands during rush hour.
1969: The Stonewall Rebellion marks beginning of the g ay rights movement.
1969: The Miracle Mets win the World Series.
1970: Knicks win their first championship.
1970: First New York City Marathon is run.
1971: World Trade Center opens.
1975: Ford to City: Drop Dead.
1977: Thousands arrested in various mischief during a city wide blackout.
1977: Ed Koch elected mayor to the first of three terms.
1987: Black Monday—stock market plunges
1993: Giuliani elected mayor.
1993: A bomb explodes in the parking garage of the World Trade Center, killing 5.
1994: Rangers win the Stanley Cup after a 40-year drought.
1999: NFT publishes its first edition.
2000: Yankees win their 26th World Championship.
2001: The World Trade Center is destroyed in a terrorist attack; New Yorkers vow to rebuild.
2003: Tokens are no longer accepted in subway turnstiles.

Television

2	WCBS (CBS)	www.cbsnewyork.com
4	WNBC (NBC)	www.wnbc.com
5	WNYW (FOX)	www.fox5ny.com
7	WABC (ABC)	abclocal.go.com/wabc/
9	WWOR (UPN)	www.upn9.com
11	WPIX (WB)	www.wb11.com
13	WNET (PBS)	www.thirteen.org
21	WLIW (Long Island Public)	www.wliw.org
25	WNY (Public)	www.wnye.nycenet.edu/
31	PXN (Pax)	www.paxson.com/wpxn/
41	WXTV (Univision)	www.univision.com
47	WNJU (Telemundo)	www.telemundo.com
49	CPTV (Conn. Public)	www.cptv.org
50	WNJN (NJ Public)	www.njn.net
55	WLNY (Public)	www.wlnytv.com
63	WMBC (Religious)	www.wmbctv.com

AM Stations

570	WFME	Religious
620	WSNR	Sports
660	WFAN	Sports
710	WOR	Talk
770	WABC	Talk
820	WNYC	Talk
880	WCBS	Talk
930	WPAT	Talk
1010	WINS	News
1050	WEVD	Sports
1130	WBBR	Talk
1190	WLIB	Talk
1280	WADO	Sports
1600	WWRL	Talk
1660	WWRU	Talk

FM Stations

88.3	WBGO	Jazz
88.9	WSIA	College
89.1	WFDU	College
89.1	WNYU	College
89.5	WSOU	Alternative/Hard Rock
89.9	WKCR	Jazz
90.3	WHCR	College
90.3	WHPC	College
90.7	WFUV	Adult Alternative
90.9	WKPB	College
91.1	WFMU	College
91.5	WNYE	Talk
92.3	WXRK	Alternative/Hard Rock
92.7	WLIR	Latin
93.1	WPAT	Latin
93.9	WNYC	Talk
94.7	WFME	Religious
95.5	WPLJ	Top 40
96.3	WQXR	Classical
97.1	WQHT	Hip-Hop/R&B
97.9	WSKQ	Latin
98.7	WRKS	Hip-Hop/R&B
99.5	WBAI	Talk
100.3	WHTZ	Top 40
101.1	WCBS	Oldies
101.9	WQCD	Jazz
102.3	WBAB	Classic Rock
102.7	WNEW	Top 40
103.5	WKTU	Top 40/Dance
104.3	WAXQ	Classic Rock
105.1	WWPR	Hip-Hop/R&B
105.9	WWPR	Latin
106.7	WLTW	Adult Comtemporary
107.1	WCAA	Latin
107.5	WBLS	Hip-Hop/R&B

Print Media

amNY	145 W 30th St	212-239-5398	Free daily, general news.
Daily News	450 W 33rd St	212-210-2100	Daily tabloid, rival of the Post.
El Diario	345 Hudson St	212-807-4600	Daily, America's oldest Spanish language newspaper.
Metro NYC	153 E 53rd St	212-702-4669	Free daily, pick it up at the subway.
New York Observer	54 E 64th St	212-755-2400	Weekly.
New York Post	1211 Avenue of the Americas	212-997-9272	Daily tabloid, known for its headlines.
New York Sun	105 Chambers St	212-406-2000	Daily, only about a year old.
New York Times	229 W 43rd St	212-556-1234	Daily, one of the world's best known papers.
Newsday	235 Pinelawn Rd, Melville, NYC	516-843-2700	Daily, based in Long Island.
NY Press	333 7th Ave	212-244-2282	Free, mostly opinion/editorial.
The Onion	515 W 20th St	212-627-1972	Weekly, news satire.
The Village Voice	36 Cooper Sq	212-475-3300	Free, alternative weekly.
Wall Street Journal	200 Liberty St	212-416-2500	Daily, famous financial paper.
New York	444 Madison Ave	212-508-0700	Weekly, geared towards well-off, various topics.
New York Review of Books	1755 Broadway	212-757-8070	Bi-weekly, intellectual lit. review.
New Yorker	4 Times Square	212-286-5400	Weekly, intellectual news, lit. and arts.
Time Out New York	627 Broadway, 7th Fl	212-539-4444	Weekly, guide to goings on in the city.

12 Essential New York Books

A Tree Grows in Brooklyn, by Betty Smith	Coming of age story set in the slums of Brooklyn.
Bright Lights, Big City, by Jay McInerney	1980's yuppie and the temptations of the city.
Catcher in the Rye, by J.D. Salinger	Classic portrayal of teenage angst.
The Cricket in Times Square, by George Selden	Classic children's book.
The Death and Life of Great American Cities, by Jane Jacobs	Influential exposition on what matters in making cities work.
The Encyclopedia of New York City, by Kenneth T. Jackson, ed.	Huge and definitive reference work.
Gotham: A history of New York City to 1898, by Edwin G. Burrows and Mike Wallace	Authorative history of New York.
Here is New York, by E.B. White	Reflections on the city.
House of Mirth, by Edith Wharton	Climbing the social ladder in upper crust, late 19th-century NY.
Knickerbocker's History of New York, by Washington Irving	Very early (1809) whimsical "history" of NY.
The Power Broker, by Robert Caro	Biography of Robert Moses, you'll never look at the city the same way after reading it.
Washington Square, by Henry James	Love and marriage in upper-middle-class 1880s NY.

New York City is a cultural center, so finding activities to amuse children in this metropolis is easy enough with all there is to offer. From fencing classes to the funnest parks, here's our guide to finding something to entertain your little ones.

The Best of the Best

★ **Neatest Time-Honored Tradition:** Central Park Carousel (830 Fifth Ave, 212-879-0244) Open everyday during the summer and weekends in the winter months, the Central Park Carousel features the largest hand-carved figures ever constructed and has been in residence in the park since 1950. $1 will buy you a memory that will last forever.

★ **Coolest Rainy Day Activity:** Our Name is Mud (59 Greenwich Ave, 212-647-7899) A paint-your-own pottery studio with several locations throughout the city. Pick out what you want to paint and the studio will provide paint, stencils, and all the other equipment to produce a masterpiece, proving a great activity for creative kids. It's also a fantastic idea for birthday parties.

★ **Sweetest Place to Get a Cavity:** Dylan's Candy Bar (1011 Third Ave, 646-735-0078) This candy land spans two floors chock full of every confectionary delight you can think of, plus a tasty ice cream bar. Great for birthday parties, they'll provide enough candy-related activities to keep kids on a permanent sugar high. Watch out, Willy Wonka.

★ **Best Spot for Sledding:** (Central Park's Pilgrim Hill) Kids pray for a snow day for the chance to try out this slick slope. BYO sled or toboggan.

★ **Funnest Park:** Hudson River Park Playground (Pier 51, Gansevoort St) With a beautiful view of the Hudson River, water abounds in this park that boasts several sprinklers, a winding "canal" and a boat-themed area complete with prow, mast, and captain's wheel.

★ **No Tears Hair Cuts:** Whipper Snippers (106 Reade St, 212-227-2600) A children's salon sure to calm the most fearful scissor-phobe. An on-site toy store helps to distract timid tots and promises a prize for the well-behaved. The salon also offers birthday parties.

★ **Best Halloween Costume Shopping:** Halloween Adventure (104 Fourth Ave, 212-673-4546) Open year-round, this costume emporium has any disguise you can possibly imagine, along with wigs, make-up supplies, and magic tricks to complete any child's dress-up fantasy.

Rainy Day Activities

When splashing in puddles has lost its novelty and ruined far too many of their designer duds:

• **American Museum of Natural History** (Central Park West and 79th St, 212- 769-5100) Fantastic for kids of all ages, with something to suit every child's interest. From the larger-than-life dinosaur fossils and the realistic animal dioramas to the out-of-this-world Hayden Planetarium, all attention will be rapt. The hands-on exhibits of the Discovery Room and the IMAX theatre are also worth a visit.

• **Bowlmor Lanes** (110 University Pl, 212-255-8188) Great bowling alley with a retro décor that kids will love. Bumpers are available to cut down on those pesky gutter balls. Children are welcome every day before 5 pm and all day Sunday – a popular birthday spot.

• **Brooklyn Children's Museum** (145 Brooklyn Ave, 718-735-4400) The world's first museum for children (opened in 1899) engages children in educational hands-on activities and exhibits. Kids can learn about life in New York in the "Together in the City" exhibit and find out why snakes are so slimy in the "Animal Outpost."

• **Children's Museum of the Arts** (182 Lafayette St, 212-941-9198) Devoted to encouraging the creative abilities in children aged 1-12 through special exhibitions, workshops and activities, as well as after school art classes in music, ceramics, painting, and mixed media.

• **Children's Museum of Manhattan** (212 W 83rd St, 212-721-1234) As soon as you arrive at the museum, sign up for some of the day's activities. While you're waiting, check out the other exhibits in the museum. There's the Word Play area designed for the younger children in your group and the Time/Warner Media Center for the older set, where kids can produce their own television show.

• **Intrepid Sea Air Space Museum** (Pier 86, 46th St and 12th Ave, 212-245-0072) Tour *The Growler*, a real submarine that was once a top-secret missile command center, or take a virtual trip on one of the simulator rides. After you've taken a look at the authentic aircrafts on deck, visit the museum of *The Intrepid* to see an extensive model airplane collection and a Cockpit Challenge flight video game for those aspiring pilots.

• **Lower East Side Tenement Museum** (90 Orchard St, 212-431-0402) Visit this hands-on museum for an insight into life in the historic tenements of the Lower East Side. One tour called "Visit the Confino Family" is led by "Victoria," a young girl dressed in authentic costume who teaches children about the lives of immigrants in the early 1900s.

• **The Metropolitan Museum of Art** (1000 Fifth Ave, 212-535-7710) A great museum to explore with audio guides designed specifically for children. From the armor exhibits to the Egyptian Wing, there are exhibits from all historical periods.

• **Sydney's Playground** (66 White St, 212-431-9125) An indoor playground featuring a giant sandbox, climbing play town, and a book nook. There's also a Womb Room, a quiet, dimly lit space with a view of the play area for moms who need to quiet baby while big brother plays.

Shopping Essentials

Kid's designer couture sounds like an oxymoron with the threat of grass stains and dirt around every corner, but it sure exists nonetheless (eg. Julian & Sara). buybuyBaby has nursing rooms which are very helpful. Here's a list of shops for the best party clothes and party gifts and everything in between:

- **American Girl Place** • 609 Fifth Ave • 877-AGPLACE• dolls
- **Art & Tapisserie•** 1242 Madison Ave • 212-722-3222 • clothing & knick knacks
- **Bambini** • 1088 Madison Ave • 212-717-6742 • European clothing
- **A Bear's Place** • 789 Lexington Ave • 212-826-6465 • furniture & toys
- **Bellini** • 1305 Second Ave • 212-517-9233 • furniture
- **Betwixt** • 245 W 10th St • 212-243-8590 • pre-teen clothing
- **Big Fun** • 636 Hudson St • 212-414-4138 • toys & trinkets
- **Bombalulus** • 101 W 10th St • 212-463-0897 • unique clothing & toys
- **Bonpoint** • pricey clothing
  • 1269 Madison Ave • 212-722-7720
  • 811 68th St • 212-879-0900
- **Books of Wonder** • 16 W 18th St • 212- 989-3270 • books
- **Boomerang Toys** • 173 West Broadway • 212-226-7650 • infant toys
- **Bu and the Duck** • 106 Franklin St • 212-431-9226 • vintage-inspired clothing/toys
- **buybuyBABY** • 270 Seventh Ave • 917-344-1555 • furniture/clothing/toys
- **Calypso Enfant & Bebe** • 426 Broome St • 212-966-3234 • hand-made clothing
- **Catimini** • 1284 Madison Ave • 212-987-0688 • French clothing
- **The Children's General Store** • Central Passage Grand Central Terminal • 212-682-0004 • toys
- **The Children's Place** • chain clothing store
  • 1460 Broadway • 212-398-4416
  • 901 Sixth Ave • 212-268-7696
  • 173 E 86th St • 212-831-5100
  • 22 W 34th St • 212-904-1190
  • 2039 Broadway • 917-441-2374
  • 2187 Broadway • 917-441-9807
  • 36 Union Sq E • 212-529-2201
  • 600 W 181 St • 212-923-7244
  • 1164 Third Ave • 212-717-7187
  • 248 W 125th St • 212-866-9616
  • 650 Sixth Ave • 917-305-1348
  • 163 E 125th St • 212-348-3607
  • 142 Delancey St • 212-979-5071
- **Classic Toys** • 218 Sullivan St • 212-674-4434 • toys
- **Dinosaur Hill** • 306 E 9th St • 212-473-5850 • toys & clothes
- **Disney Store** • 711 Fifth Ave • 212-702-0702 • Disney merchandise
- **Discovery Channel Store** • 107 E 42nd St • 212-808-9144 • educational toys
- **East Side Kids** • 1298 Madison Ave • 212-360-5000 • shoes
- **EAT Gifts** • 1062 Madison Ave • 212-861-2544 • toys & trinkets
- **Enchanted Forest** • 85 Mercer St • 212-925-6677 • toys
- **Estella** • 493 Sixth Ave • 212-255-3553 • boutique clothing
- **FAO Schwarz** • 767 Fifth Ave • 212-644-9400 • toy land
- **Funky Fresh Children's Boutique** • 9 Clinton St • 212-254-5584 • unique clothing
- **GapKids/baby Gap** • chain clothing store
  • 11 Fulton St • 212-374-1051
  • 1535 Third Ave • 212-423-0033
  • 2300 Broadway • 212-873-2044
  • 354 Sixth Ave • 212-777-2420
  • 341 Columbus Ave • 212-875-9196
  • 1037 Lexington Ave • 212-327-2614
  • 1988 Broadway • 212-721-5304
  • 122 Fifth Ave • 917-408-5580
  • 250 W 57th St • 212-315-2250
  • 545 Madison Ave • 212-980-2570
  • 657 Third Ave • 212-697-3590
  • 680 Fifth Ave • 212-977-7023
  • 60 W 34th St • 212-760-1268
  • 1212 Sixth Ave • 212-730-1087
  • 1466 Broadway • 212-382-4500
- **Geppetto's Toy Box** • 10 Christopher St • 212 620-7511 • toys
- **Granny-Made** • 381 Amsterdam Ave • 212-496-1222 • hand-made sweaters
- **Greenstone's** • hats & clothing
  • 442 Columbus Ave • 212-580-4322
  • 1184 Madison Ave • 212-427-1665
- **Gymboree** • chain clothing store
  • 1049 Third Ave • 212- 688-4044
  • 2015 Broadway • 212- 595-7662
  • 1332 Third Ave • 212-517-5548
  • 2271 Broadway • 212- 595-9071
  • 1120 Madison Ave • 212-717-6702
- **Halloween Adventure** • 104 Fourth Ave • 212-673-4546 • costumes & magic tricks
- **Ibiza Kids** • 42 University Pl • 212-505-9907 • clothing & toys
- **Jacadi** • expensive French clothing
  • 1296 Madison Ave • 212-369-1616
  • 787 Madison Ave • 212-535-3200
  • 1260 Third Ave • 212-717-9292
- **Jane's Exchange** • 207 Avenue A • 212-674-6268 • consignment clothing
- **Jay Kos** • boys' clothing
  • 986 Lexington Ave • 212-327-2382
  • 475 Park Ave • 212-319-2770
- **Julian & Sara** • 103 Mercer St • 212-226-1989 • European clothing
- **Just for Tykes** • 83 Mercer St • 212-274-9121 • clothing & furniture
- **KB Toys** • chain toy store
  • 901 Sixth Ave • 212-629-5386
  • 2411 Broadway • 212-595-4389
  • 1411 St Nicholas Ave • 212-928-4816
- **Karin Alexis** • 490 Amsterdam Ave • 212-769-9550 • clothing & toys
- **Kendal's Closet** • 162 W 84th St • 212-501-8911 • clothing
- **Kidding Around** • 60 W 15th St • 212-645-6337 • toy store
- **Kidrobot** • 126 Prince St • 212-966-6688 • toy store
- **Leeper Kids** • 79 Grand Central Terminal • 212-499-9111 • pricey clothing & toys
- **Lester's** • clothing • 1522 Second Ave • 212-734-9292
- **Lilliput** • pricey clothing
  • 240 Lafayette St • 212-965-9201
  • 265 Lafayette St • 212-965-9567
- **Little Eric** • 1118 Madison Ave • 212-717-1513 • shoes
- **Magic Windows** • 1186 Madison Ave • 212-289-0181 • clothing
- **Manhattan Dollhouse Shop** • 428 Second Ave • 212-725-4520 • dolls
- **Mary Arnold Toys** • 1010 Lexington Ave • 212-744-8510 • toys
- **Oilily** • unique clothing
  • 820 Madison Ave • 212-772-8686
  • 870 Madison Ave • 212-628-0100
- **Oshkosh B'Gosh** • 586 Fifth Ave • 212-827-0098 • play clothes
- **Papoose** • 311 E 81st St • 212-639-9577 • European clothing
- **Peanut Butter and Jane** • 617 Hudson St • 212-620-7952 • clothing & toys
- **Penny Whistle Toys** • toys & trinkets
  • 448 Columbus Ave • 212-873-9090
  • 1283 Madison Ave • 212-369-3868
- **Pipsqueak** • 248 Mott St • 212-226-8824 • clothing
- **Planet Kids** • infant gear
  • 247 E 86th St • 212-426-2040
  • 2688 Broadway • 212-864-8705
- **Pokemon Center** • 10 Rockefeller Plz • 212-307-0900 • Pokemon
- **Promises Fulfilled** • 1592 Second Ave • 212-472-1600 • toys & trinkets
- **ShooFly** • shoes & accessories
  • 465 Amsterdam Ave • 212-580-4390
  • 42 Hudson St • 212-406-3270
- **Space Kiddets** • 46 E 21st St • 212-420-9878 • girls' clothing
- **Spring Flowers** • shoes & clothes
  • 538 Madison Ave • 212-207-4606
  • 905 Madison Ave • 212-717-8182
  • 1050 Third Ave • 212-758-2669
- **Stinky & Minky** • 171 Sullivan St • 212-253-2530 • vintage clothing
- **Talbot's Kids and Babies** • clothing
  • 527 Madison Ave • 212-758-4152
  • 1523 Second Ave • 212-570-1630
- **Tannen's Magical Development Co** • 24 W 25th St, 2nd Fl • 212-929-4500 • magic shop
- **The Scholastic Store** • 557 Broadway • 212-343-6166 • books & toys
- **Tigers, Tutu's and Toes** • fun clothing & shoes
  • 128 Second Ave • 212-228-7990
  • 56 University Pl • 212-375-9985
- **Tiny Doll House** • 1179 Lexington Ave • 212-744-3719 • dolls
- **Toys R Us** • toy superstore
  • 1514 Broadway • 800-869-7787
  • 24-30 Union Sq • 212-674-8697
- **West Side Kids** • 498 Amsterdam Ave • 212-496-7282 • toys
- **Yoya** • 636 Hudson St • 646-336-6844 • clothing
- **Z'baby** • clothing
  • 976 Lexington Ave • 212-879-4900
  • 100 W 72nd St • 212-579-BABY
  • 996 Lexington Ave • 212-472-BABY
- **Zittles** • 969 Madison Ave, 3rd Fl • 212-737-2040 • toys & books

Outdoor *and* Educational

They can't learn *everything* from the Discovery Channel.

• **Central Park Zoo** • 830 Fifth Ave, 212-439-6500 • Houses more than 1400 animals including some endangered species. Take a walk through the arctic habitat of the polar bears and penguins to the steamy tropical Rain Forest Pavilion. The Tisch Children's Zoo nearby is more suited for the younger crowd with its smaller, cuddlier animals.

• **Fort Washington Park** • W 155 St to Dyckman, at the Hudson River • 212-304-2365 Call the Urban Park Rangers to arrange a tour of the little red lighthouse located at the base of the George Washington Bridge. The lighthouse affords some spectacular views—better than anything they'd see from atop dad's shoulders.

• **Historic Richmond Town** • 441 Clarke Ave, Staten Island, 718-351-1611 • A 100-acre complex with over 40 points of interest and a museum that covers over three centuries of the history of Staten Island. People dressed in authentic period garb give demonstrations and tours.

Classes

The children of New York City are some of the most well-rounded in the country with all the after school classes and camps available to participate in. Help them beef up their college applications with some fancy extracurriculars. It's never too early...

- **92nd Street Y Afterschool Programs** • 1395 Lexington Ave, 212-415-5500 • The center provides children of all ages with tons of activities ranging from music lessons and chess to flamenco and yoga. 92nd St is known as "the Y to beat all Y's."
- **Abrons Arts Center/Henry Street Settlement** • 466 Grand St, 212-598-0400 • The Arts Center offers classes and workshops for children of all ages in music, dance, theater, and visual arts.
- **Archikids** • 44 E 32 St, 718-768-6123 • Afterschool classes and summer camp for children ages 5 and up that teach kids all about architecture through hands-on building projects.
- **The Art Farm** • 419 E 91st St, 631-537-1634 • "Mommy & Me" art and music classes, baking courses and small animal care for the very young.
- **Asphalt Green** • 1750 York Ave, 212-369-8890 • Swimming and diving lessons, gymnastics, teams sports and art classes. They've got it all for kids one and up.
- **Baby Moves** • 139 Perry St, 212-255-1685 • A developmental play space that offers classes for infants to 6 year olds in movement, music and play.
- **Children and Art** • 747 Amsterdam Ave, 917-841-9651 Afterschool art lessons for children ages 5 and up that focus on art history and developing the skills to create masterpieces.
- **The Children's Studio** • 307 E 84th St, 212-737-3344 • The Studio offers hands-on courses in art, science and yoga with an emphasis on process and discovery.
- **Church Street School for Music and Art** • 74 Warren St, 212-571-7290 • This community arts center offers a variety of classes in music and art involving several different media, along with private lessons and courses for parent and child.
- **Claremont Riding Academy** • 175 W 89th St, 212-724-5100 • Horseback riding lessons offered by the oldest continuously operating stable in the United States.
- **Dieu Donné Papermill** • 433 Broome St, 212-226-0573 • Workshops in hand papermaking offered for children ages 7 and up.
- **free2be** • 24 Fifth Ave, 212-598-9760 • A holistic enrichment program that combines yoga, art, drama, storytelling, music, and poetry in classes where children are encouraged to be unabashedly creative and free with their own self-expression.
- **Greenwich House Music School** • 27 Barrow St, 212-242-4140 Group classes and private lessons provided for children of all ages in music and ballet.
- **Greenwich Village Center** • 219 Sullivan St, 212-254-3074 • Run by the Children's Aid Society, the center provides arts and afterschool classes ranging from gymnastics to origami, as well as an early childhood program and nursery school.
- **Hamilton Fish Recreation Center** • 128 Pitt St, 212-387-7687 The center offers free swimming lessons in two outdoor pools along with a free afterschool program with classes like astronomy and photography.
- **Hi Art!** • 601 W 26th St, Studio 1425I, 212-362-8190 • For children ages 2-12, the classes focus on the exploration of art in museums and galleries in the city and giving children ages 2-12 the freedom to develop what they've seen into new concepts in a spacious studio setting.
- **Institute of Culinary Education** • 50 W 23rd St, 212-847-0700 • Hands-on cooking classes.
- **Irish Arts Center** • 553 W 51st St, 212-757-3318 • Introductory Irish step dancing classes for children over the age of five.
- **Jewish Community Center** • 334 Amsterdam Ave, 646-505-4444 • The center offers swimming lessons, team sports, and courses in arts and cooking, and there's even a rooftop playground.
- **Kids at Art** • 1349 Lexington Ave, 212-410-9780 • This art program focuses on the basics in a non-competitive environment for kids ages 2-11.
- **Marshall Chess Club** • 23 W 10th St, 212-477-3716 • Membership to the club offers access to Weekend chess classes, summer camp, and tournaments for children ages five and up.
- **Metropolis Fencing** • 45 W 19st St, 212-463-8044 • Fencing classes offered for children ages 7 and up.
- **Tannen's Magical Development Co** • 24 W 25th St, 2nd Fl, 212-929-4500 • Private magic lessons for children over the age of 8 on weekday evenings, or group lessons of 3-4 teens on Monday nights. Their week-long summer sleep-away camp is also very popular.
- **The Mixing Bowl** • 243 E 82nd St, 212-585-2433 • Cooking classes for the aspiring young chef, ages 2 and up.
- **The Techno Team** • 160 Columbus Ave, 212-501-1425 • Computer technology classes for children ages 3-12.
- **Trapeze School** • West St, south of Canal, 917-797-1872 • Kids ages 6 and up can learn how to fly through the air with the greatest of ease.

Babysitting/Nanny Services

Baby Sitter's Guild • 60 E 42nd St, 212-682-0227
Barnard College of Babysitting Services • 11 Milbank Hall, 212-854-7678
My Child's Best Friend • 239 E 73rd St, 212-396-4090
New York City Explorers • 212-591-2619
The NYC Babysitters Club • 212-396-4090

Where to go for more info

www.gocitykids.com

Whether you never miss a Friday/Saturday/Sunday worship, or see religion as an archaic bastion of hypocrisy, there may be a time when you need to find a place of worship in the city. Maybe because it's Easter and it'd make your mom feel better if you went, or your nephew is getting bar mitzvahed, or because they'll probably let you use the bathroom...

The faiths practiced in New York are, unsurprisingly, as diverse as the people who live here, ranging from Catholic and Protestant churches to Buddhist temples to quasi-religious fringe freak faiths. In other words, for the many people on a spiritual quest, there are plenty of options. If none of the below places attract you in a religious way, many are worth a visit for their significant historical, cultural or architectural appeal. Some notable places of worship:

Abyssinian Baptist Church—famous politically active Harlem church. Previous pastors include Adam Clayton Powell Sr. and Jr. [Map 22]

African Methodist Episcopal—first African American church in the city, played a crucial role in the Underground Railroad. [Map 22]

Brooklyn Tabernacle—home of the famous Brooklyn Tabernacle Choir. [Map 30]

Cathedral of St. John the Divine—largest Gothic cathedral in the world. [Map 18]

Mosque no. 7/Masjid Malcolm Shabazz—Malcolm X served as imam here from 1954-1965. [Map 19]

Riverside Church—boasts the world's largest carillon bell tower. [Map 18]

St. Patrick's Cathedral—largest Roman Catholic cathedral in the US. [Map 12]

St. Paul's Chapel—NY's only church built before the Revolution; relief center during 9/11 aftermath. [Map 1]

Temple Emanu-El—largest Jewish house of worship in the world. [Map 15]

Trinity Church—downtown landmark since 1698; current building dates to1846. [Map 1]

The Watchtower—international headquarters of the Jehovah's Witness. [Map 30]

Denomination Key:

B=*Baptist*	M=*Methodist*
Bu=*Buddhist*	Mu=*Muslim*
C=*Catholic*	ND=*Non-denominational*
E=*Episcopal*	O=*Eastern Orthodox*
J=*Jewish*	OP=*Other Protestant*
L=*Lutheran*	P=*Presbyterian*
	Pe=*Pentacostal*

Map 1 • Financial District

Bu	True Buddha Diamond Temple	105 Washington St
C	Our Lady of Victory Church	60 William St
C	St Elizabeth Ann Seton Shrine	7 State St
C	St Joseph's Chapel	385 South End Ave
E	St Paul's Chapel	209 Broadway
E	Trinity Church	Broadway & Wall St
M	St John's United Methodist Church	44 John St

Map 3 • City Hall / Chinatown

B	Chinese Conservative Baptist	103 Madison St
B	Mariners' Temple Baptist Church	3 Henry St
Bu	Eastern States Buddhist Temple	64 Mott St
Bu	Faith Vow Ded Buddhist Association	130 Lafayette St
Bu	Mahayana Temple Buddhist Association	133 Canal St
Bu	Society of Buddhist Studies	214 Centre St
Bu	Transworld Buddhist Association	7 East Broadway
C	Most Precious Blood Church	113 Baxter St
C	St Andrew's Roman Catholic Church	20 Cardinal Hayes Pl
C	St Joseph's Church	5 Monroe St
C	Transfiguration Catholic Church	29 Mott St
E	Church Our Saviour	48 Henry St
E	Seamen's Church	241 Water St
J	Civic Center Synagogue (Orthodox)	49 White St
L	True Light Lutheran Church	195 Worth St
M	Chinese United Methodist Church	69 Madison St
O	St Barbara Greek Orthodox Church	27 Forsyth St
P	First Chinese Presbyterian Church	61 Henry St
-	Church of Jesus Christ of Latter Day Saints (Mormon)	401 Broadway

Map 4 • Lower East Side

C	St Mary's Church	440 Grand St
C	St Teresa's Church	141 Henry St
E	St Augustine's Episcopal Church	333 Madison St
J	Mesivtha Tifereth Jerusalem (Orthodox)	145 East Broadway
J	Young Israel Synagogue (Orthodox)	225 East Broadway
Pe	Primitive Christian Church	207 East Broadway

Map 5 • West Village

B	Legree Baptist Church	362 W 125th St
C	Our Lady of Guadalupe Catholic Church	328 W 14th St
C	Our Lady of Pompeii Church	25 Carmine St
E	St John's in the Village	224 Waverly Pl
E	St Luke in the Fields Church	487 Hudson St
J	A Greenwich Village Synagogue	53 Charles St
L	St John's Lutheran Church	81 Christopher St
M	Metropolitan-Duane United Church	201 W 13th St
ND	Village Church	232 W 11th St
OP	Manhattan Seventh Day Adventist Church	232 W 11th St

Map 6 • Washington Sq / NYU / SoHo

B	Judson Memorial Church	55 Washington Sq
C	Nativity Church	44 Second Ave
C	Old St Patrick's Cathedral	263 Mulberry St
C	Our Lady of Loreto	18 Bleecker St
C	St Cyril's Church	62 St Mark's Pl
C	St George's Ukrainian Catholic	30 E 7th St
E	Church of the Ascension	Fifth Ave & 10th St
E	Grace Church	802 Broadway
P	First Presbyterian Church	12 W 12th St

Map 6 • *continued*

J	Conservative Synagogue-Fifth Ave (Conservative)	11 E 11th St
M	Church of All Nations	48 St Mark's Pl
M	Washington Square United Methodist	135 W 4th St
ND	Abounding Grace	9 E 7th St
O	Russian Orthodox Cathedral of the Holy Virgin Protection	59 E 2nd St
OP	Christian Science Church 10th	171 MacDougal St
OP	Middle Church (Dutch Reformed)	50 E 7th St
OP	NY Chinese Alliance Church	162 Eldridge St
-	Baha'i Faith (Independent)	53 E 11th St
-	Dianetics Foundation Hubbard (Scientology)	4 W 43th St

Map 7 • East Village

B	Greater New Hope Missionary Baptist Church of Christ	507 E 11th St
C	Church of Mary Help-Christians	440 E 12th St
C	Immaculate Conception Church	414 E 14th St
C	Most Holy Redeemer Church	173 E 3rd St
C	St Emeric's Church	740 E 13th St
C	St Stanislaus B & M Church	101 E 7th St
J	Congregation Meseritz Synagogue (Orthodox)	451 E 6th st
L	Trinity Lower East Side Lutheran	602 E 9th St
ND	East Side Tabernacle	6163 Rivington St
ND	Father's Heart Church	545 E 11th St
OP	Church of Christ	257 E 10th St
OP	De Witt Reformed Church	280 Rivington St
Pe	Citylight Church	121 E 7th St
-	Islamic Council of America (Islamic)	401 E 11th St

Map 8 • Chelsea

C	St Columba Church	343 W 25th St
C	St Michael's Catholic Church	424 W 34th St
E	Holy Apostles Episcopal Church	296 Ninth Ave
E	St Peter's Episcopal Church	346 W 20th St
J	Congregation Beth Israel (Modern Orthodox)	347 W 34th St
ND	Chelsea Community Church	346 W 20th St
ND	Metropolitan Community Church	446 W 36th St

Map 9 • Flatiron / Lower Midtown

B	Madison Ave Baptist Church	129 Madison Ave
Bu	Shambhala Meditation Center of NY (Tibetan)	118 W 22nd St
C	Church of Holy Innocents	128 W 37th St
C	St Francis Church	135 W 31st St
C	St Francis Xavier Church	30 W 16th St
C	St Vincent de Paul Church	116 W 24th St
E	Church of the Incarnation	209 Madison Ave
J	Congregation Emunath Israel (Orthodox)	236 W 23rd St
J	Metropolitan Synagogue of NY (Reformed)	40 E 35th St
J	United Synagogue of America (Conservative)	155 Fifth Ave
J	Young Israel of 5th Ave (Orthodox)	3 W 16th St
M	Japanese American United Church	255 Seventh Ave
ND	Aquarian Foundation	139 W 35th St
OP	Community Church of New York (Unitarian)	40 E 35th St
OP	French Evangelical Church	126 W 16th St
OP	Unity Church of New York	230 W 29th St

Map 10 • Murray Hill / Gramercy

C	Church of Our Saviour	59 Park Ave
C	Our Lady of the Scapular & St Stephen's Church	149 E 29th St
C	Sacred Hearts Church	307 E 33rd St
E	St Ann's Church for the Deaf	209 E 16th St
J	East End Temple (Reformed)	245 E 17th St
J	Society of Jewish Science (Reformed)	109 E 39th St
L	Christ Lutheran Church (Evangelical)	355 E 19th St
L	Lutheran Church of Gustavus	155 E 22nd St
O	Diocese of the Armenian Church	630 Second Ave
O	Greek Orthodox Church of St John the Baptist	143 E 17th St
O	St Illuminators Cathedral (Armenian)	221 E 27th St
OP	Armenian Evangelical Church	152 E 34th St
OP	First Moravian Church	154 Lexington Ave
OP	Manhattan Mennonite Fellowship	15th St & Second Ave
P	Remnant Presbyterian Church	206 E 29th St

Map 11 • Hell's Kitchen

B	Metro Baptist Church	410 W 40th St
C	Church of the Sacred Heart of Jesus	457 W 51st St
C	St Paul the Apostle Church	415 W 59th St
E	St Clement's Episcopal Church	423 W 46th St
J	Congregation Ezrath Israel (Conservative)	339 W 47th St
ND	Rauschenbusch Memorial United Church in Christ	422 W 57th St
OP	Crossroads Seventh Day Church	410 W 45th St
P	First Prebyterian Church	424 W 51st St
P	Trinity Presbyterian Church	422 W 57th St

Map 12 • Midtown

B	First Corinthian Baptist Church	1912 Seventh Ave
B	Shiloh Baptist Church	2226 Seventh Ave
C	St Patrick's Cathedral	460 Fifth Ave
E	St Mary the Virgin Church	145 W 46th St
E	St Thomas Church Fifth Ave	1 W 53rd St
J	Chabad Lubavitch of Midtown (Orthodox)	509 Fifth Ave
J	Garment Center Congregation (Modern Orthodox)	205 W 40th St
L	St Luke's Lutheran Church	308 W 46th St
L	Swedish Seamen's Church	5 E 48th St
M	Salem United Methodist Church	2190 Seventh Ave
ND	Harvest Christian Fellowship	130 W 56th St
O	St George Greek Orthodox Church	307 W 54th St
OP	Christian Science Church	9 E 43rd St
OP	First Church of Religious Science (Metaphysical)	14 E 48th St
OP	Lamb's Church of the Nazarene	130 W 44th St
P	Fifth Ave Presbyterian Church	7 W 55th St

Map 13 • East Midtown

C	Church of St Agnes	143 E 43rd St
C	Holy Family Church	315 E 47th St
C	St John Evangelist Church	348 E 55th St
E	St Bartholomew's	109 E 50th St
J	Central Synagogue (Reformed)	123 E 55th St
J	Conservative Synagogue (Conservative)	308 E 55th St
L	St Peter's Lutheran Church	619 Lexington Ave
OP	Sacred Center for Spiritual Living (New Thought Church)	111 E 59th St

Map 14 • Upper West Side (Lower)

B	First Baptist Church	265 W 79th St
Bu	Karma Thegwum Choling	412 West End Ave
C	Blessed Sacrament Church	152 W 71st St
C	Holy Trinity Roman Catholic	213 W 82nd St
E	All Angels Church	251 W 80th St
E	St Matthew & St Timothy Church	26 W 84th St
J	Congregation Habonim (Conservative)	44 W 66th St
J	Congregation Rodeph Sholom (Reformed)	7 W 83rd St
J	Congregation Shearith Israel (Sephardic Orthodox)	8 W 70th St
J	Lincoln Square Synagogue (Modern Orthodox)	200 Amsterdam Ave
J	West End Synagogue (Reconstructionist)	190 Amsterdam Ave
J	West Side Synagogue (Modern Orthodox)	120 W 76th St
L	Holy Trinity Lutheran Church	3 W 65th St
L	Lutheran Church of the Holy Trinity	65 Central Park W
ND	Church of Humanism & Humanist	250 W 85th St
ND	Vision Church	2 W 64th St
OP	Christian Science Church	10 W 68th St
OP	Collegiate Reformed Church	368 West End Ave
OP	World Wide Church of God (Evangelical)	2 W 64th St
P	Good Shepherd of Faith Church	152 W 66th St
P	Rutgers Church	236 W 73rd St

Map 15 • Upper East Side (Lower)

B	Trinity Baptist Church	250 E 61st St
Bu	Zen Studies Society	223 E 67th St
C	Our Lady of Peace	237 E 62nd St
C	St Catherine of Siena Church	411 E 68th St
C	St Ignatius Church (Jesuit)	53 E 83rd St
C	St Jean Baptiste Church	184 E 76th St
C	St John Nepomucene Church	411 E 66th St
C	St Monica's Church	413 E 79th St
C	St Stephens of Hungary Church	414 E 82nd St
E	Church of the Epiphany	1393 York Ave
E	Church of the Resurrection	115 E 74th St
E	St James' Episcopal Church	865 Madison Ave
J	Congregation of Zarua (Conservative Traditional)	127 E 82nd St
J	Congregation Zichron Ephraim (Orthodox)	164 E 68th St
J	Fifth Avenue Synagogue (Modern Orthodox)	5 E 62nd St
J	Lisker Congregation (Orthodox)	163 E 69th St
J	Manhattan Sephardic Congregation (Orthodox)	325 E 75th St
J	Temple Emanu-El (Reformed)	1 E 65th St
J	Temple Israel of the City of NY (Reformed)	112 E 75th St
J	Temple Shaaray Tefila (Reformed)	250 E 79th St
J	Temple-Universal Judaism (Reformed)	1010 Park Ave
L	Zion St Marks Church	424 E 84th St
M	Christ Church United Methodist	520 Park Ave
M	Lexington United Methodist Church	150 E 62nd St
O	Greek Orthodox Cathedral	319 E 74th St
OP	Christian Science Church	103 E 77th St
OP	Christian Science Church	583 Park Ave
OP	Unitarian Church of All Souls	1157 Lexington Ave
P	Madison Ave Presbyterian Church	921 Madison Ave
-	Dianetics Foundation Hubbard (Scientology)	65 E 82nd St

Map 16 • Upper West Side (Upper)

B	Central Baptist Church of NY	166 W 92nd St
B	Southern Baptist Church	12 W 108th St
Bu	New York Buddhist Church	332 Riverside Dr
C	Ascension Catholic Church	221 W 107th St
C	Church of St Gregory	144 W 90th St
E	St Ignatius Episcopal Church	552 West End Ave
J	Ansche Chesed Temple (Conservative)	251 W 100th St
J	Congregation Ohab Zedek (Orthodox)	118 W 95th St
J	Congregation Shaare Zedek (Conservative)	212 W 93rd St
L	Advent Lutheran Church	2504 Broadway
L	Trinity Lutheran Church	168 W 100th St
M	St Paul & St Andrew Methodist	West End Ave & W 86th St
O	Evangelismos Greek Orthodox	302 W 91st St
O	Greek Orthodox Community	149 W 105th St
P	Second Presbyterian Church	6 W 96th St
P	West End Presbyterian Church	165 W 105th St
P	West Park Presbyterian Church	165 W 86th St

Map 17 • Upper East Side / East Harlem

B	East Ward Missionary Baptist	2011 First Ave
C	Church of St Thomas More	65 E 89th St
C	Church of the Holy Agony	1834 Third Ave
C	Our Lady of Good Counsel Church	230 E 90th St
C	St Cecilia's Parish Service	125 E 105th St
C	St Francis De Sales Church	135 E 96th St
C	St Joseph's Church	404 W 87th St
C	St Lucy Catholic Church	344 E 104th St
E	Church of the Heavenly Rest	2 E 90th St
E	Church of the Holy Trinity	316 E 88th St
E	St Edward the Martyr	14 E 109th St
J	Park Avenue Synagogue (Conservative)	50 E 87th St
L	Immanuel Lutheran Church	122 E 88th St
M	Park Avenue Church	106 E 86th St
ND	Church of the Resurrection	325 E 101st St
ND	City Church New York	111 E 87th St
O	Synod of Bishops Russian Church	75 E 93rd St
OP	Bethany Christian Church (Spanish-speaking Assembly of God)	131 E 103rd St
OP	Church of Advent Hope (Seventh Day Adventist)	111 E 87th St
OP	Church of the Living Hope (United Church of Christ)	161 E 104th St
Pe	Healing Stream Deliverance Church	121 E 106th St
P	Brick Presbyterian Church	62 E 92nd St
-	Ramakrishna-Vivekananda Center (Hindu)	17 E 94th St

Map 18 • Columbia / Morningside Hts

B	Antioch Baptist Church	515 W 125th St
B	St Luke Baptist Church	103 Morningside Ave
C	Annunciation Rectory	88 Convent Ave
C	Church of Notre Dame	405 W 114th St
C	Corpus Christi Catholic Church	529 W 121st St
C	Timplo Biblico Church	503 W 126th St
E	Cathedral of St John the Divine	1047 Amsterdam Ave
E	St Mary's Episcopal Church	521 W 126th St
J	Congregation Ramath Orah (Orthodox)	550 W 110th St
M	Emanuel African Methodist Episcopal Church	3741 W 119th St
M	Korean Methodist Church	633 W 115th St
ND	Manhattan Grace Tabernacle	2929 Broadway
ND	Riverside Church	409 Riverside Dr
Pe	Gethsemane Revival Holiness	463 W 125th St
Pe	Manhattan Pentecostal Church	541 W 125th St
P	Broadway Presbyterian Church	601 W 114th St

Map 19 • Harlem (Lower)

B	Beulah Baptist Church	125 W 130th St
B	Canaan Baptist Church	132 W 116th St
B	Christ Temple Baptist Church	161 W 131st St
B	Friendship Baptist Church	144 W 131st St
B	Greater Central Baptist Church	2152 Fifth Ave
B	Greater Metropolitan Baptist Church	147 W 123rd St
B	Memorial Baptist Church	141 W 115th St
B	Metropolitan Baptist Church	151 W 128th St
B	Mt Nebo Baptist Church	1883 Seventh Ave
B	Mt Pisgah Baptist Church	30 W 126th St
B	Second Canaan Baptist Church	10 Lenox Ave
B	Second Providence Baptist Church	11 W 116th St
C	St Thomas the Apostle	262 W 118th St
E	All Souls Church	88 St Nicholas Ave
E	St Ambrose Episcopal Church	9 W 130th St
E	St Andrew's Episcopal Church	2067 Fifth Ave
E	St Martin's Episcopal Church	230 Lenox Ave
E	St Philips Church	204 W 134th St
L	Lutheran Church of Transfiguration	74 W 126th St
M	Bethel African Methodist Episcopal Church	60 W 132nd St
M	St James African Methodist Episcopal Church	2010 Fifth Ave
Mu	Masjid Malcolm Shabazz Mosque	102 W 116th St
ND	Bethelite Community Church	38 W 123rd St
ND	Faith Mission Christian Church	160 W 129th St
ND	Harlem Grace Tabernacle	180 W 135th St
ND	New Covenent Life Christian	2433 Eighth Ave
ND	Salvation & Deliverance Church	37 W 116th St
OP	Ephesus 7th Day Adventist Church of Harlem	101 W 123rd St
OP	Lively Stone Church-Apostolic	161 W 122nd St
OP	NY United Sabbath Day Church (Seventh Day Adventist)	145 W 110th St
OP	Shiloh Church of Christ	5 W 128th St #7
OP	Tabernacle of Prayer	139 W 126th St
Pe	Kelly Temple Church of God in Christ	8 E 130th St
Pe	Pilgrim Cathedral of Harlem	15 W 126th St
Pe	Refuge Temple Church	2081 Seventh Ave
Pe	United House of Prayer For All	2320 Eighth Ave

Map 20 • El Barrio

B	Church of the Crucified Christ	350 E 120th St
C	All Saints Church	47 E 129th St
C	Church of Our Lady of Mt Carmel	448 E 116th St
C	St Ann's Roman Catholic Church	312 E 110th St
M	Madison Ave United Methodist Church	1723 Madison Ave
M	Metropolitan Community Church	1975 Madison Ave
ND	Holy Tabernacle Church	407 E 114th St
ND	Hosanna City Church	240 E 123rd St
ND	United Moravian Church	200 E 127th St
OP	Elmendorf Reformed Church	171 E 121st St
OP	Kingdom Hall of Jehovah's Witness	1763 Madison Ave
Pe	Christ Apostolic Church	160 E 112th St
Pe	Community Pentecostal Church	214 E 111th St
Pe	Greater Highway Church of Christ	132 E 111th St
-	Church of Scientology	2250 Third Ave

Map 21 • Manhattanville / Hamilton Hts

B	Convent Avenue Baptist Church	420 W 145th St
B	Jehovah-Jireh Baptist Church	536 W 148th St
B	Macedonia Baptist Church	452 W 147th St
B	St John Baptist Church	448 W 152nd St
C	Church of Our Lady of Esperanza (Spanish speaking)	624 W 156th St
C	Our Lady of Lourdes Church	463 W 142nd St
E	Church of the Intercession	550 W 155th St
E	St Luke's Episcopal Church	435 W 141st St
M	Mt Calvary Methodist Church	116 Edgecombe Ave
M	United Methodist Church	53 Edgecombe Ave
O	Russian Holy Fathers Church	524 W 153rd St
OP	Christian Science Church	555 W 141st St
Pe	Bethel Holy Church of Mt Sinai	922 St Nicholas Ave
P	North Presbyterian Church	525 W 155th St
P	St James Presbyterian Church	409 W 141st St

Map 22 • Harlem (Upper)

B	Abyssinian Baptist Church	132 W 138th St
B	Bethany Baptist Church	303 W 153rd St
B	Mt Calvary Baptist Church	231 W 142nd St
C	Church of St Mark	65 W 138th St
C	Resurrection Roman Catholic Church	276 W 151st St
C	St Charles Church	211 W 141st St
C	St Mark Evangelist Catholic	65 W 138th St
C	St Thomas Liberal Catholic Church	147 W 144th St
E	African Methodist Episcopal	140 W 137th St
ND	Calvery Christian Fellowship	2350 Fifth Ave
Pe	First Emmanuel Church of Jesus	270 W 153rd St
P	Rendall Memorial Presbyterian	59 W 137th St

Map 23 • Washington Heights

B	Primera Iglesia Baptista	96 Wadsworth Ave
C	Christ United Church & the United Palace	4140 Broadway
C	Church of the Incarnation	1290 St Nicholas Ave
C	St Rose of Lima Church	510 W 165th St
J	Congregation Shaare (Orthodox)	711 W 179th St
M	Christ United Church	4140 Broadway
O	Washington Heights Hellenic Orthodox (Greek)	124 Wadsworth Ave
OP	Collegiate Reformed Church	729 W 181st St
OP	Correa Miguel (Evangelical)	507 W 159th St

Map 24 • Fort George / Fort Tryon

B	Wadsworth Ave Baptist Church	210 Wadsworth Ave
C	Our Lady Queen of Martyrs	71 Arden St
C	St Elizabeth's Church	268 Wadsworth Ave
J	Congregation K'Hal Adath Jeshurun (Orthodox)	85 Bennett Ave
J	Fort Tyron Jewish Center (Reformed)	524 Ft Washington Ave
L	Our Saviors Atonement	178 Bennett Ave

Map 25 • Inwood

C	Church of the Good Shepherd	4967 Broadway
C	St Jude's Roman Catholic Church	431 W 204th St
E	Holy Trinity Episcopal Church	20 Cumming St
ND	Manhattan Bible Church	3816 Ninth Ave
Pe	Narrow Door Church	161 Sherman Ave

Map 30 • Brooklyn Heights/ DUMBO / Downtown

ND	Brooklyn Tabernacle	17 Smith St
-	The Watchtower (Jehovah's Witness)	360 Furman St

Roosevelt Island

C	Sacred Heart of Jesus Church	206 Main St
C	St Mary's Roman Catholic Church	201 Main St

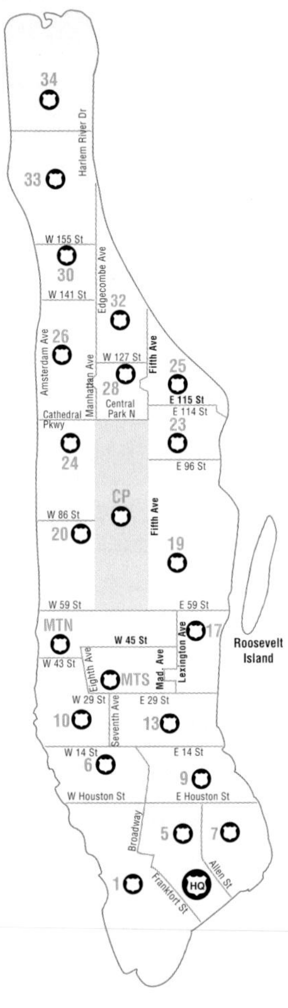

Important Phone Numbers

All Emergencies: 911
Non-Emergencies: 311
Terrorism Hot Line: 888-NYC-SAFE
Crime Stoppers: 800-577-TIPS
Crime Stoppers (Spanish): 888-57-PISTA
Sex Crimes Report Line: 212-267-RAPE
Crime Victims Hotline: 212-577-7777
Cop Shot: 800-COP-SHOT
Quality of Life Hotline: 888-677-LIFE
Missing Persons Case Status: 646-610-6914
Missing Persons Squad: 212-473-2042
Operation Gun Stop: 866-GUNSTOP
Organized Crime Control Bureau Drug line: 888-374-DRUG
Noise Complaints (EPA): 718-337-4357 or local precinct
Complaints (Internal Affairs): 212-741-8401
website: www.ci.nyc.ny.us/html/nypd/home.html

Statistics	*2003*	*2002*	*2001*	*2000*
Uniformed Personnel	37,200			39,778
Murders	596	584	643	671
Rapes	1,877	2,013	1,917	2,067
Robberies	25,890	27,124	27,863	32,231
Felony Assaults	18,717	20,700	22,994	25,854
Burglaries	29,120	31,250	32,663	38,241
Grand Larcenies	46,518	45,461	46,115	49,381
Grand Larcenies (cars)	23,144	26,339	29,619	35,602
Rank (in crime, of US cities with over 100,000 in pop.)			160/217	165/217

Precinct	*Address*	*Phone*	*Map*
1	16 Ericsson Pl	212-334-0611	2
5	19 Elizabeth St	212-334-0711	3
6	233 W 10th St	212-741-4811	5
7	19 1/2 Pitt St	212-477-7311	4
9	321 East 5th St	212-477-7811	7
10	230 W 20th St	212-741-8211	9
13	230 E 21st St	212-477-7411	10
Mid-Town S.	357 W 35th St	212-239-9811	8
17	167 E 51st St	212-826-3211	13
Mid-Town N.	306 W 54th St	212-760-8300	11
19	153 E 67th St	212-452-0600	15
20	120 W 82nd St	212-580-6411	14
Central Park	86th St & Transverse Rd	212-570-4820	C. Pk
23	162 E 102nd St	212-860-6411	17
24	151 W 100th St	212-678-1811	16
25	120 E 119th St	212-860-6511	20
26	520 W 126th St	212-678-1311	18
28	2271 Eighth Ave	212-678-1611	19
30	451 W 151st St	212-690-8811	21
32	250 W 135th St	212-690-6311	19
33	2120 Amsterdam Ave	212-927-3200	23
34	4295 Broadway	212-927-9711	24
Headquarters	1 Police Plaza	646-610-5000	3

Since its inception in 1648 (when "prowlers" walked the streets with buckets, hooks, and ladders, looking for fires), the FDNY has grown to include more than 11,400 Fire Officers and fire-fighters, 2,800 Emergency Medical Technicians, Paramedics and Supervisors, and 1,200 civilian employees.

In 2003, for example, the FDNY responded to 27,105 structural fires, 24,015 non-structural fires, and 173,694 medical emergencies, as well as 41,018 malicious false alarms. The Fire Department is overseen by the Fire Commissioner, who is appointed by and reports to the Mayor. The Fire Officers and fire-fighters are under the command of the Chief of Department. Each of the companies listed here (and all of the companies disbanded) has a history on the informative FDNY website at www.ci.nyc.ny.us/html/fdny/home.html. Also check out the very interesting history of the fire service at nyc.gov/html/fdny/html/history/index.shtml.

An "engine" company runs the smaller trucks with the hoses, and a "ladder" company has the bigger trucks with the large (you guessed it) ladders on the back. An engine and a ladder company may be located together or separately, but cooperation between them is the key to fighting the fires.

Map 1 • Financial District

Engine 10, Ladder 10	124 Liberty St
Engine 4, Ladder 15	42 South St

Map 2 • TriBeCa

Ladder 8	14 N Moore St

Map 3 • City Hall / Chinatown

Engine 55	363 Broome St
Engine 6	49 Beekman St
Engine 7, Ladder 1	100 Duane St
Engine 9, Ladder 6	75 Canal St

Map 4 • Lower East Side

Engine 15	269 Henry St
Ladder 18	25 (19 1/2) Pitt St

Map 5 • West Village

Engine 24, Ladder 5	227 Sixth Ave

Map 6 • Washington Sq / NYU / SoHo

Engine 33, Ladder 9	42 Great Jones St
Engine 5	340 E 14th St
Ladder 20	251 Lafayette St
Ladder 3	108 E 13th St

Map 7 • East Village

Engine 28, Ladder 11	222 E 2nd St

Map 8 • Chelsea

Engine 34, Ladder 21	440 W 38th St

Map 9 • Flatiron / Lower Midtown

Engine 1, Ladder 24	142 W 31st St
Engine 14	14 E 18th St
Engine 26	220 W 37th St
Engine 3, Ladder 12	146 W 19th St

Map 10 • Murray Hill / Gramercy

Engine 16, Ladder 7	234 E 29th St

Map 11 • Hell's Kitchen

Rescue 1	530 W 43rd St

Map 12 • Midtown

Engine 23	215 W 58th St
Engine 54, Ladder 4	782 Eighth Ave
Engine 65	33 W 43rd St

Map 13 • East Midtown

Engine 21	238 E 40th St
Engine 8, Ladder 2	165 E 51st St

Map 14 • Upper West Side (Lower)

Engine 40, Ladder 35	133 Amsterdam Ave
Engine 74	120 W 83rd St
Ladder 25	205 W 77th St

Map 15 • Upper East Side (Lower)

Engine 22, Ladder 13	159 E 85th St
Engine 39, Ladder 16	157 E 67th St
Engine 44	221 E 75th St

Map 16 • Upper West Side (Upper)

Engine 76, Ladder 22	145 W 100th St

Map 17 • Upper East Side / East Harlem

Engine 53, Ladder 43	1836 Third Ave

Map 18 • Columbia/Morningside Heights

Engine 37, Ladder 40	415 W 125th St
Engine 47	502 W 113th St

Map 19 • Harlem (Lower)

Engine 58, Ladder 26	1367 Fifth Ave
Engine 59, Ladder 30	111 W 133rd St

Map 20 • El Barrio

Engine 35, Ladder 14	2282 Third Ave
Engine 36	120 E 125th St
Engine 91	244 E 111th St

Map 21 • Manhattanville/Hamilton Heights

Engine 80, Ladder 23	503 W 139th St

Map 22 • Harlem (Upper)

Engine 69, Ladder 28	248 W 143rd St

Map 23 • Washington Heights

Engine 67	518 W 170th St
Engine 84, Ladder 34	513 W 161st St
Engine 93, Ladder 45	515 W 181st St

Map 25 • Inwood

Engine 95, Ladder 36	29 Vermilyea Ave

Generally, if you have to get to a hospital, it's best to go to the closest one. As a quick reference, this is a list of largest hospitals by neighborhood. Obviously, we recommend going to the map page for your neighborhood to see the location of these and all hospitals in your area:

Lower Manhattan: NYU Downtown Hospital • William and Beekman Sts, just south of the Brooklyn Bridge • [Map 3]
West Village/Chelsea: St Vincent's • Seventh Ave & 12th St [Map 5]
East Village: Beth Israel Medical Center • 14th St & Broadway/Union Square • [Map 10]
Murray Hill: Bellevue Hospital Center • First Ave & 27th St [Map 10]
Hell's Kitchen/Upper West Side: St Luke's Roosevelt Hospital • 10th Ave & 58th St [Map 10]
East Side: New York Presbyterian • York Ave & 68th St; Lenox Hill Hospital • Lexington Ave & 77th St; Mt. Sinai Medical Center • Madison Ave & 101st St [Map 15]
Columbia/Morningside Heights: St Luke's Hospital Center • Amsterdam Ave & 114th St [Map 18]
El Barrio: North General Hospital • Madison Ave & 125th St [Map 20]
Farther uptown: Columbia Presbyterian Medical Center • 168th St & Broadway [Map 23]

If you have a condition that isn't immediately threatening, certain hospitals in New York specialize and excel in specific areas of medicine.

Cancer: Memorial Sloan-Kettering
Birthing Center/Labor & Delivery: St Luke's Roosevelt
Digestive Disorders: Mt Sinai
Ear, Nose and Throat: Mt Sinai
Eyes: New York Eye and Ear Infirmary
Geriatrics: Mt Sinai, New York Presbyterian
Heart: New York Presbyterian
Hormonal Disorders: New York Presbyterian
Kidney Disease: New York Presbyterian
Mental Health: Bellevue
Neurology: New York Presbyterian, NYU Medical Center
Orthopedics: Hospital for Special Surgery, New York Presbyterian
Pediatrics: Children's Hospital of New York Presbyterian
Psychiatry: New York Presbyterian, NYU Medical Center
Rheumatology: Hospital for Special Surgery, Hospital for Joint Diseases Orthopedic Institute, NYU Medical Center

Hospital	*Address*	*Phone*	*Map*
American Association for Bikur Cholim Hospital	156 Fifth Ave	212-989-2525	9
American Friends of Laniado Hospital	18 W 45th St	212-944-2690	12
Bellevue Hospital Center	462 First Ave	212-562-4141	10
Beth Israel Medical Center	281 First Ave	212-420-2000	10
Beth Israel Medical Center: Phillips Ambulatory/Cancer Center	10 Union Sq E	212-844-8000	10
Beth Israel Medical Center: Singer Division	170 East End Ave	212-870-9000	17
Cabrini Medical Center	227 E 19th St	212-995-6000	10
Columbia-Presbyterian Allen Pavilion	5141 Broadway	212-932-4000	25
Columbia-Presbyterian Medical Center	622 W 168th St	212-305-2500	23
Gouverneur Hospital	227 Madison St	212-238-7000	4
Gracie Square Hospital	420 E 76th St	212-988-4400	15
Harlem Hospital Center	506 Lenox Ave	212-939-1000	22
Hospital for Joint Diseases	301 E 17th St	212-598-6000	10
Hospital for Special Surgery	535 E 70th St	212-606-1000	15
Lenox Hill Hospital	100 E 77th St	212-434-2000	15
Manhattan Eye, Ear & Throat Hospital	210 E 64th St	212-838-9200	15
Manhattan Eye, Ear & Throat Hospital	55 E 124th St	212-987-1360	20
Memorial Sloan-Kettering Cancer Center	1275 York Ave	212-639-2000	15
Metropolitan Hospital	1901 First Ave	212-423-6262	17
Morgan Stanley Children's Hospital	3959 Broadway	800-245-5437	23
Mt Sinai Medical Center	1190 Fifth Ave	212-241-6500	17
National Jewish Center For Immunology	450 Seventh Ave	212-868-3062	9
National Jewish Center for Immunology & Respiratory	535 Fifth Ave	212-297-0857	12
New York Eye & Ear Infirmary	310 E 14th St	212-979-4000	6
New York Hospital - Cornell Medical Center	525 E 68th St	212-746-5454	15
North General Hospital	1879 Madison Ave	212-423-4000	20
NYU Downtown Hospital	170 William St	212-312-5000	3
NYU Medical Center: Tisch Hospital	560 First Ave	212-263-7300	10
Renaissance Health Care Network	215 W 125th St	212-932-6500	19
St Clare's Hospital & Health Center	426 W 52nd St	212-586-1500	11
St Luke's Hospital Center	1111 Amsterdam Ave	212-523-4000	18
St Lukes Roosevelt Hospital Center	1000 Tenth Ave	212-523-4000	11
St Vincent's AIDS Center	412 Sixth Ave	212-604-1576	5
St Vincent's Hospital & Medical Center	153 W 11th St	212-604-7000	5
The Floating Hospital	Pier 11	212-514-7447	1
VA Hospital	423 E 23rd St	212-686-7500	10

In addition to the regular branch system of the New York Public Library, there are several specialized "research" libraries in Manhattan. The **Schomburg Center for Research in Black Culture** contains an incredible amount of material relating to the history of African Americans. The **Science, Industry, and Business Library** is perhaps the newest and swankiest of all Manhattan's libraries. **The Library for the Performing Arts** contains a wonderful archive of New York City theater on film and tape. **The Early Childhood Resource and Information Center** runs workshops for parenting and reading programs for children. And, of course, the main branch of the **New York Public Library** (one of Manhattan's architectural treasures designed by Carrere and Hastings in 1897) has several special collections and services, such as the Humanities and Social Sciences Library, the Map Division, Exhibition galleries, and divisions dedicated to various ethnic groups. It contains 88 miles of shelves and has over 10,000 current periodicals from almost 150 countries. There is also the **Andrew Heiskell Library for the Blind and Physically Handicapped** designed to be barrier-free. It contains large collections of special format materials and audio equipment for listening to recorded books and magazines. You can check out the full system online at www.nypl.org.

Library	*Address*	*Phone*	*Map*
125th St	224 E 125th St	212-534-5050	20
58th St	127 E 58th St	212-759-7358	13
67th St	328 E 67th St	212-734-1717	15
96th St	112 E 96th St	212-289-0908	17
Aguilar	174 E 110th St	212-534-2930	20
Andrew Heiskell Library for the Blind	40 W 20th St	212-206-5400	9
Bloomingdale	150 W 100th St	212-222-8030	16
Chatham Square	33 East Broadway	212-964-6598	3
Columbus	742 Tenth Ave	212-586-5098	11
Countee Cullen	104 W 136th St	212-491-2070	22
Donnell Library Center	20 W 53rd St	212-621-0618	12
Early Childhood Resource & Information Center	66 Leroy St	212-929-0815	5
Epiphany	228 E 23rd St	212-679-2645	10
Ft Washington	535 W 179th St	212-927-3533	23
George Bruce	518 W 125th St	212-662-9727	18
Hamilton Fish Park	415 E Houston St	212-673-2290	7
Hamilton Grange	704 St Nicholas Ave	212-926-2147	21
Harlem	2011 Adam Clayton Powell Jr Blvd	212-666-9393	19
Hudson Park	66 Leroy St	212-243-6876	5
Humanities & Social Sciences Library	42nd St & Fifth Ave	212-930-0830	12
Inwood	4790 Broadway	212-942-2445	25
Jefferson Market	425 Sixth Ave	212-243-4334	5
Kips Bay	446 Third Ave	212-683-2520	10
Macomb's Bridge	2650 Adam Clayton Powell Jr Blvd	212-281-4900	22
Mid-Manhattan Library	455 Fifth Ave	212-340-0833	12
Morningside Heights Library	2900 Broadway	212-864-2530	18
Muhlenberg	209 W 23rd St	212-924-1585	9
New Amsterdam	9 Murray St	212-732-8186	3
New York Academy of Medicine Library	1216 Fifth Ave	212-822-7200	17
New York Public Library for the Performing Arts	40 Lincoln Center Plz	212-870-1630	14
New York Society Library	53 E 79th St	212-288-6900	15
NYC Municipal Archives	31 Chambers St	212-788-8580	3
Ottendorfer	135 Second Ave	212-674-0947	6
Riverside	127 Amsterdam Ave	212-870-1810	14
Roosevelt Island	524 Main St	212-308-6243	Roosevelt Island
Schomburg Center for Research in Black Culture	515 Malcolm X Blvd	212-491-2200	22
Science, Industry, and Business Library	188 Madison Ave	212-592-7000	9
Seward Park	192 East Broadway	212-477-6770	4
St Agnes	444 Amsterdam Ave	212-877-4380	14
Terence Cardinal Cooke-Cathedral	560 Lexington Ave	212-752-3824	13
Tompkins Square	331 E 10th St	212-228-4747	7
Washington Heights	1000 St Nicholas Ave	212-923-6054	23
Webster	1465 York Ave	212-288-5049	15
Yorkville	222 E 79th St	212-744-5824	15

From the "Muscle Marys" of Chelsea to the grungy rock-and-roll homos of the East Village, New York offers a diverse range of men and the places they play. Strangely, the gay scene in NYC is barely visible in daylight, as most clubs don't get busy before midnight. To see the boys during the day, check out the **Big Cup** coffee shop on Eighth Avenue and 22nd Street. Otherwise, enjoy the museums and shopping before taking your disco-nap to explore the city that never sleeps—perhaps as a result of all the "Tina" in this town.

If you're a lesbian venturing into New York City with the high hopes of finding a hot soccer mom, turn around, girlfriend, because they live on the other side of the tunnel. And even if you think you might find her sipping on a Miller Light at old **Henrietta Hudson**, stay away, because the bar is notorious for its intolerable bathroom line. There are few venues in Manhattan that cater to the lesbian crowd full-time—instead you'll need to hit the weeknight girl parties dotted around the island. Check out **Starlight** on Sunday nights for the hotties. For an up-to-the-minute list, visit www.gonyc.magazine.com. In Brooklyn, check out the patio at **Ginger's**.

Websites

Lesbian and Gay Community Services Center: www.gaycenter.org —
Information about center programs, meetings, publications, and events.

Out and About: www.outandabout.com —
Travel website for gays and lesbians including destination information, a gay travel calendar, health information, and listings of gay tour operators.

Gayellow Pages: www.gayellowpages.com —
Yellow pages of gay- and lesbian-owned and gay- and lesbian-friendly businesses in the US and Canada.

Dyke TV: www.dyketv.org —
Whether you're interested in viewing or contributing, this website has all the info you'll need.

Edwina.com: www.edwina.com —
A New York online meeting place for gays and lesbians looking for love, lust, or just friendship.

Publications

Free at gay and lesbian venues and shops and available at some street corners.

HX — Weekly magazines featuring information about bars, clubs, restaurants, events, and meetings and loads of personals. www.hx.com

Gay City News (formerly LGNY) — Newspaper for lesbian and gay New Yorkers including current local and national news items. www.gaycitynews.com

Blade News — Free monthly listings and features magazine that offers comprehensive arts and entertainment listings, weekly cultural and special event picks, as well as extensive information on community organizations and lesbian/gay owned and lesbian/gay-friendly businesses.www.gonyc magazine.com

GO NYC — Free monthly listings and features magazine that offers comprehensive arts and entertainment listings, weekly cultural and special event picks, as well as extensive information on community organizations, lesbian/gay owned and lesbian/gay-friendly businesses. www.gonycmagazine.com

Bookshops

Creative Visions, 548 Hudson St (212-255-5756) — Gay and lesbian magazines and videos.

Blue Stockings, 172 Allen St (212-777-6028) — Lesbian/radical bookstore with regular readings and book signings. www.bluestockings.com

Health Centers and Support Organizations

Michael Callen-Audre Lorde Community Health Center, 356 W 18th St b/w Eighth & Ninth Ave (212-271-7200) — Primary Care Center for gay, lesbian, bisexual, and transgender New Yorkers. www.callen-lorde.org

Gay Men's Health Crisis, 129 W 24th St btw 6th and 7th Ave (212-367-1000) www.gmhc.org

AIDS advice hotline (212-807-6655)

Lesbian and Gay Community Services Center, 208 W 13th St between 7th & 8th Ave (212-620-7310) www.gaycenter.org

Gay and Lesbian Switchboard — (212-620-7310) Switchboard for referrals, advice, counseling. www.glnh.org

PFLAG – Parents, Families, and Friends of Lesbians and Gays (212-463-0629) www.pflagnyc.org

Lesbian/Gay Immigration Rights Task Force (LGIRTF) – (212-714-2904) Advocates for changing US policy on immigration of permanent partners. www.lgirtf.org

GLAAD — Gay and Lesbian Alliance Against Defamation — (212-629-3322) These are the folks who go to bat for you in the media. www.glaad.org

Annual Events

Pride Week — Usually the last full week in June; www.hopinc.org (212-807-7433)

New York Lesbian and Gay Film Festival — Showcase of International gay and lesbian films, May/June; www.newfestival.org (212-254-8504)

AIDS Action Ride — Replacing the old NY to Boston Aids ride, this version is a 3-day, 225-mile ride across Massachusetts. The ride begins in Pittsfield and finishes in Salem, mid-August; www.aidsactionride.org (617-450-1100)

Venues — Lesbian

- **Cubbyhole** • 281 W 12th St & W 4th St • 212-243-9041
- **Henrietta Hudson** • 438 Hudson St b/w Barrow & Morton • 212-924-3347 • henriettahudsons.com
- **Meow Mix** • 269 E Houston St & Suffolk St • 212-254-0688 • meowmixchix.com
- **Rubyfruit** • 531 Hudson St • 212-929-3343
- **Wonderbar** • 505 6th St & Avenue A • 212-777-9105 • wonderbarnyc.com
- **Bar d'O** (Mon) • 29 Bedford St • 212-627-1580
- **Halo** (first Mon) • 49 Grove St • 212-243-8885
- **Nowhere** (Mon) • 322 E 14th St & First Ave • 212-477-4744
- **Slipper Room** (Tues) • 167 Orchard St • 212-253-7246
- **Hell** (second Tues) • 59 Gansevoort St b/w Ninth Ave & Washington • 212-727-1666
- **Heaven** (Wed, Fri, Sat) • 579 Sixth Ave b/w 16th & 17th Sts • 212-243-6100
- **Club Fahrenheit** (2nd, 4th Fri) • 95 Leonard St b/w Broadway & Church • 917-299-1975
- **Escuelita** (Fri) • 301 W 39th St & Eighth Ave • 212-631-1093
- **Opaline** (Fri) • 85 Avenue A b/w 5th & 6th Sts • 212-995-8684
- **Starlight** (Sun) • 167 Avenue A • 212-475-2172

Venues — Gay

- **219 Flamingo** • 219 Second Ave • 212-533-2860
- **Avalon** • Sixth Ave & 20th St • 212-807-7780 • jblair.com
- **Babalu** • 117 Seventh Ave S • 212-675-0350
- **Barracuda** • 275 W 22nd St off Eighth Ave • 212-645-8613
- **Barrage** • 401 W 47th St between Ninth & Tenth Aves • 212-586-9390
- **Bridge Bar** • 309 E 60th St & Second Ave • 212-223-9104
- **Boots & Saddle** • 76 Christopher St & Seventh Ave S • 212-929-9684
- **Boysroom** • Ninth Ave & Houston St • 212-358-1440
- **Candle Bar** • 309 Amsterdam Ave • 212-874-9155
- **Chances Are** • 143 Christopher St • 212-255-8252
- **Chi Chiz** • 135 Christopher St & Hudson St • 212-462-0027
- **Cleo's Ninth Avenue Salon** • 656 Ninth Ave • 212-307-1503
- **The Cock** • 188 Avenue A • 212-777-9105
- **Code** • 255 W 55th St • 212-265-5555
- **Crobar** • 530 W 28th St, between Tenth & Eleventh Aves • 212-629-9000 • crobar.com
- **Dick Bar** • 192 Second Ave • 212-475-2071
- **The Dugout** • 185 Christopher St • 212-242-9113 • metrobears.org
- **The Duplex** • 61 Christopher St & Seventh Ave • 212-255-5438 • theduplex.com
- **The Eagle** • 554 W 28th St • 646-473-1866 • eaglenyc.com
- **Edelweiss Bar** • 137 Seventh Ave • 212-929-5155
- **Escuelita** • 301 W 39th St & Eighth Ave • 212-631-0588
- **G Lounge** • 225 W 19th St b/w Seventh & Eighth Aves • 212-929-1085 • glounge.com
- **Hangar Bar** • 115 Christopher St & Bleecker St • 212-627-2044 • hangarbar.us
- **Heaven** • 579 Sixth Ave • 243-6100
- **Hell** • 59 Gansevoort St b/w Ninth Ave & Washington • 212-727-1666
- **The Hole** • 29 Second Ave • 212-946-1871
- **Julius** • 159 W 10th St • 212-929-9672
- **La Fleur's** • 355 W 41st St • 212-947-1188 • lafleursbar.com
- **Marie's Crisis** • 59 Grove St • 212-243-9323
- **The Monster** • 80 Grove St • 212-924-3558 • manhattan-monster.com
- **Nocturne** • 144 Bleecker St • 212-979-8434
- **The Now Bar** • 22 Seventh Ave S • 212-802-9502
- **Nowhere** • 322 E 14th St & First Ave • 212-477-4744
- **O. W. Bar** • 221 E 58th St & Second Ave • 212-355-3395 • owbar.com
- **Pegasus** • 119 E 60th St & Lexington Ave • 212-888-4702
- **The Phoenix** • 447 E 13th St • 212-477-9979
- **Pieces Bar** • 8 Christopher St • 212-929-9291 • piecesbar.com
- **Posh** • 405 W 51st St • 212-957-2222
- **Pyramid Club** • 101 Avenue A & 6th St • 212-473-7184
- **Rawhide** • 212 Eighth Ave & 21st • 212-242-9332
- **Regents** • 317 E 53rd St • 212-593-3091
- **Roxy** • 515 W 18th St, b/w Tenth & Eleventh Aves • 212-645-5156
- **Saints** • 992 Amsterdam Ave & 109th St • 212-961-0599
- **SBNY (Splash)** • 50 W 17th St near Sixth Ave • 212-691-0073 • splashbar.com
- **The Slide** • 356 Bowery & 4th St • 212-420-8885
- **Sneakers** • 382 West St • 212-242-9830
- **Starlight** • 167 Avenue A • 212-475-2172 • starlightbarlounge.com
- **Stonewall** • 53 Christopher St • 212-463-0950 • stonewall-place.com
- **Tenth Avenue Lounge** • 642 Tenth Ave • 212-245-9088
- **Therapy** • 348 W 52nd St • 212-397-1700 • therapy-nyc.com
- **Tool Box** • 1742 Second Ave & 91st St • 212-348-1288
- **Townhouse** • 236 E 58th St • 212-754-4649 • townhouseny.com
- **Ty's** • 114 Christopher St • 212-741-9641
- **Urge** • 33 Second Ave & 2nd St • 212-533-5757 • urgenyc.com
- **View Bar** • 232 Eighth Ave • 212-929-2243
- **The Web** • 40 E 58th St • 212-308-1546
- **Wonder Bar** • 505 E 6th St • 212-465-7571 • wonderbarny.com
- **XL** • 357 W 16th St & Ninth Ave • 646-336-5574 • XLnewyork.com

New York has more landmarks than you can shake a foam Statue of Liberty crown at, which is good because it means that New Yorkers can enjoy some of them without tackling a crowd of out-of-towners. The landmarks discussed are highly idiosyncratic choices, and this list is by no means complete or even logical, but we've included an array of places, from world famous to little known, all worth visiting.

Coolest Skyscrapers

The **Empire State Building** doesn't need a description—even jaded New Yorkers can't help but feel awed by it. The **Chrysler Building** is a more sublime pleasure. Other midtown highlights include the **Citicorp Center**, an example of a building that could have been another banal office tower but for a very simple yet effective design choice. The **RCA Building** is one of the steepest looking skyscrapers in the city. The financial district offers its share of spectacular structures, including the **Woolworth Building**, the **AIG Building** at 70 Pine Street (with private spire rooms that you can only access if you're connected), **40 Wall Street,** the **Bankers Trust Company Building** and **20 Exchange Place.**

Best Bridges

The **Brooklyn Bridge** is undoubtedly the best bridge in New York—aesthetically, historically, and practically (as the constant flow of walkers and bikers proves). The **George Washington Bridge**, connecting New Jersey and New York City, is a stunning steel structure that carries over 53 million cars per year. The **Henry Hudson Bridge** expresses the tranquility of that part of the island, jutting out of Inwood Hill Park in a graceful swoon over to Spuyten Duyvil. The **Verrazano-Narrows Bridge**'s role in transforming Staten Island is controversial, but standing under it and seeing it span across the bay is an awe-inspiring endeavor. It also makes a cool gateway to the harbor.

Great Architecture

Grand Central Terminal stands as New York's great transit hub and is more famous for its interior than its exterior. The **Singer Building** in SoHo is a good example of cast iron architecture. The **Flatiron,** once among the tallest buildings in NY, remains one of the most distinctive. The **Lever House**, the **Seagram's Building**, and the **Marine Midland Bank Building** are great examples of Modernism. The **Guggenheim** is one of New York's most unique and distinctive buildings. The **Cathedral of St. John the Divine** is the world's largest and coolest unfinished cathedral—a much better destination than the hordes clamoring to get in to see St. Pat's.

Great Public Buildings

Once upon a time, the city felt that public architecture should aspire to be great architecture. Accordingly, most landmark public buildings are older. **City Hall** was built in 1812, the **Tweed Courthouse** in 1880, the **Jefferson Market Courthouse** (now a library) in 1877, the **Municipal Building** in 1914, and a host of other courthouses around the city were built in the early 20th century. The **Old Police Headquarters** would probably be a more celebrated building if it weren't located in a forgotten corner of Little Italy/Chinatown. And what are the chances that new firehouse built today would have the same charm as the **Great Jones Firehouse**?

Outdoor Spaces

Central Park, obviously. **Madison Square Park** is not as well known as many other central city parks, but it succeeds in being a peaceful respite from the city, which is more than you can say for Tompkins or Washington Square. For better or worse, **Washington Square** is a landmark (the arch is nice to look at), although there's a ton of other parks we'd rather spend time in. In addition to **Union Square** housing a bunch of great statues (Gandhi, Washington, Lincoln), it also offers an amazing Farmer's Market (Mon, Wed, Fri, & Sat) and is close to great shopping. **Duane Park** is tiny, but a perfect place to read a book on a nice day. The same goes for **Bryant Park**, plus they've got movies in the summer. Right next door, the **NY Public Library** steps are a classic NY set piece. **Rockerfeller Center** tends to get overrun by tourists, but it's still a neat place to visit, especially with all the Art Deco stylings. **Trinity Church** is a nice building and the view of it from along Wall Street is really cool. The graveyard next door has some famous names and is worth a stroll too. The **Cloisters** and **Inwood Hill Park** are great escapes. Thanks to Stuyvesant Street's diagonal path, **St. Marks-in-the-Bowery** has a nice little corner of land in front for a park, which gives a hint of its rural past. **Yankee Stadium**—less for the architecture and more for the gargoyles within.

Lowbrow Landmarks

The **Chinatown Ice Cream Factory** is worth a slog through Chinatown crowds on a hot day. Just around the corner is **Doyers Street**, which retains the slight air of danger from its gang war past. **CBGB's** is dingy, dark, and loud, among other positive attributes. Finally, there are some classic and historic New York bars, often known for their famous patrons of drinks past: **Pete's Tavern**, the **White Horse Tavern**, **Chumleys**, and the **Ear Inn**.

Lame, Bad & Overrated Landmarks

Even the most cynical New Yorker would have to admit that **Times Square** is a unique place, but the truth is it sucks to go there. **South Street Seaport,** in the end, is essentially a lame mall with some old ships parked nearby. **Madison Square Garden** is often given vaunted status as a great sports arena, but the accolades aren't really deserved. Aside from a few highlights, the teams there have stunk and the architecture is mostly banal. The worst part is that the gorgeous old Penn Station was torn down to make room for it. You can see pictures of the old station when you walk through the new **Penn Station**, which is famous not for its totally drab and depressing environs, but because of the sheer volume of traffic it handles. The **Cross Bronx Expressway** gets a mention as the worst highway ever.

Underrated Landmarks

Many of these get overlooked because they are uptown. **Grant's Tomb** was once one of New York's most famous attractions, but these days it's mostly a destination for history buffs. The **City College** campus is quite beautiful, even though a few newer buildings muck things up. Further up you'll find **Sylvan Terrace** and the **Morris Jumel Mansion**, a unique block of small row houses and a revolutionary war era house. While certainly not awe-inspiring, they offer a truer glimpse of old New York than the Seaport or Fraunces Tavern.

Map 1 • Financial District

American International Building	70 Pine St	Great Art Deco skyscraper.
Battery Maritime Building	11 South St	Ready-to-be-converted riverfront building.
Bowling Green	Broadway & State St	Watch the tourists take pics of the bull. New York's first park.
Cunard Building	25 Broadway • 212-363-9490	Great mosaics on the ceiling.
Customs House/Museum of the American Indian	1 Bowling Green • 212-514-3700	Stately Cass Gilbert building; check out the oval staircases.
Federal Hall	26 Wall St • 212-825-6888	Where George the First was inaugurated.
New York Stock Exchange	20 Broad St • 212-656-5168	Where *Wall Street* took place.
South Street Seaport	South St • 212-732-7678	Go late and check out the fishmongers.
St Paul's Chapel & Cemetery	Broadway & Fulton St • 212-602-0874	Old-time NYC church and cemetery.
The Federal Reserve Bank	33 Liberty St • 212-720-6130	Where *Die Hard 3* took place.
Trinity Church & Cemetery	Broadway & Wall St	Formerly the tallest building in New York.
Vietnam Veterans Plaza	Coenties Slip & Water St	A nice quiet spot to contemplate our faded dreams of empire.
World Trade Center Site	World Trade Center site	We still can't believe what happened.

Map 2 • TriBeCa

Duane Park	Duane St & Hudson St	One of the nicest spots in all of New York.
Harrison St Row Houses	Harrison St & Greenwich St	Some old houses.
The Dream House	275 Church St • 212-925-8270	Cool sound + light installation by LaMonte Young. Closed during summer.
Washington Market Park	Greenwich St • 212-274-8447	One of the city's oldest marketplaces.

Map 3 • City Hall / Chinatown

African Burial Ground	Duane St & Broadway	Just recently discovered.
Bridge Cafe	279 Water St • 212-227-3344	The oldest bar in NYC. Great vibe, good food too.
Chinatown Ice Cream Factory	65 Bayard St • 212-608-4170	The best mango ice cream, ever.
City Hall	Park Row & Broadway • 212-788-6879	Beautiful and now heavily barricaded.
Doyers St (Bloody Angle)	Doyers St	One of the few angled streets in New York. Has a decidedly otherworldly feel.
Eastern States Buddhist Temple	64 Mott St • 212-966-6229	The oldest Chinese Buddhist temple on the East Coast.
Hall of Records/Surrogate's Court	Chambers St & Park Row	Great lobby and zodiac-themed mosaics.
Municipal Building	Chambers St & Park Row	Wonderful McKim, Mead & White masterpiece.
Not For Tourists	2 East Broadway • 900-BUY-NFTS	Where the sh*t goes down!
Tweed Courthouse	Chambers St & Broadway	Great interior dome, but will we ever see it?
Woolworth Building	233 Broadway	A Cass Gilbert classic. Now partly condominium.

Map 4 • Lower East Side

Bialystoker Synagogue	7 Bialystoker Pl • 212-475-0165	The oldest building in NY to currently house a synagogue. Once a stop on the Underground Railroad.
Eldridge St Synagogue	12 Eldridge St	The first large-scale building constructed by Eastern European immigrants in NY!
Gouverneur Hospital	Gouverneur Slip & Water St	One of the oldest hospital buildings in the world.
Lower East Side Tenement Museum	90 Orchard St • 212-431-0233	Great illustration of turn-of-the-century (20th, that is) life.

Map 5 • West Village

Chumley's	86 Bedford St • 212-675-4449	Former speakeasy; still one of the coolest bars around.
Jefferson Market Courthouse	425 Sixth Ave • 212-243-4334	Now a library.
Stonewall	53 Christopher St • 212-463-0950	Site of a very important uprising in the late '60s.
The Ear Inn	Washington & Spring Sts • 212-226-9060	Second-oldest bar in New York; great space.
Westbeth Building	Washington St & Bethune St • 212-989-4650	Cool multifunctional arts center.
White Horse Tavern	567 Hudson St • 212-243-9260	Another old, cool bar. Dylan Thomas drank here (too much).

Map 6 • Washington Square / NYU / SoHo

Bayard-Condict Building	65 Bleecker St	Louis Sullivan's only New York building.
CBGB & OMFUG	315 Bowery • 212-982-4052	Stands for: Country, BlueGrass, Blues, and Other Music For Uplifting Gourmandizers.
Colonnade Row	428 Lafayette St	Remains of a very different era.

Map 6 • Washington Square / NYU / SoHo *— continued*

Con Edison Building	145 E 14th St	Cool top.
Cooper Union	30 Cooper Sq • 212-353-4195	Great brownstone-covered building.
Grace Church	802 Broadway • 212-254-2000	Another old, small, comfortable church.
Great Jones Fire House	Great Jones St & Bowery	The coolest firehouse in NYC.
Milano's	51 E Houston St • 212-226-8844	One of our favorite bars. An utter dump.
Old Merchant's House	29 E 4th St	The merchant is now dead.
Salmagundi Club	47 Fifth Ave • 212-255-7740	Cool building.
Singer Building	561 Broadway	Now houses Kate's Paperie; a fine building by Ernest Flagg.
St Mark's-in-the-Bowery Church	131 E 10th St • 212-674-6377	Old church with lots of community ties.
The Public Theater	425 Lafayette St • 212-260-2400	Great building, great shows.
The Strand Bookstore	828 Broadway • 212-473-1452	One of a kind. All others are imitations.
Washington Mews	University Pl (entrance)	Where horses and servants used to live. Now coveted NYU space.
Washington Square Park	Washington Sq	Dime bag, anyone?

Map 7 • East Village

Charlie Parker House	151 Avenue B & Tompkins Sq Pk	The Bird lived here. Great festival every summer in Tompkins Square.
Nuyorican Poets Cafe	236 E 3rd St • 212-505-8183	Home of the poetry slam, among other things.
Tompkins Square Park	Avenue A & E 9th St • 212-387-7685	Home to many.

Map 8 • Chelsea

J A Farley Post Office	441 Eighth Ave • 212-967-2781	Another McKim, Mead & White masterpiece.
Jacob K Javits Convention Center	36th St & Eleventh Ave • 212-216-2000	I M Pei's attempt to make sense out of New York. Love the location.

Map 9 • Flatiron / Lower Midtown

Chelsea Hotel	23rd St b/w Seventh & Eighth Aves • 212-243-3700	The scene of many, many crimes.
Empire State Building	34th St & Fifth Ave • 212-736-3100	The roof deck at night is unmatched by any other view of New York.
Flatiron Building	175 Fifth Ave • 212-633-0200	A lesson for all architects: design for the actual space.
Flower District	28th St b/w Sixth & Seventh Aves	Lots of flowers by day, lots of nothing by night.
Garment District	West 30s south of Herald Sq	Clothing racks by day, nothing by night. Gritty, grimy.
Macy's Herald Square	151 W 34th St • 212-494-4662	13 floors of wall-to-wall tourists! Sound like fun?
Madison Square Garden	4 Penn Plz • 212-465-6000	Crappy, uninspired venue for Knicks, Rangers, Liberty, and over-the-hill rock bands.
Madison Square Park	23rd St & Broadway • 212-360-8111	One of the most underrated parks in the city. Lots of great weird sculpture.
Metropolitan Life Insurance Co	1 Madison Ave • 212-578-3700	Cool top, recently refurbished.
Penn Station	31st St & Eighth Ave	Well, the old one was a landmark, anyway...
Theodore Roosevelt Birthplace	28 E 20th St • 212-645-1242	Teddy was born here, apparently.
Union Square	14th St & Broadway	Famous park for protests and rallys. Now bordered on all sides by chain stores.

Map 10 • Murray Hill / Gramercy

Gramercy Park	Irving Pl & 20th St	New York's only keyed park. This is where the revolution will doubtlessly start.
National Arts Club	15 Gramercy Park S • 212-477-2389	One of two beautiful buildings on Gramercy Park South.
Pete's Tavern	129 E 18th St • 212-473-7676	Where O Henry hung out. And so should you, at least once.
Sniffen Court	36th St & Third Ave	Great little space.
The Players	16 Gramercy Park S	The other cool building on Gramercy Park South.

Map 11 • Hell's Kitchen

Intrepid Sea, Air, and Space Museum	Twelfth Ave & 45th St • 212-957-3700	Lots of tourists.
Theater Row	42nd St b/w Ninth & Tenth Aves	This is that "Broadway" place that everyone keeps talking about, isn't it?

Map 12 • Midtown

Carnegie Hall	154 W 57th St • 212-247-7800	Great classic performance space. The Velvet Underground's first gig was here.
Museum of Modern Art (MoMA)	11 W 53rd St • 212-708-9400	Moved to Queens for three years in a vain attempt to get some street cred.
New York Public Library	Fifth Ave & 42nd St • 212-930-0787	A wonderful Beaux Arts building. Great park behind it. The map room rules.
Plaza Hotel	768 Fifth Ave • 212-759-3000	The best lobby and bars of any hotel in New York .
Rockefeller Center	600 Fifth Ave • 212-632-3975	Sculpture, ice skating, and a mall!
Royalton Hotel	44th St b/w Fifth Ave & Sixth Ave • 212-869-4400	Starck + Schrager = cool.
St Patrick's Cathedral	Fifth Ave & 50th St • 212-753-2261	NYC's classic cathedral. Always empty.
Times Square	42nd St & Broadway	It looks even cooler than it does on TV!

Map 13 • East Midtown

Chrysler Building	405 Lexington Ave • 212-682-3070	The stuff of Art Deco dreams. Wish the Cloud Club were public.
Citicorp Center	153 E 53rd St	How does it stand up?.
Grand Central Terminal	42nd St • 212-340-2583	Another Beaux Arts masterpiece by Warren & Wetmore. Ceiling, staircases, tiles, clock, Oyster Bar, all great.
Seagram Building	375 Park Ave	Or, "how to be a modernist in 3 easy steps!"
United Nations	First Ave b/w 42nd & 48th Sts • 212-963-8687	The diplomatic version of the World Cup.
Waldorf-Astoria	301 Park Ave • 212-355-3000	Great hotel, although the public spaces aren't up to the Plaza's.

Map 14 • Upper West Side (Lower)

Ansonia Hotel	2109 Broadway & 73rd St • 212-724-2600	Truly unique residence on Broadway.
Lincoln Center	Broadway & 64th St • 212-875-5000	A rich and wonderful complex. Highly recommended--movies, theater, music, opera.
Museum of Natural History	Central Park W & 79th St • 212-769-5100	Includes the new Planetarium and lots and lots of stuffed animals.
New-York Historical Society	2 W 77th St • 212-873-3400	Oldest museum in New York City. And most bizarre hyphenation.
The Dakota	Central Park W & 72nd St	Classic Central Park West apartment building, designed by Henry J Hardenbergh.
The Dorilton	Broadway & 71st St	Cool, weird arch. Flashy facade.
The Majestic	115 Central Park W	Great brick by Chanin.
The San Remo	Central Park W & 74th St • 212-877-0300	Emery Roth's contribution to the Upper West Side skyline.

Map 15 • Upper East Side (Lower)

Abigail Adams Smith Museum	421 E 61st St • 212-838-6878	Nice old building.
Asia Society	725 Park Ave • 212-288-6400	Small-scale modernism.
Frick Collection	1 E 70th St • 212-288-0700	Lots of furniture.
Metropolitan Museum of Art	1000 Fifth Ave • 212-879-5500	The mother of all art musuems. Check out: temple, roof garden, Clyfford Still room, baseball cards.
New York Society Library	53 E 79th St • 212-288-6900	A 250-year-old library. Wow!
Temple Emanu-El	1 E 65th St • 212-744-1400	Way cool building.
Whitney Museum of American Art	945 Madison Ave • 212-570-3676	It almost always has something to talk about—not the least of which is their typically controversial Biennial.

Map 16 • Upper West Side (Upper)

Pomander Walk	261 W 94th St	Great little hideaway.
Soldiers and Sailors Monument	Riverside Dr & 89th St	It's been seen in "Law & Order," along with everything else in New York.

Map 17 • Upper East Side (Upper)

Cooper-Hewitt Museum	2 E 91st St • 212-860-8400	Great design shows; run by the Smithsonian.
Gracie Mansion	Carl Schulz Park & 88th St • 212-570-4751	Our own Buckingham Palace, and right above the FDR Dr.
Jewish Museum	1109 Fifth Ave • 212-423-3200	A musem devoted to Jewish history and culture.
Museo del Barrio	Fifth Ave & 104th St • 212-831-7272	NY's only Latino museum.
Museum of the City of New York	Fifth Ave & 103rd St • 212-534-1672	Nice space, but we were excited when they were going to move to the Tweed Courthouse.
Solomon R Guggenheim Museum	1071 Fifth Ave • 212-423-3500	Wright's only building in NYC, but it's one of the best.
St Nicholas Russian Orthodox Cathedral	15 E 97th St	This UES Cathedral, built in 1902, remains the center of Russion Orthodoxy in the US.

Map 18 • Columbia / Morningside Heights

Cathedral of St John the Divine	112th St & Amsterdam Ave • 212-316-7540	Our favorite cathedral. Completely unfinished and usually in disarray—just the way we like it. Go for the vertical tour.
City College	138th St & Convent Ave • 212-650-7000	Once known for academic excellence and free tuition, now has open admissions and hefty fees. Peaceful gothic campus.
Columbia University	116th St & Broadway • 212-854-1754	A nice little sanctuary amid the roiling masses.
Grant's Tomb	122nd St & Riverside Dr • 212-666-1640	A totally underrated experience—interesting, great grounds.
Riverside Church	490 Riverside Dr	Gothic, great views from 392-foot tower.

Map 19 • Harlem (Lower)

Apollo Theater	253 W 125th St • 212-749-5838	Live: the Hardest Working Man in Show Business, Mr. James Brown!
Duke Ellington Circle	110th St & Fifth Ave	Nice monument to a jazz great.
Harlem YMCA	180 W 135th St • 212-281-4100	Sidney Poitier, James Earl Jones, and Eartha Kitt have performed at this Y's "Little Theatre".
Langston Hughes Place	20 E 127th St • 212-534-5992	Where the prolific poet lived & worked.
Marcus Garvey Park	E 120-124th Sts & Madison Ave • 212-201-PARK	Appeallingly mountainous park.
Sylvia's	328 Lenox Ave • 212-996-0660	It's worth the trip.

Map 20 • El Barrio

Church of Our Lady of Mt Carmel	448 E 115th St • 212-534-0681	The first Italian parish in NYC.
Harlem Courthouse	170 E 121st St	Great Romanesque Revival architecture.
Keith Haring "Crack is Wack" Mural	Second Ave & 127th St	Keith was right.
Harlem Fire Watch Tower	Marcus Garvey Park	It's tall.

Map 21 • Manhattanville / Hamilton Heights

Audubon Terrace	Broadway & W 155th St	American Academy and Institute of Arts and Letters, American Numismatic Museum, Hispanic Society of America. Pleasant, if lonely, Beaux Arts complex. What's it doing here?
Hamilton Grange National Memorial	287 Convent Ave • 212-368-9133	Elegant buildings on a serene street.
Hamilton Heights Historic District	W 141st- W 145th Sts & Convent Ave	Hamilton's old dig moved here from its original location and now facing the wrong way. Damn those Jeffersonians.
Trinity Church Cemetery's Graveyard of Heroes	3699 Broadway	Hilly, almost countryish cemetery.

Map 22 • Harlem (Upper)

Abyssinian Baptist Church	132 Odell Clark Pl • 212-862-7474	NY's oldest black congregation.
St Nicholas Historic District	202 W 138th St	Beautiful neo-Georgian townhouses.
The Dunbar Houses	Frederick Douglass Blvd & W 149th St	Historic multi-family houses.

Map 23 • Washington Heights

George Washington Bridge	W 178th St	Try to see it when it's lit up. Drive down from Riverdale on the Henry Hudson at night and you'll understand.
Morris-Jumel Mansion	Edgecombe Ave & 161st St • 212-923-8008	The oldest building in New York, at least until someone changes it again.
Sylvan Terrace	b/w Jumel Ter & St Nicholas Ave	The most un-Manhattanlike place in all the world.
The Little Red Lighthouse	under the George Washington Bridge 212-304-2365	It's there, really!

Map 24 • Fort George / Fort Tryon

Fort Tyron Park	Ft Washington Ave	A totally beautiful and scenic park on New York's north edge.

Map 25 • Inwood

Dyckman House	4881 Broadway • 212-643-1527	Needs some work.
The Cloisters	Ft Tryon Park • 212-923-3700	The Met's storehouse of medieval art. Great herb garden, nice views.

Map 26 • Astoria

Socrates Sculpture Park	Broadway & Vernon Blvd	Constantly revolving sculpture collection resides on this former illegal dump. Great view of the Manhattan skyline from the river.

Map 27 • Long Island City

American Museum of the Moving Image	35th Ave & 36th St • 718-784-4520	Educates about the art, history, technique, and technology of film, television, and digital media.
Center for the Holographic Arts	45-10 Court Sq • 718-784-5065	Promotes the art of holography.
Citicorp Building	1 Court Sq	This 48-story structure in blue glass is the tallest New York building outside of Manhattan.
Kaufman-Astoria Studios	34-12 36th St • 718-706-5300	The US's largest studio outside of Los Angeles sits on a 13-acre plot with 8 sound stages. Films made here include *Scent of a Woman* and *The Secret of My Success*. Television's *The Cosby Show* and *Sesame Street* were also taped here.
MoMA QNS	33rd St & Queens Blvd • 212-708-9400	Temporary location of MoMA while its better half was renovated.
NY Center for Media Arts	45-12 Davis St • 718-472-9414	Educates on traditional and modern artistic methods.
PS1	22-25 Jackson Ave • 718-784-2084	A contemporary art center partly owned by MoMA.
Silvercup Studios	42-22 22nd St • 718-906-2000	Former bakery that now produces hundreds of commercials, films, television shows, and music videos.
The Isamu Noguchi Museum	36-01 43rd Ave • 718-204-7088	Showcases the work of Isamu Noguchi.
The Space	42-16 West St • 718-706-6697	Organization to encourage public arts in Long Island City.

Map 30 • Brooklyn Heights / DUMBO / Downtown

Brooklyn Borough Hall	209 Joralemon St • 718-802-3700	Built in the 1940s, this Greek Revival landmark was employed as the official City Hall when Brooklyn was an independent city.
Brooklyn Bridge	Adams St & East River	Opened in 1883, the Brooklyn Bridge is the oldest NYC bridge open to vehicles and pedestrians and is still considered one of the most beautiful bridges ever built.

Brooklyn Conservatory of Music	58 17th Ave • 718-622-3957	This five-story Victorian Gothic brownstone in Park Slope is home to the conservatory of music, which hosts regular performances by its students and guest artists.
Brooklyn Heights Promenade		Killer views of lower Manhattan.
Brooklyn Historical Society	128 Pierrepoint St • 718-254-9830	This newly renovated historical landmark building houses a new exhibition, *Brooklyn Works: 300 Years of Making a Living in Brooklyn*.
Brooklyn Ice Cream Factory	Fulton Ferry Pier • 718-246-3963	Old fashioned ice cream beneath the bridge.
Juniors Cheesecakes	386 Flatbush Ave • 1-800-458-6467	With cheesecake and serving 4,000 Brooklyn patrons daily.
New York Transit Museum	Boerum Pl & Schermerhorn St • 718-243-8601	Housed appropriately in an old subway station, the museum exhibits old subway cars, photographs and maps from bygone eras.
Plymouth Church of Pilgrims	56 Cranberry St • 718-624-4743	The original site of the pilgrim church in Brooklyn.

Map 31 • Fort Greene

Brooklyn Academy of Music	30 Lafayette Ave • 718-636-4100	BAM holds the title of America's oldest continuously operating performing arts center. Performances include opera, music, dance, drama and film.
Fort Greene Park	Dekalb Ave & Washington Park	It just has a great feel!
Long Island Railroad Station	Hanson Pl & Flatbush Ave • 718-217-5477	A low red brick building which is used by more than 20 million passengers annually.
Williamsburg Savings Bank Building	1 Hanson Pl	Completed in 1929, it is still the tallest structure in Brooklyn.

Map 32 • Cobble Hill / Boerum Hill / Carroll Gardens

Gowanus Canal		Brooklyn's answer to the Seine.
Red Hook Grain Terminal		Abandoned grain terminal that looks really cool.

Map 33 • Park Slope / Prospect Heights

Brooklyn Botanic Garden	900 Washington Ave • 718-623-7200	More than 12 individual gardens and 12,000 species of plants inhabit this peaceful public garden.
Brooklyn Museum of Art	200 Eastern Pkwy • 718-638-5000	Excellent permanent collection including a highly regarded collection of American paintings. Check the website for temporary exhibitions - www.brooklynart.org
Brooklyn Tabernacle	290 Flatbush Ave • 718-783-0942	Home of the Grammy Award-winning Brooklyn Tabernacle Choir.
Grand Army Plaza	Flatbush Ave & Plaza St	Site of John H. Duncan's Soldiers' and Sailors' Memorial Arch. At the northern entrance to Prospect Park.
Park Slope Food Co-op	782 Union St • 718-622-0560	One of the largest food co-ops in the country. Best place to buy groceries in all of New York!
Prospect Park Wildlife Center	450 Flatbush Ave • 718-399-7339	Originally a menagerie at the site in the late 1800s, the newly refurbished wildlife center was opened in 1993 and is home to approximately 400 animals.
The Old Stone House	336 3rd St • 718-768-3195	A 1930s replica of a Dutch stone farmhouse tells the story

Map 34 • Hoboken

First recorded baseball game	Elysian Fields	On 19 June 1846, the first officially recorded, organized baseball match was played on Hoboken's Elysian Fields with the New York Base Ball Club defeating the Knickerbockers 23-1.
Frank Sinatra's Childhood House Location	415 Monroe St	A brick arch built by fans marks the spot where Sinatra spent his childhood.
Hoboken Historical Museum	1301 Hudson St • 201-656-2240	The zipper was invented in Hoboken.

Map 35 • Jersey City

Colgate Clock	105 Hudson St	The world's largest clock's dial is 50 feet in diameter and has a minute hand weighing 2,200 pounds.
Powerhouse	344 Washington Blvd	This coal-powered railway powerhouse connected New York to New Jersey by train via Hudson River tunnels. Today the Powerhouse is being considered for residential development.

Battery Park City

Manhattan Sailing Club	North Cove • 212-786-3323	Membership required.
Mercantile Exchange	1 North End Ave	A great, big financial building in Battery Park.
Police Memorial	Liberty St & South End Ave	A fountain commemorating the career of a policeman and those killed in the line of duty.
The Irish Hunger Memorial	corner of Vesey St & North End Ave	A memorial to the "The Great Irish Famine & Migration" to the US in the mid-1800s.
The Real World		Tom Otterness sculptures of a tiny, whimsical society. Cooler than Smurfs.
Winter Garden	37 Vesey St	A cavernous marble and glass atrium.

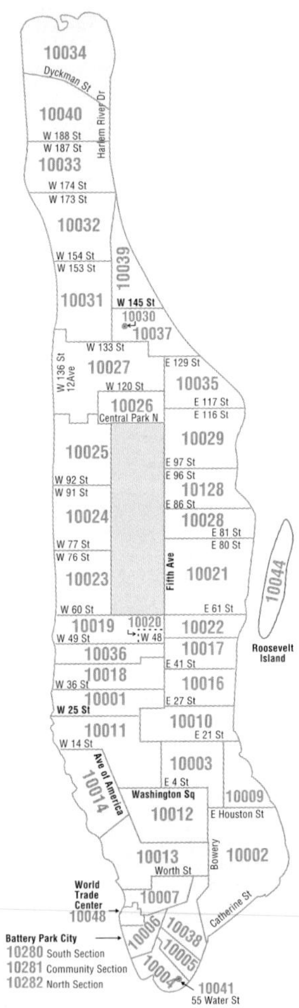

The phone number for all branches is now one central number: 800-275-8777.

Branch	Address	Zip	Map
Ansonia	178 Columbus Ave	10023	14
Audubon	511 W 165th St	10032	23
Bowling Green	25 Broadway	10004	1
Bryant	23 W 43rd St	10036	12
Canal Street	350 Canal St	10013	2
Canal Street Retail	6 Doyers St	10013	3
Cathedral	215 W 104th St	10025	16
Cherokee	1483 York Ave	10021	15
College Station	217 W 140th St	10030	22
Colonial Park	99 Macombs Pl	10039	22
Columbia University	534 W 112th St	10025	18
Columbus Circle	27 W 60th St	10023	14
Cooper	93 Fourth Ave	10003	6
Dag Hammarskjold	884 Second Ave	10017	13
Empire State	19 W 33rd St	10118	9
Filmfest Contract Unit	1594 York Ave	10028	15
Fort George	4558 Broadway	10040	24
Fort Washington	556 W 158th St	10032	21
Franklin D Roosevelt	909 Third Ave	10022	13
Gracie	229 E 85th St	10028	15
Grand Central Station	450 Lexington Ave	10017	13
Greeley Square	39 W 31st St	10001	9
Hamilton Grange	521 W 146th St	10031	21
Hell Gate	153 E 110th St	10029	20
Inwood Post Office	90 Vermilyea Ave	10034	25
J A Farley General	441 Eighth Ave	10001	8
Knickerbocker	128 East Broadway	10002	4
Lenox Hill	217 E 70th St	10021	15
Lincolnton	2266 Fifth Ave	10037	22
Madison Square	149 E 23rd St	10010	10
Manhattanville	365 W 125th St	10027	18
Midtown	223 W 38th St	10018	9
Morningside	232 W 116th St	10026	19
Murray Hill	205 E 36th St	10016	10
Murray Hill Finance	115 E 34th St	10016	10
Old Chelsea	217 W 18th St	10011	9
Park West	693 Columbus Ave	10025	16
Patchin	70 W 10th St	10011	6
Peck Slip	1 Peck Slip	10038	3
Peter Stuyvesant	432 E 14th St	10009	7
Pitt Station	185 Clinton St	10002	4
Planetarium	127 W 83rd St	10024	14
Port Authority Station	76 Ninth Ave	10011	8
Prince Station	124 Greene St	10012	6
Radio City	322 W 52nd St	10019	11
Rockefeller Center	610 Fifth Ave	10020	12
Roosevelt Island	694 Main St	10044	p202
Times Square	340 W 42nd St	10036	11
Tompkins Square	244 E 3rd St	10009	7
Triborough	167 E 124th St	10035	20
Village	201 Varick St	10014	5
Wall Street	73 Pine St	10005	1
Washington Bridge	555 W 180th St	10033	23
West Village	527 Hudson St	10014	5
Yorkville	1617 Third Ave	10128	17

General Information • **Shipping Locations**

The latest FedEx dropoffs are at 9:30 pm Monday-Friday at 880 Third Ave (Map 13), 606 W 49th St and 621 W 48th St (Map 11), 130 Leroy (Map 5) and 537 W 33rd St (Map 8). However, many Manhattan FedEx delivery trucks have a drop-off slot on the side of the truck itself, in case you're on your way to a service center at 9:15 pm and see one. For UPS dropoffs, try one of the UPS Centers located at 79 Madison Ave (Map 9), 1410 Broadway (Map 9) or 80 Broad St (Map 1). All three are open until 9 pm. The latest Airborne Express/DHL drop-offs can be made at 33 E 33rd St (Map 9) and Pier 40 (Map 5), which both close at 9 pm. Please note that locations, hours of operation, and pickup times may change. If in doubt, call 1-800-Go-FedEx or visit www.fedex.com for Fedex services, call 1-800-PICKUPS or visit www.ups.com for UPS services. Airborne Express and DHL recently joined forces, so for information you should call 1-800-CALL-DHL or visit www.dhl-usa.com.

The column marked with a * is pick-up time (pm). Where multiple pick-up times appear, they correspond to the order of the columns.

Map 1 • Financial District

Map 1 • Financial District		*	F	U	A
Drop Box	125 Maiden Ln	8:00/7:30	■		■
Drop Box	20 Exchange Pl	7:45			■
Drop Box	90 William St	9:00/5:00		■	■
Drop Box	1 Battery Park Plz	8:30	■		
Drop Box	17 Battery Pl	8:30/8:00/7:00	■	■	■
FedEx Service Center	40 Broad St	9:15	■		
Drop Box	85 Broad St	8:30	■		
Drop Box	90 Broad St	8:30	■		
Drop Box	11 Broadway	8:00	■		
Drop Box	26 Broadway	8:30/8:00/7:00	■	■	■
FedEx Service Center	55 Broadway	9:00	■		
Drop Box	120 Broadway	8:00	■		
Drop Box	150 Broadway	8:30	■		
Drop Box	1 Chase Manhattan Plz	8:00	■		
Drop Box	2 Chase Manhattan Plz	8:00	■		
Drop Box	40 Exchange Pl	8:00/7:45	■	■	
Global Express	50 Fulton St	6:00	■		
Drop Box	7 Hanover Sq	8:00/6:30	■	■	
Drop Box	10 Hanover Sq	8:30	■		
Postnet	29 John St	6:00	■	■	
Drop Box	33 Liberty St	7:30	■		
Drop Box	180 Maiden Lane	8:00	■		
Drop Box	1 New York Plz	8:30	■		
Drop Box	4 New York Plz	8:00	■		■
Drop Box	32 Old Slip	8:30	■		
Post Office	73 Pine St	5:00	■		
Drop Box	88 Pine St	8:30/7:30	■	■	
Drop Box	40 Rector St	7:30	■		
Drop Box	1 State St Plz	8:30	■		
Complete Mail Centers	28 Vesey St	6:30/7:00	■		■
Drop Box	200 Vesey St	7:00			■
Drop Box	14 Wall St	8:30/8:00	■	■	
Drop Box	60 Wall St	8:00/7:00	■		■
Drop Box	67 Wall St	8:30	■		
Drop Box	95 Wall St	8:00	■		
Kinko's	100 Wall St	8:00	■		
FedEx Service Center	110 Wall St	9:00	■		
Drop Box	175 Water St	7:00	■		
FedEx Service Center	100 William	9:00	■		
Kinko's	110 William St	7:30	■		
UPS Air Service Center	80 Broad St	9:00		■	
Drop Box	42 Broadway	8:00		■	
Drop Box	111 Broadway	8:00		■	
Drop Box	115 Broadway	8:00		■	
Drop Box	243 Pearl St	7:00		■	
Drop Box	45 Wall St	8:00		■	
Drop Box	130 William St	7:45		■	

Map 2 • TriBeCa

Map 2 • TriBeCa		*	F	U	A
Drop Box	100 Sixth Ave	8:00	■	■	
Drop Box	32 Sixth Ave	9:00	■		
Mail Boxes Etc	295 Greenwich St	5:30/6:30/6:00	■	■	■
Drop Box	443 Greenwich St	8:00		■	
Drop Box	145 Hudson St	7:30	■	■	
Drop Box	75 Varick St	8:30		■	
Express Color	285 West Broadway	6:00	■		
Mail Boxes Etc	305 West Broadway	5:30		■	

Map 3 • City Hall / Chinatown

Map 3 • City Hall / Chinatown		*	F	U	A
FedEx Service Center	4 Barclay St	9:00	■		
Drop Box	225 Broadway	8:00		■	
Drop Box	299 Broadway	7:00		■	
Drop Box	361 Broadway	6:30/7:00/8:00	■	■	■
Billion Fortune Corp	383 Broadway	6:00		■	
JAC Services	387 Broadway	7:00		■	
Drop Box	401 Broadway	8:30/8:30/7:00	■	■	■
Drop Box	434 Broadway	8:00	■		
Staples	488 Broadway	6:00	■		
Post Office	6 Doyers St	4:30	■		
Kinko's	105 Duane St	8:00	■		
Grand Postal Center	115 Eldridge St & Grand St	5:30/5:30/6:00	■	■	■
Q's Global	25 Howard St	6:00	■		
Howard Shipping & Trading	33 Howard St	6:00	■		
Speedy Shipping Svs	150 Lafayette St	8:00		■	■
Drop Box	11 Park Pl	8:30	■	■	
Post Office	1 Peck Slip	4:30	■		

Map 4 • Lower East Side

Map 4 • Lower East Side		*	F	U	A
Kinko's	191 Madison St	7:00	■		

Map 5 • West Village

Map 5 • West Village		*	F	U	A
Airborne Svc Ctr	Pier 40 Westside Hwy	9:00			■
Mail Boxes Etc	511 Sixth Ave	6:00/6:30/6:00	■	■	■
Drop Box	80 Eighth Ave	8:00	■	■	
Mail Boxes Etc	315 Bleecker St	6:00/7:00/5:00	■	■	■
Your Neighborhood Office	332 Bleecker St	7:00	■	■	
Drop Box	139 Charles St	7:30	■		
UPS Customer Counter	522 Greenwich St	8:00		■	
Drop Box	315 Hudson St	7:30	■	■	
Drop Box	350 Hudson St	8:30/8:00	■	■	
Drop Box	375 Hudson St	8:30/8:00	■	■	
Drop Box	421 Hudson St	7:00		■	
Village Copy & Computer	520 Hudson St	7:00/6:00	■	■	
FedEx Service Center	130 Leroy St	9:30	■		
Drop Box	95 Morton St	8:00	■		
Drop Box	12 Vandam St	6:30		■	
Drop Box	180 Varick St	8:00	■		
Drop Box	201 Varick St	8:00	■		
Mail Boxes Etc	302 W 12th St	5:00/6:30	■	■	
FedEx Service Center	229 W 4th St	9:00	■		

Map 6 • Washington Sq./SoHo

Map 6 • Washington Sq./SoHo		*	F	U	A
Mail Boxes Etc	168 Second Ave	5:30		■	
Readers Stationery	61 Fourth Ave	5:00	■		
Staples	5-9 Union Sq W	7:00	■		
Kinko's	21 Astor Place	8:00	■		
Drop Box	580 Broadway	8:00	■		
Drop Box	588 Broadway	7:00		■	
Office Depot	686 Broadway	6:00		■	
Drop Box	715 Broadway	9:00		■	
Drop Box	799 Broadway	8:00	■	■	
United Shipping & Packaging	200 E 10th St	6:00/6:30		■	■
Mail Boxes Etc	111 E 14th St	6:00		■	
Drop Box	9 E 4th St	8:00	■		

Map 6 • Washington Sq./SoHo – continued

Location	Address	*	F	U	A
Mail Boxes Etc	7 E 8th St	7:00/6:00		■	
Post All	61 E 8th St	6:00		■	
Drop Box - Yeshiva Univ	55 Fifth Ave	8:00		■	
Drop Box	92 Greene St	8:00		■	
Post Office	124 Greene St	4:30	■		
Drop Box	252 Greene St	7:00	■		
Drop Box	225 Lafayette St	8:00/7:00		■	
Drop Box	270 Lafayette St	8:00	■	■	
Postal	341 Lafayette St	5:00		■	
Drop Box	375 Lafayette St	8:30	■		
Village Postal Center	532 LaGuardia Pl	5:30		■	
Drop Box	547 LaGuardia Pl	9:00		■	
Drop Box	196 Mercer St	7:00		■	
FedEx Service Center	70 Spring St	9:00	■		
Drop Box	4 Washington Pl	9:00		■	
Drop Box - NYU	14A Washington Pl	8:00		■	
Drop Box	70 Washington Sq S	9:00		■	

Map 7 • East Village

Location	Address	*	F	U	A
Little Village Postal	151 First Ave	6:00/5:00	■		
FedEx Service Center	250 E Houston St	9:00	■		
Kinko's	250 E Houston St	8:30	■		

Map 8 • Chelsea

Location	Address	*	F	U	A
Post Office	234 Tenth Ave	4:30	■		
Drop Box	111 Eighth Ave	8:00/7:00/8:00	■		
Mail Boxes Etc	245 Eighth Ave	6:00/5:00	■	■	
Drop Box	322 Eighth Ave	8:00/7:00	■	■	
Drop Box	421 Eighth Ave	8:00	■		
Drop Box	505 Eighth Ave	8:00	■		
Drop Box	519 Eighth Ave	8:00	■		
Drop Box	520 Eighth Ave	8:00	■		
Drop Box	545 Eighth Ave	8:00	■	■	
Drop Box	75 Ninth Ave	8:00	■		
Drop Box	88 Tenth Ave	7:00		■	
Drop Box	450 W 15th St	8:30	■		
Drop Box	437 W 16th St	7:00		■	
Drop Box	508 W 26th St	8:00	■		
Drop Box	547 W 27th St	7:30	■		
Drop Box	360 W 31st St	7:00/8:00		■	■
Drop Box	380 W 33rd St	8:00	■		
Drop Box	450 W 33rd St	6:00	■		
FedEx Service Center	537 W 33rd St	9:30	■		
Drop Box	460 W 34th St	7:00		■	
Drop Box	538 W 34th St	9:00	■		
Mail Boxes Etc	655 W 34th St	5:00	■		

Map 9 • Flatiron

Location	Address	*	F	U	A
Drop Box	45 W 18th St	8:00	■	■	
Post Office	223-241 W 38th St	5:00	■		
Drop Box	220 Fifth Ave	8:00/7:00	■	■	
Drop Box	230 Fifth Ave	8:00/7:30	■	■	
Drop Box	330 Fifth Ave	6:00	■		
FedEx Service Center	350 Fifth Ave	9:00/7:30	■		■
Drop Box	366 Fifth Ave	6:00	■	■	
Drop Box	390 Fifth Ave	8:00	■		
Kinko's	650 Sixth Ave	8:00	■		
Drop Box	875 Sixth Ave	8:00	■		
Mail Boxes Etc	130 Seventh Ave	6:45		■	
Kinko's	245 Seventh Ave	8:00	■		
FedEx Service Center	326 Seventh Ave	9:00	■		
FedEx Service Center	390 Seventh Ave	9:00	■		
Drop Box	450 Seventh Ave	8:00	■	■	
Drop Box	463 Seventh Ave	8:00	■	■	
Drop Box	469 Seventh Ave	8:00	■		
Drop Box	485 Seventh Ave	8:00	■		
FedEx Service Center	500 Seventh Ave	9:00	■		
FedEx Service Center	525 Seventh Ave	9:00	■		
Mobile Car (Air only)	Seventh Ave & 33rd St	6:00		■	
Mobile Car (Air only)	Seventh Ave b/w 34th & 35th	7:30		■	
Drop Box	1133 Broadway	8:00	■	■	
Drop Box	1182 Broadway	7:00		■	
Drop Box	1225 Broadway	8:00		■	
Drop Box	1250 Broadway	7:00	■	■	
FedEx Service Center	1350 Broadway	9:00	■		
Drop Box	1370 Broadway	7:30/7:00	■	■	
Drop Box	1372 Broadway	6:00			■
Drop Box	1385 Broadway	7:30/7:00	■	■	
Drop Box	1407 Broadway	7:00	■	■	
UPS Air Service Center	1410 Broadway	9:00		■	
FedEx Service Center	20 E 20th St	9:00	■		
FedEx Service Center	8 E 23rd St	9:00	■		
Drop Box	4 E 24th St	8:00	■		
Drop Box	28 E 28th St	7:00	■		
Drop Box	37 E 28th St	7:00	■		
Drop Box	10 E 30th St	7:00		■	
Drop Box	35 E 32nd St	7:00		■	
Drop Box	44 E 32nd St	7:00		■	
Drop Box	33 E 33rd St	9:00			■
Staples	16 E 34th St	6:00	■		
Drop Box	225 Fifth Ave	8:00		■	
Drop Box	11 Madison Ave	8:00		■	
Drop Box	41 Madison Ave	8:00	■		
UPS Air Service Center	79 Madison Ave	9:00		■	
FedEx Service Center	149 Madison Ave	9:00	■		
Kinko's	191 Madison Ave	9:00	■		
Mail Boxes Etc	244 Madison Ave	5:30		■	
FedEx Service Center	261 Madison Ave	9:00	■		
Drop Box	315 Park Ave S	7:30		■	
Drop Box	21 Penn Plz	8:00	■		
FedEx Service Center	1 Penn Plz	9:00	■		
Drop Box	5 Penn Plz	7:30/8:00/8:00	■	■	■
Drop Box	275 Seventh Ave	7:00		■	
Drop Box	499 Seventh Ave	7:00		■	
Drop Box	625 Sixth Ave	8:00		■	
Sidney Bernstein	855 Sixth Ave	8:00		■	
Post Office	217 W 18th St	5:00	■		
Drop Box	233 W 18th St	5:00	■		
Drop Box	220 W 19th St	5:00/7:00	■	■	
Drop Box	16 W 22nd St	7:00		■	
Mail Boxes Etc	101 W 23rd St	5:00		■	
Drop Box	207 W 25th St	8:00	■		
Drop Box	121 W 27th St	8:00/7:00	■	■	
Drop Box	39 W 31st St	4:30	■		
Drop Box	132 W 31st St	7:30/7:00	■	■	
Shipping Factory	22 W 32nd St	6:00		■	
Post Office	19 W 33rd St	4:30	■		
Drop Box	100 W 33rd St	7:00	■	■	
FedEx Service Center	125 W 33rd St	9:00	■		
Drop Box	19 W 34th St	8:00/7:00		■	■
Drop Box	50 W 34th St	7:00	■	■	
Drop Box	225 W 34th St	8:00	■		
FedEx Service Center	157 W 35th St	9:00	■		
Drop Box	213 W 35th St	7:00		■	
Drop Box	5 W 37th St	7:30	■		
FedEx Service Center	112 W 39th St	9:00	■		
Drop Box	45 W18th St	7:30	■		

Map 10 • Murray Hill

Location	Address	*	F	U	A
The Villager	338 First Ave	7:00	■		
Emerald Too	346 First Ave	7:00/6:00	■	■	
Drop Box - NYU	530 First Ave	8:00	■	■	
Drop Box	545 First Ave	8:00/7:30/8:00	■	■	■
Drop Box	550 First Ave	8:00		■	
Drop Box	660 First Ave	6:00	■		
Mail Boxes Etc	163 Third Ave	6:00	■	■	
Mail Boxes Etc	350 Third Ave	6:00	■	■	
Mail Boxes Etc	527 Third Ave	6:00	■		
FedEx Service Center	600 Third Ave	9:00	■		
Drop Box	111 E 18th St	8:00	■		
Back Office NYC	345 E 18th St	7:00/5:00	■	■	
Drop Box	220 E 23rd St	8:00	■		
Drop Box	425 E 25th St	7:30	■		
FedEx Service Center	108 E 28th St	9:00	■		
Drop Box	227 E 30th St	5:00		■	
Drop Box	192 Lexington Ave	7:00	■		
Drop Box	200 Lexington Ave	8:00/7:00	■	■	
Drop Box	215 Lexington Ave	7:00		■	
FedEx Service Center	2 Park Ave	9:00/8:00	■	■	
Drop Box	3 Park Ave	7:00/8:00	■	■	
FedEx Service Center	90 Park Ave	9:00	■		
Pak Mail	99 Park Ave	6:00		■	
FedEx Service Center	230 Park Ave	8:30	■		
Drop Box	200 Park Ave S	8:15	■		
Drop Box	225 Park Ave S	7:30		■	
Drop Box	257 Park Ave S	8:00	■		
Mail Boxes Etc	303 Park Ave S	6:30/7:15	■	■	
Drop Box	345 Park Ave S	8:00	■		
Staples	345 Park Ave S	6:00	■		
Drop Box	444 Park Ave S	7:00		■	

Location	Address	Hours	F	U	A
Drop Box	475 Park Ave S	8:00	■	■	
Office Depot	542 Second Ave	8:00		■	
FedEx Service Center	4 Union Sq E	9:00	■		
Drop Box	30 Waterside Plz	8:00/7:00	■	■	

Map 11 • Hell's Kitchen

Location	Address	*	F	U	A
Drop Box	630 Ninth Ave	8:00/7:00/8:00	■	■	■
Mail Boxes Etc	676 A Ninth Ave	5:00/6:30/5:30	■	■	■
Drop Box	330 W 42nd St	8:00		■	
Post Office	340 W 42nd St	4:30	■		
FedEx Service Center	560 W 42nd St	9:30	■		
Drop Box	315 W 43rd St	6:00		■	
UPS Service Center	601 W 43rd St	8:00		■	
FedEx Service Center	606 W 49th St	9:30	■		
FedEx Service Center	621 W 48th St	9:30	■		
Post Office	322 W 52nd St	7:00	■		
Drop Box	429 W 53rd St	8:00	■		
Drop Box	411 W 55th St	7:00		■	
Mail Boxes Etc	331 W 57th St	6:00/6:30	■	■	
Drop Box	432 W 58th St	6:00	■		

Map 12 • Midtown

Location	Address	*	F	U	A
Drop Box	489 Fifth Ave	7:00		■	
Drop Box	500 Fifth Ave	8:00		■	
Post Office	610 Fifth Ave	4:30	■		
Mail Boxes Etc	666 Fifth Ave	5:30/7:00/6:00	■	■	■
Drop Box	712 Fifth Ave	8:00	■		
Drop Box	745 Fifth Ave	8:30/8:00	■	■	
Staples	1065 Sixth Ave	7:00	■	■	
Drop Box	1095 Sixth Ave	8:00			■
FedEx Service Center	1120 Sixth Ave	9:00	■		
Drop Box	1133 Sixth Ave	7:00		■	
FedEx Service Center	1211 Sixth Ave	9:00	■		
Kinko's	1211 Sixth Ave	8:30/8:00	■		■
FedEx Service Center	1221 Sixth Ave	9:00/8:00	■		■
Drop Box	1230 Sixth Ave	8:30	■		
Drop Box	1285 Sixth Ave	8:00	■		
FedEx Service Center	1290 Sixth Ave	9:00/8:00	■	■	
Drop Box	1325 Sixth Ave	8:30	■		
Drop Box	1350 Sixth Ave	8:00	■		
Drop Box	1370 Sixth Ave	8:00	■	■	
Drop Box	787 Seventh Ave	7:45	■		
Drop Box	825 Eighth Ave	8:00/7:45	■	■	
FedEx Service Center	980 Eighth Ave	9:00	■		
Mobile Car Fashion (Air)	Seventh Ave & 40th St	7:00		■	
FedEx Service Center	1440 Broadway	9:00	■		
Drop Box	1441 Broadway	7:00		■	
Drop Box	1466 Broadway	8:00	■	■	
Drop Box	1500 Broadway	8:00/7:00/8:00	■	■	■
Drop Box	1501 Broadway	8:00	■		
Drop Box	1515 Broadway	8:30	■		
Drop Box	1619 Broadway	7:00		■	
Drop Box	1700 Broadway	8:00	■	■	
Drop Box	1775 Broadway	8:00	■		■
Drop Box	1790 Broadway	8:00		■	
Kinko's	240 Central Park S	8:00	■		
Drop Box	10 E 40th St	8:00/7:00	■	■	
Drop Box	12 E 41st St	6:30		■	
Drop Box	6 E 43rd St	8:00	■	■	
FedEx Service Center	51 E 44th St	9:00	■		
Kinko's	16 E 52nd St	8:30/7:30	■	■	
FedEx Service Center	10 E 53rd St	9:00	■		
Drop Box	3 E 54th St	8:00	■		
La Boutique	2 E 55th St	7:00	■		
Office Depot	521 Fifth Ave	6:30		■	
Drop Box	575 Fifth Ave	8:00		■	
Drop Box	767 Fifth Ave	8:00		■	
Drop Box	330 Madison Ave	7:00		■	
Drop Box	335 Madison Ave	8:00/7:00	■	■	
FedEx Service Center	437 Madison Ave	9:00	■		
Drop Box	444 Madison Ave	8:30	■	■	
Drop Box	477 Madison Ave	8:00	■		
Drop Box	488 Madison Ave	8:30	■		
Drop Box	550 Madison Ave	7:30	■		
Drop Box	555 Madison Ave	8:00	■		
Drop Box	575 Madison Ave	8:00/7:30	■	■	
Drop Box	590 Madison Ave	7:30/8:00	■	■	
Drop Box	600 Madison Ave	8:30/7:00	■	■	
The UPS Store	1 Rockefeller Plz	8:00		■	
Drop Box	1155 Sixth Ave	7:00		■	
FedEx Service Center	60 W 40th St	9:00	■		
Drop Box	218 W 40th St	7:00		■	
FedEx Service Center	43 W 42nd St	9:00	■		
Post Office	23 W 43rd St	4:30	■		
Airborne Staffed Facility	108 W 43rd St	8:00			■
Drop Box	120 W 45th St	8:00	■		
FedEx Service Center	6 W 48th St	9:00	■		
Drop Box	10 W 48th St	7:00		■	
FedEx Service Center	135 W 50th St	9:00	■		
Drop Box	51 W 52nd St	8:00	■		
FedEx Service Center	233 W 54th St	9:00	■		
Drop Box	156 W 56th St	7:30	■		
Staples	57 W 57th St	7:00	■		
Drop Box	152 W 57th St	8:00	■	■	■
FedEx Service Center	200 W 57th St	9:00	■		
Drop Box	224 W 57th St	6:00	■		
Drop Box	162 W 58th St	7:00		■	

Map 13 • East Midtown

Location	Address	*	F	U	A
Mail Boxes Etc	1040 First Ave	4:00/5:00	■	■	
Mail Boxes Etc	847A Second Ave	5:00/6:00	■	■	
Drop Box	630 Third Ave	8:00/7:30	■	■	
Drop Box	633 Third Ave	8:00/7:00	■	■	
FedEx Service Center	685 Third Ave	9:00	■		
Kinko's	747 Third Ave	8:00	■		
FedEx Service Center	750 Third Ave	7:00	■		
Drop Box	780 Third Ave	7:00		■	
Drop Box	805 Third Ave	5:00/8:00	■	■	
FedEx Service Center	880 Third Ave	9:30	■		
Drop Box	885 Third Ave	8:00	■		■
Post Office	909 Third Ave	6:30	■		
Drop Box	979 Third Ave	7:00	■	■	
Drop Box	60 E 42nd St	8:00		■	■
Drop Box	150 E 42nd St	7:00	■		
Staples	205 E 42nd St	6:00/6:30	■	■	
Drop Box	220 E 42nd St	7:30/7:00/8:00	■	■	■
Drop Box	211 E 43rd St	8:00/7:00	■	■	
Drop Box	228 E 45th St	7:00		■	
FedEx Service Center	305 E 46th St	9:00	■		
Kinko's	305 E 46th St	8:00	■		
Drop Box	45 E 49th St	5:00	■		
Kinko's	153 E 53rd St	7:00	■		
Drop Box	115 E 57th St	8:00		■	
Drop Box	135 E 57th St	7:00		■	
Drop Box	150 E 58th St	8:30/5:30	■	■	
Drop Box	55 E 59th St	8:00	■		
Drop Box	110 E 59th St	8:00	■		
Post Office	450 Lexington Ave	8:00	■		
Drop Box	353 Lexington Ave	7:30	■		
Drop Box	420 Lexington Ave	8:00	■	■	■
FedEx Service Center	480 Lexington Ave	9:00	■		
Drop Box	575 Lexington Ave	7:00	■	■	
FedEx Service Center	641 Lexington Ave	9:00	■		
Shoppers Parking	750 Lexington Ave	7:30		■	
Drop Box	100 Park Ave	8:00/7:00	■	■	
Drop Box	270 Park Ave	8:30	■		
Drop Box	280 Park Ave	8:30/8:00	■	■	
Drop Box	299 Park Ave	8:30	■		
Drop Box	300 Park Ave	8:00			■
Drop Box	350 Park Ave	7:30	■		
FedEx Service Center	405 Park Ave	9:00	■		
Staples	425 Park Ave	6:00	■		
Drop Box	450 Park Ave	7:00		■	
Drop Box	500 Park Ave	7:00	■	■	
Drop Box	622 Third Ave	7:30		■	
Drop Box	800 Third Ave	7:00		■	
Drop Box	875 Third Ave	7:30		■	
Drop Box	919 Third Ave	8:00		■	
Drop Box	809 United Nations Plz	7:00	■		
Drop Box	866 United Nations Plz	8:00/8:00/6:00	■	■	■

Map 14 • Upper West Side (Lower)

Name	Address	*	F	U	A
Mail Boxes Etc	163 Amsterdam Ave	6:00/6:00/5:30	■	■	■
Drop Box	517 Amsterdam Ave	7:00/7:00	■		
Drop Box	1995 Broadway	7:00		■	
Drop Box	2112 Broadway	7:30	■	■	
FedEx	2211 Broadway	9:00	■		
Copy Experts	2240 Broadway	7:30	■		
Mail Boxes Etc	2244 Broadway	6:00	■		■
Staples	2248 Broadway	5:00	■		
Post Office	168 Columbus Ave	6:30	■		
Mail Boxes Etc	459 Columbus Ave	6:00	■		
Post Office	27 W 60th St	3:30	■		
Drop Box	113 W 60th St	7:00		■	
Drop Box	211 W 61st St	6:00	■		
FedEx Service Center	156 W 72 St	9:00	■		
Mail Boxes Etc	119 W 72nd St	6:45		■	
Matrix Copy & Printing	140 W 72nd St	5:00		■	
Drop Box	155 W 72nd St	8:00		■	
Kinko's	221 W 72nd St	6:30	■		
Post Office	127 W 83rd St	6:00	■		
The Padded Wagon	215 W 85th St	5:00	■		
Drop Box	101 West End Ave	6:00	■		

Map 15 • Upper East Side (Lower)

Name	Address	*	F	U	A
Mail Boxes Etc	1275 First Ave	5:30/6:30	■	■	
Mail Boxes Etc	1461 First Ave	5:30	■	■	
Mail Boxes Etc	1562 First Ave	7:00		■	
Mail Boxes Etc	1173 Second Ave	6:00/5:00	■	■	
Drop Box	1343 Second Ave	8:30	■		
Big Apple Business Ctr	1467 Second Ave	6:00	■		
The Padded Wagon	1569 Second Ave	6:00	■		
Postal Express Bus	1382 Third Ave	6:00/4:30/6:30	■	■	■
Drop Box	425 E 61st St	5:30	■		
Drop Box	525 E 68th St	8:00	■		
Drop Box	201 E 69th St	7:00		■	
Drop Box	445 E 69th St	5:30	■		
Post Office	217 E 70th St	6:00	■		
Drop Box	428 E 72nd St	6:00	■		
Post Office	229 E 85th St	7:00	■		
Mail Boxes Etc	954 Lexington Ave	5:45/6:00	■	■	
Drop Box	968 Lexington Ave	6:00	■		
Kinko's	1122 Lexington Ave	8:30	■		
Mail Boxes Etc	1202 Lexington Ave	5:00/5:30	■	■	
Drop Box	650 Madison Ave	7:30	■		
Drop Box	667 Madison Ave	8:30/8:30/8:00	■	■	■
Drop Box	695 Park Ave	7:30	■		
Senderos	1471 Third Ave	5:00	■		
Drop Box	1275 York Ave	8:30	■		
Drop Box	1300 York Ave	8:30/7:00	■		■
Drop Box	1334 York Ave	7:15		■	
The Padded Wagon	1431 York Ave	6:00	■		

Map 16 • Upper West Side (Upper)

Name	Address	*	F	U	A
Copy Experts	2440 Broadway	7:30	■		
Mail Boxes Etc	2565 Broadway	6:00	■	■	
Mail Boxes Etc	2753 Broadway	6:30		■	
Columbia Copy Center	2790 Broadway	5:00		■	
Drop Box - Rapid Park	205 W 101st St	7:00		■	
Post Office	215 W 104th St	4:00	■		
Drop Box	70 W 86th St	8:00	■		
Foxy Graphic Services	211 W 92nd St	6:30	■		

Map 17 • Upper E Side/E Harlem

Name	Address	*	F	U	A
Mail Boxes Etc	1710 First Ave	6:00	■	■	
Compu Sign Plus	1598 Third Ave	5:00	■		
Post Office	1619 Third Ave	5:00	■		
Mail Boxes Etc	1636 Third Ave	9:00		■	
Drop Box	1 E 104th St	6:30	■		
FedEx Service Center	208 E 86th St	9:00	■		
Mail Boxes Etc	217 E 86th St	5:30		■	
Drop Box	225 E 95th St	8:30	■		
Staples	1280 Lexington Ave	8:00	■		
Mail Boxes Etc	1369 Madison Ave	6:00	■	■	

Map 18 • Morningside Heights

Name	Address	*	F	U	A
Mail Boxes Etc	2840 Broadway	6:00	■	■	
Drop Box - Lerner Hall	2920 Broadway	5:00		■	
Drop Box	3022 Broadway	8:00	■		
Drop Box	412 Low Library	7:00			■
Drop Box	475 Riverside Dr	6:30/7:30	■	■	
Drop Box	435 W 116th St	8:00/7:00	■		■
FedEx Service Center	600 W 116th St	9:00	■		
Drop Box	420 W 118th St	7:00			■
Drop Box	525 W 120th St	8:00	■		

Map 19 • Harlem (Lower)

Name	Address	*	F	U	A
Drop Box	2261 Adam C Powell Jr Blvd	7:30	■		
Mail Boxes Etc	55 W 116th St	6:30		■	
Drop Box	55 W 125th St	7:30/7:00	■	■	
Drop Box	163 W 125th St	7:30/7:00	■	■	

Map 20 • El Barrio

Name	Address	*	F	U	A
Drop Box	1879 Madison Ave	6:45	■		

Map 22 • Harlem (Upper)

Name	Address	*	F	U	A
Drop Box	402 W 145th St	4:00	■		

Map 23 • Washington Heights

Name	Address	*	F	U	A
Rel Express	2140 Amsterdam Ave	6:00	■		
Doc Q Pack	2201 Amsterdam Ave	7:00	■		
Drop Box	3960 Broadway	7:00/7:30	■	■	
Drop Box	161 Ft Washington Ave	7:00/6:00	■	■	
Drop Box	177 Ft Washington Ave	7:00	■		
Drop Box	60 Haven Ave	7:00	■	■	
Drop Box	100 Haven Ave	7:00	■		
Drop Box	1051 Riverside Dr	7:30/6:30	■	■	
Drop Box	1150 St Nicholas Ave	6:30/7:00	■	■	
Drop Box	622 W 168th St	7:00	■		
Drop Box	630 W 168th St	7:00	■		
Mail Boxes Etc	809 W 181st St	6:30		■	

Map 24 • Ft George / Ft Tryon

Name	Address	*	F	U	A
Drop Box	2495 Amsterdam Ave	7:30		■	
Quisqueyana Express	4468 Broadway	6:30	■		
Drop Box	701 W 168th St	5:30	■		
Drop Box	710 W 168th St	7:00	■		■
Drop Box	722 W 168th St	5:00/7:00	■		■
Drop Box - Furst Hall	500 W 185th St	7:00		■	

Map 25 • Inwood

Name	Address	*	F	U	A
Atlas Travel Group	4742 Broadway	5:00	■		
La Nacional	566 W 207th St	3:00	■		

Battery Park City

Name	Address	*	F	U	A
Drop Box	333 Rector St	7:00		■	

Randalls Island

Name	Address	*	F	U	A
Randall's Island	600 E 125th St	5:00	■	■	

Pharmacies

Pharmacies	Address	Phone	Map
CVS	342 E 23rd St	212-473-5750	10
CVS	1 Columbus Pl	212-245-0611	11
CVS	305 E 72nd St	212-249-5699	15
CVS	630 Lexington Ave	917-369-8687	13
CVS	1396 Second Ave	212-249-5062	15
CVS	342 E 23rd St	212-505-8919	10
CVS	1622 Third Ave	212-876-7016	17
Duane Reade	224 W 57th St	212-541-9708	12
Duane Reade (*8 pm)	405 Lexington Av	212-808-4743	13
Duane Reade (*8 pm M-F, 7 pm Sat, 6 pm Sun)	300 Park Ave S	212-533-7580	10
Duane Reade (*9 pm M-Sat, 6 pm Sun)	1191 Second Ave	212-355-5944	15
Duane Reade	2465 Broadway	212-799-3172	16
Duane Reade (*9 pm M-F, 8 pm Sat 6, pm Sun)	378 Sixth Ave	212-674-5357	6
Duane Reade	1279 Third Ave	212-744-2668	15
Duane Reade(*8:30 pm M-F, 6 pm Sat, 5 pm Sun)	485 Lexington Ave	212-682-5338	13
Duane Reade (*9 pm)	866 Third Ave	212-759-9412	13
Duane Reade (*10 pm)	155 E 34th St	212-683-3042	10
Duane Reade (*9 pm)	1231 Madison Ave	212-360-6586	17
Duane Reade (*8:45 pm)	2025 Broadway	212-579 9955	14
Duane Reade (*10 pm)	24 E 14th St	212-989-3632	6
Duane Reade (*9:30 pm)	661 Eighth Ave	212-977-1562	12
Rite Aid	2833 Broadway	212-663-3135	18
Rite Aid	408 Grand St	212-529-7115	4
Rite Aid	144 E 86th St	212-876-0600	17
Rite Aid (*9 pm)	210 Amsterdam Ave	212-787-2903	14
Rite Aid (*10 pm)	542 Second Ave	212-213-9887	10
Rite Aid	303 W 50th St	212-247-8384	12

* These stores are open 24 hours, but the pharmacy in the store closes at this time.

Veterinary

Veterinary	Address	Phone	Map
Animal Medical Center	510 E 62nd St	212-838-8100	15
Animal Emergency Clinic	240 E 80th St	212-988-1000	15
Park East Animal Hospital	52 E 64th St	212-832-8417	15
St Marks Veterinary Hospital	348 E 9th St	212-446-0102	6
Center for Veterinary Care	236 E 75th St	212-734-7480	15

Locksmiths

Locksmiths	Phone
A&M Locksmith	212-242-4733
A&V Locksmith	212-226-0011
Aaron-Hotz Locksmith	212-243-7166
Abbey Locksmiths	212-535-2289
Always Ready Locksmith	888-490-4900
American Locksmiths	212-888-8888
CBS Locksmith	212-410-0090
Champion Locksmiths	212-362-7000
East Manhattan Locksmith	212-369-9063
Emergency Locksmith 24 Hours	212-231-7627
KC Manhattan Locksmith	212-398-5500
LockDoctors	212-935-6600
Lockmasters Locksmith	212-690-4018
Night and Day Locksmith	212-722-1017
Paragon Security & Locksmith	212-620-9000
Speedway Locksmith	877-917-6500

Plumbers

Plumbers	Address	Phone	Map
New York Plumbing & Heating Service	244 Fifth Ave	212-496-9191	9
Sanitary Plumbing & Heating	211 E 117th St	212-734-5000	20
Effective Plumbing	Multiple locations	212-545-0100	
Roto-Rooter Plumbing	Multiple locations	212-687-1661	
Express Plumbing, Heating & Gas	183 E 104th St	212-427-9000	17

Post Office

Post Office	Address	Phone	Map
J A Farley GPO	421 Eighth Ave	212-330-5557	8

Delivery and Messengers

Delivery and Messengers	Phone		Phone
Moonlite Courier	212-473-2246	Need It Now	212-989-1919
Alliance Courier & Freight	212-302-3422	Urban Express	212-855-5555
Same Day Express	800-982-5910	Parkes Messenger Service	212-997-9023

Private Investigators

Private Investigators	Phone		Phone
American Eagle Investigations	212-344-1566	Matthew T. Cloth, P.I.	718-449-4100
Skipp Porteous, Wiretap & Bug Detection	212-579-4302/ 888-354-2174	North American Investigations	800-724-8080

Copying

Copying	Address	Phone	Map
ADS Copying	29 W 38th St	212-398-6166	12
MCD Print & Document	222 E 45th St	212-687-6699	13
Kinko's	105 Duane St	212-406-1220	3
Kinko's	1122 Lexington Ave	212-628-5500	15
Kinko's	1211 Sixth Ave	212-391-2679	12
Kinko's	16 E 52nd St	212-308-2679	12
Kinko's	191 Madison Ave	212-685-3449	9
Kinko's	233 W 54th St	212-977-2679	12
Kinko's	240 Central Park	212-258-3750	12
Kinko's	245 Seventh Ave	212-929-0623	9
Kinko's	2081 Broadway	212-362-5288	14
Kinko's	2872 Broadway	212-316-3390	18
Kinko's	60 W 40th St	212-921-1060	12
Kinko's	641 Lexington Ave	212-572-9995	13
Kinko's	650 Sixth Ave	646-638-9238	9
Kinko's	747 Third Ave	212-753-7778	13
On-Site Sourcing	443 Park Ave S	212-252-9700	9
The Village Copier	420 Lexington Ave	212-599-3344	13
The Village Copier	25 W 43rd St	212-924-3456	12
The Village Copier	20 E 13th St	212-924-3456	6
The Village Copier	10 E 39th St	212-869-9665	13
The Village Copier	601 W 115th St	212-666-0600	18

Gyms

Gyms	Address	Phone	Map
Crunch (Mon–Sat only)	Lafayette St & 4th St	212-614-0120	6

Laundromats

Laundromats	Address	Phone	Map
106 Audubon Avenue Laundromat	106 Audubon Ave	212-795-8717	23
69 Avenue C Laundromat	69 Avenue C	212-388-9933	7
Clean Action Laundromat	3476 Broadway	212-491-0392	21
Clean Rite Center	262 W 145th St	917-507-4865	22
D&D Laundromat	568 W 184th St	212-923-3409	24
Pearl Laundry & Dry Cleaner	2130 Broadway	917-335-8895	14
Stavros Laundromat	78 W 3rd St	212-475-3408	6

Hardware Store

Hardware Store	Address	Phone Number	Map
HomeFront	202 E 29th St	212-545-1447	10

Newsstands

Newsstands	Map		Map
49th St and Eighth Ave	12	Broadway & 50th St	12
42nd St and Seventh Ave	12	59th St & Third Ave	13
23rd St and Third Ave	10	Second Ave (60th/61st Sts)	15
Third Ave (34th/35th Sts)	10	72nd St & Broadway	14
Sixth Ave (South of 8th St)	5	76th St & Broadway	14
St Marks Pl(8th St)/Bowery (Third Ave)	6	79th St & York (First Ave)	15
Sixth Ave and 3rd St	5	86th St & Lexington Ave	17
Second Ave and St Marks Pl	6	First Ave 7 63rd St	15
Delancey and Essex Sts	7	Columbus Ave & 81st St	14
First Ave and 57th St	13	Broadway & 116th St	18

Car Rental

Car Rental	Address	Phone	Map
Avis	217 E 43rd St	212-593-8378	13

Car Washes

Car Washes	Address	Phone	Map
Broadway Car Wash	614 Broadway (Houston St)	212-673-5115	6
Eastside Car Wash	1770 First Ave (92nd St)	212-722-2222	17
Westside Highway Car Wash	638 W 47th St	212-757-1141	11
Cars A-Poppin Carwash	124 Sixth Ave	212-925-3911	5

Gas Stations

Gas Stations		Map			Map
Amoco	Broadway & Houston St	6	Gulf	Tenth Ave & 23rd St	8
Amoco	Eighth Ave & 110th St	19	Jerusalem	Tenth Ave & 201st St	25
Amoco	Amsterdam Ave & 165th St	23	Merit	Seventh Ave & 145th St	22
Amoco	Tenth Ave & 207th St	25	Mobil	Allen St & Division St	4
Citgo	Bowery & 3rd St	6	Mobil	Sixth Ave & Spring St	5
Exxon	110th St & Central Park W	19	Mobil	Houston St& Avenue C	7
Gaseteria	Houston & Lafayette Sts	6	Mobil	Eleventh Ave & 51st St	11
Gaseteria	West End Ave & 59th St	11	Mobil	Eleventh Ave & 57th St	11
Gaseteria	Broadway & 193rd St	24	Mobil	Seventh Ave & 145th St	22
Getty	Eighth Ave & 13th St	5	Shell	Amsterdam Ave & 167th St	23
Getty	Tenth Ave & 20th St	8	Shell	Amsterdam Ave & 181st St	23

Useful websites: www.doglaw.com, www.nycparks.org, www.allny.com/pets.html, www.nyc.dogslife.com, www.nycpetinfoline.com/home_page/

NYC is full of dog runs—both formal and informal—scattered throughout the city's parks and neighborhood community spaces. The city, while not actually administrating the runs, does provide space to community groups who then manage them. The runs are eager for help (volunteer time or financial contributions) and most post volunteer information on park bulletin boards. The formal runs are probably your safest bet, as most are enclosed and maintained for cleanliness and order. When your dog is in a run, it is important to remove any choke or pronged collars, as they may get tangled with another dog's collar or a fence (both of which can severely injure your dog). Do leave your dog's flat collar and identification tag on. Most runs prohibit dogs in heat, aggressive dogs, and dogs without inoculations. Many do not allow toys, balls, or Frisbees.

Map	*Name • Address • Comments*
2	**P.S. 234** • 300 Greenwich St at Chambers St • Private run. $50/year membership.
3	**Fish Bridge Park** • Pearl and Dover Sts • Concrete-surfaced run. Features water hose, wading pool, and lock box with newspapers.
5	**West Village D.O.G. Run** • Little W 12th St • Features benches, water hose, and drink bowl. Membership costs $40 annually, but there's a waiting list.
6	**Washington Square Park** • MacDougal St at W 4th St • Located in the southwest corner of the park, this is a large, gravel-surfaced run with many spectators. This popular run gets very crowded, but is well-maintained nonetheless.
6	**LaGuardia Place** • Mercer St at Houston St • This is a private run with a membership (and a waiting list). The benefits to this run include running water and a plastic wading pool for your dog to splash in.
6	**Union Square** • Broadway at 16th St • Crushed stone surface.
7	**Tompkins Square Park** • Avenue B at 10th St • New York City's first dog run is quite large and has a wood chip surface. Toys, balls, frisbees, and dogs in heat are all prohibited. This community-centered run offers lots of shade, benches, and running water.
8	**Thomas Smith Triangle** • Eleventh Ave at 23rd St • Concrete-surfaced run.
8	**Chelsea** • 18th St at the West Side Hwy
10	**Madison Square Park** • Madison Ave at 25th St • Medium-sized run with gravel surface and plenty of trees.
11	**DeWitt Clinton Park** • Eleventh Ave at 52nd & 54th Sts • Two small concrete-surfaced runs.
11	**Hell's Kitchen/Clinton Dog Run** • W 39th St at Tenth Ave • A private dog run (membership costs $15 a year) featuring chairs, umbrellas, fenced garden, and woodchip surface.
13	**E 60th Street Pavilion** • 60th St at the East River • Concrete-surfaced run.
13	**Peter Detmold Park** • Beekman Pl at 51st St • Large well-maintained run with cement and dirt surfaces and many trees.
13	**Robert Moses Park** • First Ave and 42nd St • Concrete surface.
14	**Theodore Roosevelt Park** • Central Park W at W 81st St • Gravel surface.
14	**Riverside Park** • Riverside Dr at 72nd St
14	**Margaret Mead Park** • Columbus Ave at 81st St
15	**Balto Dog Monument** • Fifth Ave at E 67th St (Central Park)
15,17	**Carl Shurz Park** • East End Ave at 85/86th Sts • Medium-sized enclosed run with pebbled surface and separate space for small dogs. This run has benches and shady trees, and running water is available in the bathrooms.
15	**Riverside Park** • Riverside Dr at 77/78th Sts
16	**Riverside Park** • Riverside Dr at 87th St • Medium-sized run with gravel surface.
16	**Riverside Park** • Riverside Dr at 105/106th Sts • Medium-sized run with gravel surface.
20	**Thomas Jefferson Park** • E 112nd St at First Ave • Woodchips surface.
21	**Harlem** • Riverside Dr at 140th St
23	**J. Hood Wright Park** • Haven Ave at W 173rd St • An enclosed dirt-surfaced run.
25	**Inwood Hill Dog Run** • W 207th St • Gravel surface.
BPC	**Battery Park City (south end)** • Third Pl at Battery Pl • This long, narrow, concrete-surfaced enclosed run is located along the West Side Highway and offers a pleasant view of the river and some shade.
BPC	**Battery Park City** • Along River Ter between Park Pl W and Murray St • Concrete-surfaced run with a view of the river.

Obviously, these listings will be of limited use to New Yorkers, but should prove useful if cousin Becky's coming to town, or if you really, really can't make it back home after a long night, or perhaps if you want to make a romantic (or slightly less than romantic) getaway. In the case of the latter, see the hotels with hourly rates. Rates are ballpark and subject to change—go to one of the many websites (Hotels.com, Priceline, Hotwire, Travelocity, Expedia, etc.) to get the best rates. Prices are generally highest during the holiday season and the summer, and lowest in the times in-between. Not all hotels have a star rating, and those that do are sometimes inaccurate. The rates quoted will give you a pretty good idea of the quality of each hotel.

Map 1 • Financial District	*Address*	*Phone*	*Rate $*	*Rating*
Hilton Millenium Hotel	55 Church St	212-693-2001	159-299	★★★★
Holiday Inn Wall Street	15 Gold St	212-232-7700	169-269	★★★1/2
Manhattan Seaport Suites	129 Front St	212-742-0003	179-229	
New York Marriott Financial Center	85 West St	212-385-4900	165-265	★★★★
Wall Street Inn	9 S William St	212-747-1500	169-249	★★★★
Map 2 • TriBeCa				
Cosmopolitan Hotel	95 West Broadway	212-566-1900	119-149	★★★
Soho Grand Hotel	310 West Broadway	212-965-3000	239-259	
Tribeca Grand Hotel	2 Sixth Ave	212-519-6600	269-319	★★★★
Map 3 • City Hall / Chinatown				
Best Western Seaport Inn	33 Peck Slip	212-766-6600	159	★★★
Holiday Inn Downtown	138 Lafayette St	212-966-8898	189-199	★★★
Pioneer of Soho Hotel	341 Broome St	212-226-1482	80-91	
Windsor Hotel	108 Forsyth St	212-226-3009	155	
Map 5 • West Village				
Abingdon Guest House	13 Eighth Ave	212-243-5384	137-212	
Chelsea Pines Inn	317 W 14th St	212-929-1023	79-119	
Hotel Gansevoort	18 Ninth Ave	212-206-6700	325-395	
Hotel Riverview	113 Jane St	212-929-0060	40	
Incentra Village House	32 Eighth Ave	212-206-0007	119	
Liberty Inn	51 Tenth Ave	212-741-2333	150	
Rooms to Let	83 Horatio St	212-675-5481	110	
Map 6 • Washington Square / NYU / SoHo				
60 Thompson	60 Thompson St	877-431-0400	370	★★★★
Howard Johnson Express Inn	135 E Houston St	212-358-8844	129-149	
Larchmont Hotel	27 W 11th St	212-989-9333	70-80	
Off Soho Suites Hotel	11 Rivington St	212-353-0860	149	
Second Home on Second Avenue	221 Second Ave	212-677-3161	75-145	
St Marks Hotel	2 St Mark's Pl	212-674-2192	110	
Union Square Inn	209 E 14th St	212-614-0500	140	
Village House	45 W 9th St	212-473-5500	115-135	
Washington Square Hotel	103 Waverly Pl	212-777-9515	130-150	
White House Hotel	340 Bowery	212-477-5623	32	
Map 7 • East Village				
East Village Bed & Coffee	110 Avenue C	212-533-4175	60-90	
Surface - The Hotel	107 Rivington St	212-246-2371		
Map 8 • Chelsea				
Allerton Hotel	302 W 22nd St	212-243-6017	68	
Best Western Convention Center Hotel	522 W 38th St	212-405-1700	99-199	
Chelsea Inn	184 Eleventh Ave	212-929-4096	45	
Chelsea International Hostel	251 W 20th St	212-647-0010	65	
Chelsea Lodge Suites	318 W 20th St	212-243-4499	90	
Chelsea Star Hotel	300 W 30th St	212-244-7827	69-99	
Colonial House Inn	318 W 22nd St	212-243-9669	125–140	
Manhattan East Suite Hotels	500 W 37th St	212-465-3690	189-219	
Manhattan Inn	303 W 30th St	212-629-4064	92-120	
New Yorker Ramada Hotel	481 Eighth Ave	212-971-0101	130	★★★

Map 9 • Flatiron / Lower Midtown

Map 9 • Flatiron / Lower Midtown	Address	Phone	Rate $	Rating
Americana Inn	69 W 38th St	212-840-2019	60-70	★★
Arlington Hotel	18 W 25th St	212-645-3990	85-100	★★
As You Like It Bed & Breakfast	244 Fifth Ave	212-695-7143	125	
Avalon, The	16 E 32nd St	212-299-7000	195	★★★★
Best Western Inn Manhattan	17 W 32nd St	212-736-1600	119	★★★
Broadway Plaza Hotel	1155 Broadway	877-50-HOTEL	99-169	★★★1/2
Carlton Hotel	22 E 29th St	212-532-4100	129-159	★★★
Chelsea Grand Hotel	160 W 25th St	212-627-1888	139	★★★
Chelsea Hotel	222 W 23rd St	212-243-3700	150-165	
Chelsea Inn	46 E 17th St	212-645-8989	139	
Chelsea Savoy Hotel	204 W 23rd St	212-929-9353	99-150	
Comfort Inn Manhattan	42 W 35th St	212-947-0200	129	★★★
Comfort Inn Midtown	129 W 32nd St	212-221-2600	119-139	★★★
Comfort Inn New York	442 W 36th St	212-714-6699	99-159	
Gershwin Hotel	7 E 27th St	212-545-8000	99-119	
Hampton Inn Manhattan/Chelsea	108 W 24th St	212-414-1000	159	
Herald Square Hotel	19 W 31st St	212-279-4017	85-99	
Holiday Inn Martinique on Broadway	49 W 32nd St	212-736-3800	129-189	★★★1/2
Hotel Grand Union	34 E 32nd St	212-683-5890	120	★★1/2
Hotel Metro	45 W 35th St	212-947-2500	170	★★★
Hotel Stanford	43 W 32nd St	212-563-1500	120	
Hotel Thirty Thirty	29 E 29th St	212-689-1900	120-150	★★★
Howard Johnson Penn Station	215 W 34th St	212-947-5050	125	★1/2
Inn on 23rd	131 W 23rd St	212-463-0330	189	
Jolly Hotel Madison Towers	22 E 38th St	212-802-0600	169-199	★★★
La Quinta Inn - Manhattan	17 W 32nd St	212-790-2710	89-119	★★★
La Samanna	25 W 24th St	212-255-5944	139, 169	
Le Marquis New York	12 E 31st St	212-889-6363	219-239	★★★★
Madison Hotel on the Park	21 E 27th St	212-532-7373	64	
Morgan's Hotel	237 Madison Ave	212-686-0300	210-290	★★★★
New York Hotel Pennsylvania	401 Seventh Ave	212-736-5000	119, 200	★★★★
Red Roof Inn	6 W 32nd St	212-643-7100	99-119	★★
Roger Williams Hotel	131 Madison Ave	212-448-7000	200	★★★
Senton Hotel	39 W 27th St	212-684-5800	78	
Southgate Tower Hotel	371 Seventh Ave	212-563-1800	189-209	★★★
Wolcott Hotel	4 W 31st St	212-268-2900	100-140	★★

Map 10 • Murray Hill / Gramercy

Map 10 • Murray Hill / Gramercy	Address	Phone	Rate $	Rating
Carlton Arms Hotel	160 E 25th St	212-679-0680	75	
Clarion Park Avenue	429 Park Ave S	212-532-4860	139	★★
Deauville Hotel	103 E 29th St	212-683-0990	99	★★
Doral Park Avenue Hotel	70 Park Ave	212-687-7050	179	★★★
Dumont Plaza	150 E 34th St	212-481-7600	199-229	★★★1/2
Eastgate Tower Suite Hotel	222 E 39th St	212-687-8000	179-199	★★★
Gramercy Park Hotel	2 Lexington Ave	212-475-4320	165	★★★
Hotel 17	225 E 17th St	212-475-2845	65	★★★
Hotel 31	120 E 31st St	212-685-3060	100	
Hotel Giraffe	365 Park Ave S	212-685-7700	265-325	★★★★
Inn at Irving Place	56 Irving Pl	212-533-4600	325	★★★★
Kitano Hotel New York	66 Park Ave	212-885-7000	210-230	★★★★
Marcel Hotel	201 E 24th St	888-664-6835	180-200	★★★
Maritime Hotel	363 16th St	212-242-4300	155-245	
Murray Hill East Suites	149 E 39th St	212-661-2100	199	★★★
Murray Hill Inn	143 E 30th St	212-545-0879	79-119	
Oakwood Montrose	300 E 38th St	602-687-3322	220	
Park South Hotel	122 E 28th St	212-448-0888	189-229	★★★1/2
Ramada Inn Eastside	161 Lexington Ave	212-545-1800	99-109	★★★
Shelburne	303 Lexington Ave	212-689-5200	150-219	★★★
Sheraton Russell Hotel	45 Park Ave	212-685-7676	199-239	★★★
W New York - The Court	130 E 39th St	212-685-1100	209-229	★★★
W New York - The Tuscany	120 E 39th St	212-686-1600	229-249	
W Union Square	201 Park Ave S	212-253-9119	319-339	

Map 11 • Hell's Kitchen	*Address*	*Phone*	*Rate $*	*Rating*
414 Inn New York	414 W 46th St	212-399-0006	120-140	★★★
Belvedere Hotel	319 W 48th St	212-245-7000	160-170	★★★
Elk Hotel	360 W 42nd St	212-563-2864	40	
Holiday Inn Midtown	440 W 57th St	212-581-8100	159-214	★★★
Hudson Hotel	356 W 58th St	212-554-6000	165-210	★★★
Skyline Hotel	725 Tenth Ave	212-586-3400	119-159	★★★
Travel Inn	515 W 42nd St	212-695-7171	125	★★★
Washington Jefferson Hotel	318 W 51st St	212-246-7550	139	★★★
Westpark Hotel	308 W 58th St	866-937-8727	119-149	★★1/2

Map 12 • Midtown				
Algonquin Hotel	59 W 44th St	212-840-6800	209-229	★★★★
Ameritania Hotel	230 W 54th St	212-247-5000	139-189	★★★★
Amsterdam Court Hotel	226 W 50th St	212-459-1000	125-185	★★★
Best Western Ambassador	132 W 45th St	212-921-7600	129	
Best Western President Hotel	234 W 48th St	212-246-8800	129	★★★
Big Apple Hostel	119 W 45th St	212-302-2603	90	
Broadway Bed & Breakfast Inn	264 W 46th St	212-997-9200	100-120	★★★★
Bryant Park Hotel	40 W 40th St	212-869-0100	245-265	★★★★
Buckingham Hotel	101 W 57th St	212-246-1500	169	
Carnegie Hotel	229 W 58th St	212-245-4000	170-250	★★★★
Carter Hotel	250 W 43rd St	212-944-6000	90	
Casablanca Hotel	147 W 43rd St	212 869-1212	160-225	
Chambers Hotel	15 W 56th St	212-974-5656	235-275	★★★★
City Club Hotel	55 W 44th St	212-921-5500	199-225	
Clarion Hotel	3 E 40th St	212-447-1500	160-180	★★★
Comfort Inn (Remington) Midtown	129 W 46th St	212-221-2600	120-140	★★★
Courtyard by Marriott Times Square South	114 W 40th St	212-391-0088	150-220	★★★
Crowne Plaza Times Square	1605 Broadway	212-977-4000	210, 170	★★★★
Da Vinci Hotel	244 W 56th St	212-489-4100	105-125	★★★
Days Inn Hotel Manhattan Midtown	790 Eighth Ave	212-581-7000	129-149	★★1/2
Doubletree Guest Suites	1568 Broadway	212-719-1600	240-270	★★★★
Dylan Hotel	52 E 41st St	212-338-0500	209-259	★★★★
Flatotel International	135 W 52nd St	212-887-9400	270	★★★★
Four Seasons Hotel	57 E 57th St	212-758-5700	525-675	★★★★★
Gorham Hotel	136 W 55th St	212-245-1800	219	★★★★
Hampshire Hotel Suites	157 W 47th St	212-768-3700	110-140	★★1/2
Helmsley Park Lane Hotel	36 Central Park S	212-371-4000	219-379	★★★★
Hilton New York	1335 Sixth Ave	212-586-7000	275-300	★★★★
Hilton Times Square	234 W 42nd St	212-840-8222	250-280	★★★★
Hotel 41	206 W 41st St	212 703-8600	149	
Hotel Edison	228 W 47th St	212-840-5000	150	★★★
Hotel Shoreham	33 W 55th St	212-247-6700	180-210	★★★
Hotel St James	109 W 45th St	212-221-3600	100	
Howard Johnson	851 Eighth Ave	212-581-4100	160-180	★★★
Inter-Continental Central Park South	112 Central Park S	212-757-1900	189-229	★★★★
Iroquois Hotel	49 W 44th St	212-840-3080	239-269	★★★★
LC Essex House St Regis Club	120 Central Park S	212-247-0300	229-269	★★★★
Le Parker Meridien	118 W 57th St	212-245-5000	275-295	★★★★
Library Hotel	299 Madison Ave	212-983-4500	199-285	
Majestic, The	210 W 55th St	212-247-2000	129-159	★★★
Mansfield Hotel	12 W 44th St	212-944-6050	159-189	★★★
Mayfair Hotel	242 W 49th St	212-586-0300	120	
Michelangelo	152 W 51st St	212-765-1900	195-245	★★★★
Milford Plaza	700 Eighth Ave	212-536-2200	119	★★★1/2
Milford Plaza Hotel	270 W 45th St	212-869-3600	155	★★★
Millennium Broadway	145 W 44th St	212-768-4400	209	★★★★
Moderne Hotel	243 W 55th St	212-397-6767	175-185	★★★
Muse, The	130 W 46th St	877-692-6873	229-259	★★★★
New York Inn	765 Eighth Ave	212-247-5400	85	
New York Marriott Marquis	1535 Broadway	212-398-1900	200	★★★
New York Palace Hotel	455 Madison Ave	212-888-7000	275-325	★★★★
Novotel New York	226 W 52nd St	212-315-0100	219	★★★1/2

Map 12 • Midtown

Map 12 • Midtown	Address	Phone	Rate $	Rating
Omni Berkshire Place	21 E 52nd St	212-753-5800	179-289	★★★★
Paramount Hotel	235 W 46th St	212-764-5500	120-180	★★★★
Park Central Hotel	870 Seventh Ave	212-247-8000	129-239	★★★1/2
Park Savoy Hotel	158 W 58th St	212-245-5755	95-105	
Peninsula New York	700 Fifth Ave	212-956-2888	325	★★★★
Plaza Hotel	Fifth Ave & Central Park S	212-759-3000	249-289	★★★★
Portland Square Hotel	132 W 47th St	212-382-0600	85-110	
Premier, The	133 W 44th St	212-789-7670	179-295	★★★★
Renaissance New York Times Square	714 Seventh Ave	212-765-7676	219-249	★★★★
Rihga Royal New York	151 W 54th St	212-468-8888	275-300	★★★★
Royalton Hotel	44 W 44th St	212-869-4400	205-260	★★★★
Salisbury Hotel	123 W 57th St	212-246-1300	90-139	★★★
Sheraton Manhattan	790 Seventh Ave	212-621-8500	179-379	★★★
Sheraton New York Hotel and Towers	811 Seventh Ave	212-581-1000	179-379	★★★
Sherry Netherland Hotel	781 Fifth Ave	212-355-2800	350-450	★★★★★
Sofitel	45 W 44th St	212-354-8844	209-229	★★★★1/2
St Moritz Hotel/Ritz Carlton Central Park	50 Central Park S	212-308-9100	415-465	
St Regis	2 E 55th St	212-753-4500	550-610	★★★★★
Super 8 Times Square	59 W 46th St	212-719-2300	119	★★★
Time Hotel	224 W 49th St	212-246-5252	179-199	★★★★
W New York Times Square	1567 Broadway	212-930-7400	279-299	★★★★
Wellington Hotel	871 Seventh Ave	212-247-3900	110-190	★★★
West Park Hotel	6 Columbus Cir	212-445-0200	120	★★
Westin Essex House	160 Central Park S	212-247-0300	289-339	★★★★
Westin New York at Times Square	270 W 43rd St	212-201-2700	249-279	
Wyndham Hotels & Resorts	42 W 58th St	212-753-3500	140-155	

Map 13 • East Midtown

Name	Address	Phone	Rate $	Rating
Alex Hotel	205 E 45th St	212-867-5100	239	
Bedford Hotel	118 E 40th St	212-697-4800	125	★★★1/2
Beekman Tower Suite Hotel	3 Mitchell Pl	212-355-7300	160-290	★★★
Best Western	145 E 49th St	212-753-8781	175-240	★★★
Churchill Residence Suites	234 E 46th St	877-424-7848	170-250	★★★
Courtyard by Marriot Midtown East	866 Third Ave	212-644-1300	159-209	★★★★★
Crowne Plaza at the United Nations	304 E 42nd St	212-986-8800	239-269	★★★★
Fitzpatrick Grand Central Hotel	141 E 44th St	212-351-6800	229-325	★★★★1/2
Fitzpatrick Manhattan Hotel	687 Lexington Ave	212-355-0100	199-239	★★★★
Grand Hyatt Hotel	109 E 42nd St	212-883-1234	310-355	★★★★
Habitat Hotel	130 E 57th St	212-753-8841	75-125	★
Helmsley Middletowne Hotel	148 E 48th St	212-755-3000	159-289	★★★
Hotel Elysee	60 E 54th St	212-753-1066	195-265	
Hotel Inter-Continental - The Barclay	111 E 48th St	212-755-5900	239-259	★★★★★
Kimberly Hotel	145 E 50th St	212-755-0400	189-209	★★★★
Marriott New York City East Side	525 Lexington Ave	212-755-4000	149-219	★★★★
Metropolitan Hotel	569 Lexington Ave	212-752-7000	99-159	★★★
Millenium Hotel NY UN Plaza Hotel	1 United Nations Plz	212-758-1234	199-229	
New York Helmsley Park	212 E 42nd St	212-490-8900	179-189	★★★
Pickwick Arms Hotel	230 E 51st St	212-355-0300	109-129	
Plaza Fifty Suite Hotel	155 E 50th St	212-751-5710	199-249	★★★
Radisson Hotel East Side	511 Lexington Ave	212-755-4400	159-189	★★★
Roger Smith Hotel	501 Lexington Ave	212-755-1400	215-235	★★★
Roosevelt Hotel	45 E 45th St	212-661-9600	149-199	★★★★
San Carlos Hotel	150 E 50th St	212-755-1800	179	
Seton Hotel	144 E 40th St	212-889-5301	95	
Swissotel New York	440 Park Ave	212-421-0900	249-299	★★★
W New York	541 Lexington Ave	212-755-1200	239-289	★★★★
Waldorf Astoria	301 Park Ave	212-872-4534	199-249	★★★★★
Waldorf Towers	100 E 50th St	212-355-3100	199	★★★★
YMCA Vanderbilt Hotel	224 E 47th St	212-756-9600	115	

Map 14 • Upper West Side (Lower)

Name	Address	Phone	Rate $	Rating
Amsterdam Inn	340 Amsterdam Ave	212-579-7500	110	
Amsterdam Residence	207 W 85th St	212-873-9402	100	

Map 14 • Upper West Side (Lower)

	Address	Phone	Rate $	Rating
Comfort Inn Central Park West	31 W 71st St	212-721-4770	100-130	★★★
Country in the City	270 W 77th St	212-580-4183	150-210	
Excelsior Hotel	45 W 81st St	212-362-9200	129-169	★★★1/2
Hayden Hall Hotel	117 W 79th St	212-787-4900	115	
Hotel Beacon	2130 Broadway	212-787-1100	145-175	★★★
Hotel Lucerne	201 W 79th St	212-875-1000	150 -180	★★★★
Hotel Riverside Studios	342 W 71st St	212-873-5999	60	
Inn New York City	266 W 71st St	212-580-1900	295-375	
Mandarin Oriental New York	80 W 60th St	212-805-8800	429-615	★★★★★
Mayflower Hotel	15 Central Park W	212-265-0060	139-215	★★★
Milburn Hotel	242 W 76th St	212-362-1006	149-159	
On the Ave Hotel	2178 Broadway	212-362-1100	139-159	★★★1/2
Phillips Club	155 W 66th St	212-835-8800	310	
Riverside Tower Hotel	80 Riverside Dr	212-877-5200	84	★★
Trump International	1 Central Park W	212-299-1000	395-595	★★★★★
YMCA West Side Branch	5 W 63rd St	212-875-4100	100	

Map 15 • Upper East Side (Lower)

Barbizon Melrose Hotel	140 E 63rd St	212-838-5700	199-229	★★★★
Bentley Hotel	500 E 62nd St	888-66-HOTEL	129-255	★★★★
Carlyle Hotel	35 E 76th St	212-744-1600	360-420	★★★★
Gracie Inn	502 E 81st St	212-628-1700	129	
Helmsley Carlton	680 Madison Ave	212 838-3000	255	★★★★
Hotel Plaza Athenee	37 E 64th St	212-734-9100	329-515	★★★★
Lowell Hotel	28 E 63rd St	212-838-1400	415-445	★★★★
Lyden Gardens Suite Hotel	215 E 64th St	212-355-1230	199-209	★★★
Mark New York, The	25 E 77th St	212-744-4300	299-400	★★★★
Pierre Four Seasons, The	2 E 61st St	212-838-8000	380-495	★★★★
Regency Hotel	540 Park Ave	212-759-4100	269-319	★★★★
Stanhope Park Hyatt Hotel	995 Fifth Ave	212-774-1234	279-305	★★★★
Surrey Suite Hotel	20 E 76th St	212-288-3700	259-289	★★★

Map 16 • Upper West Side (Upper)

Astor on the Park	465 Central Park W	212-866-1880	95-125, 145	
Belnord Residence Hotel	209 W 87th St	212-873-5222	175	★
Central Park Hostel	19 W 103rd St	212-678-0491	75	
Hostelling International New York	891 Amsterdam Ave	212-932-2300	35	
Hotel Belleclaire	250 W 77th St	212-362-7700	99-149	★★
Hotel Dexter House	345 W 86th St	212-873-9600	60	
Hotel Newton	2528 Broadway	212-678-6500	95	★★
Malibu Hotel	2688 Broadway	212-222-2954	89	
Morningside Inn	235 W 107th St	212-316-0055	95	
Quality Hotel on Broadway	215 W 94th St	212-866-6400	149-159	★★★
Riverside Inn	319 W 94th St	212-316-0656	80-90	
West End Studios	850 West End Ave	212-749-7104	69	
West Side Inn	237 W 107th St	212-866-0061	60-70	★1/2

Map 17 • Upper East Side (Upper)

92nd Steeet Y de Hirch Residence	1395 Lexington Ave	212-415-5650	30	
Franklin Hotel	164 E 87th St	212-369-1000	179-219	
Wales Hotel	1295 Madison Ave	212-876-6000	189-219	★★★

Map 19 • Harlem (Lower)

Efuru Bed & Breakfast	106 W 120th St	212-961-9855	95-125	
Urban Jem Guest House	2005 Fifth Ave	212-831-6029	130	

Map 21 • Manhattanville / Hamilton Heights

Blue Rabbit International House	730 St Nicholas Ave	212-491-3892	25	

Battery Park City

Embassy Suites New York City	102 North End Ave	212-945-0100	280, 200	★★★★
Ritz-Carlton New York Battery Park	2 West St	212-344-0800	289-395	★★★★

Internet

A variety of establishments offer Internet access. In the list below you'll find everything from copy centers to milkshake stores, as well as traditional "cyber-cafés." All Kinko's offer Internet access for 30-45 cents per minute depending on which Kinko's you go to and which machine you use ($18-$27 per hour). Due to this variety, it is possible that there are other places to access the Internet in New York, hiding in seemingly unlikely places…

Internet Café	*Map*
@cafe • 12 St Marks Pl	6
alt.Coffee • 139 Avenue A • 212-529-CAFÉ	7
Bistro 2 Go • 316 Lexington Ave	10
Bistro New York • 100 Park Ave	13
Brooklyn Bagel Café • 319 Fifth Ave	9
Café Pick Me Up • 145 Avenue A	7
Café Vienna • 161 Lexington Ave	10
Coffee Pot • 350 W 49th St	11
Coffee Pot • 41 Avenue A • 212-614-0815	7
Cyber Café • www.cyber-cafe.com • 273A Lafayette St • 212-334-5140	3
Cyber Café Times Square • 250 W 49th St • 212-333-4109	12
Cyberfelds • 20 E 13th St • 212-647-8830	6
Cyber Station Internet Cafe • 2255 31st St	26
Ditto Internet Cafe • 48 W 20th St • 212-242-0841	9
easyInternetcafe • www.easyeverything.com/map/nyc.html:	
• 101 Park Ave	13
• 16 W 48th St	12
• 234 W 42nd St • 212-398-0775	12
ECT • www.ectcafe.com • 417 Fifth Ave • 212-684-8088	9
Game Player Station • www.gameplayerstation.com • 28 Elizabeth St • 212-619-1019 •	3
Gametime Nation • 111 E 12th St	6
Grammercy Hotel • 2 Lexington Ave	16
Hotel Grand Union • 34 E 32nd St	9
Internet Cafe NYC • www.internetcafenyc.com • 17 John St • 212-217-6043	1
Internet Café • 82 E 3rd St • 212-614-0747	7
Internet Cyber Café • 32 Third Ave • 212-777-5544	6
Juice & Java • 581 Broadway	6
Keelum Broadband Internet Cafe • 273 W 38th St • 212-921-9791	8
Kinko's • www.kinkos.com:	
• 110 William St • 212-766-4646	1
• 100 Wall St • 212-269-0024	1
• 105 Duane St • 212-406-1220	3
• 250 E Houston St • 212-253-9020	7
• 21 Astor Pl • 212-228-9511	6
• 257 Park Ave S • 646-602-0074	10
• 650 Sixth Ave • 646-638-9238	9

Internet Café	*Map*
Kinko's • www.kinkos.com:	
• 245 Seventh Ave • 212-929-0623	9
• 230 Park Ave • 212-949-2534	13
• 350 Fifth Ave • 212-279-3556	9
• 191 Madison Ave • 212-685-3449	9
• 600 Third Ave • 212-599-2679	10
• 500 Seventh Ave • 646-366-9166	9
• 60 W 40th St • 212-921-1060	12
• 305 E 46th St • 212-319-6600	13
• 747 Third Ave • 212-753-7778	13
• 1211 Sixth Ave • 212-391-2679	12
• 153 E 53rd St • 212-753-7580	13
• 16 E 52nd St • 212-308-2679	12
• 641 Lexington Ave • 212-572-9995	13
• 233 W 54th St • 212-977-2679	12
• 240 Central Park S • 212-258-3750	12
• 1122 Lexington Ave • 212-628-5500	15
• 221 W 72nd St • 212-362-5288	14
Kudo Beans • 49½ First Ave • 212-353-1477	7
Le Petit Dejeuner • 333 Sixth Ave	5
Little Caesars • 40 W 14th St	6
LNC Sunshine • 230 E 25th St	10
New York Computer Place • 247 E 57th St • 212-872-1704	13
News Bar 19th • 2 W 19th St	9
Original New York Milkshake Co • 1037 St Marks Pl • 212-505-5200	6
Oxford Catering Café • 399 Third Ave	10
Rick's Cyber Café at the Casablanca Hotel • 147 W 43rd St • 212-869-1212	12
Rainbow Pizza • 347 E 14th St	6
Rocket Wrapps • 81 Third Ave	6
Six and Twelve • 469 Sixth Ave	5
Spin City • 180 Avenue B	7
Spin City • 345 E 204th St	25
Village Juice Bar • 200 E 14th St • 673-0005	6
William Christy Internet Cafe • 159 Avenue C • 212-477-6000	7
Web2zone • www.web2zone.com • 54 Cooper Sq • 212-614-7300	6
Ziggie's Café • 1817 Second Ave	17

Wi-Fi

For those with a laptop or PDA that has wireless access (WiFi 802.11b enabled), there are a ton of free public "Wi-Fi" connections available. The NYC Wireless' website at www.nycwireless.net has a listing and map of these locations. The majority of hotspots on this page are run by private citizens, though a few are run by the Downtown Alliance. Specific information on the DA hotspot locations and signing on can be found at www.downtownny.com/wireless.asp.

T-Mobile Hotspot subscribers ($6 per hour or $30 per month unlimited) can find access at most Kinko's, Borders, and Starbucks locations.

McDonald's offers free Wi-Fi access at more than 50 locations in Manhattan; www.mcdwireless.com.

If you're the kind of person who likes to talk on your cell phone in restaurants, then you'll probably be partial to doing some emailing or Web browsing too. A number of New York restaurants & hotels offer Wi-Fi; www.subscriberdirect.com/the_new_yorker/zagat/ny.cfm.

On their website http://intel.jiwire.com, Intel has a Hotspot Search function, where you can search for locations throughout the city.

Free Wi-Fi is also offered in Penn Station for AT&T Wireless customers, and to anyone else for $9.99 per 24 hrs. Finally, fifty-three branches of the NY Public Library offer Wi-Fi access, a number that is sure to increase. Info can be found at www.nypl.org/branch/services/wifi.html.

Overview

We haven't checked (why should we?) but we're willing to bet that the highest concentration of art galleries in the world is contained in a rough box you can draw around Chelsea, Williamsburg, Dumbo, and SoHo. At any given time, more than 500 galleries are showing artwork done in every conceivable medium with, of course, varying levels of quality. But most galleries, especially in Chelsea and in Williamsburg, are almost always showing something that's at least *provocative*, if not actually *good*. And since you can always hike up to the Met or the MoMA if you want to see comfortable, familiar masterworks, we're more than happy for the gallery scene to continue to provoke us.

SoHo Area

Five years ago, there were still hundreds of art galleries in SoHo. Now, it's swiftly becoming a very nice mall. However, there are still some permanent artworks in gallery spaces, such as Walter DeMaria's excellent **"The Broken Kilometer"** (a Dia-sponsored space at 393 West Broadway), and his sublime **New York Earth Room** at 141 Wooster Street. And a short jaunt down to TriBeCa will land you in LaMonte Young's awesome aural experience **"The Dream House"** at the **Mela Foundation.**

For revolving artworks, the **Edward Carter Gallery** has a great collection of photography, **HERE Art** usually has some interesting things going on, and **Ace Gallery** almost never fails to disappoint (favorite recent show: *The Überorgan* by Tim Hawkinson).

Chelsea

In case you weren't sure where all the galleries went after SoHo prices exploded, this is it. Over 200 galleries now reside here, and there is always something to see. Our recommendation is to hit at least two streets—W 24th Street between Tenth and Eleventh Avenues, and W 22nd Street between Tenth and Eleventh Avenues. W 24th Street is anchored by the almost-always-brilliant **Gagosian Gallery** and also includes the **Luhring Augustine**, **Charles Cowles, Mary Boone**, and **Matthew Marks** galleries. W 22nd has the brilliant **Dia Center for the Arts** as well as the architecture-friendly **Max Protech** gallery, and the **Julie Saul, Leslie Tonkonow, Marianne Boesky,** and **Yancey Richardson** galleries. Also check out the famous "artists" bookstore **Printed Matter** (535 W 22nd Street).

If you're not tired from all that, there are tons more galleries on W 20th Street and W 26th Street. Take a cruise through the massive and cool **Starrett-Lehigh Building** not only for the art but also for the great pillars, windows, and converted freight elevators (some big enough to fit trucks!).

Perhaps the final lid in the coffin for SoHo was **Exit Art**'s move to 475 Tenth Avenue last year. It's a truly original gallery that does everything from album covers to multimedia installations, and it's highly recommended.

Map 1 • Financial District

Water Street Gallery	241 Water St	212-349-9090

Map 2 • TriBeCa

123 Watts Gallery	123 Watts St	212-219-1482
A Taste of Art	147 Duane St	212-964-5493
Adelphi University	75 Varick St, 2nd Fl	212-965-8340
Anthem Gallery	41 Wooster St	212-334-9364
Apex Art	291 Church St	212-431-5270
Arcadia Gallery	51 Greene St	212-965-1387
Art at Format	50 Wooster St	212-941-7995
Artists Space	38 Greene St, 3rd Fl	212-226-3970
Atlantic Gallery, The	40 Wooster St, 4th Fl	212-219-3183
Brooke Alexander Gallery	59 Wooster St	212-925-4338
Capeluto Arts	147 Reade St	212-964-1340
Cheryl Pelavin Fine Art	13 Jay St	212-925-9424
Coda Gallery	472 Broome St	212-334-0407
Dactyl Foundation for the Arts & Humanities	64 Grand St	212-219-2344
Deitch Projects	76 Grand St	212-343-7300
DFN Gallery	176 Franklin St	212-334-3400
Drawing Center, The	35 Wooster St	212-219-2166
Ethan Cohen Fine Arts	37 Walker St	212-625-1250
Gallery Viet Nam	345 Greenwich St	212-431-8889
Jack Tilton	49 Greene St	212-941-1775
Kristen Frederickson Contemporary Art	149 Reade St	212-566-7787
Latincollector	153 Hudson St	212-334-7813
Location One	26 Greene St	212-334-3347
Mela Foundation	275 Church St, 3rd Fl	212-925-8270
Michael Perez Gallery	11 Harrison St	212-966-7278
Organization of Independent Artists	19 Hudson St	212-219-9213
Painting Center, The	52 Greene St	212-343-1060
PPOW	476 Broome St, 3rd Fl	212-941-8642
Spencer Brownstone Gallery	39 Wooster St	212-334-3455
Woodward Gallery	476 Broome St, 5th Fl	212-966-3411

Map 3 • City Hall / Chinatown

55 Mercer Gallery	55 Mercer St	212-226-8513
Agora Gallery	415 West Broadway	212-226-4151
Animazing Art	461 Broome St	212-226-7374
Art in General	79 Walker St	212-219-0473
Bronwyn Keenan Gallery	3 Crosby St	212-431-5083
Broome Street Gallery	498 Broome St	212-226-6085
Canada	55 Chrystie St	212-925-4631
Gallery 456	456 Broadway, 3rd Fl	212-431-9740
Globe Institute Gallery	291 Broadway	212-349-4330
Grant Gallery	7 Mercer St	212-343-2919
KS Art	73 Leonard St	212-219-9918
Leo Koenig	249 Centre St	212-334-9255
Paul Sharpe Contemporary Art	86 Walker St, 6th Fl	646-613-1252
Rhonda Schaller Studio	59 Franklin St	212-226-0166
Ronald Feldman Fine Arts	31 Mercer St	212-226-3232
S E Feinman Fine Arts	448 Broome St	212-431-6820
Studio 18 Gallery	18 Warren St	212-385-6734
Swiss Institute Contemporary Art	495 Broadway, 3rd Fl	212-925-2035
Synagogue for the Arts	49 White St	212-966-7141
The Gallery at Dieu Donne Papermill	433 Broome St	212-226-0573

Map 4 • Lower East Side

maccarone	45 Canal St	212-431-4977

Map 5 • West Village

Akira Ikeda	17 Cornelia St, #1C	212-366-5449
Baron/Boisante	421 Hudson St	212-924-9940
Casey Kaplan	416 W 14th St	212-645-7335
Clockwork Apple	32B Gansevoort St	212-229-1187
Cooper Classics Collection	137 Perry St	212-929-3909
DOMA	17 Perry St	212-929-4339

Map 5 • West Village *continued*

Gavin Brown's Enterprise	620 Greenwich St	212-627-5258
Hal Katzen Gallery	459 Washington St	212-925-9777
Heller Gallery	420 W 14th St	212-414-4014
HERE Art	145 Sixth Ave	212-647-0202
Jane Hartsook Gallery at Greenwich House Pottery	16 Jones St	212-242-4106
Long Fine Art	427 W 14th St, 2nd Fl	212-337-1940
MGoldstrom Gallery/CVB Space	407 W 13th St	212-941-9175
Parkett Editions	155 Sixth Ave, 2nd Fl	212-673-2660
Plane Space	102 Charles St	917-606-1268
Pratt Manhattan Gallery	144 W 14th St, 2nd Fl	212-647-7778
Sperone Westwater	415 W 13th St	212-999-7337
Synchronicity Fine Arts	106 W 13th St	646-230-8199
Van Brunt Gallery New York	819 Washington St	917-971-0176
Westbeth Gallery	155 Bank St	212-989-4650
White Columns	320 W 13th St	212-924-4212
Wooster Projects	421 W 14th St	646-336-1999

Map 6 • Washington Sq/NYU/SoHo

A/D	560 Broadway	212-966-5154
Ace Gallery	275 Hudson St	212-255-5599
Agora	415 West Broadway, 5th Fl	212-226-4151
American Indian Community House Gallery	708 Broadway	212-598-0100
American Primitive	594 Broadway #205	212-966-1530
Ariel Meyerowitz Gallery	580 Broadway #1203	212-414-2770
Axelle Fine Arts Ltd	148 Spring St	212-226-2262
Big Cat Gallery	28 E 2nd St	212-982-6210
Bottom Feeders Studio Gallery	195 Chrystie St, 2nd Fl	917-974-9664
Broadway Windows	Broadway & E 10th St	212-998-5751
Broken Kilometer, The	393 West Broadway	212-925-9397
Bronfman Center Gallery at NYU	7 E 10th St	212-998-4114
Caldwell Snyder Gallery	451 West Broadway	212-387-0208
Cavin-Morris	560 Broadway #405B	212-226-3768
CFM	112 Greene St	212-966-3864
Chaim Gross Studio	526 LaGuardia Pl	212-529-4906
Dia Center for the Arts	141 Wooster St, 2nd Fl	212-989-5566
Dia Center for the Arts	393 West Broadway	212-989-5566
Edward Carter Gallery	560 Broadway #406	212-966-1933
Eleanor Ettinger	119 Spring St	212-925-7474
Emily Harvey Gallery	537 Broadway, 2nd Fl	212-925-7651
Entree Libree	66 Crosby St	212-431-5279
Exhibit A	160 Mercer St	212-343-0230
Franklin Bowles Galleries	431 West Broadway	212-226-1616
Gallery Juno	568 Broadway #604B	212-431-1515
Gallery Revel	96 Spring St	212-925-0600
Gracie Mansion Gallery	407 E 6th St #2	212-505-9577
Grey Art Gallery	100 Washington Sq E	212-998-6780
Hebrew Union College - Jewish Institute of Religion	1 W 4th St	212-824-2205
Inframundo	106 Spring St	212-925-3126
ISE Foundation	555 Broadway	212-925-1649
Jacques Carcanagues	106 Spring St	212-925-8110
Janet Borden	560 Broadway	212-431-0166
John Szoke Editions	591 Broadway, 3rd Fl	212-219-8300
June Kelly	591 Broadway	212-226-1660
Kent Gallery	67 Prince St	212-966-4500
Kerrigan Campell Art + Projects	317 E 9th St	212-505-7196
Lance Fung Gallery	537 Broadway, 2nd Fl	212-334-6242
Lennon, Weinberg	560 Broadway #308	212-941-0012
Leslie-Lohman Gay Art Foundation	127B Prince St	212-673-7007
Locus Media Gallery	594 Broadway	212-334-6424
Louis K Meisel	141 Prince St	212-677-1340
Luise Ross	568 Broadway #402	212-343-2161
Margarete Roeder Gallery	545 Broadway, 4th Fl	212-925-6098
Martin Lawrence	457 West Broadway	212-995-8865
Michael Ingbar Gallery of Architectural Art	568 Broadway	212-334-1100
Mimi Ferzt	114 Prince St	212-343-9377
Montserrat	584 Broadway	212-941-8899
Multiple Impressions	128 Spring St	212-925-1313
Nancy Hoffman	429 West Broadway	212-966-6676
National Association of Women Artists Fifth Avenue Gallery	80 Fifth Ave #1405	212-675-1616
New York Earth Room	141 Wooster St	212-473-8072
New York Studio School	8 W 8th St	212-673-6466
Nolan/Eckman	560 Broadway #604	212-925-6190
OK Harris Works of Art	383 West Broadway	212-431-3600
Opera Gallery	115 Spring St	212-966-6675
Parsons School of Design Exhibitions	2 W 13th St	212-229-8987
Pen & Brush, The	16 E 10th St	212-475-3669
Peter Blum Gallery	99 Wooster St	212-343-0441
Peter Freeman	560 Broadway #602	212-966-5154
Phoenix	568 Broadway #607	212-226-8711
Phyllis Kind Gallery	136 Greene St	212-925-1200
pop international galleries	473 West Broadway	212-533-4262
Rosenberg Gallery	34 Stuyvesant St	212-998-5702
Rosenberg + Kaufman Fine Art	115 Wooster St	212-431-4838
Salmagundi Club	47 Fifth Ave	212-255-7740
Sculptors Guild	110 Greene St #603	212-431-5669
Soho Black and White Photo	216 Lafayette St	212-431-7100
Sragow	73 Spring St	212-219-1793
Staley-Wise Gallery	560 Broadway #305	212-966-6223
Storefront for Art and Architecture	97 Kenmare St	212-431-5795
Suite 106/Popiashvili Newman Gallery	112 Mercer St	212-274-9166
Sundaram Tagore Gallery	137 Greene St	212-677-4520
Susan Teller Gallery	568 Broadway #103A	212-941-7335
Tenri Cultural Institute	43A W 13th St	212-645-2800
Terrain Gallery	141 Greene St	212-777-4490
Tobey Fine Arts	580 Broadway #902	212-431-7878
Visual Arts Gallery	137 Wooster St	212-598-0221
Walter Wickiser Gallery	568 Broadway #104B	212-941-1817
Ward-Nasse Gallery	178 Prince St	212-925-6951
Washington Square Windows	80 Washington Sq E	212-998-5748
Westwood Gallery	578 Broadway	212-925-5700
Wooster Arts Space	147 Wooster St	212-777-6338
Work Space Gallery, The	96 Spring St, 8th Fl	212-219-2790

Map 7 • East Village

ATM Gallery	170 Avenue B	212-375-0349
Gallery Onetwentyeight	128 Rivington St	212-674-0244
Rivington Arms	102 Rivington St	646-654-3213
The Phatory	618 E 9th St	212-777-7922
Transplant	139 Orchard St, 2nd Fl	212-505-0994

Map 8 • Chelsea

303 Gallery	525 W 22nd St	212-255-1121
ACA Galleries	529 W 20th St, 5th Fl	212-206-8080
AIR Gallery	511 W 25th St	212-255-6651
Alexander and Bonin	132 Tenth Ave	212-367-7474
Allen Sheppard Gallery	530 W 25th St	212-989-9919
Alona Kagan Gallery	540 W 29th St	212-343-4293
American Fine Arts at PHAG	530 W 22nd St	212-727-7366
Amos Eno Gallery	530 W 25th St, 6th Fl	212-226-5342
Amsterdam Whitney	511 W 25th St	212-255-9050
Andre Zarre Gallery	529 W 20th St, 7th Fl	212-255-0202
Andrea Rosen Gallery	525 W 24th St	212-627-6000
Andrew Edlin Gallery	529 W 20th St, 6th Fl	212-206-9723
Andrew Kreps	516 W 20th St	212-741-8849
Annina Nosei	530 W 22nd St, 2nd Fl	212-741-8695

Anton Kern	532 W 20th St	212-367-9663
Ariel Meyerowitz Gallery	120 Eleventh Ave, 2nd Fl	212-414-2770
Art of this Century	530 W 25th St, 6th Fl	212-352-8131
Art Resources Transfer	511 W 23rd St #3B	212-691-5956
Art @ Urban Architecture	210 Eleventh Ave, 4th Fl	212-924-1688
Aurora Gallery	515 W 29th St, 2nd Fl	212-643-1700
Axel Raben Gallery	526 W 26th St #304	212-647-9064
Axis Gallery	453 W 17th St, 4th Fl	212-741-2582
Barbara Gladstone Gallery	515 W 24th St	212-206-9300
Bill Maynes	529 W 20th St, 8th Fl	212-741-3318
Bitforms	529 W 20th St, 2nd Fl	212-366-6939
Blue Mountain Gallery	530 W 25th St, 4th Fl	646-486-4730
Bose Pacia Modern	508 W 26th St, 11th Fl	212-989-7074
Bound & Unbound	601 W 26th St #1201	212-463-7348
Bowery Gallery	530 W 25th St, 4th Fl	646-230-6655
Brent Sikkema	530 W 22nd St	212-929-2262
Briggs Robinson Gallery	527 W 29th St	212-560-9075
Bruce Silverstein Gallery	504 W 22nd St	212-627-3930
Bryce Wolkowitz Gallery	601 W 26th St #1240	212-243-8830
Caelum Gallery	526 W 26th St, #315	212-924-4161
Camhy Studio Gallery	526 W 26th St	212-741-9183
Caren Golden Fine Art	526 W 26th St, #215	212-727-8304
Ceres	547 W 27th St, 2nd Fl	212-947-6100
Chambers Fine Art	210 Eleventh Ave, 2nd Fl	212-414-1169
Chappell Gallery	526 W 26th St, #317	212-414-2673
Charles Cowles Gallery	537 W 24th St	212-925-3500
Cheim & Read	547 W 25th St	212-242-7727
Clementine Gallery	526 W 26th St, 2nd Fl	212-243-5937
COFA/Claire Oliver Fine Art	529 W 20th St #2W	212-929-5949
Cohan and Leslie	138 Tenth Ave	212-206-8710
CRG Gallery	535 W 22nd St, 3rd Fl	212-229-2766
Cristinerose/Josee Bienvenu Gallery	529 W 20th St, 2nd Fl	212-206-0297
Cue Art Foundation	511 W 25th St	212-206-3583
D'Amelio Terras	525 W 22nd St	212-352-9460
Daniel Silverstein Gallery	520 W 21st St	212-929-4300
David Krut Fine Art	526 W 20th St #816	212-255-0394
David Zwirner	525 W 19th St	212-727-2070
DCA Gallery	525 W 22nd St	212-255-5511
Debs & Co	525 W 26th St, 2nd Fl	212-643-2070
Denise Bibro Fine Art	529 W 20th St, 4th Fl	212-647-7030
Derek Eller Gallery	526 W 25th St, 2nd Fl	212-206-6411
Dia Center for the Arts	548 W 22nd St	212-989-5566
DJT Fine Art/Dom Taglialatella	511 W 25th St, 2nd Fl	212-367-0881
Dorfman Projects	529 W 20th St, 7th Fl	212-352-2272
Edition Schellmann	210 Eleventh Ave, 8th Fl	212-219-1821
Edward Thorp	210 Eleventh Ave, 6th Fl	212-691-6565
Elizabeth Dee Gallery	545 W 20th St	212-924-7545
Elizabeth Harris	529 W 20th St	212-463-9666
Esso Gallery	531 W 26th St	212-560-9728
Exit Art	475 Tenth Ave	212-966-7745
Eyebeam	540 W 21st St	212-252-5193
Feature	530 W 25th St	212-675-7772
Feigen Contemporary	535 W 20th St	212-929-0500
First Street Gallery	526 W 26th St #915	646-336-8053
Fischbach Gallery	210 Eleventh Ave #801	212-759-2345
Florence Lynch Gallery	539 W 25th St	212-924-3290
Fredericks Freiser Gallery	504 W 22nd St	212-633-6555
Frederieke Taylor Gallery	535 W 22nd St, 6th Fl	646-230-0992
Friedrich Petzel	535 W 22nd St	212-680-9467
Gagosian Gallery	555 W 24th St	212-741-1111
Gale-Martin Fine Arts	134 Tenth Ave	646-638-2525
Galeria Ramis Barquet	532 W 24th St	212-675-3421
Galerie Lelong	528 W 26th St	212-315-0470
Gallery Henoch	555 W 25th St	917-305-0003
Gary Tatintsian Gallery	531 W 25th St	212-633-0110
Gavin Brown's Enterprise	436 W 15th St	212-627-5258
Generous Miracles	529 W 20th St #8F	212-352-2858
George Billis Gallery	511 W 25th St	212-645-2621
Gorney Bravin & Lee	534 W 26th St	212-352-8372
Greene Naftali	526 W 26th St, 8th Fl	212-463-7770
Haim Chanin Fine Arts	210 Eleventh Ave #201	646-230-7200
Heidi Cho Gallery	522 W 23rd St	212-255-6783
Henry Urbach Architecture	526 W 26th St	212-627-0974
Howard Scott	529 W 20th St, 7th Fl	646-486-7004
I-20 Gallery	529 W 20th St	212-645-1100
In Camera	511 W 25th St #401	212-647-7667
International Poster Center	601 W 26th St	212-787-4000
International Print Center New York	526 W 26th St #824	212-989-5090
J Cacciola Galleries	531 W 25th St	212-462-4646
Jack Shainman Gallery	513 W 20th St	212-645-1701
James Cohan	533 W 26th St	212-714-9500
Jan Van Der Donk Rare Books	601 W 26th St #1201	212-691-5973
Jeff Bailey Gallery	511 W 25th St #808	212-989-0156
Jeffrey Coploff	508 W 26th St #318	212-741-1149
JG Contemporary/James Graham & Sons	505 W 28th St	212-564-7662
Jim Kempner Fine Art	501 W 23rd St	212-206-6872
John Connelly Presents	526 W 26th St, 10th Fl	212-337-9563
John Elder Gallery	529 W 20th St #7W	212-462-2600
John Stevenson Gallery	338 W 23rd St	212-352-0070
Joseph Helman	601 W 26th St	212-929-1545
Julie Saul Gallery	535 W 22nd St, 6th Fl	212-627-2410
Kashya Hildebrand Gallery	531 W 25th St	212-366-5757
Katherine Markel Fine Arts	529 W 20th St	212-366-5368
Kim Foster	529 W 20th St	212-229-0044
Kimcherova	532 W 25th St	212-929-9720
Kitchen Gallery, The	512 W 19th St	212-255-5793
Klemens Gasser & Tanja Grunert	524 W 19th St, 2nd Fl	212-807-9494
Klotz Sirmon Gallery	511 W 25th St	212-741-4764
Kravets/Wehby Gallery	521 W 21st St	212-352-2238
Lehmann Maupin	540 W 26th St	212-255-2923
Leslie Tonkonow Artworks and Projects	535 W 22nd St, 6th Fl	212-255-8450
LFL Gallery	530 W 24th St	212-989-7700
Linda Durham Contemporary Art	210 Eleventh Ave, 8th Fl	212-337-0025
Lohin Geduld Gallery	531 W 25th St	212-675-2656
Lombard-Freid Fine Arts	531 W 26th St	212-967-8040
Lost Art	515 W 29th St PH	212-594-5450
Lucas Schoormans	508 W 26th St #11B	212-243-3159
Luhring Augustine	531 W 24th St	212-206-9100
Lyons Wier Gallery	511 W 25th St #205	212-242-6220
Margaret Thatcher Projects	511 W 25th St #404	212-675-0222
Marianne Boesky Gallery	535 W 22nd St	212-680-9889
Marvelli Gallery	526 W 26th St	212-627-3363
Mary Boone Gallery	541 W 24th St	212-752-2929
Massimo Audiello	526 W 26th St #519	212-675-9082
Matthew Marks Gallery	522 W 22nd St	212-243-0200
Matthew Marks Gallery	523 W 24th St	212-243-0200
Matthew Marks Gallery	529 W 21st St	212-243-0200
Max Protech	511 W 22nd St	212-633-6999
McKenzie Fine Art	511 W 25th St, 2nd Fl	212-989-5467
Medialia: Rack & Hamper Gallery	335 W 38th St, 4th Fl	212-971-0953
Messineo Wyman Projects	525 W 22nd St	212-414-0827
Metro Pictures	519 W 24th St	212-206-7100
Mike Weiss Gallery	520 W 24th St	212-691-6899
Miller/Geisler Gallery	511 W 25th St, 3rd Fl	212-255-2885
Mixed Greens	601 W 26th St, 11th Fl	212-331-8888
Murray Guy	453 W 17th St	212-463-7372

Map 8 • Chelsea *continued*

MY Art Prospects	547 W 27th St, 2nd Fl	212-268-7132
Nancy Margolis Gallery	523 W 25th St	212-343-9523
New Century Artists	530 W 25th St #406	212-367-7072
Nicole Klagsbrun Gallery	526 W 26th St #213	212-243-3335
NoHo Gallery in SoHo	530 W 25th St, 4th Fl	212-367-7063
PaceWildenstein	534 W 25th St	212-929-7000
Paint Box Gallery	170 Ninth Ave	212-675-1680
Paul Kasmin Gallery	293 Tenth Ave	212-563-4474
Paul Morris Gallery	465 W 23rd St	212-727-2752
Paul Rodgers/9W	529 W 20th St, 9th Fl	212-414-9810
Paula Cooper Gallery	534 W 21st St	212-255-1105
Pavel Zoubok Gallery	533 W 23rd St	917-364-3293
Perimeter Gallery	511 W 25th St #402	212-675-1585
Perry Rubenstein	521 W 23rd St	212-206-7348
Pleiades Gallery	530 W 25th St	646-230-0056
Plum Blossoms Gallery	555 W 25th St	212-719-7008
Postmasters Gallery	459 W 19th St	212-727-3323
PPOW	555 W 25th St, 2nd Fl	212-647-1044
Prince Street Gallery	530 W 25th St, 4th Fl	646-230-0246
Printed Matter	535 W 22nd St	212-925-0325
Rare	521 W 26th St	212-268-1520
Reeves Contemporary	535 W 24th St, 2nd Fl	212-714-0044
Ricco/Maresca Gallery	529 W 20th St, 3rd Fl	212-627-4819
Riva Gallery	529 W 20th St, 11th Fl	212-242-3434
Robert Mann Gallery	210 Eleventh Ave	212-989-7600
Robert Miller	524 W 26th St	212-366-4774
Robert Steele Gallery	511 W 25th St	212-243-0165
Rush Arts Gallery & Resource Center	526 W 26th St #311	212-691-9552
Sandra Gering Gallery	534 W 22nd St	646-336-7183
Sara Meltzer Gallery	516 W 20th St	212-727-9330
Sean Kelly Gallery	528 W 29th St	212-239-1181
Sears-Peyton Gallery	210 Eleventh Ave #802	212-966-7469
Sherry French	601 W 26th St	212-647-8867
Silas Seandel Studio	551 W 22nd St	212-645-5286
Skoto Gallery	529 W 20th St	212-352-8058
SoHo 20 Chelsea	511 W 25th St #605	212-367-8994
Solo Impression	601 W 26th St	212-229-9595
Sonnabend	536 W 22nd St	212-627-1018
Spike Gallery	547 W 20th St	212-627-4100
Stefan Stux Gallery	529 W 20th St #9E	212-352-1600
Stephen Haller	542 W 26th St	212-741-7777
Stricoff Fine Art	564 W 25th St	212-219-3977
Studio 601	511 W 25th St	212-367-7300
Susan Inglett Gallery	535 W 22nd St, 6th Fl	212-647-9111
Tanya Bonakdar Gallery	521 W 21st St	212-414-4144
Team	527 W 26th St	212-279-9219
The Proposition: Ellen Donahue & Ronald Sosinski Art	559 W 22nd St	212-242-0035
Thomas Erben Gallery	516 W 20th St	212-645-8701
Thomas Werner Gallery	526 W 26th St #712	646-638-2883
Universal Concepts Unlimited	507 W 24th St	212-727-7575
Van De Weghe Fine Art	521 W 23rd St	212-929-6633
Viridian Artists	530 W 25th St #407	212-414-4040
Von Lintel Gallery	555 W 25th St, 2nd Fl	212-242-0599
WhiteBox	525 W 26th St	212-714-2347
Yancey Richardson Gallery	535 W 22nd St	646-230-9610
Yossi Milo Gallery	552 W 24th St	212-414-0370
Yvon Lambert	564 W 25th St	212-242-3611
Ziehersmith	531 W 25th St	212-229-1088

Map 9 • Flatiron / Lower Midtown

A Ramona Studio	65 W 37th St	212-398-1904
Alp Galleries	291 Seventh Ave, 5th Fl	212-206-9108
Art Center of the Graduate Center CUNY	365 Fifth Ave	212-817-7386
Avalanche	39 E 31st St, 3rd Fl	212-447-9485
Christine Burgin Gallery	243 W 18th St	212-462-2668
H Heather Edelman Gallery	141 W 20th St	646-230-1104
Illustration House	110 W 25th St	212-966-9444
Kavehaz	37 W 26th St	212-343-0612
Limner	870 Sixth Ave	212-725-0999
Marlborough Chelsea	211 W 19th St	212-463-8634
Merton D Simpson Gallery	38 W 28th St, 5th Fl	212-686-6735
Nabi Gallery	137 W 25th St	212-929-6063
Rachel Adler Fine Art	1200 Broadway	212-308-0511
School of Visual Arts Westside Gallery	141 W 21st St	212-592-2145
Senior & Shopmaker	21 E 26th St	212-213-6767
Sepia International	148 W 24th St	212-645-9444
Studio Annex at Madison Industries	279 Fifth Ave	212-652-0629
Terrapin Art Gallery	121 W 15th St	212-645-3041
The Museum at the Fashion Institute of Technology	227 W 27th St	212-217-5800
Tibet House Museum	22 W 15th St	212-807-0563
Ursus Books Chelsea	132 W 21st St	212-627-5370
Yeshiva University Museum	15 W 16th St	212-294-8330

Map 10 • Murray Hill / Gramercy

Baruch College/Sidney Mishkin Gallery	135 E 22nd St	212-802-2690
Blue Heron Arts Center	123 E 24th St	212-979-5000
SVA Main Gallery	209 E 23rd St	212-592-2145
Swann Galleries	104 E 25th St	212-254-4710
Talwar Gallery	108 E 16th St	212-673-3096
Tepper Galleries	110 E 25th St	212-677-5300

Map 11 • Hell's Kitchen

Art for Healing NYC / Art for Healing Gallery	405 W 50th St	212-977-1165
Fountain Gallery	702 Ninth Ave	212-262-2756
Gallery @49	322 W 49th St	212-767-0855
Hunter College/Times Square Gallery	450 W 41st St	212-772-4991
Jadite	413 W 50th St	212-315-2740

Map 12 • Midtown

Alexandre Gallery	41 E 57th St, 13th Fl	212-755-2828
Ameringer & Yohe Fine Art	20 W 57th St, 2nd Fl	212-445-0051
Anthony Grant	37 W 57th St, 2nd Fl	212-755-0434
Art Students League of NY	215 W 57th St, 2nd Fl	212-247-4510
Artemis Greenberg Van Doren Gallery	730 Fifth Ave, 7th Fl	212-445-0444
Austrian Cultural Forum	11 E 52nd St	212-319-5300
AXA Gallery	787 Seventh Ave	212-554-4818
Babcock	724 Fifth Ave, 11th Fl	212-767-1852
Barbara Mathes	41 E 57th St, 3rd Fl	212-752-5135
Bernarducci - Meisel	37 W 57th St, 6th Fl	212-593-3757
China 2000 Fine Art	5 E 57th St	212-588-1198
Dai Ichi Gallery, Julian Jadow Ceramics	24 W 57th St #601	212-757-6660
Danese	41 E 57th St, 6th Fl	212-223-2227
David Findlay Jr Fine Art	41 E 57th St #1120	212-486-7660
DC Moore	724 Fifth Ave, 8th Fl	212-247-2111
Edwynn Houk	745 Fifth Ave, 4th Fl	212-750-7070
Fitch-Febvrel	5 E 57th St, 12th Fl	212-688-8522
Forum	745 Fifth Ave, 5th Fl	212-355-4545
Franklin Parrasch	20 W 57th St	212-246-5360
Frederick Schultz Ancient Art	41 E 57th St, 11th Fl	212-758-6007
Galeria Ramis Barquet	41 E 57th St, 5th Fl	212-644-9090
Galerie St Etienne	24 W 57th St #802	212-245-6734
Gallery: Gertrude Stein	56 W 57th St, 3rd Fl	212-535-0600
Garth Clark	24 W 57th St #305	212-246-2205
Gemini GEL	58 W 58th St #21-B	212-308-0924

at Joni Moisant Weyl		
George Adams	41 W 57th St, 7th Fl	212-644-5665
Grant Selwyn Fine Art	37 W 57th St, 2nd Fl	212-755-0434
Hammer Galleries	33 W 57th St	212-644-4400
Herbert Arnot	250 W 57th St	212-245-8287
Howard Greenberg	41 E 57th St, 14th Fl	212-334-0010
International Center of Photography	1133 Sixth Ave	212-857-0000
Jain Marunouchi	24 W 57th St, 6th Fl	212-969-9660
James Goodman	41 E 57th St, 8th Fl	212-593-3737
Jan Krugier	41 E 57th St, 6th Fl	212-755-7288
Joan T Washburn	20 W 57th St, 8th Fl	212-397-6780
Joan Whalen Fine Art	24 W 57th St #507	212-397-9700
Katharina Rich Perlow	41 E 57th St, 13th Fl	212-644-7171
Kennedy Galleries	730 Fifth Ave	212-541-9600
Kraushaar	724 Fifth Ave	212-307-5730
Laurence Miller	20 W 57th St	212-397-3930
Leo Kaplan Modern	41 E 57th St, 7th Fl	212-872-1616
Leonard Hutton	41 E 57th St, 3rd Fl	212-751-7373
Littlejohn Contemporary	41 E 57th St, 7th Fl	212-980-2323
Lori Bookstein Fine Art	37 W 57th St	212-439-9605
Marian Goodman	24 W 57th St, 4th Fl	212-977-7160
Marlborough	40 W 57th St, 2nd Fl	212-541-4900
Mary Boone	745 Fifth Ave, 4th Fl	212-752-2929
Mary Ryan	24 W 57th St, 2nd Fl	212-397-0669
Maxwell Davidson	724 Fifth Ave	212-759-7555
McKee	745 Fifth Ave, 4th Fl	212-688-5951
Meridian Gallery - Rita Krauss	41 E 57th St, 8th Fl	212-980-2400
Michael Rosenfeld	24 W 57th St, 7th Fl	212-247-0082
Museum of Arts & Design	40 W 53rd St	212-956-3535
Neuhoff	41 E 57th St, 4th Fl	212-838-1122
New Art Center	580 Eighth Ave	212-354-2999
Nohra Haime	41 E 57th St, 6th Fl	212-888-3550
O'Hara	41 E 57th St, 13th Fl	212-355-3330
Pace MacGill	32 E 57th St, 9th Fl	212-759-7999
Pace Primitive	32 E 57th St, 7th Fl	212-421-3688
Pace Prints	32 E 57th St, 3rd Fl	212-421-3237
Pace Wildenstein	32 E 57th St	212-421-3292
Peter Findlay	41 E 57th St, 3rd Fl	212-644-4433
Reece	24 W 57th St #304	212-333-5830
Rehs Galleries	5 E 57th St	212-355-5710
Scholten Japanese Art	145 W 58th St #2H	212-585-0474
So Hyun Gallery	41 W 57th St	212-355-6669
Susan Sheehan	20 W 57th St, 7th Fl	212-489-3331
The Project	37 W 57th St, 3rd Fl	212-688-4673
Tibor de Nagy	724 Fifth Ave, 12th Fl	212-262-5050
Tina Kim Fine Art	41 W 57th St, 2nd Fl	212-716-1100
UBS Art Gallery	1285 Sixth Ave	212-713-2885
UMA Gallery	30 W 57th St, 6th Fl	212-757-7240
Zabriskie	41 E 57th St, 4th Fl	212-752-1223

Map 13 • East Midtown

Dai Ichi Arts	249 E 48th St	212-230-1680
Gallery Korea	460 Park Ave, 6th Fl	212-759-9550
Japan Society	333 E 47th St	212-832-1155
National Sculpture Society	237 Park Ave	212-764-5645
Spanierman Gallery	45 E 58th St	212-832-0208
St Peter's Lutheran Church	619 Lexington Ave	212-935-2200
Throckmorton Fine Art	145 E 57th St, 3rd Fl	212-223-1059
Trygve Lie Gallery	317 E 52nd St	212-319-0370
Ubu Gallery	416 E 59th St	212-753-4444
Wally Findlay Galleries	124 E 57th St	212-421-5390

Map 14 • Upper West Side (Lower)

Linda Hyman Fine Arts	25 Central Park W	212-399-0112

Map 15 • Upper East Side (Lower)

Achim Moeller Fine Art	167 E 73rd St	212-988-4500
Acquavella	18 E 79th St	212-734-6300
Adam Baumgold	74 E 79th St	212-861-7338
Adelson Galleries	25 E 77th St, 3rd Fl	212-439-6800
American Illustrators Gallery	18 E 77th St #1A	212-744-5190
Anita Friedman Fine Arts	980 Madison Ave	212-472-1527
Anita Shapolsky	152 E 65th St	212-452-1094
Barry Friedman, LTD	32 E 67th St	212-794-8950
Berry-Hill	11 E 70th St	212-744-2300
Bonni Benrubi	52 E 76th St	212-517-3766
Bruton	40 E 61st St	212-980-1640
C&M Arts	45 E 78th St	212-861-0020
Carosso Fine Art	42 E 76th St	212-744-5400
CDS	76 E 79th St	212-772-9555
Conner & Rosenkranz	16 E 73rd St	212-517-3710
Cook Fine Art	1063 Madison Ave	212-737-3550
D Wigmore Fine Art	22 E 76th St	212-794-2128
David Finlay	984 Madison Ave	212-249-2909
Davis & Langdale	231 E 60th St	212-838-0333
Debra Force Fine Art	14 E 73rd St #4B	212-734-3636
Diane Upright Fine Arts	188 E 76th St	212-734-3072
Dickinson Roundell	19 E 66th St	212-772-8083
Ekstrom & Ekstrom	417 E 75th St	212-988-8857
Elkon Gallery	18 E 81st St	212-535-3940
Evan Janis Fine Art	70 E 79th St	212-639-1501
Ezair	905 Madison Ave	212-628-2224
Flowers	1000 Madison Ave, 2nd Fl	212-439-1700
Frick Collection, The	1 E 70th St	212-288-0700
Frost & Reed	21 E 67th St	212-717-2201
Gagosian	980 Madison Ave	212-744-2313
Galerie Rienzo	20 E 69th St #4C	212-288-2226
Gallery 71	974 Lexington Ave	212-744-7779
Gallery Pahk	988 Madison Ave	212-861-3303
Gallery Schlesinger	24 E 73rd St, 2nd Fl	212-734-3600
Gerald Peters	24 E 78th St	212-628-9760
Godel & Co	39A E 72nd St	212-288-7272
Goedhuis Contemporary	42 E 76th St	212-535-6954
Hall & Knight	21 E 67th St	212-772-2266
Hilde Gerst	987 Madison Ave	212-288-3400
Hirschl & Adler Galleries	21 E 70th St	212-535-8810
Hollis Taggart Galleries	48 E 73rd St	212-628-4000
Hoorn-Ashby	766 Madison Ave, 2nd Fl	212-628-3199
Hubert Gallery	1046 Madison Ave	212-628-2922
Hunter College/Bertha & Karl Leubsdorf Gallery	E 68th St & Lexington	212-772-4991
Irena Hochman Fine Art	1100 Madison Ave	212-772-2227
Jacobson Howard	19 E 76th St	212-570-2362
James Francis Trezza	39 E 78th St #603	212-327-2218
James Graham & Sons	1014 Madison Ave	212-535-5767
Jane Kahan	922 Madison Ave, 2nd Fl	212-744-1490
Janos Gat Gallery	1100 Madison Ave	212-327-0441
Kate Ganz USA	25 E 73rd St	212-535-1977
Keith De Lellis	47 E 68th St	212-327-1482
Kimberly Venardos & Co	1014 Madison Ave	212-879-5858
Knoedler & Co	19 E 70th St	212-794-0550
Kouros	23 E 73rd St	212-288-5888
L'Arc En Seine	15 E 82nd St	212-585-2587
Lawrence Markay	42 E 76th St, 4th Fl	212-517-9892
Leo Castelli	18 E 77th St	212-249-4470
Leon Tovar Gallery	16 E 71st St	212-585-2400
M Sutherland Fine Arts	55 E 80th St, 2nd Fl	212-249-0428
Mark Murray Fine Paintings	39 E 72nd St	212-585-2380
Martha Parrish & James Reinish	25 E 73rd St, 2nd Fl	212-734-7332
Mary-Anne Martin Fine Art	23 E 73rd St	212-288-2213
McGrath Galleries	9 E 77th St	212-737-7396
Menconi & Schoelkopt Fine Art	13 E 69th St	212-879-8815
Michael Werner	4 E 77th St	212-988-1623
Michail-Lombardo Gallery	19 E 69th St #302	212-472-2400
Michelle Rosenfeld	16 E 79th St	212-734-0900
Mitchell-Innes & Nash	1018 Madison Ave, 5th Fl	212-744-7400

Map 15 • Upper E Side (Lower) *continued*

AMMC Gallery	221 E 71st St	212-517-0692
Neptune Fine Art & Brand X Projects	50 E 72nd St	212-628-0501
Pat Kery Fine Arts	61 E 66th St	212-535-0741
Peter Hay Halpert Fine Art	515 E 72nd St #26D	212-988-3662
Praxis International Art	25 E 73rd St, 4th Fl	212-772-9478
Questroyal Fine Art	903 Park Ave #3A & B	212-744-3586
Randel Gallery	49 E 78th St	212-861-6650
Richard Gray	1018 Madison Ave, 4th Fl	212-472-8787
Richard L Feigen & Co	34 E 69th St	212-628-0700
Richard York	21 E 65th St, 2nd Fl	212-772-9155
Roth Horowitz	160A E 70th St	212-717-9067
Salander-O'Reilly	20 E 79th St	212-879-6606
Sayer Fine Arts Gallery	129 E 71st St	212-517-8811
Schiller & Bodo	19 E 74th St	212-772-8627
Shepherd & Derom Galleries	58 E 79th St	212-861-4050
Skarstedt Fine Art	1018 Madison Ave, 3rd Fl	212-737-2060
Solomon & Co Fine Art	959 Madison Ave	212-737-8200
Soufer	1015 Madison Ave	212-628-3225
Ukrainian Institute of America	2 E 79th St	212-288-8660
Ursus Prints	981 Madison Ave	212-772-8787
Vivian Horan Fine Art	35 E 67th St, 2nd Fl	212-517-9410
Wildenstein	19 E 64th St	212-879-0500
William Secord	52 E 76th St	212-249-0075
Winston Wachter Mayer Fine Art	39 E 78th St #301	212-327-2526
Yoshii	17 E 76th St #1R	212-744-5550
Zwirner & Wirth	32 E 69th St	212-517-8677

Map 17 • Upper E Side / E Harlem

Allan Stone Gallery	113 E 90th St	212-987-4997
Casa Linda Galleries	300 E 95th St	212-860-8016
Doyle New York	175 E 87th St	212-427-2730
Gallery at the Marmara-Manhattan	301 E 94th St	212-427-3100
Gallery Evan	300 E 95th St	212-534-1867
Jeffrey Myers Primitive & Fine Art	12 E 86th St	212-472-0115
Neue Galerie New York	1048 Fifth Ave	212-628-6200
Samson Fine Arts	1150 Fifth Ave	212-369-6677
Uptown Gallery	1194 Madison Ave	212-722-3677

Map 18 • Columbia/Morningside Hts

Galleries at the Interchurch Ctr	475 Riverside Dr	212-870-2200
Miriam & Ira D Wallach Art Gallery	116th & Broadway, Schermerhorn Hall, 8th Fl	212-854-7288

Map 19 • Harlem (Lower)

PCOG Gallery	1902 AC Powell Jr Blvd	212-932-9669
Studio Museum in Harlem	144 W 125th St	212-864-4500

Map 27 • Long Island City

Dorsky Gallery	11-03 45th Ave	718-937-6317
Fisher Landau Center for Art	38-27 30th St	718-937-0727
Garth Clark Gallery's Project Space	45-46 21st St	718-706-2491
La Guardia Community College, CUNY	31-10 Thomson Ave	718-482-5696
Ro Gallery	47-15 36th St	800-888-1063
Sculpture Center	44-19 Purves St	718-361-1750
Socrates Sculpture Park	Broadway & Vernon Blvd	718-956-1819

Map 28 • Greenpoint

Art-Lore	1155 Manhattan Ave	718-389-7100
Galeria Janet	205 Norman Ave	718-383-9380
GV/AS	140 Franklin St	718-389-6847
Martinez Gallery	37 Greenpoint Ave	718-706-0606

Map 29 • Williamsburg

31 Grand	31 Grand St	718-388-2858
531 Artspace	531 Graham Ave	718-388-6087
Artpage	781 N 7th St	718-302-1534
Barthelemy	329 Grand St	718-599-9772
Bench Dogs	60 Broadway	718-486-7338
Bicycle Paintings	35 Broadway	718-486-5490
Bingo Hall	212 Berry St	718-599-0844
Black & White	483 Driggs Ave	718-599-8775
Dollhaus	37 Broadway	917-667-2332
Elaint Kayne	475 Keap St	718-387-4123
EX	872 Kent Ave	718-783-0060
Fishtank	93 N 6th St	718-387-4320
Fluxcore	340 Grand St	718-599-8640
Good/Bad	383 S 1st St	718-599-4962
Hogar	111 Grand St	718-388-5022
Jack the Pelican	487 Driggs Ave	718-782-0183
Jessica Murray Projects	210 N 6th St	718-384-9606
Landing	242 Wythe Ave	718-218-6743
Lunarbase	197 Grand St	718-599-9205
Modern Mediums	104 Roebling St	718-302-9507
Naked Duck	66 Jackson St	718-609-4096
National Gallery of Brooklyn	90 Berry St	718-384-3913
Open Ground	252 Grand St	718-387-8226
Photo Gallery of Williamsburg	425 Keap St	718-782-3433
Priska C. Jushka	97 N 9th St	718-782-4100
Roebling Hall	390 Wythe Ave	718-599-5352
S1	242 S 1st St	718-302-1521
Studio	84 S 1st St	718-302-4863

Map 30 • Brooklyn Heights / DUMBO

Antiquarius	183 Concord St	718-222-2434
Artisan's Gallery	221 Court St	718-330-3432
DUMBO Arts Center	30 Washington St	718-694-0831
Engels Galerie	45 State St	718-596-0850
Faith Art	393 Bridge St	718-852-1558
Howard Schickler	100 Water St	718-431-6363
Jubilee	117 Henry St	718-596-1499
Momose Art Studio	68 Jay St	718-403-9007
SouthFirst	60 N 6th St	718-599-2500
Spring	126 Front St	718-222-1054

Map 31• Fort Greene

DEMU	761 Fulton St	718-596-8484
Sarafina	411 Myrtle Ave	718-522-1083

Map 32 • Cobble Hill / Carroll Gardens

Artez'N	444 Atlantic Ave	718-596-2649
Axelle	312 Atlantic Ave	718-246-1800
David Allen	331 Smith St	718-488-5568
East End Ensemble	273 Smith St	718-624-8878
Felice Amara	121 3rd St	718-797-4414

Map 33 • Park Slope/Prospect Heights

JK Flynn	471 Sixth Ave	718-369-8934
Praxis	610 Dean St	718-398-0894

Map 34 • Hoboken

AJ Lederman	901 Hudson St	201-659-3570
Andrew Edlin Fine Arts	1308 Garden St	201-795-0292
Rodriguez-Valdes Art Gallery	720 Monroe St	201-222-8773

Map 35 • Jersey City

Chamot Gallery	111 First St	201-610-1468
Cooper Gallery	295 Grove St	201-451-1074
Kearon-Hempenstall Gallery	536 Bergen Ave	201-333-8855
New Jersey City University	2039 Kennedy Blvd	201-200-3246
Shoe-String Gallery	111 First St	201-420-5018
Trans Hudson Gallery	160 First St	201-222-3030

Battery Park City

World Financial Center Courtyard Gallery	220 Vesey St	212-945-2600

Without a doubt, New York City boasts the best assortment of bars per square foot on the planet. How many you ask? A lot—a whole lot. Luckily for you, we've narrowed it down to the best of the best. While more and more places are opening up throughout the isle of Manhattan and its outer boroughs, the majority of bars are still parked between14th and Canal Street. This is particularly evident in the East Village/ Lower East Side area, where new bars are sprouting like weeds east of Avenue A and south of Houston. Faced with so many options, how do you choose where to go? We've taken the liberty of selecting a few choice destinations for your basic bar variables: the dive, best beer selection, outdoor space, décor, jukebox, and smoker-friendly. Happy drinking!

Dive Bars

There are A LOT of dumps in this city, but we've done our best to single out the darkest and the dirtiest. A popular choice among our staff is the oh-so derelict **Mars Bar**—clean-freaks beware of the bathroom! Other favorites include **Milano's**, **The Subway Inn**, **Welcome to the Johnson's**, **International Bar**, and **The Hole**. If you need to get down and dirty in Brooklyn check out the **Turkey's Nest** in Williamsburg.

Best Beer Selection

When it comes to range of beer, there are a number of worthy contenders. The heavily-trodden **Peculiar Pub** offers an expensive, yet extensive beer list. Visit this one on a weekday if you want some genuine one-on-one time with the bartender. **The Ginger Man** in lower Midtown stocks over 100 kinds of bottled brew, and has over 60 options on tap. **Vol de Nuit** has a large number of Belgian beers and a warm but reclusive atmosphere that sucks you in. Other places to try are **d.b.a.**, **Blind Tiger Ale House** and **The Waterfront Ale House** (located in both Manhattan and Brooklyn).

Outdoor Spaces

What could be better than sipping a cocktail under the stars? How about sipping a cocktail *with a smoke* under the stars? That's right; bars with outdoor patios have circumvented the no-smoking legislation. Not only do these outdoor spaces offer solace to cranky smokers, they provide us all with a short intermission from the commotion and clamor of city life...that is until the next fire truck screams by. We love the aptly named **Gowanus Yacht Club** in Carroll Gardens. This intimate beer garden serves up cold ones with dogs and burgers in a cook-out setting. Other patios to check out are **The Porch**, **Barramundi**, the **Bowery Bar**, **Sweet & Vicious**, the **Heights Bar & Grill** and the **High Bar** on top of the Gramercy Park Hotel.

Best Décor

We all have different styles, so let's break this down a little further. For class and sophistication try **Pravda** or **The Royalton**. For funky and unique, check out the space at **Happy Ending**, **Motor City** or **Korova Milk Bar**. For cozy and comfortable visit **Chumley's** or **Molly's**. For dark and romantic try **Decibel** or **Chez es Saada**.

Best Jukebox

Again, this is truly a matter of personal opinion, but here is a condensed list of NFT picks. For Manhattan: **Ace Bar** (indie rock/punk), **Cherry Tavern** (punk/rock), **Lakeside Lounge** (a little something for everybody), **7B** (rock all the way), **Rudy's Bar & Grill** (blues) and **The Village Idiot** (country). For Brooklyn: **The Charleston** (Williamsburg—old school), **Sweetwater Tavern** (Williamsburg—punk), **Great Lakes** (Park Slope—indie rock), and **The Boat** (Carroll Gardens—indie rock).

Smoker-Friendly

Despite Bloomberg's efforts to create a smoker-free New York, there are a few loopholes in the current legislation. You can still light up in cigar bars and hookah bars, bars with outdoor spaces, and privately owned establishments. Another exception is the separate smoking room which is tightly sealed off from the rest of the bar and specially ventilated. Unless you bring a bottle of Febreze with you, we don't recommend this last option. Good places to puff are **Circa Tabac** (cigar bar) and **Swan's Bar & Grill**.

Map 1 • Financial District

Beckett's Bar & Grill	78 Pearl St	212-269-1001	Decent downtown Irish pub.
John Street Bar & Grill	17 John St	212-349-3278	Nightmarish underground nonsense.
Liquid Assets @ Millennium Hilton Hotel	55 Church St	212-693-2001	Plush seating and soft lighting.
Ryan Maguire's Ale House	28 Cliff St	212-566-6906	Decent Irish pub.
Ryan's Sports Bar & Restaurant	46 Gold St	212-385-6044	Downtown sports bar.
Swan's Bar & Grill	213 Pearl St	212-952-0266	Recommended.
Ulysses	95 Pearl St	212-482-0400	Slightly hipper downtown bar.
White Horse Tavern	25 Bridge St	212-668-9046	Downtown dive.

Map 2 • TriBeCa

Bubble Lounge	228 West Broadway	212-431-3433	Champagne bar.
Circa Tabac	32 Watts St	212-941-1781	Smoker-friendly lounge.
Lucky Strike	59 Grand St	212-941-0772	Hipsters, locals, ex-smoky.
Nancy Whisky Pub	1 Lispenard St	212-226-9943	Good dive.
Puffy's Tavern	81 Hudson St	212-766-9159	Locals, hipsters.
Raccoon Lodge	59 Warren St	212-766-9656	Cruddy, standard.
Tribeca Tavern	247 West Broadway	212-941-7671	Good enough for us.
Walker's	16 N Moore St	212-941-0142	Where old and new Tribeca neighbors mix.

Map 3 • City Hall / Chinatown

The Beekman	15 Beekman St	212-732-7333	Guinness on tap and karaoke nights.
Double Happiness	173 Mott St	212-941-1282	Downstairs hipster bar.
Happy Ending	302 Broome St	212-334-9676	Still taking the edge off.
Knitting Factory	74 Leonard St	212-219-3006	Great downstairs bar.
Metropolitan Improvement Company	3 Madison St	212-962-8219	Where the cops drink.
Milk & Honey	134 Eldridge St		Good luck finding the phone number.
Paris Cafe	119 South St	212-240-9797	New Orleans-feel old-time pub.
Winnie's	104 Bayard St	212-732-2384	Chinese gangster karaoke!

Map 4 • Lower East Side

Bar 169	169 East Broadway	212-473-8866	Sometimes good, sometimes not.
Lolita	266 Broome St	212-966-7223	Hipster-haven.

Map 5 • West Village

Art Bar	52 Eighth Ave	212-727-0244	Great spaces, cool crowd.
Automatic Slims	733 Washington St	212-645-8660	LOUD. Yes, that loud.
Blind Tiger Ale House	518 Hudson St	212-675-3848	Excellent beer selection.
Chumley's	86 Bedford St	212-675-4449	Former speakeasy. Top 10 bar.
Duplex	61 Christopher St	212-255-5438	Everything's still fun.
Ear Inn	326 Spring St	212-226-9060	2nd oldest bar. A great place.
Henrietta Hudson	438 Hudson St	212-924-3347	Good lesbian vibe.
Red Light Bistro	50 Ninth Ave	212-675-2400	Great mix of everything.
Trust	421 W 13th St	212-645-7775	Large, laid-back lounge.
Village Idiot	355 W 14th St	212-989-7334	The mother of all neighborhood bars.
West	425 West St	212-242-4375	Lounge with a view.
White Horse Tavern	567 Hudson St	212-243-9360	Another NYC classic.

Map 6 • Washington Square / NYU / SoHo

Bar 89	89 Mercer St	212-274-0989	Cool bathrooms.
Beauty Bar	231 E 14th St	212-539-1389	Just a little off the top, dahling?
Blue & Gold	74 E 7th St	212-473-8918	Another fine East Village establishment.
Burp Castle	41 E 7th St	212-982-4576	One of a kind. Faux monks.

Cedar Tavern	82 University Pl	212-741-9754	Classic NYU/actor hangout.
Chez Es Saada	42 E 1st St	212-777-5617	Cavernous space with rose petals lining the stairwell.
Decibel	240 E 9th St	212-979-2733	Go for the sake and the space.
Detour	349 E 13th St	212-533-6212	No cover jazz.
Fanelli's	94 Prince St	212-226-9412	Old-time SoHo haunt. Nice tiles.
Fez	380 Lafayette St	212-533-7000	Great hangout space, gets crowded.
Hole, The	29 Second Ave	212-473-9406	Dark and smoky.
Holiday Lounge	75 St Mark's Pl	212-777-9637	Where to go to lose your soul.
Josie Wood's Pub	11 Waverly Pl	212-228-9909	Friendly underground pub.
KGB	85 E 4th St	212-460-0982	Former CP HQ. Meet your comrades.
Mars Bar	25 E 1st St	212-473-9842	The king of grungy bars. Recommended.
McSorley' s Old Ale House	15 E 7th St	212-473-9148	Lights or darks?
Milano's	51 E Houston St	212-226-8844	Grungy, narrow, awesome.
Nevada Smith's	74 Third Ave	212-982-2591	GooooaaaaaaLLL!
Peculiar Pub	145 Bleecker St	212-353-1327	Large beer selection. NYU.
Pravda	281 Lafayette St	212-226-4696	Sophisticated lounge serving up inventive martinis.
Red Bench	107 Sullivan St	212-274-9120	Tiny, classy, quiet (sometimes).
The Room	144 Sullivan St	212-477-2102	Candle-lit lounge with excellent beer selection.
Spring Lounge	48 Spring St	212-965-1774	Packed but still a classic.
Sweet & Vicious	5 Spring St	212-334-7915	Great outdoor space.

Map 7 • East Village

11th Street Bar	510 E 11th St	212-982-3929	Darts, Irish, excellent.
2A	25 Avenue A	212-505-2466	Great upstairs space.
7B	108 Avenue B	212-473-8840	*Godfather II* shot here. What can be bad?
Ace Bar	531 E 5th St	212-979-8476	Loud, headbanger-y, good.
Barramundi	147 Ludlow St	212-529-6900	Great garden in summer.
Bouche Bar	540 E 5th St	212-475-1673	Small, intimate, cool.
Cherry Tavern	441 E 6th St	212-777-1448	Get the Tijuana Special.
Clubhouse	700 E 9th St	212-260-7970	2A + 7B = 9C, right?
d.b.a.	41 First Ave	212-475-5097	Lots of beers and hipsters.
The Edge	95 E 3rd St	212-477-2940	Biker hangout. Don't bring your camera.
International Bar	120 1/2 First Ave	212-777-9244	Small and unique.
Joe's Bar	520 E 6th St	212-473-9093	Classic neighborhood hangout. A favorite.
Korova Milk Bar	200 Avenue A	212-254-8838	Everyone goes here.
Lakeside Lounge	162 Avenue B	212-529-8463	Great jukebox, live music, décor, everything.
Lansky Lounge	104 Norfolk St	212-677-9489	Great space, packed with hyenas.
Max Fish	178 Ludlow St	212-253-1922	Where the musicians go.
Meow Mix	269 E Houston St	212-254-0688	2-story lesbian lovefest! Recommended.
Mona's	224 Avenue B	212-353-3780	Depressing. Recommended.
Motor City	127 Ludlow St	212-358-1595	Faux biker bar. Still good, though.
Parkside Lounge	317 E Houston St	212-673-6270	Good basic bar.
The Phoenix	447 E 13th St	212-477-9979	$1 Wednesdays!
The Porch	115 Avenue C	212-982-4034	Just like back at home.
Sophie's	507 E 5th St	212-228-5680	More crowded counterpart to Joe's.
WCOU Radio Bar	115 First Ave	212-254-4317	Great small neighborhood bar.
Welcome to the Johnsons	123 Rivington St	212-420-4317	Great décor, but too crowded mostly.
Zum Schneider	107 Avenue C	212-598-1098	Get weisse, man.

Map 8 • Chelsea

Billymark's West	332 Ninth Ave	212-629-0118	Down and dirty dive.
Blarney Stone	340 Ninth Ave	212-502-4656	The only bar in purgatory.
Blarney Stone	410 Eighth Ave	212-997-9248	The only bar in purgatory.
Chelsea Brewing Company	Pier 59	212-336-6440	When you're done playing basketball.
Chelsea Commons	242 Tenth Ave	212-929-9424	Basic local pub.
Freight	410 W 16th St	212-242-6555	Huge lounge. Small crowds.
Glass	287 Tenth Ave	212-904-1580	Trendy. Whatever that means.
Kanvas	219 Ninth Ave	212-727-2616	Bi-level Chelsea haven.
Openair	559 W 22nd St	212-243-1851	Minimal Chelsea goodness.
The Park	118 Tenth Ave	212-352-3313	Good patio.
Red Rock West	457 W 17th St	212-366-5359	F--king loud!
West Side Tavern	360 W 23rd St	212-366-3738	Local mixture.

Map 9 • Flatiron / Lower Midtown

Blarney Stone	106 W 32nd St	212-502-5139	The only bar in purgatory.
Cutting Room	19 W 24th St	212-691-4065	Large, usually mellow vibe.
Dusk of Miami	147 W 24th St	212-924-4490	Raw, post-hip, good.
Ginger Man	11 E 36th St	212-532-3740	Excellent beer selection.
Heartland Brewery	35 Union Sq W	212-645-3400	Heartland HeartLAND HEARTLAND!
Live Bait	14 E 23rd St	212-353-2400	Still a great feel. A mainstay.
Merchants	112 Seventh Ave	212-366-7267	Good mixed space.
Old Town Bar & Restaurant	45 E 18th St	212-529-6732	Excellent old-NY pub. Skip the food.
Tir Na Nog	5 Penn Plz	212-630-0249	Penn Station hangout.
Under The Volcano	12 E 36th St	212-213-0093	Relaxed, subdued; large selection of tequilas.

Map 10 • Murray Hill / Gramercy

Abbey Tavern	354 Third Ave	212-532-1978	Only decent place in the neighborhood? Yes!
Bar 515	515 Third Ave	212-532-3300	Local pseudo-frat hangout.
Galaxy	15 Irving Pl	212-777-3631	Good drinks, space-age décor.
High Bar @ Gramercy Park Hotel	2 Lexington Ave	212-475-4320	Cocktails under the stars.
Joshua Tree	513 Third Ave	212-689-0058	Murray Hill meat market.
Mercury Bar	493 Third Ave	212-683-2645	Lots of TVs for sports. You make the call.
Molly's	287 Third Ave	212-889-3361	Great Irish pub with a fireplace.
Revival	129 E 15th St	212-253-8061	Low maintenance beer drinking.
Waterfront Ale House	540 Second Ave	212-696-4104	Decent local vibe.

Map 11 • Hell's Kitchen

Bellevue Bar	538 Ninth Ave	212-760-0660	How low can you go?
Bull Moose Saloon	354 W 44th St	212-956-5625	Good local hangout.
Hudson Hotel Library	356 W 58th St	212-554-6000	Super-super-super pretentious.
Landmark Tavern	626 Eleventh Ave	212-757-8595	Worth the trek to Eleventh Ave…
Otis	754 Ninth Ave	212-246-4417	Good, laid-back feel.
Rudy's Bar & Grill	627 Ninth Ave	212-974-9169	Classic Hell's Kitchen. Recommended.
Siberia Bar	356 W 40th St	212-333-4141	Brrrr...it's cold out there.
Xth	642 Tenth Ave	212-245-9088	Good local vibe.

Map 12 • Midtown

Heartland Brewery	127 W 43rd St	646-366-0235	Heartland HeartLAND HEARTLAND!
Heartland Brewery	1285 Sixth Ave	212-582-8244	Heartland HeartLAND HEARTLAND!
Howard Johnson's	1551 Broadway	212-354-1445	A Times Square haven in a sea of madness.
Oak Bar @ Plaza Hotel	768 Fifth Ave	212-546-5330	Where Cary gets abducted. A classic.
Paramount Bar	235 W 46th St	212-764-5500	Tiny, pretentious, unavoidable.
Russian Vodka Room	265 W 52nd St	212-307-5835	Russian molls and cranberry vodka. Awesome.
Scruffy Duffy's	743 Eighth Ave	212-245-9126	We like this place, unfortunately.
The Royalton	44 W 44th St	212-768-5000	Phillippe Starcke is the SH--!

Map 13 • East Midtown

Blarney Stone	710 Third Ave	212-490-0457	The only bar in purgatory.
The Campbell Apartment	Grand Central Terminal	212-953-0409	Awesome space, awesomely snooty!
Metro 53	307 E 53rd St	212-838-0007	Celebrites and suits.
PJ Clarke's	915 Third Ave	212-759-1650	An old-timer, resuscitated.
Tammany Hall	218 E 53rd St	212-355-6607	Decent Midtown oasis.

Map 14 • Upper West Side (Lower)

All State Café	250 W 72nd St	212-874-1883	Great underground space.
Dead Poet	450 Amsterdam Ave	212-595-5670	Good Irish feel.
Dublin House	225 W 79th St	212-874-9528	Great dingy Irish pub. Recommended.
Emerald Inn	220 Columbus Ave	212-874-8840	Another good Irish pub!
Jake's Dilemma	430 Amsterdam Ave	212-580-0556	Sort of okay sometimes.
P&G	279 Amsterdam Ave	212-874-8568	Depressing dive. Recommended.
Prohibition	503 Columbus Ave	212-579-3100	Cool space, music, people, etc.

Raccoon Lodge	480 Amsterdam Ave	212-874-9984	Everyone knows what these are like.
Shalel Lounge	65 W 70th St	212-799-9030	Very cool, semi-hidden lounge.

Map 15 • Upper East Side (Lower)

Banshee Pub	1373 First Ave	212-717-8177	Good, fun Upper East Sider.
Brother Jimmy's	1485 Second Ave	212-288-0999	Crowded meat market.
Finnegan's Wake	1361 First Ave	212-737-3664	Standard Irish pub. Therefore, good.
Hi-Life	1340 First Ave	212-249-3600	Pseudo-retro, okay.
Raccoon Lodge	1439 York Ave	212-650-1775	You get what you pay for.
Session 73	1359 First Ave	212-517-4445	Live music and yuppies.
Subway Inn	143 E 60th St	212-223-8929	Sad, bad, glare, worn-out, ugh. Totally great.

Map 16 • Upper West Side (Upper)

Abbey Pub	237 W 105th St	212-222-8713	Cozy Columbia hangout.
Broadway Dive	2662 Broadway	212-865-2662	Where everyone who reads this book goes.
Dive Bar	732 Amsterdam Ave	212-749-4358	Columbia hangout.
The Parlour	250 W 86th St	212-580-8923	Irish pub, two spaces, good hangout.
Sip	998 Amsterdam Ave	212-749-5100	New, good tunes.
Smoke	2751 Broadway	212-864-6662	Local jazz hangout.
SOHA	988 Amsterdam Ave	212-678-0098	Dark, pool tables, cozy.

Map 17 • Upper East Side (Upper)

Auction House	300 E 89th St	212-427-4458	Stylin' uptown lounge.
Big Easy	1768 Second Ave	212-348-0879	Cheap college dive. Beer pong anyone?
Kinsale Tavern	1672 Third Ave	212-348-4370	Right-off-the-boat Irish staff. Good beers.
Rathbones Pub	1702 Second Ave	212-369-7361	Basic pub.
Ruby's Tap House	1754 Second Ave	212-987-8179	Lots of beer, lots of meat.
Who's on First?	1683 First Ave	212-410-2780	Funneling fratboy crud.

Map 18 • Columbia / Morningside Heights

1020 Amsterdam	1020 Amsterdam Ave	212-961-9224	A nice break from the frat bars around Columbia.
Cotton Club	666 W 125th St	212-663-7980	Good, fun swingin' uptown joint.
Heights Bar & Grill	2867 Broadway	212-866-7035	Fun rooftop bar in summer.
Nacho Mama's Kitchen Bar	2893 Broadway	212-665-2800	Get your nacho on.
West End	2911 Broadway	212-662-8830	Long-time Columbia hangout.

Map 19 • Harlem (Lower)

Lenox Lounge	288 Lenox Ave	212-427-0253	Old-time Harlem hangout, recenty redone.

Map 21 • Manhattanville / Hamilton Heights

St Nick's Pub	773 St Nicholas Ave	212-283-9728	Great vibe, cool jazz.

Map 25 • Inwood

Piper's Kilt	4944 Broadway	212-569-7071	Irish pub and sports bar.
Tubby Hook Cafe	348 Dyckman St	212-567-8086	Nice view on the Hudson.

Map 26 • Astoria

Amnesia	3203 Broadway	718-204-7010	Greek night club.
Bohemian Hall	29-19 24th Ave	718-274-4925	More than 90 years old, this bar is run by the Bohemia Citizens' Benevolent Society. Check out the Czech beers. Beer garden seats more than 500!
Brick Café	30-95 33rd St	718-267-2735	Great atmosphere with European lounge music piping through the speakers quiet enough so you can still chat.
Byzantio	28-31 31st St	718-956-5600	Greek-style café and bar.
Café Bar	32-90 34th Ave	718-204-5273	Serves Cypriot cuisine and often features live jazz performances.
Gibneys	32-01 Broadway	718-545-8567	Authentic Irish pub.
McCann's Pub & Grill	3615 Ditmars Blvd	718-278-2621	Where the young and the Greek hang out.
McLoughlin's Bar	31-06 Broadway	718-278-9714	Another Irish local bar.

Map 27 • Long Island City

Café Athens	32-07 30th St	718-626-2164	Greek bar, thin menu.
Club XL	25-22 34th Ave	718-784-1822	Loud. Dancing.
Krash	34-48 Steinway St	718-937-2400	Performers, DJs, lots of butt shaking.
Tupelo	34-18 34th Ave	718-707-9588	Eclectic music played by a host of DJs—don't expect to hear top 40s hits here and be prepared to yell your conversations!

Map 28 • Greenpoint

Enid's	560 Manhattan Ave	718-349-3859	Trendy drinking space.
Europa	765 Manhattan Ave	718-383-5723	Strobe light extravaganza.
Pencil Factory	142 Franklin St	718-609-5858	Promising newcomer.
Splendid	132 Greenpoint Ave	718-383-1900	Roomy drinking space.

Map 29 • Williamsburg

The Abbey	536 Driggs Ave	718-599-4400	Great jukebox and staff.
Black Betty	366 Metropolitan Ave	718-599-0243	Get the Black Betty Margarita...yum!
Boogaloo	168 Marcy Ave	718-599-8900	Intimate dancing to live music and DJs.
BQE	300 N 6th St	718-388-2211	Live music and great views of the BQE.
Brooklyn Ale House	103 Berry St	718-302-9811	When you just want to drink some beer.
Brooklyn Brewery	79 N 11th St	718-486-7422	Open Friday nights only. Tours on Saturdays.
Charleston	174 Bedford Ave	718-782-8717	Old school bar with pizza.
Galapagos	70 N 6th St	718-782-5188	Reflecting pools, candles and attractive people.
Greenpoint Tavern	188 Bedford Ave	718-384-9539	Cheap beer in Styrofoam cups.
Iona	180 Grand St	718-384-5008	Plenty of choices on tap.
Pete's Candy Store	709 Lorimer St	718-302-3770	Cozy space—Scrabble on Saturdays!
Stinger Club	241 Grand St	718-218-6662	Good bands from time to time.
Sweetwater Tavern	105 N 6th St	718-963-0608	Punk dive.
Toybox	256 Grand St	718-599-1000	Formerly Luxx.
Turkey's Nest	94 Bedford Ave	718-384-9774	Best dive in Williamsburg.
Union Pool	484 Union Ave	718-609-0484	Good starting point or finishing point.

Map 30 • Brooklyn Heights / DUMBO / Downtown

Henry Street Ale House	62 Henry St	718-522-4801	Cozy, dark space with good selections on tap.
Water Street Bar	66 Water St	718-625-9352	Roomy Irish pub.

Map 31 • Fort Greene

BAM Café	30 Lafayette Ave	718-636-4100	Highly recommended.
Frank's Lounge	660 Fulton St	718-625-9339	When you need to get funky.
Moe's	80 Lafayette Ave	718-797-9536	Fort Green default.

Map 32 • Cobble Hill / Boerum Hill / Carroll Gardens

Boat	175 Smith St	718-254-0607	Nice and dark with great tunes.
Brazen Head	228 Atlantic Ave	718-488-0430	Decent beer—mixed crowd.
Brooklyn Inn	148 Hoyt St	718-625-9741	When you're feeling nostalgic.
Gowanus Yacht Club	323 Smith St	718-246-1321	Dogs, burgers and beer.
Kili	81 Hoyt St	718-855-5574	Nice space & cool vibe.
Last Exit	136 Atlantic Ave	718-222-9198	Still trying to win trivia night....pails of PBR for $10.
Magnetic Field	97 Atlantic Ave	718-834-0069	Great decor—even better beer specials.
PJ Hanely's	449 Court St	718-834-8223	Great patio.
Quench	282 Smith St	718-875-1500	Mod space with fun drink specials.
Sunny's	253 Conover St	718-625-8211	No longer pay what you wish, but still cheap and good.
Waterfront Ale House	155 Atlantic Ave	718-522-3794	Go for the beer and the great service.
Zombie Hut	263 Smith St	718-875-3433	Drinks with bamboo umbrellas.

Map 33 • Park Slope / Prospect Heights

Bar 4	444 7th Ave	718-832-9800	Replaced its previous glitz with stoop-sale furniture and (gulp) video poker.
Barbes	376 9th St	718-965-9177	Best entertainment in the Slope, from accordian trios to Delta Blues to McSweeney's-sponsored readings.
Freddy's	485 Dean St	718-622-7035	Music and readings and way-coolness.

The Gate	321 5th Ave	718-768-4329	THE best place to drink outdoors in the Slope, plus 20 great beers on tap.
Ginger's	363 5th Ave	718-788-0924	Nice and casual for center Slope.
Great Lakes	284 5th Ave	718-499-3710	Great, great bar.
Loki Lounge	304 5th Ave	718-965-9600	Darts and billiards tone down the classic wood bar. Good music.
Mooney's Pub	353 Flatbush Ave	718-783-6406	The real old Brooklyn deal—smells of many spilt beers.
O'Connor's	39 5th Ave	718-783-9721	The brick face and tiny windows say, "Run away!" but the friendly locals say, "Pull up a stool."
Park Slope Ale House	356 6th Ave	718-788-1756	The brewpub is gone, replaced with non-micro beers, but the bar food remains excellent.
Up Over Jazz Café	351 Flatbush Ave	718-398-5413	Serious jazz at late hours.

Map 34 • Hoboken

Black Bear	205 Washington St	201-656-5511	Ordinary food, but the bands and atmosphere compensate.
City Bistro	56 14th St	201-963-8200	Great summer scene, rooftop views to the city.
Leo's Grandezvous	200 Grand St	201-659-9467	Hoboken's Rat Pack bar. Bring a dame and have some booze.
Louise & Jerry's	329 Washington St	201-656-9698	Old stlye Hoboken saloon. A real throwback.
Martini Blue	1300 Park Ave	201-653-2583	Quiet lounge, enjoy a cocktail on the sofa. Sophisticated elegance.
Maxwell's	1039 Washington St	201-653-1703	Interesting bands, relax in the lounge with friends or grab a bite to eat.
Mile Square	221 Washington St	201-420-0222	Preppy bar where the food is good and the scene is lively.
Moran's	501 Garden St	201-795-2025	Classic Irish tavern; darts, pool and a garrulous bartender.
Oddfellows	80 River St	201-656-9009	Happening happy hour. Close to the PATH, so it catches the commuter crowd.
Sinatra Park Café	529 Sinatra Dr	201-420-9900	Small bar and boardwalk-style food, but one of the top ten views on the planet.
Texas Arizona	76 River St	201-420-0304	You can eat, you can drink, you can catch a band.

Map 35 • Jersey City

Coles Street Café	174 Coles St	201-656-9240	Neighborhood bar with an eclectic mix of regulars. Avoid the food and enjoy the outdoor seating in the warmer months.
Dennis and Maria's Bar	322 1/2 7th St	201-217-6607	Popular with the locals.
LITM	140 Newark Ave	201-536-5557	Artsy, laid-back lounge.
Lamp Post Bar and Grille	382 2nd St	201-222-1331	Look for the lamp post on the street to find this friendly neighborhood bar. If you're going to order food, do it from the front bar.
Markers	Harborside Financial Ctr, Plz II	201-433-6275	Happy hour heaven. The upscale after-work crowd selects from excellent beers on tap.
PJ Ryan's	172 First St	201-239-7373	A real Irish pub. Guaranteed to see your favorite sporting event. Enjoy a pint and watch the live entertainment.
White Star	230 Brunswick St	201-653-9234	Great bar & good eats.

Battery Park City

Rise Bar @ the Ritz	2 West St	212-344-0800	Great harbor and park views.

They don't call New York the city that never sleeps for nothing. There are a million reasons to stay out late in this town. On any given night you can choose from over a hundred musical acts ranging from jazz to punk or you can practice your moves on some of the finest dance floors in the country. Although the New York club scene is in a state of constant flux, there are a few steady venues that we highly recommend.

Music

For smaller venues we love **Arlene's Grocery**, **CB's**, **Tonic**, the **Mercury Lounge**, **Sin-é**, and **Magnetic Field** (Brooklyn). For larger clubs, we like the space at **Bowery Ballroom**, **Hammerstein Ballroom**, **Northsix** (Brooklyn), and **Warsaw** (Brooklyn). The best jazz is still at the **Village Vanguard**, **Birdland**, **Iridium,** and **Small's**. **The Knitting Factory** still, on many occasions, serves up the best of all of the above.

Dancing

For those of you who don't believe in paying to dance there are a number of great places where you can boogie for free. We like **Lit**, **Good World**, **Jack Rabbit Slims**, **Rififi** (free-$5), the **APT** (sometimes free, sometimes $5), and **Cielo**. If you're feeling adventurous, check out the pants-free party on Saturday nights at **Opaline**—that's right, no pants allowed!

If you don't mind shelling out some dough, definitely check out the cozy dance space at **Sapphire Lounge** ($5 after 10:30 pm) and the new gargantuan-sized **Crobar** ($25). We also highly recommend the newfangled **Coral Room** ($10-$20 on the weekends). This space is completely decked out in an under-the-sea theme, replete with a 9,000-gallon aquarium filled with exotic fish and the occasional mermaid. Aside from these suggestions, there are a few major openings worth mentioning: **Avalon** (formerly Limelight), **Capitale** (located in the old Bowery Savings Bank), and **Spirit** (formerly Twilo). If you visit these clubs on the weekend, you're sure to run into long lines and pricey cover charges ($20-$30), but many of them have reduced rates on weeknights. If you need to shake your tail feather in Brooklyn, we suggest checking out the lively dance scene at **Boogaloo** ($5-Williamsburg).

Venue	*Address*	*Phone*	*Map*
101	70 Grove St	212-620-4000	9
1050 Lounge	735 Tenth Ave	212-445-0149	11
13	35 E 13th St	212-979-6677	6
219 Flamingo	219 Second Ave	212-533-2860	6
2i's	248 W 14th St	212-807-1775	5
46 Grand	46 Grand St	212-219-9311	2
55 Bar	55 Christopher St	212-929-9883	5
59 Canal	59 Canal St		4
9 1/2	35 E 21st St	212-239-0222	9
Abaya	244 E Houston St	212-777-7467	7
ABC No Rio	156 Rivington St	212-254-3697	7
Acme Underground	9 Great Jones St	212-420-1934	6
Alchymy	12 Avenue A	212-477-9050	7
Alibi	116 MacDougal St	212-254-9996	6
Alphabet Lounge	104 Avenue C	212-780-0202	7
Anatomy	511 E 6th St	212-995-8889	7
Angel Bar	174 Orchard St	212-780-0313	7
Anyway Cafe	32 E 2nd St	212-533-3412	6
Apollo Theatre	253 W 125th St	212-749-5838	19
APT	419 W 13th St	212-414-4245	5
Arc	6 Hubert St	212-226-9212	2
Arci's Place	450 Park Ave S	212-532-4370	10
Aria	539 W 21st St	212-229-1618	8
Arlene Grocery	95 Stanton St	212-358-1633	7
Arshile	166 First Ave	212-228-0444	7
Aubette	119 E 27th St	212-686-5500	10
Avalon	660 Sixth Ave	212-807-7780	9
B Bar	358 Bowery	212-475-2220	6
B3	33 Avenue B	212-614-9755	7
Back Fence	155 Bleecker St	212-475-9221	6
Baggot Inn	82 W 3rd St	212-477-0622	6
Bar 169	169 East Broadway	212-473-8866	4
Bar Code	1540 Broadway	212-869-9397	12
Bar d'O	34 Downing St	212-627-1580	5
Baraza	133 Avenue C	212-539-0811	7
Bauhaus	196 Orchard St	212-477-1550	7
BB King Blues Club	237 W 42nd St	212-997-4144	12
Beauty Bar	231 E 14th St	212-539-1389	6
Belmont Lounge	117 E 15th St	212-533-0009	10
Belt, The	336 W 37th St	212-971-2442	8
Big Six Bar and Lounge	97 Bowery	212-219-9955	3
Birdland	315 W 44th St	212-581-3080	11
The Bitter End	147 Bleecker St	212-673-7030	6
Black Star Lounge	92 Second Ave	212-254-4747	6

Venue	*Address*	*Phone*	*Map*
Blarney Star	43 Murray St	212-732-2873	2
Blue Note	131 W 3rd St	212-475-2462	6
Blur	286 Spring St	212-929-4941	5
Botanica	47 E Houston St	212-343-7251	6
Bouche Bar	540 E 5th St	212-475-1673	7
Bowery Ballroom	6 Delancey St	212-533-2111	6
Bowlmor Lanes	110 University Pl	212-255-8188	6
Brandy's Piano Bar	235 E 84th St	212-650-1944	15
Brite Bar	297 Tenth Ave	212-279-9706	8
Bubble Lounge	228 West Broadway	212-431-3433	2
Buddha	36 E 20th St	212-674-1111	9
C-Note	157 Avenue C	212-677-8142	7
Caché	221 W 46th St	212-719-5799	12
Cafe Carlyle and Bemelmans Bar	35 E 76th St	212-744-1600	15
Cafe Deville	105 Third Ave	212-477-4500	6
Cafe Novecento	343 West Broadway	212-925-4706	2
Cafe Wha?	115 MacDougal St	212-254-3706	6
Cajun	129 Eighth Ave	212-691-6174	8
Capitale	130 Bowery	212-334-5500	3
CB's 313 Gallery	313 Bowery	212-677-0455	6
CBGB and OMFUG	315 Bowery	212-982-4052	6
Centro-Fly	45 W 21st St	212-627-7770	9
Chaos	223 E Houston St	212-475-3200	7
Chazal	41 Madison Ave	212-545-8555	9
Cheetah	12 W 21st St	212-206-7770	9
Chez Es Saada	42 E 1st St	212-777-5617	6
China Club	268 W 47th St	212-398-3800	12
China White	143 Madison Ave	212-684-0004	9
Church Lounge at the Tribeca Grand Hotel	25 Walker St	212-519-6600	2
Cielo	18 Little W 12th St	212-645-5700	5
Club Masa	802 Columbus Ave	212-663-1154	16
Club New York	252 W 43rd St	212-997-9510	12
Club Privilege	565 W 23rd St	212-243-6888	8
Club Shelter	20 W 39th St	212-719-4479	9
Clubhouse	700 E 9th St	212-260-7970	7
Cock, The	188 Avenue A	212-777-6254	7
Coffee Shop	29 Union Sq W	212-243-7969	9
Connolly's Pub and Restaurant	14 E 47th St	212-867-3767	12
Continental	25 Third Ave	212-529-6924	6
Copacabana	560 W 34th St	212-239-2672	11
Coral Room	512 W 29th St	212-244-1965	8
Cornelia Street Cafe	29 Cornelia St	212-989-9319	5

Venue	Address	Phone	Map
Cotton Club	666 W 125th St	212-663-7980	18
Coz	511 E 6th St	212-995-8889	7
Cream	246 Columbus Ave	212-712-1666	14
Crobar	530 W 28th St	212-629-9000	8
Culture Club	179 Varick St	212-243-1999	5
The Cutting Room	19 W 24th St	212-691-1900	9
De Lounge	73 Thompson St	212-966-7299	6
Decade	1117 First Ave	212-835-5979	15
Deep	16 W 22nd St	212-229-2000	9
Delft	14 Ave B	212-260-7100	7
Demerara	215 W 28th St	212-643-1199	9
Dempsey's Pub	61 Second Ave	212-388-0662	6
Dinerbar	1569 Lexington Ave	212-348-0200	17
Discotheque	17 W 19th St	212-352-9999	9
Don Hill's	511 Greenwich St	212-334-1390	5
Don't Tell Mama	343 W 46th St	212-757-0788	11
Downtime	251 W 30th St	212-695-2747	9
Duplex Cabaret & Piano Bar	61 Christopher St	212-255-5438	5
The East Side Company	49 Essex St		4
Eight Mile Creek	240 Mulberry St	212-431-4635	6
El Flamingo	547 W 21st St	212-243-2121	8
Ellie Club	390 Eighth Ave	212-947-1970	8
Eugene	27 W 24th St	212-462-0999	9
Exit2	610 W 56th St	212-582-8282	11
Falucka	162 Bleecker St	212-777-5154	6
Feinstein's at the Regency	540 Park Ave	212-339-4095	15
Fez	380 Lafayette St	212-533-2680	6
Filter 14	432 W 14th St	212-366-5680	5
Finally Fred's	765 Washington St	212-255-5101	5
Flow	150 Varick St	212-929-9444	5
Garage	99 Seventh Ave	212-645-0600	9
Gonzalez y Gonzalez	625 Broadway	212-533-4645	6
Good World	3 Orchard St	212-925-9975	4
Groove	125 MacDougal St	212-254-9393	6
Guernica	25 Ave B	212-674-0984	7
Hammerstein Ballroom	311 W 34th St	212-279-7740	8
Hard Rock Cafe	221 W 57th St	212-459-9320	12
Hogs & Heifers Uptown	1843 First Ave	212-722-8635	17
Idlewild	145 E Houston St	212-477-5005	6
Iridium	1650 Broadway	212-582-2121	14
Irving Plaza	17 Irving Pl	212-777-6800	10
Jack Rabbit Slims	226 E 10th St	212-677-1717	7
Jack Rose	771 Eighth Ave	212-247-7518	12
Jazz Gallery	290 Hudson St	212-242-1063	5
The Jazz Standard	116 E 27th St	212-576-2232	10
Joe's Pub	425 Lafayette St	212-539-8776	6
Kaplan Penthouse	Lincoln Center, 65th St at Columbus	212-721-6500	14
Karma	51 First Ave	212-677-3160	7
Kate Kearney's	251 E 50th St	212-935-2045	13
Kavehaz	37 W 26th St	212-343-0612	9
Kenny's Castaways	157 Bleecker St	212-473-9870	6
Kiko's	279 Church St	212-219-0225	2
Knitting Factory	74 Leonard St	212-219-3055	3
La Belle Epoque	827 Broadway	212-254-6436	6
La Linea	15 First Ave	212-592-3138	7
Lakeside Lounge	162 Ave B	212-529-8463	7
Lansky Lounge	104 Norfolk St	212-677-9489	7
Le Bar Bat	311 W 57th St	212-307-7228	11
Lei Bar	139 1/2 E 7th St	212-420-9517	7
Leopard Lounge	85 Second Ave	212-253-2222	6
Lickwed	113 Ludlow St	646-372-2896	7
Lightship Frying Pan	Pier 63	212-989-6363	8

Venue	Address	Phone	Map
Lion's Den	214 Sullivan St	212-477-2782	6
Liquids	266 E 10th St	212-677-1717	7
Lit	93 Second Ave	212-777-7987	6
Living Room	84 Stanton St	212-533-7235	7
Lobby	330 W 38th St	212-465-2200	8
Local 138	138 Ludlow St	212-477-0280	7
Lotus	409 W 14th St	212-243-4420	5
Lotus Music	109 W 27th St	212-627-1076	9
Lu Lu's Cafe Lounge	493 Tenth Ave	212-244-4521	8
Luahn	59 Fifth Ave	212-242-9710	6
Ludlow Bar	165 Ludlow St	212-353-0536	7
Luke & Leroy	21 Seventh Ave S	212-366-6312	5
Luna Lounge	171 Ludlow St	212-260-2323	7
Lush	110 Duane St	212-766-1295	3
M & R	354 Bowery	212-226-0559	6
Madame X	94 W Houston St	212-539-0808	6
Makor	35 W 67th St	212-601-1000	14
Man Ray	147 W 15th St	212-929-5000	9
Manitoba's	99 Ave B	212-982-2511	7
Mannahatta	316 Bowery	212-253-8644	6
Marion's Continental	354 Bowery	212-475-7621	6
Meow Mix	269 E Houston St	212-254-0688	7
Mercury Lounge	217 E Houston St	212-260-4700	7
Metronome	915 Broadway	212-505-7400	9
Mission	217 Bowery	212-473-3113	6
Naked Lunch	17 Thompson St	212-343-0828	2
Nells	246 W 14th St	212-675-1567	5
Niagara	112 Ave A	212-420-9517	7
Nicholson	323 E 58th St	212-355-6769	13
Nightingale Bar	213 Second Ave	212-473-9398	6
No Moore	234 West Broadway	212-925-2595	2
Nowbar	22 Seventh Ave	212-293-0323	5
Nublu	62 Ave C	212-979-9925	7
NV	304 Hudson St	212-929-6868	5
The Oak Room	59 W 44th St	212-840-6800	12
Octagon	555 W 33rd St	212-947-0400	8
Opaline	85 Ave A	212-995-8684	7
Openair	121 St Mark's Pl	212-979-1459	7
Opium Den	29 E 3rd St	212-505-7344	6
Orange Bear	47 Murray St	212-566-3705	2
Orchard Bar	200 Orchard St	212-673-5350	7
Otto's Shrunken Head	538 E 14th St	212-228-2240	7
Paddy Reilly's	519 Second Ave	212-686-1210	10
Paisley	49 E 21st St	212-353-8833	9
Parkside Lounge	317 E Houston St	212-673-6270	7
Parlay	206 Ave A	212-228-6231	7
Plant Bar	217 E 3rd St	212-375-9066	7
Play	49 Grove St	212-243-8885	5
Polly Esther's	186 W 4th St	212-924-5707	5
Potion	370 Columbus Ave	212-721-4386	14
Powder Deep Studio	431 W 16th St	212-229-9119	8
Pressure	110 University Pl	212-255-8188	6
Pulse, The	226 E 54th St	212-688-5577	13
Punch	913 Broadway	212-673-6333	9
Pyramid	101 Ave A	212-228-4888	7
Rainbow & Stars	30 Rockefeller Plz, 65th Fl	212-632-5000	12
Rare	416 W 14th St	212-675-2220	5
Rare	416 W 14th St	212-675-2220	5
Raven	194 Ave A	212-529-4712	7
The Red Lion	151 Bleecker St	212-260-9797	6
Rififi	332 E 11th St	212-677-6309	6

Venue	Address	Phone	Map
Rivertown Lounge	187 Orchard St	212-388-1288	7
Rocky Sullivan's	129 Lexington Ave	212-725-3871	10
Rodeo Bar & Grill	375 Third Ave	212-683-6500	10
Roseland	239 W 52nd St	212-247-0200	12
Roulette	228 West Broadway	212-219-8242	2
Route 85A	85 Avenue A	212-673-1775	7
Roxy	515 W 18th St	212-645-5156	8
Rubber Monkey	279 Church St	212-625-8220	2
Rue-B	188 Avenue B	212-358-1700	7
Sala	344 Bowery	212-979-6606	6
Sapphire Lounge	249 Eldridge St	212-777-5153	6
Satalla	37 W 26th St	212-576-1155	9
Serena	222 W 23rd St	212-255-4646	9
Shine	285 West Broadway	212-941-0900	2
Show	135 W 41st St	212-278-0988	12
Sidewalk	94 Avenue A	212-473-7373	7
Sin Sin	248 E 5th St	212-253-2222	6
Sin-e	150 Attorney St	212-388-0077	7
Slipper Room	167 Orchard St	212-253-7246	7
Small's	183 W 10th St	212-929-7565	5
Smithfields	115 Essex St	212-475-9997	7
Smoke	2751 Broadway	212-864-6662	16
SOB'S	200 Varick St	212-243-4940	5
SoHo Grand Hotel	310 West Broadway	212-965-3000	2
Solas	232 E 9th St	212-375-0297	6
Speeed	20 W 39th St	212-719-9867	9
Spirit	530 W 27th St	212-268-9477	8
Splash Bar	50 W 17th St	212-691-0073	9
St Nick's Pub	773 St Nicholas Ave	212-283-9728	21
Standard Bar and Listening Room	158 First Ave	212-387-0239	7
Starlight Bar & Lounge	167 Avenue A	212-475-2172	7
Suede	161 W 23rd St	212-633-2113	9
Suite 16	127 Eighth Ave	212-627-1680	8
Sullivan Room	218 Sullivan St	212-252-2151	6
Supper Club	240 W 47th St	212-921-1940	12
Swim	146 Orchard St	212-673-0799	7
Swing 46	349 W 46th St	212-262-9554	11
Tapis Rouge	9 Avenue A	646-602-2590	7
Tavaru	192 Third Ave	212-471-9807	10
Terra Blues	149 Bleecker St	212-777-7776	6
Three of Cups Lounge	83 First Ave	212-388-0059	7
Tonic	107 Norfolk St	212-358-7501	7
Top of the Tower	3 Mitchell Pl, Beekman Tower	212-355-7300	13
Triad	158 W 72nd St	212-362-2590	14
Tribeca Blues	16 Warren St	212-766-1070	3
Trust	421 W 13th St	212-645-7775	5
Twirl	208 W 23rd St	212-691-7685	9
Upstairs at Rosa's Turn	55 Grove St	212-366-5438	5
Velvet Lounge	223 Mulberry St	212-965-0439	6
Veruka	525 Broome St	212-625-1717	6
Village Underground	130 W 3rd St	212-777-7745	6
Village Vanguard	178 Seventh Ave S	212-255-4037	9
Vinyl	157 Hudson St	212-343-1379	2
Void	16 Mercer St	212-941-6492	3
Vudu	1487 First Ave	212-249-9540	15
Webster Hall	125 E 11th St	212-353-1600	6
Westbeth Theatre Center	111 W 17th St	212-691-2272	5
Wonderbar	505 E 6th St	212-777-9105	7
Xth Avenue Lounge	642 Tenth Ave	212-245-9088	11
Zinc Bar	90 W Houston St	212-477-8337	6

Brooklyn

Brooklyn	Address	Phone	Neighborhood	Map
BAMcafe	30 Lafayette Ave	718-636-4139	Fort Green	31
Barbes	376 9th St	718-965-9177	Park Slope / Prospect Heights	33
Boogaloo	168 Marcy Ave	718-599-8900	Williamsburg	29
The Charleston Bar and Grill	174 Bedford Ave	718-782-8717	Williamsburg	29
Cafe 111	111 Court St	718-858-2806	Cobble Hill / Boerum Hill / Carroll Gardens	32
3032Dumba	57 Jay St	718-670-3719	Brooklyn Heights / DUMBO / Downtown	30
Frank's Lounge	660 Fulton St	718-625-9339	Fort Greene	31
Galapagos	70 N 6th St	718-782-5188	Williamsburg	29
The Good Coffee House	53 Prospect Park W	718-768-2972	Park Slope / Prospect Heights	33
The Hook	18 Commerce St	718-797-3007	Cobble Hill / Boerum Hill / Carroll Gardens	32
Laila Lounge	113 N 7th St	718-486-6791	Williamsburg	29
Liberty Heights Tap Room	34 Van Dyke St	718-246-1793	Cobble Hill / Boerum Hill / Carroll Gardens	32
Magnetic Field	97 Atlantic Ave	718-834-0069	Cobble Hill / Boerum Hill / Carroll Gardens	32
The Nest	88 Front St	646-489-7380	Brooklyn Heights / DUMBO / Downtown	30
Northsix	66 N 6th St	718-599-5103	Williamsburg	29
Pete's Candy Store	709 Lorimer St	718-302-3770	Williamsburg	29
Southpaw	125 Fifth Ave	no phone	Park Slope / Prospect Heights	33
St Ann's Warehouse	38 Water St	718-858-2424	Brooklyn Heights / DUMBO / Downtown	30
Stinger Club	241 Grand St	718-218-6662	Williamsburg	29
Toybox	256 Grand St	718-599-1000	Williamsburg	29
Two Boots Park Slope	514 2nd St	718-499-3253	Park Slope / Prospect Heights	33
Union Pool	484 Union Ave	718-609-0484	Williamsburg	29
Up Over Jazz Café	351 Flatbush Ave	718-398-5413	Park Slope / Prospect Heights	33
Warsaw	261 Driggs Ave	718-387-5252	Williamsburg	29

The New York City book scene has taken a sharp decline in terms of diversity in recent years, with many excellent bookshops—including A Different Light, Academy, A Photographer's Place, Rizzoli Soho, Tower Books, Brentano's, Pageant, Spring Street Books, Shortwave—all going the way of the dodo. The remaining stores are now the last outposts before everything interesting or alternative disappears altogether. And some of NYC's richest cultural neighborhoods—such as the East Village and the Lower East Side—don't have enough bookstores to even come close to properly serving their populations of literate hipsters. But we thought we'd take this opportunity to list some of our favorite remaining shops...

General New/Used

The Strand is still the mother of all general bookshops, with three locations and an astounding selection. Finding specific things, of course, always remains a challenge, but it can't be beat for browsing. **Gotham Book Mart** remains midtown Manhattan's major literary watering hole, and **St. Mark's Books** anchors the border between the NYU crowd and the East Village hipster contingent. Both Gotham and St. Mark's have excellent literary journal selections. **Argosy Book Store** on 57th Street is still a great destination for books and prints. Uptown, **Papyrus** and **Labyrinth** serve the Columbia area well. The best local chain is the quite punchy **Shakespeare & Company**, with four locations. Incursions by the chains have made Shakespeare a great alternative destination. In the West Village, **Three Lives and Co.** should be your destination. The **Barnes & Noble** on Union Square is their signature store, and has a great feel. The **Housing Works Used Book Café** is one of our favorite bookstores—and when you support your cerebral habit, you're also helping out some people in need!

Small Used

Fortunately there are still a lot of these tucked away all over the city. **Mercer Street Books** serves NYU, **Last Word** covers Columbia, **East Village Books** takes care of hipster heaven, **Skyline** is a good Chelsea destination, and many others still lurk in corners all over the city.

Travel

The city's travel book selection is possibly its greatest strength—from the two **Hagstrom Map & Travel** locations (one near Bryant Park and the other downtown), to several independents—including the elegant **Complete Traveller Bookstore**, **SoHo's Traveler's Choice Bookstore**, and the **Civilized Traveler** on Broadway.

Artists Books/Art Books

Printed Matter has one of the best collections of artist's books in the world and is highly recommended. Across the street, the **DIA** bookstore has a fantastic selection of books about art with a special case reserved for artist's books. The store's worth a visit for the Jorge Pardo design alone! The **New Museum Bookstore** also has a brilliant selection of both artists and art books. If you aren't on a budget and have a new coffee table to populate, try **Ursus** in Chelsea.

Independent

Soft Skull Press' excellent bookshop has moved from its location on the Lower East Side to slightly more spacious, fancier digs in Brooklyn, at 71 Bond Street.

NYC/Government

The City Store in the Municipal Building is small, but has a good selection (and the only place we've seen that sells old taxicab medallions!). The **Civil Service Bookstore** on Chambers Street has all your study guides when you want to change careers and start driving a bus. The **UN Bookshop** has a great range of international and governmental titles. The **New York Transit Museum** shop at Grand Central also has an excellent range of books on NYC.

Specialty

Books of Wonder in Chelsea has long been a downtown haven for children's books. Mystery shops **Murder Ink**, **Mysterious Book Shop**, and **Partners & Crime** slake the need for whodunits. **Biography Bookshop** and **Bluestockings Women's Bookstore** speak for themselves. **Urban Center Books** has a great architecture collection.

Map 1 • Financial District

Borders Books, Music, & Cafe	100 Broadway	212-964-1988	Chain
Hagstrom Map and Travel Center	125 Maiden Ln	212-785-5343	Specialty - Travel/Maps
Shakespeare & Co	1 Whitehall St	212-742-7025	Chain
Strand	95 Fulton St	212-732-6070	Used; Remainders
Trinity	74 Trinity Pl	212-349-0376	Specialty - Spiritual

Map 2 • TriBeCa

College of Insurance	101 Murray St	212-962-4111	Academic - Business/Insurance
Manhattan Books	150 Chambers St	212-385-7395	General Interest
Posman Collegiate Bookstores at Manhattan Community College	199 Chambers St	212-608-1023	Academic - General
Ruby's Book Sale	119 Chambers St	212-732-8676	General Interest
Sufi Books	225 West Broadway	212-334-5212	Specialty - Spiritual
Traveler's Choice	2 Wooster St	212-941-1535	Specialty - Travel

Map 3 • City Hall / Chinatown

The City Store	1 Centre St	212-669-8245x8247	Specialty - NYC
Civil Service Book Shop	89 Worth St	212-226-9506	Specialty - Civil Services
Computer Book Works	78 Reade St	212-385-1616	Specialty - Computer
Good Field Trading Co	74B Mott St	212-966-3338	Specialty - Chinese
K-Mei	81 Bayard St	212-693-1989	Specialty - Chinese
Ming Fay Book Store	42 Mott St	212-406-1957	Specialty - Military
Oriental Books, Stationery, & Arts Co	29 East Broadway	212-962-3634	Specialty - Chinese
Oriental Culture Enterprises	13 Elizabeth St	212-226-8461	Specialty - Chinese
Pace University Bookstore	41 Park Row	212-349-8580	Academic - General
United States Government Printing Office Bookstore	26 Federal Plz, Room 2-120	212-264-3825	Specialty - Federal Publications
Zakka	147 Grand St	212-431-3961	Specialty - Graphic design books

Map 4 • Lower East Side

Eastern Books	15 Pike St	212-964-6869	Specialty - Chinese

Map 5 • West Village

Barnes & Noble	396 Sixth Ave	212-674-8780	Chain
Biography Book Shop	400 Bleecker St	212-807-8655	Specialty - Biography
Bookleaves	304 W 4th St	212-924-5638	Used; Antiquarian
Creative Visions	548 Hudson St	212-645-7573	Specialty - Gay/Lesbian
Drougas Books	34 Carmine St	212-229-0079	Used, political, Eastern religious, etc.
Joanne Hendricks Cookbooks	488 Greenwich St	212-226-5731	Specialty - Wine & Cooking
Lectorum	137 W 14th St	212-741-0220	Specialty - Spanish
Macondo Books	221 W 14th St	212-741-3108	Specialty - Spanish
Oscar Wilde Memorial Bookshop	15 Christopher St	212-255-8097	Specialty - Gay/Lesbian
Partners & Crime Mystery	44 Greenwich Ave	212-243-0440	Specialty - Mystery
Three Lives and Co	154 W 10th St	212-741-2069	General Interest

Map 6 • Washington Square / NYU / SoHo

12th Street Books & Records	11 E 12th St	212-645-4340	Used
Alabaster	122 Fourth Ave	212-982-3550	Used
Barnes & Noble	4 Astor Pl	212-420-1322	Chain
Benjamin Cardozo School of Law Bookstore	55 Fifth Ave	212-790-0339/0200	Academic - Law
Bilingual Publications	270 Lafayette St	212-431-3500	Specialty - Spanish
Copernicus Books	37 E 7th St	212-228-0175	Specialty - Science
East West Books	78 Fifth Ave	212-243-5994	Specialty - Spirituality; Self-Help
Fine Art In Print	159 Prince St	212-982-2088	Specialty - Fine Art
Forbidden Planet	840 Broadway	212-473-1576/ 212-475-6161	Specialty - Fantasy/Sci-fi
Housing Works Used Book Cafe	126 Crosby St	212-334-3324	Used
Mercer Street Books and Records	206 Mercer St	212-505-8615	Used
New Museum of Contemporary Art Bookshop	583 Broadway	212-219-1222	Specialty - Art/ Artists Books
New York Open Center	83 Spring St	212-219-2527x109	Specialty - New Age; Spiritual
New York University Book Center-Main Branch	18 Washington Pl	212-998-4667	Academic - General
New York University Book Center-Professional Bookstore	530 LaGuardia Pl	212-998-4680	Academic - Management
Perimeter Books On Architecture	21 Cleveland Pl	212-334-6559	Specialty - Architecture
Scholastic Store	557 Broadway	212-343-6166	Specialty - Education
Science Fiction Shop	214 Sullivan St	212-473-3010	Specialty - Sci-Fi
Shakespeare & Co	716 Broadway	212-529-1330	Chain
St Mark's Bookshop	31 Third Ave	212-260-7853/ 212-260-0443	General Interest
Strand	828 Broadway	212-473-1452	Used; Remainders
Surma Book & Music Co	11 E 7th St	212-477-0729	Specialty - Ukrainian
Untitled	159 Prince St	212-982-2088	Specialty - Fine Art
Village Comics	214 Sullivan St	212-777-2770	Specialty - Comics
Virgin Megastore	52 E 14th St	212-598-4666	Chain

Map 7 • East Village

Bluestockings Women's Bookstore	172 Allen St	212-777-6028	Specialty - Womens/Lesbian
East Village Books and Records	101 St Mark's Pl	212-477-8647	Messy pile of used stuff

May Day Books	155 First Ave		Anarchist bookstore and collective
St Mark's Comics	11 St Mark's Pl	212-598-9439	Specialty - Comics

Map 8 • Chelsea

DIA Center Bookstore	548 W 22nd St	212-989-5566	Specialty - Art/design
Jan Van Der Donk Rare Books	601 W 26th St, 12th Fl	212-691-5973	Antiquarian
Polish American Bookstore	333 W 38th St	212-594-2386	Specialty - Polish
Printed Matter	535 W 22nd St	212-925-0325	Specialty - Artist Books

Map 9 • Flatiron / Lower Midtown

Aperture Book Center	20 E 23rd St	212-505-5555	Specialty - Photography
Barnes & Noble	33 E 17th St	212-253-0810	Chain
Barnes & Noble	675 Sixth Ave	212-727-1227	Chain
Barnes & Noble College	6 E 18th St	212-675-5500	Textbook mayhem.
Books of Wonder	16 W 18th St	212-989-3270	Specialty - Children's
Center for Book Arts	28 W 27th St, 3rd Fl	212-481-0295	Specialty - Artist/Handmade
Compleat Strategist	11 E 33rd St	212-685-3880	Specialty - Fantasy/ Sci-Fi
Complete Traveller	199 Madison Ave	212-685-9007	Specialty - Travel
Fashion Design Books	234 W 27th St	212-633-9646	Specialty - Fashion design
Hudson News	Penn Station	212-971-6800	Chain
Jim Hanley's Universe	4 W 33rd St	212-268-7088	Specialty - Comics; Sci-Fi
Koryo Books	35 W 32nd St	212-564-1844	Specialty - Korean
Longitude	115 W 30th St	212-904-1144	Specialty - Travel Related
Longitude	27 W 20th St	212-463-8464	Specialty - Travel Related
Manhattan Comics and Cards	228 W 23rd St	212-243-9349	Specialty - Comics
Metropolis Comics and Collectibles	873 Broadway	212-260-4147	Specialty - Comics
Penn Station Book Store	1 Penn Plz, Seventh Ave side	212-563-6820	General Interest
Revolution Books	9 W 19th St	212-691-3345	Specialty - Political
Rudolf Steiner Bookstore	138 W 15th St	212-242-8945	Specialty - Metaphysics
Russian House	253 Fifth Ave	212-924-5477	Specialty - Russian/Russia
Skyline Books & Records	13 W 18th St	212-759-5463	Used
Ursus Books Ltd	132 W 21st St	212-627-5370	Specialty - Art

Map 10 • Murray Hill / Gramercy

Baruch College Bookstore	360 Park Ave S	646-312-4850	Academic - General
Borders Books, Music, & Cafe	550 Second Ave	212-685-3938	Chain
New York University Book Store-Health Sciences Bookstore	333 E 29th St	212-998-9990	Academic - Health Sciences
Shakespeare & Co	137 E 23rd St	212-505-2021	Chain

Map 11 • Hell's Kitchen

Dahesh Heritage Fine Books	304 W 58th St	212-265-0600	General Interest
Hudson News Bookstore	Port Authority Building, North Wing	212-563-1030	Chain

Map 12 • Midtown

AMA Management Bookstore	1601 Broadway	212-903-8286	Specialty - Management
Barnes & Noble	600 Fifth Ave	212-765-0590	Chain
Bauman Rare Books	301 Park Ave	212-759-8300	Antiquarian
Bauman Rare Books	535 Madison Ave	212-751-0011	Antiquarian
Bookoff	12 E 41st St	212-685-1410	Used
Chartwell	55 E 52nd St	212-308-0643	General Interest; Antiquarian
Coliseum Books	11 W 42nd St	212-803-5890	General Interest
Dictionary Store	610 Fifth Ave	212-581-8810	Specialty - Foreign Language
Drama Book Shop	250 W 40th St	212-944-0595	Specialty - Theater & Drama
FAO Schwarz Book Department	767 Fifth Ave	212-644-9400	Specialty - Children's
Gotham Bookmart and Gallery	41 W 47th St	212-719-4448	Used; New
Hacker Art Books	45 W 57th St, 5th Fl	212-688-7600	Specialty - Art/Design
Hagstrom Map and Travel Center	57 W 43rd St	212-398-1222	Specialty - Travel/Maps
J N Bartfield-Fine Books	30 W 57th St	212-245-8890	Used
Kinokuniya	10 W 49th St	212-765-7766	Specialty - Japanese
Librarie De France	610 Fifth Ave	212-581-8810	French and Spanish books
Metropolitan Museum of Art Bookshop at Rockefeller Center	15 W 49th St	212-332-1360	Specialty - Art books
Michelin Guides & Maps	610 Fifth Ave	212-581-8810	Specialty - Guides and maps
The Mysterious Book Shop	129 W 56th St	212-765-0900	Specialty - Mystery
New York Transit Museum	Grand Central Station	212-682-7572	Specialty - NYC/Transit
Oan-Oceanie Afrique Noire Books	15 W 39th St	212-840-8844	Specialty - Africa; Australia
Rizzoli	31 W 57th St	212-759-2424/ 800-52-BOOKS	Specialty - Art/Design

Map 12 • Midtown *continued*

Urban Center Books	457 Madison Ave	212-935-3595	Specialty - Architecture; Urban Planning
Virgin Megastore	1540 Broadway, Level B-2	212-921-1020x296	Chain

Map 13 • East Midtown

Argosy Book Store	116 E 59th St	212-753-4455	Used
Asahiya Bookstores New York	52 Vanderbilt Ave	212-883-0011	Specialty - Japanese
Barnes & Noble	160 E 54th St	212-750-8033	Chain
Barnes & Noble	750 Third Ave	212-697-2251	Chain
Borders Books, Music, & Cafe	461 Park Ave	212-980-6785	Chain
Come Again	353 E 53rd St	212-308-9394	Specialty - Erotica; Gay/Lesbian
Hudson News Bookstore	89 E 42nd St, Grand Central Station	212-687-4580	Chain
Posman Books	9 Grand Central Terminal	212-983-1111	General Interest
Potterton Books	979 Third Ave	212-644-2292	Specialty - Decorative Arts/ Architecture/Design
Quest Book Shop	240 E 53rd St	212-758-5521	Specialty - New Age
United Nations Bookshop	General Assembly Building, Rm 32	212-963-7680/ 800-553-3210	Good range of everything

Map 14 • Upper West Side (Lower)

Applause Theater Books	211 W 71st St	212-496-7511	Specialty - Theater & Drama
Barnes & Noble	1972 Broadway	212-595-6859	Chain
Barnes & Noble	2289 Broadway	212-362-8835	Chain
The Book Ark	173 W 81st St	212-787-3914	Used; Antiquarian
The Civilized Traveler	2003 Broadway	212-875-0306	Specialty - Travel
Fordham University Bookstore	113 W 60th St	212-636-6079/6080	Academic - General
Gryphon Book Shop	2246 Broadway	212-362-0706	Used; Antiquarian
Juillard School Bookstore	60 Lincoln Center Plz	212-799-5000	Academic - Music
New York Institute of Technology Bookstore	1855 Broadway	212-261-1551	Specialty - Technical

Map 15 • Upper East Side (Lower)

Asia Society Bookstore	725 Park Ave	212-288-6400	Specialty - Asian
The Black Orchid Bookshop	303 E 81st St	212-734-5908	Specialty - Mystery/Crime
Bookberries	983 Lexington Ave	212-794-9400	General Interest
Bookstore of the NY Psychoanalytic Institution	247 E 82nd St	212-772-8282	Specialty - Psychoanalysis
Choices Bookshop - Recovery	220 E 78th St	212-794-3858	Specialty - Self-help and recovery
Cornell University Medical College Bookstore	424 E 70th St	212-988-0400	Academic - Medical
Crawford Doyle Booksellers	1082 Madison Ave	212-288-6300	General Interest
Glenn Horowitz Book Dealers	19 E 76th St	212-327-3538	Antiquarian
Green Booksellers	944 Madison Ave	212-439-9194	Art and architecture
Hunter College Bookstore	695 Park Ave	212-650-3970	Academic - General
Imperial Fine Books	790 Madison Ave	212-861-6620	Antiquarian
James Cummins Book Seller	699 Madison Ave, 7th Fl	212-688-6441	Antiquarian
Lenox Hill Bookstore	1018 Lexington Ave	212-472-7170	General Interest
Metropolitan Museum of Art Bookshop	1000 Fifth Ave	212-650-2911	Specialty - Art books
Shakespeare & Co	939 Lexington Ave	212-570-0201	Chain
Strand Books Kiosk	Fifth Ave @ 60th St	646-284-5506	Used; Remainders
Ursus Books	981 Madison Ave	212-772-8787	Specialty - Art
Whitney Museum of American Art Bookstore	945 Madison Ave	212-570-3614	Specialty - Art/ Artists Books

Map 16 • Upper West Side (Upper)

Funny Business Comics	660B Amsterdam Ave	212-799-9477	Specialty - Comics
Murder Ink	2486 Broadway	212-362-8905/ 800-488-8123	Specialty - Mystery

Map 17 • Upper East Side / East Harlem

Barnes & Noble	1280 Lexington Ave	212-423-9900	Chain
Barnes & Noble	240 E 86th St	212-794-1962	Chain
Corner Bookstore	1313 Madison Ave	212-831-3554	General Interest
The Military Bookman	29 E 93rd St	212-348-1280	Specialty - Military
Mt Sinai Medical Bookstore	1 Gustave Levy Pl	212-241-2665	Specialty - Medical

Map 18 • Columbia / Morningside Heights

Augsburg Fortress	3041 Broadway	212-280-1554	Specialty - Spiritual and theological
Bank Street College Bookstore	610 W 112th St	212-678-1654	Academic - Education/Children
Columbia University Bookstore	2922 Broadway	212-854-4131	Academic - General
Labyrinth	536 W 112th St	212-865-1588	General Interest
Last Word Used Books	1181 Amsterdam Ave	212-864-0013	Used
Papyrus	2915 Broadway	212-222-3350	General Interest; Used
Teachers College Bookstore (Columbia University Graduate School of Education)	1224 Amsterdam Ave	212-678-3920	Academic - Education

Map 19 • Harlem (Lower)

Hue-Man	2319 Frederick Douglass Blvd	212-665-7400	African-American
Liberation	421 Lenox Ave	212-281-4615	General Interest

Map 20 • El Barrio

J P Medical Books	53 E 124th St	212-410-0593	Academic - Medical

Map 21 • Manhattanville / Hamilton Heights

La Boheme	3441 Broadway	212-862-5500	Specialty - Spanish
Sisters Uptown	1942 Amsterdam Ave	212-862-3680	General Interest

Map 23 • Washington Heights

Columbia Medical Books	3954 Broadway	212-923-2149	Academic - Medical

Map 24 • Fort George / Fort Tryon

Metropolitan Museum of Art Bookshop-Cloisters Branch	Ft Tyron Park	212-923-3700	Specialty - Art books

Map 28 • Greenpoint

Exlibris Polish Book Gallery	140 Nassau Ave	718-349-0468	Polish
Polish American Bookstore	946 Manhattan Ave	718-389-7790	Polish
Polish Bookstore	739 Manhattan Ave	718-383-0739	Polish
Polish Bookstore & Publishing	161 Java St	718-349-2738	Polish
Polonia Book Store	882 Manhattan Ave	718-389-1684	Polish

Map 29 • Williamsburg

Clovis Press	229 Bedford Ave	718-302-3751	Indie
Spoonbill & Sugartown	218 Bedford Ave	718-387-7322	General

Map 30 • Brooklyn Heights / DUMBO / Downtown

A&B Books	146 Lawrence St	718-596-0872	General Interest
Barnes & Noble	106 Court St	718-246-4996	Chain
Heights Books Inc	109 Montague St	718-624-4876	General Interest
Long Island University Bookstore	1 University Plz	718-858-3888	Academic-General
St Mark's Comics	148 Montague St	718-935-0911	Comics

Map 31 • Fort Greene

Big Deal Books	973 Fulton St	718-622-4420	Remainder books
Dare Books	33 Lafayette Ave	718-625-4651	Culture books
Indigo Cafe & Books	672 Fulton St	718-488-5934	Indie

Map 32 • Cobble Hill / Boerum Hill / Carroll Gardens

Anwaar	428 Atlantic Ave	718-875-3791	Arabic books
Bookcourt	163 Court St	718-875-3677	Indie-General Interest
Community Book Store	212 Court St	718-834-9494	Used
Freebird Books	123 Columbia St	718-643-8484	Used

Map 33 • Park Slope / Prospect Heights

Seventh Avenue Kid's Books	202 7th Ave	718-840-0020	Children's books
Barnes & Noble	267 7th Ave	718-832-9066	Chain
Comics Plus	302 7th Ave	718-768-5681	Comics
Community Book Store	143 7th Ave	718-783-3075	Used
Nkiru International Book	732 Washington Ave	718-783-6306	Cultural books.
Park Slope Books	200 7th Ave	718-499-3064	Used

Multiplexes abound in NYC, but, unlike everywhere else, you'll need to cash in a savings bond to cover the steep $10.25 ticket price, the ridiculously over-priced popcorn doused in artificial grease, and exorbitant carbonated syrup water. Needless to say, a trip to the movies here is a very expensive affair. But hey, we don't live in the Big Apple 'cause it's cheap! New York City multiplexes come in many shapes and sizes—not surprisingly, some are definitely better than others. If you're after a first-run Hollywood blockbuster, we highly recommend the **Regal 16** in Battery Park City. It has spacious theaters with large screens, big sound, comfortable seats, plenty of aisle room, and most importantly, fewer people! The **Regal/United Artists Union Square** is gargantuan too, but is frequently so packed that the lines spill out onto the sidewalk. **Loews Lincoln Square** is a great theater to catch a huge film, with stadium seating and an IMAX theater. It's in a great location, so you can find loads of after-movie options—we recommend grabbing a bite at the Whole Foods Market in the fancy new Time-Warner Center.

For the independent or foreign film, the **Landmark Sunshine** on Houston and Forsyth has surpassed the **Angelika** as the better downtown movie house. Angelika still plays some great movies, but the theater itself is a far cry from the Sunshine. Either way, viewing a flick below 14th Street requires you to be attired completely in black! Speaking of hip venues, check out the **Two Boots Pioneer** and **Den of Cin**, both operated by the Two Boots folks. The Den of Cin is a tiny, tiny space showing the most eclectic sampling of rarely screened underground, avant-garde, and cult films. The Pioneer Theater, a more traditional single screen venue, specializes in the independent scene, screening documentaries, short films, cool film series and festivals (www.twoboots.com/pioneer). The best revival houses are **Cinema Classics**, the **Cine-Noir Society**, and the **Film Forum**—especially with the Screening Room (now **Tribeca Cinemas**) gone.

The most decadent and enjoyable movie experiences can be had at the theaters that feel the most "New York." The **Cinepelex Odeon Beekman** on the Upper East Side, while small, is in some of the best scenes in Annie Hall, so put on your big tie and vest and impress your date! **Clearview's Ziegfeld** on 54th Street is a vestige from a time long past when theaters were works of art. This venue is so posh with its gilding and red velvet, you feel like you're crossing the Atlantic on an expensive ocean liner. The **Paris Theater** on 58th Street is one of our favorite theaters in the city—it has the best balcony, hands down!

Oh, and don't forget to use Moviefone (777-film; www.moviefone.com) or Fandango (www.fandango.com) to reserve your tickets ahead of time on an opening weekend!

Manhattan	*Address*	*Phone*	*Map*	
92nd Street Y	Lexington Ave & 92nd St	212-415-5500	17	Upper East Side (Upper)
AMC Empire 25	234 W 42nd St	212-398-3939	12	Midtown
American Museum of Natural History IMAX	Central Park W & 79th St	212-769-5100	14	Upper West Side (Lower)
Angelika Film Center	18 W Houston St	777-FILM #531	6	Washington Square / NYU / SoHo
Anthology Film Archives	32 Second Ave	212-505-5181	6	Washington Square / NYU / SoHo
Asia Society	725 Park Ave	212-327-9276	15	Upper East Side (Lower)
Bryant Park Summer Film Festival (outdoors)	Bryant Park, between 40th & 42nd Sts	212-512-5700	12	Midtown
Cine-Noir Film Society	176 Ludlow St	212-253-1922	7	East Village
Cine One & Two	711 Seventh Ave	212-398-1720	12	Midtown
Cinema Classics	332 E 11th St	212-677-6309	6	Washington Square / NYU / SoHo
Cinema Village	22 E 12th St	212-924-3363	6	Washington Square / NYU / SoHo
Cineplex Odeon: Beekman Theater	1254 Second Ave	212-737-2622	15	Upper East Side (Lower)
Cineplex Odeon: Coronet Cinemas	993 Third Ave	355-1663	13	East Midtown
City Cinemas 1, 2, 3	1001 Third Ave	777-FILM #635	13	East Midtown
City Cinemas: East 86th Street	210 E 86th St	212-860-8686	17	Upper East Side (Upper)
City Cinemas: Eastside Playhouse	919 Third Ave	777-FILM #541	13	East Midtown
City Cinemas: Sutton 1 & 2	205 E 57th St	777-FILM #634	13	East Midtown
City Cinemas: Village East Cinemas	189 Second Ave	777-FILM #922	6	Washington Square / NYU / SoHo
Clearview's 59th Street East	239 E 59th St	777-FILM #615	13	East Midtown
Clearview's 62nd & Broadway	1871 Broadway	777-FILM #864	14	Upper West Side (Lower)
Clearview's Chelsea	260 W 23rd St	777-FILM #597	9	Flatiron / Lower Midtown
Clearview's Chelsea West	333 W 23rd St	777-FILM #614	8	Chelsea
Clearview's First & 62nd Street	400 E 62nd St	777-FILM #957	15	Upper East Side (Lower)
Clearview's Metro Twin	2626 Broadway	777-FILM #609	16	Upper West Side (Upper)
Clearview's Ziegfeld	141 W 54th St	777-FILM #602	12	Midtown
Common Basis Theater	750 Eighth Ave	212-302-5047	12	Midtown
Crown Theatre	1271 Second Ave	212-249-4240	15	Upper East Side (Lower)
Czech Center	1109 Madison Ave	212-288-0830	15	Upper East Side (Lower)
Den of Cin	44 Avenue A	212-254-0800	7	East Village

Film Forum	209 W Houston St	212-727-8110	5	West Village
French Institute	55 E 59th St	212-355-6160	13	East Midtown
Gavin Brown's Enterprise	436 W 15th St	212-627-5258	8	Chelsea
Goethe Institute	1014 Fifth Ave	212-439-8700	17	Upper East Side (Upper)
Hudson St Cinemas	5 Marineview Plz		34	Hoboken
Instituto Cervantes	122 E 42nd St	212-661-6011	13	East Midtown
Italian Academy	1161 Amsterdam Ave	212-854-3570	18	Columbia / Morningside Heights
Japan Society	333 E 47th St	212-752-3015	13	East Midtown
Landmark Sunshine Cinema	141 E Houston St	212-777-FILM #687	6	Washington Square / NYU / SoHo
Leonard Nimoy Thalia	2537 Broadway	212-864-5400	16	Upper West Side (Upper)
Lincoln Plaza Cinemas	30 Lincoln Plz	212-757-2280	14	Upper West Side (Lower)
Loews 19th Street East	890 Broadway	212-50-LOEWS #758	9	Flatiron / Lower Midtown
Loews 34th Street	312 W 34th St	212-244-8850	8	Chelsea
Loews 42nd Street E Walk	247 W 42nd St	212-50-LOEWS #572	12	Midtown
Loews 72nd Street East	1230 Third Ave	212-50-LOEWS #704	15	Upper East Side (Lower)
Loews 84th Street	2310 Broadway	212-50-LOEWS #701	14	Upper West Side (Lower)
Loews Astor Plaza	1515 Broadway	212-50-LOEWS #699	12	Midtown
Loews Cineplex Newport Center 11	30 Mall Dr W		34	Jersey City
Loews Cineplex Orpheum	1538 Third Ave	212-50-LOEWS #964	17	Upper East Side (Upper)
Loews Kips Bay	550 Second Ave	212-50-LOEWS #558	10	Murray Hill / Gramercy
Loews Lincoln Square & IMAX Theater	1992 Broadway	212-50-LOEWS #638	14	Upper West Side (Lower)
Loews State	1540 Broadway	212-391-0337	12	Midtown
Loews Village	66 Third Ave	212-50-LOEWS 952	6	Washington Square / NYU / SoHo
Magic Johnson Harlem USA	124th St & Frederick Douglass Blvd	212-665-8742	19	Harlem (Lower)
Makor	35 W 67th St	212-601-1000	14	Upper West Side (Lower)
Metropolitan Museum of Art	1000 Fifth Ave	212-535-7710	15	Upper East Side (Lower)
MoMA Film at the Gramercy Theater	127 E 23rd St	212-777-4900	10	Murray Hill / Gramercy
Museum of TV and Radio	25 W 52nd St	212-621-6800	12	Midtown
New York Public Library Jefferson Market Branch	425 Sixth Ave	212-243-4334	5	West Village
New York Public Library-Donnell Library Center	20 W 53rd St	212-621-0618	12	Midtown
New York Youth Theater	593 Park Ave	212-888-0696	15	Upper East Side (Lower)
NYU Cantor Film Center	36 E 8th St	212-998-4100	6	Washington Square / NYU / SoHo
Paris Theater	4 W 58th St	212-688-3800	12	Midtown
Quad Cinema	34 W 13th St	212-255-8800	6	Washington Square / NYU / SoHo
Regal Battery Park City 16	102 North End Ave			Battery Park City
Regal/UA Union Square	850 Broadway	777-FILM #777	6	Washington Square / NYU / SoHo
Regal/UA	1210 Second Ave	777-FILM #791	15	Upper East Side (Lower)
Regal/UA	1629 First Ave	777-FILM #789	15	Upper East Side (Lower)
Regal/UA	35-30 38th St		27	Long Island City
Scandinavia House	58 Park Ave	212-779-3587	10	Murray Hill / Gramercy
Guggenheim Museum, Solomon R.	1071 Fifth Ave	212-423-3500	17	Upper East Side (Upper)
Tribeca Cinemas	54 Varick St	212-334-2100	2	TriBeCa
Two Boots Pioneer Theater	155 E 3rd St	212-254-3300	7	East Village
Walter Reade Theater	70 Lincoln Plz	212-875-5600	14	Upper West Side (Lower)
Whitney Museum	945 Madison Ave	212-570-3600	15	Upper East Side (Lower)
YWCA	610 Lexington Ave	212-735-9717	13	East Midtown

Brooklyn	*Address*	*Phone*	*Map*	
BAM Rose Cinemas	30 Lafayette Ave	718-777-3456	31	Fort Greene
Cobble Hill Cinema	265 Court St	718-596-9113	32	Cobble Hill / Boerum Hill / Carroll Gardens
Pavilion Brooklyn Heights	70 Henry St	718-596-7070	30	Brooklyn Heights / DUMBO / Downtown
Pavilion Flatbush	314 Flatbush Ave	718-636-0170	33	Park Slope / Prospect Heights
Pavilion Movie Theatres	188 Prospect Park W	718-369-0838	33	Park Slope / Prospect Heights
Regal/UA Court Street	108 Court St	718-246-7995	30	Brooklyn Heights / DUMBO / Downtown

Metropolitan Museum of Art

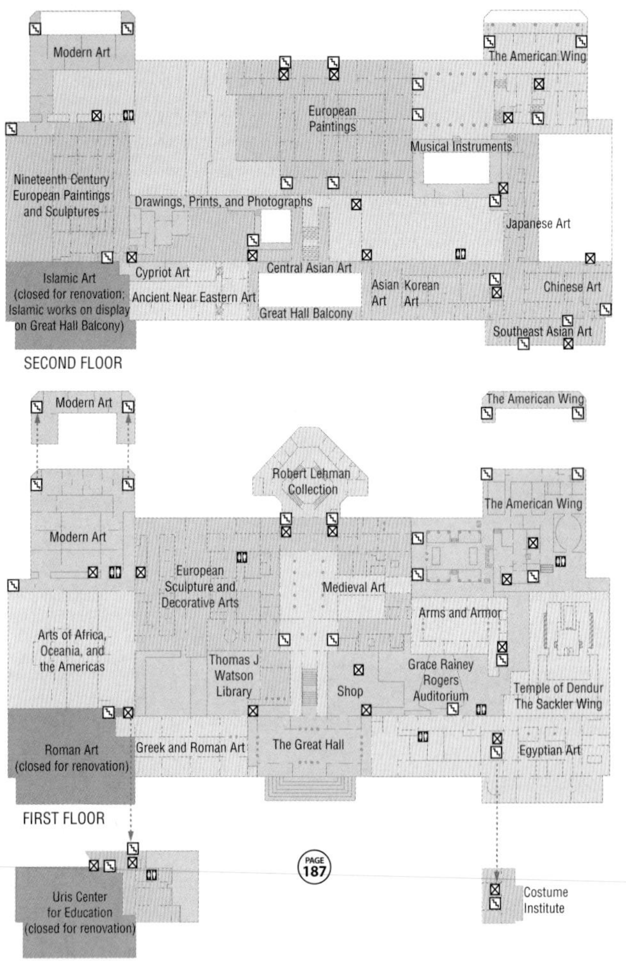

General Information

Address: 1000 Fifth Ave at 82nd St
Phone: 212-535-7710
Website: www.metmuseum.org
Hours: Sun, Tues–Thurs: 9:30 am–5:30 pm; Fri & Sat: 9:30 am–9 pm; Mon: closed
Admission: A suggested $12 donation for adults, $7 for students and senior citizens. Admission includes the Main Building and The Cloisters on the same day. Free to members and children under twelve with an adult.

Overview

The Metropolitan Museum of Art is touted as the largest and most comprehensive museum in the Western hemisphere. Established by a group of American businessmen, artists and thinkers back in 1870, the museum was created to preserve and stimulate appreciation for some of the greatest works of art in history.

In the first few years of its inception, the museum moved from its original location at 681 Fifth Avenue to the Douglas Mansion at 128 W 14th Street, and then finally to its current Central Park location in 1880.

Calvert Vaux and Jacob Wrey Mold designed the museum's Gothic Revival red-brick facade, which was later remodeled in 1926 into the grand, white-columned front entrance that you see today. Part of the original facade was left intact and can still be seen from the Robert Lehman Wing looking toward the European Sculpture and Decorative Arts galleries.
The Met's annual attendance reaches over 5 million visitors, who flock to see the more than 2 million works of art housed in the museum's permanent collection. The vast paintings anthology had a modest beginning in 1870 with a small donation of 174 European paintings and has now swelled to include works spanning 5,000 years of world culture, from the prehistoric to the present and from every corner of the globe.

The Met is broken down into a series of smaller museums within each building. For instance, the American Wing contains the most complete accumulation of American paintings, sculpture and decorative arts, including period rooms offering a look into domestic life throughout the nation's history. The Egyptian collection is the finest in the world outside of Cairo, and the Islamic art exhibition remains unparalleled, as does the mass of 2,500 European paintings and Impressionist and Post-Impressionist works. Other major collections include the arms and armor, Asian art, costumes, European sculpture and decorative arts, medieval and Renaissance art, musical instruments, drawings, prints, ancient antiquities from around the world, photography, and modern art.

The Greatest Hits

You can, of course, spend countless hours in the Met. But if you're rushed for time, check out the sublime space that houses the **Temple of Dendur** in the Sackler Wing, the elegant **Frank Lloyd Wright Room** in the American Wing, the fabulous **Tiffany Glass** and **Tiffany Mosaics**, also in the American Wing, the **Arms and Armor** exhibit, the **Caravaggios** and **Goyas** in the Renaissance Rooms, the wonderful **Clyfford Still** room in Modern Art, and that huge **canoe** in Arts of Africa and Oceania. The **Roof Garden**, when open, has killer views of Central Park, and we highly recommend it.

How to Get There–Mass Transit

Subway
Take the 4 5 6 to the 86th Street stop and walk three blocks west to Fifth Avenue.

Bus
Take the 4 bus along Fifth Avenue (from uptown locations) to 82nd Street or along Madison Avenue.

The five boroughs of New York City have over a hundred different museums of extremely varying sizes, from large world famous institutions like the **Metropolitan Museum of Art** to small historical houses and buildings. It wasn't always like this. In earlier times Manhattan grew quickly to become the capital of commerce, with culture being sorely neglected. Until the mid-1800s, most museums in the city were either small collections run by academic societies or by individuals, or entertainment-focused, profit-making ventures, such as P.T. Barnum's American Museum.

The second half of the 19th century saw the founding of the **American Museum of Natural History** and the **Met** with money donated by wealthy industrialists. This trend continued into the 20th century, with large donations of paintings to the Met by J.P. Morgan and B. Altman, the opening of **The Cloisters** with money from John D. Rockefeller, and the opening of galleries based on the collections of Morgan and Henry Clay Frick. Other notable openings of this time include the **Brooklyn Children's Museum**, the **Museum of the City of New York**, and **Hayden Planetarium**.

Museums devoted to modern art such as the **Whitney Museum of American Art**, the **Museum of Modern Art**, and the **Guggenheim** were founded in the 1920s and '30s. Museum openings continued into the middle of the century with the **International Center of Photography**, the **American Folk Art Museum**, and the **Museum of Television and Radio**. This was also a period that saw spaces open with a focus on an ethnicity including the **Asia Society** and the **Museo Del Bario**. Alternative spaces, such as **P.S. 1**, also began to have a greater presence. In the last half of the 20th century, the increased interest in historical structures in the city after the destruction of Penn Station led to many small museums opening in historic houses across all five boroughs. The conversion of obsolete buildings into museums such as the transformation of the Custom House into the **National Museum of the American Indian** also happened during this period. Quite a few large museums have been recently renovated, or will be in the next few years, including the Museum of Natural History (which now has a new planetarium), MoMA, and the Met.

Just about every museum in the city is worth a visit, and the major ones have so many exhibits and special collections that making the trek to them a few times a year isn't unreasonable. A few favorites include the **Transit Museum** (Brooklyn), the Museum of Television and Radio, the **Morgan Library** (closed until early 2006—has copies of Guttenburg's Bible on display), the **American Museum of the Moving Image** (Queens), the **Frick Collection**, the Cloisters, and the **Queens Museum of Art** (specifically the panorama of New York City), as well as the usual suspects—the Met, MoMA, Natural History, and the Whitney.

** All phone numbers are 212 unless otherwise denoted.*

Manhattan	*Address*	*Phone*	*Map*	
African American Institute	833 United Nations Plz	949-5666	13	East Midtown
African American Wax Museum	316 W 115th St	678-7818	18	Columbia / Morningside Heights
American Academy of Arts & Letters	633 W 155th St	368-5900	21	Manhattanville / Hamilton Heights
American Bible Society Gallery and Archives	1865 Broadway	408-1500	14	Upper West Side (Lower)
American Craft Museum	40 W 53rd St	956-6047	12	Midtown
American Folk Art Museum	45 W 53rd St	265-1040	12	Midtown
American Folk Art Museum	2 Lincoln Sq	595-9533	14	Upper West Side (Lower)
American Friends of Tel Aviv	545 Madison Ave	319-0555	12	Midtown
American Geographical Society	120 Wall St	422-5456	1	Financial District
American Institute of Graphic Arts	164 Fifth Ave	807-1990	9	Flatiron / Lower Midtown
American Museum of Natural History	Central Park W at 79th St	769-5100	15	Upper East Side (Lower)
American Numismatic Society	33 Liberty St	234-3130	21	Manhattanville / Hamilton Heights
Americas Society	680 Park Ave	249-8950	15	Upper East Side (Lower)
Anthology Film Archives	32 Second Ave	505-5181	6	Washington Square / NYU / SoHo
Arsenal Gallery	830 Fifth Ave	360-8163	15	Upper East Side (Lower)
Art in General	79 Walker St	219-0473		
Asia Society & Museum	725 Park Ave	517-ASIA	15	Upper East Side (Lower)
Asian American Art Centre	26 Bowery	233-2154	3	City Hall / Chinatown
Bard Graduate Center for Studies in the Decorative Arts	18 W 86th St	501-3000	16	Upper West Side (Upper)
Black Fashion Museum	155 W 126th St	666-1320	19	Harlem (Lower)
Chaim Gross Studio Museum	526 LaGuardia Pl	529-4906	6	Washington Square / NYU / SoHo
Chelsea Art Museum	556 W 22nd St	255-0719	8	Chelsea
Children's Galleries for Jewish Culture	515 W 20th St	924-4500	8	Chelsea
Children's Museum of Manhattan	212 W 83rd St	721-1223	14	Upper West Side (Lower)
Children's Museum of the Arts	182 Lafayette St	941-9198	3	City Hall / Chinatown
Children's Museum of the Native Americans	550 W 155th St	283-1122	21	Manhattanville / Hamilton Heights
China Institute	125 E 65th St	744-8181	15	Upper East Side (Lower)
Constitution Works	26 Wall St	785-1989	1	Financial District
Cooper Union for the Advancement of Science and Art	Foundation Building, E 7th St & Third Ave	353-4200	6	Washington Square / NYU / SoHo
Cooper-Hewitt National Design Museum	2 E 91st St	849-8300	17	Upper East Side / East Harlem
Czech Center	1109 Madison Ave	288-0830	15	Upper East Side (Lower)

Dahesh Museum	580 Madison Ave	759-0606	12	Midtown
Dia Center for the Arts	548 W 22nd St	989-5566	8	Chelsea
Drawing Center	35 Wooster St	219-2166	2	TriBeCa
Dyckman Farmhouse Museum	4881 Broadway	304-9422	25	Inwood
El Museo del Barrio	1230 Fifth Ave	831-7272	17	Upper East Side / East Harlem
Ellis Island Immigration Museum	Ellis Island, via ferry at Battery Park	363-3200	1	Financial District
Exit Art / The First World	548 Broadway	966-7745	6	Washington Square / NYU / SoHo
Eyebeam Atelier Digital Museum	115 Mercer St	431-7474	6	Washington Square / NYU / SoHo
Federal Hall	33 Liberty St	825-6870	1	Financial District
Fraunces Tavern Museum	54 Pearl St	425-1778	1	Financial District
French Institute	22 E 60th St	355-6100	15	Upper East Side (Lower)
Frick Collection	1 E 70th St	288-0700	15	Upper East Side (Lower)
Goethe-Institut	1014 Fifth Ave	439-8700	15	Upper East Side (Lower)
Gracie Mansion	East End Ave at 88th St	570-4751	17	Upper East Side / East Harlem
Grant's Tomb	W 122nd St & Riverside Dr		18	Columbia / Morningside Heights
Guggenheim Museum, Solomon R.	1071 Fifth Ave	423-3500	17	Upper East Side / East Harlem
Hayden Planetarium	175 Central Park W	769-5920	14	Upper West Side (Lower)
Hispanic Society of America	Broadway & 155th St	926-2234	21	Manhattanville / Hamilton Heights
International Center of Photography (ICP)	1133 Sixth Ave	857-0000	12	Midtown
Intrepid Sea-Air-Space Museum	Pier 86, W 46th St at the Hudson River	245-0072	12	Midtown
Japan Society	333 E 47th St	832-1155	13	East Midtown
Jewish Museum	1109 Fifth Ave	423-3200	17	Upper East Side / East Harlem
Lower East Side Tenement Museum	90 Orchard St	431-0233	4	Lower East Side
Merchant's House Museum	29 E 4th St	777-1089	6	Washington Square / NYU / SoHo
Metropolitan Museum of Art	Fifth Ave & 82nd St	535-7710	15	Upper East Side (Lower)
Morgan Library	29 E 36th St	685-0610	9	Flatiron / Lower Midtown
Morris-Jumel Mansion	65 Jumel Ter	923-8008	23	Washington Heights
Mount Vernon Hotel Museum	421 E 61st St	838-6878	15	Upper East Side (Lower)
Municipal Art Society	457 Madison Ave	935-3960	12	Midtown
Museum at the Fashion Institute of Technology	Seventh Ave & 27th St	217-5800	9	Flatiron / Lower Midtown
Museum for African Art	593 Broadway	966-1313	6	Washington Square / NYU / SoHo
Museum of African American History and Arts	352 W 71st St	873-5040	14	Upper West Side (Lower)
Museum of American Financial History	28 Broadway	908-4110	1	Financial District
Museum of American Illustration	128 E 63rd St	838-2560	15	Upper East Side (Lower)
Museum of Arts & Design	2 Columbus Cir	956-3535	12	Midtown
Museum of Chinese in the Americas	70 Mulberry St	619-4785	3	City Hall / Chinatown
Museum of Jewish Heritage	18 First Pl	968-1800	7	East Village
Museum of Modern Art (MoMA)	11 W 53rd St	708-9400	12	Midtown
Museum of Sex	233 Fifth Ave	689-6337	9	Flatiron / Lower Midtown
Museum of Television and Radio	25 W 52nd St	621-6800	12	Midtown
Museum of the American Piano	211 W 58th St	246-4823	12	Midtown
Museum of the City of New York	1220 Fifth Ave	534-1672	17	Upper East Side / East Harlem
National Academy of Design	1083 Fifth Ave	369-4880	17	Upper East Side / East Harlem
National Museum of Catholic Art & History	443 E 115th St	828-5209	12	Midtown
National Museum of the American Indian	1 Bowling Green	514-3700	1	Financial District
Neue Galerie: Museum for German and Austrian Art	1048 Fifth Ave	628-6200	17	Upper East Side / East Harlem
New Museum of Contemporary Art	556 W 22nd St	219-1222	8	Chelsea
New York City Fire Museum	278 Spring St	691-1303	5	West Village
New-York Historical Society	2 W 77th St	873-3400	14	Upper West Side (Lower)
New York Police Museum	100 Old Slip	480-3100	1	Financial District
New York Public Library for the Performing Arts	40 Lincoln Center Plz	870-1630	14	Upper West Side (Lower)
New York Unearthed	17 State St	748-8628	1	Financial District
Nicholas Roerich Museum	319 W 107th St	864-7752	16	Upper West Side (Upper)
Rose Museum	154 W 57th St	247-7800	12	Midtown
Rubin Museum of Art	138 W 17th St	620-5000	9	Flatiron / Lower Midtown

** All phone numbers are 212 unless otherwise denoted.*

Manhattan *continued*

Manhattan *continued*	Address	Phone	Map	
Scandinavia House	58 Park Ave	879-9779	10	Murray Hill / Gramercy
School of Visual Arts Museum	209 E 23rd St	592-2144	10	Murray Hill / Gramercy
Skyscraper Museum	16 Wall St	766-1324	1	Financial District
Sony Wonder Technology Lab	550 Madison Ave	833-8100	12	Midtown
South Street Seaport Museum	12 Fulton St	748-8600	1	Financial District
Statue of Liberty Museum	Liberty Island, via ferry at Battery Park	363-3200	1	Financial District
Studio Museum in Harlem	144 W 125th St	864-4500	19	Harlem (Lower)
The Cloisters	Ft Tryon Park	923-3700	24	Fort George / Fort Tryon
The New York Public Library Humanities & Social Sciences Library	Fifth Ave & 42nd St	869-8089		
The Troll Museum	122 Orchard St	560-7235	7	East Village
Tibet House	22 W 15th St	807-0563	9	Flatiron / Lower Midtown
Ukrainian Museum	203 Second Ave	228-0110	6	Washington Square / NYU / SoHo
US Archives of American Art	1285 Sixth Ave	399-5030	12	Midtown
Whitney Museum of American Art	945 Madison Ave	570-3676	15	Upper East Side (Lower)
Whitney Museum of American Art at Philip Morris	120 Park Ave	878-2550	13	East Midtown
Yeshiva University Museum	2520 Amsterdam Ave	960-5390	24	Fort George / Fort Tryon

Brooklyn

Brooklyn	Address	Phone	Map	
Brooklyn Children's Museum	145 Brooklyn Ave	718-735-4400		
Brooklyn Historical Society	128 Pierrepont St	718-222-4111	30	Brooklyn Heights / DUMBO / Downtown
Brooklyn Museum of Art	200 Eastern Pkwy	718-638-5000		
Harbor Defense Museum	101st St	718-630-4349		
Kurdish Library and Museum	144 Underhill Ave	718-783-7930	33	Park Slope / Prospect Heights
Micro Museum	123 Smith St	718-797-3116	32	Cobble Hill/Boerum Hill/Carroll Gardens
New York Aquarium	502 Surf Ave	718-265-3474		
New York Transit Museum	Boerum Pl & Schermerhorn St	718-243-8601	30	Brooklyn Heights / DUMBO / Downtown
The Old Stone House	336 Third St (b/w 4th and 5th Ave)	718-768-3195	33	Park Slope / Prospect Heights
Simmons Collection African Arts Museum	1063 Fulton St	718-230-0933	31	Fort Greene
Waterfront Museum	290 Conover St @ Pier 45	718-624-4719		
Wyckoff House	5816 Clarendon Rd	718-629-5400		

Queens

Queens	Address	Phone	Map	
P.S.1	4601 21st St	718-784-2084	27	Long Island City
American Museum of the Moving Image	35th Avenue at 36th St	718-784-4520	27	Long Island City
Queens Museum of Art	New York City Building Corona Park, Flushing Meadows	718-592-9700		

Eating out in New York. Why do we do it? Because cooking is probably only 15% cheaper. Or at least that's what we tell ourselves when we're spending $20 on a hamburger (**Union Square Café**) or $40 on pizza (**Otto**) or god knows what else. But hey—if you're into cooking, that's great. Just move where groceries are cheaper—say, Kansas.

As for the rest of us, eating out is a way of life, an art form, a topic of endless discussion. Zagat restaurant ratings, started on a photocopied sheet handed out to friends in the 1970s, is now an institution in NYC. Half the time we think it's cool to actually even *find* a restaurant that's not "Zagat Rated;" the other half of the time, it makes us very, very nervous.

But we *like* that nervous feeling, we can't wait to try a new cuisine, we don't mind eating in places that would clearly fail a Board of Health test—it's all part of eating out in New York. It never gets old....

Eating Old

Even though restaurant turnover continues at an astonishing rate, there are some old New York eateries worth checking out, for instance, the posh **'21' Club**, the former speakeasy **Chumley's**, the midtown watering hole **P.J. Clarke's**, the near-ancient **Bridge Café**, the classic Grand Central **Oyster Bar**, the Brooklyn staple **Ferdinando's Focacceria,** and the always-homey TriBeCa landmark **Walker's**.

Eating Cheap

Two words: go ethnic. Pizza, falafel, dumplings, burritos, bagels—this is what we eat to sustain ourselves on a daily basis. For pizza, check out **Two Boots**, **Joe's**, **Ben's**, **Arturo's**, **John's**, and **Patsy's**. For cheap Chinese, you can go to any place on any corner, but two cheap Dim Sum meccas in Chinatown are **Mandarin Court** and **Triple Eight Palace**. Sharing at places like **Joe's Shanghai** and **Grand Sichuan International** will also not bleed your wallet. Middle Eastern and burrito places are also a dime a dozen—for these, we simply say: choose your poison. As for bagels, go with perennial winners **Ess-a-Bagel** and **H&H Bagels**, or take our two favorites: **David's Bagels** and **Kossar's Bialys**. If you're in an insane hurry, the New York street vendor hot dog is still always an option.

Eating Hip

You mostly can't eat cool, but sometimes you can come close, especially with favorites like **First** (great décor, loud music, killer BLTs and wings), **Florent** (great diner with décor by Tibor Kallman), **Pearl Oyster Bar** (mostly bar seating and the best lobster roll south of Portland), **Norma's** (a cool room and hands-down the best brunch in town), and the relatively pretentious **Tasting Room**.

Eating Late

Kang Suh's Korean barbeque runs all night, as well as **Bereket, Odessa, Florent** (weekends only), **7A**, **Yaffa Café**, and a host of generic diners. **Blue Ribbon** and **First** are two of the best places to eat after midnight.

Eating Ethnic

New York has not only an example of every type of cuisine on the planet, but also a *good* version of every type of cuisine on the planet. To wit: **Sammy's Roumanian, Katz's Delicatessen, Carnegie Deli** (Jewish); **Shun Lee, Grand Sichuan International,** and **Joe's Shanghai** (Chinese); **Banjara, Tabla**, and **Pongal** (Indian); **Alma, Maya,** and **Rosa Mexicano** (Mexican); **Kang Suh** and **Dok Suni** (Korean); **Thailand Restaurant** (Thai); **Nobu**, **Blue Ribbon Sushi,** and about 40 others (Japanese); **Il Mulino, Il Giglio, Il Palazzo, Babbo, John's of 12th St, Il Bagatto**, and about 20 others (Italian); **Ghenet** (Ethiopian); **Eight Mile Creek** (Australian); **Balthazar, Chanterelle, La Luncheonette, Le Gamin, Jules, French Roast,** and 50 others (French); **Good World** and **Acquavit** (Scandinavian); **Hallo Berlin** (German); **Charles' Southern Style, Sylvia's,** and **Old Devil Moon** (Southern); **Stamatis** (Greek); **Village Mingala** (Burmese); etc. etc. etc.

Eating Meat

New York is of course home to perhaps the world's best steakhouse, **Peter Luger's**. But getting closer to that quality every day is the new **Mark Joseph Steakhouse**, as well as such favorites **Frank's Restaurant, Sparks, Palm, Smith & Wollensky, Angelo & Maxie's**, and, a top NFT pick, the **Strip House.** For the "all you can eat meatfest," **Churrascaria Plataforma** is the place. For poor man's steak (read: hamburger), nothing really comes close to **Corner Bistro**, although **Island Burgers 'n Shakes, 7A, Cozy Soup and Burger, Big Nick's,** and even **Jackson Hole** have many admirers.

Eating Meatless

We're not sure, but we think the first McDonald's "veggie burger" sold was in the one on St. Mark's Place and Third Avenue. However, for less disgusting fare, try the veggie burgers at **Dojos**, the great sausages at **Kate's Joint,** a whole range of vegan/macrobiotic at **Angelica's Kitchen,** the quality Indian fare at **Pongal**, and, for high-end fare, **Hangawi**.

Eating Your Wallet

Here's the rant: you can spend over $100 (per person) at any one of these places easily, without even blinking an eye. Is it worth it? Sometimes, little grasshopper, sometimes. But it's almost always at least close at: **Craft, Gotham, Gramercy Tavern, Chanterelle, Le Bernadin, Oceana, Union Square Café, March, Jean-Georges, Babbo, Danube,** and a handful of other places. But you can eat at Joe's Shanghai for a full week for the same amount of money. So here, we say: choose wisely.

Our Favorite Restaurant

It's **Blue Ribbon** on Sullivan Street. Why? A million reasons: it's open 'till 4 am, it's where the chefs of other restaurants go, it's got fondue, it's got beef marrow, it's got fried chicken, it's got pigeon, it's got a great vibe, great liquor, great service, and not-so-hellish prices. It's everything that's good and it's why we're in New York. Period.

*Key: $: Under $10 / $$: $10–$20 / $$$: $20–$30 / $$$$: $30+; * : Does not accept credit cards / † : Accepts only American Express.*

Map 1 • Financial District

Burritoville	36 Water St	212-747-1100	$	Takeout Mexican.
Cassis on Stone	52 Stone St	212-425-3663	$$	A mini European vacation.
Cosi Sandwich Bar	54 Pine St	212-809-2674	$*	Sandwiches for the masses.
Cosi Sandwich Bar	55 Broad St	212-344-5000	$*	Sandwiches for the masses.
Daily Soup	41 John St	212-791-7687	$*	Soup!
Financier Patisserie	62 Stone St	212-344-5600	$$	Have your cake and a light meal too.
Giovanni's Atrium	100 Washington St	212-513-4133	$$	Owner grows fresh herbs for meals!
The Grotto	69 New St	212-809-6990	$$	More quick, tasty Italian. Less nudity than that other grotto.
Lemongrass Grill	110 Liberty St	212-962-1370	$$	Serviceable Thai.
Les Halles	15 John St	212-285-8585	$$$	Excellent French steakhouse.
New York Pizza Factory	30 Water St	212-809-0999	$	Superior quick slices.
Red	14 Fulton St	212-571-5900	$$	Acceptable Mexican.
Rosario's	38 Pearl St	212-514-5454	$$*	Italian. Go for the small portions.
Roy's New York	130 Washington St	212-266-6262	$$$$	Hawaiian fusion seafood.
Sophie's	205 Pearl St	212-269-0909	$*	Great cheap Cuban/Carribean.
Sophie's Restaurant	73 New St	212-809-7755	$*	Great cheap Cuban/Carribean.
St Maggie's Cafe	120 Wall St	212-943-9050	$$$	Downtown lunch option.

Map 2 • TriBeCa

A&M Roadhouse	57 Murray St	212-385-9005	$$$	Down-south barbeque ribs meet Maine lobsters.
Bread Tribeca	301 Church St	212-334-8282	$$$	Country-style Italian.
Bubby's	120 Hudson St	212-219-0666	$$	Great atmosphere--good homestyle and home made pies.
Burritoville	144 Chambers St	212-571-1144	$	Mexcellent.
Cafe Noir	32 Grand St	212-431-7910	$$$	Tapas. Open 'til 4 am.
Capsuoto Freres	451 Washington St	212-966-4900	$$$	Excellent brunch, great space.
Chanterelle	2 Harrison St	212-966-6960	$$$$$	Sublime French with prices to match.
City Hall	131 Duane St	212-227-7777	$$$$	Bright, expensive, lots of suits, but still cool.
Danube	30 Hudson St	212-791-3771	$$$$	Excellent food with an Austrian twist. Go for the tasting menu.
Duane Park Cafe	157 Duane St	212-732-5555	$$$$	Underrated New American.
Edward's	136 West Broadway	212-233-6436	*	Middle-of-the-road, kid's menu, mostly locals, sometimes great.
Felix	340 West Broadway	212-431-0021	$$$	Buzzing Brazilian with French overtones, see and be seen.
Flor de Sol	361 Greenwich St	212-989-5779	$$$	Tapas with—of course—a scene.
Fresh	105 Reade St	212-406-1900	$$$$	Excellent seafood.
Il Giglio	81 Warren St	212-571-5555	$$$$	Stellar Italian.
The Harrison	355 Greenwich St	212-274-9310	$$$	Great New American—understandably popular.
Kitchenette	80 West Broadway	212-267-6740	$$	Great breakfast. Try the bacon.
Kori	253 Church St	212-334-4598	$$$	Korean.
Layla	211 West Broadway	212-431-0700	$$$	Belly dancer after 9 pm!
Le Zinc	139 Duane St	212-513-0001	$$$$	French-influenced brasserie style.
Lucky Strike	59 Grand St	212-941-0479	$$	Good bar in front, reliable food in back.
Lupe's East LA Kitchen	110 Sixth Ave	212-966-1326	$*	Tex-Mex. Quaint.
Montrachet	239 West Broadway	212-219-2777	$$$$	Wonderful French.
Nobu	105 Hudson St	212-219-0500	$$$$	Designer Japanese.
Nobu, Next Door	105 Hudson St	212-334-4445	$$$	Nobu's cheaper neighbor.
Odeon	145 West Broadway	212-233-0507	$$$	We can't agree about this one, so go and make your own decision.
Palacinka	28 Grand St	212-625-0362	$$*	A tasty load of crepe.
Petite Abeille	134 West Broadway	212-791-1360	$*	Belgian waffle chain, great beer selection. Try the stoemp.
Roc	190 Duane St	212-625-3333	$$$	Lovely Italian, good for weekend brunch.
Salaam Bombay	317 Greenwich St	212-226-9400	$$	Indian; excellent lunch buffet.
Sosa Borella	460 Greenwich St	212-431-5093	$$	Louche Argentines and brilliant french toast.
The Sporting Club	99 Hudson St	212-219-0900	$$$	Sports bar with decent food and beer to match.
Thalassa	179 Franklin St	212-941-7661	$$$	Greek. But it's cheaper and better in Astoria.
Tribeca Grill	375 Greenwich St	212-941-3900	$$$$	Are you looking at me?
Walker's	16 N Moore St	212-941-0142	$$	Surprisingly good food for a pub!
Yaffa's	353 Greenwich St	212-274-9403	$$	Cooly eclectic. Food 'til 1 am
Zutto	77 Hudson St	212-233-3287	$$$	Neighborhood Japanese.

Map 3 • City Hall / Chinatown

Bridge Cafe	279 Water St	212-227-3344	$$$$	Now extremely expensive.
Canton	45 Division St	212-226-4441	$$$*	Top-shelf Chinese.
Cup & Saucer	89 Canal St	212-925-3298	$*	Good greasy burgers.

Dim Sum Go Go	5 East Broadway	212-732-0797	$$	New, hip, inventive dim sum.
Excellent Dumpling House	111 Lafayette St	212-219-0212	*	Excellent dumplings, really.
Ferrara	195 Grand St	212-226-6150	$	Classic Little Italy patisserie.
Fuleen's	11 Division St	212-941-6888	$$†	Chinese seafood shack.
Goody's	1 East Broadway	212-577-2922	$$	Almost as good as Joe's and one-eighth as crowded. 18 different soup varieties.
Il Palazzo	151 Mulberry St	212-343-7000	$$$	Excellent mid-range Italian.
Joe's Shanghai	9 Pell St	212-233-8888	$$*	Great crab soup dumplings.
Le Pain Quotidien	100 Grand St	212-625-9009	$$*	Excellent breads.
Lily's	31 Oliver St	212-766-3336	$$*	Official Japanese/Chinese takeout of NFT management.
Mandarin Court	61 Mott St	212-608-3838	$$	Consistently good dim sum.
Mark Joseph Steakhouse	261 Water St	212-277-0020	$$$$	Luger's wannabe.
New York Noodle Town	28 1/2 Bowery	212-349-0923	$*	Cheap Chinese.
Nha Trang	87 Baxter St	212-233-5948	$$	The best cheap Vietnamese.
Pho Viet Huong	73 Mulberry St	212-233-8988	$$	Very good Vietnamese.
Ping's	22 Mott St	212-602-9988	$$	Eclectic Asian seafood.
Positano Ristorante	122 Mulberry St	212-334-9808	$$	Good northern Italian fare.
Quartino	21 Peck Slip	212-349-4433	$$†	Good, clean pizza & pasta.
Thailand Restaurant	106 Bayard St	212-349-3132	$$	Great, spicy Thai.
Triple Eight Palace	88 East Broadway	212-941-8886	$$	Dim sum madness under the Manhattan Bridge.
Umberto's Clam House	129 Mulberry St	212-431-7545	$$	Another (overpriced) Little Italy institution.
Vegetarian Paradise	33 Mott St	212-406-6988	$	A paradise indeed.
Wo Hop	17 Mott St	212-267-2536	$*	Chinatown mainstay.

Map 4 • Lower East Side

Congee Village	100 Allen St	212-941-1818	$$	Good neighborhood Asian.
Good World Bar & Grill	3 Orchard St	212-925-9975	$$	Excellent Scandinavian finger food.
Les Enfants Terribles	37 Canal St	212-777-7518	$$$	New French-African.
Pho Bang	3 Pike St	212-233-3947	$*	Vietnamese.

Map 5 • West Village

A Salt & Battery	112 Greenwich Ave	212-691-2713	$*	Great take-out fish 'n chips.
AOC	314 Bleecker St	212-675-9463	$$$	A fine French replacement for Grove.
Aquagrill	210 Spring St	212-274-0505	$$$$	Excellent seafood.
Benny's Burritos	113 Greenwich Ave	212-727-3560	$$	A NYC Mexican institution.
Blue Ribbon Bakery	33 Downing St	212-337-0404	$$$	Another Blue Ribbon success.
Café Asean	117 W 10th St	212-633-0348	$$*	Pan-Asian, via Mr. Wong.
Caffe Torino	139 W 10th St	212-675-5554	$$	Comfy, relaxed Italian.
Chez Brigitte	77 Greenwich Ave	212-929-6736	*	You never thought a chicken sandwich could be this good.
Chumley's	86 Bedford St	212-675-4449	$$	Former speakeasy, great atmosphere & food.
Corner Bistro	331 W 4th St	212-242-9502	$*	Top NYC burgers. Open 'til 4.
Cowgirl Hall of Fame	519 Hudson St	212-633-5133	$$	Good chicken fried steak.
Crispo	240 W 14th St	212-229-1818	*	
Day-O	103 Greenwich Ave	212-924-3160	$$	Island fave, great cocktails.
Dragonfly	47 Seventh Ave	212-255-2848	$$	Try the Filipino specialties.
Florent	69 Gansevoort St	212-989-5779	$$*	One of the best places on the planet.
Grey Dog's Coffee	33 Carmine St	212-462-0041	$$*	Happy coffee, huge sandwiches.
Home	20 Cornelia St	212-243-9579	$$$	There's no place like it.
Ivo & Lulu	558 Broome St	212-226-4399	$$	Tiny inventive French-Caribbean (BYOB).
Jefferson	121 W 10th St	212-255-3333	$$$	Wong's American take.
Joe's Pizza	233 Bleecker St	212-366-1182	$*	Excellent slices.
John's Pizzeria	278 Bleecker St	212-243-1680	$$*	Quintessential NY pizza.
Le Gamin	27 Bedford St	212-243-2846	$$	New digs, same great food.
Lunchbox Food Company	357 West St	646-230-9466	$$*	Homemade doughnuts and ginger-sake lemonade.
Mary's Fish Camp	246 W 4th St	646-486-2185	$$$	Inventive but inconsistent seafood.
Mirchi	29 Seventh Ave S	212-414-0931	*	Spicy Indian.
Moustache	90 Bedford St	212-229-2220	$$*	Excellent sit-down falafel.
One If By Land, TIBS	17 Barrow St	212-228-0822	$$$	Exudes romance.
Pearl Oyster Bar	18 Cornelia St	212-691-8211	*	For all your lobster roll cravings.
Petite Abeille	400 W 14th St	212-727-1505	$$*	Tintin-infused waffle chain. Try the stoemp.
Petite Abeille	466 Hudson St	212-741-6479	$$*	Tintin-infused waffle chain. Try the stoemp.
Po	31 Cornelia St	212-645-2189	$$$$	Creative Italian.
Sapore	55 Greenwich Ave	212-229-0551	$$	Decent Italian, good lunch deal.
Souen	210 Sixth Ave	212-807-7421	$$$	High-end vegetarian.
Tea & Sympathy	108 Greenwich Ave	212-807-8329	$$*	Eccentric English. Cult favorite.
Two Boots	201 W 11th St	212-633-9096	$	Cajun pizza.
Yama	38 Carmine St	212-989-9330	$$$	Sushi deluxe.

*Key: $: Under $10 / $$: $10–$20 / $$$: $20–$30 / $$$$: $30+; * : Does not accept credit cards / † : Accepts only American Express.*

Map 6 • Washington Square / NYU / SoHo

Acme Bar & Grill	9 Great Jones St	212-420-1934	$$	Workmanlike Southern.
Angelica Kitchen	300 E 12th St	212-228-2909	$$*	Vegan/macrobiotic heaven.
Around The Clock	8 Stuyvesant St	212-598-0402	$$	Open 24 hours. NYU hangout.
Arturo's Pizzeria	106 W Houston St	212-677-3820	$$	Classic NYC pizza joint.
Babbo	110 Waverly Pl	212-777-0303	$$$$	Super Mario—eclectic Italian, fabulous wine list.
Balthazar	80 Spring St	212-965-1414	$$$$	Simultaneously pretentious and amazing.
Baluchi's	104 Second Ave	212-780-6000	$$	Servicable Indian.
Ben's Pizza	177 Spring St	212-966-4494	$*	Decent pizza.
Blue Hill	75 Washington Pl	212-539-1776	$$$	Wonderful food in an unexpected location.
Blue Ribbon	97 Sullivan St	212-274-0404	$$$	Open 'til 4. Everything's great.
Blue Ribbon Sushi	119 Sullivan St	212-343-0404	$$$	Great sushi.
Bond Street	6 Bond St	212-777-2500	$$$	Japanese does not get trendier or better than this...
Borgo Antico	22 E 13th St	212-807-1313	$$$	Underrated Tuscan. Usually deserted.
Cafe Colonial	73 E Houston St	212-274-0044	$$†	Excellent American/Brazilian.
Cafe Habana	17 Prince St	212-625-2001	$$	Excellent Cuban takeout joint.
Cafe Spice	72 University Pl	212-253-6999	$$$	Designer Indian.
Canteen	142 Mercer St	212-431-7676	$$$	New American in the heart of SoHo.
Chez Es Saada	42 E 1st St	212-777-5617	$$$	Dark and mysterious Moroccan.
Cozy Soup & Burger	739 Broadway	212-477-5566	$	Great Burgers!
Dojo	14 W 4th St	212-505-8934	$	Cheap and cheerful in Studentville.
Dojo	24 St Mark's Pl	212-674-9821	$$*	Cheap and cheerful in Studentville.
Eight Mile Creek	240 Mulberry St	212-431-4635	$$$$	Awesome Australian.
Frank	88 Second Ave	212-420-0202	$$*	Good food, great breakfast.
French Roast	78 W 11th St	212-533-2233	$$	Open 24 hours. French comfort food.
Ghenet	284 Mulberry St	212-343-1888	$$$	Excellent, unpretentious Ethiopian.
Gotham Bar & Grill	12 E 12th St	212-620-4020	$$$$	Excellent New American—one of the best.
Great Jones Cafe	54 Great Jones St	212-674-9304	$$	Classic soul food. Sort of.
Green Papaya	185 Sullivan St	212-253-5469	$$	Good neighborhood Thai.
Hampton Chutney Co	68 Prince St	212-226-9996	$*	Good take-out dosas.
Haveli	100 Second Ave	212-982-0533	$$$	Most expensive of the 6th Street Indians. Good dosas.
Holy Basil	149 Second Ave	212-460-5557	$$	Holy sh*t this is good Thai!
Il Buco	47 Bond St	212-533-1932	$$$	Lovely Italian food. Great wines by the glass.
Iso	175 Second Ave	212-777-0361	$$$$	Crowded Japanese.
Jane	100 W Houston St	212-254-7000	$$$	Good all-around!
John's of 12th Street	302 E 12th St	212-475-9531	$$*	Classic Italian. Get the rollatini.
Jules	65 St Mark's Pl	212-477-5560	$$$	Small French bistro with live unimposing Jazz.
Kelley & Ping	127 Greene St	212-228-1212	$$	Noodles and killer tea selection.
Khyber Pass	34 St Mark's Pl	212-473-0989	$$	Good Afghani.
Lupa	170 Thompson St	212-982-5089	$$$$	Italian, get reservations.
Melampo Imported Foods	105 Sullivan St	212-334-5179	$*	Excellent sandwiches.
Mingala Burmese	21 E 7th St	212-529-3656	$$	Burmese.
Otto	1 Fifth Ave	212-995-9559	$$$	$45 pizza? Absolutely!
Peep	177 Prince St	212-254-7337	$$$	Stylin' Thai. See-through bathroom mirrors.
Penang	109 Spring St	212-274-8883	$$$	Snooty but good Malaysian.
Pravda	281 Lafayette St	212-226-4696	$$$	Scene at the bar, tiny food.
Sammy's Roumanian	157 Chrystie St	212-673-0330	$$$$	An experience not to be missed.
Shabu-Tatsu	216 E 10th St	212-472-3322	$$	Affordable, homey sushi joint.
Snack	105 Thompson St	212-925-1040	$$*	Great Greek salads & spinach pie.
Soho Steak	90 Thompson St	212-226-0602	$$$	Excellent mid-range steakhouse.
Spice	60 University Pl	212-982-3758	$$	Trendy Thai.
Strip House	13 E 12th St	212-328-0000	$$$$	Super downtown steakhouse.
Time Cafe / Fez	380 Lafayette St	212-533-7000	$$	Consistently good, great indoor & outdoor spaces.
Tomoe Sushi	172 Thompson St	212-777-9346	$$$	Good sushi, long line.
Zoe	90 Prince St	212-966-6722	$$$$	Excellent New American, great desserts, a scene of course.

Map 7 • East Village

1492 Food	60 Clinton St	646-654-1114	$$$	Tapas. It's cool.
71 Clinton Fresh Food	71 Clinton St	212-614-6960	$$$$	We still can't get in.
7A	E 7th St & Avenue A	212-475-9001	$$	Open 24 hours. Great burgers.
B3	33 Avenue B	212-614-9755	$$$	Great default date restaurant.
Banjara	97 First Ave	212-477-5956	$$$	Best Indian on 6th Street, hands-down.
Benny's Burritos	93 Avenue A	212-254-2054	$	A NYC Mexican institution.
Bereket Turkish Kebab House	187 E Houston St	212-475-7700	$	Middle Eastern Delights. Open late.
Boca Chica	13 First Ave	212-473-0108	$$	Excellent, fun South American.
Café Mogador	101 St Mark's Pl	212-677-2226	$$*	Perfect place for hummus and a latte.
Crooked Tree Creperie	110 St Mark's Pl	212-533-3299	$*	Casual restaurant crepes.
Dish	165 Allen St	212-253-8840	$$	Home cooking in a hip locale. Recommended.

Dok Suni's	119 First Ave	212-477-9506	$$$*	Excellent Korean fusion.
El Castillo de Jaqua	113 Rivington St	212-982-6412	$*	Great cheap Dominican.
Esashi	32 Avenue A	212-505-6740	$$	Good low-key, friendly sushi.
Essex Restaurant	120 Essex St	212-533-9616	$$$	Great space, OK food.
First	87 First Ave	212-674-3823	$$	The best BLT on the planet.
Flea Market Cafe	131 Avenue A	212-358-9280	$$†	French, good brunch.
Flor's Kitchen	149 First Ave	212-387-8849	$$*	Authentic South American.
Grilled Cheese NYC	168 Ludlow St	212-982-6600	$*	Official selection of NFT interns.
Il Bagatto	192 E 2nd St	212-228-0977	$$$*	Packed Italian.
Kate's Joint	58 Avenue B	212-777-7059	$$	Inventive vegetarian and vegan.
Katz's Delicatessen	205 E Houston St	212-254-2246	$$	Great corned beef and fries.
Kuma Inn	113 Ludlow St	212-353-8866	$$*	Spicy southeast Asian tapas.
Kura Sushi	67 First Ave	212-979-6646	$$	Good sushi, good atmosphere, good music.
La Focacceria	128 First Ave	212-254-4946	$$	Simple Italian neighborhood joint.
Lavagna	545 E 5th St	212-979-1005	$$$	We hear it's great!
Le Gamin	536 E 5th St	212-254-8409	$$†	Great French Toast, overall brunch, etc.
Mama's Food Shop	200 E 3rd St	212-777-4425	$*	Great home-cooking and take-out.
Moustache	265 E 10th St	212-228-2022	$*	Excellent Middle Eastern.
Odessa	119 Avenue A	212-253-1470	$	Open 24 hours. Diner.
Old Devil Moon	511 E 12th St	212-475-4357	$$	Good southern food. Great biscuits.
Pylos	128 E 7th St	212-473-0220	$$	Delicious Greek, cool hanging-pot ceiling.
Raga	433 E 6th St	212-388-0957	$$$	Good Indian fusion.
Takahachi	85 Avenue A	212-505-6524	$$$	Super-good Japanese and sushi.
Tasting Room	72 E 1st St	212-358-7831	$$$$	Relatively pretentious.
Teany	90 Rivington St	212-475-9190	$$	Cute café-vegan-drinks-whatever.
The Hat (Sombrero)	108 Stanton St	212-254-4188	$$*	Cheap margaritas.
The Lite Touch Restaurant	151 Avenue A	420-8574	$	Authentic Morrocan and Middle Eastern.
Two Boots	42 Avenue A	212-505-2276	$	Cajun Pizza.
Yaffa Cafe	97 St Mark's Pl	212-674-9302	$$	Eclectic food/decor. Open 24 hours.
Zum Schneider	107 Avenue C	212-598-1098	$$*	Finally some downtown wurst.

Map 8 • Chelsea

Blue Moon Mexican Cafe	150 Eighth Ave	212-463-0560	$$	Great Mexican.
Bottino	246 Tenth Ave	212-206-6766	$$$	Good, clean Italian.
Bright Food Shop	216 Eighth Ave	212-243-4433	$$	Small, Asian-Mexican experience.
Burritoville	352 W 39th St	212-563-9088	$	Takeout Mexican.
Chelsea Bistro & Bar	358 W 23rd St	212-727-2026	$$$$	Charming French.
Cupcake Cafe	522 Ninth Ave	212-465-1530	$*	Three words: sweet potato doughnuts.
El Cid	322 W 15th St	212-929-9332	$$$	Spanish/tapas.
Empire Diner	210 Tenth Ave	212-243-2736	$$	A Chelsea institution. 24 Hours.
Frank's Restaurant	85 Tenth Ave	212-243-1349	$$$$	Noisy beef-fest.
Grand Sichuan Int'l	229 Ninth Ave	212-620-5200	$$	Some of the best Chinese in NYC.
Havana Chelsea	190 Eighth Ave	212-243-9421	$$*	Great Cuban sandwiches.
La Lunchonette	130 Tenth Ave	212-675-0342	$$$$	A truly great French restaurant. Recommended.
La Taza de Oro	96 Eighth Ave	212-243-9946	$$*	Great local Puerto Rican.
Le Gamin	183 Ninth Ave	212-243-8864	$$	Great French toast.
Moonstruck Diner	400 W 23rd St	212-924-3709	$$	24-hours on weekends only.
Pepe Giallo	253 Tenth Ave	212-242-6055	$$	Takeout Italian.
The Red Cat	227 Tenth Ave	212-242-1122	$$$$	Hip and expensive.
Salon Mexico	509 Ninth Ave	212-685-9400	$$*	Grimy authentic Mexican.
Sandwich Planet	534 Ninth Ave	212-273-9768	$*	Unlimited sandwich selection.
Skylight Diner	402 W 34th St	212-244-0395	$	24-hour diner.
Spice	199 Eighth Ave	212-989-1116	$$	Good, straightforward Thai.
Tick Tock Diner	481 Eighth Ave	212-268-8444	$	24-hour diner.
Viceroy	160 Eighth Ave	212-633-8484	$$$	Stargazin' American.

Map 9 • Flatiron / Lower Midtown

Basta Pasta	37 W 17th St	212-366-0888	$$$	Pac-rim Italian.
Blue Water Grill	31 Union Sq W	212-675-9500	$$$$	Seafood. Overrated.
Burritoville	264 W 23rd St	212-367-9844	$	Mexcellent and cheap.
Cafeteria	119 Seventh Ave	212-414-1717	$$$	Comfort food, open all night.
Chat 'n Chew	10 E 16th St	212-243-1616	$$	Home cookin'.
City Bakery	3 W 18th St	212-366-1414	$$	Stellar baked goods.
Coffee Shop	Union Sq W	212-243-7969	$$	Open 24 hours. Diner.
Craft	43 E 19th St	212-780-0880	$$$$	Outstanding. A top-end place worth the $.
Eisenberg Sandwich Shop	174 Fifth Ave	212-675-5096	$$	Old-school corned beef and pastrami.
Eleven Madison Park	11 Madison Ave	212-889-0905	$$$$	Where the elite meet to greet.
Francisco's Centro Vasco	159 W 23rd St	212-645-6224	$$$	Fun Spanish.
Gramercy Tavern	42 E 20th St	212-477-0777	$$$$	Expensive, but good, New American
Hangawi	12 E 32nd St	212-213-0077	$$$$	Serene Korean.

*Key: $: Under $10 / $$: $10–$20 / $$$: $20–$30 / $$$$: $30+; * : Does not accept credit cards / † : Accepts only American Express.*

Map 9 • Flatiron / Lower Midtown — *continued*

Kang Suh	1250 Broadway	212-564-6645	$$$	Late-night Korean.
Kum Gang San	49 W 32nd St	212-967-0909	$$$	Another late-night Korean paradise.
Le Madri	168 W 18th St	212-727-8022	$$$$	Chelsea Tuscan Class.
Le Pain Quotidien	38 E 19th St	212-673-7900	$*	Excellent breads & such.
Le Zie 2000	172 Seventh Ave	212-206-8686	$$$*	Venetian. That means it's Italian.
Luna Park	50 E 17th St	212-475-8464	$$$	Have meals May-October in Union Square Park.
Mesa Grill	102 Fifth Ave	212-807-7400	$$$$	Southwest heaven.
Periyali	35 W 20th St	212-463-7890	$$$$	Upscale Greek.
Petite Abeille	107 W 18th St	212-604-9350	$$*	Tintin-infused waffle chain. Try the stoemp.
Republic	37 Union Sq W	212-627-7172	$$	Noisy noodles.
Silver Swan	41 E 20th St	212-254-3611	$$	Beer, brats, 'n schnitzel.
Tabla	11 Madison Ave	212-889-0667	$$$$	Inventive Indian-inspired American.
Toledo	6 E 36th St	212-696-5036	$$$$	Classy Spanish.
Uncle Moe's	14 W 19th St	212-727-9400	$*	Solid lunchtime burrito joint.
Union Square Cafe	21 E 16th St	212-243-4020	$$$$	Someday we'll get in and like it.
Woo Chon	8 W 36th St	212-695-0676	$$$	All-night Korean.

Map 10 • Murray Hill / Gramercy

Angelo & Maxie's	233 Park Ave S	212-220-9200	$$$	Excellent steaks, burgers, etc.
Artisanal	2 Park Ave	212-725-8585	$$$	Eat the fondue and leave.
Blockheads Burritos	499 Third Ave	212-213-3332	$$*	Damn good burritos, a little pricey.
Coppola's	378 Third Ave	212-679-0070	$$	Neighborhood Italian.
El Parador Cafe	325 E 34th St	212-679-6812	$$$	NY's oldest and friendliest Mexican.
Gemini Restaurant	641 Second Ave	212-532-2143	$$	Open 24 hours. Diner.
Gramercy Restaurant	184 Third Ave	212-982-2121	$$	Open 24 hours. Diner.
Haandi	113 Lexington Ave	212-685-5200	$$*	Stellar Pakistani grilled meats.
I Trulli	122 E 27th St	212-481-7372	$$$$	Italian. Great garden.
Jackson Hole	521 Third Ave	212-679-3264	$$	Extremely large burgers.
Jaiya Thai	396 Third Ave	212-889-1330	$$$	Inventive, spicy Thai.
L'Express	249 Park Ave S	212-254-5858	$$	Always open French bistro.
Park Avenue Country Club	381 Park Ave S	212-685-3636	$$	Somewhat bearable sports bar.
Patria	250 Park Ave S	212-777-6211	$$$$	Expensive and inventive.
Patsy's Pizza	509 Third Ave	212-689-7500	$$*	Classic NY pizza.
Pete's Tavern	129 E 18th St	212-473-7676	$$$*	Good pub food, especially after drinking!
Pongal	110 Lexington Ave	212-696-9458	$$	Possibly NY's best Indian.
Pongsri Thai	311 Second Ave	212-477-4100	$$	Great, spicy Thai.
Sarge's Deli	548 Third Ave	212-679-0442	$$	Open 24 hours. Jewish deli.
Tatany	380 Third Ave	212-686-1871	$$$	Japanese.
Union Pacific	111 E 22nd St	212-995-8500	$$$$	Top-end American.
Verbena	54 Irving Pl	212-260-5454	$$$$	Another top-end American.
Via Emilia	240 Park Ave S	212-505-3072	$$$	Emilia-Romagnan specialties.
Water Club	500 E 30th St	212-683-3333	$$$$	Romantic, good brunch.
Yama	122 E 17th St	212-475-0969	$$$	Sushi deluxe.
Zen Palate	34 Union Sq E	212-614-9291	$$$	Dependable vegetarian.

Map 11 • Hell's Kitchen

Afghan Kebab House	764 Ninth Ave	212-307-1612	$$	Great kebabs.
Ariana Afghan Kebab	787 Ninth Ave	212-262-2323	$	Afghan.
Burritoville	625 Ninth Ave	212-333-5352	$	Takeout Mexican.
Churruscaria Plataforma	316 W 49th St	212-245-0505	$$$$	Popular but uneven Brazilian.
Grand Sichuan Int'l	745 Ninth Ave	212-582-2288	$$	Excellent weird Szechuan.
Hallo Berlin	402 W 51st St	212-541-6248	$$	Indeed the best wurst.
Island Burgers 'n Shakes	766 Ninth Ave	212-307-7934	$$*	Aptly named.
Jezebel	630 Ninth Ave	212-582-1045	$$$	Southern charm.
Joe Allen	326 W 46th St	212-581-6464	$$$	De riguer stargazing, open late.
Les Sans Culottes	347 W 46th St	212-247-4284	$$$	Friendly French.
Meskerem	468 W 47th St	212-664-0520	$$	Standard Ethiopian.
Old San Juan	765 Ninth Ave	212-262-6761	$$	Good, Puerto Rican-Argentinian fare.
Orso	322 W 46th St	212-489-7212	$$$$	Popular busy Italian.
Ralph's	862 Ninth Ave	212-581-2283	$$	Classic Italian cuisine.
Soul Cafe	444 W 42nd St	212-244-7685	$$$	Large, noisy soul.
Uncle Nick's	747 Ninth Ave	212-245-7992	$$$	Greek, noisy.
Zen Palate	663 Ninth Ave	212-582-1669	$$$	Dependable vegetarian.

Map 12 • Midtown

'21' Club	21 W 52nd St	212-582-7200	$$$$	Old, clubby New York.
Angelo & Maxie's	1285 Sixth Ave	212-459-1222	$$$	Excellent steaks, burgers, etc.
Aquavit	13 W 54th St	212-307-7311	$$$$	Top-drawer Scandinavian.
Baluchi's	240 W 56th St	212-397-0707	$$	Slightly above-average Indian.
Carnegie Deli	854 Seventh Ave	212-757-2245	$$$*	Still good.
Cosi Sandwich Bar	11 W 42nd St	212-398-6660	$*	Sandwiches for the masses.
Cosi Sandwich Bar	1633 Broadway	212-397-2674	$*	Sandwiches for the masses.
Cosi Sandwich Bar	61 W 48th St	212-265-2674	$*	Sandwiches for the masses.
Haru	205 W 43rd St	212-398-9810	$$	Excellent mid-range Japanese. Loud, good.
Joe's Shanghai	24 W 56th St	212-333-3868	$$*	Uptown version of killer dumpling factory.
Le Bernardin	155 W 51st St	212-554-1515	$$$$$	Top NYC seafood.
Molyvos	871 Seventh Ave	212-582-7500	$$$$	Top Greek.
Nation Restaurant & Bar	12 W 45th St	212-391-8053	$$$$	Loud, pretentious, good.
Norma's	118 W 57th St	212-708-7460	$$$	Inventive and upscale brunch.
Pongsri Thai	244 W 48th St	212-582-3392	$$	Great, spicy Thai.
Pret a Manger	1350 Sixth Ave	212-307-6100	$*	British sandwich chain.
The Pump Energy Food	40 W 55th St	212-246-6844	$*	Just what you think it is.
Redeye Grill	890 Seventh Ave	212-541-9000	$$$	Sprawling and diverse.
Virgil's Real BBQ	152 W 44th St	212-921-9494	$$$	It's real.

Map 13 • East Midtown

Cosi Sandwich Bar	165 E 52nd St	212-758-7800	$*	Sandwiches for the masses.
Cosi Sandwich Bar	60 E 56th St	212-588-0888	$*	Sandwiches for the masses.
Dawat	210 E 58th St	212-355-7555	$$$$	Top-end Indian.
Docks Oyster Bar	633 Third Ave	212-986-8080	$$$	Great seafood, good atmosphere.
Felidia	243 E 58th St	212-758-1479	$$$$	Top Northern Italian.
Four Seasons	99 E 52nd St	212-754-9494	$$$$	Designer everything.
Lutece	249 E 50th St	212-752-2225	$$$$	$32 prix fixe lunch.
March	405 E 58th St	212-754-6272	$$$$	Lovely. It's actually 8 dollar signs.
Menchanko-tei	131 E 45th St	212-986-6805	$$	Japanese noodle shop.
Oceana	55 E 54th St	212-759-5941	$$$$$	Le Bernadin Jr.
Organic Harvest Café	235 E 53rd St	212-421-6444	$$	Vegetarian
Oyster Bar	Grand Central, Lower Level	212-490-6650	$$$	Classic New York seafood joint.
Palm	837 Second Ave	212-687-2953	$$$$	Steak.
Pershing Square	90 E 42nd St	212-286-9600	$$$	Excellent food and awesome space.
PJ Clarke's	915 Third Ave	212-317-1616	$$$	Pub grub.
Rosa Mexicano	1063 First Ave	212-977-7700	$$$$	Inventive Mexican. Great guac.
Shun Lee Palace	155 E 55th St	212-371-8844	$$$$	Top-end Chinese.
Smith & Wollensky	797 Third Ave	212-753-1530	$$$$	Don't order the fish.
Sparks Steak House	210 E 46th St	212-687-4855	$$$$	If you can't go to Luger's.
Vong	200 E 54th St	212-486-9592	$$$$	$38 pre-theater menu. Top Pan-Asian.

Map 14 • Upper West Side (Lower)

All-State Cafe	250 W 72nd St	212-874-1883	$$	Very comfy and friendly joint.
Avenue	520 Columbus Ave	212-579-3194	$$$	Good friendly bistro.
Baluchi's	283 Columbus Ave	212-579-3900	$$	Slightly above-average Indian.
Big Nick's	2175 Broadway	212-362-9238	$$	Death by burger.
Cafe Des Artistes	1 W 67th St	212-877-3500	$$$$	A fine romance.
Cafe Lalo	201 W 83rd St	212-496-6031	$$	Packed dessert & coffee destination.
Cafe Luxembourg	200 W 70th St	212 873 7411	$$$$	Top-end bistro.
Caprice	199 Columbus Ave	212-580-6948	$$$	Spanish, Italian, African, whatever.
China Fun	246 Columbus Ave	212-580-1516	$$	Uptown dim sum option.
Edgar's Cafe	255 W 84th St	212-496-6126	$$*	24-hour desserts and atmosphere.
EJ's Luncheonette	447 Amsterdam Ave	212-873-3444	$$*	Homey diner.
Fairway Cafe	2127 Broadway	212-595-1888	$$	When it is all too much.
The Firehouse	522 Columbus Ave	212-595-3139	$$	Where to go for after-softball wings.
French Roast	2340 Broadway	212-799-1533	$$	Open 24 hours. Good C. Monsieur.
Gray's Papaya	2090 Broadway	212-799-0243	$*	Open 24 hours. An institution.
Harry's Burrito Junction	241 Columbus Ave	212-580-9494	$$	What could they possibly serve here?
Hunan Park	235 Columbus Ave	212-724-4411	$$	Dependable Chinese.
Jackson Hole	517 Columbus Ave	212-362-5177	$$	Extremely large burgers.
Jean Georges	1 Central Park W	212-299-3900	$$$$	$20 prix fixe summer lunch!
Jean-Luc	507 Columbus Ave	212-712-1700	$$$$	Classy, expensive bistro.
Josie's	300 Amsterdam Ave	212-769-1212	$$$	Good vegetarian option.
Krispy Kreme	141 W 72nd St	212-724-1100	$*	Health-food mecca.
La Caridad 78	2197 Broadway	212-874-2780	$$*	Cheap Cuban paradise.
La Fenice	2014 Broadway	212-989-3071	$$$	Good Italian.

*Key: $: Under $10 / $$: $10–$20 / $$$: $20–$30 / $$$$: $30+; * : Does not accept credit cards / † : Accepts only American Express.*

Map 14 • Upper West Side (Lower) — *continued*

Le Pain Quotidien	50 W 72nd St	212-712-9700	$*	Good breads & such.
Lenge	200 Columbus Ave	212-799-9188	$$	Serviceable Japanese.
Manhattan Diner	2180 Broadway	212-877-7252	$	Diner.
Penang	240 Columbus Ave	212-769-3988	$$$	Snooty but good Malaysian.
Picholine	35 W 64th St	212-724-8585	$$$$	Go for the cheese.
Planet Sushi	380 Amsterdam Ave	212-712-2162	$$	Decent sushi in a cheap raw fish no-man's land.
Rosa Mexicano	51 Columbus Ave	212-753-7407	$$$$	Inventive Mexican. Great guac.
Ruby Foo's Dim Sum & Sushi Palace	2182 Broadway	212-724-6700	$$$	Your parents will love it.
Santa Fe	72 W 69th St	212-724-0822	$$$	Calm Southwest.
Sarabeth's	423 Amsterdam Ave	212-496-6280	$$	Go for brunch.
Shun Lee	43 W 65th St	212-595-8895	$$$$	Top Chinese.
Taco Grill	146 W 72nd St	212-501-8888	$*	Mexican.
Vince and Eddie's	70 W 68th St	212-721-0068	$$$$	Cosy comfort food.
Vinnie's Pizza	285 Amsterdam Ave	212-874-4382	$*	Good slice of pizza.

Map 15 • Upper East Side (Lower)

Afghan Kebab House	1345 Second Ave	212-517-2776	$$	Great kebabs.
Atlantic Grill	1341 Third Ave	212-988-9200	$$$$	Seafood galore.
Aureole	34 E 61st St	212-319-1660	$$$$	Well-done but unimaginative
Baluchi's	1149 First Ave	212-371-3535	$$	Slightly above-average Indian.
Baluchi's	1565 Second Ave	212-288-4810	$$	Slightly above-average Indian.
Barking Dog Luncheonette	1453 York Ave	212-861-3600	$$*	Good diner/café food.
Brunelli	1409 York Ave	212-744-8899	$$$	Old-world Italian.
Canyon Road	1470 First Ave	212-734-1600	$$$	Southwest haven.
Daniel	60 E 65th St	212-288-0033	$$$$	Overrated $150+ meal.
EJ's Luncheonette	1271 Third Ave	212-472-0600	$$*	Homey diner.
Haru	1329 Third Ave	212-452-2230	$$	Sushi. Takeout recommended.
Jackson Hole	1611 Second Ave	212-737-8788	$$	Extremely large burgers.
Jackson Hole	232 E 64th St	212-371-7187	$$	Extremely large burgers. Cozy.
JG Melon	1291 Third Ave	212-744-0585	$$*	Burgers. Open till 2:30 am.
Jo Jo	160 E 64th St	212-223-5656	$$$$	Charming.
John's Pizzeria	408 E 64th St	212-935-2895	$$	Quintessential NY pizza.
Le Pain Quotidien	1131 Madison Ave	212-327-4900	$*	Great breads & such.
Le Pain Quotidien	1336 First Ave	212-717-4800	$*	Great breads & such.
Le Pain Quotidien	833 Lexington Ave	212-755-5810	$*	Great breads & such.
Mary Ann's	1503 Second Ave	212-249-6165	$$	Good Mex, order margaritas.
Maya	1191 First Ave	212-585-1818	$$$$	Top-drawer Mexican.
Our Place	1444 Third Ave	212-288-4888	$$$	Next level Chinese.
Park Avenue Cafe	100 E 63rd St	212-644-1900	$$$$	Wonderful expensive American.
Pearson's Texas Barbecue	170 E 81st St	212-288-2700	$$$*	Stick with the brisket. For ribs you have to go to Memphis.
Penang	1596 Second Ave	212-585-3838	$$$	Snooty but good Malaysian.
Pintaile's Pizza	1237 Second Ave	212-752-6222	$	Tasty thin-crust stuff
Pintaile's Pizza	1443 York Ave	212-717-4990	$	Tasty thin-crust stuff.
Pintaile's Pizza	1577 York Ave	212-396-3479	$	Tasty thin-crust stuff.
Post House	28 E 63rd St	212-935-2888	$$$$	Good bet: steak.
Rain	1059 Third Ave	212-223-3669	$$$	Pan-Asian.
RM	33 E 60th St	212-319-3800	$$$$$	Simply excellent.
Serafina Fabulous Grill	29 E 61st St	212-702-9898	$$	Good pizza and pasta.
Spada	1431 Third Ave	212-650-0850	$$$	Good basic Italian.
Totonno Pizzeria Napolitano	1544 Second Ave	212-327-2800	$$	Quality pizza.
Viand	1011 Madison Ave	212-249-8250	$$	This one closes at 10 pm.
Viand	673 Madison Ave	212-751-6622	$$*	This one closes at 10 pm.

Map 16 • Upper West Side (Upper)

A	947 Columbus Ave	212-531-1643	$$*	French-Carribean café.
Afghan Kebob House	2680 Broadway	212-280-3500	$$	Kebobs for you!
Bella Luna	584 Columbus Ave	212-877-2267	$$$	Italian.
Cafe Con Leche	726 Amsterdam Ave	212-678-7000	$$	Cuban-Dominican haven.
Carmine's	2450 Broadway	212-362-2200	$$$	Large-portion Italian.
City Diner	2441 Broadway	212-877-2720	$$	Neighborhood joint.
Docks Oyster Bar	2427 Broadway	212-724-5588	$$$	Consistently good seafood.
Flor de Mayo	2651 Broadway	212-595-2525	$$	Cuban-Chinese-Chicken-Chow.
Gabriela's	685 Amsterdam Ave	212-961-0574	$$	Cheery Mexican.
Gennaro	665 Amsterdam Ave	212-665-5348	$$$*	Crowded Italian.

Henry's	2745 Broadway	212-866-0600	$$$	Friendly uptown joint.
Lemongrass Grill	2534 Broadway	212-666-0888	$$	Serviceable Thai.
Mary Ann's	2452 Broadway	212-877-0132	$$	Good Mex, order margaritas.
Pampa	768 Amsterdam Ave	212-865-2929	$$$*	Good Argentinian.
Popover Cafe	551 Amsterdam Ave	212-595-8555	$$	Kind of fun. Whatever.
Saigon Grill	2381 Broadway	212-875-9072	$$	Vietnamese.
Trattoria Pesce Pasta	625 Columbus Ave	212-579-7970	$$$	Italian.

Map 17 • Upper East Side / East Harlem

Barking Dog Luncheonette	1678 Third Ave	212-831-1800	$$*	Good diner/café food.
Blue Grotto	1576 Third Ave	212-426-3200	$$	Progressive Mediterannean, hip scene.
Burritoville	1606 Third Ave	212-410-2255	$	Takeout Mexican.
Dinerbar	1569 Lexington Ave	212-348-0200	$$	Upscale comfort food, open late.
El Paso Taqueria	1642 Lexington Ave	212-831-9831	$*	Mexican
Elaine's	1703 Second Ave	212-534-8103	$$$$	It's still there.
Jackson Hole	1270 Madison Ave	212-427-2820	$$	Extremely large burgers.
La Fonda Boricua	169 E 106th St	212-410-7292	$$	Puerto Rican home-cookin'.
Saigon Grill	1700 Second Ave	212-996-4600	$$	Vietnamese.
Sarabeth's	1295 Madison Ave	212-410-7335	$$$	Good breakfast, if you can get in.
Viand	300 E 86th St	212-879-9425	$$	Open all night.

Map 18 • Columbia / Morningside Heights

Bistro Ten 18	1018 Amsterdam Ave	212-662-7600	$$$	Excellent uptown American bistro.
Hungarian Pastry Shop	1030 Amsterdam Ave	212-866-4230	$*	Exactly what it is—and excellent.
Kitchenette Uptown	1272 Amsterdam Ave	212 531 7600	$$	Good for everything.
Le Monde	2885 Broadway	212-531-3939	$$	Student brasserie.
M&G Soul Food Diner	383 W 125th St	212-864-7326	$$*	A soulful diner.
Massawa	1239 Amsterdam Ave	212-663-0505	$$	Neighborhood joint.
Max SoHa	1274 Amsterdam Ave	212 531 2221	$$	The Italian genius of Max, uptown.
The Mill Korean Restaurant	2895 Broadway	212-666-7653	$$	Great neighborhood Korean.
Ollie's	2957 Broadway	212-932-3300	$$	Only if you must.
Pisticci	125 La Salle St	212-932-3500	$$	Wonderful cozy Italian.
Symposium	544 W 113th St	212-865-1011	$$*	Good traditional Greek.
Terrace in the Sky	400 W 119th St	212-666-9490	$$$$	Rooftop French.
Toast	3157 Broadway	212-662-1144	$$*	Great diverse café menu. Recommended.

Map 19 • Harlem (Lower)

Amy Ruth's	113 W 116th St	212-280-8779	$$	Soul food, incredible fried chicken.
Bayou	308 Lenox Ave	212-426-3800	$$$	Cajun, with a good bar, too.
Fifth Ave Seafood	2014 Fifth Ave	212-987-6030	$$	Takeout, eat in, good seafood.
Home Sweet Harlem Café	270 W 135th St	212-926-9616	$	Breakfast/lunch spot.
Jimmy's Uptown	2207 Seventh Ave	212-491-4000	$$$	Large, trendy, good Latin-infused cuisine.
Keur Sokhna	225 W 116th St	212-864-0081	$*	Good cheap Senegalese.
Manna's Too	486 Lenox Ave	212-234-4488	$*	Soul food buffet!
Native	161 Lenox Ave	212-665-2525	$*	Excellent soul food.
Sylvia's	328 Lenox Ave	212-996-0660	$$$	An institution. Not overrated.
Yvonne Yvonne	301 W 135th St	212-862-1223	$*	Excellent Jamaican chicken, ribs, etc.

Map 20 • El Barrio

La Hacienda	219 E 116th St	212-987-1617	$	Mexican.
Mi Mundo Bar & Restaurant	2259 Second Ave	212-860-8187	$$	Mexican.
Patsy's Pizza	2287 First Ave	212-534-9783	$$*	The original thin-crust pizza.
Rao's	455 E 114th St	212-722-6709	$$$$*	We've heard it's an institution.
Sandy's Restaurant	2261 Second Ave	212-348-8654	$$*	Neighborhood joint.

Map 21 • Manhattanville / Hamilton Heights

Copeland's	547 W 145th St	212-234-2357	$$$	Fine southern cooking.
Sugar Hill Bistro	458 W 145th St	212-491-5505	$$$	Southern with a twist.

Map 22 • Harlem (Upper)

Charles's Southern-Style Chicken	2841 Eighth Ave	212-926-4313	$*	The fried chicken they serve in heaven.
Flash Inn	107 Macombs Pl	212-283-8605	$$$	Old-timey New York Italian.
Londel's Supper Club	2620 Frederick Douglass Blvd	212-234-6114	$$$	Good Southern.
Margie's Red Rose	267 W 144th St	212-491-3665	$*	Fried chicken heaven.
Miss Mamie's/ Miss Maude's	547 Lenox Ave	212-690-3100	$$	Harlem soul food.

*Key: $: Under $10 / $$: $10–$20 / $$$: $20–$30 / $$$$: $30+; * : Does not accept credit cards / † : Accepts only American Express.*

Map 22 • Harlem (Upper) —*continued*

Sugar Shack	2611 Eighth Ave	212-491-4422	$$	Fried chicken, shrimp, catfish.

Map 23 • Washington Heights

Dallas BBQ	3956 Broadway	212-568-3700	$$	When you can't get to Virgil's.
El Malecon	4141 Broadway	212-927 3812	$	Mexican—fabulous roast chicken.
El Ranchito	4129 Broadway	212-928-0866	&&*	Central America in New York!
Empire Szechuan	4041 Broadway	212-568-1600	$$	Chinese.
Hispaniola	839 W 181st St	212-740-5222	$$	Tapas, bridge views—everything you need.
Jessie's Place	812 W 181st St	212-795-4168		Neighborhood joint.
Kismat	187 Ft Washington Ave	212-795-8633	$$	Indian.

Map 24 • Fort George / Fort Tryon

107 West	811 W 187th St	212-923-3311	*	Salads, burgers, etc.
Bleu Evolution	808 W 187th St	212-928-6006	$$	Uptown bohemian. Calm.
Caridad Restaurant	4311 Broadway	212-781-0431	*	Carribean.
Frank's Pizzeria	94 Nagle Ave	212-567 3122	$$	Pizza.
New Leaf Cafe	1 Margaret Corbin Dr	212-568-5323	$$	Uptown haven.
Rancho Jubilee	1 Nagle Ave	212-304-0100	$$	Great Dominican destination.

Map 25 • Inwood

Bobby's Fish and Seafood Market and Restaurant	3842 Ninth Ave	212-304-9440	$$†	Fish! Fresh! Open late!
Cloisters Restaurant Pizza	4754 Broadway	212-569-5035	$*	Guess what they have?
Hoppin' Jalapenos Bar & Grill	597 W 207th St	212-569-6059	$$*	Mexican bar and restaurant, good burrrrritos!

Map 26 • Astoria

Amici Amore I	29-35 Newtown Ave	718-267-2771	$$	Northern Italian.
Christos Hasapo-Taverna	41-08 23rd Ave	718-726-5195	$$$	Get your red meat here!
Elias Corner	24-02 31st St	718-932-1510	$$	Greek fish tavern.
Esperides	37-01 30th Ave	718-545-1494	$$$	Traditional Greek food, excellent place for large groups.
Kabab Café	25-12 Steinway St	718-728-9858	$$	Cheap, casual kababs.
Piccola Venezia	42-01 28th Ave	718-721-8470	$$	Old-style traditional Italian fare.
Ponticello	46-11 Broadway	718-278-4515	$$$	Italian.
S'Agapo	34-21 34th St	718-626-0303	$$$	Greek restaurant with suberb outdoor dining for the warmer months.
Stamatis	29-12 23rd Ave	718-278-9795	$$	Classic Greek dishes. Our favorite.
Taverna Kyclades	33-07 Ditmars Blvd	718-545-8666	$$	Greek seafood. Great swordfish kabobs.
Tierras Colombianas	33-01 Broadway	718-956-3012	$$	Huge platefuls of Colombian grill—not one for the veggies.
Tierras Colombianas	82-18 Roosevelt Ave	718-426-8868	$$	Huge platefuls of Colombian grill—not one for the veggies.
Ubol's Kitchen	24-42 Steinway St	718-545-2874	$$	Hyped-up Thai.
Uncle George's	33-19 Broadway	718-626-0593	$	24-hour Greek.

Map 27 • Long Island City

Brooks 1890 Restaurant	24-28 Jackson Ave	718-937-1890	$$	10% off when you show your juror's card.
Court Square Diner	45-30 23rd St	718-392-1222	$	Serves continental and Greek dishes.
Dazies	3941 Queens Blvd	718-786-7013	$$$	This Italian food will remind you of Momma.
Jackson Ave Steakhouse	12-23 Jackson Ave	718-784-1412	$$$$	Steakhouse.
La Vuelta	10-43 44th Dr	718-361-1858	$$	Lantino Bistro.
Manducatis	13-27 Jackson Ave	718-729-4602	$$$	Southern Italian.
Manetta's	10-76 Jackson Ave	718-786-6171	$$$	Brick-oven pizzas.
Sage American Kitchen	26-21 Jackson Ave	718-361-0707	$	Vegetarian-friendly American food.
Tournesol	50-12 Vernon Blvd	718-472-4355	$$$	French Bistro.
Water'sEdge	44th Dr & East River	718-482-0033	$$$$	American fare with views of the skyline.

Map 28 • Greenpoint

Amarin Café	617 Manhattan Ave	718-349-2788	$	Good, cheap Thai food.
Casanova	338 McGuinness Blvd	718-389-0990	$$	Italian fare.
Christina's	853 Manhattan Ave	718-383-4382	$	Traditional Polish food, cheap breakfasts!
Divine Follie Café	929 Manhattan Ave	718-389-6770	$$	Large selection of meats, pastas and pizza. small selection of sandwiches.
Greenpoint #1 Tex-Mex Express	681 Manhattan Ave	718-349-8216	$	Large, cheap menu, vegetarian options.
Manhattan 3 Decker Restaurant	695 Manhattan Ave	718-389-6664	$$	Greek and American fare.
Old Poland Bakery & Restaurant	192 Nassau Ave	718-389-9211	$*	Polish/American.
OTT	970 Manhattan Ave	718-609-2416	$$*	Thai.
SunView Luncheonette	221 Nassau Ave	718-383-8121	$*	Supercheap lunches.
Thai Café	925 Manhattan Ave	718-383-3562	$	Vast menu, veg options, eat in or pick up.
Valdiano	659 Manhattan Ave	718-383-1707	$$	Southern Italian.
Wasabi	638 Manhattan Ave	718-609-9368	$$*	Japanese fare.

Map 29 • Williamsburg

Acqua Santa	556 Driggs Ave	718-384-9695	$$*	Bistro Italian—amazing patio.
Allioli	291 Grand St	718-218-7338	$$*	Tapas heavy on the seafood, live Mariachi.
Anna Maria Pizza	179 Bedford Ave	718-599-4550	$	A must after late-night drinking.
Anytime	93 N 6th St	718-218-7272	$*	Greasy but good anytime, really.
Bliss	191 Bedford Ave	718-599-2547	$$*	Bland vegetarian with all vegan options.
Bonita	338 Bedford Ave	718-384-9500	$*	Inexpensive Americanized Mexican in a nice atmosphere. Bring your hot sauce.
Ciao Bella	138 N 8th St	718-599-8550	$$*	Affordable and surprisingly delicious.
Diner	85 Broadway	718-486-3077	$$	Amazing simple food like you've never tasted - never disappoints.
Miss Williamsburg Diner	206 Kent Ave	718-963-0802	$$	Creative Italian with pannacotta "to die for!"
Oznot's Dish	79 Berry St	718-599-6596	$$*	Lots of lentils and beans, Mediterranean. Good décor.
Planet Thailand	133 N 7th St	718-599-5758	$$*	Hyped-up Thai/Japanese in a trendy locale.
Relish	225 Wythe St	718-963-4546	$$*	Comfort food gone eclectic with a touch of class.
Siam Orchid	378 Metropolitan Ave	718-302-4203	$$	Yummy Thai, off-the-beaten path.
Teddy's Bar and Grill	96 Berry St	718-384-9787	$*	Best bar food ever, great beers on tap, hipster and Polish locals unite.
Vera Cruz	195 Bedford Ave	718-599-7914	$$*	Authentic Mexican. Great outdoor garden, fabulous frozen margaritas.

Map 30 • Brooklyn Heights / DUMBO / Downtown Brooklyn

Fascati Pizzeria	80 Henry St	718-237-1278	$	Inexpensive pizza.
Grimaldi's	19 Old Fulton St	718-858-4300	$	Excellent, though not the best, NY Pizza.
Henry's End	44 Henry St	718-834-1776	$$$*	Inventive, game-oriented menu.
Noodle Pudding	38 Henry St	718-625-3737	$$	Excellent Northern Italian fare.
River Café	1 Water St	718-522-5200	$$$$*	Great view, but overrated.
Superfine	126 Front St	718-243-9005	$$*	Mediterranean-inspired menu, bi-level bar, local art and music.
Yokohama	71 Clark St	718-222-0308	$$*	Sushi Express, reasonable prices.

Map 31 • Fort Greene

1 Greene Sushi and Sashimi	1 Greene Ave	718-422-1000	$$*	The only place to get sushi in the 'hood.
À Table	171 Lafayette Ave	718-935-9121	$$*	French country.
Academy Restaurant	69 Lafayette Ave	718-237-9326	$	Neighborhood diner.
BAM Café	30 Lafayette Ave	718-636-4100	$$*	Café with live music weekend evenings.
Black Iris	228 DeKalb Ave	718-852-9800	$$	Middle Eastern.
Café Lafayette	99 S Portland Ave	718-624-1605	$$	French/Asian Fusion—order the chocolate volcano!
Cambodian Cuisine	87 S Elliot Pl	718-858-3262	$$*	Cambodian/SE Asian—cheap and good!
Chez Oskar	211 DeKalb Ave	718-852-6250	$$$*	French cuisine in a good neighborhood bistro.
Good Joy Chinese Takeout	216 DeKalb Ave	718-858-8899	$	Best Chinese takeout.
Keur N' Deye Restaurant	737 Fulton St	718-875-4937	$$$	African.
Liquors	219 DeKalb Ave	718-488-7700	$$*	A great eclectic menu.
Locanda Vini & Olii	129 Gates Ave	718-622-9202	$$*	Rustic Italian, a neighborhood favorite.
Loulou	222 DeKalb Ave	718-246-0633	$$$*	The best "date place" serving wonderful French food.
Madiba	195 DeKalb Ave	718-855-9190	$$$*	South African—Bunny Chow, need we say more?
Mario's Pizzeria	224 DeKalb Ave	718-260-9520	$	The place to go for a slice.
Mo-Bay	112 DeKalb Ave	718-246-2800	$*	Caribbean/soul/bakery.
Night of the Cookers	767 Fulton St	718-797-1197	$$*	American/soul served late.
Pequeña	86 S Portland Ave	718-643-0000	$$*	Killer quesadillas.
Sol	229 DeKalb Ave	718-222-1510	$$*	Caribbean with a great bar!

*Key: $: Under $10 / $$: $10–$20 / $$$: $20–$30 / $$$$: $30+; * : Does not accept credit cards / † : Accepts only American Express.*

Map 32 • Cobble Hill / Boerum Hill / Carroll Gardens

Alma	187 Columbia St	718-643-5400	$$$	Excellent Mexican with a view.
Banania Café	241 Smith St	718-237-9100	$$$*	Great vibe and great brunch.
Bar Tabac			$$	Hands-down best vibe on Smith Street.
Cafe Luluc	214 Smith St	718-625-3815	$$$	Friendly French bistro.
Delicatessen	264 Clinton St	718-852-1991	$$	Ready to go dinners @ 3 pm, Euro deli.
El Portal	217 Smith St	718-246-1416	$	Killer breaded steak.
Faan	209 Smith St	718-694-2277	$†	Asian Fusion.
Fatoosh	330 Hicks St	718-243-0500	$	Nicely priced Middle Eastern Food.
Ferdinando's Focacceria	151 Union St	718-855-1545	$	Sicilian specialties you won't find anywhere else!
The Grocery	288 Smith St	718-596-3335	$$$$*	Modern American cuisine.
Hope & Anchor	347 Van Brunt St	718-237-0276	$$	Great upscale diner.
Joya	215 Court St	718-222-3484	$$*	Excellent but super-noisy Thai.
Leonardo's Brick Oven Pizza	383 Court St	718-624-9620	$$	Excellent pizza and terrible hours.
Liberty Heights Tap Room	34 Van Dyke St	718-246-8050	$$*	Brick oven restaurant and bar.
Margaret Palca Bakes	191 Columbia St	718-802-9771	$	Excellent sandwiches and baked goods.
Osaka	272 Court St	718-643-0044	$$	Best Sushi in BOCOCA.
Patois	255 Smith St	718-855-1535	$$$$*	French bistro. Killer brunch.
Sal's Pizzeria	305 Court St	718-852-6890	$	The neighborhood staple.
Sam's Restaurant	238 Court St	718-596-3458	$$	Classic American Italian.
Savoia	277 Smith St	718-797-2727	$$	Cozy Italian.
Schnack	122 Union St	718-855-2879	$*	Greasy goodness.
Sherwood Café/Robin des Bois	195 Smith St	718-596-1609	$$	Mellow French vibe.
Siam Garden	172 Court St	718-596-3300	$$*	One of the best Thai in Brooklyn.
Zaytoons	283 Smith St	718-875-1880	$$*	Excellent Middle Eastern pizzas and kebabs.

Map 33 • Park Slope / Prospect Heights

12th Street Bar and Grill	1123 8th Ave	718-965-9526	$$$*	Outstanding gourmet comfort fare.
2nd Street Café	189 7th Ave	718-369-6928	$$*	Clamoring brunch crowd.
Al Di La Trattoria	248 5th Ave	718-783-4565	$$$*	Chandelier, brick-walled Italian.
Beso	210 5th Ave	718-622-9894	$*	Great South American, good breakfast too.
Blue Ribbon Brooklyn	280 Fifth Ave	718-840-0404	$$$$*	The one and only!
Café Steinhof	422 7th Ave	718-369-7776	$$*	Goulash Mondays: $5! German beers.
Chip Shop	383 5th Ave	718-832-7701	$*	Brit boys dish fish, chips and The Beatles.
Convivium Osteria	68 5th Ave	718-857-1833	$$$†	Pretentious Portugese, rustic setting.
Cousin John's Café and Bakery	70 7th Ave	718-622-7333	$	Casual breakfast and lunch.
Cucina	256 5th Ave	718-230-0711	$$$	Long-time fave for upscale Italian.
El Castillo de Jagua	302 Flatbush Ave	718-638-2907	$*	Great, cheap Cuban cuisine.
Garden Café	620 Vanderbilt Ave	718-857-8863	$$$*	Small, semi-formal intimate setting with delicious food.
Geido	331 Flatbush Ave	718-638-8866	$$*	Great quality fish, arty atmosphere.
Junior's	386 Flatbush Ave	718-852-5257	$*	American with huge portions.
La Taqueria	72 7th Ave	718-398-4300	$	Popular, pennywise burritos.
Lemongrass Grill	61A Seventh Ave	718-399-7100	$$*	City-wide Thai joint.
Long Tan	196 5th Ave	718-622-8444	$$*	Spartan Vietnamese goes mod.
Luce	411 11th St	718-768-4698	$$*	Romantic, unfussy Northern Italian.
Mamma Duke	243 Flatbush Ave	718-857-8700	$	Southern take-out, tasty sides.
Mitchell's Soul Food	617 Vanderbilt Ave	718-789-3212	$	Seedy cheap soul food.
New Prospect Café	393 Flatbush Ave	718-638-2148	$$*	Try the corn and shrimp chowder.
Olive Vine Café	362 15th St	718-499-0555	$	Tasty Middle Eastern fare.
Olive Vine Pizza	131 6th Ave	718-636-4333	$	Crispy Mediterranean pizzas.
Olive Vine Pizza	81 7th Ave	718-622-2626	$	Crispy Mediterranean pizzas.
Parkside Restaurant	355 Flatbush Ave	718-636-1190	$$	Standard diner fare.
Rose Water	787 Union St	718-783-3800	$$$*	Intimate, airy Mediterranean.
Santa Fe Grill	60 7th Ave	718-636-0279	$$*	Dinner? Chips, salsa and icy pinas!
Sweets Village	702 Washington Ave	718-857-7757	$*	Cozy juicebar/café/lounge. Best and most reasonably priced brunch on weekends.
Tavern on Dean	755 Dean St	718-638-3326	$$*	Decent food, reasonable prices. Brunch from 11 am until 4 pm weekends, late night kitchen.
Tom's	782 Washington Ave	718-636-9738	$$	Old-school mom and pop diner since 1936. A cholesterol love affair.
Tutta Pasta	160 7th Ave	718-788-9500	$$*	Sidewalk seating, dependable penne.
Two Boots	514 2nd St	718-499-3253	$$*	Kid-friendly pizza and Cajun. Live music.

Map 34 • Hoboken

Amanda's	908 Washington St	201-798-0101	$$$	A touch of class in Hoboken, romantic and elegant. Catch the value-for-money early special.
Arthur's Tavern	237 Washington St	201-656-5009	$$	The best steak for the price.

Baja	104 14th St (b/w Bloomfield & Washington)	201-653-0610	$$	Good mexican food, great sangria.
Bangkok City	335 Washington St	201-792-6613	$$	A taste of Thai.
Biggies Clam Bar	318 Madison St	201-656-2161	$	Boardwalk fare and perfect raw clams. Order by the dozen.
Brass Rail	135 Washington St	201-659-7074	$$$	You can't beat the brunch deal.
Delfino's	500 Jefferson St	201-792-7457	$$	Pizza joint…Plus red checkered table cloths. BYO Chianti. The real thing.
East LA	508 Washington St	201-798-0052	$$	Knock-your-socks-off margarita's and the food's not bad.
Far Side Bar & Grill	531 Washington St	201-963-7677	$$	Hoboken's best pub food. Try the steak salad.
Frankie & Johnnie's	14th & Garden St	201-659-6202	$$$$	Power steakhouse. Keep an eye out for Tony Soprano.
Gas Light	400 Adams St	201-217-1400	$$	Off the main drag, neighbourhood Italian, cozy and cute. Quiz nights and comedy.
Gobi Grill	746 Park Ave	201-792-0003	$$	Mongolian BBQ, great value, great taste. A-la-carte or create your own, cooked before your eyes. BYOB.
Hoboken Gourmet Company	423 Washington St	201-795-0110	$$	Hoboken's one true café. Rustic, yummy, quirky
Karma Kafe	505 Washington St	201-610-0900	$$	Ultra-friendly Tibetan staff, hip Indian food with a wild mix of flavors.
La Isla	104 Washington St	201-659-8197	$$	A genuine taste of Havana.
La Scala	159 14th St	201-963-0884	$$$	An extravagant taste of old Italy. BYO. Ask the chef about his favorite opera.
La Tartuferia	1405 Grand St	201-792-2300	$$$	Modern, imaginative, Northern Italian fare, specializing in truffle dishes.
Robongi	520 Washington St	201-222-8388	$$	Consistently good sushi, friendly chefs, fun specials.
Trattoria Saporito	328 Washington St	201-533-1801	$$$	Lacks the old world Italian charm but has the old world taste and service. BYOB.
Zack's Oak Bar and Grill	232 Willow Ave	201-653-7770	$$	Relaxed, pub-style food and drink.
Zafra	301 Willow Ave	201-610-9801	$$	Cozy with authentic latino flavors. BYO wine—they'll magically turn it into sangria.

Map 35 • Jersey City

Casablanca Coffee Shop	354 Grove St	201-420-4072	$$*	Morrocan.
Ibby's Falafel	303 Grove St	201-432-2400	$	One of the few JC restaurants open after 11pm, Ibby's is owned and operated by the nephew of the owner of the great Mamoun's.
Iron Monkey	97 Greene St	201-435-5756	$$$	Quiet, romantic atmosphere. From risotto to seafood it is all savory. Enjoy the beautiful summer evenings on the rooftop terrace which is equipped with a full bar.
Kitchen Cafe	60 Sussex St	201-332-1010	$$*	The Great American breakfast.
Komegashi	103 Montgomery St	201-433-4567	$$	Authentic Japanese restaurant. Watch the chefs create a masterpiece at the open sushi bar.
Komegashi Too	99 Pavonia Ave	201-533-8888	$$	The other Komegashi.
Madame Claude Cafe	364 4th St	201-876-8800	$$**	French café.
Miss Saigon	249 Newark Ave	201-239-1988	$*	Authentic and cheap Vietnamese fare.
Nicco's Restaurant	247 Washington St	201-332-8433	$$$	Romantic and fun.
Oddfellows Restaurant	111 Montgomery St	201-433-6999	$$	It is always Mardi Gras with their happy hour specials. Enjoy authentic Cajun food served in a casual setting.
Rosie Radigans	10 Exchange Pl	201-451-5566	$	Excellent after work venue—the food is terrific and the bar draws a friendly crowd.
Saigon Café	188 Newark Ave	201 332 8711	$$	Compared to its neighbor (see above) the Saigon Café serves Southeast Asian cuisine of a quality that reflects its slightly higher prices.
Tania's	348 Grove St	201-451-6189	$$	Homecooked Eastern European food. Beware: the cold borscht is addictive.
Unlimited Pizza Café & Diner	116 Newark Ave	201-333-0053	$$*	Best slice of pizza after St Marks.
Uno Chicago Bar & Grill	286 Washington St	201-395-9500	$$	Casual, family atmosphere. All American eatery serving nachos, hamburgers and pizza. Go on an empty stomach because the sizes are large.
ZZ's Brick Oven Pizza	118 Pavonia Ave	201-626-8877	$$	They deliver!!!

Battery Park City

Cove Restaurant	2 South End Ave	212-964-1500	$$$	New American Cuisine.
Foxhounds	320 South End Ave	212-385-6199	$$	"English" pub; food, "American."
Gigino at Wagner Park	20 Battery Pl	212-528-2228	$$$*	Lady Liberty is your companion as you dine Italian.
Picasso Pizza	303 South End Ave	212-321-2616	$$	Good thin crust pizza.
Samantha's Fine Foods	235 South End Ave	212-945-555	$$	Italian take-out and catering.
Steamer's Landing	375 South End Ave	212-432-1451	$$$	Food from Italy, from the sea, and from the farms.
Grill Room	Winter Garden, World Financial Center	212-945-9400	$$$	Enter viewing palm trees; dine viewing the Hudson.
Unity	102 North End Ave	646-769-4200	$$*	Atkins-friendly food.
Wave Japanese Restaurant	21 South End Ave	212-240-9100	$$	
Zen	311 South End Ave	212-432-3634	$$	Chinese and Thai.

New York has long had a reputation as a fabulous place to shop and the reputation is well deserved. From haute couture to vintage clothing, from house and garden to cars and sporting goods, you would be hard pressed to find something you could not purchase in this town. Unlike going to a large mall, however, you might spend most of your time commuting between the stores you want to shop at. Here are a few key themes and some of the best places to give your credit card a workout:

Clothing

For the best of the haute couture labels head for the area around Madison Avenue and Fifth Avenue in the 50s, 60s, and 70s. There you will find the likes of **Chanel**, **Donna Karan**, **Armani** and **Gucci**. For department store shopping at its finest, try **Bloomingdale's**, **Macy's**, **Lord & Taylor** and (for those with a little extra cash) **Saks Fifth Avenue** and **Barney's**. If you have the patience to deal with the crowds and to sift through the merchandise to find great bargains, **Century 21** can yield great rewards of name brand clothing, shoes, make-up, accessories, and home wares at significantly discounted prices.

The past few years have seen the traditionally boutique-style SoHo welcome the larger designers such as **Prada**, **DKNY**, **Tommy Hilfiger**, **BCBG**, **Nicole Miller** and **Ralph Lauren**, as well as specialists such as **Coach**. If your wallet is a little lighter, you'll find a good cross section of "middle of the road" stores such as **Banana Republic**, **Benetton,** and **French Connection**. SoHo is a great area for browsing and strolling, with Sullivan and Thompson Streets offering a glimpse of the smaller boutiques that used to occupy the area.

For vintage clothing and up and coming designers, head to the area east of Broadway to Bowery, mainly below Houston, as well as to the East Village.

Sports

Paragon Sports in Union Square is hard to beat as a one-stop shop for everything sporting. The challenge is to find a sport that is not listed on the store directory! For outdoor gear, try **Eastern Mountain Sports**. **Sports Authority**, **Foot Locker,** and **Modell's** provide a broad range of affordable sports clothing, shoes and goods. **Blades Board & Skate** combines groovy gear for boarding (both the wheeled and the snow variety) as well as a good selection of the latest equipment for these activities.

Housewares

You can lose hours in **ABC Carpet & Home** just off of Union Square. They provide an exotic array of furniture and furnishings; much of it is antique, imported from Asia and Europe. **Crate and Barrel**, **Fish's Eddy**, **Pottery Barn**, **Portico,** and **Bed Bath & Beyond** all are good home ware stores with a wide selection of styles and prices. For cheap kitchen outfitters, try some of the restaurant supply places on Bowery. For paint, window dressings, and other home decorating supplies try **Janovic Plaza**.

Electronics

J&R provides most things electronic, including computers and accessories, games, cameras, music equipment, CDs and DVDs, and household appliances. **B&H** is another great place for photographic, audio and video equipment. Go there to witness the spectacle of how well coordinated the entire operation is as much as for the outstanding selection of gear. Other places to shop for electronics include the **Apple** store, **DataVision**, and **Best Buy**.

Food

If the way to a person's heart is through their stomach, then no wonder we all love New York! Try the tasty delights of **Myers of Keswick** in the West Village, **East Village Cheese** in the East Village, **Sullivan Street Bakery** in SoHo, **Zabar's** gourmet foods on the Upper West Side, **Dylan's Candy Bar** on the Upper East Side, and **Sette Pani** for delicious baked goods in Harlem. The introduction of online ordering and home delivery from **Fresh Direct** has brought a whole new level of convenience to New Yorkers, with the highest quality fresh food delivered to your door. You can even specify a two-hour time frame for delivery. It doesn't get a great deal better than that!

Art Supplies

Running low on Cadmium Red? Use your last stick of charcoal drawing a nude? The best art stores in NYC are scattered loosely around the SoHo area, with **Pearl Paint** being the most well-known. Located where Mercer and Canal Streets meet, the store occupies a full 6-story building with every type of art supply you can imagine, including a great separate frame shop out back on Lispenard. Closer to NYU and Cooper Union, you can find the best selection of paper at **NY Central Art Supply** on Third Avenue. On Bond Street, the shiny **Art Store** chain has a location which usually has some good sales going on and a well stocked inventory. Further north on Fourth Ave, is **Utrecht**, which sells more than just the products with their name. **SoHo Art Materials** on Grand Street is a small, traditional shop that sells super premium paints and brushes for fine artists. Don't forget to check out both **Sam Flax** and **Al Friedman** in the Flatiron area—they are both great for graphic design supplies, portfolios, and gifts.

As the art scene has made its way to Williamsburg, having an art supply store close by is as important as a good grocery store! **Artist & Craftsman** on North 8th is a good bet for supplies.

At all these stores, remember to show your student ID card as most offer a decent discount!

Music Equipment & Instruments

There are as many starving musicians as there are artists in NYC, but that doesn't keep them from finding ways to fulfill their equipment needs. New York's large and vibrant music scene supports a thriving instrument trade. To buy a new tuba or get that banjo tuned, head over to 48th

Street. You'll find the largest, most well known stores, from generalist shops such as **Manny's and Sam Ash,** to more specialized shops like **Roberto's Woodwind Repair**. Just two blocks away, on 46th, you can delight in two shops dedicated to drummers—**Manhattan Drum Shop** and **Drummer's World.**

If you can't take the bustle of the Times Square area and are looking for used, vintage, or just plain cool, then you'll want to shop elsewhere. Some of our favorites are: **East Village Music, First Flight, 30th Street Guitars, Rogue Music,** and **Ludlow Guitars.** We're surprisingly impressed with the nice salespeople at the new **Guitar Center** on 14th Street.

For an exquisite purchase, where money is no object, pick up a grand piano at **Klavierhaus,** a Strat at **Matt Umanov,** or a Strad at **Havivi Violins.**

The best remaining place for sheet music is the **Joseph Patelson Music House.**

Music - Listening

NYC is a hotbed for music lovers, and its record stores house the best and the worst of what the world has to offer. Whether you're shopping for that top 10 hit or a rare piece of 70's vinyl, your options for finding it are expansive. For those who like to dig, there's **Kim's Mediapolis**, and **Sound & Fury** to fill that void in your record collection. If you're not up for the smaller indie shops, head to **J&R Music World, Tower,** or the **Virgin Megastore** and be prepared to spend at least a good chunk of your paycheck.

The smaller stores carry the more eclectic selections and, more often than not, the staff can help you out with musical queries. Head to **Footlight** in the East Village and you'll see what we're talking about. If you're not convinced, try **Other Music** and **Earwax**—two stores with unique vibes.

If all else fails, walk along Bleecker Street for **Rebel Rebel**, **Kim's Underground**, and **Bleecker Street Records**.

Shopping "Districts"

Manhattan is famous for its shopping districts—a conglomeration of shops in one area where you go to find what you're looking for. Hit up the **Garment District** (25th to 40th Streets, Fifth to Ninth Avenues) for buttons and zippers, rick-rack and ribbons, all the ingredients you'll need to fashion your own frocks. Attention men: The **Diamond** and **Jewelry District** (W 47th between Fifth and Sixth Avenues), the world's largest market for diamonds, and the **Flower District** (26th to 29th Streets, along and off Sixth Avenue) are where to go to make her swoon. **Music Row** (48th Street between Sixth & Seventh Avenues) is where to buy that accordion you've been meaning to try. The Bowery south of Houston is another well known strip known as the **Kitchenware District** for all your culinary endeavors, the **Lighting District** (past Delancey Street) for all your illuminating needs, and the **Downtown Jewelry District** (turn the corner of Bowery to Canal Street) for the more exotic baubles you can't find uptown. The **Flatiron District** (from 14th to 34th Streets, between Sixth & Park Avenues) is a home furnishing mecca. Book Row (between 9th and 14th Streets) is sadly no more. What was once an assemblage of over 25 bookstores, now only houses the famous Strand Book Store and Alabaster Used Books, both tome troves unto themselves.

Map 1 • Financial District

Barclay Rex	75 Broad St	212-962-3355	For all your smoking needs.
Century 21	22 Cortlandt St	212-227-9092	Where most New Yorkers buy their underwear.
Flowers of the World	5 Hanover Sq	212-425-2234, 800-770-3125	Fulfill any feeling, mood, budget, or setting.
Godiva Chocolatier	33 Maiden Ln	212-809-8990	Everyone needs a fix now and then.
M. Slavin & Sons	106 South St	212-233-4522	Fresh fish at the Seaport.
Modell's	200 Broadway	212-964-4007	Generic sporting goods.
Radio Shack	114 Fulton St	212-732-1904	Kenneth, what is the frequency?
Radio Shack	75 Maiden Ln	212-785-5893	I need a multiplexer, Jim.
The World of Golf	189 Broadway	212-385-1246	Stop here on your way to Briar Cliff Manor.
Yankees Clubhouse Shop	8 Fulton St	212-514-7182	26 and counting....

Map 2 • TriBeCa

Assets London	152 Franklin St	212-219-8777	Ultra-Mod British fashions for her.
Balloon Saloon	133 West Broadway	212-227-3838	We love the name.
Bazzini	330 Greenwich St	212-334-1280	Nuts to you!
Bell Bates Natural Food	97 Reade St	212-267-4300	No MSG?
Boffi SoHo	31 1/2 Greene St	212-431-8282	Hi-end kitchen and bath design.
Canal Street Bicycles	417 Canal St	212-334-8000	Bike messenger mecca.
Commodities	117 Hudson St	212-334-8330	Get your pork bellies!
Duane Park Patisserie	179 Duane St	212-274-8447	Yummy!
Gotham Bikes	112 West Broadway	212-732-2453	Super helpful staff, good stuff.
Jack Spade	56 Greene St	212-625-1820	Barbie's got Ken, Kate's got Jack. Men's bags.
Janovic Plaza	136 Church St	212-349-0001	Top NYC paint store.
Kings Pharmacy	5 Hudson St	212-791-3100	Notary Public + discount days!
Korin Japanese Trading	57 Warren St	212-587-7021	Supplier to Japanese chefs and restaurants.

Let There Be Neon	38 White St	212-226-4883	Neon gallery and store.
Liberty Souveniers	275 Greenwich St	212-566-4604	Show your NY pride!
MarieBelle's Fine Treats & Chocolates	484 Broome St	212-925-6999	Top NYC chocolatier.
New York Nautical	140 West Broadway	212-962-4522	Armchair sailing.
Oliver Peoples	366 West Broadway	212-925-5400	Look as good as you see.
Shoofly	42 Hudson St	212-406-3270	Dressing your child for social success.
Stern's Music	71 Warren St	212-964-5455	World music.
We Are Nuts About Nuts	165 Church St	212-227-4695	They're nuts.
Willner Chemists	253 Broadway	212-682-2817	Free nutritional consultations for customers.

Map 3 • City Hall / Chinatown

Aji Ichiban	37 Mott St	212-253-7650	Japanese chain of Chinese candy.
Bangkok Center Grocery	104 Mosco St	212-349-1979	Curries, fish sauce, and other Thai products.
Bloomingdale's	504 Broadway	212-729-5900	Modern Bloomingdale's. Hottest young designers and exclusive collections.
Bowery Lighting	132 Bowery	212-941-8244	Got a match, anyone?
Catherine Street Meat Market	21 Catherine St	212-693-0494	Fresh pig deliveries every Tuesday.
Chinatown Ice Cream Factory	65 Bayard St	212-608-4170	Mango & redbean milkshakes.
Fountain Pen Hospital	10 Warren St	212-964-0580	They don't take Medicaid.
GS Food Market	250 Grand St	212-274-0990	Fresh veggies.
Hong Kong Seafood & Meat	75 Mulberry St	212-571-1445	Fresh seafood that you must eat today.
Industrial Plastic Supply	309 Canal St	212-226-2010	Plastic fantastic.
J&R Music & Computer World	33 Park Row	212-732-8600	Stereo, computer, and electronic equipment.
Kam Kuo	7 Mott St	212-349-3097	Chinese emporium.
Kate Spade	454 Broome St	212-274-1991	Downtown design mecca.
Lung Moon Bakery	83 Mulberry St	212-349-4945	Chinese bakery.
Mitchell's Place	15 Park Pl	212-267-8156	Ca-ching for bling bling.
Modell's	55 Chambers St	212-732-8484	Generic sporting goods.
New Age Designer	38 Mott St	212-349-0818	Chinese emporium.
Pearl Paint	308 Canal St	212-431-7932	Mecca for artists, designers, and people who just like art supplies.
Pearl River Mart	477 Broadway	212-431-4770	Chinese housewares and more.
Radio Shack	280 Broadway	212-233-1080	Kenneth, what is the frequency?
Soho Art Materials	127 Grand St	212-431-3938	A painter's candy store.
Tan My My Market	253 Grand St	212-966-7837	Fresh fish—some still moving!
Tent & Trails	21 Park Pl	212-227-1760	Top outfitter for gearheads.
The New York City Store	1 Centre St	212-669-8246	Great NYC stuff—manhole cover pins, subway mugs, etc.
Ting's Gift Shop	18 Doyers St	212-962-1081	Chinese emporium.
Two Lines Music	370 Broadway	212-227-9552	Music equipment.
Vespa	13 Crosby St	212-226-4410	Rosselini! Fellini! Spaghattini!
Yellow Rat Bastard	478 Broadway	877-YELL-RAT	Filled with young street clothes and skate gear.

Map 4 • Lower East Side

Doughnut Plant	379 Grand St	212-505-3700	Great, weird, recommended.
Frank's Bike Shop	553 Grand St	212-533-6332	Bikes piled to the ceiling.
Gertel's Bake Shop	53 Hester St	212-982-3250	Great chocolate babka.
Guss' Pickles	85 Orchard St	212-254-4477	Authenticity wafts out of the pickle barrels.
Hong Kong Supermarket	109 East Broadway	212-227-3388	A chance to see just how amazing food packaging can look.
Joe's Fabric Warehouse	102 Orchard St	212-674-7089	Designer fabrics and trimmings.
Kossar's Bialys	367 Grand St	212-253-2146	Oldest bialy bakery in the US.
Moishe's Kosher Bake Shop	504 Grand St	212-673-5832	Best babka, challah, hamantaschen and rualach.
Sweet Life	63 Hester St	212-598-0092	Gimme some CAN-DAY!

Map 5 • West Village

Alphabets	47 Greenwich Ave	212-229-2966	Fun miscellany store.
CO Bigelow Chemists	414 Sixth Ave	212-533-2700	Classic village pharmacy.
Faicco's Pork Store	260 Bleecker St	212-243-1974	Pork! Just for you!
Fat Beats	406 Sixth Ave	212-673-3883	Will soon be re-named "Phat Beats," undoubtedly.
Flight 001	96 Greenwich Ave	212-691-1001	Cute hipster travel shop.
Geppetto's Toy Box	10 Christopher St	212-620-7511	Excellent toys and puppets.
Integral Yoga Natural Foods	229 W 13th St	212-243-2642	Shop in the lotus position.
Janovic Plaza	161 Sixth Ave	212-627-1100	Top NYC paint store.
Leather Man, The	111 Christopher St	212-243-5339	No, you won't look like James Dean. But it'll help.
Mxyplyzyk	125 Greenwich Ave	212-989-4300	Great quirky mid-range tchochkes.
Myers of Keswick	634 Hudson St	212-691-4194	Killer English sausages, pasties, etc.
Porto Rico Importing Co	201 Bleecker St	212-477-5421	Sacks of coffee beans everywhere.
Radio Shack	49 Seventh Ave	212-727-7641	I need a multiplexer, Jim.
Scott Jordan Furniture	137 Varick St	212-620-4682	Solid hardwood furniture.

Urban Outfitters	374 Sixth Ave	212-677-9350	College cool.
Vitra	29 Ninth Ave	212-929-3626	Modern stuff, just like we like it!

Map 6 • Washington Square / NYU / SoHo

Academy Records & CDs	77 E 10th St	212-780-9166	Top Jazz/classical mecca.
Apple Store SoHo	103 Prince St	212-226-3126	Don't come looking for produce.
Blades Board and Skate	659 Broadway	212-477-7350	One-stop shop for skateboarding and inline skating gear.
Blades Downtown	659 Broadway	212-477-7350	One-stop shop for skateboarding and inline skating gear.
Burberry	131 Spring St	212-925-9300	How to dress well without having to think about it.
Canal Jean	718 Broadway	212-353-2601	Where many New Yorkers buy their jeans.
CITE Design	120 Wooster St	212-431-7272	3 cool shops on Wooster.
Daily 235	235 Elizabeth St	212-334-9728	A little tchotchke store; has great journals.
East Village Cheese	40 Third Ave	212-477-2601	Great soy cheeses, laughably bad service.
East Village Music Store	85 E 4th St	212-979-8222	Excellent wares and repairs service. NFT top pick!
EMS	591 Broadway	212-966-8730	Excellent outdoor/hiking equipment and clothing.
Footlight Records	113 E 12th St	212-533-1572	Opera.
Global Table	107 Sullivan St	212-431-5839	Quietly elegant tableware.
Jam Paper & Envelope	111 Third Ave	212-473-6666	And the envelope please...
Kar'ikter	19 Prince St	212-274-1966	Toys for kids and adults.
Kate's Paperie	561 Broadway	212-941-9816	Excellent stationery. NYC favorite.
Kiehl's	109 Third Ave	212-677-3171	Great creams, lotions, & unguents; laughably good service.
Kim's Underground	144 Bleecker St	212-260-1010	Where to blow $100 quickly.
Kim's Video	6 St Marks Pl	212-505-0311	Where to blow $100 quickly.
Leekan Designs	93 Mercer St	212-226-7226	Bead shop for aspiring jewelry-makers.
Lighting by Gregory	158 Bowery	212-226-1276	Bowery lighting mecca. Good ceiling fans.
Michael Anchin Glass	245 Elizabeth St	212-925-1470	The city's premier glassblower, still with good prices.
Moss	146 Greene St	212-226-2190	Awesome cool stuff you can't afford! Ever!
Nancy Koltes at Home	31 Spring St	212-219-2271	What's the thread-count?
National Wholesale Liquidators	632 Broadway	212-979-2400	They're not kidding.
New Museum Store	583 Broadway	212-219-1222	One of our favorite stores on the planet Earth.
New York Central Art Supply	62 Third Ave	212-473-7705	Great selection of art, papers & supplies.
Other Music	15 E 4th St	212-477-8150	An excellent range of other music.
Porto Rico Importing Co	107 Thompson St	212-966-5758	Sacks of coffee beans everywhere.
Porto Rico Importing Co	40 St Mark's Pl	212-533-1982	Sacks of coffee beans everywhere.
Prada	575 Broadway	212-334-8888	Big pretentious Rem Koolhaas-designed store!
Radio Shack	781 Broadway	212-228-6810	Kenneth, what is the frequency?
Stereo Exchange	627 Broadway	212-505-1111	Just-under-obscenely-priced audiophile equipment. Good for male depression.
Stuart Moore	128 Prince St	212-941-1023	Elegant, modern jewelry, $1000-$10,000 range.
Sullivan Street Bakery	77 Sullivan St	212-334-9435	The best bakery, period.
Surprise, Surprise	91 Third Ave	212-777-0990	Good just-moved-to-the-neighborhood store.
Tower Records	692 Broadway	212-505-1500	For all your mainstream needs.
Utrecht Art and Drafting Supplies	111 Fourth Ave	212-777-5353	Another fine downtown art store.
Veniero's	342 E 11th St	212-674-7070	Another cookie, my dear?
White Trash	304 E 5th St	212-598-5956	Retro home furnishings.

Map 7 • East Village

Alphabets	115 Avenue A	212-475-7250	Fun miscellany store.
Altman Luggage	135 Orchard St	212-254-7275	It's just you and that Samsonite gorilla, baby.
Dowel Quality Products	91 First Ave	212-979-6045	Super-cool Indian grocery. Great beer selection, too.
Earthmatters	177 Ludlow St	212-475-4180	Organic groceries with a garden out back.
Economy Candy	108 Rivington St	212-254-1531	Where Augustus Gloop can been seen hanging around late at night.
Etherea	66 Avenue A	212-358-1126	Cool East Village record store.
Exit 9	64 Avenue A	212-228-0145	Always fun and changeable hipster gift shop (The first place to sell NFT!).
First Flight Music	174 First Ave	212-539-1383	Good guitars and amps, spotty service.
Gringer & Sons	29 First Ave	212-475-0600	Kitchen appliances for every price range.
Lancelotti	66 Avenue A	212-475-6851	Fun designer housewares, not too expensive.
R&S Strauss Auto Store	644 E 14th St	212-995-8000	Sideview mirrors, tail lights, touch up paint - mecca for the urban car owner.
Russ & Daughters	179 E Houston St	212-475-4880	Get the nova, silly!
Spectra	293 E 10th St	212-529-3636	East Village photo print shop; great sepia processing.
Toys in Babeland	94 Rivington St	212-375-1701	Sex toys and more.
Yonah Schimmel's Knishery	137 E Houston St	212-477-2858	Your run-of-the-mill knishery.

Map 8 • Chelsea

B&H Photo	420 Ninth Ave	212-444-5040	Where everyone in North America buys their cameras and film. Closed Saturdays.
BuonItalia	75 Ninth Ave	212-633-9090	Imported Italian food.
Chelsea Garden Center	455 W 16th St	212-929-2477	Urban gardener's delight.
Chelsea Wholesale Flower Market	75 Ninth Ave	212-620-7500	Remember, you're in Manhattan, not Westchester.
Fat Witch Bakery	75 Ninth Ave	212-807-1335	Excellent chocolate brownies.
Kitchen Market	218 Eighth Ave	212-243-4433	Chiles, herbs, spices, hot sauces, salsas, and more.
Portico	75 Ninth Ave	212-243-8515	Minimalist, urban sophistication.

Map 9 • Flatiron / Lower Midtown

17 at 17 Thrift Shop	17 W 17th St	212-727-7516	Proceeds go to Gilda's Club.
30th St Guitars	236 W 30th St	212-868-2660	Ax heaven.
ABC Carpet & Home	888 Broadway	212-473-3000	Carpets, furniture, doodads—a NYC institution.
Abracadabra	19 W 21st St	212-627-5194	Magic, masks, costumes-presto!
Academy Records & CDs	12 W 18th St	212-242-3000	Top Jazz/classical mecca.
Adorama Camera	42 W 18th St	212-741-0052	Good camera alternative to B & H.
Ariston	69 Fifth Ave	212-929-4226, 800-422-2747	Excellent florist with orchids as well.
Bed Bath & Beyond	620 Sixth Ave	212-255-3550	De riguer destination when moving to a new apartment.
Capitol Fishing Tackle	218 W 23rd St	212-929-6132	100+ year-old fishing institution.
City Quilter, The	133 W 25th St	212-807-0390	Quilt for success!
CompUSA	420 Fifth Ave	212-764-6224	The Kmart of computer stores.
Container Store, The	629 Sixth Ave	212-366-4200	For all your container needs.
Fish's Eddy	889 Broadway	212-420-9020	The coolest used plates in the city.
Housing Works Thrift Shop	143 W 17th St	212-366-0820	Our favorite thrift store.
Jam Paper & Envelope	611 Sixth Ave	212-255-4593	And the envelope please...
Jazz Record Center	236 W 26th St	212-675-4480	All that Jazz!
Just Bulbs	936 Broadway	212-228-7820	Do you have any lamps? How about shades?
Krups Kitchen and Bath	11 W 18th St	212-243-5787	Good prices for top appliances.
Loehmann's	101 Seventh Ave	212-352-0856	Join the other thousands of bargain hunters sifting through clothing piles.
Lord & Taylor	424 Fifth Ave	212-391-3344	Classic NYC department store.
Macy's	151 W 34th St	212-695-4400	Love the wooden escalators.
Midnight Records	263 W 23rd St	212-675-2768	All-over-the-place record shop, just the way we want it.
Paper Access	23 W 18th St	212-463-7035	Relatively cheap paper and such.
Paragon Sporting Goods	867 Broadway	212-255-8036	Good all-purpose sporting goods store.
Phoenix	64 W 37th St	212-564-5656	Bead shop for aspiring jewelry-makers.
Pleasure Chest	156 Seventh Ave	212-242-2158	Always a great window display.
Radio Shack	36 E 23rd St	212-673-3670	Kenneth, what is the frequency?
Rogue Music	251 W 30th St	212-629-5073	Used equipment you probably still can't afford.
Sam Flax	12 W 20th St	212-620-3038	Portfolios, frames, furniture, and designer gifts.
Sports Authority	636 Sixth Ave	212-929-8971	Sporting goods for the masses.
Tekserve	119 W 23rd St	212-929-3645	Apple computer sales and repairs.

Map 10 • Murray Hill / Gramercy

Alkit Pro Camera	222 Park Ave S	212-674-1515	Good camera shop; developing; rentals.
City Opera Thrift Shop	222 E 23rd St	212-684-5344	They always have something or other.
Housing Works Thrift Shop	157 E 23rd St	212-529-5955	Our favorite thrift store.
Nemo Tile Company	48 E 21st St	212-505-0099	Good tile shop for small projects.
Pearl Paint	207 E 23rd St	212-592-2179	Not as big as the Canal St. store, but still very useful.
Poggenpohl U S	230 Park Ave	212-228-3334	By appointment only. $100,000 kitchens for all you grad students!
Quark Spy	537 Third Ave	212-889-4353	Spy shops are cool.
Radio Shack	270 Park Ave S	212-533-1906	Kenneth, what is the frequency?
Speedo Authentic Fitness	90 Park Ave	212-682-3830	Good gear for the pool or the gym.
Urban Angler	206 Fifth Ave	212-689-6400, 800-255-5488	We think it's for fishermen.

Map 11 • Hell's Kitchen

Just Pickles	569 Ninth Ave	212-967-7205	Do you have any artichokes?
Little Pie Company	424 W 43rd St	212-736-4780	A home-made dessert equals happiness.
Metro Bicycles	360 W 47th St	212-581-4500	New York's bicycle source.
Ninth Avenue International	543 Ninth Ave	212-279-1000	Mediterranean/Greek specialty store.

Pan Aqua Diving	460 W 43rd St	212-736-3483	SCUBA equipment and courses.
Poseidon Bakery	629 Ninth Ave	212-757-6173	Greek bakery.
Radio Shack	333 W 57th St	212-586-1909	Kenneth, what is the frequency?
Sea Breeze	541 Ninth Ave	212-563-7537	Bargains on fresh seafood.

Map 12 • Midtown

Alkit Pro Camera	830 Seventh Ave	212-262-2424	Good camera shop; developing; rentals.
Baccarat	625 Madison Ave	212-826-4100	Top glass/crystal.
Bergdorf Goodman	754 Fifth Ave	212-753-7300	The widow dressed in Bergdorf Goodman black. . .
rooks Brothers	346 Madison Ave	212-682-8800	For hip, radical fashions from the Indian subcontinent.
Bruno Magli	677 Fifth Ave	212-752-7900	Shoes to die/kill for.
Burberry	9 E 57th St	212-371-5010	How to dress well without having to think about it.
Carnegie Card & Gifts	56 W 57th St	212-977-2494	Great, diverse, always fresh.
CCS Counter Spy Shop	444 Madison Ave	212-688-8500	Spy shops are cool.
Colony Music	1619 Broadway	212-265-2050	Great sheet music store.
CompUSA	1775 Broadway	212-262-9711	The Kmart of computer stores.
Devon & Blakely	461 Fifth Ave	212-684-4321	Corporate catering and gift baskets.
Ermenegildo Zegna	743 Fifth Ave	212-421-4488	A truly stylish and classic Italian designer.
FAO Schwartz	767 Fifth Ave	212-644-9400	Noisy, crowded, overrated, awesome.
Felissimo	10 W 56th St	212-956-4438	Cool design store, great townhouse.
Henri Bendel	712 Fifth Ave	212-247-1100	Expensive, classy, and expensive.
International Cutlery	367 Madison Ave	212-924-7300	Huge, good, expensive.
Joseph Patelson Music House	160 W 56th St	212-582-5840	Where Beethoven would shop, if he wasn't dead.
Kate's Paperie	140 W 57th St	212-459-0700	Excellent stationery. NYC favorite
Manny's Music	156 W 48th St	212-819-0576	Uptown musical instruments mecca.
Manon, Le Chocolatier	754 Fifth Ave	212-753-7300	They don't carry Hershey's.
Mets Clubhouse shop	11 W 42nd St	212-768-9534	For Amazin' stuff!
MoMA Design Store	44 W 53rd St	212-767-1050	Cutting-edge, minimalist, ergonomic, offbeat, and funky everything.
Museum of Arts and Design Shop	40 W 53rd St	212-956-3535	Not your average museum store.
Orvis Company	522 Fifth Ave	212-827-0698	For the angler in all of us. Or, for Halloween.
Radio Shack	1134 Sixth Ave	212-575-2361	Kenneth, what is the frequency?
Saks Fifth Avenue	611 Fifth Ave	212-753-4000	When Bloomie's just gets to be too much...
Sam Ash	160 W 48th St	212-719-2299	The original, so not that bad.
Smythson of Bond Street	4 W 57th St	212-265-4573	High quality stationery.
Steinway and Sons	109 W 57th St	212-246-1100	Great store and free delivery!
Takashimaya	693 Fifth Ave	212-350-0100	Elegant tea, furniture, accessory store. Highly recommended.
Tiffany & Co	727 Fifth Ave	212-755-8000	Gaudy and overblown but still interesting.

Map 13 • East Midtown

Adriana's Caravan	Grand Central Station	212-972-8804	Number 1 rated herb and spice shop.
Bridge Kitchenware	214 E 52nd St	212-688-4220	A mecca.
Godiva Chocolatier	560 Lexington Ave	212-980-9810	Everyone needs a fix now and then.
Innovative Audio	150 E 58th St	212-634-4444	Quality music systems and home theaters.
Mets Clubhouse Shop	143 E 54th St	212-888-7508	For Amazin' stuff!
Modell's	51 E 42nd St	212-661-4242	Generic sporting goods.
New York Transit Museum	Grand Central, Main Concourse	212-878-0106	Great subway fun.
Radio Shack	940 Third Ave	212-750-8409	Kenneth, what is the frequency?
Sam Flax	425 Park Ave	212-935-5353	Portfolios, frames, furniture, and designer gifts.
Sports Authority	845 Third Ave	212-355-9725	Sporting goods for the masses.
Terence Conran Shop	407 E 59th St	212-755-9079	Wonderful design store--furniture, accessories, tableware, etc.
The World of Golf	147 E 47th St	212-775-9398	Stop here on your way to Briar Cliff Manor.
Yankee Clubhouse Shop	110 E 59th St	212-758-7844	26 and counting....
Zaro's Bread Basket	89 E 42nd St	212-292-0160	They've got bread. In baskets.

Map 14 • Upper West Side (Lower)

Alphabets	2284 Broadway	212-579-5702	Fun miscellany store.
Assets London	464 Columbus Ave	212-874-8253	Ultramodern British fashions for her.
Balducci's	155 W 66th St	212-653-8320	One third of the gourmet "holy trinity."
Bed Bath & Beyond	Broadway b/w W 64th St & W 65th St		De riguer destination when moving to a new apartment.
Bruce Frank	215 W 83rd St	212-595-3746	Great bead shop.
Bruno the King of Ravioli	2204 Broadway	212-580-8150	Gourmet market with a shocking specialty.
Claire's Accessories	2267 Broadway	212-877-2655	Fun for the young.
Country Rooster Flowers	70 W 71st St	212-496-2828	Floral arrangements.

EMS	20 W 61st St	212-397-4860	Excellent outdoor/hiking equipment and clothing.
Ethan Allen	103 West End Ave	212-201-9840	Furniture for the mature set.
Fish's Eddy	2176 Broadway	212-873-8819	Great used plates.
Godiva Chocolatier	245 Columbus Ave	212-787-5804	Everyone needs a fix now and then.
Gracious Home	1992 Broadway	212-231-7800	The definition of the word "emporium."
Gryphon Record Shop	233 W 72nd St	212-874-1588	Cool record store.
Harry's Shoes	2299 Broadway	212-874-2035	Mecca for reasonably priced footwear.
Housing Works Thrift Shop	306 Columbus Ave	212-579-7566	Our favorite thrift store.
Lincoln Stationers	1889 Broadway	212-459-3500	Classic stationery store.
NYCD	173 W 81st St	212-724-4466	Excellent CD shop.
Paper Access	2030 Broadway	212-799-4900	Relatively cheap papers and such.
Tumi	10 Columbus Cir	800-322-TUMI	When your luggage gets lost and insurance is paying.
Yarn Co	2274 Broadway	212-787-7878	The stories we could tell....
Zabar's	2245 Broadway	212-787-2000	The third gourmet shop in the "holy trinity."

Map 15 • Upper East Side (Lower)

A Bear's Place	789 Lexington Ave	212-826-6465	Excellent toys and children's furniture
Aveda Environmental Lifestyle Store	1122 Third Ave	212-744-3113	Pamper yourself.
Baldwin Fish Market	1584 First Ave	212-288-9032	Seafood purveyor.
Bang & Olufsen	952 Madison Ave	212-879-6161	Sleek, expensive home entertainment products.
Barneys New York	660 Madison Ave	212-826-8900	Wonderful(ly) expensive clothing.
Bed Bath & Beyond	410 E 61st St	646-215-4702	De riguer destination when moving to a new apartment.
Bloomingdale's	1000 Third Ave	212-355-5900	An upscale version of Macy's.
Dempsey & Carroll	1058 Madison Ave	212-249-6444	Upscale beautiful stationers.
Diesel	770 Lexington Ave	212-308-0055	Why spend $60 on a pair of jeans when you can spend $150?
Dylan's Candy Bar	1011 Third Ave	646-735-0078	Keeping NYC dentists in business since 2001.
Garnet Wines & Liquors	929 Lexington Ave	212-772-3211	Top NYC wine store.
Giorgio Armani	760 Madison Ave	212-988-9191	Fantastic store, fantastic clothes, fantastic(ally high) prices.
Gracious Home	1217 Third Ave	212-517-6300	The definition of the word "emporium."
Hermes	691 Madison Ave	212-751-3181	Is that an Hermes tie?
Housing Works Thrift Shop	202 E 77th St	212-772-8461	Our favorite thrift store.
Kate's Paperie	1282 Third Ave	212-396-3670	Excellent stationery. NYC favorite.
Lyric Hi-Fi	1221 Lexington Ave	212-439-1900	Friendly top-end stereo shop.
Radio Shack	925 Lexington Ave	212-249-3028	Kenneth, what is the frequency?
Steuben	667 Madison Ave	212-752-1441	Glass you can't afford.
Venture Stationers	1156 Madison Ave	212-288-7235	Great neighborhood stationers.

Map 16 • Upper West Side (Upper)

Ann Taylor	2380 Broadway	212-721-3130	For the businesswoman. Conservative, classic and clean.
Banana Republic	2360 Broadway	212-787-2064	Destination for the modern, versatile, average wardrobe.
Ben & Jerry's	2722 Broadway	212-866-6237	Cherry Garcia, Phish Food, and Half Baked.
Gothic Cabinet Craft	2652 Broadway	212-678-4368	Real wood furniture.
Gourmet Garage	2567 Broadway	212-663-0656	Less greasy food than most garages.
Health Nuts	2611 Broadway	212-678-0054	Standard health food store.
Metro Bicycles	231 W 96th St	212-663-7531	New York's bicycle source.

Map 17 • Upper East Side / East Harlem

Best Buy	1280 Lexington Ave	212-366-1373	Test the electronics before you buy.
Blades Board and Skate	120 W 72nd St	212-996-1644	One stop shop for skateboarding and inline skating gear.
Eli's Vinegar Factory	431 E 91st St	212-987-0885	Gourmet market with prepared foods, cheeses, meats, seafood, and produce.
FACE Stockholm	1263 Madison Ave	212-987-1411	Skincare & makeup.
La Tropezienne	2131 First Ave	212-860-5324	Bakery.
Piece of Cake Bakery	1370 Lexington Ave	212-987-1700	Bakery.
Steve Madden	150 E 86th St	212-426-0538	Trendy and modern, though not the highest quality.
Super Runners Shop	1337 Lexington Ave	212-369-6010	Brand name sneakers, apparel and gadgets.
Williams-Sonoma	1175 Madison Ave	212-289-6832	Fine cookware.

Map 18 • Columbia / Morningside Heights

JAS Mart	2847 Broadway	212-866-4780	Japanese Asian Specialty. Japanese imports.
Kim's Mediapolis	2906 Broadway	212-864-5321	Audiovisual heaven.
Nine West Outlet Store	282 St Nicholas St	212-665-1022	Reasonable, trendy shoes and bags.

Map 19 • Harlem (Lower)

Champs	208 W 125th St	212-280-0296	Sports and street shoes and wear.
Dr Jays Harlem NYC	256 125th Street	212-665-7795	Inner-city urban fashions.
H&M	125 W 125th St	212-665-8300	Disposable fashion.
Harlem Underground Clothing Co	2027 Fifth Ave	212-987-9385	Embroidered Harlem t-shirts.
Harlemade	174 Lenox Ave	212-987-2500	Clothes/gifts/art.
Malcolm Shabazz HarlemMarket	58 W 116th St	n/a	An open-air market for all your daishiki needs.
Sette Pani	196 Lenox Ave	917 492 4806	Lovely baked goods.
The Body Shop	1 E 125th St	212-348-4900	Naturally inspired skin and hair care products.

Map 20 • El Barrio

Gothic Cabinet Craft	2268 Third Ave	212-410-3508	Real wood furniture.
Mario's Italian Deli	2246 Second Ave	212-876-7280	Deli.
Motherhood Maternity	163 E 125th St	212-987-8808	Casual maternity wear.
Payless Shoe Source	2143 Third Ave	212-289-2251	Inexpensive shoes.
R&S Strauss Auto	2005 Third Ave	212-410-6688	Power steering fluid and windshield wipers 'till 9 pm!
The Children's Place	163 E 125th St	212-348-3607	Cute clothes for little ones.
VIM	2239 Third Ave	212-369-5055	Streetwear—-jeans, sneakers, tops—for all.

Map 21 • Manhattanville / Hamilton Heights

VIM	508 W 145th St	212-491-1143	Streetwear—jeans, sneakers, tops—for all.

Map 22 • Harlem (Upper)

Baskin-Robbins	2730 Frederick Douglass Blvd	212-862-0635	31 flavors and other frozen treats.
New York Public Library Shop	515 Malcolm X Blvd Schomburg Ctr	212-491-2206	Shop specializing in Black history and culture.

Map 23 • Washington Heights

Baskin-Robbins	728 W 181st St	212-923-9239	31 Flavors and other frozen treats.
Goodwill Industries	512 W 181st St	212-923-7910	Jeans, business attire, baby and children's clothing, housewares and appliances, furniture and more.
Modell's	606 W 181st St	212-568-3000	Generic sporting goods.
Payless Shoe Source	617 W 181st St	212-795-9183	Inexpensive shoes.
The Children's Place	600 W 181st St	212-923-7244	Cute clothes for little ones.
VIM	561 W 181st St	212-781-8801	Streetwear--jeans, sneakers, tops--for all.

Map 25 • Inwood

Payless Shoe Source	560 W 207th St	212-544-9328	Inexpensive shoes.
Tread Bicycles	225 Dyckman St	212-544-7055	Where to fix your bike after riding through Inwood Hill Park.
VIM	565 W 207th St	212-942-7478	Streetwear--jeans, sneakers, tops--for all.

Map 26 • Astoria

Bagel House	3811 Ditmars Blvd	718-726-1869	Hand-rolled bagels baked on the spot.
Book Value	3318 Broadway	718-267-7929	Bookstore.
Top Tomato	33-15 Ditmars Blvd	718-721-1400	24-Hour produce stand - you never know when you'll need fresh herbs in the wee hours.

Map 28 • Greenpoint

Dee & Dee	777 Manhattan Ave	718-389-0181	Mega-dollar store, cheap stuff.
Pop's Popular Clothing	7 Franklin St	718-349-7677	Great second-hand clothing, especially jeans.

Map 29 • Williamsburg

Artist & Craftsman	221 N 8th St	888-772-4542	Art supplies.
Beacon's Closet	88 N 11th St	718-486-0816	Rad resale with lots of gems.

Brooklyn Industries	154 Bedford Ave	718-486-6464	Bags and tops—think St Marks-esque t-shirt shop.
Crypto	152 Bedford Ave	718-486-9041	Futuristic gear from Brooklyn-based clothing co.
Domsey's Warehouse	496 Wythe Ave	718-384-6000	Ready to dig? Picked over by hipsters but bargains still abound.
Earwax Records	218 Bedford Ave	718-486-3771	Record store with all the indie classics.
Isa	88 N 6th St	718-387-3363	Fashion-forward boutique, doubles as performance/art/party space.
Otte	218 Bedford Ave	718-302-9337	Fave neighborhood boutique where the friendly staff know what makes you.
Spacial Etc.	149 N 6th St	718-599-7962	Overpriced housewares, baby clothes and knitted goods.
Spoonbill and Sugartown	218 Bedford Av	718-387-7322	Excellent indie bookstore.
The Mini-Market	218 Bedford Ave	718-302-8030	Hodge-podge of chachkis and fun clothes.
Wythe Studios	240 Wythe Ave	917-916-7215	Art gallery featuring local artists, including clothing that's tres chic.
Yarn Tree	347 Bedford Ave	718-384-8030	Knitting trend hit you yet? Visit and it will!

Map 30 • Brooklyn Heights / DUMBO / Downtown

ABC Carpet & Home	20 Jay St	718-643-7400	Carpets, furniture, doodads--a NYC institution.
Gourd Chips	113A Court St	718-797-2739	Boutique Fashion.
Heights Prime Meats	59 Clark St	718-237-0133	Butcher.
Lassen & Hennigs	114 Montague St	718-875-6272	Specialty foods and deli.
Soft Skull Press	71 Bond St	718-643-1599	Excellent indie bookstore.
SoHo Art Materials	111 Front St	718-855-2929	Art supplies.
Tapestry the Salon	107 Montague St	718-522-1202	Spa.

Map 31 • Fort Greene

Cake Man Raven Confectionary	708 Fulton St	718-694-2253	Get the red velvet cake!
Carol's Daughter	1 S Elliot Pl	718-596-1862	Skincare.
Exodus Industrial	771 Fulton St	718-246-0321	Clothing.
Indigo Café and Books	672 Fulton St	718-488-5934	Caffeine and literature.
Jacob Eyes	114 Dekalb Ave	718-625-7534	A little bit of everything, candles, bags shoes?
L'Epicerie	270 Vanderbilt Ave	718-636-0360	French Gourmet.
Malchijah Hats	225 DeKalb Ave	718-643-3269	Beautiful and unique hats.
Marquet	680 Fulton St	718-596-2018	Bakery.
My Little India	96 S Elliot Pl	718-855-5220	Furniture, candles, textiles.
Myrna's Natural Shoppe	713 Fulton St	718-858-6145	All-natural products.
The Midtown Greenhouse Garden Center	115 Flatbush Ave	718-636-0020	Fully stocked with plants and gardening supplies.
Yu Interiors	15 Greene Ave	718-237-5878	Modern furniture and accessories.

Map 32 • Cobble Hill / Boerum Hill / Carroll Gardens

Sahadi's	187 Atlantic Ave	718-624-4550	Specialty goods at bargain prices.
American Beer Distributors	256 Court St	718-875-0226	International beer merchant.
Apple Tree (24 hr deli)	312 Court St	718-624-7581	24-hour deli/farmer's market.
Astro Turf	290 Smith St	718-522-6182	Kitschy retro furniture that you'll pay top dollar for.
Caputo's Bake Shop	329 Court St	718-875-6871	Bakery.
Caputo's Fine Foods	460 Court St	718-855-8852	Italian gourmet specialties.
College Bakery	239 Court St	718-624-5534	Bakery.
Frida's Closet	296 Smith St	718-855-0031	Women's skirts, shirts and sweaters with a Frida Kahlo feel.
Granny's Attic	305 Smith St	718-624-0175	Find unique collectibles amongst the junk.
KC Art Supplies	252 Court St	718-852-1271	Pricey art supplies but good in a jam.
Kimera	366 Atlantic Ave	718-422-1147	Great pillows.
Mazzola Bakery	192 Union St	718-643-1719	Bakery.
Monte Leone's Pasticceria	355 Court St	718-624-9253	Bakery with great bread!
Olive's	434 Court St	718-243-9094	Vintage clothing.
Park Natural Foods	274 Union St	718-802-1652	Natural Foods.
Refinery	254 Smith St	718-643-7861	Great bags and accessories.
Stacia	267 Smith St	718-237-0078	Designer women's clothes by Stacy Johnson.
Staubitz Meat Market	222 Court St	718-624-0014	Best cold cuts on the block.
Swallow	361 Smith St	718-222-8201	Gallery featuring ceremic and glass products.
The Green Onion	274 Smith St	718-246-2804	Fine children's clothing.

Map 33 • Park Slope / Prospect Heights

Barnes and Noble	267 7th Ave	718-832-9066	Books and such.
Bird	430 7th Ave	718-768-4940	Unique women's clothes and accessories.
Bob and Judi's Collectibles	217 5th Ave	718-638-5770	Antiques, vintage novelties.
Boing Boing	204 Sixth Ave	718-398-0251	Boutique for mother and child.
The Bicycle Station	560 Vanderbilt Ave	718-638-0300	New, used, vintage, sales, repairs.
The Brainy Bunch	397 Flatbush Ave	718-398-7020	Educational toys and games for kids.
Castor & Pollux	76 6th Ave	718-398-4141	Slightly overpriced boutique store selling mainly fashion items and accessories.
Clay Pot	162 7th Ave	718-788-6564	Hand-crafted gift, jewelry.
Community Book Store	143 7th Ave	718-783-3075	Books, coffee, garden.
Eco-mat Cleaners	837 Union St	718-230-2990	Environmentally friendly cleaners.
Eidolon	233 5th Ave	718-638-8194	Local designer labels.
Hibiscus	564A Vandebilt Ave	718-638-6850	Flowers, plants and arrangements for all occasions.
Hooti Couture	321 Flatbush Ave	718-857-1977	Girlie vintage.
Kimera	274 5th Ave	718-965-1313	Great pillows.
Leaf and Bean	83 7th Ave	718-638-5791	Coffees and teas.
Nancy Nancy	244 Fifth Ave	718-789-5262	Cards, gifts, novelties.
Pieces	671 Vanderbilt Ave	718-857-7211	Urban clothes for sleek hip-hop crowd.
RedLipstick	64 6th Ave	718-857-9534	Luxurious hand-knitted originals. Sign up for a class.
Sound Track	119 7th Ave	718-622-1888	CDs & LPs.
Uncle Louie G's	741 Union St	718-623-6668	So many flavors, so little time.
Uprising Bread Bakery	138 7th Ave	718-499-5242	Artisanal breads, goodies.
Uprising Bread Bakery	328 7th Ave	718-499-8665	Artisanal breads, goodies.
Bagel House	3811 Ditmars Blvd	718-726-1869	Hand-rolled bagels baked on the spot.
Book Value	3318 Broadway	718-267-7929	Bookstore.
Top Tomato	33-15 Ditmars Blvd	718-721-1400	24-Hour produce stand - you never know when you'll need fresh herbs in the wee hours.

Map 34 • Hoboken

Air Studio	55 First St	201-239-1511	Cutting edge women's clothing boutique, featuring the hot designers of tomorrow.
Arts on Sixth	155 Sixth St	201-217-4311	Hand-blown glass; hand-wrought iron. Furniture and art. Screw the registry!
Basic Foods	204 Washington St	201-610-1100	Not so personal, but a good selection.
Battaglia's	319 Washington St	201-798-1122	Interesting gifts and homewares.
Big Fun Toys	602 Washington St	201-714-9575	Go for the gift wrap.. the toy's aren't bad!
City Paint & Hardware	130 Washington St	201-659-0061	Everything, including kitchen sinks.
Empire Coffee & Tea	231 Washington St	201-216-9625	Fresh roasted beans, all your java needs. Get silly with the staff.
Gallatea	1224 Washington St	201-963-1522	Elegantly luscious lingerie, chosen with an expert eye.
Hand Mad	116 Washington St	201-653-7276	"Folk, Funk, Fine Art." Plus groovy gift-wrapping.
Hoboken Farmboy	127 Washington St	201-656-0581	It doesn't come much healthier. Good advice for your health needs.
Makeovers	302 Washington St	201-420-1444	Every hair care product known to womankind. A fantasy for your follicles.
Peper	1030 Washington St	201-217-1911	Hoboken's sexiest clothing. A must for your next high school reunion.
Sobsey's Produce	92 Bloomfield St	201-795-9398	Expert greengrocer. Exotic produce and gourmet foods.
Sparrow Wine and Liquor	1224 Shipyard Ln	201-659-1500	Wine and liquor abound.
Sparrow Wine and Liquor	126 Washington St	201-659-1500	Good selection of local and imported products. Staff are helpful with selections.
Tunes New & Used CDs	225 Washington St	201-653-3355	Support your local indie music store. They'll order stuff for you.
Wishing Tree	706 Washington St	201-420-1136	Nice "girly" gifts.
Yes I Do	312 Washington St	201-659-3300	Elegant cards, stationary, invitatons, printing and gifts.

Map 35 • Jersey City

Harborside Shopping Complex			
Newport Center Mall	30 Mall Dr W	201-626-2025	

Battery Park City

Battery Park Pharmacy	327 South End Ave	212-912-0555	Best store in the 'hood.

Here is, as best as we can figure out, all the theaters in Manhattan. The difference between "Off" and "Off-Off" you ask? Size, of course. "Off-Off" is under 100 seats, "Off" is 100-500 seats.

If it's a Broadway show you're after, check out www.broadway.com for a comprehensive list of what's playing and when. You can buy tickets from their website or you can go through the usual Ticketmaster or Telecharge routes, or call the theaters directly.

If you're short on cash and long on time and patience, you might try standing in line at tkts for discounted (by 25-50%) tickets. The more popular shows such as *The Producers* (**St. James Theatre**) and *The Lion King* (**New Amsterdam Theatre**) don't offer discounts very often so be prepared to pay full price for your seats. Shows such as *42nd Street* (**Ford Center for Performing Art**), *Aida* (**Palace Theatre**), *Beauty and the Beast* (**Lunt-Fontanne Theatre**), *Chicago* (**Ambassador Theatre**), *Little Shop of Horrors* (**Virginia Theatre**), *Movin' Out* (**Richard Rodgers Theatre**), *Rent* (**Nederlander Theatre**), *The Boy from Oz* (**Imperial Theatre**), *Phantom of the Opera* (**Majestic Theatre**), and *Thoroughly Modern Millie* (**Marquis Theatre**) are featured often at the tkts booths.

Off-Broadway shows tend not to sell out either, so tkts offers discounted tickets to Off-Broadway shows too. Some long-running shows that usually have discounted tickets include *De La Guarda* (**Daryl Roth Theatre**), *Forbidden Broadway* (**Douglas Fairbanks Theatre**), *I Love You, You're Perfect, Now Change* (**Westside Theatre**), *Naked Boys Singing* (**Actors' Playhouse**), and *Stomp* (**Orpheum Theatre**).

There are two tkts booths—one in Times Square at 47th and Broadway and one at the South Street Seaport on the corner of Front and John Streets. The one at the Seaport is by far the less busy of the two, so head downtown if you can—the wait time there is usually less than half an hour compared to a couple of hours in Times Square. The Seaport opens at 11 am from Monday to Saturday and only sells evening performances. The Times Square booth starts selling tickets at 3 pm daily for evening performances, 10 am for Wednesday and Saturday matinees and 11 am for Sunday matinees.

If you're after something further off Broadway, check out the fare at some of our favorite theaters:

Pearl Theatre Company is presently located at 80 St. Mark's Place and is one of the 15 or so largest institutional theaters in New York City. 2004 marked their 20th anniversary and they continue to grow as a resident company and a classical repertory offering delights from Sheridan, Shakespeare, Aeschylus, Marivaux and Ibsen. www.pearltheatre.org

Now in its 6th season, Horse Trade continues its commitment to produce a varied program of performance series, readings, workshops, and fully realized productions. Most of its events are performed at the **Kraine Theater**, which also houses the **Proscenium Theater** on its third floor. The theaters are also available to rent for rehearsals and performances. www.httheater.org

HERE not only houses two small theaters, it also has an amazing gallery space and a cozy café that serves alcohol – perfect for a pre- or post-show snack and drinks. www.here.org

In Chelsea, **The Kitchen** literally began in the unused kitchen of the Mercer Arts Center, housed in the Broadway Central Hotel in Greenwich Village. In 1985, The Kitchen moved into its new and permanent home at 512 W 19th Street. The venue plays host to new performance artists blending music, dance, video, art, and the spoken word. www.thekitchen.org

Located in a former public school on 1st Avenue and 9th Street in the East Village, **P.S. 122** is a not-for-profit arts center serving the New York City dance and performance community. Shows rotate through on a regular basis so check the website for the latest schedule. www.ps122.org

The **Delacorte Theater** in Central Park is outdoors, so it's understandable that performances are held only in the warmer months of June, July and August. Tickets to the ridiculously popular free Shakespeare in the Park performances are given away at 1 pm at the Delacorte and also at the **Public Theate**r (425 Lafayette Street) on the day of each performance. Hopefully you enjoy camping, because people line up for days in their tents and sleeping bags just to secure tickets!

Just the other side of the Manhattan Bridge in Brooklyn is the world famous **Brooklyn Academy of Music**, better known to locals as **BAM**. A thriving urban arts center, BAM brings domestic and international performing arts and film to Brooklyn. The center includes two theaters (Harvey Lichtenstein Theater and Howard Gilman Opera House), the Bam Rose Cinemas, and the BAMcafé, a restaurant and live music venue. Our favorite season is the *Next Wave*, an annual three-month celebration of cutting-edge dance, theater, music, and opera. www.bam.org

Broadway

			Map
Ambassador Theatre	219 W 49th St	212-239-6200	12
American Airlines Theatre	227 W 42nd St	212-719-1300	12
Apollo Theater	253 W 125th St	212-749-5838	19
Belasco Theatre	111 W 44th St	212-239-6200	12
Biltmore Theatre	261 W 47th St	212-245-2266	12
Booth Theatre	222 W 45th St	212-239-6200	12
Broadhurst Theatre	235 W 44th St	212-239-6200	12
Broadway Theater	1681 Broadway	212-239-6200	12
Brooks Atkinson Theatre	256 W 47th St	212-307-4100	12
Cadillac Winter Garden Theatre	1634 Broadway	212-239-6200	12
Carnegie Hall	154 W 57th St	212-247-7800	12
Circle in the Square Theatre	1633 Broadway	212-307-0388	12
Cort Theatre	138 W 48th St	212-239-6200	12
Ethel Barrymore Theatre	243 W 47th St	608-241-2345	12
Eugene O'Neill Theatre	230 W 49th St	212-239-6200	12
Gershwin Theatre	222 W 51st St	212-307-4100	12
Golden Theatre	252 W 45th St	212-239-6200	12
Helen Hayes Theatre	240 W 44th St	212-239-6200	12
Henry Miller Theatre	124 W 43rd St	212-239-6200	12
Imperial Theater	249 W 45th St	212-239-6200	12
Longacre Theatre	220 W 48th St	212-239-6200	12
Lunt-Fontanne Theatre	205 W 46th St	212-307-4747	12
Lyceum Theatre	149 W 45th St	212-239-6200	12
Majestic Theater	245 W 44th St	212-239-6200	12
Marquis Theatre	1535 Broadway	212-307-4100	12
Minskoff Theatre	200 W 45th St	212-869-0550	12
Music Box Theatre	239 W 45th St	212-239-6200	12
Nederlander Theatre	208 W 41st St	212-307-4100	12
Neil Simon Theatre	250 W 52nd St	212-307-4100	12
New Amsterdam Theatre	214 W 42nd St	212-307-4100	12
New Victory Theatre	209 W 42nd St	212-239-6200	12
Palace Theatre	1564 Broadway	212-307-4747	12
Plymouth Theatre	236 W 45th St	212-239-6200	12
Radio City Music Hall	1260 Sixth Ave	212-247-4777	12
Richard Rodgers Theatre	226 W 46th St	212-221-1211	12
Roundabout/ Laura Pels Theatre	1530 Broadway	212-719-9300	12
Royale Theatre	242 W 45th St	212-239-6200	12
Shubert Theatre	225 W 44th St	212-239-6200	12
St James Theater	246 W 44th St	212-239-6200	12
The Theater at Madison Square Garden	2 Penn Plz	212-307-4111	9
Virginia Theatre	245 W 52nd St	212-239-6200	12
Vivian Beaumont Theatre	Lincoln Center, 150 W 65th St	212-362-7600	14
Walter Kerr Theatre	219 W 48th St	212-239-6200	12

Off- and Off-Off Broadway

			Map
13th Street Theatre	50 W 13th St	212-675-6677	6
29th Street Repertory Theatre	212 W 29th St	212-465-0575	9
45 Bleecker Theater	45 Bleecker St	212-253-7017	6
47th Street Theater	304 W 47th St	212-265-1086	12
5 C Cultural Center	68 Avenue C	212-206-1515	7
74A	E 4th St between Bowery & Second Ave	212-475-7710	6
78th Street Theatre Lab	236 W 78th St	212 873-9050	14
92nd Street Y Theatre	1395 Lexington Ave	212-996-1100	17
Abingdon Mainstage Theatre	312 W 36th St	212-206-1515	8
Access Theater	380 Broadway, 4th Fl	212-501-3909	3
Acorn Theatre	410 W 42nd St	212-279-4200	11
Actor's Playhouse	100 Seventh Ave S	212-239-6200	9
Actor's Theater Workshop	145 W 28th St	212-947-1386	8
Actors Studio Theatre	432 W 44th St	212-757-0870	11
Al Hirschfeld Theatre	302 W 45th St	212-239-6200	12
AMAS Repertory Theater	450 W 42nd St	212-563-2565	11
American Globe Theater	145 W 46th St	212-869-9809	12
American Jewish Theatre	307 W 26th St	212-633-9797	8
American Place Theatre	266 W 37th St	212-239-6200	12
American Theatre of Actors	314 W 54th St	212-239-6200	11
ArcLight Theatre	152 W 71st St	212-595-0355	14
Arno Ristorante	141 W 38th St	800-687-3374	9
Astor Place Theatre	434 Lafayette St	212-254-4370	6
Atlantic Theater Company	336 W 20th St	212-239-6200	8
Axis Theater	1 Sheridan Sq	212-807-9300	5
Beacon Theater	2124 Broadway	212-496-7070	14
Bottle Factory Theatre	195 E 3rd St	212-206-1515	6
Bouwerie Lane Theatre	330 Bowery	212-677-0060	6
Cap 21 Theatre	15 W 28th St	212-581-8896	9
Castillo Theatre	500 Greenwich St	212-941-1234	5
CBGB's 313 Gallery	313 Bowery	212-677-0455	6
Center Stage NY	48 W 21st St, 4th Fl	212-841-0326	9
Century Center	111 E 15th St	212-239-6200	10
Chashama	135 W 42nd St	212-391-8151	12
Chelsea Playhouse	125 W 22nd St	212-366-9176	9
Cherry Lane Theater	38 Commerce St	212-239-6200	5
Chicago City Limits Theatre	1105 First Ave	212-888-5233	15
Club El Flamingo	547 W 21st St	212-307-4100	8
Clurman Theatre	410 W 42nd St	212-279-4200	11
Collective: Unconscious	145 Ludlow St	212-254-5277	7
Community Service Council of Greater Harlem	207 W 133rd St	212-368-9314	19
Creative Artists Laboratory	303 W 42nd St, 3rd Fl	212-316-0400	12
Culture Club	179 Varick St	212-352-3101	5
Daryl Roth Theatre	20 Union Sq E	212-239-6200	10
Delacorte Theater	Central Park, W 81st St	212-539-8750	15
Dicapo Opera Theatre	184 E 76th St	212-288-9438	15
Dominion Theatre	428 Lafayette St	212-674-4066	6
Douglas Fairbanks Theatre	432 W 42nd St	212-239-6200	11
Duffy Theater	1553 Broadway	212-695-3401	12
Duke on 42nd Street	229 W 42nd St	212-946-1375	12
Duo Theatre	62 E 4th St	212-598-4320	6
Duplex Cabaret Theatre	61 Christopher St	212-255-5438	5
East 13th Street Theatre	136 E 13th St	212-206-1515	6
Educational Alliance—Mazer Theater	197 East Broadway	212-780-2300	4
Fez Under Time Café	380 Lafayette St	212-533-2680	6
Flatiron Theater	119 W 23rd St	212-330-7144	9
Flea Theatre	41 White St	212-226-0051	3
Fools Company Space	423 W 46th St	212-307-6000	11
Franklin Furnace	112 Franklin St	212-766-2606	2
French Institute—Florence Gould Hall	55 E 59th St	212-355-6160	13
Gene Frankel Theatre	24 Bond St	212-777-1767	6
Gertrude Stein Repertory Theater	15 W 26th St	212-725-7254	9
Gramercy Arts Theatre	138 E 27th St	212-889-2850	10
Gramercy Theatre	127 E 23rd St	212-307-4100	10
Greenwich House Theater	27 Barrow St	212-239-6200	5
Greenwich Street Theatre	547 Greenwich St	212-206-1515	5
Harold Clurman Theatre	412 W 42nd St	212-279-4200	11
Harry DeJur Playhouse	466 Grand St	212-598-0400	4
Hartley House Theater	413 W 46th St	212-246-9885	11
HERE	145 Sixth Ave	212-647-0202	5
Hudson Guild	441 W 26th St	212-760-9800	8
Hudson Theater	145 W 44th St	212-307-7171	12
Intar Theatre	508 W 53rd St	212-279-4200	11
Irish Arts Center	553 W 51st St	212-581-4125	11
Irish Repertory Theatre	133 W 22nd St	212-727-2737	9
Jane Street Theatre at the Hotel Riverview Ballroom	113 Jane St	212-239-6200	5
Jean Cocteau Repertory	330 Bowery	212-677-0060	6
John Houseman Theater	450 W 42nd St	212-239-6200	11
Jose Quintero Theatre	534 W 42nd St	212-244-7529	11
Joseph Papp Public Theater	425 Lafayette St	212-260-2400	6

Off- and Off-Off Broadway

Name	Address	Phone	Map
Judith Anderson Theater	534 W 42nd St	212-698-5429	11
Kirk Theatre	410 W 42nd St	212-279-4200	11
Knitting Factory-Alterknit Theater	74 Leonard St	212-219-3055	3
La MaMa ETC	74A E 4th St	212-475-7710	6
Lambs Theater	130 W 44th St	212-239-6200	12
Lark Theatre Studio	939 Eighth Ave, 2nd Fl	212-246-2676	12
Lillie Blake Auditorium at PS 6	45 E 81st St	212-737-9774	15
Lincoln Center for the Performing Arts	Broadway & 64th St	212-875-5456	14
Lions Theatre	410 W 42nd St	212-279-4200	11
Little Shubert Theatre	422 W 42nd St	212-239-6200	11
Lucille Lortel Theatre	121 Christopher St	212-239-6200	5
Manhattan Class Co	410 W 42nd St	212-727-7722	11
Manhattan Ensemble Theatre	549 W 52nd St	212-247-3405	11
Manhattan Theatre Source	177 MacDougal St	212-501-4751	6
Mark Goodson Theatre	2 Columbus Cir	212-841-4100	11
Martin R Kaufman Theater	534 W 42nd St	212-279-4200	11
Maverick Theatre	307 W 26th St	212-239-6200	8
MCC Theater	145 W 28th St	212-727-7722	8
McGinn/Cazale Theatre	2162 Broadway	212-279-4200	14
Medicine Show Theatre	552 W 53rd St	212-279-4200	11
Metropolitan Playhouse	220a E 4th St, 2nd Fl	212-995-5302	7
Miller Theater-Columbia University	200 Dodge Hall, Broadway & 116th St	212-854-7799	18
Minetta Lane Theatre	18 Minetta Ln	212-307-4100	6
Mint Theatre	311 W 43rd St 5th Fl	212-315-0231	11
Mitzi E Newhouse Theater	150 W 65th St	212-239-6200	14
Musical Theatre Works	440 Lafayette St	212-677-0040	6
National Arts Club	15 Gramercy Park S	212-362-2560	10
National Black Theatre	2031 Fifth Ave	212-722-3800	19
New York State Theatre	Lincoln Center, Columbus Ave at 63rd St	212-870-5570	14
New York Theatre Workshop	79 E 4th St	212-239-6200	6
Nuyorican Poets Cafe	236 E 3rd St	212-505-8183	7
Ohio Theater	66 Wooster St	800-965-4827	6
Orpheum Theater	126 Second Ave	212-477-2477	6
Ottendorfor Public Library	135 Second Ave	212-674-0947	6
Pan Asian Repertory Theater	520 Eighth Ave	212-868-4030	8
Paradise Theater	64 E 4th St	212-253-8107	6
Partners & Crime	44 Greenwich Ave	212-462-3027	5
Pearl Theatre Co	80 St Mark's Pl	212-598-9802	6
Pelican Studio Theatre	750 Eighth Ave	212-730-2030	12
People's Improvisation Theatre	154 W 29th St, 2nd Fl	212 563-7488	9
Perfoming Garage	33 Wooster St	212-966-3651	2
Players Theatre	115 MacDougal St	212-254-8138	6
Playhouse 91	316 E 91st St	212-307-4100	17
Playwrights Horizons Theater	416 W 42nd St	212-279-4200	11
Primary Stages	354 W 45th St	212-333-4052	11
Prism Theatre	4 White St	212-330-7673	2
Producers Club Times Square Theatre	300 W 43rd St	212-206-1515	12
Promenade Theatre	2162 Broadway	212-239-6200	14
Provincetown Playhouse	133 MacDougal St	212-777-2571	6
PS 122	150 First Ave	212-477-5288	7
Public Theater	425 Lafayette St	212-539-8500	6
Rattlestick Theatre	224 Waverly Pl	212-206-1515	5
Raw Space	529 W 42nd St	212-279-4200	11
Repertorio Español	138 E 27th St	212-889-2850	10
Reprise Room at Dillon's	245 W 54th St	212-239-6200	12
Riant Theatre	161 Hudson St	212-623-3488	2
Samuel Beckett Theatre	412 W 42nd St	212-307-4100	11
Sanford Meisner Theatre	164 Eleventh Ave	212-206-1764	8
Second Stage Theatre	307 W 43rd St	212-246-4422	12
Signature Theatre	555 W 42nd St	212-244-7529	11
Soho Playhouse	15 Vandam St	212-239-6200	5
Soho Repertory Theatre/ Walker Street Theater	46 Walker St	212-334-0962	3
Sol Goldman Y of the Educational Alliance	344 E 14th St	212-206-1515	6
St Lukes Church	308 W 46th St	212-239-6200	12
Stardust Theatre	1650 Broadway	212-239-6200	12
Stella Adler Theatre	419 Lafayette St	212-260-0525	6
Surf Reality	172 Allen St, 2nd Fl	212-673-4182	7
Sylvia and Danny Kaye Playhouse	695 Park Ave	212-772-5207	15
Symphony Space	2537 Broadway	212-864-5400	16
Synchronicity Space	55 Mercer St	212-925-8645	3
T Schreiber Studio	151 W 26th St	212-741-0209	9
Tenement Theater	97 Orchard St	212-431-0233	4
The Creative Place Theatre	750 Eighth Ave	212-229-7556	12
The Kitchen	512 W 19th St	212-255-5793	8
The Kraine Theater	85 E 4th St	212-868-4444	6
The Looking Glass Theatre	422 W 57th St	212-307-9467	11
The Milagro Theatre at the CSV Cultural Center	107 Suffolk St	212 279-4200	7
The Ontological Theater at St Mark's Church-in-the-Bowery	131 E 10th St	212-533-4650	6
The Pantheon Theatre	303 W 42nd St, 2nd Fl	212-479-7719	12
The Present Company Theatorium	198 Stanton St	212-946-5537	7
The Producers Club II	358 W 44th St	212-315-4743	11
The Red Room	85 E 4th St	212-539-7686	6
The World Underground Theatre at WWF	Broadway & 43rd St	212-307-4100	12
The Zipper Theatre	336 W 37th St	212-239-6200	8
Theater 3	311 W 43rd St	212-279-4200	11
Theater for the New City	155 First Ave	212-254-1109	7
Theatre 80	80 St Mark's Pl	212-598-9802	6
Theatre at St Peter's Church	619 Lexington Ave	212-239-6200	13
Theatre Studio	750 Eighth Ave	212-719-0500	12
Triad Theater	158 W 72nd St	212-239-6200	14
TriBeCa Performing Arts Center	199 Chambers St	212-220-1460	2
Trilogy Theatre	341 W 44th St	212-316-0400	11
UBU Rep	15 W 28th St	212-679-7562	9
Union Square Theater	100 E 17th St	212-307-4100	10
Urban Stages	259 W 30th St	212 695-5131	9
Variety Arts Theatre	110 Third Ave	212-239-6200	6
Victoria Five Theater	310 W 125th St	212-866-5170	5
Village Theater	158 Bleecker St	212-307-4100	6
Vineyard Theatre	108 E 15th St	212-353-0303	10
Waterloo Bridge Theatre	203 W 38th St	212-330-8879	9
West End Theatre	Church of St Paul , and St Andrew 263 W 86th St	212-279-4200	16
West End Theatre Upper West Side (Upper)	263 W 86th St	212-866-4454	16
Westbeth Theatre Center	111 W 17th St	212-691-2272	5
Westside Reportory Theater	252 W 81st St	212-874-7290	14
Westside Theatre	407 W 43rd St	212-239-6200	11
Wings Theater	154 Christopher St	212-627-2961	5
Women's Project Theatre	424 W 55th St	212-765-1706	11
WOW Cafe	59 E 4th St	212-777-4280	6

Performing Arts

			Map
Amato Opera	319 Bowery	212-228-8200	6
Beacon Theater	2124 Broadway	212-496-7070	14
CAMI Hall	165 W 57th St	212-841-9650	12
Century Center for the Performing Arts	111 E 15th St	212 239-6200	10
City Center Main Stage	131 W 55th St	212-581-7907	12
Dance Theatre Workshop	219 W 19th St	212-924-0077	9
Ford Center for the Performing Arts	214 W 43rd St	212-307-4100	12
Grace Rainey Rogers Auditorium	Metropolitan Museum, 1000 Fifth Ave	212-570-3949	15
Joyce Theater	175 Eighth Ave	212-242-0800	8
Manhattan School of Music	120 Claremont Ave	212-749-2802	18
Manhattan Theatre Club	131 W 55th St	212-581-1212	12
Merkin Concert Hall	129 W 67th St	212-501-3330	14
Music Room	Frick Museum, 1 E 70th St	212-288-0700	15
Riverside Church	490 Riverside Dr	212-870-6700	18
Town Hall	123 W 43rd St	212-840-2824	12
Warren St Performance Loft	46 Warren St	212-732-3149	2

Brooklyn

			Map	
651 Arts	651 Fulton St	718-636-4181	31	Fort Greene
BAX	421 Fifth Ave	718-832-9189	33	Park Slope / Prospect Heights
BRIC Studio	57 Rockwell Pl	718-855-7882	30	Brooklyn Heights / DUMBO / Downtown
Brick Theatre	575 Metropolitan Ave	718-907-6189	29	Williamsburg
Brooklyn Arts Council	195 Cadman Plz W	718-625-0080	30	Brooklyn Heights / DUMBO / Downtown
Brooklyn Arts Exchange	421 Fifth Ave	718-832-0018	33	Park Slope / Prospect Heights
Brooklyn Family Theatre	1012 Eighth Ave	718-670-7205	33	Park Slope / Prospect Heights
Brooklyn Lyceum	227 Fourth Ave	718-857-4816	33	Park Slope / Prospect Heights
Charlie's Pineapple Theater Company	208 N 8th St	718-907-0577	29	Williamsburg
Gallery Players Theater	199 14th St	718-595-0547	33	Park Slope / Prospect Heights
Harvey Theater (Brooklyn Academy of Music)	651 Fulton St	718-636-4100	31	Fort Greene
Heights Players	26 Willow Pl	718-237-2752	30	Brooklyn Heights / DUMBO / Downtown
Howard Gilman Opera House (Brooklyn Academy of Music)	30 Lafayette Ave	718-636-4100	31	Fort Greene
National Asian American Theater	674 President St	718-623-1672	33	Park Slope / Prospect Heights
One Arm Red	100 Water St	718-797-0046	30	Brooklyn Heights / DUMBO / Downtown
Paul Robeson Theatre	54 Greene Ave	718-783-9794	31	Fort Greene
Puppetworks	338 Sixth Ave	718-965-3391	33	Park Slope / Prospect Heights
St Ann's Warehouse	38 Water St	718-858-2424	30	Brooklyn Heights / DUMBO / Downtown
The Heights Players	26 Willow Pl	718-237-2752	30	Brooklyn Heights / DUMBO / Downtown
The Waterloo Bridge Playhouse	475 Third Ave	212-502-0796	33	Park Slope / Prospect Heights

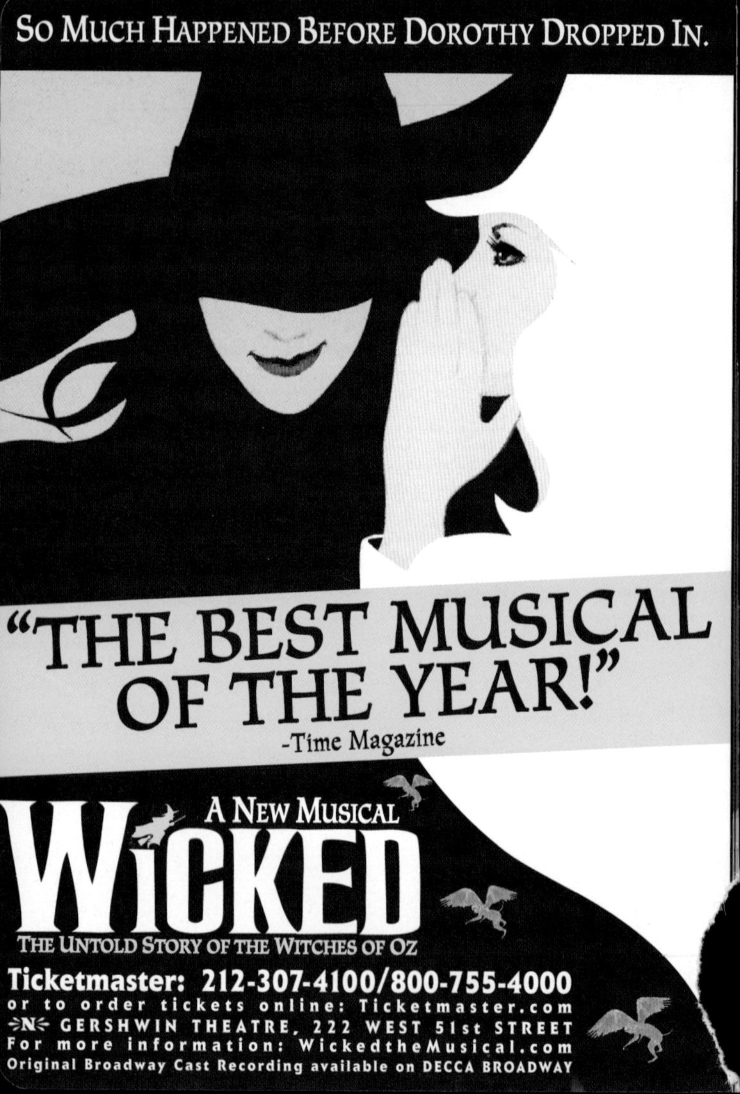
SO MUCH HAPPENED BEFORE DOROTHY DROPPED IN.
"THE BEST MUSICAL OF THE YEAR!"
-Time Magazine
A NEW MUSICAL
WICKED
THE UNTOLD STORY OF THE WITCHES OF OZ
Ticketmaster: 212-307-4100/800-755-4000
or to order tickets online: Ticketmaster.com
GERSHWIN THEATRE, 222 WEST 51st STREET
For more information: WickedtheMusical.com
Original Broadway Cast Recording available on DECCA BROADWAY

L

<THE L MAGAZINE>
PUT IT IN YOUR POCKET

every two weeks

AT A CORNER NEAR YOU
lower manhattan and brooklyn

‹THE L MAGAZINE›
events, listings, food, drink, hilarity

FREE volume II issue 11

FREE BOOZE INSIDE! ON THE CENTERFOLD

NOT FOR TOURISTS™ Custom Mapping

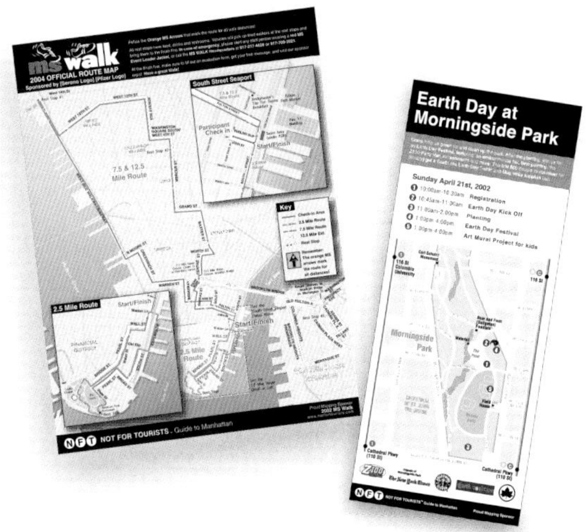

We'll map your world.

Have us make you an **NFT™** map! **Not For Tourists™** can bring its award-winning graphic functionality to helping put your organization or event and put you on the map.

The same trademark design that makes our Guidebooks stunning and unique can put your information into a clear and beautiful map package.

NFT™'s team will come up with something new or put a fresh face on something you already have.

We provide custom map-making and information design services to fit your needs—whether simply showing where your organization is located on one of our existing maps, or creating a completely new visual context for the information you wish to convey. **NFT™** will help you—and your audience—make the most of the place you're in, while you're in it.

For more information, call us at 212-965-8650 or visit www.notfortourists.com.

Not For Tourists, Inc

New York City • Los Angeles • Chicago • San Francisco • Boston • Washington DC • Brooklyn www.notfortourists.com

NOT FOR TOURISTS™ Wallmaps

Blown up and hung.

Your favorite **NFT™** map as a poster. Any **Not For Tourists™** map can be made into a 24"x 36" poster. These large wall maps are taken directly from the pages of the **Not For Tourists™** Guidebooks.

Order at www.notfortourists.com

Not For Tourists™

New York City • Los Angeles • Chicago • San Francisco • Boston • Washington DC • Brooklyn **www.notfortourists.com**

NOT FOR TOURISTS™ Online

THE MANHATTAN SKYLINE

Two detailed panoramas portraying the city prior to September 11, 2001. Drawn by John Wagner.

One of the world's most breathtaking sights is the New York City skyline, now captured as never before in two new panoramas called **The Manhattan Skyline Portraits**. Although photographic in appearance, these images are actually illustrations drawn by artist John Wagner. Using a computer as a pen and paintbrush, he carefully crafted a faithful likeness of each building based largely on thousands of photographs he took from the air as well as at ground level.

40 Months from Start to Finish

Drawing the 6.5 miles of Manhattan pictured in both portraits took Wagner more than three years to complete. He began in May 1998 and finished two weeks after the World Trade Center towers were destroyed in September 2001. More than 1,000 buildings take center stage in each drawing. Another 2,500 less-visible structures serve as the skyline's supporting cast, conveying the density of construction so characteristic of Manhattan.

The East River Portrait faithfully records the eastern side of the skyline as seen from Brooklyn and Queens across the East River. **The Hudson River Portrait** shows the west side of the city, looking across the Hudson River from the New Jersey shoreline. Each portrait is sold separately.

Drawn One Building at a Time

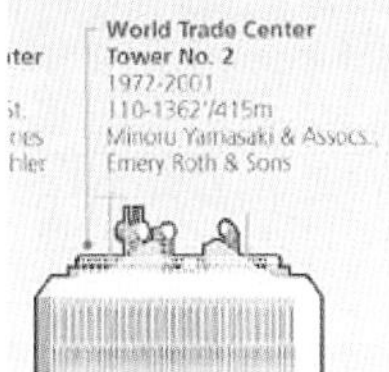

In order to fit the entire 12 feet of city depicted in each portrait on a single sheet of poster paper, the image is presented in two decks with a pause at 29th Street. Each panorama reads like a two-line sentence, left to right and top to bottom. The size of each print is 18.5 x 75 inches (47 x 190.5 cm). All buildings in the panoramas are drawn using the same scale, which means no structure is diminished in size because of its distance from you, the viewer. All skyscrapers stand tall in these group portraits, even those in the back row. How tall? The Empire State Building measures 5.75 inches tall (15 cm). More than 500 buildings in each Manhattan Skyline portrait are identified. The stories of these buildings are told in these labels, such as the date completed, the street address and the architect. Labels for skyscrapers taller than 700 feet (213 m) also list the height in stories, feet and meters. In addition, many labels include further information of historic interest.

Available at www.notfortourists.com

Street Index

Street Index

Street Index

Address Locator

Streets	Riverside	West End	Broadway	Amsterdam	Columbus	C.P.W.	Central Park
110-116	370-440	850-920	2675-2800	856-995	850-1021	419-500	
102-110	290-370	737-850	2554-2675	733-856	740-850	360-419	
96-102	240-290	620-737	2440-2554	620-733	621-740	300-360	
90-96	180-240	500-619	2321-2439	500-619	501-620	241-295	
84-90	120-180	380-499	2201-2320	380-499	381-500	239-241	
78-84	60-120	262-379	2081-2200	261-379	261-380	121-239	
72-78	1-60	122-261	1961-2079	140-260	141-260	65-115	
66-72		2-121	1791-1960	1-139	2-140	0-65	
58-66		2800-2950	995-1120				

Streets	12th Ave.	11th Ave.	Broadway	10th Ave.	9th Ave.	8th Ave.	7th Ave.	6th Ave.
52-58	710-850	741-854	1674-1791	772-889	782-907	870-992	798-921	1301-1419
46-52	600-710	625-740	1551-1673	654-770	662-781	735-869	701-797	1180-1297
40-46	480-600	503-624	1440-1550	538-653	432-662	620-734	560-701	1061-1178
34-40	360-480	405-502	Macy's-1439	430-537	431-432	480-619	442-559	1060-1061
28-34	240-360	282-404	1178-1282	314-429	314-431	362-479	322-442	815-1060
22-28	0-240	162-281	940-1177	210-313	198-313	236-361	210-321	696-814
14-22		26-161	842-940	58-209	44-197	80-235	64-209	5520-695
8-14			748-842	0-58	0-44	0-80	2-64	420-520
Houston-8			610-748					244-402

The address locator below is formatted north-south, from 116th Street to Houston Street. For east-west addresses, simply remember that Fifth Ave. is the dividing line-2 E. 54th would be right off of Fifth, while 200 E. 54th would be around Third Ave.

5th Ave.	Madison	Park	Lexington	3rd Ave.	2nd Ave.	1st Ave.	York	Streets
1280-1400	1630-1770	1489-1617	1766-1857	1981-2103	2109-2241	2175-2238		110-116
1209-1280	1500-1630	1350-1489	1612-1766	1820-1981	1880-2109	1975-2175		102-110
1148-1209	1379-1500	1236-1350	1486-1612	1709-1820	1854-1880	1855-1975		96-102
1090-1148	1254-1379	1120-1236	1361-1486	1601-1709	1736-1854	1740-1855	1700-end	90-96
1030-1089	1130-1250	1000-1114	1248-1355	1490-1602	1624-1739	1618-1735	1560-1700	84-90
970-1028	1012-1128	878-993	1120-1248	1374-1489	1498-1623	1495-1617	1477-1560	78-84
910-969	896-1006	760-877	1004-1116	1250-1373	1389-1497	1344-1494	1353-1477	72-78
850-907	772-872	640-755	900-993	1130-1249	1260-1363	1222-1343	1212-1353	66-72
755-849	621-771	476-639	722-886	972-1129	1101-1260	1063-1222	1100-1212	58-66

5th Ave.	Madison	Park	Lexington	3rd Ave.	2nd Ave.	1st Ave.	Avenue A	Streets
656-754	500-611	360-475	721	741-855	862-983	827-944		46-52
562-655	377-488	240-350	476-593	622-735	746-860	701-827		40-46
460-561	284-375	99-240	354-475	508-621	622-747	599-701		34-40
352-459	188-283	5-99	240-353	394-507	500-621	478-598		28-34
250-351	79-184	4-404	120-239	282-393	382-499	390-478		22-28
172-249	1-78	286-403	9-119	126-281	230-381	240-389		14-22
69-170	University	0-285	1-8	59-126	138-230	134-240	129-210	8-14
9-69	0-120			1-59	0-138	0-134	0-129	Houston - 8
0-9		596-	856-968	984-1101	945-1063		52-58	